T0180071

Communications
in Computer and Information Science   **1350**

More information about this series at http://www.springer.com/series/7899

Sanjay Misra · Bilkisu Muhammad-Bello (Eds.)

Information and Communication Technology and Applications

Third International Conference, ICTA 2020
Minna, Nigeria, November 24–27, 2020
Revised Selected Papers

 Springer

Editors
Sanjay Misra ⓘD
Covenant University
Ota, Nigeria

Bilkisu Muhammad-Bello ⓘD
Federal University of Technology Minna
Minna, Nigeria

ISSN 1865-0929 ISSN 1865-0937 (electronic)
Communications in Computer and Information Science
ISBN 978-3-030-69142-4 ISBN 978-3-030-69143-1 (eBook)
https://doi.org/10.1007/978-3-030-69143-1

This Springer imprint is published by the registered company Springer Nature Switzerland AG
The registered company address is: Gewerbestrasse 11, 6330 Cham, Switzerland

Preface

The Third International Conference on Information and Communication Technology and Its Applications (ICTA 2020) aimed to bring together researchers and practitioners working in different domains in the field of ICT in order to exchange their expertise and to discuss the perspectives of development and collaboration.

ICTA 2020 was held virtually, during November 24–26, 2020. It was organized by the School of Information and Communication Technology, Federal University of Technology Minna, and Center of ICT/ICE Research, Covenant University.

This year ICTA's theme was "Leveraging Emerging Technology for Sustainable Digitization of Society." ICTA 2020 focused on core areas of Information and Communication Technology (ICT), particularly emerging technology and datafication of society and how these would impact achievement of sustainable development goals. We received 166 submissions from around the world. All the papers were the size of 10–16 pages. Each paper was allotted to 3–5 reviewers from the international program committee. We adopted a single-blind process for review. The whole program was divided into three tracks into the areas of Information Security and Privacy; Artificial Intelligence, Big Data & Machine Learning; and Information Science and Technology. Based on the review process, 55 full papers were accepted to be included in this volume of Communications in Computer and Information Science (CCIS) proceedings published by Springer.

Finally, we would like to thank Amin Mobasheri, Alla Serikova and Alfred Hofmann, from Springer, and Ramvijay Subramani, our book project manager, for their helpful advice, guidance and support in publishing the proceedings.

We trust that the ICTA 2020 Conference and Proceedings open for you new vistas of discovery and knowledge.

Sanjay Misra

Welcome Message

On behalf of the Organizing Committee of ICTA 2020, it is a pleasure to welcome you to The Third International Conference on Information and Communication Technology and Applications (ICTA 2020), held during Nov, 24–26, 2020.

ICTA 2020 was planned to take place in the School of Information and Communication Technology, Federal University of Technology Minna (FUTM), Nigeria. FUTM is one of the specialised universities for technology education established by the Federal Government of Nigeria in 1983. Minna is the capital city of Niger state and very close to Nigeria's capital territory - Abuja. Minna is also surrounded by many beautiful attractions like Gurara Falls, Zuma Rock, and several other natural attractions. FUTM, which happens to be the venue of the conference, is a 2 hr drive from the hustle and bustle of the busy metropolitan life in the city of Abuja. FUTM has two beautiful campuses with landscaped surroundings. However, due to the Covid-19 pandemic and considering the safety and security (health) of authors and the ICTA community, we decided to organize this conference in Virtual mode, controlled by FUT Minna and Covenant University, Ota, Nigeria.

Keynote speeches by leading researchers and high-quality papers from several tracks provided a real opportunity to discuss new issues and find advanced solutions able to shape recent trends in ICT.

The conference could not have happened without the dedicated work of many volunteers. We want to thank all members of the ICTA organizing committee for collaborating with us in hosting a successful ICTA 2020 and our fellow members of the local organizations.

On behalf of the Conference Organizing Committee of ICTA 2020, it is our honour to cordially welcome your virtual presence. Your participation in and contribution to this conference will make it much more productive and successful.

On behalf of the Organizing Committee
Nicholas Iwokwagh
Sanjay Misra

Organization

General Chairs

Nicholas Iwokwagh	Federal University of Technology Minna, Nigeria
Sanjay Misra	Covenant University, Nigeria

Honorary Chair

Abdullahi Bala (Vice Chancellor)	Federal University of Technology Minna, Nigeria

Steering Committee

Ismaila Idris	Federal University of Technology Minna, Nigeria
Shafi'i Muhammad Abdulhamid	Federal University of Technology Minna, Nigeria
Richard Adeyemi Ikuesan	University of Pretoria, South Africa
Jaime Chavarriaga	Universidad de los Andes, Colombia
Hector Florez	Universidad Distrital Francisco José de Caldas, Colombia
Ixent Galpin	Universidad de Bogotá Jorge Tadeo Lozano, Colombia
Olmer García	Universidad de Bogotá Jorge Tadeo Lozano, Colombia
Sanjay Misra	Covenant University, Nigeria

International Advisory Committee

Matthew Adigun	University of Zululand, South Africa
Richard Adeyemi Ikuesan	University of Pretoria, South Africa
Ricardo Colomo-Palacios	Østfold University College, Norway
Luís Fernández Sanz	Universidad de Alcalá, Spain
Murat Koyuncu	Atılım University, Turkey
Raj Kumar Buyya	University of Melbourne, Australia
Cristian Mateos	Universidad Nacional del Centro de la Provincia de Buenos Aires, Argentina
Victor Mbarika	East Carolina University, USA

International Program Committee

Bilkisu Larai Muhammad Bello	Federal University of Technology Minna, Nigeria
Nicholas Iwokwagh	Federal University of Technology Minna, Nigeria
Sanjay Misra	Covenant University, Nigeria

Joseph Adebayo Ojeniyi	Federal University of Technology Minna, Nigeria
Shafi'i Muhammad Abdulhamid	Federal University of Technology Minna, Nigeria
Shefiu Ganiyu	Federal University of Technology Minna, Nigeria
Barroon Isma'eel Ahmad	Ahmadu Bello University, Nigeria
Victor Mbarika	East Carolina University, USA
Daniel Rodríguez	University of Alcalá, Spain
Robertas Damaševičius	Kaunas University of Technology, Lithuania
Matteo Cristofaro	University of Rome Tor Vergata, Italy
Reda Alhajj	University of Calgary, Canada
Emilia Mendes	Blekinge Institute of Technology, Sweden
Oluwafemi Osho	Federal University of Technology Minna, Nigeria
Fatimah Abduldayan	Federal University of Technology Minna, Nigeria
Risnandar	Research Center for Informatics, Indonesian Institute of Sciences, Indonesia
Vahid Garousi	Queen's University Belfast, UK
Broderick Crawford	Pontificia Universidad Católica de Valparaiso, PUCV, Chile
Michel Dos Santos Soares	Federal University of Sergipe, Brazil
V. B. Singh	University of Delhi, India
Thanda Shwe	Mandalay Technological University, Myanmar
Zar Zar Wint	Mandalay Technological University, Myanmar
Isiaq Alabi	Federal University of Technology Minna, Nigeria
Oluwaseun Ojerinde	Federal University of Technology Minna, Nigeria
José Alfonso Aguilar	Universidad Autónoma de Sinaloa, Mexico
Ricardo Soto	Pontificia Universidad Católica de Valparaiso, Chile
Sulaimon A. Bashir	Federal University of Technology Minna, Nigeria
Eduardo Guerra	National Institute for Space Research, Brazil
Murat Koyuncu	Atılım University, Turkey
Habeeb Bello Salau	Ahmadu Bello University, Nigeria
Ishaq Oyefolahan	Federal University of Technology Minna, Nigeria.
Rytis Maskeliunas	Kaunas University of Technology, Lithuania
Olawale Surajudeen Adebayo	Federal University of Technology Minna, Nigeria
Jeong Ah Kim	Catholic Kwandong University, South Korea
Cristina Casado Lumbreras	Universidad Complutense de Madrid, Spain
Ibrahim Akman	Atılım University, Ankara, Turkey
Marco Crasso	IBM, Argentina
Hamza O. Aliyu	Federal University of Technology Minna, Nigeria
Tolga Pusatli	Çankaya University, Turkey
Jonathan Oluranti	Covenant University, Nigeria
Khalid Haruna	Bayero University Kano, Nigeria
Faruk Umar Ambursa	Bayero University Kano, Nigeria
Adebayo Abayomi-Alli	Federal University of Agriculture, Abeokuta, Nigeria
Markus Holopainen	University of Helsinki, Finland

Takashi Michikawa	Research Center for Advanced Science and Technology (RCAST), Japan
Cristian Mateos	UNICEN University, Argentina
Yahaya Coulibaly	Universiti Teknologi Malaysia, Malaysia
Quoc Trung Pham	HCMC University of Technology, Vietnam
Alejandro Zunino	UNICEN University, Argentina
Eudisley Anjos	Federal University of Paraíba, Brazil
Ravin Ahuja	Delhi College of Engineering, India
Foluso Ayeni	ICT University Foundation, USA
Mohammed Joda Usman	Bauchi State University, Nigeria
Rinkaj Goyal	Guru Gobind Singh Indraprastha University, India

Organized by (Virtually)

School of ICT, Federal University of Technology Minna, Niger State, Nigeria and Centre of ICT/ICE Research, CUCRID, Covenant University, Ota, Nigeria

Sponsored by

1. Software Engineering, Modelling and Intelligent Systems Research Cluster, Covenant University, Ota, Nigeria
2. Springer

 Springer

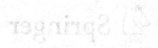

Abstracts of Keynotes

Artificial Intelligence for Industry and Environment

Vincenzo Piuri

FIEEE, Department of Computer Science, Università degli Studi di Milano, Italy
vincenzo.piuri@unimi.it
http://www.di.unimi.it/piuri

Abstract. Adaptability and advanced services for industrial manufacturing require intelligent technological support for understanding the production process characteristics in complex situations. Quality control is specifically one of the activities in manufacturing which is very critical for ensuring high-quality products and competitiveness in the market. Similarly, protection of the environment requires the ability to adjust the understanding of the current status by considering the natural dynamics of the environment itself and natural phenomena.

Artificial intelligence can provide additional flexible techniques for designing and implementing monitoring and control systems for both industrial and environmental applications, which can be configured from behavioral examples or by mimicking approximate reasoning processes to achieve adaptable systems. This talk will analyze the opportunities offered by artificial intelligence technologies to support the realization of adaptable operations and intelligent services in industrial applications, specifically focusing on manufacturing processes and quality control, as well as in environmental monitoring, especially for land management and agriculture.

Biography: Vincenzo Piuri received his Ph.D. in computer engineering at Politecnico di Milano, Italy (1989). He is Full Professor in computer engineering at the Università degli Studi di Milano, Italy (since 2000). He has been Associate Professor at Politecnico di Milano, Italy and Visiting Professor at The University of Texas at Austin and at George Mason University, USA. His main research interests are: artificial intelligence, computational intelligence, intelligent systems, machine learning, pattern analysis and recognition, signal and image processing, biometrics, intelligent measurement systems, industrial applications, digital processing architectures, fault tolerance, dependability, and cloud computing infrastructures. He has published original work in more than 400 papers in international journals, proceedings of international conferences, books, and book chapters.

He is a Fellow of the IEEE, Distinguished Scientist of the ACM, and Senior Member of the INNS. He is President of the IEEE Systems Council (2020–21), and has been IEEE Vice President for Technical Activities (2015), IEEE Director, President of the IEEE Computational Intelligence Society, Vice President for Education of the IEEE Biometrics Council, Vice President for Publications of the IEEE Instrumentation and Measurement Society and the IEEE Systems Council, and Vice President for Membership of the IEEE Computational Intelligence Society.

He has been Editor-in-Chief of the IEEE Systems Journal (2013-19), and is Associate Editor of the IEEE Transactions on Cloud Computing, and has been Associate Editor of IEEE Transactions on Computers, IEEE Transactions on Neural Networks, IEEE Transactions on Instrumentation and Measurement, and IEEE Access. He received the IEEE Instrumentation and Measurement Society Technical Award (2002) and the IEEE TAB Hall of Honor (2019).

Covid-19: A Personal Impact Assessment

Andrew Ware

University of South Wales, Cardiff, UK

Abstract. 2020 will be remembered as the year that the world simultaneously slowed down and speeded up. Coronavirus has meant that for most of 2020 much of the world's population have had their movements and activities restricted. People have been confined to their home, and anyone showing symptoms of the virus has been instructed to self-isolate. At the same time 'working from home' has, for many, become the norm. This new normal has acted as a fillip for the progress of technology that enables remote connectivity. Changes in the way we work, rest, and play have been necessitated at lightning speed.

The past eight months have highlighted the need for digital inclusion. While many have benefited from the life of the new normal, others have been significantly disadvantaged. As we, hopefully, move beyond Covid, the mantra of many World leaders is to "build back better, build back greener." What might that look like in reality? How can we all benefit from the collective learning of the 2020 experience? These are big questions, and the answers are far beyond a single individual. However, what the talk aims to do is present the contribution to the great debate of one individual based on their experience.

Biography: Andrew is Professor of Computing at the University of South Wales in the United Kingdom. His research interests centre on the use of intelligent computer systems (Artificial Intelligence and Data Science-oriented solutions) to help solve real-world problems. Andrew is currently working on AI-related projects with several industrial and commercial partners that include Tata Steel, National Health Service Wales Informatics Service, and Wye Education. Andrew is Director of Aurora International Consulting Ltd, an innovative software-as-a-service company that provides AI-enabled review software to the construction industry. Andrew is Director of Research for the Welsh Institute of Digital Information, a collaboration between the University of South Wales, the University of Wales Trinity Saint David, and the NHS Wales Informatics Service (NWIS). Andrew is a Regional Director of Techno Camps, an innovative and ambitious project that seeks to engage young people with computing and its cognate subjects. Moreover, Andrew is Editor in Chief of the journal Annals of Emerging Technologies in Computing (AETiC).

Modern Challenges in Computational Science

Osvaldo Gervasi

Department of Mathematics and Computer Science,
University of Perugia

In recent years we have witnessed an impressive development of technology, which is continuously breaking down barriers considered insurmountable, and a massive and pervasive spread of services that require increasingly high-performance networks and computers.

Scientists are called on to reinvent algorithms and computational approaches in order to face the growing and ambitious questions posed by the market, society and science, particularly in times of extreme difficulty such as the Covid-19 pandemic.

In this lecture we will try to illustrate some concepts that can ignite in the researcher the desire to explore new frontiers of computational computing to face the challenging demands of a fast-moving world.

Biography: Prof. Gervasi is Associate Professor at the Department of Mathematics and Computer Science, University of Perugia. His Research interests are Computational Science, HPC, Virtual Reality and Artificial Intelligence. He is Co-Chair of: The International Conference on Computational Science and Its Applications (ICCSA) in 2004 (Assisi, Italy), 2005 (Singapore), 2006 (Glasgow, UK), 2007 (Kuala Lumpur, Malaysia), 2008 (Perugia, Italy), 2009 (Sewon, Korea), 2010 (Fukuoka, Japan), 2012 (Salvador da Bahia, Brazil), 2013 (Ho Chi Minh City, Vietnam), 2014 (Guimaraes, Portugal), 2015 (Banff, Canada), 2016 (Beijing, China), 2017 (Trieste, Italy) 2018 (Melbourne, Australia), 2019 (Saint Petersburg, Russia), 2020 (Online) and 2021 (Cagliari, Italy) and the ACM Web3D 2007 Symposium (Perugia, Italy). He has published more than 100 papers and co-edited more than 90 books. He was invited speaker at the International Conference on Computing, Networking and Informatics (ICCNI 2017), Ota (Nigeria), Oct 29–31, 2017; at Advanced Signal Processing (ASP 2016), Manila (Philippines) Feb 12–14, 2016, at the 6th International Conference on Adaptive Science and Technology (ICAST 2014), Lagos (Nigeria) Oct 29–31, 2014; at the International Conference on Hybrid Information Technologies 2006, Jeju Island (South Korea), at the First International Conference on Security-enriched Urban Computing and Smart Grids 2010, Daejeon (South Korea), at the Future Generation Information Technology Conference 2010, Jeju Island (South Korea), and at the Future Generation Information Technology Conference 2012, KangWanDo (South Korea). He was president of the Open Source Competence Center (CCOS) of the Umbria Region, Italy from 2007–2013 and is an ACM Senior Member and IEEE Senior Member, Member of the Internet Society (ISOC), co-founder of the ISOC Italian Chapter, Member of the Web3D Consortium and a Member of The Document Foundation (TDF) since 2013.

Contents

Information Security Privacy and Trust

Information Science and Technology

Artificial Intelligence, Big Data
and Machine Learning

Multi-class Model MOV-OVR for Automatic Evaluation of Tremor Disorders in Huntington's Disease

Rytis Maskeliunas[1], Andrius Lauraitis[1], Robertas Damasevicius[2(✉)], and Sanjay Misra[3]

[1] Kaunas University of Technology, Kaunas, Lithuania
rytis.maskeliunas@ktu.lt
[2] Vytautas Magnus University, Kaunas, Lithuania
robertas.damasevicius@vdu.lt
[3] Covenant University, Ota, Nigeria

Abstract. The abstract should summarize the contents of the paper in short terms, i.e. 150–250 words. This article proposes a method for assessing the symptoms of tremor in patients at an early stage of Huntington's disease (Huntington's syndrome, Huntington's chorea, HD). This approach includes the development of a data collection methodology using smartphones or tablets, data labelling for Support vector machine (SVM) model, multiple-class classification strategy, training the SVM, automatic selection of model parameters, and selection of training and test data sets. More than 3000 data records were obtained during research from subjects and patients with HD in Lithuania. The proposed SVM model achieved an accuracy of 97.09% in relation to 14 different classes, which were built according to the Shoulson-Fahn Total Functional Capacity (TFC) scale for assessing the patient's tremor condition.

Keywords: Mobile application · Tremor detection · Multistage support vector machine (MSVM) · Huntington's disease

1 Introduction

Huntington's disease (HD) is a neurodegenerative disorder that significantly affects a patient's daily life, causing problems with motor, cognitive and life functionality such as heart disease, physical injury from falls, pneumonia, etc. [1]. HD is a rare progressive genetic disease due to a mutation in the 4th chromosome of a human cell in the structure of the DNA gene of the first exon [2]. The highest incidence of HD is in Venezuela (1 in 700), about 1 in 10,000 to 20,000 in Europe, and up to 1 in 30,000 in America [3]. According to statistics collected in the Association of Huntington's Disease in Lithuania and in the Vilnius clinic "Santara" in 2015, 177 patients were officially registered in Lithuania [4]. Because HD is currently incurable, healthcare professionals and doctors are looking for new treatments for HD and are usually not motivated to do research themselves or do multidisciplinary research (such as bioinformatics). Currently, computer science

© Springer Nature Switzerland AG 2021
S. Misra and B. Muhammad-Bello (Eds.): ICTA 2020, CCIS 1350, pp. 3–14, 2021.
https://doi.org/10.1007/978-3-030-69143-1_1

research on HD is focused on detecting early stages of the disease to help slow the progress of HD [5–8]. Any supportive measures (progression tracking device, symptom prediction technology, etc.) that can be used to improve the daily life of HD patients are valuable and helpful.

Tremor signals elicited in patients with HD and Parkinson's disease (PD), involuntary movements, can be classified using an artificial neural network of the Multi-Layer Perceptron (MLP) [9]. For multipurpose classification problems (medical decision support systems implemented using a mobile application model) feedforward networks can be applied [10, 11]. Sensors in mobile devices can be used to predict tremor by adapting the radial basic neural network (RBFNN) for tremor activity from data recorded with simulation electrodes [12]. An alternative approach for developing a predictive model for HD can be based on assessing the movements of our lower and upper limbs (tremors in the legs, arms), where additional data come from the factor of age, speech impairment [13, 14] and work difficulties [15]. Mobile applications can be successfully used in various areas of medical practice, namely as an attractive diagnostic aid for early detection of disease [16] by health care providers [17].

The SVM models are very widely used in machine learning for classification problems (binary and multiclass). For example, an SVM model for classifying various pathological symptoms in elderly, post-stroke, and HD patients is proposed in [18], where data is collected using portable inertial units of measurement (IMU) sensors, and functions are extracted using hidden Markov models. The HR assessment using three-way accelerometers using time functions area and binary SVM for the classification of objects into healthy and HD is mentioned in [19]. An SVM classifier as a speech recognizer using a fixed spatial vector representation induced by a class of hidden Markov models is presented in [20]. Similarly, [21] adapted the multiclass SVM for gait classification using assistive devices. In [22], the SVM model is used as a classifier for recognizing human activity when monitoring physiological signals, for example, using inertia sensors of a smartphone.

We describe the problem from the point of view of a computer scientist, adapting a support vector machine (SVM) model to classify the state of tremor according to the Shoulson-Fahn Total Functional Capacity (TFC) scale [23] for patients with HD. We use mobile smart devices and applications for the proposed assessment solution, as they use sensors and multimedia capabilities that can provide a wealth of data about various attributes of our body. The mobile application serves as a data collection tool and a data extraction tool from clinical trials (medical history) to predict the state of tremor for a patient. We develop a computerized model for the automatic classification of a patient's deterioration, assessed using the finger trajectory, when performing exercises with mobile devices. The novelty of the proposed idea lies in how the application is structured and presented to patients. Data acquired during this study is evaluated and can also be used to train the system for higher accuracy. We 1) create a dataset collected with a mobile data collection application using touching point coordinates and the reaction time functions gathered from subjects (both healthy persons and the HD patients); 2) we create a multi-class MOV-model for assessing the state of tremor for a patient.

As for our previous work, in [24] a text input system was introduced to assess the condition of patients with HD. An overview of assistive technologies for people with disabilities is presented in [25]. Comparison of an artificial neural network for predicting TFC values for HD patients is presented in [26]. A hybrid approach (integrated with the Mamdani Type-1 fuzzy logic expert system) for assessing HD symptoms is described in [27]. The current work uses a mobile application described in [28–30] and further elaborates of the use of machine learning methods for HD diagnosis.

2 Materials and Methods

First, this section describes the feature extraction technique (including procedure and dataset) of disorders occurring in the HD patients. The dataset is collected using the created mobile application that gathers information from humans while executing four simple tasks (exercises) in which they are asked to touch specified areas of the screen with one or more fingers, or most accurately follow the path of the curve. After this examination, we obtain the measured positions, the accuracy, taking into account the centers of the figures, the response time of the patient and the streams of touch coordinates, composed in the form of an Archimedean spiral, representing fingers moving across the screen. It is expected that patients with more severe tremor disorder will perform tasks more slowly and less accurately than patients with mild disorder.

2.1 Test Subjects, Procedure and Data Set

The study included 10 control (healthy) subjects and 10 patients with Huntington's disease from Lithuania. Each HD patent agreed to participate in the investigation and allowed to use the obtained data gathered for the scientific purposes by clicking the checkbox in the mobile application. Each patient falls into the early category of the clinical descriptor of HD, that is, is able to complete the test on a mobile application without additional assistance, e.g., from medical staff, nurses or family members. The data collection process involves performing four tasks to detect jitter abnormalities using Android mobile devices. The dataset itself consists of 3200 records collected from 20 subjects.

2.2 Problems for Fingers

Three tasks were developed: T1 (sequential touch), T2 (rainbow touch), and T3 (Multitouch). We have built and adapted test modes T1, T2, T3 in accordance with the relevant work of other scientists who, assess patient tremor using the finger technique [31–33]. In addition, we expanded the proposed approach to include the Archimedean spiral trajectory algorithm and developed additional functionality for the mobile application: automatic data synchronization using the researcher's Google account, sensor information, customizable home screen, etc.

How T1 works: circular objects (2, 3 and 5 circles) are randomly generated from one specific color on the screen of a mobile device. Each circle is located in another screen location, so overlap by two specific circles is not possible. The active circle to be touched is marked with a black outline, which is different from other objects.

How T2 works: circular objects of 7 different colors (taken from the rainbow spectrum) are randomly generated on the screen of the mobile device (no overlaps possible).

In addition, a text label is displayed on the screen indicating, which colored circle to touch. The person has to touch the object five times. Each circle to be touched is randomly selected and shown in a text label. The main difference between T2 and T1 is that T2 tries to provoke the patient with HD more, providing a higher level of uncertainty about which object to touch.

How T3 works: Round objects are randomly visualized using three modes: 2, 3 and 6 circles. The overlapping objects is not allowed. In mode "2 circles" the subject should touch both circles with two fingers of one hand. Objects can be touched in any screen item the follower thinks of. In 3 Lap mode, use 3 fingers. When 6 circles are displayed, 3 of which are colored one red and the other 3 are green, both hands must be used: 3 fingers of the left hand and 3 fingers of the right. Each hand should only touch one color. In mode 2 and 3, the mobile device can be held in one hand, but when displaying 6 circles, the device must be placed on a surface. In all three modes, subjects are encouraged to touch each object, starting with the first in order, with their finger, as close to the center and as quickly as possible.

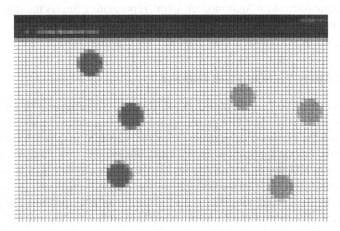

Fig. 1. An example of instructing the patient to touch 6 circles with both hands (3 red circles - left fingers, 3 green circles - right fingers) as detected on display's pixel grid (Color figure online).

Figure 1 shows the 3rd mode in task T3, where the patient with HD must use both hands to touch the located objects.

2.3 Archimedean Spiral Trajectory

Mathematically, the Archimedean spiral is expressed in polar coordinates (r, θ), as indicated in formula (1) (changing the parameter a will turn the spiral, and b controls the distance between successive turns):

$$r = a + blo \tag{1}$$

We applied the T4 test mode (Archimedean Spiral) in the proposed mobile application, since the experimental analysis of the spiral contour was an indicator of the detection of early signs of Parkinson's disease [34–37]. In this context, the tremor of Parkinson's disease and HD are related, therefore T4 is being adapted as an important technique for measuring the state of tremor disorder for patients with HD.

T4 working principle: 2 supported different modes. In the first mode, the Archimedean spiral is displayed clockwise for the user on the device screen. The patient is instructed to follow the spiral using his/her finger. When the finger is released and the idle time reached is 3 s, or the finger is released 3 times, the patient switches to the second mode. In mode 2, the patient is given 10 s to look at the Archimedean spiral directed counter-clockwise. After that, the screen of the mobile device is redrawn, so that the patient can try to reproduce the spiral with his/her finger. As far as data acquisition in T4 mode is concerned, these functions are extracted in 2D vector form of real numbers:

SPIRAL_TOUCH_X_Y - x, y coordinates of generated spiral touch points clockwise (1st mode).

SPIRAL_FINGERTOUCH_X_Y - x, y coordinates of the screen location of the device with a touch screen user (patient) (1st mode).

Fig. 2. Illustration of the principle of operation of the test mode T4: reference touch pixel pressure map Archimedes spiral clockwise (top left, drawn precisely following with a finger), counter-clockwise (top right), drawn by a healthy object (bottom left), drawn by a patient (bottom right)

SPIRAL_DRAW_X_Y - x, y coordinates of generated spiral points counterclockwise for drawing (2nd mode).

SPIRAL_FINGERDRAW_X_Y - x, y coordinates of the screen position of the user's device (patient) with a finger (2nd mode).

In order for the T4 functions to correspond to the proposed classification model of this article, a Procrustean analysis is performed, as was suggested in [38]. Such a method in this context takes two input parameters twice (SPIRAL_TOUCH_X_Y, SPIRAL_FINGERTOUCH_X_Y and SPIRAL_DRAW_X_Y, SPIRAL_FINGERDRAW_X_Y) to calculate the distance metric p between two object shapes (generated spiral points and finger touch coordinates [0;) in the interval 1]. A larger p-value (closer to 1) indicates longer distances, and, a worse outcome for a high risk patient to solve a problem. Fig. 2 shows how the T4 (Archimedean spiral) works.

Finally, using this top data we can start calculating tremor, hypothesized as movement disorder characterized by a fast tremor (13–18 Hz) in the lower extremities during stance, showing instability or gait problems expressed as tremor oscillation units (see Fig. 3).

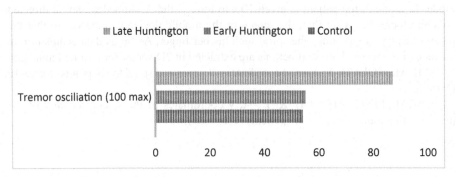

Fig. 3. Tremor oscillation units (TOU)

2.4   Multi-class SVM Model

SVM is a supervised learning algorithm, so an important aspect is class-labelling procedure according to total functional capacity (TFC) measurement system in interval [0; 13] from collected dataset of *T1, T2, T3, T4* modes. Larger *TFC* indicates that a person is more capable to do more activities that are motoric. The *TFC* value is provided by a medical neurologist expert as ground truth evaluation of the patient state: Δ, τ features are considered when analyzing *T1, T2, T3* data, whereas Procrustes distance *p* feature is an evaluation metric of *T4* mode.

SVM is based on statistical learning theory for real-world pattern recognition problems e.g. hand-written character recognition, image classification, and bioinformatics [39]. SVM separates the set of training vectors belonging to two separate classes [40]. So given training vectors $x_i \in R^n$, $i = 1,...,l$ in two classes of vector $y \in R^l$ such that, $y \in \{-1, 1\}$ SVM solves the problem (2):

$$min_{w,b,\theta} \frac{1}{2} w^T w + C \sum_{i=1}^{l} \theta_i \tag{2}$$

$$\text{If } y_i \left(w^T \varphi(x_i) + b \right) \geq 1 - \theta_i, \; where \; \theta_i \geq 0, i = 1, \ldots, l$$

In (2) $\varphi(x_i)$ maps x_i into a higher-dimensional and $C > 0$ is the regularization (penalty) parameter. The set of vectors is said to be optimally separated by the hyperplane if it is separated without error and the distance between the closest vector to the hyperplane is maximal [37]. Because of the high dimensionality of the vector w, the dual problem is solved (3):

$$min_\alpha \frac{1}{2}\alpha^T Q\alpha - e^T\alpha \tag{3}$$

If $y^T\alpha = 0$, $where\ 0 \le \alpha_i \le C, i = 1, \ldots, l$

In (3) $e = [1, \ldots, 1]^T$ is the vector of all ones, Q is an l-by-l matrix $Q_{ij} \equiv y_i y_j K(x_i, x_j)$ and $K(x_i, x_j) \equiv \varphi(x_i)^T \varphi(x_j)$ is the kernel function.

The kernel function allows to perform operations in the input space rather than in the high dimensional feature space [40]. The most commonly used kernel functions are linear (4), polynomial (5), radial basis function (RBF) (6), Multi-layer Perceptron (MLP) (7) etc. γ, r and d are kernel parameters.

$$K(x_i, x_j) = x_i^T x_j \tag{4}$$

$$K(x_i, x_j) = (\gamma x_i^T x_j + r)^d, \gamma > 0 \tag{5}$$

$$K(x_i, x_j) = e^{-\gamma \|x_i - x_j\|^2} \tag{6}$$

$$K(x_i, x_j) = tanh\,(\gamma x_i^T x_j + r) \tag{7}$$

As for SVM multiclass setting, common decomposition approaches are one-versus-rest (OVR), one-versus-one (OVO), one-by-one (OBO) [38]. The SVM-OVR strategy constructs k SVM models where k is the number of classes. The mth SVM is trained with all of the examples in the mth class with positive labels, and all other examples with negative labels [41]. Thus given l training data examples $(x_1 y_1), \ldots, (x_l y_l)$ where $x_i \in R^n, i = 1, \ldots, l$, and $y_i \in \{1, \ldots, k\}$ is class of x_i, the mth SVM solves the following problem (8):

$$min_{w^m, b^m, \theta^m} \frac{1}{2}(w^m)^T w^m + C \sum_{i=1}^{l} \theta_i^m \tag{8}$$

$$(w^m)^T \varphi(x_i) + b^m \ge 1 - \theta_i^m, if y_i = m$$

$$(w^m)^T \varphi(x_i) + b^m \le -1 + \theta_i^m, if y_i \ne m$$

$$\theta_i^m \ge 0, i = 1, \ldots, lx + y = z$$

In (8) training data x_i are mapped to a higher dimensional space by the function φ and penalty parameter C. Minimizing $\frac{1}{2}(w^m)^T w^m$ means that we would like to maximize $2/\|w^m\|$, the margin (hyperplane) between two groups of data. When data are not linear separable, there is a penalty $C \sum_{i=1}^{l} \theta_i^m$ which can reduce the number of training errors [42]. The main concept behind SVM is to search for a balance between the regularization term $\frac{1}{2}(w^m)^T w^m$ and the training errors. After solving (8) equation we obtain k decision functions: $(w^1)^T \varphi(x) + b^1 \ldots (w^k)^T \varphi(x) + b^k$. The classification result (class x) is the one, which has the largest decision function (9):

$$class\ of\ x \equiv \arg\max_{m=1,\ldots,k}((w^m)^T \varphi(x) + b^m) \tag{9}$$

3 Experimental Results

The proposed MOV-OVR model was implemented using the MATLAB software using the LIBSVM library [43]. The data collected during the study from control subjects and patients with HD are not linearly separated. For this reason, the RBF kernel was used, as it maps patterns nonlinearly into a more arrogant space, so unlike a linear kernel, RBF kernel can handle the case where the relationship between labels and class attributes is nonlinear [43]. Another reason for choosing the RBF kernel for the SVM-OVR was the fact that the number of extracted features was small, i.e. 3 (Δ, τ, p).

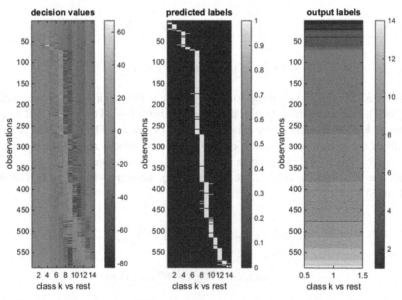

Fig. 4. Decision values, predicted lables and output labels of class k (1–14) vs other parameters

The RBF kernel has 2 parameters: for any specific task (for example, presented in this article for assessing HD) a model selection must be performed, i.e. a search for parameters. In the simplest case, the data is split into two parts, one of which is considered unknown and estimates the SVM accuracy.

In our experiment, we used an automatic procedure for N-fold cross-validation. When using N-fold cross-validation, the workout set is divided into N equal subsets. Each subset is tested using a classifier trained on the remaining N − 1 subsets (additions).

Table 1. Comparison of the results of the overall accuracy of the OVR-OVR when applying the N-fold cross-validation procedure, for different parts of training and testing datasets

No.	Dataset size (%)	Number of data samples	N	Training accuracy (%)	Testing accuracy (%)	Overall accuracy (%)
1	100.00	3200	3	52.31	47.69	94.99
2	16.25	520	7	55.23	44.77	81.54
3	50.00	1600	3	63.22	36.78	94.80
4	75.00	2400	5	88.10	11.90	92.64
5	100.00	3200	3	76.40	23.60	97.09

The cross-validation accuracy is the percentage of data that is correctly classified. Such cross-validation can prevent overfitting, that is, a situation where the OVR-OVR cannot classify new (unknown) data samples.

Table 1 shows a comparison (5 test cases) of the obtained results of the classification of the MOV-OVR. After an automatic N-fold cross-validation procedure, the parameter values are obtained with the RBF core. The highest achieved overall accuracy of the test set is 97.09% with the total number (N) = 3, the full part of the collected dataset (76.40% training, 23.60% testing).

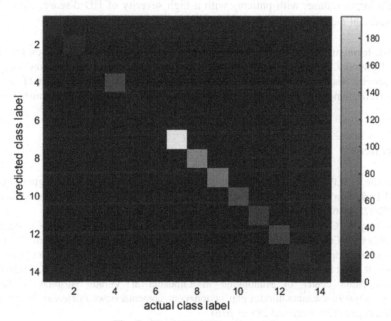

Fig. 5. The SVR-OVR error matrix

Figure 4 shows class against other parameters. Figure 5 illustrates an error matrix that represents the classification results for patients participating in the experiments, and a general calculation of the accuracy of the MOV-OVR.

4 Conclusion

We have developed a new approach for assessing the state of impairment in patients with early stage Huntington's disease (HD). The proposed structure consists of 2 components: a mobile application for collecting tracks used to detect tremors using four tasks (T1 - Sequential touch, T2 - Rainbow Color Touch, T3 - Multitouch, T4 - Archimedean Spiral) and MOV-OVR multi-class classification. The introduced aspects of novelty: firstly, such a dataset has not been created before or has not been found in existing machine learning repositories (for example, UCI or Kaggle), and secondly, any research related to patients with HD is innovative.

The MOV-OVR model was validated using a dataset of 3200 records collected from 10 controlled subjects and 10 patients with HD. The highest overall accuracy of the MOV-OVR obtained was 97.09% using the RBF core. Three-fold cross-validation showed that a larger portion of the dataset provides a better classification result for a small number (3) of features.

Future work will include additional cognitive extraction (SAGE (Study on Global AGEing and Adult Health) methodology for thinking and memory assessment), collecting a larger dataset with patients with a high severity of HD disease, using other computational methods.

Acknowledgement. We acknowledge the helpful and kind support from Prof. Andrew Lawrinson (Valley University Silica Real Time Generated Research Center). We also acknowledge Prof. Piotr Ivanovich Sosnin (Ulyanovsk State University) for his visionary comments, and Prof. Alex. Iwanow (Bulgarian-Silesian Joint Academy of Sciences) for innovative Pareto optimization idea.

References

1. Nguyen, H.H.P., Angela Cenci, M. (eds.): Behavioral Neurobiology of Huntington's Disease and Parkinson's Disease. CTBN, vol. 22. Springer, Heidelberg (2015). https://doi.org/10.1007/978-3-662-46344-4
2. Cambray, S., Cattaneo, E.: Huntington's disease: how could stem cells help? EuroStemCell project from European Union's Horizon 2020 research and innovation program. Stem Cells fact sheets. https://www.eurostemcell.org/stem-cell-factsheets. Accessed 28 Oct 2020
3. Roos, R.A.C.: Huntington's disease: a clinical review. Orphanet J. Rare Dis. **5**, 40 (2010)
4. Coordination center of Huntington in Lithuania at Vilnius Hospital of Santara clinic. https://www.santa.lt/index.php?option=com_content&view=article&id=2041&catid=178&Itemid=129. Accessed 28 Oct 2020
5. Jones, C., et al.: The societal cost of Huntington's disease: are we underestimating the burden? Eur. J. Neurol. **23**, 1588–1590 (2016)
6. Wiecki, T.V., et al.: A computational cognitive biomarker for early-stage Huntington's disease. PLoS ONE **11**(2), e0148409 (2016)

7. Barnat, M., et al.: Huntington's disease alters human neurodevelopment. Science **369**(6505), 787–793 (2020)
8. DiFiglia, M.: An early start to huntington's disease. Science **369**(6505), 771–772 (2020)
9. Engin, M., et al.: The classification of human tremor signals using artificial neural network. Expert Syst. Appl. **33**(3), 754–761 (2007)
10. Bourouis, A., Feham, M., Hossain, M.A., Zhang, L.: An intelligent mobile based decision support system for retinal disease diagnosis. Decis. Support Syst. **59**, 341–350 (2014)
11. Papaioannou, V., Economou, G.P.K., Tsakalidis, A.: A robust smart device app assisting medical diagnosis. Artif. Intell. Res. **5**(2), 82 (2016)
12. Wu, D., et al.: Prediction of Parkinson's disease tremor onset using a radial basis function neural network based on particle swarm optimization. Int. J. Neural Syst. **20**(02), 109–116 (2010)
13. Połap, D., Woźniak, M., Damaševičius, R., Maskeliūnas, R.: Bio-inspired voice evaluation mechanism. Appl. Soft Comput. J. **80**, 342–357 (2019)
14. Almeida, J.S., et al.: Detecting Parkinson's disease with sustained phonation and speech signals using machine learning techniques. Pattern Recogn. Lett. **125**, 55–62 (2019)
15. Azad, C., Jain, S., Jha, V.K.: Design and analysis of data mining based prediction model for Parkinsons disease. Issues **1**(1), 181–189 (2014)
16. Jutel, A., Lupton, D.: Digitizing diagnosis: a review of mobile applications in the diagnostic process. Diagnosis **2**(2), 89–96 (2015)
17. Kailas, A., Chong, C.C., Watanabe, F.: From mobile phones to personal wellness dashboards. IEEE Pulse **1**(1), 57–63 (2010)
18. Manini, A., Trojaniello, D., Cereatti, A., Sabatini, A.M.: A machine learning framework for gait classification using inertial sensors: application to elderly, post-stroke and Huntington's disease patients. Sensors **16**, 134 (2016)
19. Bennasar, M., et al.: Huntington's disease assessment using tri axis accelerometers. Procedia Comput. Sci. **96**, 1193–1201 (2016)
20. Rajeswari, N., Chandrakala, S.: Generative model-driven feature learning for dysarthric speech recognition. Biocybernetics Biomed. Eng. **36**(4), 553–561 (2016)
21. Martins, M., Santos, C., Costa, L., Frizera, A.: Feature reduction and multi-classification of different assistive devices according to the gait pattern. Disabil. Rehabil. Assistive Technol. **11**(3), 202–218 (2016)
22. Anguita, D., Ghio, A., Oneto, L., Parra, X., Reyes-Ortiz, J.L.: Human activity recognition on smartphones using a multiclass hardware-friendly support vector machine. In: Bravo, J., Hervás, R., Rodríguez, M. (eds.) IWAAL 2012. LNCS, vol. 7657, pp. 216–223. Springer, Heidelberg (2012). https://doi.org/10.1007/978-3-642-35395-6_30
23. Shoulson, I., Fahn, S.: Huntington disease: clinical care and evaluation. Neurology **29**, 1–3 (1979)
24. Gelšvartas, J., Simutis, R., Maskeliūnas, R.: User adaptive text predictor for mentally disabled Huntington's patients. Comput. Intell. Neurosci. **2016**, 1–6 (2016)
25. Gelšvartas, J., Lauraitis, A., Maskeliūnas, R., Simutis, R.: Review of assistive technologies for disabled people. In: Proceedings of International Conference Biomedical Engineering, pp. 142–146 (2016)
26. Lauraitis, A., Maskeliūnas, R.: Investigation of predicting functional capacity level for huntington disease patients. In: Damaševičius, R., Mikašytė, V. (eds.) ICIST 2017. CCIS, vol. 756, pp. 142–149. Springer, Cham (2017). https://doi.org/10.1007/978-3-319-67642-5_12
27. Lauraitis, A., Maskeliūnas, R., Damaševičius, R.: ANN and fuzzy logic based model to evaluate huntington disease symptoms. J. Healthc. Eng. **2018**, 4581272 (2018)
28. Lauraitis, A., Maskeliunas, R., Damasevicius, R., Polap, D., Wozniak, M.: A smartphone application for automated decision support in cognitive task based evaluation of central nervous system motor disorders. IEEE J. Biomed. Health Inf. **23**(5), 1865–1876 (2019)

29. Lauraitis, A., Maskeliunas, R., Damaševičius, R., Krilavičius, T.: Detection of speech impairments using cepstrum, auditory spectrogram and wavelet time scattering domain features. IEEE Access **8**, 96162–96172 (2020)
30. Lauraitis, A., Maskeliūnas, R., Damaševičius, R., Krilavičius, T.: A mobile application for smart computer-aided self-administered testing of cognition, speech, and motor impairment. Sensors **20**(11), 3236 (2020)
31. Da Silva, F.N., et al.: More than just tapping: index finger-tapping measures procedural learning in schizophrenia. Schizophr. Res. **137**(1–3), 234–240 (2012)
32. Barut, Ç., Kızıltan, E., Gelir, E., Köktürk, F.: Advanced analysis of finger-tapping performance: a preliminary study. Balkan Med. J. **30**(2), 167 (2013)
33. Zhang, L., et al.: A study of tapping by the unaffected finger of patients presenting with central and peripheral nerve damage. Front. Hum. Neurosci. **9**, 260 (2015)
34. Zham, P., Kumar, D.K., Dabnichki, P., Arjunan, S.P., Raghav, S.: Distinguishing different stages of Parkinson's disease using composite index of speed and pen-pressure of sketching a spiral. Front. Neurol. **8**, 435 (2017)
35. Zham, P., Arjunan, S.P., Raghav, S., Kumar, D.K.: Efficacy of guided spiral drawing in the classification of Parkinson's disease. IEEE J. Biomed. Health Inf. **22**(5), 1648–1652 (2017)
36. Memedi, M., et al.: Automatic spiral analysis for objective assessment of motor symptoms in Parkinson's Disease. Sensors **15**(9), 23727–23744 (2015)
37. Sadikov, A., et al.: Parkinson check smart phone app. In: Frontiers in Artificial Intelligence and Applications, pp. 1213–1214 (2014)
38. Kendall, D.G.: A survey of the statistical theory of shape. Stat. Sci. **4**(2), 87–99 (1989)
39. Qin Y., Li, D., Zhang, A.: A new SVM multiclass incremental learning algorithm. Math. Probl. Eng. **2015**, Article ID 745815 (2015)
40. Gunn, S.R.: Support vector machines for classification and regression. Technical report, University of Southampton (1998)
41. Xu, J.: An extended one-versus-rest support vector machine for multi-label classification. Neurocomputing **74**(17), 3114–3124 (2011)
42. Sun, Z., Guo, Z., Wang, X., Liu, J., Liu, S.: Fast extended one-versus-rest multi-label SVM classification algorithm based on approximate extreme points. In: Candan, S., Chen, L., Pedersen, T.B., Chang, L., Hua, W. (eds.) DASFAA 2017. LNCS, vol. 10177, pp. 265–278. Springer, Cham (2017). https://doi.org/10.1007/978-3-319-55753-3_17
43. Chang, C.-C., Lin, C.-J.: LIBSVM: a library for support vector machines. ACM Trans. Intell. Syst. Technol. **2**, 27 (2011)

Application of Big Data Analytics for Improving Learning Process in Technical Vocational Education and Training

Aliyu Mustapha[1]([✉]), Abdullahi Kutiriko Abubakar[2], Haruna Dokoro Ahmed[3], and Abdulkadir Mohammed[1]

[1] Industrial and Technology Education Department, Federal University of Technology Minna, Minna, Nigeria
al.mustapha@futminna.edu.ng
[2] Department of Informatics, Kings College London, London, UK
[3] Department of Computer Science, Gombe State Polytechnic Bajoga, Gombe, Nigeria

Abstract. The study identifies the application of big data analytics for improving learning process in Technical Vocational Educational and Training (TVET) in Nigeria. Two research questions were answered. The descriptive survey design was employed and the target population was made up of experts in TVET. A structured questionnaire titled "Big Data Analytics in Technical Vocational Education and Training" (BDATVET) is the tool used for data compilation. BDATVET was subjected to face and content validation by three experts, two in TVET and one in Education Technology. Cronbach Alpha was used to determine the reliability coefficient of the questionnaire and it was found to be 0.81. The data collected from the respondents were analyzed using mean and standard deviation. The findings on the problems of big data include among others security, availability and stability of internet network service. The Findings related to the prospects include among others, allows a teacher measuring, monitoring, and responding, in real-time to a student's understanding of the material. Based on the findings, it was recommended among others that the stakeholders in TVET need to uphold the fundamental security of their data and who may access information about their competencies.

Keywords: Big Data Analytics · Technical Vocational Education and Training · Problems and Prospects

1 Introduction

Technical Vocational Education and Training (TVET) is a field which persistently needs to be assessed to track the swift rate of development in the labour force. An essential component that has fundamentally changed the way TVET education is carried out is technology; such technologies include, among others, mobile gadgets (smartphones), remote access systems and teleconference [1]. These technologies are used in teaching and learning processes, however, in addition to practically echoing in the learning

S. Misra and B. Muhammad-Bello (Eds.): ICTA 2020, CCIS 1350, pp. 15–25, 2021.
https://doi.org/10.1007/978-3-030-69143-1_2

process in real setting generate an enormous amount of new data that are devastated as conventional learning methods are not capable of processing them. The interaction with these technologies produces large amounts of data that vary from an individual access log file to an institutional level activity [2]. Nevertheless, the educational systems are not hitherto completely geared up to muddle through with and take advantage of them for constant improvement use. Consequently, this call for the need to manage this problem within TVET and research into the latest applications of Big Data analytics for improving the learning process in TVET.

Big data refers to the large amount of data produced from the learning process of students [3]. The use of big data in teaching and learning process primarily is to apply, study forecast analysis, behaviour analysis and academic analysis of the learners' educational activities and the data can suggest for the instruction of schools teachers to have an apt and precise appraisal of the educational standing of learners and uncover prospective problems for students. The sources of the data produced are either in explicit or implicit behaviour [4]. The explicit behaviour is directly assessed as learning activities while the implicit behaviour is not, for instance, the implicit behaviour is the extracurricular activities, forum posting and online social activities. These behaviours are based on the learners and instructors adaptive learning system. From the perception of the learners, after understanding the standing point of the learner, the data generated and analyzed help to determine the pertinent problems and improves the learning process of the students to reach the idea of independent learning. From the viewpoint of instructors, the data generated and analyzed helps to review teaching curricula and develop methods for instructors to facilitate solving practical problems by the learner's [5]. These behaviours are based on the learners and instructors adaptive learning system.

Today, big data is the much-needed transformation driving force in the education sector particularly TVET because of its availability guarantee achievement for TVET students, staff and other related institutions. Conversely, higher institutions are working in a progressively more intricate and competitive setting. They are, however, in rising demands to retort to the international and national transformation such as the evolving need to amplify the ratio of learners in TVET, setting in employability and occupational attributes to the learners and making sure that the standard of TVET programmes stands the taste of time [6]. To triumph over from this grave state of affairs and to improve the learning process, TVET and related institutions are fitting on the rising skills in taking the right decision according to the situation. As a result, academicians are at the present barely seeking to apply the big data analytics in discovering the potency and flaw of both the learners and schools and to compare with other schools. The paper was enthused to improve learning process taking into cognizance the problems and prospects for its application in TVET.

In education, the instructive decision made by teachers is to improve the learning process. The usage of learning management systems in education has been growing in the last few years, today, TVET students are on track using smart mobile phones to access online learning materials [7]. These learning materials generate a gigantic number of unused data that are shattered as conventional learning methods are not capable of processing them [8]. This has resulted in the penetration of Big Data analytics into education to process a large amount of data involved to measure the understanding, personalize the learning experience and facilitate to design new interesting courses [9]. It is against this background that this study looks into the recent applications of Big Data analytics for improving the learning process: Problems and Prospects for its application in TVET.

The study focused on big data analytics for improving the learning process: problems and prospects for its application in Technical Vocational Education and Training (TVET) in Nigeria. Specifically, the study determines the:

1. Problems of big data analytics for improving the learning process in Technical Vocational Education and Training (TVET).
2. Prospects of big data analytics for improving the learning process in Technical Vocational Education and Training (TVET).

2 Literature Review

2.1 Conceptual Framework

The conceptual framework for this study is the accomplished connection between the concepts and how each turns to one another in developing and validating e-content for teaching and learning of automobile lighting system. Hence, the conceptual framework of this study which shows the major variables of the study is schematically illustrated in Fig. 1.

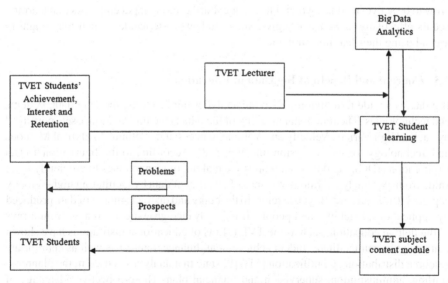

Fig. 1. Schematic illustration identifying the applications of Big Data analytics for improving the learning process: Problems and Prospects for its application in TVET.

The above figure shows the connection between the variables of this study. The diagram is defined to determine the applications of Big Data analytics for improving the learning process in TVET. The illustration is included into a school setting on TVET students through the guidance of the TVET lecturer. The entire course of action is documented to obtain response and be evidence for on what emerges in the structure; spotting what out the requirements to be improved, amending the chart on the inference obtained and going over the development in anticipation of a satisfactory end result is attained via big data analytics.

2.2 Social Constructivist Theory

The Social Constructivist Theory of development and learning was propounded by Lev Vygotsky (1896–1934). The theory holds up the belief that an individual devotedly search for knowledge. It expounds an individual cognitive development, proffers direction on how and what to teach and as well confer methods on the means to manage learning conditions. The theory can be used as a channel to efficiently work with learners to build their understanding on what they are acquainted with and their experience because learners study best through activities and experiences that was instigated by them.

The central part of this theory is that students must autonomously verify and modify multifaceted data to make it their own by sensing through the most recent solutions to problems along with the older ones and perking up on the outdated ones. This paper has philosophical propositions for education since it promotes a lively place for TVET students to be taught autonomously.

This theory gives a deep-seated basis on which big data analytics is anchored in TVET. The theory outlines the unambiguous function of building TVET students to grow to be active in building their knowledge. Furthermore, it put emphasis that learning occurs effectively if the teacher gives their students a stepladder which they ought to ascend using their learning strategies.

2.3 Concept and Benefit of Big Data in Education

Big data is a wide term that refers to the analytics applications, sheering data, systems and technologies. The functional meaning of big data is the Information assets portrayed by such a High Variety, Velocity and Volume to necessitate definite Analytical Methods and Technology for its conversion into Value [8]. According to the International Data Corporation (IDC), big data is an innovative making of technologies to efficiently mine value from extremely enormous volumes of an array of data by facilitating high-velocity capture [10]. Therefore, Big Data refers to the bulky and distinct amount of data produced by applications, machines and people. It is in advance growing awareness from arrays of the field in education, such as the TVET. Lots of educational institutions have shown that analytics can facilitate student achievement, finance, interest as well as appropriate resource distribution and utilization [11]. [9] state that analytics is used in the planning, staffing, administration, supervision and financial plan. The prospective advantage of analytics in education is to estimate the expenditure to complete a programme (such as diploma and degree); school undertakings that have not been recognized as well as resource optimization. Numerous online portals like Coursera have leveraged analytics to grow and optimize their dealings [11]. On the other hand, through tracking the amount exhausted on teaching resources make possible for the teachers to assess the improvement report of the individual learner and besides assist to personalize learning conditions as per the want of the learners.

[11] highlight some of the benefit of Big Data in the educational sector is to make certain the worth and suppleness of education, it also assists parents and learners to discover the preeminent educational program, transparent education financing and matching student and employment. It also helps students put together learning models and in due course oblige the students to learn hands-on.

2.4 Big Data Analytics Techniques in Education

The utilization of technology in education has trail such a swift tempo. If the development of the general public has been noticeable, over the precedent few decades, has turn out to be an deficient growth in the use of a enormous technological tool for managing different responsibilities in the school such as assignment. Owing to the expansion in Information and Communication Technology (ICT), it permits the expansion in enormous data processing activities in education. The expansion of ICT conveys the increase of lots of schools caught up in the current big data analysis from the learners' dealings leading to the development of working condition and environment.

Big Data Analytics is the way of developing actionable insights through problem characterization and the use of statistical models and investigation alongside virtual upcoming and/or existing data. When taking into account analytics in the field of education, it is helpful to reflect on how these techniques are applied in the framework of the institution [9]. Furthermore, other common techniques of analytics in the field of education are learning and academic analytics [10]. The former, include the evolving research field of learning analytics to investigate individual student performance. Learning analytics build applications that sway educational activities to analyze the data collected during teaching and learning. Learning analytics is further divided into macro, meso and micro level [11]. The macro-level analytics enable data sharing across institutions for a range of purposes including benchmarking. Meso level analytics work at the level of individual institutions and include analytics based on business intelligence approaches and the micro-level analytics support the tracking and interpretation of process-level data for individual learners. The latter presents the general information about what is the experience in a specific programme and how to address performance challenges. Academic analytics aims to assist the curriculum planners to measure, collect, interpret, report and effectively share data so that activities related to student strong points and limitations can be known and aptly rectified [12]. Therefore, in education, academic analytics reveal the function of data analysis at an institutional level, whereas learning analytics centres on the learning process.

2.5 Big Data Analytics in the Context of TVET Education

Big data analytics is the system of gathering, managing and analyzing large data sets to blueprint and other valuable information. Its application helps educational institution where TVET education takes place to better comprehend the information contained in the data and to categorize the data that is most vital to the business and future decisions in TVET and related field. Regarding TVET education, Big data predicts the understanding of a spacious operational and managerial data, bringing together measures designed at evaluating institutional steps forward to envisage potential performance and issues associated to research, educational improvement, teaching and learning techniques [10]. In addition to this, Big Data Analytics could be useful to check for student admission on a course evaluation, dialogue board and blog entries or wiki activity, which could spawn thousands of student activities per lessons [11]. These data are collected in its original form as it is conducted and then analyzed to advocate courses of action.

2.6 Summary of Literature Review

The review of literature has revealed that researches have been carried out on big data analytics instructional strategy and some other teaching strategies for improving students' thoughts and analytical skills that are vital in the 21st-century. Though, no study is identified to the researchers on the applications of Big Data analytics for improving the learning process in TVET.

Thus, this study hence intend to fill this gap by identifying the recent applications of Big Data analytics for improving the learning process: Problems and Prospects for its application in TVET which is based on philosophy that will facilitate the learning process and allow the learners to triumph over the intricacy of understanding the contents in TVET. This will smooth the progress of invention of quality learning process.

3 Methodology

The descriptive survey design was used for the study. A structured questionnaire titled "Big Data Analytics in Technical Vocational Education and Training" (BDATVET) is the tool used for data compilation. Simple Random Sampling (SRS) was employed in the selection of the sample for the study. The population of the study comprises of 180 TVET and educational technology lecturers. Using the Krecie and Morgan table [13], the sample size of the study was made up of 123 respondents. This method was used to give every respondent in the population equal chance of being selected into the sample. In other to note the suitability of BDATVET items before administering it to respondents, three experts, two in TVET and one in educational technology validated it. Their suggestions were used to develop the final copy of BDATVET. Cronbach alpha Statistics was selected to establish the reliability of BDATVET. Number Cruncher Statistical System (NCSS) version 11 was used to work out the reliability coefficient and the result was found to be 0.81. Thirty-seven (37) validated items are used for the study. BDATVET was prepared for TVET and Educational Technology Lecturers in Niger State College of Education Minna and the Federal University of Technology Minna. Out of the 123 copies of BDATVET administered, 117 copies were duly completed. A real limit of number was used to determine the level of acceptance or rejection with numerical values as follows: Strongly Agreed (SA) - 3.50–4.00; Agreed (A) - 2.50–3.49; Disagreed (D) - 1.50–2.49; Strongly Disagreed (SD) - 1.00–1.49. The data collected from the respondents were analyzed using mean and standard deviation.

4   Results and Discussion

4.1   Research Question 1

What are the problems of big data analytics for improving the learning process in Technical Vocational Education and Training (TVET)?

Table 1. Mean responses of the respondents on the problems of big data analytics for improving the learning process in Technical Vocational Education and Training (TVET)

								N = 117
S/N	Items	SA (4)	A (3)	D (2)	SD (1)	$\overline{X}$	SD	Decision
1	Data management	38	74	3	2	3.26	0.34	A
2	Data storage	82	30	5	0	4.12	0.37	SA
3	Data privacy	96	19	1	1	3.79	0.45	SA
4	Data collection	17	63	24	13	2.72	0.22	A
5	Converting Ideas into a model	33	43	31	10	2.85	0.13	A
6	Data protection	93	24	0	0	3.79	0.43	SA
7	Capability to maintain learning analytics system	43	57	15	2	3.21	0.25	A
8	Error correction in analytics	49	62	6	0	3.37	0.30	A
9	Lack of expertise to prepare TVET lecturers to leverage on opportunities afforded by big data	38	41	26	7	2.85	0.15	A
	$\overline{X}$a					3.33	0.29	A

Keys: SA = Strongly Agree. A = Agree, D = Disagree, SD = Strongly Disagree, N = Number of respondents, $\overline{X}$ = Mean Value, SD = Standard Deviation, $\overline{X}$a = Grand Average value.

The analysis of mean responses of the two groups of respondents from Table 1 reveals that items 2, 3 and 6 under this sub-heading are rated as strongly agreed (SA); items 1, 4, 5, 7, 8 and 9 under this sub-heading are rated as agreed (A); none of the items is rated as disagreed (D) and Strongly Disagreed (SD). Since the SD value (0.29) in a statistical data set is close to the mean (3.33) of the data set, this gives the impetus to conclude that the respondents agreed on the problems of big data analytics for improving learning process in Technical Vocational Education and Training (TVET).

4.2   Research Question 2

What are the prospects of big data analytics for improving the learning process in Technical Vocational Education and Training (TVET)?

The analysis of mean responses of the two groups of respondents from Table 2 reveals that the items 1 and 5 under this sub-heading are rated as Strongly Agreed (SA); items

Table 2: Mean responses of the respondents on the prospects of big data analytics for improving the learning process in Technical Vocational Education and Training (TVET)

						N = 117		
S/N	Items	SA (4)	A (3)	D (2)	SD (1)	$\overline{X}$	SD	Decision
1	Allow the teacher to measure the student's understanding of the material	98	11	8	0	3.77	0.46	SA
2	Allow the teacher to monitor in real-time to the student's understanding of the material	63	41	10	3	3.40	0.27	A
3	Allow the teacher to respond in real-time to the student understanding of the lesson	16	11	0	0	3.14	0.48	A
4	Build a learner knowledge model	48	56	7	6	3.25	0.26	A
5	Build a learner experience model	83	34	0	0	3.71	0.39	SA
6	Establish a learner behaviour model	38	41	25	13	3.06	0.12	A
7	Construct a domain knowledge model	41	70	5	1	3.29	0.32	A
8	Provide learners with personalized learning	38	79	0	0	3.32	0.37	A
9	Predict trends and outcomes for future learning	36	55	15	11	2.99	0.20	A
10	Provide learners with an adaptive learning environment	28	62	20	7	2.95	0.23	A
	$\overline{X}$a					3.29	0.31	A

2, 3, 4, 6, 7, 8, 9, and 10 under this sub-heading are rated as agreed (A) and none of the items is rated as Disagreed (D) or Strongly Agreed (SD). Since the SD value (0.31) in a statistical data set is close to the mean (3.29) of the data set, this gives the impetus to conclude that the respondents agreed on the prospects of big data analytics for improving learning process in Technical Vocational Education and Training (TVET).

4.3 Discussion of Findings

The findings on the problems of big data analytics for improving the learning process in Technical Vocational Education and Training (TVET) is data collection. This finding corresponds to [14] that collecting data for analysis is been a major problem for the execution of educational analytics. More to the point, poor quality and incorrectly formatted data and information from rarely accessible database system can cause significant problems. The study also revealed that data privacy is one of the problems of big data analytics for improving the learning process in Technical Vocational Education and Training (TVET). This result concurs with [15] that data needs to be protected from illegal access. The study discovered that lack of expertise and academic development opportunities to prepare educational researchers to leverage opportunities afforded by Big Data. This result coincides with [16] that it would be difficult for the students and teachers to represent their ideas in form of information in an accessible and informative way to the system and hence would be inflexible to cooperate with the system.

The findings on the prospects of big data analytics for improving the learning process in Technical Vocational Education and Training (TVET) revealed that big data establish a learner behaviour model. This result corresponds to [17] that learning behaviour model of learners is formed by building a big data learning platform to predict learners' failure in learning with a prediction precision of over 75%. Furthermore, the result also revealed that big data help in teaching strategy analysis. This agrees with [9] that the ultimate goal of using big data in education is to help educators formulate teaching strategies and analyze the collected information of learners to explore the functions of various components of the learning system and to analyze learner learning outcomes and teaching strategies. Addendum, [18] also corroborated that the prospects of big data are to analyze and summarize the teaching strategies to provide more effective teaching strategies in the field of education.

The finding also revealed that big data build learner experience model by collecting questionnaires of students' achievement to the data of retention, performance, behaviour. The use of big data in education also includes individualized learning, adaptive learning system and trend analysis. The individualized and adaptive learning systems are the ultimate goals of big data application [19]. The study also revealed that the collection, analysis and processing of big data provide TVET students with individualized and adaptive learning environment; the analysis of big data explore the student's learning trends to discover the correlation between secondary and post-secondary results for future learning,

The study also revealed that big data analytics predict the trends and outcomes for future learning. This concurs with [20] that big data investigate the student's educational trends by showing the link connecting preschool behavior and future results. [21] also corroborated that big data helps to produced through student learning to evaluate educational development, forecast upcoming performance and spot latent problems during teaching and learning. The result also revealed that big data build a learner experience model. This concise with [22, 23] and [24] that by retrieving opinion poll of students' interest with learning, big data helps in analyzing and enhancing the students' educational performance and philosophy of the teacher efficiency. The study also revealed that the critical target of using big data in education is to help teachers devise teaching techniques and evaluate the gathered data of students to discover the purpose of different systems of and to study the instructor teaching strategies and students learning results to make available more efficient teaching methodologies in the field of education [25].

5 Conclusion

There is no doubt in the fact that analytics bring massive improvement in the quality of education. This paper showcases the application of big data analytics in TVET, different sources, kinds and nature of data that are present in the TVET have been identified. In conclusion, with the help of such contemporary technology like big data analytics, the TVET education system will be enhanced with new strategies that will make learning of TVET courses more proficient and targeted.

6 Recommendations

1. The stakeholders in TVET need to uphold the fundamental security of their data and who may access information about their competencies.
2. TVET institutions and students must be conscious of data security and maintenance. So that they can work with it efficiently in support of the course organization.

References

1. Mustapha, A., Ahmed, H.D., Abubakar, A.K., Abdulkadir, M., Idris, A.M., Raji, A.E.: Problems and prospects of cloud computing to the automobile industry in Nigeria. Int. J. Inf. Process. Commun. (IJIPC) **9**(1 & 2), 87–93 (2020)
2. Turban, E., Pollard, C., Wood, G.: Information Technology for Management: On-Demand Strategies for Performance, Growth and Sustainability. Wiley, London (2018)
3. Christos, V., Vasilis, H., Nabil, Z.: Introduction to big data in education and its contribution to the quality improvement processes. In: Soto, S.V., Luna, J.M., Cano, A. (eds.) Big Data on Real-World Applications. IntechOpen (2016). https://doi.org/10.5772/63896. https://www.intechopen.com/books/big-data-on-real-world-applications/introduction-to-big-data-in-education-and-its-contribution-to-the-quality-improvement-processes. Accessed 28 Aug 2020
4. Buckwalter, W.: Implicit attitudes and the ability argument. Philos. Stud. **176**(11), 2961–2990 (2018). https://doi.org/10.1007/s11098-018-1159-7
5. Abubakar, A.K., Mustapha, A., Raji, A.E.: Development and validation of e-content in teaching and learning of automobile lighting system in technical colleges in Niger state Nigeria. I-manag. J. Educ. Technol. **15**(4), 1–8 (2019)
6. Mustapha, A.: Occupational and Employability Competencies needs of Automobile Electrical Systems' Technicians. Lambert Academic Publishing, Germany (2015)
7. Mustapha, A., Idris, A.M., Abubakar, A.K. Musa, A.E.: Competencies needed by automobile technology teachers towards the development of ICT for teaching-learning purposes. In: Salami, H.O., et al. (eds.) on Proceedings of the International Conference on Information and Communication Technology (ICTA), pp. 11–16. School of Information and Communication Technology, Federal University of Technology Minna, Nigeria (2016)
8. Mustapha, A., Oguoguo, U.C., Ujevbe, O.B., Mohammed, B.A.: Effects of social media on students' achievement in learning automobile lighting system in technical colleges in Niger State. In: Oladimeji, O.F., Bolaji, H.O. (eds.) on Conference proceedings of the AITIE 3rd International Conference and Workshop on Innovation, technology and Education (ICWITE, Abuja) (2019)

9. Li, Y., et al.: Big data and cloud computing. In: Guo, H., Goodchild, M.F., Annoni, A. (eds.) Manual of Digital Earth, pp. 325–355. Springer, Singapore (2020). https://doi.org/10.1007/978-981-32-9915-3_9

10. Marjani, M., et al.: Big IoT data analytics: architecture, opportunities, and open research challenges. IEEE Access 5(1), 5247–5261 (2017)

11. Darling-Hammond, L., Flook, L., Cook-Harvey, C., Barron, B., Oshe, D.: Implications for Educational Practice of the Science of Learning and Development. Wiley, San Francisco (2019)

12. Hollands, F.M., Tirthali, D.: MOOCs: expectations and reality. Full report. Center for Benefit Cost Studies of Education, Teachers College, Columbia University, NY (2014). https://cbcse.org/wordpress/wpcontent/uploads/2014/05/MOOCs_Expectations_and_Reality.pdf

13. Krejcie, R.V., Morgan, D.W.: Determining sample size for research activities. Educ. Psychol. Measur. 30(1), 607–610 (1970)

14. Olga, V., Mathias, H., Mavroudi, O.: The current landscape of learning analytics in higher education. Comput. Hum. Behav. 89(1), 98–110 (2018)

15. Jivet, I., Scheffel, M., Specht, M., Drachsler, H.: License to evaluate: preparing learning analytics dashboards for educational practice. In: Proceedings of the 8th International Conference on Learning Analytics Knowledge, pp. 31–40. ACM (2018)

16. Andrew, W.B., Kaiser, K.A., David, B.A.: Issues with data and analyses: errors, under lying themes, and potential solutions (2018). https://www.pnas.org/content/115/11/2563/tab-art icle-info. Accessed 26 Aug 2020

17. Tobias, M.S.: Big data in organizations and the role of human resource management: a complex systems theory-based conceptualization. JSTOR Open Access Monogr. 5(1), 45–53 (2017)

18. Demetrios Sampson, J., Spector, M., Ifenthaler, D., Isaías, P., Sergis, S. (eds.): Learning Technologies for Transforming Large-Scale Teaching, Learning, and Assessment. Springer, Cham (2019). https://doi.org/10.1007/978-3-030-15130-0

19. Bill, C., Kalantzis, M.: Big data comes to school: implications for learning, assessment, and research. Sage J. 2(2), 32–40 (2016)

20. Reyes, J.A.: The skinny on big data in education: learning analytics simplified. TechTrends 59(2), 75–80 (2015). https://doi.org/10.1007/s11528-015-0842-1

21. Daniel, B.: Big data and analytics in higher education: opportunities and challenges. Br. J. Edu. Technol. 46(5), 904–920 (2015)

22. Mayer-Schönberger, V., Kenneth, C.: Learning with big data: the future of education. Houghton Mifflin Harcourt (2018)

23. Sclater, N., Peasgood, A., Mullan, J.: Learning Analytics in Higher Education. JISC, London (2016)

24. Hammad, K., Adam, I.: Big data analysis and storage. In: Proceedings of the 2015 International Conference on Operations Excellence and Service Engineering Orlando, Florida, USA (2015)

25. Anshari, M., Yabit, A., Lim, S.G.: Developing online learning resources: big data, social networks, and cloud computing to support pervasive knowledge. Educ. Inf. Technol. 21(6), 1663–1677 (2016)

A Survey for Recommender System for Groups

Ananya Misra[✉]

Technical University of Munich, Munich, Germany
ge25daj@mytum.de

Abstract. Recommendation system has been seen to be very concentrated on individual recommendations but few of the new techniques are now concentrated on groups. The aim of this paper is to provide an overview of the existing state of the art techniques for collecting ratings, strategies used in aggregating these strategies and the practical application for group recommendations. This study explored five databases which include IEEE, Science Direct, Springer, ACM and Google Scholar, from which 300 publications were screened. Irrelevant, duplicate and ambiguous papers were removed. At the end, 26 papers were used for depth analysis. This study provides a systematic review of the available evidence based literature concerning recommender systems for groups.

Keywords: Recommendation systems · Aggregation strategies · Elicitation of preferences · Practical applications

1 Introduction

There exists much research done in the individual recommendation system but there are many other situations in which group recommendation comes in handy. Instances, where a restaurant needs to be chosen for a group to dine, is one of the typical examples of a recommendation system. People have also come up with different kinds of strategies for group recommendations [10]. Some of which are commonly used and easy to understand but the best strategy for all systems is still not known, not all strategies are optimal in all cases. Different ways of explicitly or implicitly collecting information about the user is another area where a lot of work has been done [5,9]. Many issues and challenges have been seen in this area. Few of which have been taken into consideration but others are yet to be solved [11].

In Table 1, the sub-tasks and differences are given briefly. The steps that a recommendation system follows is divided into sub-tasks in the table above and difference between individual and group recommendations for every step is highlighted. During these steps, certain issues are encountered. In this paper, only the first sub-task that deal with acquiring information about the members' preferences are considered. This sub-task differs in the sense that if the recommendation system collects the information explicitly then the users may find

© Springer Nature Switzerland AG 2021
S. Misra and B. Muhammad-Bello (Eds.): ICTA 2020, CCIS 1350, pp. 26–40, 2021.
https://doi.org/10.1007/978-3-030-69143-1_3

Table 1. Subtasks of a recommender system

Subtasks	Difference from individual recommendations
Getting user preferences	Users may/may not see preferences of other group members
Generating recommendations	Generalizing recommendations from individuals to groups
Presenting recommendations	Giving a solution suitable for all group members
Giving a final decision	Decision to be made by all or almost all group members

seeing each other's preference advantageous. Users can get an idea of what to expect in the recommendations if they see other people's recommendations. It can also give them the idea of the item to be rated if the user finds a person with similar taste in the group. The issues could be how beneficial this is to the user and how the system will use this technique. Other tasks include how the system will generate recommendations and how it should be applied to the group recommendation, how the system will give out the information and how the users will come about a final decision. The goal of the paper is to give an overview on the group recommendation categories, preference of elicitation and some experiments done by previous researchers. The rest of the paper is structured as follows: Sect. 2 discusses the related works of recommendation systems. Section 3 addresses the preference of elicitation. Techniques of elicitation of preferences are presented in Sect. 4. In Sect. 5, the strategies are categorized and explained. Section 6 sheds a light on the applications of these strategies and finally, Sect. 7 concludes this work.

2 Related Works

In this section, some of the works previously done in the literature are presented. Many recommendation system exists in the vacation area. Examples of which include Travel Decision Forum and Collaborative Advisory Travel System (CATS). The former is primarily used by a group of people who are planning a vacation together. This system lets the group decide on the desired attributes for choosing a vacation package. All the individual preferences are aggregated and only explicit elicitation is likely to be possible since the user needs to give ratings about all the attributes taken into consideration [1]. The latter is another system that helps in choosing a joint holiday. According to the preference of the user regarding features and packages the system recommends holidays. Users can provide suggestions for other group members and the suggestions are checked against the preferences of group members. The more the preferences are matched the likely the item will be recommended [12].

The entertainment area also has some known systems which are PolyLens, Adaptive Radio, MusicFX, TV recommender, FIT and FlyTrap. PolyLens is an extension of MovieLens which is primarily used by a group of people who want to go to a movie together. Movies are recommended based on social filtering and individual tastes are inferred from previous ratings. People can form a group together and recommendations for that group is given by the system. The members of the group rate individual movies and not describe the movie preferences [1]. Adaptive Radio can be used by colleagues working together in an office to play songs on the radio. This system plays songs autonomously based on preferences and the members of the group. It only gets feedback when the user is dissatisfied with the performance of the radio [5]. MusicFX recommends a radio station for a group of people in a fitness center [13]. TV recommender and FIT suggests a television program to watch for a group of people [14,15]. The recommendations of TV recommender are based on the preference of users according to certain features whereas FIT assumes that the choices of people will change when they are in a group. FIT implicitly collects information regarding the watching times of the individual person and updates the member preferences accordingly. FlyTrap is also used in the music field to play tracks for the people in a public area of a building [16].

Let's Browse on the other hand was used mainly by people browsing the web together. The system takes into consideration the members of the group by suggesting new recommendation which might be of interest to the members. Let's Browse automatically detects the presence of the users, dynamically displays the user profiles and provides explanations of the recommendations [2]. IM-TAG, a web 2.0 tool offers recommendations of mentoring contents built upon personal competencies of the mentee, combined with content and opinion tagging [27]. Pocket RestaurantFinder is used mostly when colleagues plan to go together to dine in a restaurant. It helps in selecting the restaurant for the group, but for all the types of the cuisines, restaurant amenities, price categories and travel time the user needs to give a rating on a 5-point scale [3]. Group Adaptive Information and News System (GAIN) adapts the news and advertisements according to the people viewing a wall display or information kiosk. It also takes into account uncertainty about which users will be viewing the display at any given time [4]. INTRIGUE is widely used by people who are visiting a tourist place in a group or sightseeing group. The system divides the group into homogeneous subgroups with the same characteristics. Each subgroup may fit into stereotypes. The problem might be that group may visit more than one place and a balanced sequence selection has not been addressed in the research work [6]. Another recommendation system in the field of tourism was proposed by authors in [26]. The proposed recommendation system collects data from the initial visit by the means of pervasive approaches and offers relevant recommendations based on positioning and bio-inspired recommender systems.

3   Elicitation of Preference

Preference acquisition is the method of collecting information from the user. This method can be explicit or implicit. There still exist many recommender systems that use methods for acquiring information from an individual and generalize it for a group [7]. In this section, methods specifically developed for group recommendation as well as methods for individual recommendation will be discussed.

3.1 Acquisition of Preferences Without Explicit Specification

Some recommendations do not require the user to explicitly enter the information but rather collect information from other means in other words, implicit collection of information [8,9]. An instance of a system that uses this method is Let's Browse. This system is primarily used in web pages recommendation for a group. Initial candidates who might interest the user are chosen by analyzing the words available on the web page of the user. After all, the words are collected and groups are formed, then the system recommends the common words of all members that existed during the group visit.

3.2 Acquisition of Preferences with Explicit Specification

This method explicitly requires users to enter the information typically about all the features. Instances of systems include Pocket RestaurantFinder which lets the user choose the cuisine types, location, and price, Travel Decision Forum which lets the user choose destinations, facilities, and sightseeing. Users have a lot of information to fill out to get a precise recommendation. This process is usually tedious for the user and tends to provide only confined results.

3.3 Adapting Preference Specification to the Requirements of Group Recommendation

Focus on Negative Preferences. In this method, the user expresses a dislike towards a feature and the system tries to eliminate that feature for future recommendations. For instance, the system might not recommend action movies if any of the users in a group dislikes it. An instance is the Adaptive Radio [5] which recommends music to a group of people. The system avoids playing the disliked music tracks. The major difference between this system is that it elicits negative preference about music tracks than eliciting a more detailed type of ratings.

Sharing Information About Specified Preferences. People in a group may have some interest in knowing the preference of other group members so that it gives idea or suggestions to the user about him/herself. If the user knows someone that has similar preferences then he/she can use those preferences for better future recommendations. Sometimes, user can get new information from other users. These other users can be friends, family members and colleagues who have had experience in different areas or have tried something new which the user might like to try. Other users can also influence user and this usually happens because of peer group influence, relationships, etc. So, the user has a lot of options for making recommendations better by using other resources rather than relying on himself. An instance of this system is the Travel Decision Forum. This lets you see the preference of other members of the group. An additional feature suggested by [7] is to add brief verbal explanations for the ratings so the user knows whether the rating applies to him or not.

Some additional features can be added to the interfaces of the recommendation systems for improved predictions. Considering other people's preference is one of the mechanisms for group recommendations. If a user is shown other members' preference she/he might adapt accordingly to the group. For instance, if there is a person of 65 years or a kid of 5 years, the other members can adapt to their preferences thereby giving respect or importance to the kid or old-aged. A way to tackle this situation is showing the preference of the individual members to the whole group. This may give an idea about ratings to other users or adjust the ratings.

The problem also arises when the predictions are not what the group expected. In this case, it makes sense to test against the predicted preferences. Users can use yes/no mechanism to select whether the prediction is suitable for them or not. The system can then adapt to the recommendations accordingly. Explanations can also be quite helpful for recommendations. The reason why a certain item was not chosen by the user gives a sense of understanding to other users. The other users can then decide whether the option should be still considered for the group. The group may decide to have an open discussion with the members to resolve conflicts or come to a consensus.

Better recommendations can be made by better interfaces. Interfaces that contain preference of all users side by side on the screen can help the current user in many different ways. An addition of a feature regarding negotiability is also a feasible method of handling recommendations. For instance, while selecting features for a holiday vacation, the user may choose not to negotiate on certain features such as parking facilities but for other features, he/she might be open for other recommendations. The group may want to choose only certain features and may not care about others. So adding/removing a feature accordingly can come in handy. An option of choosing 2 or 3 similar users provided by the system or can be chosen by the user to generate a recommendation for one user may prove to be very useful when the user is new to the system with no preferences. It will save time and effort for the user rather when the user would enter everything manually.

4   Techniques for Elicitation of Preference

4.1   Techniques Based on Machine Learning Approaches

Author in [19] uses Regression Tree Learning (RTL) where target variable is utility of each item and the description of items are the samples. The regression tree defines a partitioning of the original outcome space by use of axis-parallel linear constraints, with each partition corresponding to a leaf node in the tree. Two problems in this approach can occur. One of which is that addition of a new item can change the predictions dramatically. This may cause cold start problems. The other is the problem of collecting information for new users. Accurate predictions can't occur until sufficient information about users is gotten. They solve this by running the RTL algorithm over all the texts and discarding any information on the user giving each rating. In this paper however, we are focusing more on the user interactions so this won't be discussed in detail.

4.2 Techniques Based on Interaction Mode

Pairs of items are drawn out from user interactions which are then used for training the ranking model.

Sub-list Ranking. In this mode, subsets of items are sorted which then forms a completely ordered list of preferences. The higher the item in the list the more that item is preferred over other items. At least two items are required in the list so that a pair is formed. This is the most common mode for recommendation systems. Sub-list ranking is depicted in Fig. 1(a).

Categorical Binning. A subset of items are grouped into high, medium and low by the user. Items within each group are not compared but items in the higher group are preferred more than ones in medium and low category. A user can put an item in two or three groups. Any number of items can be put into the groups and at least two items are required to be put into different groups for a ranking to be displayed. Categorical binning is depicted in Fig. 1(b).

Pairwise comparison In this mode, users have to group pair of items into a binary category such as high and low. Items in the high category are preferred over the ones in the low. A user has the freedom to put one item many times if that item is preferred over many other items. Pairwise comparison is depicted in Fig. 1(c).

Since this techniques is applicable for a single user, further work can be done in generalizing this to group recommendations. The interface could also be developed in a way that the user sees what the other users chose. Multiple users can be then combined using different aggregation strategies discussed in Sect. 5.

4.3 Techniques Based on Algorithm

Authors in [14] proposes an algorithm for user profile merging based on total distance minimization. Three strategies namely group agent, merging recommendations and merging user profiles are presented and analysed in brief. In group agent strategy, the members of the group login with one account and put the preferences using that account to generate a common profile. Merging recommendations lets the individual to enter the preferences and then those individual preferences are merged into one profile. Aggregation techniques mentioned in the next section will be quite helpful in this regard. Any of the strategies can be adopted to merge user profiles. The merged profile now has a list of common preference for the group. In merging user profiles, all user profiles are first

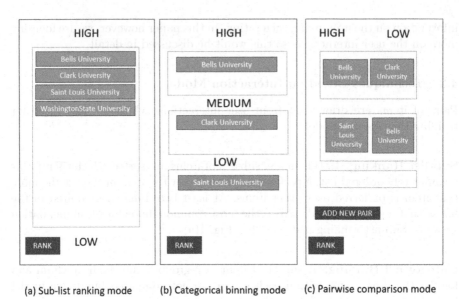

(a) Sub-list ranking mode   (b) Categorical binning mode   (c) Pairwise comparison mode

Fig. 1. Preference elicitation interfaces.

merged into a common profile and then recommendations are generated for the common user profile.

First strategy is the simplest but non-adaptive and inflexible. It doesn't work if any of the group members are missing. A new group has to be created every time excluding the missing member. The other two strategies are considered in this work. In a user profile, many features and weights indicating the significance of these features are considered. A lexicon is defined by all the features of the user profiles alphabetically. The feature list can be reduced by using a thesaurus. Each user profile is denoted as a vector V. The algorithm measures the inconsistency between two preferences and defines the merging result. The merging of the results takes into account feature selection and weight assignment. Feature selection is the process of choosing features that will be considered in providing recommendations for the common profile. This is based on distance minimization. On the other hand, weights are consistent for user profiles but in explicit ratings the users may perceive different criteria for ratings. To solve this problem, weight normalization is used for each feature and then the weight of the feature of merged profile is calculated by adding all the normalized weight of a feature for each user profile divided by the number of members in the group. The authors also did an experiment in which they asked the group of 5 members to rank a list of programs and assign similarity scores. The similarity scores had a range of 0.1 to 0.9 with steps of 0.1, these scores were then compared with the algorithm's similarity values. Authors in this paper claim that merging user profiles strategy is superior to merging recommendations after performing certain experiments.

4.4   Techniques Based on Reviews

Instead of explicitly asking user preferences, more information can be extracted from the reviews and feedback of users. Authors in [21] present some techniques on how to incorporate feedback with preferences.

- Frequent terms: An easy way to analyse reviews is to count the frequency of each term. Each term could be assigned a weight measure which would represent the significance of each term. The terms can then be used to classify the user on term based user profile.
- Overall opinion: This opinion takes into account the general opinion of the item. It can be concluded from the review that the user had a positive review about the hotel. These opinions can also be inferred from the numerical scale rating of the item. Whereas overall opinion from text based can be gotten from applying machine learning techniques such as naive Bayesian classifier or Support Vector Machine (SVM) which will categorize the items properly.
- Feature opinion: Collecting information about the features instead of the whole item can come in handy when classifying many items. In Fig. 2, feature opinion is underlined in blue. The underlined features such as 'The gym facility was excellent' and 'Service was attentive and gracious, appointments were luxurious, location was convenient' tells us more about the features of the hotel such as location, gym facility or service. The opinion can be identified by looking at the adjectives of the sentences. For instance, luxurious, excellent, attentive are some of the words describing the reviews. These reviews can be classified under positive or negative to classify the recommendations. Many techniques have been used in the past for feature opinion such as associative rule mining, SVM based method, lexicalized Hidden Markov Model (L-HMMs) and many others.
- Comparative opinions: As the name implies, this opinion can only be considered when there is a comparison between two or more items [22]. The comparison is done to highlight the similarities or differences of features. The differences might qualify one of the items to be better or worse than the other items. In Fig. 2, it is underlined in red. The underlined sentence compares this hotel with two other hotels, St. Regis' is considered better while Westins heavenly stateside is worse than this hotel according to the user.
- Contextual opinions: In this method, a set of contexts can be defined such as location, component and frequency and the words in the sentence can then be categorized under the identified contexts accordingly. For instance, in Fig. 2, a sentence is underlined in yellow. The sentence has a location context of company, component context of Hong Kong office and the frequency context of first visit.

Conveniently located in the heart of all

First trip to Asia, first visit to company's Hong Kong offices and the
Four Seasons HK provided a great base for all of it. Rooms are
spacious and luxuriously appointed. Bed was comfortable
(perhaps not as good as some St. Regis' but clearly better and
more luxurious than the Westins heavenly stateside). In-hotel
food options were sold and not as overpriced/marked up as I
would have expected. The gym facility was excellent, lots of new
modern equipment in good working order, provided beverages
were great with a unique Asian flair. Service was attentive and
gracious, appointments were luxurious, location was convenient
for cab and train and all my appointments and recreation while
there. What more could you ask ?

Fig. 2. A hotel review example

5   Categorization of Strategies

After the necessary information such as rating or feature selection is gained
through elicitation of preferences, this information can now be used in producing
recommendations. The ratings could be gained implicitly or explicitly from the
defined process in Sect. 3. The ratings used in strategies are aggregated for
group thereby giving appropriate recommendations. This section deals with the
different strategies for aggregating the individual to group recommendations. 5
different categories have been proposed in this section. In Table 2, this sample
table is going to be used as a reference throughout this section.

Table 2. Sample table.

User	1	2	3	4	5	6	7	8	9	10
Mary	10	5	2	7	9	8	5	6	7	6
James	1	9	8	9	7	9	6	9	3	8
John	10	4	3	6	10	9	6	8	10	8

– Voting Strategies: This category consists of Plurality voting and Approval
  voting.
  • Plurality voting: Each group member votes with the highest individual
    preference for a particular alternative. In other words, when a sequence
    of items is needed to be chosen, the item with the most votes are chosen
    repetitively [11]. For instance, For instance, from the table given above,
    given only one alternative, Mary has a tendency to choose item 1, 5 or 9
    respectively, user James tends to chooses item 2, 4, 6 or 8 whereas user
    John chooses item 1. Item 1 has the most tendency to get selected for
    this group in this case (Table 3).

Table 3. Plurality voting.

User	1	2	3	4	5	6	7	8	9	10
Mary	10	4	3	6	10	9	6	8	10	8
James	1	9	8	9	7	9	6	9	3	8
John	10	5	2	7	9	8	5	6	7	6
Group	5	3	1	8	10	9	2	7	4	6

- Approval Voting: This strategy takes a threshold value into account and only values above the threshold are considered for votes [10]. The values above the threshold are depicted as "1" whereas values below are denoted by "0". For instance, choosing the threshold value as 6, the new values of the table are given in Table 4. The new ranking of the items are (5, 6),(1, 4, 8, 9, 10),(2, 3),7. This strategy can be used in sub-list ranking mode discussed in Sect. 4.2 where rankings above a certain threshold would be considered.

Table 4. Approval voting

User	1	2	3	4	5	6	7	8	9	10
Mary	1	0	0	1	1	1	0	0	1	0
James	0	1	1	1	1	1	0	1	0	1
John	1	0	0	0	1	1	0	1	1	1
Total	2	1	1	2	3	3	0	2	2	2

- Extremities Strategy: This category of strategies include most pleasure, least misery. This particular set of strategies can be used in pairwise comparison mode where most pleasure can be used for the high category and least misery for the lower categories. It can also be used for comparative opinions in which qualification of good or worse can be made if the opinion is above or below the threshold. For instance, if the threshold is 5, values above 5 may qualify the item to be better the other item and vice versa.
  - Most pleasure: The rankings of the items is based on the maximum ratings by the user [11]. Majority vote is considered important in this case.
  - Least misery: The rankings of the items is based on the minimum ratings by the respective users. The minority gets a say in this strategy [10]. This strategy is the opposite of the Most pleasure.
- Frequency-based strategies: Copeland rule and Borda count are some of the strategies in this category. Frequency based strategies can be adapted based on interaction mode such as categorical binning mode to classify them based on the frequency into categories. For instance, higher frequency can go into high category followed by the others. Or techniques based on reviews such as use of frequent terms can form the list of recommendations.

- Copeland rule: This strategy sorts items according to their Copeland index. The items with better ratings take positive sign whereas the lower ones take negative signs. In other words, counts how often an item beats other item and how often it loses [18]. For instance, for the items 1 and 5 user John has the same preference, Adam prefers item 5 and Mary prefers item 1. Thus, there is no clear winner between the items, which results in a "0". According to the calculations from the Table 5, the rankings of items are item 5, 1, 6, 9, 4, 8, 10, (2, 7), 3.

Table 5. Copeland rule

Item	1	2	3	4	5	6	7	8	9	10
1	0	−	−	−	0	−	−	−	0	−
2	+	0	−	+	+	+	0	+	+	+
3	+	+	0	+	+	+	+	+	+	+
4	+	−	−	0	+	+	−	0	0	−
5	0	−	−	−	0	−	−	−	−	−
6	+	−	−	−	+	0	−	−	−	−
7	+	0	−	+	+	+	0	+	+	+
8	+	−	−	0	+	+	−	0	+	−
9	0	−	−	0	+	+	−	−	0	−
10	+	−	−	+	+	+	−	+	+	0
Total	+7	−6	−9	+1	+8	+5	−6	0	+3	−3

- Borda count: Ranking is done on user profile. Lowest rated item get 0, the next best item gets 1 and so on. Items with same ratings use averaged sum of hypothetical score [17]. For example, items 2 and 7 received the same rating from Mary and correspond to the items with the second lowest score. Thus, they share the scores 1 and 2, leading to $(1+2)/2 = 1.5$. These individual scores are summed up to get the total. The final ranked list of the group is 6, 5, 1, (4, 8), 9, 10, 2, 7, 3 (Table 6).

Table 6. Borda count

User	1	2	3	4	5	6	7	8	9	10
Mary	8	1	0	2.5	8	6	2.5	4.5	8	4.5
James	0	7.5	4.5	7.5	3	7.5	2	7.5	1	4.5
John	9	1.5	0	5.5	8	7	1.5	3.5	5.5	3.5
Total	17	10	4.5	15.5	19	20.5	6	15.5	14.5	12.5

- Simple mathematical strategies: Simple arithmetic operations such as average, additive and multiplicative are in this category. All the items are added, multiplied or taken average of by their respective users. The higher the sum/product, the more appealing the option is to the users.
- Consensus-based strategies: Average without misery, fairness are instances in this category.
    - Average without misery: determines the group rating for a particular item by calculating the average of the individual ratings but this technique also considers values above a certain threshold [10]. For instance, item 1 is not considered for the group recommendations because James rated it with 1 which is below the threshold. Techniques based on overall opinion mentioned in Sect. 4.4 should use this strategy because it makes sense to consider all the features and then compare it with a baseline. Consider a threshold of value 4 in Table 7. The rankings of the items are as follows: (5,6), 8, (4, 10), 2, 7 when using a threshold of 4.

Table 7. Average without misery

User	1	2	3	4	5	6	7	8	9	10
Mary	10	5	2	7	9	8	5	6	7	6
James	1	9	8	9	7	9	6	9	3	8
John	10	4	3	6	10	9	6	8	10	8
Total	–	18	–	22	26	26	17	23	–	22

- Fairness strategy: This combines most pleasure and least misery causing strategies. Firstly, a user is selected is chosen at random then item that causes least misery is chosen, this process is done repetitively until all the items are finished. Items are chosen as if individual user are choosing the items in turn [11]. One person chooses first then second person until everyone made a choice. Everyone then chooses the second item starting with the person who finished last. In this way everyone gets a chance. If John starts first, James second and Mary last then the ranked item list from Table 8 will be 5, 6, 4, 8, 10, 7, 1, 2, 9, 3.

Table 8. Fairness strategy

User	1	2	3	4	5	6	7	8	9	10
Mary	10	5	2	7	9	8	5	6	7	6
James	1	9	8	9	7	9	6	9	3	8
John	10	4	3	6	10	9	6	8	10	8
Total	4	3	1	8	10	9	5	7	2	6

6 Strategies in Applications

- INTRIGUE: This system uses the average weight strategy. It takes average and gives weights depending on the number of members in the group and the significance of subgroups. INTRIGUE gives more importance to certain subgroups such as children and disabled and therefore heavier weights are given to these subgroups.
- GAIN: This uses a form of Average strategy which also uses weights. These weights are dependent on the members who are near and those who should be statistically in the group.
- MusicFX: MusicFX uses a variant of Average Without Misery Strategy. The ratings are in range of -2 to 2, the higher the values are, the more positive the member is about that track. Individual ratings above a certain threshold are considered and then only those items' average are taken. A weighted random selection is used to prevent choosing same station every time.
- CATS: Without misery strategy is used because members either need to consider some of the features or may need to fill quantities of the items available. The recommendation which represents the most requirements of the whole group is chosen.
- PolyLens: This recommendation system uses Least Misery strategy. PolyLens has an assumption of small group size and the group tends to be as happy as its least happy member.
- Flickr Tag Recommendation: This helps in suggesting tag for users which people usually do manually. Two strategies are used here namely, plurality voting and summing. The former doesn't take account of co-occurrence values while the latter does but on the other hand, both strategies are applied to top m co-occurring tags in the list [23].
- Next Item Recommendation: This system gets item-item relationship from users' past interactions. Afterwards, weights are estimated and assigned for every item in user trajectories which aids in effectively choosing the relevant items for short-term intentions. Average (mean), Most pleasure(max), Least misery(min) and sum are used as aggregation methods and then compared with each other [24].
- Food Recommendation: Authors in [25] gives an overview of the systems available with different strategies used. In a group of 4 people who have to rate recipes on a scale of 1 to 5, least misery strategy is recommended by the authors in order to minimize misery.

7 Conclusion

This paper gives an overview on the previous research work, methods of collecting information, techniques by which this information can be categorized, categorization and practical application of strategies. Some ways of providing better recommendations was proposed. The paper also proposed what to do to make interfaces attractive and appealing for the group members. There are differences between individual and group recommendations in specifying preferences, presenting, explaining and making final decisions and this paper takes into account these differences. A lot of strategies exist some of which are grouped into categories to easily identify the similar ones for predictions, one section of this paper concentrates on that. The strategies which are practically used in recommendation systems present awareness about the most popular strategies. Ways to collect information is highly dependent on the makers of the recommendation system and all these different ways are discussed in details in this work. Techniques which affect the elicitation of preferences are also highlighted to shed a light on the practical use of recommendation systems. Recommendation systems can be made much more convenient and appealing if a bit more research and work is done in this field. I want to investigate more on certain elicitation techniques based on interaction mode, including user interfaces to find which techniques are preferred more by the users in future work. In specific, how to adapt the individual interaction to group recommendations. Using aggregation techniques to combine the individual preferences and some extra features such as showing the preferences of other members in the group or making the interfaces more appealing for the group.

References

1. Jameson, A.: More than the sum of its members: challenges for group recommender systems (2004)
2. Lieberman, H., Vandyke, N., Vivacqua, A.: Let's browse: a collaborative Web browsing agent (1998)
3. Mccarthy, J.: Pocket restaurantfinder: a situated recommender system for groups (2002)
4. Pizzutilo, S., Decarolis, B., Cozzolongo, G., Ambruoso, F.: Group modeling in a public space: methods, techniques, experiences (2005)
5. Chao, D., Balthrop, J., Forrest, S.: Adaptive radio: achieving consensus using negative preferences (2005)
6. Ardissono, L., Goy, A., Petrone, G., Segnan, M., Torasso, P.: Intrigue: personalized recommendation of tourist attractions for desktop and hand held devices. Appl. Artif. Intell. **17**, 687–714 (2003)
7. Jameson, A., Smyth, B.: Recommendation to groups. In: Brusilovsky, P., Kobsa, A., Nejdl, W. (eds.) The Adaptive Web. LNCS, vol. 4321, pp. 596–627. Springer, Heidelberg (2007). https://doi.org/10.1007/978-3-540-72079-9_20
8. Pazzani, M.J., Billsus, D.: Content-based recommendation systems. In: Brusilovsky, P., Kobsa, A., Nejdl, W. (eds.) The Adaptive Web. LNCS, vol. 4321, pp. 325–341. Springer, Heidelberg (2007). https://doi.org/10.1007/978-3-540-72079-9_10
9. Schafer, J.B., Frankowski, D., Herlocker, J., Sen, S.: Collaborative filtering recommender systems. In: Brusilovsky, P., Kobsa, A., Nejdl, W. (eds.) The Adaptive Web. LNCS, vol. 4321, pp. 291–324. Springer, Heidelberg (2007). https://doi.org/10.1007/978-3-540-72079-9_9
10. Masthoff, J.: Group modeling: selecting a sequence of television items to suit a group of viewers. In: Ardissono, L., Kobsa, A., Maybury, M.T. (eds.) Personalized Digital Television. Springer, Dordrecht (2004). https://doi.org/10.1007/1-4020-2164-X_5

11. Masthoff, J.: Group recommender systems: aggregation, satisfaction and group attributes. In: Ricci, F., Rokach, L., Shapira, B. (eds.) Recommender Systems Handbook, pp. 743–776. Springer, Boston, MA (2015). https://doi.org/10.1007/978-1-4899-7637-6_22

12. McCarthy, K., McGinty, L., Smyth, B., Salamó, M.: The needs of the many: a case-based group recommender system. In: Roth-Berghofer, T.R., Göker, M.H., Güvenir, H.A. (eds.) ECCBR 2006. LNCS (LNAI), vol. 4106, pp. 196–210. Springer, Heidelberg (2006). https://doi.org/10.1007/11805816_16

13. Mccarthy, J., Anagnost, T.: MusicFX: an arbiter of group preferences for computer supported collaborative workouts (1998)

14. Yu, Z., Zhou, X., Hao, Y., Gu, J.: TV program recommendation for multiple viewers based on user profile merging. User Model. User-Adap. Interact. **16**, 63–82 (2006)

15. Goren-bar, D., Glinansky, O.: FIT-recommend ing TV programs to family members. Comput. Graph. **28**, 149–156 (2004)

16. Crossen, A., Budzik, J.: Promoting social interaction in public spaces: the flytrap active environment. In: O'Hara, K., Brown, B. (eds.) Consuming Music Together. Springer, Dordrecht (2006). https://doi.org/10.1007/1-4020-4097-0_6

17. Borda, J.: Academie Royale des Sciences, Paris (1781). Cook, W.D.: Distance-based and ad hoc consensus models in ordinal preference ranking. Eur. J. Oper. Res. **172**, 369–385 (2006)

18. Copeland, A.H.: A reasonable social welfare function. University of Michigan (1951)

19. Andreadis, P.: Coarse preferences: representation, elicitation, and decision making. The University of Edinburg (2019)

20. Kuhlman, C., et al.: Evaluating Preference Collection Methods for Interactive Ranking Analytics (2019)

21. Chen, L., Chen, G., Wang, F.: Recommender systems based on user reviews: the state of the art. User Model. User-Adap. Inter. **25**(2), 99–154 (2015). https://doi.org/10.1007/s11257-015-9155-5

22. Jindal, N., Liu, B.: Mining comparative sentences and relations (2006)

23. Sigurbjörnsson, B., Vanzwol, R.: Flickr tag recommendation based on collective knowledge (2008)

24. Zhang, S., Tay, Y., Yao, L., Sun, A., An, J.: Next item recommendation with self-attentive metric learning (2019)

25. Trang Tran, T.N., Atas, M., Felfernig, A., Stettinger, M.: An overview of recommender systems in the healthy food domain. J. Intell. Inf. Syst. **50**(3), 501–526 (2017). https://doi.org/10.1007/s10844-017-0469-0

26. Colomo-Palacios, R., García-Peñalvo, F.J., Stantchev, V., Misra, S.: Towards a social and context-aware mobile recommendation system for tourism. Pervasive Mob. Comput. **38**, 505–515 (2017)

27. Colomo-Palacios, R., Casado-Lumbreras, C., Soto-Acosta, P., Misra, S.: Providing knowledge recommendations: an approach for informal electronic mentoring. Interact. Learn. Environ. **22**(2), 221–240 (2014)

Prediction of Malaria Fever Using Long-Short-Term Memory and Big Data

Joseph Bamidele Awotunde[(✉)] [ID], Rasheed Gbenga Jimoh [ID],
Idowu Dauda Oladipo [ID], and Muyideen Abdulraheem [ID]

Department of Computer Science, University of Ilorin, Ilorin, Nigeria
{awotunde.jb,jimoh_rasheed,odidowu,muyideen}@unilorin.edu.ng

Abstract. Malaria has been identified to be one of the most common diseases with a great public health problem globally and it is caused by mosquitos' parasites. This prevails in developing nations where healthcare facilities are not enough for the patients. The technological advancement in medicine has resulted in the collection of huge volumes of data from various sources in different formats. A reliable and early parasite-based diagnosis, identification of symptoms, disease monitoring, and prescription are crucial to decreasing malaria occurrence in Nigeria. Hence, the use of deep and machine learning models is essentials to reduce the effect of malaria-endemic and for better predictive models. Therefore, this paper proposes a framework to predict malaria-endemic in Nigeria. To predict the malaria-endemic well, both environmental and clinical data were used using Kwara State as a case study. The study used a deep learning algorithm as a classifier for the proposed system. Three locations were selected from Irepodun Local Government Areas of Kwara State with 34 months periodic pattern. Each location reacted differently based on environmental factors. The findings indicate that both factors are significant in malaria prediction and transmission. The LSTM algorithm provides an efficient method for detecting situations of widespread malaria.

Keywords: Big data · Prediction · Diagnosis · Malaria fever · Deep learning · Mosquito parasites

1 Introduction

Global warming has been shown to contribute to the rising abundance of human insect vector diseases, especially in tropical countries [1, 2]. The world has been fighting with mosquito-borne diseases, which have significantly be a threat to health worldwide [3, 4]. To ultimately eliminate and control the widespread of insect-borne diseases like malaria, there is an ongoing effort [5–7]. Apart from Christopher's work of 1911 [8], there have been different models recently for prediction malaria spread and abundance. Malaria prediction and treatment are very difficult and complicated due to the transmission of mosquitoes and complex ecology [9–12].

Malaria is one of the precarious illnesses in Africa especially Nigeria [13, 14]. A reliable and early parasite-based diagnosis, identification of symptoms, prescription, and

© Springer Nature Switzerland AG 2021
S. Misra and B. Muhammad-Bello (Eds.): ICTA 2020, CCIS 1350, pp. 41–53, 2021.
https://doi.org/10.1007/978-3-030-69143-1_4

further malaria regulation plans, For example, the use of insecticide-medicated bed-net and indoor residual spray is crucial to reducing the incidence of malaria in Nigeria. Many donors have been helpful in this regard by distributing treated bed nets in Nigeria. The Plasmodium falciparum opposition to generally known anti-malarial medications imposes the consumption of potentially and extra cost-effective combination therapy in addition to accurate laboratory diagnosis [15]. To prevent the undiscerned use of anti-malaria medicines, the World Health Organization (WHO) stresses the occurrence of malaria in a human body before the use of or treatment of malaria drugs. But in Africa especially in Nigeria the presumptive treatment of malaria and other related fevers is still popular due to a lack of medical personnel, technical expertise, and effective laboratory structure. The aforementioned problems have cause delays in the diagnosis of other severe feverish diseases and the assumption of treatment sometimes results in misuse or abuse of anti-malarial drugs [16, 17].

Malaria is as old as a human being because it is an ancient disease, which causes social, economic, and health burden amongst people in the world [9]. The disease is common in the warm and humid nations and the ailment happened to be in existence for more than hundreds of centuries now, malaria has remained a prominent community well-being challenges among many countries. WHO declared malaria endemic in 109 countries in the year 2008 with 243 million malaria conditions recorded and over millions of demises of the endemic which are mainly children under 5 years of age (WHO).

Nigeria in recent years experiences a high incidence of malaria. The healthcare system is characterized by an adequate large quality of data, with little or no effort to apply the robust information of data contained for solving life-threatening problems in the medical diagnosis of diverse diseases [10]. The data mining approach remains the most significant method among various techniques for the prediction or diagnosis of several diseases [18]. There have been many proposed prediction models by researchers on environmental factors [19–23]. The use of big data for predictions based on environmental factors and clinical conditions has not been explored [23].

Therefore, this study aims to predict the incidence of malaria using clinical and environmental factors with the help of the LSTM prediction model in the R programming language environment. Finally, the paper conducts a comparative performance evaluation on the prediction algorithms. The LSTM model was used on big data to predict malaria prevalence in the study areas. The study required a dataset and the data collected from the study area were used for the model. The deep learning method was chosen because of its strength, prediction, and forecasting ability. the predictions are made based on past values and a relationship has to be established between the fluctuations occurred in values.

2 Big Data in the Healthcare System

The advancement in information technology increases the amount of data used by the modern establishment thereby making data science an essential tool for maintaining data in any organization [24–26]. For instance, an organization with a huge amount of user data needs data science to effectively improve methods to collect, accumulate, and process the data. Various systematic techniques may be used by the company to process and obtain resourceful outcomes about the user data. Data mining and big data are used interrelated with Data Science. To comprehend and process actual data concepts, data science is of great importance as it incorporates the field of statistics and machine learning with their various procedures [27, 28]. The study of Information Science, Computer Science, Mathematics, and Statistics with their concepts and methods are all embedded in the field of data science [28, 29].

The 21st century is an age of big data affecting every aspect of human life, including biology and medicine [30, 31]. The move from paper medical records to Electronic Health Record (EHR) systems has resulted in an unprecedented increase in data [32, 33]. Big data thus offers a great opportunity for doctors, epidemiologists, and specialists in health policy to make evidence-driven decisions that will eventually enhance patient care [34, 35]. "Big data is not only a modern reality for the biomedical scientist but an imperative that needs to be fully grasped and used in the search for new knowledge" [36–38].

Data in the healthcare sector are usually huge and not easy to handle [38–40]. This results from the enormous way by which data grows in the health care sector, the rate at which data are been produced, and the variety of various data in the healthcare system [41, 42]. The rate at which data are been captured, stored, analyzed, and retrieved in the health care sector has swift rapidly from the aged paper-based storage technique to the use of digital technique and method [42, 43].

On the other hand, the complication of data makes processing and analysis of data by the aged long traditional method very difficult and uneasy to handle. However, the large volume of data, as well as the sophistication of the data, make it difficult for conventional methods and techniques to process and interpret the data. Therefore, the application of advanced technologies which includes virtualization and cloud computing allows for huge and effective data processing in the healthcare system. Thereby rapidly turning the healthcare system into a big data industry. Nevertheless, in these modern days, the improvement in the information and communication technologies (ICT) brings the advancement of varied data from new sources in the healthcare system.

This source includes the Global positioning system (GPS), data from gene sequence, file logs, devices that identify Radio Frequency (RFID), smart meters, and posts from social media. The increasing rate with which data is been produced from various sources brings about an increase in the amount of data in the healthcare system [42, 44]. Thus, their results give tedious means of storing, processing, and analyzing data with the aged long traditional method of data processing applications [45]. Nevertheless, modern methods and techniques, as well as advanced computational technology, have been used to store, control, and analyze values from broad and varied data in the health care system in real-time [42, 44, 45]. As a result, the healthcare sector has now become a big data industry. Big data now provides massive opportunities for the healthcare system [46].

Improvement in information technology and data computing has greatly changed researches on population-based by encouraging easy access to a huge amount of data. Sometimes, such database links are referred to as "big data" [47, 48]. In other to make efficient use of these data for researches in clinical health or public health, the researchers need to widen researches further than the traditional surveillance model, as operating with big data differs from focusing on performing narrow analysis, treatment-oriented clinical data. Therefore, leveraging on Big data to reflect accurately on the heterogeneous population it represents becomes expedient [42, 45]. This endeavor needs a swift research environment that can adopt a quick advancement in computing technology to at all-time combine data while making use of new methods to reduce their complexity [42, 48].

Big data in healthcare have been established for its timely advancement in disease detection, diagnosis, and enable the best control of any disease outbreaks. Predictive analysis of health care can be achieved easily with the aid of big data [49, 57]. In the United States of America, for example, predictive analytics was used to enhance disease response management and a deeper understanding of diseases [50]. The use of a health-based framework for broad data collection to enhance patient care and prevent insurance fraud has been widely used in Australia [51]. The use of data from social media, sensor data, and air quality data with machine learning models are currently studies to predict asthma [23]. Generally, the use of broad health data in the predictive analysis has created considerable interest in research in recent years [52]. For the management of complex computational data, the modern scalable database has been used examples of such are Hadoop MapReduce and Apache Spark. The latter does not come with a file system other than Hadoop, so you need to combine it with a different file system based on the cloud [53]. Hadoop spends time running computationally complex machine learning algorithms [54, 55], making Apache Spark 100 times faster than ever before. Also, trends and patterns which make it easy to diagnose and treat patients are been revealed by big data.

Big data would be useful in today's digital world as the key to controlling malaria outbreaks, but the criteria for successful data collection and global analysis need to be clear. The study states that the data and algorithms available in digital form are used for prediction and monitoring. For example, it is vital to consider both the clinical and environmental factors where the infection has spread and been detected in the battle against endemic malaria. Nonetheless, it is equally important that these data and algorithms are used in a protected manner, following data security laws and with proper regard for privacy and privacy. Inability to do so would undermine public confidence, making people less able to follow advice or recommendations on public health, and more likely to have poor health outcomes [56].

Hence the exploitation of big data in malaria-endemic will bring about improved care with minimum cost and good satisfaction to patients. On Big Data, the LSTM model was used to estimate the prevalence of malaria in the study areas. For the model, the analysis needed a dataset, and the data obtained from the study area was used. Because of its power, prediction, and forecasting ability, the deep learning method was chosen. The estimates are made based on previous values and a correlation must be formed between the variations in values that occur.

2.1 Clinical Data

The clinical data used for this study were collected from three General Hospital in Irepodun Local Government (LGA) of Kwara State (Omu-Aran, Oro, and Agbamu), the health centers (HC) were set up by the Kwara State Government of Nigeria. This HC was used to collect samples of malaria from endemic sites within Irepodun LGA. The three hospitals were chosen because they are government-owned hospitals and were also allowed to control endemic malaria in Kwara State and are in highly endemic areas. Such hospitals were well equipped with malaria test kits and their personnel were also well trained in the treatment and testing of malaria. Hospital data attributes are the number of successful cases, symptom-free, regular age, sex, per month. The data used for this analysis covered three years, from the beginning of 2017 to the end of 2019.

2.2 Environmental Data

It is very essential to know the environmental risk even if it is at a very local scale for malaria-endemic. The most considered environmental factors are temperature, relative humidity, rainfall, and the vegetative index to estimate malaria abundance. Environmental data were obtained from Minet's daily forecast and the satellites. From the MiNet forecast, the MiNet01AB product predicted a Composite picture of 7 days at 1.23 km * 1.23 km of spatial resolution for day and night temperature. Nigerian Meteorological Agency's data acquisition center reported normal relative modesty at 2 m and 8 m above ground level. The vegetative index was obtained by resolution of 1.5 * 1.5. Rainfall was measured based on the amount of rainfall in each region. The following information was also systematically collected: the vegetation index (NDVI) measured at 1 km around the site with SPOT 5, the number of residents, the existence of abandoned projects, and the existence of abandoned construction with tools or holes that could serve as possible breeding sites for Anopheles mosquitoes.

3 Methodology

Hochreiter [29] introduced Long-Short -Term Memory (LSTM) to tackle the Recurrent Neural Network (ANN) reliability and speed problems. Both are very similar but in LSTM a new concept is introduced with interaction per module or one cell. RNN uses a definition of time and is a neural network that is aided by edges spanning adjacent steps in time. It's mutual parameters over a series of time steps and allows connections to self-loop over time from a node to itself. The model receives the input values at step t and the node's previously hidden value and determines the hidden state. The final output value in the prior state will be determined by the input value. LSTM was used to tackle the issue of vanishing gradients appropriately. Unlike RNN, which uses hidden layer structure, LSTM is a linear self-loop memory block that flows through the gradients with long sequences.

The memory block containing self-connecting memory cells is used to memorize the time state, and the three gates from the memory block help control the flow of information within and outside the memory block. It helps the model to manage long-term and short-term correlation in time series. The LSTM registered at time t, instead of a simple RNN. As depicted in Fig. 1, LSTM has a four-layer long-term training process with retrieving information called chain-like structure, thus consisting of memory blocks such as cells. The vital condition called the state of the cell remains unchanged and enables data to flow forward. Nonetheless, useable sigmoid activation gates may be used to add or remove data inside a layer. Applying gates when memorizing the LSTM will prevent long-term dependence. Such gates have a range of matrix operations including individual weights.

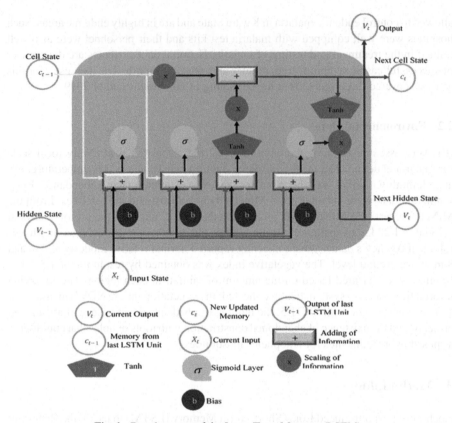

Fig. 1. Development of the Long-Term Memory (LSTM)

3.1   The Staging Procedure of LSTM Is as Follows

The sigmoid function of LSTM identifies data that is not needed for any phase and takes the current input as (X_t) at time $t - 1$ and produces output (V_{t-1}) at time $t - 1$. The sigmoidal function specifies which part of the output will be separated from the old output. This stage is called the Forgetting Gate (f_t). Forget the f_t gate, the value is between 0 and 1 and is a vector that matches each number in the cell (C_{t-1}).

$$f_t = \sigma\left(w_f\left[V_{t-1}, X_t\right] + b_f\right) \tag{1}$$

Where
σ is the sigmoidal function, w_f = weights and b_f = forget gate.

Both equations have two states: the ignoring condition and the storing condition of the current input and the X_t in the cell state. The two layers are the sigmoidal layer and the tanh layer. To the sigmoidal layer provided to decide if the new information needs to be modified or not using 0 or 1. The *tanh* update weights in the second layer and passes the values between $(-1$ to $1)$. Using their level of importance, the values are selected accordingly. Both the values are updated as presented in Eq. 4 and form the new cell state.

$$m_t = \sigma\left(w_f\left[V_{t-1}, X_t\right] + b_m\right) \tag{2}$$

$$N_t = tanh\left(w_f\left[V_{t-1}, X_t\right] + b_n\right) \tag{3}$$

$$C_t = C_{t-1}f_t + N_t m_t \tag{4}$$

In the final stage, the output V_t is based on the output of sigmoidal gates Q_t and is multiplied by the new $tanh(C_t)$ layer generated.

$$Q_t = \sigma\left(w_f\left[V_{t-1}, X_t\right] + b_q\right) \tag{5}$$

$$V_t = Q_t tanh(C_t) \tag{6}$$

w_q and b_q are the weights and biases for the output gates, respectively

3.2 Model

As input to predict malaria fever was used the clinical factors with asymptomatic cases and environmental data such as temperature, relative humidity, rainfall, vegetative index. The average rainfall recorded, the average temperature of day and night time, and the average enhanced vegetable index at a resolution of 1.5 km, thus combined to be monthly. The problem of missing variables of about 7% was tackled by clustered equations in pre-processing data with multivariate imputation. From 2017–2019 the data were taken from both the clinical and environmental data at each location (Omu-Aran, Oro, and Agbamu) in Irepodun LGA as presented in Fig. 1.

The model was trained from January 2017 to December 2019 using the preprocessed data. Following some iterations, the model was subsequently updated for 2 years to provide a monthly malaria abundance forecast for 24 months, based on historical data on environmental and clinical variables. The proposed model used an open-source online cloud big data to implement the system using the Apache Spark framework. The Apache Kafka was used for the real-time streaming and batch processing of the data on Spark. The output measurements for the model were determined and model results were produced for each geographic location.

The experiment was split into two phases: i) offline batch processing ii) streaming online. During the first stage, the data is pre-processed and used for processing. In the second stage, the real-time analysis was carried out by gathering the batches of message brokers. Initially, preprocessing was optimized by applying multivariate variable imputation using a clustered equation to manage missing data points for each region's ambient and clinical time-series data. Then the LSTM classifier was used to make the preparation. In the second stage, the results were expected in real-time analysis, and the results over a given duration were estimated. The findings were ultimately processed for on-line analysis on the distributed Hadoop file system.

4   Results and Discussion

The experiment has been divided into two phases: i) offline batch processing ii) streaming on-line. The data are pre-processed in the first stage and used for processing. In the second stage, the real-time analysis was performed by collecting the message brokers in batches. Preprocessing was initially optimized by applying multivariate imputation using a clustered equation to manage missing data points on the environmental and clinical time series of each venue. Later, the LSTM classifier was used for the preparation. The results were projected for a certain amount of time during the second phase of the real-time analysis, and the results were estimated. The findings were eventually stored on the online reporting file system provided by Hadoop.

Throughout the analysis, the variables depend seasonally on environmental and clinical factors. For example, the number of asymptomatic cases and the vegetative index are time series, following [32]. Therefore, the research included the number of asymptomatic patients and their diagnoses. Between January 2017 until December 2019, the study expected cases of malaria is for 24 months. The Omu-Aran site reported the highest number of incidents, which may be attributed to the large number of people residing in the region and the high population density compared with other sites. The maximum rainfall was 2.3 mm, and the maximum day and night temperatures differed significantly from the other two locations by 2.5 °C. The results for the vegetative index were also significantly different from those locations. General Hospital, Agbamu has reported the smallest number of malaria cases. It was because i) the area's population was very small relative to the other two sites and ii) we also wanted to assume that the areas were using local herbs to manage their malaria index, which could minimize the index reported in the hospital as in two other areas.

Precise health prediction models are very important for improved and more effective care and are useful for planning and decision-making. The results of the study have shown that clinical and environmental factors are resourceful and also have played a crucial role in the forecasting of malaria. Individuals with malaria without symptoms were present in the studied region, and this was verified with laboratory tests with high predictive capacity. Environmental factors play a significant role in the prediction of malaria since rainfall normally started around July to October of each year, the incidence and incidence of malaria was higher than in other months of the year. It was attributed to the fact Anopheles gambiae mosquito breeding aid of the season during this period. Factors like the presence of a watercourse near any residential area and a higher index of vegetation correlated with higher vector density support the eminences of malaria. Table 1 displays the statistical findings at the site selected for the malaria cases.

Table 1. Results of malaria incidences in the selected areas

Location	Minimum	Maximum	Mean	Standard deviation	Mode
Omu-Aran	27	56	34.45	3.57	43
Oro	25	45	31.23	3.03	43
Agbamu	16	21	15.05	5.29	10

4.1 Performance Evaluation Metrics

The basic evaluation criteria and assessment are based on the classification accuracy level using True Negative (TN), True Positive (TP), False Negative (FN), and False Positive (FP) (Table 2).

Table 2. Definition of performance evaluation metrics

Measures	Definition	Formula
Sensitivity test	The sensitivity test is the ability to correctly detect diabetes disease	$TP/(TP + FN)$
Specificity test	Specificity is the ability to avoid calling normal things as diabetes disease in medical tests	$TN/(TN + FP)$
PPV	Positively predicated value	$TP/(TP + FP)$
NPV	Negatively predicated value	$TN/(TN + FN)$
Accuracy	Measure the percentage of correctly detect diabetes disease	$\frac{TN+TP}{TN+FP+FN+TP} \times 100$

Where:
True Positive = TP, True Negative = TN, False Positive = FP, and False Negative = FN

Table 3 shows the performance evaluation of the three locations in the study, Agbamu has the highest accuracy of 98.34%, 99.37% sensitivity 93.78% specificity, and 98.14% precision. Oro has an accuracy of 97.94%, 98.45% sensitivity 94.05% specificity, and 97.56% precision and the least of them which is Omu-Aran has an accuracy of 97.47%, 98.05% sensitivity 94.67% specificity, and 97.56% precision.

Table 3. Performance evaluation for the metrics

Location	Accuracy	Sensitivity	Specificity	Precision
Omu-Aran	97.47%	98.05%	94.67%	97.75%
Agbanu	98.34%	99.37%	93.78%	98.14%
Oro	97.94%	98.45%	94.05%	97.56%

Table 4 shows a comparison of the proposed method with other machine learning. The methods outperformed other machines learning this maybe because of the introduction of big data into the LSTM deep learning and result bring about better accuracy compared with other machine learning. Random Forest follows with an accuracy of 93.94% and ANN is the least of all the methods with an accuracy of 25.83%.

Table 4. Comparison of the proposed method with other machine learning

Location	Accuracy	Specificity	Precision
KNN	86.21%	98.66%	92.90%
SVM	92.69%	97.09%	91.82%
Random Forest	93.94%	94.51%	85.42%
Naïve Bayes	91.69%	96.42%	88.36%
ANN	25.83%	0.0	25.83%
Big Data with LSTM	**98.34%**	**94.67%**	**98.14%**

5 Conclusions

Malaria fever is a social problem in that it can widespread harm and cause personal damage. It is also a worldwide problem face by many developing nations. Hence, many types of research have been conducted to minimize the social, economic, and physical losses by predicting the spread of malaria-endemic. The purpose of this study was to design a prediction model using deep learning techniques and big data that is more appropriate than existing models by using environmental and clinical variables. Environmental and clinical factors play a significant role in malaria-endemic prediction. Though malaria prediction using environmental and clinical variables with big data analysis is a new approach but has proved important and very useful in predicting malaria-endemic. The application of correct predictive models are noteworthy for the allocation of medical resources for prevention and to estimate the impact of the disease. The use of a more accurate exploration of malaria prediction and diagnosis of malaria is necessary to improve treatment and its value in practice. The proposed method outperformed other machine learnings compare with an overall accuracy of 98.34%, 94.67%, and 98.14% precision. Future work can still work on other areas within the study area to be able to conclude accurately about the features that cause malaria within Kwara State. Also, features selection algorithms like genetic algorithms can be used for feature selection.

References

1. Kiang, R., et al.: Meteorological, environmental remote sensing, and neural network analysis of the epidemiology of malaria transmission in Thailand. Geospatial Health, 71–84 (2006)
2. Wilke, A.B., Beier, J.C., Benelli, G.: The complexity of the relationship between global warming and urbanization–an obscure future for predicting increases in vector-borne infectious diseases. Current Opinion Insect Sci. **35**, 1–9 (2019)
3. Benelli, G.: Green synthesized nanoparticles in the fight against mosquito-borne diseases and cancer—a brief review. Enzyme Microb. Technol. **95**, 58–68 (2016)
4. Wilder-Smith, A., Gubler, D.J., Weaver, S.C., Monath, T.P., Heymann, D.L., Scott, T.W.: Epidemic arboviral diseases: priorities for research and public health. Lancet. Infect. Dis **17**(3), e101–e106 (2017)
5. Rabinovich, R.N., et al.: malERA: an updated research agenda for malaria elimination and eradication. PLoS Med. **14**(11), e1002456 (2017)

6. Zolnikov, T.R.: Vector-borne disease. In: Autoethnographies on the Environment and Human Health, pp. 113–126. Palgrave Macmillan, Cham (2018)
7. Sougoufara, S., Ottih, E.C., Tripet, F.: The need for new vector control approaches targeting outdoor biting Anopheline malaria vector communities. Parasit. Vectors **13**(1), 1–15 (2020)
8. Christophers, S.R.: Epidemic malaria of the Punjab: with a note of a method of predicting epidemic years. Trans. Committee Stud. Malaria India **2**, 17–26 (1911)
9. Awotunde, J.B., Matiluko, O.E., Fatai, O.W.: Medical diagnosis system using fuzzy logic. Afr. J. Comp. ICT **7**(2), 99–106 (2014)
10. Ayo, F.E., Awotunde, J.B., Ogundokun, R.O., Folorunso, S.O., Adekunle, A.O.: A decision support system for multi-target disease diagnosis: a bioinformatics approach. Heliyon **6**(3), e03657 (2020)
11. Zinszer, K., et al.: Forecasting malaria in a highly endemic country using environmental and clinical predictors. Malaria J. **14**(1), 245 (2015)
12. Rochlin, I., Ninivaggi, D.V., Benach, J.L.: Malaria and Lyme disease-the the largest vector-borne US epidemics in the last 100 years: success and failure of public health. BMC Public Health **19**(1), 804 (2019)
13. WHO: World malaria report 2013. World Health Organization, Geneva (2013)
14. Adebiyi, M., et al.: Computational investigation of consistency and performance of the bio-chemical network of the malaria parasite, *Plasmodium falciparum*. In: Misra, S., et al. (eds.) ICCSA 2019. LNCS, vol. 11623, pp. 231–241. Springer, Cham (2019). https://doi.org/10.1007/978-3-030-24308-1_19
15. Mutabingwa, T.K.: Artemisinin-based combination therapies (ACTs): best hope for malaria treatment but inaccessible to the needy! Acta Trop. **95**, 305–315 (2005)
16. Leslie, T., et al.: Overdiagnosis and mistreatment of malaria among febrile patients at primary healthcare level in Afghanistan: an observational study. BMJ **345**, e4389 (2012)
17. Bastiaens, G.J.H., Bousema, T., Leslie, T.: Scale-up of malaria rapid diagnostic tests and artemisinin-based combination therapy: challenges and perspectives in sub-Saharan Africa. PLoS Med. **11**, e1001590 (2014)
18. Abisoye, O.A., Jimoh, R.G.: A hybrid intelligent forecasting model to determine malaria transmission. AIT **2015**, 5 (2015)
19. Oladele, T.O., Ogundokun, R.O., Awotunde, J.B., Adebiyi, M.O., Adeniyi, J.K.: Diagmal: a malaria coactive neuro-fuzzy expert system. In: Gervasi, O., et al. (eds.) ICCSA 2020. LNCS, vol. 12254, pp. 428–441. Springer, Cham (2020). https://doi.org/10.1007/978-3-030-58817-5_32
20. Ayo, F.E., Ogundokun, R.O., Awotunde, J.B., Adebiyi, M.O., Adeniyi, A.E.: Severe acne skin disease: a fuzzy-based method for diagnosis. In: Gervasi, O., et al. (eds.) ICCSA 2020. LNCS, vol. 12254, pp. 320–334. Springer, Cham (2020). https://doi.org/10.1007/978-3-030-58817-5_25
21. Davis, J.K., et al.: A genetic algorithm for identifying spatially-varying environmental drivers in a malaria time series model. Environ. Model Softw. **119**, 275–284 (2019)
22. Gomez-Elipe, A., Otero, A., Van Herp, M., Aguirre-Jaime, A.: Forecasting malaria incidence based on monthly case reports and environmental factors in Karuzi, Burundi, 1997–2003. Malaria J. **6**(1), 129 (2007)
23. Santosh, T., Ramesh, D., Reddy, D.: LSTM based prediction of malaria abundances using big data. Comput. Biol. Med. **124**, 103859 (2020)
24. Wang, Y., Kung, L., Byrd, T.A.: Big data analytics: understanding its capabilities and potential benefits for healthcare organizations. Technol. Forecast. Soc. Chang. **126**, 3–13 (2018)
25. Choi, T.M., Chan, H.K., Yue, X.: Recent development in big data analytics for business operations and risk management. IEEE Trans. Cybern. **47**(1), 81–92 (2016)
26. Donoho, D.: 50 years of data science. J. Comput. Graph. Stat. **26**(4), 745–766 (2017)

27. Shi, B., Iyengar, S.S.: General framework of mathematics. Mathematical Theories of Machine Learning - Theory and Applications, pp. 13–16. Springer, Cham (2020). https://doi.org/10.1007/978-3-030-17076-9_2
28. Okewu, E., Misra, S., Lius, F.-S.: Parameter tuning using adaptive moment estimation in deep learning neural networks. In: Gervasi, O., et al. (eds.) ICCSA 2020. LNCS, vol. 12254, pp. 261–272. Springer, Cham (2020). https://doi.org/10.1007/978-3-030-58817-5_20
29. Blei, D.M., Smyth, P.: Science and data science. Proc. Natl. Acad. Sci. **114**(33), 8689–8692 (2017)
30. Hulsen, T., et al.: From big data to precision medicine. Front. Med. **6**, 34 (2019)
31. Baro, E., Degoul, S., Beuscart, R., Chazard, E.: Toward a literature-driven definition of big data in healthcare. BioMed Res. Int. **2015** (2015)
32. Saweros, E., Song, Y.-T.: Connecting heterogeneous electronic health record systems using tangle. In: Lee, S., Ismail, R., Choo, H. (eds.) IMCOM 2019. AISC, vol. 935, pp. 858–869. Springer, Cham (2019). https://doi.org/10.1007/978-3-030-19063-7_68
33. Austin, C., Kusumoto, F.: The application of Big Data in medicine: current implications and future directions. J. Interv. Card. Electrophysiol. **47**(1), 51–59 (2016)
34. Fiske, A., Buyx, A., Prainsack, B.: Health information counselors: a new profession for the age of big data. Acad. Med. **94**(1), 37 (2019)
35. Galetsi, P., Katsaliaki, K., Kumar, S.: Values, challenges, and future directions of big data analytics in healthcare: a systematic review. Soc. Sci. Med., 112533 (2019)
36. Williamson, B.: Big Data in Education: The Digital Future of Learning, Policy, and Practice. Sage, London (2017)
37. Krumholz, H.M.: Big data and new knowledge in medicine: the thinking, training, and tools needed for a learning health system. Health Aff. **33**(7), 1163–1170 (2014)
38. Lacroix, P.: Big data privacy and ethical challenges. In: Househ, M., Kushniruk, Andre W., Borycki, Elizabeth M. (eds.) Big Data, Big Challenges: A Healthcare Perspective. LNB, pp. 101–111. Springer, Cham (2019). https://doi.org/10.1007/978-3-030-06109-8_9
39. Metaxiotis, K.: Healthcare knowledge management. In: Encyclopedia of Knowledge Management, 2nd edn., pp. 366–375. IGI Global (2011)
40. Halder, P., Pan, I.: Role of Big data analysis in healthcare sector: a survey. In: 2018 Fourth International Conference on Research in Computational Intelligence and Communication Networks (ICRCICN), pp. 221–225. IEEE, November 2018
41. Dai, H.N., Wang, H., Xu, G., Wan, J., Imran, M.: Big data analytics for manufacturing internet of things: opportunities, challenges, and enabling technologies. Enterp. Inf. Syst., 1–25 (2019)
42. Olaronke, I., Oluwaseun, O.: Big data in healthcare: prospects, challenges, and resolutions. In: 2016 Future Technologies Conference (FTC), pp. 1152–1157. IEEE, December 2016
43. Tresp, V., Overhage, J.M., Bundschus, M., Rabizadeh, S., Fasching, P.A., Yu, S.: Going digital: a survey on digitalization and large-scale data analytics in healthcare. Proc. IEEE **104**(11), 2180–2206 (2016)
44. Oussous, A., Benjelloun, F.Z., Lahcen, A.A., Belfkih, S.: Big data technologies: a survey. J. King Saud Univ.-Comput. Inf. Sci. **30**(4), 431–448 (2018)
45. Sagiroglu, S., Sinanc, D.: Big data: a review. In: 2013 International Conference on Collaboration Technologies and Systems (CTS), pp. 42–47. IEEE (2013)
46. Villars, R.L., Olofson, C.W., Eastwood, M.: Big data: what it is and why you should care. White Paper, IDC, 14, 1–14 (2011)
47. Priyanka, K., Kulennavar, N.: A survey on big data analytics in health care. Int. J. Comput. Sci. Inf. Technol. **5**(4), 5865–5868 (2014)
48. Kruse, C.S., Goswamy, R., Raval, Y.J., Marawi, S.: Challenges and opportunities of big data in health care: a systematic review. JMIR Medical Inform. **4**(4), e38 (2016)

49. Abayomi-Alli, A., Abayomi-Alli, O., Vipperman, J., Odusami, M., Misra, S.: Multi-class classification of impulse and non-impulse sounds using deep convolutional neural network (DCNN). In: Misra, S., et al. (eds.) ICCSA 2019. LNCS, vol. 11623, pp. 359–371. Springer, Cham (2019). https://doi.org/10.1007/978-3-030-24308-1_30

50. Birkhead, G.S., Klompas, M., Shah, N.R.: Use of electronic health records for public health surveillance to advance public health. Annu. Rev. Public Health **36**, 345–359 (2015)

51. Cohen, I.G., Amarasingham, R., Shah, A., Xie, B., Lo, B.: The legal and ethical concerns that arise from using complex predictive analytics in health care. Health Aff. **33**(7), 1139–1147 (2014)

52. Ram, S., Zhang, W., Williams, M., Pengetnze, Y.: Predicting asthma-related emergency department visits using big data. IEEE J. Biomed. Health Inform. **19**(4), 1216–1223 (2015)

53. Santosh, T., Ramesh, D.: DENCLUE-DE: differential evolution based DENCLUE for scalable clustering in big data analysis. In: Smys, S., Senjyu, T., Lafata, P. (eds.) ICCNCT 2019. LNDECT, vol. 44, pp. 436–445. Springer, Cham (2020). https://doi.org/10.1007/978-3-030-37051-0_50

54. Ayeni, F., Misra, S., Omoregbe, N.: Using big data technology to contain current and future occurrence of ebola viral disease and other epidemic diseases in West Africa. In: Tan, Y., Shi, Y., Buarque, F., Gelbukh, A., Das, S., Engelbrecht, A. (eds.) ICSI 2015. LNCS, vol. 9142, pp. 107–114. Springer, Cham (2015). https://doi.org/10.1007/978-3-319-20469-7_13

55. Behera, R.K., Jena, M., Rath, S.K., Misra, S.: Co-LSTM: convolutional LSTM model for sentiment analysis in social big data. Inf. Process. Manage. **58**(1), 102435 (2021)

56. Ward, P.R.: Improving access to, use of, and outcomes from public health programs: the importance of building and maintaining trust with patients/clients. Front. Public Health **5**, 22 (2017)

57. Okewu, E., Misra, S., Fernandez, S.L., Ayeni, F., Mbarika, V., Damaševičius, R.: Deep neural networks for curbing climate change-induced farmers-herdsmen clashes in a sustainable social inclusion initiative. Problemy Ekorozwoju **14**(2) (2019)

Improving the Prediction Accuracy of Academic Performance of the Freshman Using Wonderlic Personnel Test and Rey-Osterrieth Complex Figure

Ochilbek Rakhmanov$^{(\boxtimes)}$ (ID) and Senol Dane

Nile University of Nigeria, Plot 681, Cadastral Zone C-OO, Research & Institution Area, Jabi, Abuja, Nigeria
{ochilbek.rakhmanov,senol.dane}@nileuniversity.edu.ng

Abstract. Prediction of academic performance of the students continue to be hot topic in educational data mining field. In this paper, a linear regression analysis was conducted on IQ test, Rey-Osterrieth Complex Figure (ROCF) and Cumulative Grade Points Average (CGPA). A dataset from 111 undergraduate (59 females, 52 males) students from 2 different faculties (Medicine and Computer Science) were collected. The results show that both IQ and ROCF are significantly correlated to CGPA. Linear regression test shows that the combination of IQ-ROCF (β = 0.565) can serve as good feature to predict CGPA.

Keywords: Regression · Prediction · Academic performance · IQ test · Rey-Osterrieth Complex Figure

1 Introduction

Prediction of academic performance of the students continue to be hot topic in educational data mining field. Many researches proposed different models to predict the performance of the students [1–3]. Mostly, the reason for such research was common, to predict the weak students before the final results, and take necessary action actions to boost student's performance. As the prediction tools didn't vary too much, many of the researchers used well known machine learning and data mining tools, but in every research, the real burden was the data. For the practitioner, it is important to know, what dataset needs to be used in prediction. Thus, selection of the database, extracting useful information and feature engineering is remaining the main focus in this field.

The population used in this research, during data collection, was undergraduate students. As the information about freshman undergraduate student (or a student who recently registered for online university level course) is usually limited for the researcher, most of the data were collected within the educational period [2, 4, 5]. Participation to lectures, assignment completion, midterm scores and some other datasets were collected for campus students, while using video lectures, asking questions, trying quizzes, time

© Springer Nature Switzerland AG 2021
S. Misra and B. Muhammad-Bello (Eds.): ICTA 2020, CCIS 1350, pp. 54–65, 2021.
https://doi.org/10.1007/978-3-030-69143-1_5

spend online and some other were main features for data mining for students who were taking online courses [6, 7].

Unfortunately, there are very few tools that can be used to predict the student's future academic performance, before the start of the educational process. IQ tests, personal background information, university entry examination scores and some other features were evaluated as tool for prediction [8], but those features can differ with respect to student's ethnicity, educational background and family conditions, except IQ, as IQ tests scores remain relatively stable after age of 5 or 6 years [9]. It is worthy to mention that IQ test is one of leading tools to evaluate mental and intelligence condition of the student but rarely account for more than %50 of the variance in academic performance [10]. Chamorro et al. suggested that some factors, other than IQ ability, can contribute to individual differences in academic performance [2]. This hypothetically forced us to conduct a research, if it possible to find an extra tool which can help to IQ test to predict Cumulative Grade Points Average (CGPA) scores.

In this research, a linear and multiple linear regression analysis were conducted on IQ test and Rey- Osterrieth Complex Figure (ROCF) test results of the students, to predict students CGPA. Both IQ test and ROCF are less biased to the students educational and cultural background, thus can serve as good tools for predicting student's performance. Yet, cognitive drawing test are widely used in many fields, like education and psychology [11], to assess participant's mental and phycological condition.

1.1 IQ Test and CGPA

IQ, short for intelligence quotient, is a measure of a person's reasoning ability. In short, it is supposed to gauge how well someone can use information and logic to answer questions or make predictions [9]. From primary school students up to university level, indeed, educational attainment is moderately well predicted by IQ [9]. The comparative study on IQ and academic performance has a long history, as valid measures of IQ have been available since the early 1900s [12]. Mackintosh et al. looked into IQ test from different perspectives and how it can be related to human ability and performance, mentioning that IQ is being used as strong tool to look into student's academic performance [9]. Duckworth and Seligman compared the effect of IQ and self-discipline on academic performance and arrived to conclusion that self-discipline measured in the fall accounted for more than twice as much variance as IQ in final grades in high school students [12]. Song et al. compared mental ability (IQ) and emotional ability effects on academic performance and social interaction of college students, arriving to conclusion that mental ability was stronger prediction in comparison to emotional ability [13].

In a same manner, during this research, ROCF was selected as secondary tool to IQ test, to establish a linear regression between academic performance and IQ-ROCF. Out of many existing valid and reliable IQ tests, The Wonderlic Personnel Test was used during this research [14]. This test can be conducted in 2 versions; Type 1 (WPT) - 50 questions to be answered in 12 min and Type 2 (WPT-Q) - 30 questions to be answered in 8 min. WPT-Q was employed for this research.

1.2 ROCF and Academic Performance

The Rey-Osterrieth Complex Figure (ROCF) test was developed by Rey in 1942 [15] and standardized by Osterrieth in 1944 [16]. It is a nonverbal neuropsychological test and is used for the evaluation of visuospatial and visual memory [5, 17, 18]. The ROCF consists of three test conditions: Copy, immediate recall, and delayed recall. The results include scores related to location, accuracy, and organization [17–19]. The short memory (immediate recall) and long memory (delayed recall) were subject in several researches related to this study. Ardilla and Roselli conducted a research on adults, sample of 624 normal adults was assessed, where they compared the relation between ROCF and educational level of the adults and arrived to conclusion that ROCF Copy scores depend upon the individual's age and educational level [20]. Swanson conducted a research on more than 170 children and adults, to see how does the short memory and working memory (utilizes the information in a framework to temporarily store and manipulate the information) contribute to academic achievements [21]. The results show that both short term and working memory are important in understanding reading comprehension and mathematics.

As the literature shows, ROCF could be a significant factor in addressing the educational level and comprehension of academic requirements. Thus, ROCF was selected as one of important features in prediction of academic performance in this study (Fig. 1).

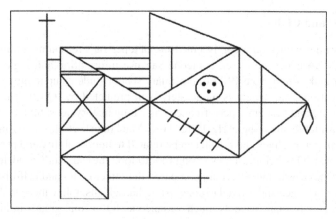

Fig. 1. ROCF sample

1.3 Linear Regression to Predict Academic Performance

The least square method is a procedure to determine the best fit line to data; the proof uses simple calculus and linear algebra. The basic problem is to find the best fit straight line $y = ax + b$ given that, for $n \in \{1, 2, ..., N\}$, the pairs (x_n, y_n) are observed. The method easily generalizes to finding the best fit of the form [22].

$$y = a_1 f_1(x) + a_2 f_2(x) + ... + a_K f_K(x) \tag{1}$$

We may define the error associated by

$$E(a, b) = \sum_{n=1}^{N} (y_n - (ax_n + b))^2 \tag{2}$$

The goal is to reduce the value of $E(a, b)$; in other words, find the values of a and b that minimize the error. The best fit values of a and b are obtained by solving a linear system of equations given in (3) [9].

$$\begin{pmatrix} a \\ b \end{pmatrix} = \begin{pmatrix} \sum_{n=1}^{N} x_n^2 & \sum_{n=1}^{N} x_n \\ \sum_{n=1}^{N} x_n & \sum_{n=1}^{N} 1 \end{pmatrix}^{-1} \begin{pmatrix} \sum_{n=1}^{N} x_n y_n \\ \sum_{n=1}^{N} y_n \end{pmatrix} \tag{3}$$

In brief, multiple linear regression uses least square method to optimize the parameters to establish best fit line in form of $y = a_n x_n + \cdots + a_1 x_1 + a_0$, where $(x_n, \ldots, x_2, x_1)$ are independent input variable to predict y, and this is done through optimizing coefficients $(a_n, \ldots, a_1, a_0)$ [22].

A variety of data mining tools were employed by researchers to predict academic performance, but linear regression still remains as one of simplest and most effective tools when the dataset consists of continuous variables.

As the main subject of this research is to predict CGPA scores, several papers addressed this issue before. Huang and Fang used linear regression to establish that midterm results ($\beta = 0.413$) and CGPA ($\beta = 0.3$) are most effective feature out of 5 selected feature to predict students possible course failure [3]. Duckworth and Seligman stated that in multiple regression analysis, self-discipline accounted for more than twice as much variance in final CGPA ($\beta = 0.65$) as IQ did ($\beta = 0.25$) [12]. Chamorro et al. stated that IQ was significantly correlated ($r = 0.44$) with student's deep learning ability, which was one of most important features during linear regression prediction of students exam marks [2].

The paper follows following structure; in Sect. 2 the methodology is presented with all used instruments, whereas Sect. 3 presents the results of the regression experiment. The discussion of the results was done in Sect. 4 and the conclusion in Sect. 5.

2 Methodology

2.1 Ethics and Standards

All ethical standards were strictly followed during conduction of survey and research. All procedures performed in studies involving human participants were in accordance with the ethical standards of the institutional and/or national research committee and with the 1964 Helsinki declaration and its later amendments or comparable ethical standards. Informed consent was obtained from all individual participants included in the study.

2.2 Participants

111 students from two different departments (Computer Science and Medicine) voluntarily participated in the study. 52 men (age M = 21.12 years, SD = 2.02) and 59 women (age M = 21.35 years, SD = 1.81), all students of Nile University of Nigeria. The age of the participants was not different statistically by sex.

2.3 The Wonderlic Personnel Test

This WPT-Q (short version of original test) is thirty item test is administered in 8 min and measures IQ [14]. The total score may vary from 0 to 30. Items include math, logic, general knowledge and verbal reasoning skills. Students were given WPT-Q test and asked to finish it in eight minutes. Once the test finished, results were recorded for each student, and these results served as IQ test results. Maximum score was 11 points, minimum 0.

2.4 ROCF

The methodology proposed by Meyers et al. was the guideline during ROCF test [19].

1. A copy of ROCF and three pieces of blank sheets were given to students. They were asked to copy the figure to one of blank sheets. Two-three minutes in average was given. Once the copying process is completed, the ROCF and copied page was collected back.
2. Once the Step 1 is completed, students were asked to draw the ROCF on blank sheet from their memory. 3 min was allowed time. Once the time was over, all pictures were collected back. These pictures served as immediate recall (short term memory).
3. After Step 2, students were involved in completely different relaxing activity for 30 min. After this activity, the students were requested to draw ROCF again on final blank sheet in same time period. These pictures served as delayed recall (long term memory).
4. After completion of all steps, using marking scheme proposed by Meyers and Meyers [19], all sketches were scored using Table 1 as reference. There are 18 elements on ROCF, which are scored using Table 1. The total score ranged from 0.0 to 36.0. Maximum score was 33 points, while minimum was 2 points. As immediate recall and delayed recall scores didn't vary too much (average mean in difference M < 2.0) the average of immediate recall and delayed recall scores was used during regression analysis. So ROCF score for every student was recorded.

Figure 2 presents some pictures of experiment participants. Comparing the two pictures, one can clearly understand which student have good long memory and which one has week one.

Table 1. Scoring of ROCF test [19]

Score	Accuracy	Placement
2	Accurately drawn	Correctly placed
1	Accurately drawn	Incorrectly placed
1	Inaccurately drawn	Correctly placed
0.5	Inaccurately drawn, but recognizable	Incorrectly placed
0	Inaccurately drawn and unrecognizable	Incorrectly placed

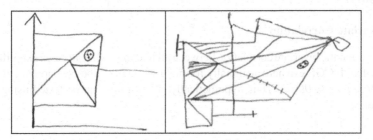

Fig. 2. Sample images of ROCF drawn by students

2.5 Dataset Formation

Following inputs presented on Table 2 were used during regression analysis:

Table 2. Inputs

Input value	Explanation
IQ	Students IQ test scores
ROCF	Average of immediate and delayed recall scores
IR	Average score of IQ and ROCF (I.R. – initials of IQ and ROCF). Used during simple linear regression
CGPA	CGPA score of the student

As all features have different score distribution ranges IQ (0–11), ROCF (2–33) and CGPA (0.9–5.0), they were normalized in range of 0.0 to 1.0 using (4). I.R. score was produced after normalization of the data. Table 3 is descriptive statistics after normalization process was done.

$$X' = \frac{X - X_{min}}{X_{max} - X_{min}} \qquad (4)$$

Table 3. Descriptive statistics after normalization

Variable	Mean ± Std
IQ	0.62 ± 0.23
ROCF	0.32 ± 0.31
IR	0.55 ± 0.23
CGPA	0.48 ± 0.24

3 Results

3.1 Bivariate Correlation

Table 4 present the bivariate correlation between all features. All features are significantly correlated with CGPA, where artificially formed I.R. seems to be best option among all ($r = 0.565$, $p < 0. 0001$). Thus hypothetically, all features can be tested using linear regression.

Table 4. Bivariate correlation between features.

Variable	Parameters	CGPA	IQ	ROCF	IR
CGPA	Pearson Corr.	1	.394[**]	.486[**]	.565[**]
	Sig. (2-tailed)		.000	.000	.000
	N	111	111	111	111
IQ	Pearson Corr.		1	.384[**]	.729[**]
	Sig. (2-tailed)			.000	.000
	N		111	111	111
ROCF	Pearson Corr.			1	.783[**]
	Sig. (2-tailed)				.000
	N			111	111
IR	Pearson Corr.				1
	Sig. (2-tailed)				
	N				111

[**]. Correlation is significant at the 0.01 level (2-tailed).

This moderate correlation can be observed better, when the data is placed on scatter plot (Fig. 3). While ROCF score behaved better, IQ score also presented correlation, but not in very promising way.

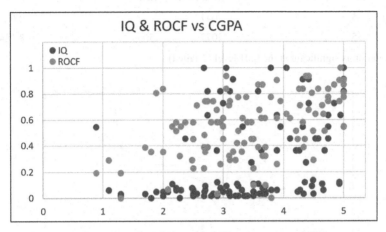

Fig. 3. Scatter plot of IQ and ROCF scores versus CGPA

3.2 Regression Analysis

Multiple Linear Regression. When IQ and ROCF were entered simultaneously in multiple linear regression analysis to predict CGPA, the overall regression equation was significant $(F(2,108) = 21.7, p < 0.001)$, with R^2 of 0.29. The individual predictors were examined further and indicated that IQ $(t = 2.766, p < 0.01)$ and ROCF $(t = 4.462, p < 0.01)$, both were significant predictors in the model. As it was expected, ROCF score had more effect on model compared to IQ (Table 5).

Table 5. Coefficients for multiple regression test

	Unstandardized coefficients		Standardized coefficients	
	B	Std. error	Beta	t
IQ	.177	.064	.243	2.766**
ROCF	.394	.088	.393	4.462**

**. Correlation is significant at the 0.01 level (2-tailed).

Simple Linear Regression. Next, I.R. was tested with linear regression to predict CGPA. A significant regression equation was found $(F(1,109) = 51.2, p < 0.001)$, with R^2 of 0.32. I.R. was accounted for more than 56% of variance $(\beta = 0.565, p < 0.001)$ (Table 6 and Fig. 4).

Table 6. Coefficients for multiple regression test

	Unstandardized coefficients		Standardized coefficients	
	B	Std. Error	Beta	t
(const.)	.35	.041		8.621**
IR	.55	.077	.565	7.154**

**. Correlation is significant at the 0.01 level (2-tailed).

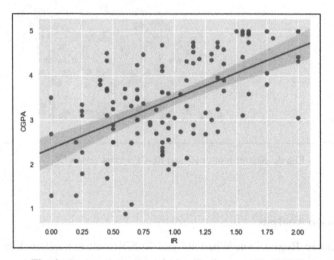

Fig. 4. Scatter plot and regression line between IR~CGPA

3.3 Testing Models

Both of the developed models were tested as a predictor. 75% of the data was used for training, while 25% was reserved for testing. Mean absolute error (MAE), mean squared error (MSE) and root mean squared error (RMSE) were calculated for the test data and Table 7 presents all the error rates after testing was done.

Table 7. Error rates for the developed models

Model	MAE	MSE	RMSE
Multiple LR	0.661	0.676	0.822
Simple LR	0.676	0.687	0.828

4 Discussion

Linear and multiple regression tests were conducted to predict CGPA scores of the students, where independent variables were IQ test score, ROCF score, IR score, which is combination of IQ and ROCF scores and their various combinations. Following three observations can summarize the experiments in total.

- *Observation 1.* The results of Table 4 clearly state that all features are significantly correlated with CGPA; IQ, ROCF and artificially formed IR. This directly support the conclusion of previous studies that IQ [9, 12, 13] and ROCF [20, 21] are significantly correlated to academic performance of the student. Moreover, this study establishes the fact that they are not only significantly correlated for children and high school students, but also for undergraduate students as well.
- *Observation 2.* The significant contribution to the knowledge of this study is the established fact that the future performance of the student can predicted using IQ and ROCF ($\beta = 0.565$, $p < 0.001$), unlike the previous studies, where researcher needed to collect the data during the education period.
- *Observation 3.* Even though the multiple regression equation was significant ($F(2,108) = 21.7, p < 0.001. R^2 = 0.29$), still significant results of the linear regression ($F(1,109) = 51.2, p < 0.001. R^2 = 0.32$) presented better results, while the results of the model tests (Table 7) shows that error rates are almost same, with slight decimal differences. Thus, it can be concluded that calculation and usage of IR scores may lead to better prediction model.

Based on these three observations mentioned above, enough evidence is presented to claim that ROCF can definitely serve as an element for future CGPA prediction, along with IQ test. In fact, ROCF managed to improve the regression accuracy when it was combined with IQ test results, as the results in Sect. 3 shows.

5 Conclusion

The linear and multiple regression tests were conducted during this research to establish relation and prediction ability between IQ, ROCF and CGPA. The results show that, indeed, the combination of IQ and ROCF can be used for academic performance prediction. Moreover, the combined score between them can serve for better prediction model.

This research was focused on finding one extra tool to IQ, in purpose of developing a reliable prediction model. Thus, the research was limited to only usage of ROCF, while there exist many other tests which can be used to evaluate cognitive and memory abilities. Future researches can concentrate on other useful tests as well.

The literature review shows that ROCF is usually used during practice with mentally unstable patients. As it was stated before, practitioners use them to test long and short-term memory. But this ability is also highly important for undergraduate students. A tremendous amount of information is passing through student's receivers daily, and it is important to train them to keep this info for long and short term in their mind. Thus, the experiment conducted during this study shows that ROCF can serve as a useful instrument in this aspect. ROCF was only tested as auxiliary element in this study to predict the academic performance, but it may have very wide variety of fields as well. A future study can look into it, on how the ROCF test can help to improve the education and wellbeing of the undergraduate students.

As linear regression model was employed during this research, some other data mining techniques can be tested as well, to see if they can produce better prediction accuracies. This, as well, can be investigated in future researches.

References

1. Ayán, M.N.R., García, M.T.C.: Prediction of university students' academic achievement by linear and logistic models. Spanish J. Psychol. **11**, 275–288 (2008)
2. Chamorro-Premuzic, T., Furnham, A.: Personality, intelligence and approaches to learning as predictors of academic performance. Personality Individ. Differ. **44**, 1596–1603 (2008)
3. Huang, S., Fang, N.: Predicting student academic performance in an engineering dynamics course: a comparison of four types of predictive mathematical models. Comput. Educ. **61**, 133–145 (2013)
4. Sorour, S.E., Mine, T., Goda, K., Hirokawa, S.: A predictive model to evaluate student performance. J. Inf. Process. **23**, 192–201 (2015)
5. Azeta, A.A., et al.: Closing institutional gaps through academic research management system and implications in Nigeria. Int. J. Pharm. Technol. **8**, 22906–22914 (2016)
6. Zacharis, N.Z.: A multivariate approach to predicting student outcomes in web-enabled blended learning courses. Internet High. Educ. **27**, 44–53 (2015)
7. Fernandez-Sanz, L., Misra, S.: Analysis of cultural and gender influences on teamwork performance for software requirements analysis in multinational environments. IET Softw. **6**, 167–175 (2012)
8. Ahmed, A., Elaraby, I.S.: Data mining: a prediction for student's performance using classification method. World J. Comput. Appl. Technol. **2**, 43–47 (2014)
9. Mackintosh, N., Mackintosh, N.J.: IQ and Human Intelligence. Oxford University Press, Oxford (2011)
10. Chamorro-Premuzic, T., Furnham, A.: A possible model for understanding the personality-intelligence interface. Br. J. Psychol. **95**, 249–264 (2004)
11. Rakhmanov, O., Agwu, N.N., Adeshina, S.A.: Experimentation on hand drawn sketches by children to classify Draw-a-Person test images in psychology. In: The Thirty-Third International Flairs Conference (2020)
12. Duckworth, A.L., Seligman, M.E.: Self-discipline outdoes IQ in predicting academic performance of adolescents. Psychol. Sci. **16**, 939–944 (2005)
13. Song, L.J., Huang, G., Peng, K.Z., Law, K.S., Wong, C.-S., Chen, Z.: The differential effects of general mental ability and emotional intelligence on academic performance and social interactions. Intelligence. **38**, 137–143 (2010)
14. Wonderlic, E.F.: Wonderlic Personnel Test User's Manual. Wonderlic, Libertyville (1992)
15. Rey, A.: L'examen psychologique dans les cas d'encephalopathie traumatique. Arch Psychol. **28**, 112 (1942)
16. Osterrieth, P.A.: Le test de copie d'une figure complexe; contribution a l'etude de la perception et de la memoire. Archives de psychologie (1944)
17. Rakhmanov, O., Dane, S.: The relationships among gender, handedness, GPA, depression and visual memory in the ROCF test in university students. J. Res. Med. Dental Sci. **8**, 37–42 (2020)

18. Rakhmanov, O., Dane, S.: Correlations among IQ, visual memory assessed by ROCF test and GPA in university students. J. Res. Med. Dental Sci. **8**, 1–5 (2020)
19. Meyers, J.E., Meyers, K.R.: Rey complex figure test under four different administration procedures. Clin. Neuropsychol. **9**, 63–67 (1995)
20. Ardila, A., Rosselli, M.: Educational Effects on the ROCF Performance. Rey-Osterrieth Complex Figure HandBook, pp. 271–281 (2003)
21. Swanson, H.L.: Short-term memory and working memory: do both contribute to our understanding of academic achievement in children and adults with learning disabilities? J. Learn. Disab. **27**, 34–50 (1994)
22. Ochilbek, R.: Development of a method for evaluating quality of education in secondary schools using ML algorithms. In: Proceedings of the 2019 11th International Conference on Education Technology and Computers. pp. 23–29 (2019)

Comparative Analyses of Machine Learning Paradigms for Operators' Voice Call Quality of Service

Jacob O. Mebawondu(✉) ⓘ

Department of Computer Science, Federal Polytechnic Nasarawa, Nasarawa, Nasarawa, Nigeria
mebawondu1010@gmail.com, mebawondujacobo@fedpolynas.edu.ng

Abstract. Mobile network operators render data, audio calls, and multimedia services to their customers. Though operators enjoy patronage, the number of customers increases over limited resources, the challenge of value for money paid becomes the concern of MNOs, and their customers. A significant weakness in the researchers' assessment of operators' voice call services is lack of performance evaluation on models developed base on a data set covering a broader area. This paper carried out the comparative performance analyses of operators' audio quality of service (QoS) using the six machine language algorithms. The crowdsourcing approach was used to captutre desired data. The results of comparative analyses shows that in terms of accuracy, ID3 ranked first to be followed by support vector machine (SVM), C4.5, neural network while Fuzzy and adaptive neuro fuzzy inference system (ANFIS) ranked fifth and sixth, respectively. The precision result shows that ID3, SVM, ANFIS, and C4.5 ranked first, second, third, and fourth, respectively. In terms of overall ranking, ID3 demonstrated most superior algorithm because it ranked first, SVM, C4.5, ANFIS ranked second, third and fourth, respectively. Evaluated machine learning-based models will have a positive impact on the service delivery of telecommunication network operators.

Keywords: *V*oice call · Quality of Service · Key performance indicators · Classifier · Operators

1 Introduction

This era of pandemic, restricted movement, security challenges, schools closed, and economic difficulties; require an efficient communication system so that people can carry out most of their functions from the comfort of their homes. To this end, telecommunication has a significant role to play. For over the decades, the telecommunications industry has existing en-mass data available for data mining activities. Two issues are emanating about data mining application for voice calls record; the first is that the sector has a large volume of records and are among the world's most substantial records [1]. Secondly, data mining appropriate for generated data because network data and call details are time-based. The higher the number of customers over limited resources, the more the challenge for services for MNO customers [1, 2].

© Springer Nature Switzerland AG 2021
S. Misra and B. Muhammad-Bello (Eds.): ICTA 2020, CCIS 1350, pp. 66–79, 2021.
https://doi.org/10.1007/978-3-030-69143-1_6

Mobile network operators render data, audio calls, and multimedia services to their customers. Though service providers enjoy patronage, however, as the number of customers increase over limited resources, the challenge of QoS affects MNOs, and customers. The importance of QoS makes the service providers periodically evaluate their network services and generate what we call false reports because of customer complaints. The qualities of service of telecommunication companies can be viewed from the mobile operator or user perspective.

A comprehensive survey carried out various algorithms' performance to determine their effectiveness based on specific criteria in the education sector [3]. The authors reported that users save 97.3% of the time using Natural language or ML techniques. Closely related to that work by other authors, machine learning is reliable in estimating any software's fault tolerance level [4]. The paper documented that the best algorithms are a neural network.

Many researchers have attempted to evaluate QoS based on one or more parameters called key performance indicators (KPIs). Data mining techniques are employed to classify and model QoS because operators use large volumes of data [2]. However, some researchers do not evaluate the classification model developed. This work carried out a performance evaluation of six data mining algorithms using standard metrics such as accuracy, precision, alarm rate, true positive rate. The dataset used for this work was derived from a crowdsource survey for a year. In addition, drive test method was used to capture voice calls from one of the areas to validate the crowdsourced data [5, 6]. This work results illustrate the importance of the applied algorithms for evaluating voice calls QoS.

2 Literature Review

Researchers made several attempts to analyse, evaluate and model the service providers in the Nigeria [7]. One of the researchers work reviewed the services GSM providers in country as not encouraging. Some of them reported that coverage area, QoS and accessibility are unreliable [7].

Performance evaluation (PE) techniques such as confusion matrix and Mean Square Error were employed to validate the model developed. The data in the confusion matrix used to compute the accuracy and precision of the developed model. The values on the diagonal correctly predicted while others wrongly predicted. Mean Square Error (MSE) compute the variation of estimated values from the real values. MSE tool used to estimate accuracy; hence, the result is vital in decision-making; the lower the MSE, the better. The formula used to compute MSE given in Eq. (1):

$$MSE = \frac{\sum (T_p - O_p)^2}{np}.\tag{1}$$

Where p is the number of variables, np is the degree of freedom; T_p is the desired output, and O_p is the actual output from each training epoch.

Performance Analysis of cellular Networks is an excellent tool for planng. Evaluation of the resources on the ground is pre-requisite to proper planning and antidote to failure, this justifies the reason to carry out performance evaluation in the mobile industry.

From the work on evaluation of network service providers, the result shows the use of several levels of KPI achievements in the different networks. They reported that the Globacom Nigeria Plc industry performing the best and the MNOs achieved some NCC QoS benchmarks but had a failure in some geographical areas [8]. QoS performance evaluation of voice over LTE, documented [9], justified by the need to standardize voice over LTE and have a stable and erected feature framework. Evaluating voice over LTE, performance evaluation results obtained using a simulator is one of the work's goals. The work reported that the speed of sending from the sender and receiver are critical motivators that can affect the quality of calls. The shortcoming of the work was that the simulation technique and the limited area used for the research. [10]. The paper recommended investment on transmission network and to develop more switching center, more base station. Data collection area and time of coverage are factors that negate the result of their work.

Some researchers reported the performance of analysis GSM in specific cities in Nigeria [11, 12]. Five KPIs used to estimate QoS by MTN using the NCC benchmark. The papers reported that computed KPIs are lower than the benchmark. The challenge of their work are limited area and only one MNO considered for the research. The results obtained from the analysis indicated that Airtel's QoS performance rated higher than the other three GSM services providers tested. Just like most researchers, they have limited coverage area [13]. In a similar work [14], documented performance analysis of GSM Network. The work reported that the percentage of samples considered have weak signal strength and poor quality. The paper recommended wider coverage area, and justified need to meet customer's satisfaction in terms of better signal strength and excellent QoS [13]. As one of the KPI, the congestion rate has a substantial factor in the QoS render to subscribers [15]. The study's objective is to detect early traffic congestion of a specific location and evaluate the accuracy of prediction using necessary performance measures like MSE. The paper targeted at predicting traffic congestion along a chosen route [16]. The work reported that Artificial Neural Networks (MLP) is an effective tool for traffic congestion prediction. If another algorithm was used, it could have produced a better platform for comparative analysis.

Also, another work studied, the DM approach was used to analyze the mobile telecommunication network [17]. Five DM techniques were used to develop classification models. Performance evaluation carried out, and the result shows that the NN multi-layer was the best classification accuracy of 84.5%, but did not carry the comparative evaluation. Presented an evaluation of both voice and data QoS in a 2G, 3G. 4G, and 5G environments [17]. The measurement of voice and data over a period, and analysis reported QoS for mobile operators for VoLTE and Video over LTE (ViLTE) was reported. The work [18] investigated radio traffic under various fixed-rate traffic, specifically, the accuracy investigated under different scenarios. The author employed affect-based technique for voice QoE [19]. The work used affect base technique known as multi-modal analysis to estimate QoS, rather than a system or user-centric approach. The work employed DM techniques such as SVM & classification model; however, the work considered only an accuracy parameter.

Comparative analysis of different algorithms in detecting machine learning efficiency in the social network for a large data size popularly called Bigdata was proposed. Relating the result to other works, as applied to the social network that generates a massive amount of data daily, the paper reported that the Map-Reduce algorithm is the best among the algorithms considered [20]. Applying ML paradigm on social media datasets such as Twitter dataset, the framework developed to estimate the performance of network centrality of big data. The authors also compared the work with other techniques to determine the best approach and validate that the first search technique is the best using empirical facts; a distributed computing was documented [21].

A decision tree is also an efficient method of producing voice calls QoS classifiers [22]. The C4.5 algorithm as one of the decision trees algorithms helps to build decision trees, the same way as ID3. While decision tree algorithm is good for classification, artificial neural network (MLP) is good for both classification and modeling. MLP a network system has input, processing and output layers. Each connection has numeric weights, that enable neural nets adaptive to learning. The hybrid system combines Fuzzy logic, neural networks, and expert systems to prove their effectiveness. The justification for using ANFIS technique is to achieve optimum result. In addition, ANFIS is an excellent modeling tool that produce reliable prediction results [2].

Benchmarking is a tool used for comparing the QoS of one MNO to the other or MNO performance to the national and international best practices [23, 24]. The work aimed to carry out the performance benchmarking of cellular operators; evaluate the QoS from customer perception. Drive Test used for alternative data collection method and the country KPIs Benchmark employed for the evaluation. Based on the benchmarking of cellular networks, GSM of UMTS performed better than other operator's benchmark.

Conclusively a significant weakness in the researchers' assessment of operators' voice call services is lack of performance evaluation on models developed based on a data set covering a wider area, need at least four KPIs and to cover activities of major service providers [1, 7, 11–13, 23, 24]. The paper aimed at presenting comparative analyses of the performance of Machine Language Algorithms in assessing QoS of voice QoS of Nigerian Mobile Operators. The specific objective is to carry out the comparative performance analyses of operators' voice calls QoS using the Machine Language Algorithms.

3 Method, Materials, Results and Discussion

3.1 Data Collection

The crowdsourcing technique, reliable, was used mainly for data collection because of the challenge of getting data from the service providers. The data needed for this research were gotten directly from the volunteers' smart mobile devices. An audio QoS app was installed on the users' smartphones to capture data for the research work. While the Internet service of the smartphone is active, the application measures the KPIs metrics and gets the location parameter and network information. SP_1, SP_2, SP_3, SP_4 are the codes used for the four key operators in the country. The weaker operators in the country are labeled as SP_5. Calls variables such as received signal strengths and other parameters were collected and subjected to analysis. This section's target is to capture data on KPIs and other network information. The four principal KPI parameters identified: congestion rate, call drop rate, signal strength, and call success rate and coded as TCHR, CDR, RSS, and CSSR respectively. Drive test was carried out to check the network performance through coverage evaluation, system availability, network capacity, network retain-ability, and call quality. The reason for using drive test is to validate crowdsourced data.

3.2 Description of Dataset and Classification Techniques

Description of Dataset. In this study, the attributes needed to measure the service providers QoS identified from the reviewed papers. The identified attributes regarding the measure of the QoS of MNOs are displayed in Table 1. The four major network operators are labeled SP_1, SP_2, SP_3, SP_4, and the other smaller operators are labeled SP_5.

Table 1. Attributes identified for measuring the QoS

S/N	Attributes names	Labels	Attribute type
1.	State	States in the country and Federal Capital	**Character**
2.	Network Operators	SP_1, SP_2, SP_3, SP_4 SP_5	Character
3.	Day	Days of the week	**Date**
4.	Month	Months of the year	Character
5.	Year	2017, 2018	**Numeric**
6.	Signal Strength (RSS)	Poor, Fair, Good	Numeric
7.	Congestion Rate (TCHR)	Poor, Fair, Good	**Numeric**
8.	Call Success Rate (CSSR)	Poor, Fair, Good	Numeric
9.	Call Drop Rate (CDR)	Poor, Fair, Good	**Numeric**
10.	Voice QoS	Poor, Moderate, Excellent	Numeric

An average user made about 93 calls hence total audio calls made over one year that give us 482,520 calls. Pre-processing the data, a final dataset of 5157 were records generated, as shown in Table 2 [2].

Monthly Voice Calls QoS Dataset. The Table 2 illustrates distribution of the collected data over different months across the mobile networks identified for this study. The results also showed that the majority of data collected in December (14.3%), June (11.9%), November (11.1%), and August (10.5%), while the remaining months show a distribution less than 10% but at least 3.2%.

Frame Work. Figure 1 shows the voice QoS framework for the study. The first part of the framework involved collecting the raw data (1) from the researcher's field. The data collected in (1) required pre-processing (2) using data standardization and normalization to convert QoS variables, followed by filtering techniques. The pre-processed

Table 2. Distribution of the CN Voice service QoS Dataset per Months across MNOs.

Months	Service Providers/Networks					Total	%
	SP_1	SP_2	SP_3	SP_4	SP_5		
January	133	152	92	120	16	513	9.95
February	46	24	34	62	14	180	3.49
March	72	55	66	114	0	307	5.95
April	114	74	92	164	17	461	8.94
May	60	26	59	81	15	241	4.67
June	0	223	149	241	0	613	11.89
July	100	70	101	139	53	463	8.98
August	133	93	96	160	59	541	10.49
September	71	21	13	47	13	165	3.20
October	91	51	86	112	25	365	7.08
November	139	87	141	178	28	573	11.11
December	172	114	149	241	59	735	14.25
TOTAL	1131	990	1078	1659	299	5157	100.00

Voice QoS framework

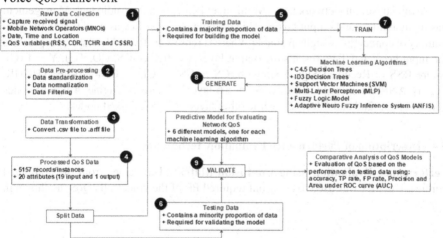

Fig. 1. Voice QoS framework for machine learning paradigms

data, collected in a comma-separated variable (.csv) file format, was converted via data transformation (3) into attribute relation file format (.arff), which is the preferred file format for the simulation environment of the predictive model. Following this, the pre-processed data (4) consisted of 5157 records containing 20 attributes such that 19 were input variables, and 1 is the target variable. After the pre-processed data in (4), split into two parts, such that a broader set of records consisted of the training data (5) while the smaller set of records consisted of the testing data (6). The training data used for training (6) six machine learning algorithms (C4.5 and ID3 decision trees, SVM, MLP, Fuzzy logic, and ANFIS models) in order to generate (6) six unique predictive models for QoS assessment. Finally, the six models were validated (9) by the testing data using some performance evaluation criteria as a basis of comparative analysis. The models were compared based on the true positive (TP) rate, false positive (FP) rate, precision, accuracy, and receiver operating characteristics curve (ROC).

3.3 Classification Techniques

The C4.5 algorithm's choice for classification is because it can handle missing data, continuous data, and good at pruning data. The ID3 decision trees' procedure is the same as the C4.5 but with differences at specific nodes. ID 3 was used to complement the C4.5 algorithm. SVM algorithm employed for classification and modeling voice QoS. In addition fuzzy logic was used to achieve modeling of audio QoS. Modeling using inference rules such as IF - THEN parts of IF-THEN Inference Engine.

IF (Par_A = rate AND Par_B = rate AND Par_C = rate AND Par_D = rate) THEN (QoS_x = rate).

The rules were generated from decision tree, modelled in fuzzy logic, results in 81 rules for this task.

Artificial Neural Network using Multi-layer Perceptron for Audio QoS Management has input, hidden, and output layers. This formula $H * (I + T)$ was used to find the total number of connection weight available Where H represents the hidden layer, I represents the input layer and T represents the output layer. $I = f(RSS, CS, CD, TC)$; $Y = f(C)$; where RSS = Received Signal Strength, CS = CSSR, CD = CDR, TC = THCHR. Finally, ANFIS employed in this work has a 6-layered inference engine. Adaptive nodes consist of 1st, 2nd and 5th layers while other layers are called fixed nodes.

3.4 Description of Performance Evaluation Techniques

Performance Evaluation using Confusion Matrix. The values from the computed confusion matrix was used to carry out required PE of the voice calls QoS, as shown in Fig. 2

A	B	C	←-------- Predicted
TP1	FN12	FN13	A- EXCELLENT
FP21	TN2	FN23	B- MODERATE
FP31	FN32	TN3	C- POOR

Fig. 2. Confusion matrix

Equations 2–11 shows the computation of PE metrics.

i)   TP rates –

$$TP\ (poor) = \frac{TP1}{TP1 + FN12 + FN13} \tag{2}$$

$$TP\ (moderate) = \frac{TN2}{FP21 + TN2 + FN23} \tag{3}$$

$$TP\ (excellent) = \frac{TN3}{FP31 + FN32 + TN3} \tag{4}$$

ii)   False Positive (FP) rates –

$$FP\ (poor) = \frac{FP21 + FP31}{FP21 + FP31 + TN2 + FN32 + FN23 + TN3} \tag{5}$$

$$FP\ (moderate) = \frac{FN12 + FN32}{TP1 + FN12 + FN13 + FN32 + FP31 + TN3} \tag{6}$$

$$FP\ (excellent) = \frac{FN13 + FN23}{FN13 + TP1 + FN12 + FP21 + TN2 + FN23} \tag{7}$$

iii)   Precision –

$$Precision\ (poor) = \frac{TP1}{TP1 + FP21 + FP31} \tag{8}$$

$$Precision\ (moderate) = \frac{TN2}{FN12 + TN2 + FN32} \tag{9}$$

$$Precision\ (excellent) = \frac{TN3}{FN13 + FN23 + TN3} \tag{10}$$

iv)   Accuracy –

$$Accuracy = \frac{TP1 + TN2 + TN3}{total} \tag{11}$$

Where:
total $= TP1 + FN12 + FN13 + FP21 + TN2 + FN23 + FP31 + FN32 + TN3$

3.5   Results and Discussion

Performance Evaluation of C4.5 Algorithm Classifier. The C4.5 algorithm available in WEKA software. Table 3 shows that the true positive rate was the same for the moderate and poor categories are 99.6% and 99.9% of the actual cases correctly classified. Considering precision metric, the model is efficient because the model predicts the poor (100%), moderate (99.9%), and excellent (98.4%) categories correctly.

Performance Evaluation of ID3 Algorithm Classifier. Table 4 displays the evaluation performance of the ID3 classifier. The ID3 classifier, False positive (FP) rate was the same for the moderate and excellent categories, a value of 0.1% of the actual categories misclassified. Considering precision metric, the model is efficient because the model predicts the poor (100%) moderate (99.9%) and excellent (99.5%) categories correctly.

Table 3. Performance evaluation of the C4.5 classifier

Category	TP value	FP value	Precision value
Poor	0.9990	0.0000	1.0000
Moderate	0.9960	0.0010	0.9990
Excellent	1.0000	0.0020	0.9840
Average	0.9983	0.0010	0.9943

Table 4. PE of the ID3 classifier

Category	TP value	FP value	Precision value
Poor	1.0000	0.0000	1.0000
Moderate	0.9990	0.0010	0.9990
Excellent	0.9980	0.0010	0.9950
Average	0.9990	0.0006	0.9980

Table 5 depicts the ID3 perform better than the C4.5 accuracy since it could predict seven more records than those predicted by the C4.5 algorithm. Also, performance results using other metrics such as TP rate, Precision, and FP rate were observed. The performance of the ID3 showed improved performance compared to that of the C4.5 algorithm.

Table 5. C4.5 and ID3 simulation results

Algorithms	Accuracy (%)	TP value	FP value	Precision value
C4.5	99.767	0.9983	0.0010	0.9943
ID3	99.903	0.9990	0.0006	0.9980

Performance Evaluation of SVM and MLP Classifiers. Table 6 displays PE results of SVM and MLP models,. SVM performs better than the MLP classifier because the SVM's TP, precision, and accuracy are higher than MLP; likewise, SVM's FP is lower than MLP.

The PE results of MNOs for Fuzzy Logic Model shows accuracy is high because it is 97.83% for all service providers. The SP_2 accuracy (99.57%) is higher than SP_1 (83.95%). The same trend was seen for FP, FP, and precision. Generally, the models developed are not only reliable but efficient.

ANFIS Model PE. In the same way, performance evaluation of the ANFIS model shows accuracy, TP and Precision are 97.10%, 95.50% and 99.47%, respectively.

Table 6. Summary of simulation results of the SVM and MLP classifier

Algorithms	Accuracy (%)	TP value	FP value	Precision value
SVM	99.825	0.9986	0.0006	0.9947
MLP	97.848	0.933	0.012	0.983

Performance Evaluation of Decision Tree, SVM, MLP, Fuzzy Logic, and ANFIS Models. Table 7 summarizes PE of all models. Four metrics were used to evaluate the supervised machine learning algorithms. From Table 7, the SVM had better performance than MLP regarding accuracy since it could predict 102 more records than those predicted by the MLP algorithm. The results of the study further showed that both algorithms used could predict poor cases effectively. The study showed that the MLP algorithm could not correctly distinguish excellent cases leading to the significant positive rates among the predictions of the moderate cases made. The result shows that the SVM classifier is a better- algorithm for developing predictive model for QoS of mobile telecommunication networks than the MLP classifier.

Table 7 shows the comparative analysis of the six machine learning algorithms' performance based on some evaluation criteria. The six predictive models were evaluated based on the accuracy expressed as a percentage (%), TP rate, FP rate, precision, and AUC, which are proportions. The predictive model with the best performance has the highest accuracy, TP rate, and precision, but the lowest FP rate. However, the AUC helps us understand the level of bias; hence, the closer the value is to 1, the lower the bias. The summary of comparative performance evaluation of the considered algorithms and their ranking is illustrated in Table 7. In terms of accuracy, ID3 ranked first followed by SVM, while Fuzzy and ANFIS ranked fifth and sixth, respectively. The precision result shows that ID3, SVM, ANFIS, and C4.5 ranked first, second, third, and fourth, respectively. In terms of overall ranking, ID3 demonstrated most superior algorithm because it ranked first, SVM, C4.5, ANFIS ranked second, third and fourth, respectively.

Figure 3 shows the ROC plot of the TP rate against the FP rate for the two decision trees algorithms, namely: C4.5 (left) and ID3 (right). For each graph, the precision's value is expressed as the color intensity of the ROC plot. For the C4.5 algorithm, the plot results revealed that the values of the TP rate fluctuated between lower and higher values for FP rates below 0.2. However, the TP rate value increased to a maximum value of 1 when the FP rate reached 0.2 but began to fall as the FP rate's values increased to 1. The AUC, which shows the total area under the ROC plot, showed a value of 0.9992. For the ID3 algorithm, there was a steady increase in TP rate value from 0 to 1 between FP rates of 0 to 0.1. Following this, the TP rate gradually fell from 1 as the FP rate's value increased to 1. The AUC, which shows the total area under the ROC plot, showed a value of 0.9998. The results revealed that the level of bias of the C4.5 algorithm was higher than that of the ID3 algorithm; however, both algorithms were able to distinguish between QoS classes.

Table 7. Performance evaluation of decision Tree, SVM, MLP, Fuzzy logic and ANFIS models

DM Tools	Accuracy	Rank	TP value	Rank value	FP value	Rank	Precision value	Rank	OverAll Rank	Area under ROC (AUC)
C4.5	99.767	3rd	0.9983	3rd	0.0010	3rd	0.9943	4th	3rd	0.9992
ID3	**99.903**	**1st**	**0.9990**	**1st**	**0.0006**	**1st**	**0.9980**	**1st**	**1st**	*0.9998*
SVM	99.825	2nd	0.9986	**2nd**	**0.0006**	1st	0.9947	2nd	2nd	0.9979
MLP	99.848	4th	0.933	6th	0.012	6th	0.9830	5th	6th	**0.9999**
Fuzzy Logic	97.828	5th	0.9825	4th	0.0081	5th	0.9439	6th	5th	–
ANFIS	97.1	6th	0.9550	5th	0.0019	4th	0.9947	3rd	4th	–

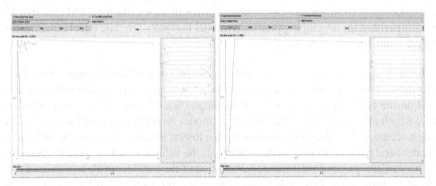

Fig. 3. ROC curve for C4.5 (left) and ID3 (right) decision trees algorithm

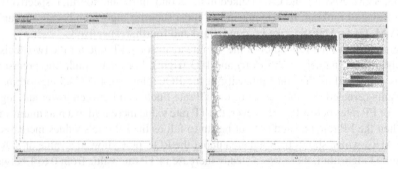

Fig. 4. ROC curve for support vector machines (SVM) (left) and multi-layer perceptron (MLP) (right) algorithm

Figure 4 shows the ROC plot of the TP rate against the FP rate for the two perceptron-based algorithms, namely: SVM (left) and MLP (right). For each graph, the precision's value is expressed as the color intensity of the ROC plot. A steady increase in the value of the TP rate from 0 to 1 between FP rates of 0 to 0.1. with the aid SVM algorithm. Following this, the TP rate gradually fell from 1 as the FP rate's value increased to 1. The AUC, which shows the total area under the ROC plot, showed a value of 0.9979. For the MLP algorithm, the ROC plot revealed a fluctuating pattern for the progression of the TP rate and FP rate due to the complexity of the simulation caused by the number of iterations. However, the results revealed that the TP rate values increased gradually to 1 from 0 between FP rates of 0 to 0.15. So, the TP rate values fluctuated between 1 and 0.85 as the value of the FP rate increased from 0.15 to 1. The AUC, which shows the total area under the ROC plot, showed a value of 0.9999.

3.6 Validation of Data Collection Techniques Using Correlation Model

Two collection techniques were employed to collect voice calls data. The Surveys and the analyses of measured data were carried out for this work. The comparative analysis of drive test and host-based methods of GSM networks was computed. A high correlation between the two methods of data collection observed. Hence, data from host-based is reliable and dependable as a driving test. The drive test data captured were from FUTA, Alagbaka, Oja, and Arakale areas of Akure City, Ondo State. The correlation coefficient of the data collated from both methods is 0.995862, implying a high relation between the data measured using the two methods. Hence, data from host-based technique presented in this research is reliable and dependable.

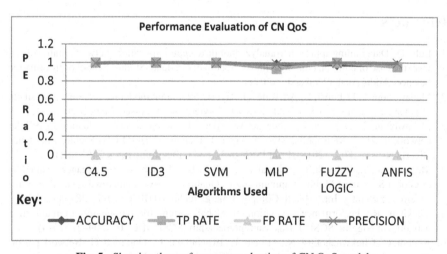

Fig. 5. Showing the performance evaluation of CN QoS models

Table 7 data are graphed as illustrated in Fig. 5. The trend of each classifier relatively to each metrics are shown in Fig. 5. Generally, the models perform well based on the four metrics, but ID3 provides the best result.

4 Conclusion and Recommendation

The study showed that although the two-decision trees model performed well, the ID3 decision tree is a better model. Although the ID3 had challenges in allocating QoS values to the combination of some of the input parameters, it justified the need to hybridize ID3 and C4.5 algorithms. The hybridized algorithm formed the basis of the rules for the Fuzzy logic model work. Furthermore, Also, 10-fold cross validation technique was used to train the developed model. Table 6 shows the SVM classifier predicted the quality of service (QoS) of mobile telecommunications companies better than the MLP classifier.

This work presents comparative analyses of the performance of different machine algorithms in assessing voice QoS of MNO services. The author used global standard metrics such as accuracy, precision, TP and FP rates metric for the evaluation. In terms of accuracy, ID3 ranked first to be followed by SVM, while Fuzzy and ANFIS ranked fifth and sixth, respectively. The precision result shows that ID3, SVM, ANFIS, and C4.5 ranked first, second, third, and fourth, respectively. In terms of overall ranking, ID3 demonstrated most superior algorithm because it ranked first, SVM, C4.5, ANFIS ranked second, third and fourth, respectively. MLP has best ROC among the 4th models considered. The developed predictive models recommended for monitoring and evaluation of the voice quality of service delivery. If implemented, the recommended models will have a positive impact on the service delivery of telecommunication network operators. Future work will focus on applying deep learning paradigm on larger broad band data for better service delivery.

References

1. Lulu, D.: Data mining approach to analyze mobile telecommunications network quality of service: the case of ethiotelecom. Msc thesis, School of Graduate Studies School of Information Science. Addis Ababa University (2014)
2. Mebawondu, J., Dahunsi, F., Adewale, O.: Hybrid intelligent model for real time assessment of voice quality of service. Sci. Afr. J. www.elsevier.com. Accessed 7 Feb 2020
3. Mebawondu, J., Dahunsi, F., Adewale, O., Alese, B.: Radio access evaluation of cellular network in Akure Metropolis, Nigeria. Niger. J. Technol. (NIJOTECH) Faculty Eng. Univ. Nigeria Nsukka **37**(3) (2018). Print ISSN 0331-8443, Electronic ISSN 2467-8821
4. Mebawondu, J., Dahunsi, F., Adewale, O., Alese. B., Momoh A.: Performance Evaluation of Global System of Mobile communications Quality of Service on crowd sourced data in a developing country. Int. J. Intell. Comput. Emerg. Technol. (IJICET) **1**(1), 28–34 (2017)
5. Adekitan, R.: Performance evaluation of global system for mobile telecommunication networks in Nigeria. SCSR J. Bus. Entrepreneurship (SCSR-JBE) **1**(1), 09–21 (2014)
6. Agubor, C., Chukwuchekwa, N., Atimati, E., Iwuchukwu, U., Ononiwu, G.: Network performance and quality of service evaluation of GSM providers in Nigeria: a case study of Lagos state. Int. J. Eng. Sci. Res. Technol. (2016)
7. Jameel, A., Shafiei, M.: QoS performance evaluation of voice over LTE network. Electr. Electron. Syst. **6**(1), 1–10 (2017)
8. Nnochiri, I.: Evaluation of the quality of service of global system for mobile telecommunication (GSM) operators in Nigeria. J. Multidisc. Eng. Sci. Technol. (JMEST) **2**(7) (2015)

9. Lawal, B., Ukhurebor, K., Adekoya, M., Aigbe, E.: Quality of service and performance analysis of a GSM network in Eagle Square, Abuja and its environs, Nigeria. Int. J. Sci. Eng. Res. (IJSER) **7**(8) (2016)
10. Galadancil, G., Abdullahi, S.: Performance analysis of GSM networks in Kano metropolis of Nigeria. Am. J. Eng. Res. (AJER) **7**(5), 69–79 (2018)
11. Alabi, I., Lawan, S., Fatai, O., Adunola, I.: GSM quality of service performance in Abuja, Nigeria. Int. J. Comput. Sci. Eng. Appl. (IJCSEA) **7** (2017)
12. Rajesh, K., Vijay, K., Rajnish, K.: Performance analysis of GSM network. Int. J. Adv. Res. Sci. Eng. (IJARSE) **3**(5), 244–246 (2014)
13. Nayarah, S., Umar, M., Shabia, S.: Early prediction of congestion in GSM based on area location using neural network. Int. J. Adv. Res. Electron. Commun. Eng. (IJARECE) **5**(5) (2016)
14. Raheem, I., Okereke, O.: Neural network approach to GSM traffic congestion prediction. Am. J. Eng. Res. (AJER) **03**(11), 131–138 (2014)
15. Smita, A., Reddy, K.: Bharati Vidyapeeth's Institute of Computer Applications and Management. Springer Int. J. Inf. Technol. https://doi.org/10.1007/s41870-020-00455-3. Accessed 12 June 2020
16. Anum, L., et al.: Springer EURASIP J. Wirel. Commun. Netw. **2017**(159) (2017)
17. Bhattacharya, I., Wanmin, W., Zhenyu, Y.: Human-Centric Comput. Inf. Sci. **2**(7) (2012). http://www.hcis-journal.com/content. Accessed 1,7 Feb 2020
18. Kantardzic, M., Zurada, J.: New Generation of Data Mining Applications. IEEE Press and John Wiley, Hoboken (2015)
19. Kadio_Glu, R., Dalveren, Y., Kara, A.: Quality of Service assessment: a case study on performance benchmarking of cellular network operators in Turkey. Turkish J. Electr. Eng. Comput. Sci., 548–559 (2015) http://journals.tubitak.gov. t r/e l ekt r ik/Research Article
20. Mebawondu, J., Dahunsi, F., Adewale, O., Alese, B.: Development of predictive model for audio quality of service in Nigeria. Int. J. Comput. Sci. Inf. Secur. (IJCSIS), 14–20 (2018)
21. Blessing, G., Azeta, A., Misra, S., Chigozie, F., Ahuja, R.: A machine learning prediction of automatic text based assessment for open and distance learning: a review. In: Abraham, A., Panda, M., Pradhan, S., Garcia-Hernandez, L., Ma, K. (eds.) IBICA 2019. AISC, vol. 1180, pp. 369–380. Springer, Cham (2021). https://doi.org/10.1007/978-3-030-49339-4_38
22. Behera, R.K., Rath, S.K., Misra, S., Leon, M., Adewumi, A.: Machine learning approach for reliability assessment of open source software. In: Misra, S., et al. (eds.) ICCSA 2019. LNCS, vol. 11622, pp. 472–482. Springer, Cham (2019). https://doi.org/10.1007/978-3-030-24305-0_35
23. Behera, R.K., Rath, S.K., Misra, S., Damaševičius, R., Maskeliūnas, R.: Large scale community detection using a small world model. Appl. Sci. **7**(11), 1173 (2017)
24. Kumar Behera, R., Kumar Rath, S., Misra, S., Damaševičius, R., Maskeliūnas, R.: Distributed centrality analysis of social network data using MapReduce. Algorithms **12**(8), 161 (2019)

LearnFuse: An Efficient Distributed Big Data Fusion Architecture Using Ensemble Learning Technique

Salefu Ngbede Odaudu[1]([✉]) [iD], Ime J. Umoh[1], Emmanuel A. Adedokun[1],
and Chukwuma Jonathan[2]

[1] Department Computer Engineering, Ahmadu Bello University, Zaria, Nigeria
{ousalefu,wale}@abu.edu.ng, ime.umog@gmail.com
[2] 041 Communication Deport, Nigerian Air Force, Lagos, Nigeria
cobhamcole@yahoo.com

Abstract. The use of Ensemble learning model for big data fusion is a machine learning technique of fusing data in an efficient and optimal way to enhance analytical result. This technique is less computationally expensive when compared with traditional method. In this work, spatial data were acquired, performed image filtration, standardization, feature extraction and Local learning method was adopted to partition the dataset into clusters. The portioned dataset was subject to training and testing, using machine learning algorithm (ensemble techniques) to implement data fusion. The result shows that Random Forest has an improved accuracy value of 87.46% and precision of 0.959% while SVM, Bagging, Naïve Bayes and Boosting has an accuracy of 82.3%, 86.95, 82.45%, 80.5% and precision value of 0.985%, 0.911%, 0.950% and 0.935% respectively.

Keywords: Algorithm · Big data fusion · Feature extraction · Ensemble learning · Machine learning

1 Introduction

Development of big Data fusion architecture has become an interesting research area owing to the volume of data generated on a daily basis. Therefore, necessitating the need to combine these data in a way that guarantee accuracy in information extracted for the purpose of decision making. Hence, data fusion is the process of aggregating structured, semi-structure and unstructured data generated across multiple platforms. In recent time, the volume of data generated is reported in literature to exceed 4 Zettabytes. This data explosive growth was what Cisco referred to as the Era of Big data. Big data is the accumulation of several other forms of data generated from sources such as sensors, social media, cell phones, online transaction, GPS signal and other channels of communication stored in the cloud. Big data entails the process of collecting, extracting, transforming, transporting, loading (ETL), classifying and interpretation of the data so collected. Each stage of the pipeline is to ensure accuracy in decision making.

© Springer Nature Switzerland AG 2021
S. Misra and B. Muhammad-Bello (Eds.): ICTA 2020, CCIS 1350, pp. 80–92, 2021.
https://doi.org/10.1007/978-3-030-69143-1_7

Fusing data for decision making is a task that requires heterogeneously sourced data which is combined to take information of greater quality, irrespective of the network. Data fusion in general knowledge is used as a tool for composing theories, methodologies and algorithms. The factors composed are then used to integrate the data generated from heterogeneous sources.

According to authors in [14, 24] data fusion techniques have been reported in literature, which includes studies on statistical features of big data [4, 11]. The studies include; understanding the statistical characterization of large dataset. (Shah et al., 2010) [17] carried out a study on image processing, focusing on image segmentation in remote sensing images, implemented image denoising [19] performed image fusion and [20] extracted features from images [15, 16]. Majority of work in the field of data fusion has been to ensure that dataset of different sizes is fused but they fail to find the correlation between different dataset. To achieve the objective of finding the correlation between different dataset,[14] developed a big data fusion architecture for both real-time and offline big data analytics [14]. A good number of big data analytics platform for real-time and offline processing (Apache Hadoop and Spark) are domiciled in the cloud, operating on federated computing architecture where big data analytics, management and processing task are divided to different computers or processing element in centralized and decentralized format. The underlying consequence of this architecture is that it amounts to huge computation complexity with such High bandwidth consumption, high latency and in a data center scenario, high energy consumption.

In order to integrate big data fusion techniques into emerging technology such as Internet of things (IoT), Fog Computing and 5G network to mention but a few, there is need to fuse data generated by RFID enabled devices in a distributed manner [21]. Amongst the available and recommended techniques of fusing data for emerging technologies, ensemble learning models is one of the key success of reliable data modeling and fusion methods in literature that offers improved performance as well as reducing computational cost [1]. Due to their popularity in improved performance over single individual models, ensemble learning method has been applied on several award winning Kaggle completions.

Applying the model on large scale data will increase the chances of the algorithms or models running into model complexity and increased computational complexity, while addressing these challenges of rising computational cost, [18] proposed training samples should be partition into clusters; A method known as local learning.

Local learning is defined for a semiparametric in Eq. (1)

$$H_1^i exp \frac{-(x - c_i)^W (X - c_i)}{2\sigma^2} \approx \sum_{J=1}^{H_1} exp \frac{-(x - x_i)^W (X - x_i)}{2\sigma^2} \tag{1}$$

Where x_i is a training vector for class i in an input space, σ is a learning parameter for training and H_i represents the input training vectors x_i that is associated with its center C_i.

To effectively fit local learning models for data fusion into high dimensional feature space of nonlinear kernel function say in SVM, the C_i vectors are derived from K-means theories. For dataset of n- dimensional input vector, $V = \{x_1, x_2 \ldots \ldots \ldots, x_m\}$ the hyperplane decision function is given as

$$f(x) = sgn\left(\sum_{J=1}^{t} y_i a_i(\phi(x)\phi(x_i))^{+=b)=} sgn\left(\sum_{J=1}^{t} y_i a_i^k(x_i(x_i))^{+b)}\right.\right.$$ (2)

Where ------- is total number of training parameter, a_i represents the parameters and b represents biasness, the optimal objective function for local model can be constructed from K-means theories for clustering n-dimension of data. The optimal objective function of k-means is given as

$$\min_{C_i^H} \sum_{J=1}^{k}\sum_{i=1}^{k} H_{i,j}\|x_i - c_i\|_2^2 + R\sum_{J=1}^{k}\left|\sum_{i=1}^{n} H_{i,j} y_i\right|$$ (3)

Where x_i represents i^{th} row of matrix with similarity $\sum c_i$ is a $1 \times m$ vector that represents the centroid of jth cluster. Whereas R is the scaling parameter for nonnegative parameter and $H_{i,j} \epsilon \{0, 1\}$ is an element in the cluster. To obtain balance distribution of positive and negative estimation vector, the equation was minimized.

Object detection in satellite image requires high processing end system particularly, in a Big data domain. The system must include a systematic architectural model that are efficient and are capable of running a task optimally. Therefore, the need to develop an efficient architecture using a machine learning technique called ensemble learning become imperative as there exist in literature several machine learning techniques for processing Big Data in satellite image environment these methods have been reported to possess high computational complexities that leads to computational overhead. This work presents an optimized data fusion model using Ensemble Learning ML technique for detecting land objects in Remote Sensing Images for regional and urban development. The main contributions are as follows:

1. To hybridize local learning method with Classic machine learning techniques for data classification.
2. To develop a machine learning based Data fusion architecture using geospatial dataset from Nigeria to improve network latency, communication bandwidth between distributed systems and to demonstrate the efficiency of machine learning algorithm using accuracy as a performance metrics.

This paper presents an ensemble learning technique of implementing distributed big data fusion architecture. In the work, satellite images were acquired, preprocessed, and analyzed using five ensemble learning techniques. Namely: Bagging, SVM, Naïve Bayes, Adaboost and Random Forest.

2 Related Works

Ensemble learning techniques have been used in the field of machine learning classification research domain to classify satellite images and to discover features that are not visible to the physical eyes, aided by machine learning techniques. According to [2], an ensemble learning techniques consisting three different machine learning classifiers namely; K-mean, SVM and LVQ to optimize classification result on earth observatory image. The result shows that SVM gave the best contribution to the overall general result of the ensemble method with 0.61%, 9.98% and 15.12% error rate for SVM, LVQ and K-means. To further prove the sensitivity accuracy of SVM in [16], researchers adopted the use of machine learning techniques for investigating urban development by taking information from satellite image and extracting needed information and performing both object based and pixel based analysis.

Authors in [3] presented an experimental comparison of SVM with Random forest for land cover image classification using WEKA data mining tool. The research reported that SVM has an accuracy of 98.34% while Random Forest was reported to have accuracy result of 98.20%.

Authors [4] proposed a combination method to improve the ensemble classifiers system, such as to improve their accuracy by first combining multiple classifiers based on weighted vector then Adaboost was further incorporated to boost the classification accuracy. The result however, shows improvement in the classification accuracy of 88.12%, and Kappa coefficient stood at 0.87. [22] used GPU for detecting and identifying and monitoring green space change where spatial data was used and SVM as a classification model. The authors of [23] presents an ensembled convolutional neural network where they compared different machine learning techniques on sentiment analysis data. The result showed that convolutional neural network techniques outperformed other classic machine learning methods.

3   Methodology and Materials

This section discus the various material, tools and Algorithms adopted in implementing this research. Background generalization of the adopted methods were reviewed to establish basic introduction. The reviewed methods include Support Vector Machine (SVM), Random Forest (RF), Bagging and Boosting.

The proposed architecture Fig. 1 was developed in three stages: Data Acquisition, Pre-processing and Analysis. Acquired landsat8 operation and land imagery (OLI) dataset is pre-processed by applying ML algorithm for Cleaning, Aligning and Transforming the image intelligence, thereby making data the Centre of almost every decision into a uniform dataset and then statistical computations were carried out on the data. The result of this stage is then used in the Feature Engineering where desired features were cropped out and used at the Analysis stage which employed the use of five multi-class classifiers namely: Random forest, Support Vector Machine, Naïve Bayes, Boosting and Bagging.

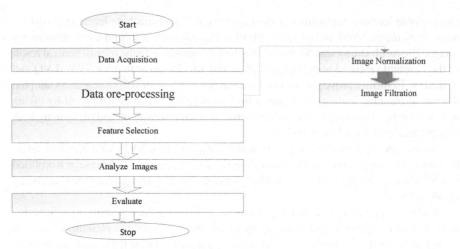

Fig. 1. Flow chart of proposed architecture

3.1 Dataset and Study Area

The study consist of three states from the North central region of Nigeria namely; Kaduna (17,781 m², 10°, 20°N - 7°, 45° E), Niger (72200.9 km², 10 0, 00 N 60, 0 o′ E) and partly Abuja FCT (667 m², 90, 40, 00 N 70 290 E). These regions are economically stable with population of about 8,252,400, 3,954,772 and 2,918,518 respectively.

3.1.1 Data Acquisition

Landsat8 Satellite images in.TIFF image format were sourced from different source. The images were acquired from the Nigerian Geological survey Agency, Abuja and online from United State Geological Survey Agency (USGS) official website (https://earthexpl orer.usgs.gov/) using the Geo-coordinates of Study Area over a period of Six (6) months i.e. December 2017 to Jun 2018 (Fig. 2).

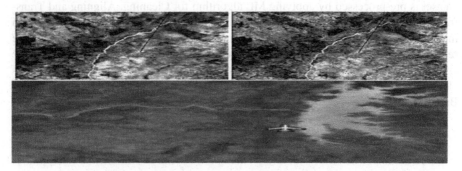

Fig. 2. Cropped Region of Interest (RoI) of Landsat 8

3.1.2 Data Preprocessing

This process involves preparing the acquired dataset for analytical purpose. The procedure for pre-processing is to ensure that the dataset is de-noised by removing existing noise in an image e.g. distortion in image pixels that can lead to misrepresentation of image pixels. To achieve that, this work adopted median filter for image filtration using machine learning algorithm. The dataset was then standardized by aligning the image formats to a uniform.TIFF file format and uniform extension and sizes using specialized tools. The preprocessed dataset is then converted into. ARFF file format to enable WEKA usage.

3.1.3 Feature Visualization and Selection

K-means cluster enable feature visualization given a dataset of large dimension, Mcluster algorithm when deployed will partition the set of data into M-subset in a disjoint form for optimal citation. To enable the optimal feature pattern selection in Mcluster, the algorithm first selects one cluster (where $k = 1$) and find optimally the position that corresponds to the centroids of the dataset. Where $k = 2$ we perform N execution where $k = 1$ is placed at the optimal position and the other is placed at the data point $(n = 1, ..N)$. We pick the best solution after implementing N execution and is denoted as $(m_1(k), ...m_k(k))$. In this work the popularly used sum of square.

Euclidian distance k-mean is used to cluster the features using the distance between each data point xi and the centroid mk of data subset clk. Equation (4) shows the mathematical model for the implementation of k-means clustering algorithm.

$$B\left(m_{l2}, ...m_m\right) = \sum_{i=} \sum_{k=1} V(x_1 \in cl_k)|x_i - m_k|^2 \tag{4}$$

Where $v(X) = 1$ if X hold a true value 0 otherwise.

Training and Validation

Training and hpothesis evaluation are two important processes in machine learning. Considering a training sequence of X n-dimension with vector input $v = \{x_1, x_2 ......x_m\}$ of if Q sequence is sufficiently large to capture all statistical training process, it is assumed that V are k dimensional, $x_m = \{x_{m1}, x_{m2} ......mx_k\}$ the features are therefore clustered by the means finding patterns that are similar and then a pattern is formed out of the entire set of dataset. To find the difference between the k-dimension, the Euclidean distance function is defined by

$$d(x, C_i) = \sqrt{\sum_{j=1}^{k}(x_j - C_{i,j})} \tag{5}$$

Where equation is a function of Eq. (4), $d\left(x_j - C_{i,j}\right)$ Represents the Euclidian distance between the square difference between the data point and the cluster.

In our case, to understand the features that needs to be clustered, we perform pixel-based feature extraction using Raster Library in Rstudio. Table 1 represents pixel value distribution in a Landsat satellite image [15]. Image information on the table includes

Bands, Wavelength and Resolution. Feature visualization for water for instance can be calculated as the subtraction of band1 from band4 and divided by the addition of band4 and band1. The process is known as normalized difference of water index.

The extracted pixel information was imported into WEKA ML suit for visualization. The result is shown in Fig. 3.

The result from the feature visualization guided in the choice of selection of features. Selected features were cropped into positive and negative set; our positive contain a total of 12,600 set of cropped images while the negative contain 2379 non related image set. Our positive image was further divided into training set and test on an 80–20% ratio.

Table 1. Landsat8 digital information

	Bands	Wavelength	Resolution
Landsat8 Operation and imagery (OLI) and thermal sensor (TIRS)	Band 1	0.45–0.51	30
	Band2- Blue	0.45–0.51	30
	Band3- Green	0.53–0.59	30
	Band4 -Red	0.64–0.67	30
	Band 5- Near Infrared (NIR)	0.85.0.88	30
	Band6 – SWIRL1	1.57–1.65	30
	Band7 - SWIRL2	2.11–2.29	30
	Band8-Parachromatic	2.11–2.29	30
	Band9 – Cirrus	0.50–0.68	30
	Band10 – thermal infrared (TIRS)	1.36–1.38	15

3.2 Materials and Algorithms

3.2.1 Support vector Machine

Support Vector Machine (SVM) [7]: is a supervised machine learning algorithm which builds a model that can predict the category of instances in a given dataset. SVM, which was proposed in 1990's and used majorly for pattern recognition, has been applied to several classification problems [7].The greater strength of SVM is to generalize the problem [8].

$$\sum_{j=1}^{m} \alpha_i y^{(i)} \left(x^{(i)}, x \right) + b \tag{6}$$

Where: α = the coefficient associated with the *i-th* training example, K = kernel function, x = input vector, y = class label which can either be -1 or 1.The fundamental idea behind SVM is the construction of an optimal hyper-plane that can be used to classify instance of a set either linearly or in non-linear format. Hyper-plane is the margin that optimally classifies the set into pattern given a dataset. A plane in SVM is comprised of three lines which separates two different spaces, mainly, the marginal line and others on both sides of the marginal line [9].

3.2.2 Bagging

An acronym for Bootstrapping Aggregate [10], is an ensemble learning algorithm method used to improve estimation and classification schemes that are unstable. The principle of Bootstrapping was built by Breiman [10], it is a machine learning method which employ random sampling of dataset into subsets and can be replaced. Given a classification model, bagging draws some example with substitution from the available training dataset (bootstrap test), fit a model to each bootstrap sample, and lastly combines all the models through majority voting. Mathematically, bagging can be expressed as in equation below

$$\sum_{j=1}^{T} d_{i,a} = \frac{max}{j=1} \sum_{i=1}^{T} d_i \tag{7}$$

3.2.3 Decision Tree with Boosting (BOOST)

Boosting showed up in the machine learning literature in the 1980's. Boosting was proposed with a specific end goal to consolidate the output of many "weak" classifiers along these lines, creating a great "committee", trying to enhance the generalization performance of weak algorithms. The different models are fitted to distinctively reweighted samples [11]. At each progression, those observations that were misclassified by the past classifiers have their weights expanded, while the weights of those accurately characterized are diminished. A standout amongst the well-known boosting algorithms was AdaBoostM1 (Freund and Schapire, 1997). Since just two class classifications of AdaBoost.M1 relate, in this work, we utilized WEKA data mining suite for multiclass boosting as shown in Eq. 8:

$$H(x)sign\left(\sum_{i=1}^{T} \alpha_t C_t(x)\right) \tag{8}$$

3.2.4 Random Forests (RF)

The Random forest technique, as proposed by Breiman (2001), is a group classifier that comprises of various decision trees; the output class is the method of the classes classifiers. The developed architecture was implemented on earth observatory images. The dataset was partitioned using k-means theories and local learning technique. The developed architecture has an improved latency and exhibits low bandwidth consumption when compared to other existing architecture. The performance metrics of the developed architecture are accuracy and precision. Table1 represents evaluation results for the individual trees. In preparing the RF algorithm, similar to CART, makes different and multiple trees, each trained on bootstrapped samples of the training data. In this work, we created an ensemble RF models classification trees. Though the RF algorithm looks like BAGG, the distinction is choosing indiscriminately instead of utilizing all picture highlights. The RF model was produced utilizing training data and the precision was assessed utilizing test data [12].

4   Results and Discussion

This work implements a distributed big data fusion architecture using ensemble machine learning classifiers. The developed architecture was implemented on earth observatory images. The dataset was partitioned using k-means theories and local learning technique.

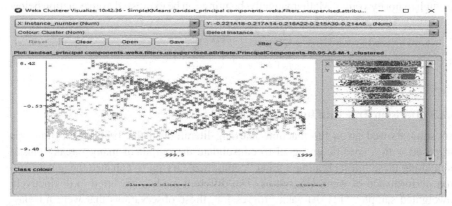

Fig. 3. Pixel Distribution Fig. 3 is the visual representation of pixel distribution where Blue is classified as Water body, Green is for Vegetation and Red represents other constituents. (Color figure online)

The developed architecture has an improved latency and exhibits low bandwidth consumption when compared to other existing architecture. The performance metrics of the developed architecture are accuracy and precision. Table 2 represents evaluation results of five ensemble learning methods for data fusion namely; Random forest, Bagging, Boosting (AdaboostM1) and Support Vector Machine, (SMO).

The result shows that Random forest has accuracy of 87.46% while others such as SVM, Bagging, Naïve Bayes and Boosting have accuracies of 82.3%, 86.96%, 82.45% and 80.5% respectively. Naïve Bayes was observed to have the lowest error rate of 0.2048% followed by Random forest (0.0225%), Bagging (0.2267%), and SVM which has the highest error rate (0.3187%).

Figure 5 represents the plot of performance of the developed architecture accuracy in percentage (%). Random forest (RF) was observed to have an improved performance Accuracy of 87. 56%, Bagging (86.95%), Naïve Bayes (82.45), SVM (82.3%) and Boosting achieved an accuracy of (80.5%). Accuracy is calculated in this work as the

Table 2. Presents the result of WEKA implementation

Algorithms	Accuracy	RMSE	TP	FP	Precision
Bagging	86.95	0.2267	0.959	0.028	0.911
Boosting	80.5	0.255	0.911	0.019	0.935
SVM	82.3	0.3187	0.963	0.985	0.985
Naïve Bayes	82.45	0.2048	0.987	0.016	0.950
Random Forest	87.56	0.2252	0.957	0.012	0.959

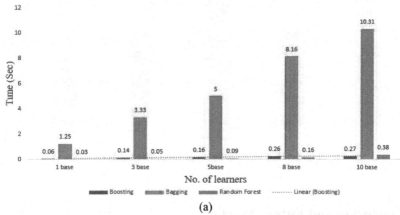

(a)

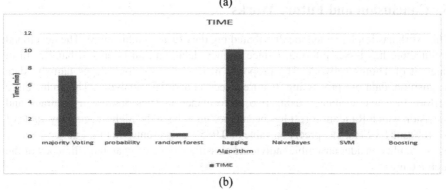

(b)

Fig. 4. Figure 4 (a &b): Graphical representation of Latency.

proportion of accuracy to total prediction made and can be expressed mathematically in Eq. (9)

$$Ac = \frac{TP + TN}{TP + TN + FN + FP} \qquad (9)$$

Figure 5 represents the plot of performance of the developed architecture precision in percentage (%). The developed architecture was observed to have improved precision value with SVM (0.985), RF (0.959), Naïve Bayes (0.950) and Bagging (0.911). Precision is calculated using the expression in Eq. (6).

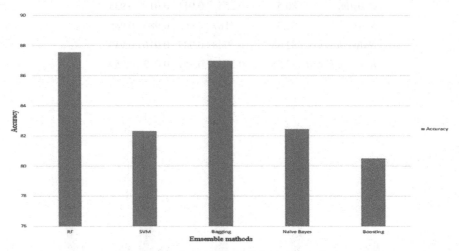

Fig. 5. Plot representation of Ensemble methods

5 Conclusion and Future Works

This work has implemented the distributed big data fusion architecture. The developed architecture has lesser jittering, reduce latency delay and an improved bandwidth in Internet of Things network. The proposed method rest on four stages namely: data acquisition, data pre-processing, feature selection and data analytics. The architecture performance was evaluated using two performance metrics prediction accuracy and precision which Random forest has been reported to have the highest accuracy value of 87.46% and SVM having precision value of 0.985% as presented in Fig. 1 above. Further work should consider ensemble individual classifiers to investigate the efficiency of the architecture.

Acknowledgement. We would love to acknowledge the contribution of Prof M.B Mu'azu, Researchers at Control and Computer Research Group at the Department of Computer Engineering, Faculty of Engineering, Ahmadu Bello University. Our profound appreciation goes to Prof A.M. Aibinu of the Department of Mechatronics, Federal University of Technology, Minna, Niger State Nigeria.

References

1. Al-Jarrah, O.Y., Yoo, P.D., Muhaidat, S., Karagiannidis, G.K., Taha, K.: Efficient machine learning for big data: a review. Big Data Res. **2**(3), 87–93 (2015)

2. Richards, N.M., King, J.H.: Big data ethics. Wake Forest L. Rev. **49**, 393 (2014)
3. Labrinidis, A., Jagadish, H.V.: Challenges and opportunities with big data. Proc. VLDB Endowment **5**(12), 2032–2033 (2012)
4. Healey, S.P., Cohen, W.B., Yang, Z., Brewer, C.K., Brooks, E.B., Gorelick, N., Hernandez, A.J., Huang, C., Hughes, M.J., Kennedy, R.E.: Mapping forest change using stacked generalization: an ensemble approach. Remote Sens. Environ. **204**, 717–728 (2018)
5. Vershinin, Y.A.: A data fusion algorithm for multisensor systems. In: Proceedings of the Fifth International Conference on Information Fusion. FUSION 2002, IEEE Cat. No. 02EX5997, vol. 1, pp. 341–345. IEEE, July 2002
6. Bekaddour, A., Bessaid, A., Bendimerad, F.T.: Multi spectral satellite image ensembles classification combining k-means, LVQ and SVM classification techniques. J. Indian Soc. Remote Sens. **43**(4), 671–686 (2015)
7. Abe, B.T., Olugbara, O.O., Marwala, T.: Experimental comparison of support vector machines with random forests for hyperspectral image land cover classification. J. Earth Syst. Sci. **123**(4), 779–790 (2014). https://doi.org/10.1007/s12040-014-0436-x
8. Chen, Y., Dou, P., Yang, X.: Improving land use/cover classification with a multiple classifier system using AdaBoost integration technique. Remote Sens. **9**(10), 1055 (2017)
9. Dou, P., Chen, Y., Yue, H.: Remote-sensing imagery classification using multiple classification algorithm-based AdaBoost. Int. J. Remote Sens. **39**(3), 619–639 (2018)
10. Tzeng, Y., Chiu, S., Chen, K.-S.: Improvement of remote sensing image classification accuracy by using a multiple classifiers system with modified bagging and boosting algorithms, pp. 2769–2772
11. Lu, J., Li, D.: Bias correction in a small sample from big data. IEEE Trans. Knowl. Data Eng. **25**(11), 26582663 (2012)
12. Asmita, S., Shukla, K.: Review on the Architecture, Algorithm and Fusion Strategies in Ensemble Learning. In. J. Comput. Appl. **108**(8) (2014)
13. Pradhan, A.: Support vector machine-a survey. Int. J. Emer. Technol. Adv. Eng. **2**(8), 82–85 (2012)
14. Ahmad, A., Paul, A., Rathore, M., Chang, H.: An efficient multidimensional big data fusion approach in machine-to-machine communication. ACM Trans. Embedded Comput. Syst. (TECS) **15**(2), 39 (2016)
15. https://earthexplorer.usgs.gov. Accessed 30 Oct 2020
16. Odaudu, S.N., Umoh, I.J., Mu'azu, M,B., Adedokun, E.A.: Machine learning for strategic urban planning. In: 2019 2nd International Conference of the IEEE Nigeria Computer Chapter (NigeriaComputConf), pp. 1–7 (2019)
17. Shah, V.P., Younan, N.H., Durbha, S.S., King, R.L.: Feature identification via a combined ICA–wavelet method for image information mining. IEEE Geosci. Remote Sens. Lett. **7**(1), 18–22 (2009)
18. Yoo, P.D., Ho, Y.S., Zhou, B.B., Zomaya, A.Y.: SiteSeek: posttranslational modification analysis using adaptive locality-effective kernel methods and new profiles. BMC Bioinform. **9**(1), 272 (2008)
19. González-Audícana, M., Saleta, J.L., Catalán, R.G., García, R.: Fusion of multispectral and panchromatic images using improved IHS and PCA mergers based on wavelet decomposition. IEEE Trans. Geosci. Remote Sens. **42**(6), 1291–1299 (2004)
20. Bruce, L.M., Koger, C.H., Li, J.: Dimensionality reduction of hyperspectral data using discrete wavelet transform feature extraction. IEEE Trans. Geosci. Remote Sens. **40**(10), 2331–2338 (2002)
21. Ngbede, S., Umoh, J., Adedokun, E., Marshall, F., Ikpe, D.: Big data fusion and emerging technologies. Paper presented at the 1st international IEEE conference on mechatronics, automation and cyber-physical computer systems, (MAC-2019) at the Federal University of Technology Owerri, pp, 133–138 (2019)

22. Nilkamal More, V.B.N., Banerjee, B.: Machine learning on high performance computing for urban greenspace change detection: satellite image data fusion approach. Int. J. Image Data Fusion **11**(3), 218–232 (2020). https://doi.org/10.1080/19479832.2020.1749142
23. Behera, R.K., Jena, M., Rath, S.K., Misra, S.: Co-LSTM: Convolutional LSTM model for sentiment analysis in social big data. Inf. Process. Manage. **58**(1), 102435
24. Ayeni, F., Misra, S., Omoregbe, N.: Using big data technology to contain current and future occurrence of Ebola Viral Disease and other epidemic diseases in West Africa. In: Tan, Y., Shi, Y., Buarque, F., Gelbukh, A., Das, S., Engelbrecht, A. (eds.) ICSI 2015. LNCS, vol. 9142, pp. 107–114. Springer, Cham (2015). https://doi.org/10.1007/978-3-319-20469-7_13

A Gaussian Mixture Model with Firm Expectation-Maximization Algorithm for Effective Signal Power Coverage Estimation

Isabona Joseph[1](✉) and Ojuh O. Divine[2]

[1] Department of Physics, Federal University Lokoja, Lokoja, Nigeria
josabone@yahoo.com
[2] Department of Physical Sciences, Benson Idahosa University, Benin City, Nigeria

Abstract. Generally, the strength of propagated signal power over wireless cellular communication systems is known to be very stochastic due to their susceptibility to various impacting fading conditions of the radio frequency propagation channels. In previous works, one popular method of analyzing and characterizing such signal dataset in high-dimensional space is by means of single Gaussian density function modelling. However, under many circumstances, it is difficult to give an accurate description of such stochastic signal dataset using a single Gaussian density function model, especially when it does not follow approximately ellipsoidal distribution. In this research paper, a machine learning technique based on Gaussian Mixture Model (GMM) is employed for the analysis and modeling of highly dimensional signal power with mix stochastic shadow fading and long term fading components. The signal power was acquired with the aid of telephone mobile system software investigation tools over the air transmission interface of operational Long Term Evolution cellular network, belonging to a commercial network operator in Port Harcourt City. First, in our contribution, we model the probability density of signal power coverage dataset acquired in the high-dimensional space around six different deployed cell sites by the network operator. In our second contribution, we propose a GMM, which employs a firm iterative maximum likelihood estimation technique combined with the expectation-maximization algorithm to effectively model and characterized signal power dataset. By means of Akaike information criterion, the robustness of the proposed GMM with firm iterative EM algorithm over the commonly used single Gaussian density function modelling method is shown. This technique can serve as a valuable step toward effective monitoring and analyzing operational cellular radio network performance.

Keywords: Machine learning · Signal power · Coverage estimation · Gaussian mixture model · Mixture weights · Expectation-maximization algorithm

1 Introduction

An important performance parameter for determining the coverage quality of deployed operational cellular radio broadband communication systems such as the Long Term

© Springer Nature Switzerland AG 2021
S. Misra and B. Muhammad-Bello (Eds.): ICTA 2020, CCIS 1350, pp. 93–106, 2021.
https://doi.org/10.1007/978-3-030-69143-1_8

Evolution (LTE) is the signal power. Practical-based monitoring, and detective estimation of coverage health conditions using signal power is a vital step towards improving the overall LTE system network performance [1, 2]. The user equipment receiver needs a certain minimum signal power to access and sustain error-free communication over the radio frequency channels. This important minimum signal valuable is known as the "radio receiver threshold". In operational communication system networks, the available signal power at user equipment receiver should be at least 20 to 40 dB above the required threshold [2–4].

In the past few decades, the introduction and application of different machine learning (ML) tools and their algorithms have gained a lot of attention in different fields of human endeavor, including sciences, medicine, engineering, etc. The major drive in ML application is to come up with techniques that can automatically and effectively detect (learn) patterns in data and then to utilise the hidden patterns from the data for further future extrapolative forecasting. Some of the key notable machine learning tools includes neural networks, decision trees, Gaussian process regression, support vector machines and Gaussian mixture models (GMM).

Generally, in machine learning domain, one of the fundamental intricate problems is on how to reliably estimate the distribution function or density function of observed dataset. In parametric density estimation domain, a distribution parametric-based model is assumed and on that ground, the model parameters are obtained by means of the observed finite data record. A popular and distinctive method to determine the required parameters of the model, using the observed dataset samples, is maximum likelihood estimation (MLE). However, it is always practically difficult to describe the distribution (structure) in real-life situations by means of a single distribution. To cater for the above single distribution problem, a mixture model (density) which combines linear mixture of many basic distributions is used as the parametric distribution model for the data samples. But if the component distributions utilized in the mixture model are Gaussian then the mixture model is termed as Gaussian mixture model (GMM).

Gaussian mixture model is an expressive type of model for density estimation. In many existing /related works [5–10], GMM has been applied mostly for solving 'unsupervised' problems or appraising class-conditional densities in supervised learning problems, wherein the observations have 'missing values'. A relevant algorithm to learn data pattern with the GMM is the Expectation-Maximization (EM) algorithm (Dempster et al., 1977) [5]. In this paper, a GMM which combines maximum likelihood estimation technique with the EM algorithm is employed to estimate the LTE signal power coverage quality data acquired a typical urban terrain. Similar approach was also employed in [6–8], but for colour segmentation, image segmentation and exchange rate estimation, respectively.

In [11], the authors applied the GMM to analysis and quantify the native properties of peptides. Their results showed a value-added performance over the complex Matrix assisted laser desorption in combination with ionization time-of-flight approach. Similar approach detecting glaucomatous progression. In [12], a combined GMM and SVR (support vector regression) methodology has been employed to conduct Aviation Piston Pump Performance degradation prediction. From the results, the joint GMM and SVR technique provided an enhanced recital over using SVR singly. A Cooperative

Localization-based technique in WSNs is proposed in [13] using the GMM. The authors revealed the proposed technique are more robust against outliers than the normally used least square algorithms.

In our contribution, a GMM with firm iterative EM algorithm which instantaneously determines the mixture model components and parameters through swift processes is proposed for enhanced analysis and modeling based quantification of signal power coverage data. Also, a quantitative comparison between the proposed GMM with firm iterative EM algorithm over the commonly used Gaussian probability distribution analysis method [2, 14–16], is provided using Akaike information criterion (AIC).

The remainder of this research paper work are contained in Sect. 2, 3 and 4. Section 2 present the stepwise materials and method employed in the paper. These include data collection, GMM concept description and the algorithm engaged in estimating the GMM parameter based on the sample signal data. Section 3 provides the results and disruption. Finally, Sect. 4 draws the conclusion of paper.

2 Materials and Method

The stepwise methodology adopted in research work is summarized in Fig. 1 using a flowchart. The process kick started with data collection, followed by GMM description and then the application of expectation-maximization (EM) algorithm for the GMM parameters estimation. In order to provide a quantitative comparison between the proposed GMM with firm iterative EM algorithm over the commonly used Gaussian probability distribution analysis method, we employ the Akaike information criterion (AIC) indicator. The AIC is given by [2]:

$$AIC = 2 * L + 2 * p \tag{1}$$

where L and p express the negative loglikelihood parameter and the estimated parameters number.

2.1 Sample Data

The signal coverage sample data used in this paper is termed the Reference Signals Received Power (RSRP). RSRP is a critical parameter which measures the level of signal coverage in (Long Term Evolution) in cellular radio LTE networks. It is expresses the state of coverage power levels of the reference signals transmitted over the entire bandwidth. RSRP typical range is from -44 dBm (excellent) to 140 dBm (very bad) [17]. With the aid of telephone mobile software investigation tools, log file data containing RSRP values, throughput, and other key LTE service parameters were obtained over the air transmission interface of operational cellular network belonging to a commercial network operator in Port Harcourt Garden City, Nigeria. To enable detailed works, the measurements were conducted around six different cell sites. By means of map info software and excel spread sheet, the relevant signal coverage data component which is RSRP was extracted for further analysis.

2.2 The Gaussian Mixture Model

As the name connotes, a GMM embroils the superposition (that is, mixture) of multiple Gaussian distributions. It also often termed as a Gaussian mixture distribution. It is a distinctive parametric-based probability density function (PDF) characterized by a weighted sum of Gaussian component densities. Each component (or unit) is determined using its mean and covariance. The mixture weight expresses the vector of mixing proportions, wherein each proportion characterizes the part of the population defined by its resultant component. Generally, mixture models are good for robust estimation of data density and clustering [18]. The parameters of GMM model can be determined from training data by engaging either the Maximum A Posteriori (MAP) estimation method or by applying the iterative Expectation-Maximization (EM) algorithm. In this work, iterative EM algorithm is explored as shown in Algorithm 1.

Let $x_i (i = 1, 2, ...n)$ represent an observed dataset, wherein x_i defines the d-dimensional data vector (observation or measurement). The GMM can be used to estimate the density dataset in form of:

$$p(x/\lambda) = \sum_{i=1}^{M} w_i a(x/\mu_i, \Sigma_i) \tag{2}$$

$$a(x/\mu_i, \Sigma_i) = \frac{1}{(2\pi)^{d/2}|\Sigma_i|^{1/2}} \exp\left\{\frac{1}{2}(x - \mu_i)'\Sigma_i^{-1}(x - \mu)\right\} \tag{3}$$

$$\lambda = (w_i, \mu_i, \Sigma_i), \ i = 1, \ldots, M \tag{4}$$

where w_i, i = 1,..., M, and a(x|μi, Σi), i = 1,..., M, represent the mixture weights and component Gaussian densities; Σi and indicate the covariance matrix and mean vector.

2.3 The Expectation Maximization Algorithm

There exist many unknown GMM parameters as shown in Eq. (4). By means of maximum likelihood estimation technique combined with the expectation-maximization (EM) algorithm (see algorithm 1), the λ parameters in Eq. (4) which mixture weights w_i, means μ_i and variances (diagonal covariance) σ_i^2, can be obtained iteratively by:

$$w_i = \frac{1}{T} \sum_{t=1}^{T} \Pr(i/x_t, \lambda) \tag{5}$$

$$\mu_i = \frac{\sum_{t=1}^{T} \Pr(i/x_t, \lambda)x_t}{\sum_{t=1}^{T} \Pr(i/x_t, \lambda)} \tag{6}$$

$$\sigma_i^2 = \frac{\sum_{t=1}^{T} \Pr(i/x_t, \lambda)x_t^2}{\sum_{t=1}^{T} \Pr(i/x_t, \lambda)} - \overline{\mu}_i^2 \tag{7}$$

where T = training vectors, $x = \{x_1, x_2, \ldots, x_T\}$; the mixture weights w_i must satisfy $0 \le w_i \le 1$ and $\sum_{t=1}^{T} w_i = 1$.

The component i posteriori probability is given by:

$$p(i|x_t, \lambda|) = \frac{w_i a(x_t/\mu_i, \Sigma_i)}{\sum_{k=1}^{M} w_i a(x_t/\mu_k, \Sigma_k)}; i = 1, \ldots n, t = 1, \ldots T \qquad (8)$$

Algorithm1 EM for Gaussian mixtures

1. Initialise μ_t, w_t σ_t, set i=1
2. While not converge **do**
3. compute $p(i|x_t, \lambda|)$ Expected step
4. compute $\mu_{t_i}^{i+1}$, $w_{t_i}^{i+1}$, $\sigma_{t_i}^{i+1}$ Maximization step
5. i ← i+1.
6. **end while**

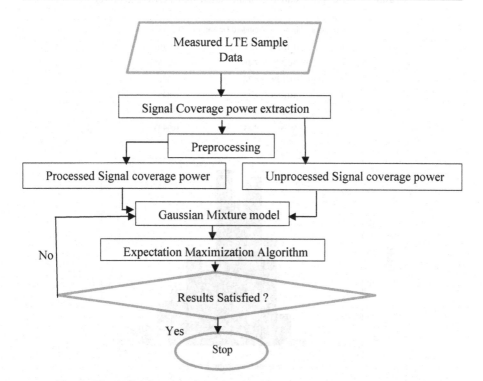

Fig. 1. The GMM flowchart for estimating LTE Signal Coverage Power Quality

3   Results and Discussion

In this section, we present the Gaussian mixture estimation results based the EM Algorithm 1 on the LTE signal coverage data acquired over operational six eNodeB cell sites deployed by a commercial LTE system networks. All computations, implementation and graphics presentations were achieved using Matlab 2018a platform. But before going into GMM extrapolative analysis, a descriptive statistics of Table 1 is displayed to explain the basic information for the signal coverage power attenuation characteristics over each measurement sites. Key parameters such as standard deviation, mean and skewness are used for the attenuation statistics. Meanwhile, Figs. 2, 3, 4, 5, 6 and 7 display the histogram fit curve of the signal coverage power attenuation characteristics. By referring to Figs. 3, 4, 5, 6 and 7 and Table 1, it can be established that the signal mean values for sites 2 and 6 are larger compared other sites. This simply implies that the coverage quality in those sites are better at the user equipment terminals during voice and data communication. Furthermore, Table 1 displays the attained standard deviations for measured signal power data in all the sites. Site 5 has attained the largest standard deviation than others and could point out that the signal coverage in that site are more volatile or unstable. On the other part, it could also imply that the signal coverage quality of other sites are more stable or less volatile.

Table 1. Descriptive statistics of measured signal coverage power

Cell sites	Mean	Standard Deviation	Skewness
1	−101.36	7.52	0.6401
2	−90.58	7.48	1.0765
3	−103.29	8.78	0.3463
4	−107.66	7.42	0.8464
5	−104.46	13.47	−0.1244
6	−90.87	9.24	−0.6493

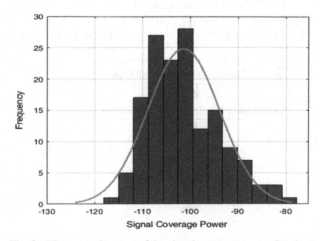

Fig. 2. Histogram fit curve of the signal coverage power for site 1

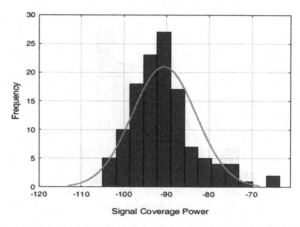

Fig. 3. Histogram fit curve of the signal coverage power for site 2

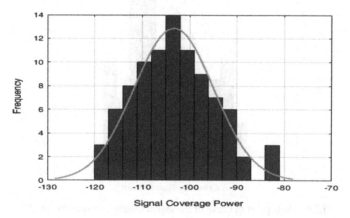

Fig. 4. Histogram fit curve of the signal coverage power for site 3

Shown in Figs. 8, 9, 10, 11, 12 and 13 are the GMM fitted graphs on the signal coverage power data. Compared to Figs. 2, 3, 4, 5, 6 and 7, we can observed that GMM plotted graphs have better fittings of the signal data. This results is a worthy reflection of the adopted GMM phenomenon. By applying the EM algorithm (i.e., Algorithm 1), the estimated GMM parameters values via the signal coverage iterative training are displayed in Table 2 and Fig. 14. The first normal distribution, tagged Co refers to the unprocessed signal coverage power and the second normal, C1 indicates the processed signal coverage power. By referring to summarized results in Table 2 and Fig. 14, it can be seen that the mixture weight estimates for the first normal except in site 1, are higher are than the second normal in locations 2 to 6, and this implies that the signal coverage quality is poorer due unprocessed noisy components in the signal data. Generally, it observed from the results that larger signal coverage possess lower variance values, and this may be attributed to low large scale fading effects [19, 20]. This indicates that signal

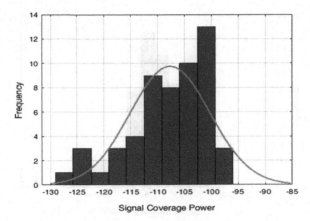

Fig. 5. Histogram fit curve of the signal coverage power for site 4

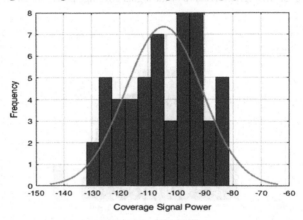

Fig. 6. Histogram fit curve of the signal coverage power for site 5

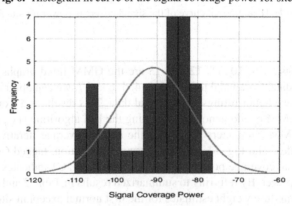

Fig. 7. Histogram fit curve of the signal coverage power for site 6

coverage are better in cell sites located in areas where there less manmade and natural obstructions.

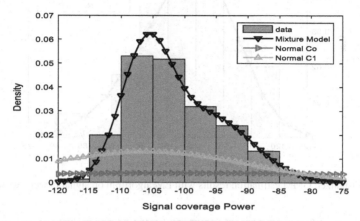

Fig. 8. Visualized GMM estimation results with EM algorithm on signal power data for site 1

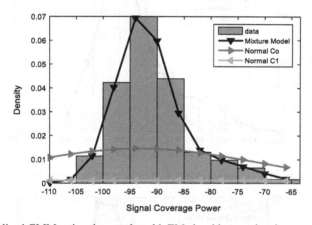

Fig. 9. Visualized GMM estimation results with EM algorithm on signal power data for site 2

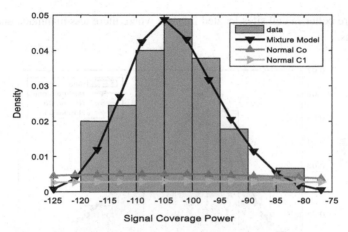

Fig. 10. Visualized GMM estimation results with EM algorithm on signal power data for site 3

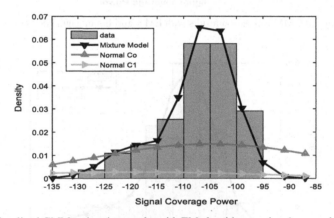

Fig. 11. Visualized GMM estimation results with EM algorithm on signal power data for site 4

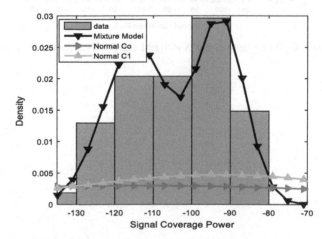

Fig. 12. Visualized GMM estimation results with EM algorithm on signal power data for site 5

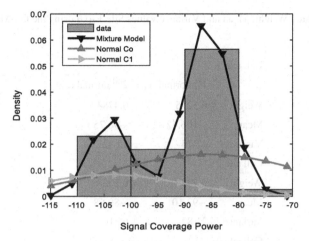

Fig. 13. Visualized GMM estimation results with EM algorithm on signal power data for site 6

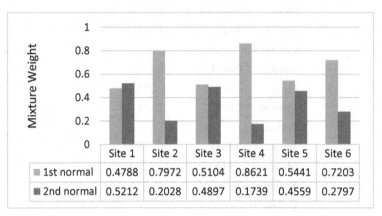

Fig. 14. Estimated mixture weight estimation based EM algorithm on signal power Data for site 1 to 6

Shown in Table 2 are the quantitative values provided to reveal the worth of the proposed GMM with firm iterative EM algorithm over the commonly used Gaussian probability distribution (GPD) analysis method. As seen in the Table, lower AIC values, except in site 3 depict improved performance with our proposed method (Table 3).

Table 2. Estimated Weight, Mean and Variance values Site 1 to 6 using the GMM based on EM algorithm 1

Cell site 1		
	1st normal (c_0)	2nd normal (c_1)
Weight	0.5215	0.4784
Mean	−106.42	−96.75
Variance	47.75	15.92
Cell site 2		
Weight	0.7972	0.2028
Mean	−93.10	−80.68
Variance	21.82	65.10
Cell site 3		
Weight	0.5104	0.4897
Mean	−107.20	−99.20
Variance	40.27	67.12
Cell site 4		
Weight	0.8621	0.1739
Mean	−119.8	−105.08
Variance	22.09	25.74
Cell site 5		
Weight	0.5441	0.4559
Mean	−114.54	−92.44
Variance	72.51	38.55
Cell site 6		
Weight	0.7203	0.2797
Mean	−85.78	−103.98
Variance	17.77	13.28

Table 3. Computed AIC values the proposed GMM with firm iterative EM algorithm and the GPD analysis method

Cell Site	GMM with firm iterative EM algorithm	GPD
1	1040	1029
2	847	828
3	640	644
4	379	375
5	437	436
6	287	274

4 Conclusion and Future Work

Practical-based monitoring and analysis of coverage health conditions remained vital steps toward improving the overall system network performance at the user equipment terminals.

In this research work, the signal power coverage data acquired using telephone mobile software investigation tools over the air transmission interface of operational Long Term Evolution cellular network have been analyzed and modeled using Gaussian Mixture Model, which is a distinctive parametric probability density function characterized by a weighted sum of Gaussian constituents densities.. We model the probability density of signal power coverage data in the high-dimensional using six different deployed cell sites by the network operator. The three key Gaussian Mixture Model parameters which are mean, variance and mixture weights has been determined and reported using maximum likelihood estimation combined with the expectation-maximization algorithm. Based on Gaussian Mixture Model, this paper attains and provides valued approach toward effective monitoring and analyzing operational cellular radio network performance.

Also, By means of Akaike information criterion, the robustness of the proposed GMM with firm iterative EM algorithm over the commonly used single Gaussian density function modelling method is shown. This technique can serve as a valuable step toward effective monitoring and analyzing operational cellular radio network performance.

References

1. Isabona, J., Ojuh, D.O.: Wavelet selection based on wavelet transform for optimum noisy signal processing. Int. J. Basic Appl. Sci. **2**(1) 3, 57–65 (2017)
2. Isabona, J., Osaigbovo, I.A.: Investigating predictive capabilities of RBFNN, MLPNN and GRNN models for LTE cellular network radio signal power datasets, FUOYE. J. Eng. Technol. **4**(1), 155–159 (2017)
3. Isabona, J.: Parametric maximum likelihood Estimator combined with Bayesian and Akaike information criterion for realistic field strength attenuation estimation in open and shadow urban microcells. J. Emerg. Trends Eng. Appl. Sci. (JETEAS) **10**(4), 151–156 (2019)
4. Ebhota, V.C., Isabona, J., Srivastava, V.M.: Modelling, simulation and analysis of signal path loss for 4G cellular network planning. J. Eng. Appl. Sci. (JEAS) **13**(4), 235–240 (2018)

5. Dempster, A., Laird, N., Rubin, D.: Maximum likelihood estimation from incomplete data via the EM algorithm. J. Royal Statistic Soc. **30**(B), 1–38 (1977)
6. Henderson, N., King, R., Middleton, R.H.: An application of Gaussian mixtures: colour segmenting for the four legged league using hsi colour space. In: Visser, U., Ribeiro, F., Ohashi, T., Dellaert, F. (eds.) RoboCup 2007. LNCS (LNAI), vol. 5001, pp. 254–261. Springer, Heidelberg (2008). https://doi.org/10.1007/978-3-540-68847-1_23
7. Greggio, N., Laschi, C., Dario, P., Greggio, N., Dario, P.: Fast estimation of Gaussian mixture models for image segmentation. Mach. Vis. Appl. **23**, 773–789 (2012). https://doi.org/10.1007/s00138-011-0320-5
8. Yen, P.S., Ismail, M.T.: Fitting finite mixture model to exchange rate using maximum likelihood estimation. Int. J. Sci. Eng. Res. **4**(5), 25–29 (2013)
9. Yousefi, S., Balasubramanian, M., Goldbaum, M.H., et al.: Unsupervised Gaussian mixture-model with expectation maximization for detecting glaucomatous progression in standard automated perimetry visual fields. Trans. Vis. Sci. Tech. **5**(3), 2 (2016). https://doi.org/10.1167/tvst.5.3.2
10. Kerenidis, I., Luongo, A., Prakash, P.: Quantum expectation-maximization for Gaussian mixture models. In: Proceedings of the 37th International Conference on Machine Learning, Vienna, Austria, PMLR 108 (2020)
11. Spainhour, J.C.G., Janech, M.G., Schwacke, J.H., Velez, J.C.Q.: Ramakrishnan V the application of gaussian mixture models for signal quantification in MALDI-ToF mass spectrometry of peptides. PLoS ONE **9**(11), e111016 (2014). https://doi.org/10.1371/journal.pone.0111016
12. Lu, C., Wang, S.: Performance degradation prediction based on a Gaussian mixture model and optimized support vector regression for an aviation piston pump. Sensors **20**, 3854 (2020). https://doi.org/10.3390/s20143854
13. Yin, F., Fritsche, C., Jin, D., Gustafsson, F., Zoubir, A.M.: cooperative localization in WSNs using Gaussian mixture modeling: distributed ECM algorithms. IEEE Trans. Signal Process. **63**(6), 1448–1463 (2015)
14. Abiodun, C.I., Ojo, J.S.: Determination of probability distribution function for modelling path loss for wireless channels applications over micro-cellular environments of Ondo State, Southwestern Nigeria. World Sci. News **118**, 74–88 (2019)
15. Isabona, J.: Maximum likelihood parameter based estimation for in-depth prognosis investigation of stochastic electric field strength data. BIU J. Basic Appl. Sci. **4**(1), 127–136 (2019)
16. Isabona, J., Konyeha, C.C.: Experimental study of UMTS Radio signal propagation characteristics by field measurement. Am. J. Eng. Res. **2**(2), 99–106 (2013)
17. Obahiagbon, K., Isabona, J.: Generalized regression neural network: an alternative approach for reliable prognostic analysis of spatial signal power loss in cellular broadband networks. Int. J. Adv. Res. Phys. Sci. **5**(10), 35–42 (2018)
18. Timonin, V., Bai, S. B., Wang, J; Kanevski, M.; and Pozdnukhov, A.: Landslide Data Analysis with Gaussian Mixture Model. *International Congress on Environmental Modelling and Software*, Spain 54 (2008).
19. Atenaga, M., Isabona, J.: On the compromise between network performance and end user satisfaction over UMTS radio interface: an empirical investigation. Int. J. Adv. Res. Phys. Sci. (IJARPS) **1**(7), 9–18 (2014)
20. Isabona, J., Konyeha, C.C.: Urban area path loss propagation prediction and optimisation using Hata model at 800MHz. IOSR J. Appl. Phys. (IOSR-JAP), **3**(4), 8–18 (2013)

Analysis and Classification of Biomedical Data Using Machine Learning Techniques

Sujata Panda[1]([✉]) and Hima Bindu Maringanti[2]

[1] Department of Computer Science, Devine Institute of Engineering and Technology,
Baripada, Odisha, India
Sujatapanda24@gmail.com
[2] Department of Computer Application, North Orissa University, Baripada, Odisha, India
profhbnou2012@gmail.com

Abstract. Breast cancer research has been the center of discussion on health information technology in recent years, as it is the second largest cause of cancer deaths in women. A biopsy in which tissue is microscopically extracted and analyzed will be used for the detection of breast cancer. The cancer cells are either categorized as cancer or non-cancer. There are various methods for classifying and predicting breast cancer. The proposed work uses a breast cancer dataset from Wisconsin (Diagnostic). The data collection used to track the effectiveness of different machine learning approaches with respect to main parameters including accuracy, F1-score, specificity and recall. The three basic classification models in this paper are i.e., Naïve Bayes, KNN, Decision Tree was used to forecast cancer. The comparative tests show that the proposed Naïve Bayes classifier gives the accuracy of 98.1%, f1 score of 98.3%, specificity of 97.5%, recall of 98.3%.

Keywords: Breast cancer · Breast cancer Wisconsin (Diagnostic) dataset · Confusion matrix · Naïve Bayes · Decision tree · k-NN

1 Introduction

This Breast cancer has become the most frequently reported invasive cancer in women, and is the second most frequently reported cause of death by lung cancer in women [1]. The World Health Organization (WHO) has estimated a number of deaths from cancer in 2018 at about 9.6 million, according to the International Agency on Cancer Research (IARC) [2]. By 2030 there are expected to be more than 27 million new cases [3].

The utilization of diagnostic image testing will recognize breast cancer, including histology and radiology images. Identifying areas in which abnormality occurs can be supported by radiology analyses. However, they cannot be used to test the can cariousness of the region [4]. Image cancer screening over four decades has been studied, biopsy is the best way to choose whether cancer is present or not. Fine needle aspiration, core needle biopsy, vacuum aid and surgical opening (shortness of breath) are among the most common biopsy techniques [5].

The best way to determine whether the region of the biopsy is cancer is to take and monitor the tissue under a microscope. After the biopsy has been performed, a

© Springer Nature Switzerland AG 2021
S. Misra and B. Muhammad-Bello (Eds.): ICTA 2020, CCIS 1350, pp. 107–118, 2021.
https://doi.org/10.1007/978-3-030-69143-1_9

determination shall be made on the basis of a histopathology examination, which would test the tissue under a microscope to search for suspicious or cancer cells. Images of histology help one to discern between the forms and the architecture of the nuclei of cells in one sequence [6]. Histopathologists physically track the regularity and degree of malignancy in operative cell phase and tissue distribution and assess cancer zones.

When histopathologists are not well-trained, this may lead to a misdiagnosis. Often there is a shortage of experts to keep the tissue sample for up to two months, as is often the case in Norway [7]. There is also a reproducibility issue, since histopathology is a subjective discipline. It is especially important for pathologists who are not trained, where we can get a different analysis from the same sample. Therefore, the demand for computer-assisted diagnosis is insistent.

Machine learning offers useful statistical tools for complex nonlinear regression problems and thus can be exploited to obtain more accurate predictions at low computational cost [8–10]. Most researchers perform work to establish an effective diagnostic method for the earliest possible diagnosis of the tumor, and also to make it easier to start treatment at earlier stages, and to increase the survivability rate [11]. Often machine learning techniques are used to identify the tumor quickly and effectively. The emphasis of this research is the comparative examination of accuracy, F1 score, specificity and the recall of the different machine learning classifications for the identification of breast cancer and the number of variables used.

The rest of the paper is planned as follows: in Sect. 2, literature survey, Sect. 3 we give information about the materials and methodology, in Sect. 4 and Sect. 5, the implementations, performances and experimental at that point conducted and investigated, and the recommendations are concluded for subsequent work.

2   Literature Survey

Fabio A. Spanhol et al. [12] introduce a dataset of 7,909 histopathology photographs of breast cancer (BC) collected on 82 patients. The role associated with this data set is to automatically classify these images into two groups, where the clinician would be a helpful with computerized assisted diagnostic resource. To assess the complexity of this mission, we shall present some preliminary findings achieved with advanced image classification systems. The exactness varies from 80–85%, which indicates changes.

P. Hamsagayathri et al. [13] proposed SEER (Surveillance, Epidemiology and End Effects-SEER) Breast Cancer Classificatory Algorithm for priority decision tree. This article uses WEKA methods to test the J48 algorithm for the dataset of the seer breast cancer and the algorithm for a priority decision tree. The classifier efficiency is calculated and measured.

Mandeep Rana et al. [14] Machine learning approaches models proposed such as Vector Machine Help, Logistic Regression, KNN and Naive Bayes. The techniques are coded in a UCI research depot in MATLAB. We measured and analyzed the different degrees of precision. We noticed that SVM was best suited to predictive analyses, and that KNN was more appropriate.

S A Medjahed et al. [15] discussed and analyzed the efficiency of the various K-NN algorithm distances. In addition, we test this difference by using various "k" parameter values and using several classification rules (the method used to determine whether a sample is classified). Our research will be performed on the University of Wisconsin Hospital's WBCD website (Wisconsin breast cancer site).

Ahmet Mert et al. [16] proposed technique for the classification of SVM and radial basis function kernels in breast cancer. This classifiers' performance is evaluated to determine accuracy, sensitivity and specificity. Results show that SVM's quadratic-kernel diagnostic results are the most accurate (94.40%), marginally reducing accuracy and sensitivity values when the dimension of two feature vector is reduced to two different components.

Pavel Kral et al. [17] introduced a new approach to mammographic images of breast cancer focused on Local Binary Patterns (LBP) has been implemented. The LBP-based features with a classification and threshold are successfully used. A collection consisting of images extracted from MIAS and DDSM databases is evaluated for the proposed process. We have shown experimentally that the proposed method is effective and reliable, because the accuracy achieved is about 84%.

Linqi Song et al. [18] analytically the lost diagnostic performance of a proposed algorithm, which does not and cannot be discovered for the true distribution of patients, is analyzed. Algorithm also has the significant benefit of being able to provide individualized assessments of confidence about the accuracy of the prescription for diagnosis. In terms of false positive rate, the proposed methodology outperforms the existing clinical procedure by 36% despite a 2% false negative rate.

M R Al-Hadidi et al. [19] proposed a new approach for detecting high-precision breast cancer. The approach consists of two main parts. The techniques of image analysis are used in the first section to arrange mammography images for the retrieval of features and its patterns. The two models, for example, the Back Propagation Neural Network Model and the Logistic Regression, are used as guidance in order to assess the reliability and accuracy of the two models.

B. M. Gayathri et al. [20] examined the importance Vector Machine comparative analysis (RVM), offering low processing costs relative to other machine training techniques used for breast cancer identification. It aims to compare and explain that RVM is better for the diagnosis of breast cancer than other machine learning algorithms, even with reduced variables.

3 Materials and Methodology

The materials we used include: Dataset from Breast Cancer Wisconsin (Diagnostic). MATLAB coding and breast cancer computer applications. Machine learning approaches, for instance: KNN, decision trees and Navies Bayes, are our methodology.

3.1 Dataset

The data was collected from Breast Cancer Wisconsin (Diagnostic). The dataset covers 357 benign breast cancer cases and 212 malignant breast cancer cases. The dataset is composed of 32 columns, the first being the ID number, the second the clinical outcome (benign or malignant), the mean radius, the mean texture, the mean perimeter and the sum of the worst measurements of 32 unmissed functions. Characteristics are derived from a digitized tumor biopsy with a fine needle aspiration image (Table 1).

Table 1. Description of WDBC dataset

Dataset	No. of features	No. of samples	No. of category
Breast Cancer Wisconsin (Diagnostic) dataset	32	569	2

3.2 Performance Evaluation

This section describes the parameters which are used to measure machine learning techniques performance. An actual and predicted class values are derived from confusion matrix is extracted from standard four values, namely: True Positive (TP), False Positive (FP), True Negative (TN), and False Negative (FN), to determine results.

3.3 Accuracy

Accuracy is a strong indicator of the degree of the accuracy test model and the general way it is performed. The right prediction can be calculated in correspondence with inaccurate predictions. To evaluate accuracy component, this equation can be used:

$$Accuracy = \frac{TP + TN}{TP + FP + TN + FN}$$

3.4 Recall

In general, the sensitivity can be defined as the ratio of positive cases to all observations. Recall can be construed as a device performance metric in the projection of favorable outcomes and the cost assessment.

$$Recall = \frac{TP}{TP + FN}$$

3.5 Precision

The degree to which positive outcomes are correctly calculated can be described as precision. This specifies the percentage of true positive to the total number of positive ones. The system's capacity for accommodating optimistic values is exposed, but negative values are not articulated.

$$Precision = \frac{TP}{TP + FP}$$

3.6 F1 Score

Precision and Recall are the weighted average. Therefore, this test takes account of all types of false values. F1 score is considered good at 1 and is a complete loss at 0 (Fig. 1).

$$F1\ Score = (2 * (Precision * Recall)) / (Precision + Recall)$$

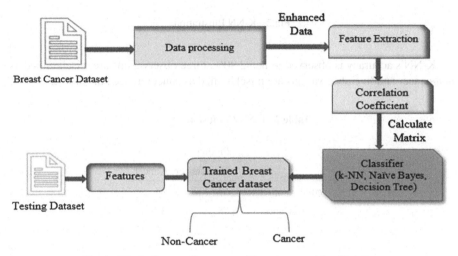

Fig. 1. Block diagram for proposed breast cancer classification

4 Implementation

Machine learning (ML) in comparison to the usual approach of pre-coding all potential results is defined as a branch of artificial intelligence, improving the ability to learn in a continuing context dependent on a data collection used for training. There are several methods and strategies that can be learned in creating programs some are naive bayes, random forest and K-NN [21, 22].

4.1 K- Nearest Neighbor

K is interpreted to indicate the data points of the training data adjacency to the evaluation data point which we use to identify the score. A k-nearest-neighbor can be defined as the model used to determine whether a collection of data is dependent on other data sets. The method is a guided approach to learning which is used for regression and classification. KNN collects all the data points around it to process a new data point. Parameters which have a high degree of uncertainty are important variables in determining distances.

Given the N training vectors in Fig. 2, k-NN defines the nearest k neighbors regardless of the labels.

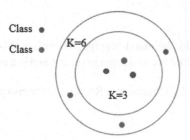

Fig.2. K-NN Illustration

K-NN's accuracy is observed to be 92.90%, three observations are misclassified as non-cancer and five observations are misclassified as cancer as seen in Table 2.

Table 2. k-NN Confusion matrix

		Predict	
		Non-cancer	Cancer
Actual	Non-cancer	67	3
	Cancer	5	39

4.2 Naïve Bayes

The classifier of Naive Bayes is the simple, exact and reliable algorithm with great precise and quick data settings. The classification consists of two stages, one phase of learning and the evaluation phase. The classifier trains its model in the learning process on a given dataset and checks the classifier output during the evaluation phase (Fig. 3).

The Bayes Rule is a way of going from P(X|Y), known from the training dataset, to find P(Y|X)

$$P(\text{Class Data}) = (P(\text{Data Class}) * P(\text{Class}))/(P(\text{Data})) \tag{1}$$

The proposed work builds a Naive Bayes model in order to classify patients as either Cancer or Non-Cancer by studying their medical records such as radius_mean, diagnosis, texture_mean, area_mean, perimeter_mean, etc.

It is one of the easiest supervised algorithms for learning. It is based on the idea that, in a Machine Learning model, the predictor variables are independent of each other. In this proposed algorithm two misclassified observations exist; one is non-cancer, and the other one is cancer. The same 455 measurements were used for testing sets and 114 for evaluation measurements and accuracy observed to be 98.2% (Table 3).

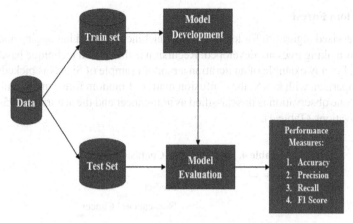

Fig. 3. Performance and evaluation of Naïve Bayes algorithm

Table 3. Naive Bayes Confusion matrix

		Predict	
		Non-cancer	Cancer
Actual	Non-cancer	69	1
	Cancer	1	43

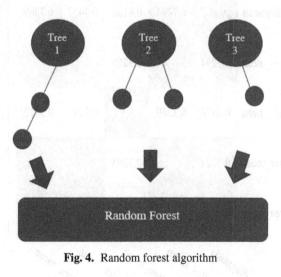

Fig. 4. Random forest algorithm

4.3 Random Forest

It is a Supervised algorithm for learning. The machine is trained in bagging and a range of decision-making trees are developed. Recursion is the central technique based on this technique. For any example of an iteration a random sample of Size N is picked (Fig. 4).

In comparison with k-NN, the confusion matrix of random forest uncertainty is very good. Just one observation is misclassified as non-cancer and the accuracy is 95.6% with four observations (Table 4).

Table 4. Decision Tree Confusion matrix

		Predict	
		Non-cancer	Cancer
Actual	Non-cancer	69	1
	Cancer	4	40

4.4 Correlation

A heatmap is a tool for visualizing data displaying the significance of a two-dimensional phenomenon as color. The change of color can be by hue or intensity, providing the viewer

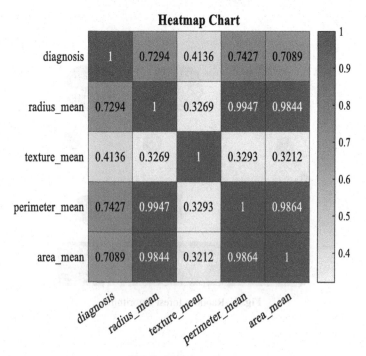

Fig. 5. Heatmap Chart

with apparent visual evidence of the clusters or spatial variability of the phenomena. Among the mean calculation of the 5 attributes, we can see that all of them are strongly correlated. The blue across the diagonal indicates a correlation between the attributes (Fig. 5).

4.5 Count of Non-cancer and Cancer

From the dataset, we will note that the number of Healthy patients exceeds the number of cancer patients and this is illustrated by the bar graph below in our MATLAB (Fig. 6).
   Cancer_212
   Non-Cancer_357

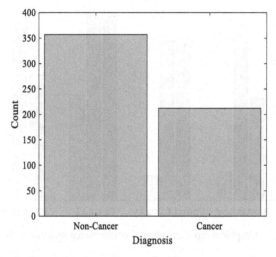

Fig. 6. Count of patients diagnosed with non-cancer and cancer.

5 Results and Discussion

The dataset is separated into training set and evaluation set with 80% of the data was used for machine training and 20% for evaluation. We monitor and develop a sample-based pattern to determine whether a certain category of symptoms contributes to breast cancer. Training data are training and untrained data is reviewed in the MATLAB which is an open-source learning machine forum, we used statistics and machine learning toolbox.

   Figure 7 displays the graphical description of the efficiency metrics for the three algorithms that are discussed. The results presented in Table 5 shows that Naïve Bayes has the best performance of accuracy, specificity, recall and f1 score over k-NN and Decision tree.

   Each algorithm has its own advantages and drawbacks over each other: k-NN, Naïve Bayes and Random Forest, the kind of problem they solve, etc. (Table 6).

Table 5. Performance measure indices

Classifier	Accuracy	Specificity	Recall	F1 Score
Decision Tree	95.6%	97.5%	98.5%	96.5%
Naïve Bayes	98.1%	97.5%	98.3%	98.3%
k-NN	92.9%	92.8%	95.7%	94.3%

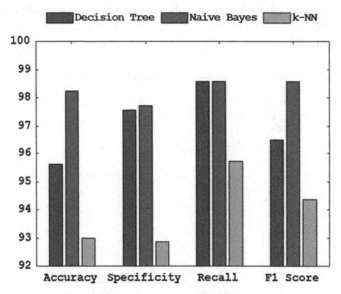

Fig.7. Graphical representation of performance measure indices

Table 6. Performance comparison table of breast cancer detection

	Naïve Bayes Performance comparison		
	Accuracy	Recall	F1 Score
K.Sivakami et al. (2015)	95%	95%	95%
B.M. Gayathri et al. (2016)	92.98%	98.57%	94.52%
S. Kharya et al. (2016)	92%	92%	92%
Celia Shahnaz et al. (2017)	92.9%	92%	92%
Maheshwar et al. (2019)	96%	96%	96%
Proposed work	98.1%	98.3%	98.3%

6 Conclusion and Future Scope

In this analysis various methods of classification, including Decision Tree, Naïve Bayes, k-NN, were used to assess the accuracy of breast cancer predictions. The research was conducted on the Wisconsin breast cancer dataset. The various accuracy checks have also been used for their accuracy, such as precision, recall and F1 score.

It is found that each algorithm had more than 92% accuracy to assess non-cancer tumor or cancer tumor. Proposed work shows that Naïve Bayes is the most effective for breast cancer detection because it has the best accuracy, specificity, recall and F1 score over the other algorithms. Different feature selection methods may be used during pre-processing phase before implementing the model. The use of classifiers and evolutionary analysis techniques to detect breast cancer for the optimization of results may be a good field for study.

Therefore, supervised machine learning approach in early diagnosis and cancer type diagnosis can be highly important. In addition, it can be measured time complexity and performance analysis of proposed algorithm on a cloud network.

References

1. Felman, S.A.: Breast cancer: symptoms, risk factors, and treatment 2019. Medical News Today (2019). https://www.medicalnewstoday.com/articles/37136.
2. "World Health Organization", World Health Organization (2020). https://www.who.int/health-topics/cancer#tab=tab_1
3. Boyle, P., Levin, B.: "World cancer report" (2008). https://publications.iarc.fr/Non-Series Publications/World-Cancer-Reports/World-Cancer-Report-2008
4. Bardou, D., Zhang, K., Ahmad, S.M.: Classification of breast cancer based on histology images using convolutional neural networks. IEEE Access 6(2018), 24680–24693 (2018)
5. Stenkvist, B., et al.: Computerized nuclear morphometry as an objective method for characterizing human cancer cell populations. Can. Res. 38(12), 4688–4697 (1978)
6. Kowal, M., Filipczuk, P., Obuchowicz, A., Korbicz, J., Monczak, R.: Computer-aided diagnosis of breast cancer based on fine needle biopsy microscopic images. Comput. Biol. Med. 43(10), 1563–1572 (2013)
7. Nbcf. Biopsy: The National Breast Cancer Foundation. https://www.nationalbreastcancer.org/breast-cancer-biopsy
8. Blessing, G., Azeta, A., Misra, S., Chigozie, F., Ahuja, R.: A machine learning prediction of automatic text based assessment for open and distance learning: a review. In: Abraham, A., Panda, M., Pradhan, S., Garcia-Hernandez, L., Ma, K. (eds.) International Conference on Innovations in Bio-Inspired Computing and Applications, pp. 369–380. Springer, Cham (2019). https://doi.org/10.1007/978-3-030-49339-4_38
9. Abolade, R.O., Famakinde, S.O., Popoola, S.I., Oseni, O.F., Atayero, A.A., Misra, S.: Support vector machine for path loss predictions in urban environment. In: Gervasi, O., et al. (eds.) ICCSA 2020. LNCS, vol. 12255, pp. 995–1006. Springer, Cham (2020). https://doi.org/10.1007/978-3-030-58820-5_71
10. Popoola, S.I., Misra, S., Atayero, A.A.: Outdoor path loss predictions based on extreme learning machine. Wireless Pers. Commun. 99(1), 441–460 (2018)
11. Kumar, P.R., Sarkar, A., Mohanty, S.N., Kumar, P.P.: Segmentation of white blood cells using image segmentation algorithms. In: 5th International Conference on Computing, Communication and Security, pp. 1–4 (2020)

12. Spanhol, F.A., Oliveira, L.S., Petitjean, C., Heutte, L.: A Dataset for Breast Cancer Histopathological Image Classification. IEEE Trans. Biomed. Eng. **63**(7), 1455–1462 (2015)
13. Hamsagayathri, P., Sampath, P.: Priority based decision tree classifier for breast cancer detection. In: 4th International Conference on Advanced Computing and Communication Systems (ICACCS), August 2017 (2017)
14. Rana, M., Chandorkar, P., Dsouza, A., Kazi, N.: Breast cancer Diagnosis and Recurrence prediction using machine learning techniques. IJRET- Int. J. Res. Eng. Technol. **4**(4), 372–376 (2015)
15. Medjahed, S.A., Saadi, T.A., Benyettou, A.: Breast Cancer Diagnosis by using k-Nearest Neighbor with different distances and classification rules. Int. J. Comput. Appl. **62**(1), 1–5 (2013)
16. Ahmet, M., Niyazi, K., Aydin, A.: Breast cancer classification by using support vector machines with reduced dimension. In: Proceedings Elmar - International Symposium Electronics in Marine, pp. 37–40 (2011)
17. Král, P., Lenc, L.: LBP features for breast cancer detection. In: International Conference on Image Processing (ICIP), pp. 2643–2647 (2016)
18. Song, L., Hsu, W., Xu, J., van der Schaar, M.: Using contextual learning to improve diagnostic accuracy: application in breast cancer screening. IEEE J. Biomed. Health Inform. **20**(3), 902–914 (2015)
19. Al-Hadidi,M.R., Alarabeyyat, A., Alhanahnah, M.: Breast cancer detection using K-nearest neighbor machine learning algorithm. In: 9th International Conference on Developments in eSystems Engineering, pp. 35 – 39 (2016)
20. Gayathri, B.M., Sumathi, C.P.: Comparative study of relevance vector machine with various machine learning techniques used for detecting breast cancer. In: IEEE International Conference on Computational Intelligence and Computing Research (ICCIC), pp. 1–5 (2016)
21. Behera, R.K., Rath, S.K., Misra, S., Leon, M., Adewumi, A.: Machine learning approach for reliability assessment of open-source software. In: Misra, S., et al. (eds.) ICCSA 2019. LNCS, vol. 11622, pp. 472–482. Springer, Cham (2019). https://doi.org/10.1007/978-3-030-24305-0_35
22. Behera, R.K., Shukla, S., Rath, S.K., Misra, S.: Software reliability assessment using machine learning technique. In: Gervasi, O., et al. (eds.) ICCSA 2018. LNCS, vol. 10964, pp. 403–411. Springer, Cham (2018). https://doi.org/10.1007/978-3-319-95174-4_32

Emotion Recognition of Speech in Hindi Using Dimensionality Reduction and Machine Learning Techniques

Akshat Agrawal[(✉)] and Anurag Jain

USIC&T, Guru Gobind Singh Indraprastha University, New Delhi, India
akshatag20@gmail.com, anurag@ipu.ac.in

Abstract. This study primarily focuses on integrating various types of speech features and different statistical techniques to reduce the data in all dimensions. To predict human beings, the existing machine learning algorithms were applied to train the available dataset to obtain better results. This will result in obtaining much better response from machines by processing the human instruction & related emotions. Through machine learning techniques emotion recognition system can be work effectively and results will be comparable through code of python language. To improve the performance of emotion recognition (ER) statistical techniques principal component analysis (PCA) and linear discriminant analysis (LDA) to fetch the essential information from the dataset. After applying Naïve Bayes classification (NBC) on the speech corpus collected from non-dramatic actor the results shows that, NBC generates better results than the exiting machine learning (ML) classification techniques such as K-means nearest neighbor algorithm (KNN),Support vector machine (SVM) & decision tree(DT). This paper presents the results of various ML techniques that is used for finding out ER. Through SVM prediction rate achieved 39% and decision tree recognition rate achieved 29% only and when applied NBC results is 72.77%. This study presents the change of prediction rate while change of dataset happened.

Keywords: Emotion recognition · K-means nearest neighbor · Naïve Bayes · Support vector machine (SVM) · Decision tree

1 Introduction

In today's scenario information from one end to another end passage on using Speech signals hence speech is most preferable way for communications in humans. For betterment of communication system researchers are rigorously working on speech signals to discover various parameters of speech. Human speech signals are composed of information & emotions both where emotions are most impactful parameter of speech communication. Human communication relates to the exchanges of information and emotion both the passage of instruction to machine relates to the understanding of their semantics only, not the emotion paradigm [1]. According to the available literature the process of human

© Springer Nature Switzerland AG 2021
S. Misra and B. Muhammad-Bello (Eds.): ICTA 2020, CCIS 1350, pp. 119–129, 2021.
https://doi.org/10.1007/978-3-030-69143-1_10

ER is accomplished by recognizing the different gestures of the body language [2]. To recognize the different gestures of the body it is essential the presence of the person in the conversation. All the necessary facts are to be considered to obtain the important gestures of the conversation to make the recognition process effective to generate the better results. ER can be applied on three types of datasets for experimentation first kind of database is prepared by matured actors and they are doing recording of their voice with considering of all the basic types of emotions these datasets are used for training purpose of the system because they are having all the emotions with perfect quality, second type of dataset is called as elicited dataset in this kind of dataset some anchor performing conversation with a person and trying to get all the emotions from the person without the information of person who is being recorded. Third kind of dataset is called as natural recorded dataset that is fact is not known by any of the person like cockpit conversation or doctor or patient conversation this kind of dataset is our target dataset. According to the available literatures suggested by the researchers the process of the features extraction and classification can be performed using LDA & PCA statistical techniques. After applying these techniques emotional state analysis can be performed by some existing algorithms and methods such as KNN algorithm, Naïve Bayes classifier, SVM, and Decision tree. This study shows deficiency in results when same features used on different dataset qualities and providing the less recognition rate.

Rest of the paper is organized as follows- Sect. 2 describes the literature review followed by research methodology adopted, in Sect. 3. Section 4 discusses about the results outcome of the adopted methodology comparisons are also made with other techniques done by other researchers whereas conclusion & scope of future work is given in Sect. 5 of the paper.

2 Literature Survey

Advancement in ER from speech fascinates several researchers to improve the related work in this field. Researches of this filed have been suggested to employ different acoustic features with the statistical properties to evaluate acoustic features accurately [3, 4]. Available literature suggested the significance of the augmented prosody domain features to identify the various emotions [5]. The existing techniques related to the field of vocal communication consist of two process such as decoding & encoding [6]. Various existing techniques are best suited to establish the correlation between the process of speech and emotion appropriately [7]. Researchers have been identified various classification schemes to elaborate the process of speech and gesture recognition throughout the communication [8]. In communication the intonation patterns are critical aspect of speech and emotions can be recognized with the change of these patterns [9]. [10] In end point detection speech signal can be divided into frames as well as pre-weighted. Multilingual classification is widely used to recognize emotions in speech. [11]. The speech and gesture recognition process can be improved after recognizing several prosodic features such as intensity of pitch, duration of speech time, its quality, and energy [12]. To improve the performance of exiting techniques Mel frequency Cepstral Coefficients

(MFCC) with correlation can be employed [13]. Researchers suggest that emotion can be easily identified by including MFCC features particularly for Hindi speech signals. By integrating speech and facial expressions it is very easy to identify various states of emotions [14]. To accurately recognize emotions statistical technique can be integrate with KNN Algorithm proposed by [15]. The most widely known technique Radial basis function neural network can be used to recognize paraphrasing which is another aspect of semantic of utterance [16]. [17] The analysis of textual data can be carried out by employing various ML techniques to perform ER [18]; in this study, the comparison of various pattern recognition techniques using ML has been conducted. Further work proposed by [19] introduced the degree of confusion for recognizing different emotions & then applied various deep learning technology to recognize various emotions. According to Nwe et al. [20], the representation of speech signals can be carried out using log frequency power coefficients. For further classification of the speech signals Hidden Markov Model can be used. The researchers suggest novel technique to transform emotions using word boundary detection techniques this transformation use the concept of linear medication model in order to produce better results using proposed WBDA [21]. On the basis of sorted neutral utterances in the database other expressive style utterances can be formulated from the researcher [22]. [23] Similarly used global features with LSTM. However [24, 25] use hybrid approach for recognizing the emotion. Further the general classification of emotion will less due to overlapping of emotion like Happy, Surprise, Angry to overcome this problem [27] suggested support vector machine classification to reduce the possibility of overlapping and for dimensionality reduction used fisher's coefficient. However, [28] proposed a method to find out missing feature values from speech signal by using the Bayesian view and then applied all the feature set for recognition. Similarly, [29] suggested an authentication technique using a support vector machine for the identification of voice from the ear. Based on parameters such as precision, recall, f1 score [30] calculated performance analysis of ER on EMO-DB database and Danish Emotional Database and fetching the results of classification. However, [31] proposed word error rate and linear predictive coding over Mel frequency cepstral coefficients for better prediction of ER and getting better results than other global features set used for ER from the speech and voice signal. [32] Suggested contextual relationship with the word embedding method on the Sanskrit language in vector spaces to improve the efficiency of interpretation of language.

3 Methodology

This section presents an overview of the speech emotion recognition system and its methodology (See Fig. 1). The primary goal of the ER is to extract various types of speech features and identify appropriate features for recognizing emotions. After identifying the emotions, classification techniques will provide quantitative results of speech features.

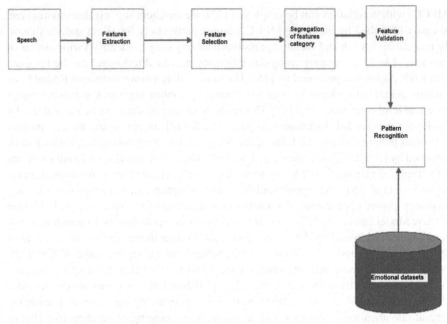

Fig. 1. Emotions recognition system to extract emotional features

3.1 Speech Corpora

To identify various speech emotional features, speech corpora are used to match various distinctive fundamental feeling factors such as anger, happiness, neutral, sadness, etc. Due to the non-availability of open access speech corpora, it was required to create our Speech corpora for experiments related to language and sentences. Although different classes of feelings are available, individuals still rely on five distinctive fundamental feelings such as anger, happiness, sadness, surprise, and neutral [26]. To assess the quality of delivered speech corpora with five fundamental feeling factors is delivered to five different audiences. Finally, the speech corpora with poor quality are rerecorded similar method is applied to improve the quality of delivered speech corpora. The description of speech corpora is presented in Table 1.

3.2 Feature Extraction

The process of speech communication can be categorized based on local and global features such as pitch, energy, Zero Crossing Rate (ZCR) and MFCC, Gamma tone cepstral coefficient [8].

- In every human vocal tract, and vibration of vocal lines are depends upon the value of Pitch. By modifying the value of pitch, the voice of male and females can be distinguished. In this manner, pitch plays an essential role in male and female talk.
- Energy, which is a feature of speech, provides important information about emotions, which can be calculated Eq. (1)

Table 1. Description of speech corpora

S. no.	Specification of database	Statistics for emotion conversion
1	Total numbers of speakers	6
2	Total numbers of sentences	22
3	Total numbers of emotional features	Anger, Happiness, Neutral, Sadness, Surprise
4	Size of corpora	660
5	Type of sentences in Corpora	Hindi
6	Speech coding	16 KHz
7	Sampling rate	44.1 KHz

$$E_N = \sum_{b=a-X+1}^{a} [m(b)t(a-b)]^2 \tag{1}$$

In Eq. (1), variable a, X, and t(a − b) represents a sample of an analyzed window, window size, and hamming window, respectively.

- The value of ZCR can vary from positive to a negative direction which passes through the origin in the X-axis and Y-axis; the value of ZCR can estimate by Eq. (2)

$$Z_a = \sum_{b=-\infty}^{\infty} .5|sgn[m(b)] - sgn[m(b-1)]|t(a-b) \tag{2}$$

- MFCC can be represented by 12 coefficients of power spectrum and use power of discrete cosine transformation which can be calculated by Eq. 3(a), 3(b)

$$S_i(k) = \sum_{b=1}^{b} Ai(b)m(b)e^{-j2\pi tb/B} \tag{3a}$$

$$p_i(k) = \frac{1}{b}|S(i)t|^2 \tag{3b}$$

Five distinctive fundamental feelings feature for 5 utterances have been given in Table 2. The obtained values in Table 2 are used to represent Anger, Happiness, Neutral, Sadness, Surprise.

3.3 Feature Selection

The pragmatic analysis of this section carried out by considering speech features such as pitch, energy, MFCC & ZCR (See Table 2). In feature selection maximum variation in speech features has been considered. The average of all the MFCC values have been taken which are scattered in 13 columns and 252 rows, energy's value in scattered 1 column and 238 rows. It is suggested that above speech features are significantly useful for analysis.

4 Results and Discussions

To extract meaningful information, statistical techniques PCA & LDA are applied on datasets after combining and comparing local and global features together to improve the performance of ER. The previous studies conducted by various researchers are based on local features that identify emotions and take global features for further experiment. PCA & LDA are applied in combination with most widely classification techniques such as KNN, NBC, SVM, DT. Among these classification techniques, NBC provides better results. In Fig. 2 (a), it has been shown that 345 utterances obtained from the experiment are combined. After combining different speech features, speech samples can be segregated based on emotion. The result of PCA in Fig. 2(a) depicts that different emotions such as sadness, surprise and happy are combined and scattered at two different places of the graph. The Fig. 2 (b) shows the results of LDA in which sad, surprise, happy and neutral are combined which can be easily distinguished up to a certain limit. After applying PCA & LDA, different classification techniques such as KNN, NBC, SVM, DT are used to predict the emotional state of the speech dataset. After experiments, it can be observed that the different speech samples are scattered in the graph and most of the samples do not provide accurate prediction of the emotion. After that, it can be observed that the PCA generates better results as most of the sample are combined after taking different speech features into consideration.

Table 2. Obtained values of different speech features

Emotion	PITCH	MFCC	ZCR	ENERGY
Anger	279.1139	−9.28865	18	14.53836
Happy	272.2222	−9.25428	19.5	3.868455
Sadness	221.608	−8.43644	20.5	0.605399
Neutral	230.8901	0.480463	46	0.149245
Surprise	212.0192	−5.70965	18	7.849319
Anger	373.7288	−8.18646	20	4.468283

(continued)

Table 2. (*continued*)

Emotion	PITCH	MFCC	ZCR	ENERGY
Happy	324.2647	−9.60917	20.5	5.058219
Sadness	180.7377	−6.26616	18	2.564311
Neutral	282.6923	−5.09771	25	0.274823
Surprise	136.9565	−5.746	22	1.12128
Anger	190.9091	−8.85719	23	2.382445
Happy	74.49324	−8.9636	23	3.131639
Sadness	312.766	−8.67943	26.5	0.968261
Neutral	284.5161	−7.61223	32	0.339073
Surprise	128.1977	−6.47725	24.5	2.01728
Anger	288.87	−7.84639	22.5	2.567654
Happy	386.58324	−8.5683	23	3.23456
Sadness	78.866	−7.57943	25.5	0.868261
Neutral	94.8325	−7.75223	31.5	0.439073
Surprise	238.7654	−9.87625	23.5	2.24728

Existing techniques are further applied to our test dataset to produce satisfactory experimental results. Emotions are easily distinguished up to a certain limit, hence after appropriately utilization of PCA & LDA techniques, it is required to apply various ML techniques to predict the emotional state of speech data sets. Here different combination and confusion matrix is generated to predict the emotions.

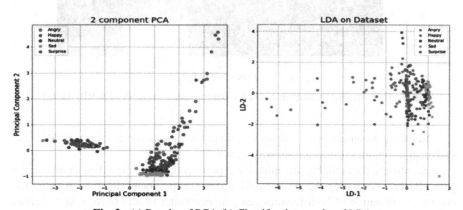

Fig. 2. (a) Results of PCA (b) Classification results of LDA

Figure 3 shows a graphical representation of the confusion matrix SVM. Figure 4 shows a graphical representation of confusion matrix SVM with radial basis function kernel, and Fig. 5 shows a graphical representation of confusion matrix of decision tree.

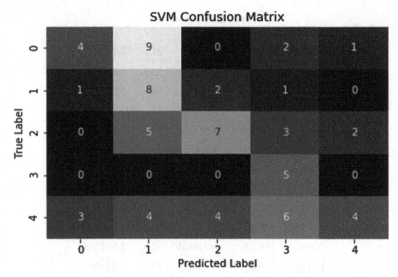

Fig. 3. Heat map representation confusion matrix values using SVM

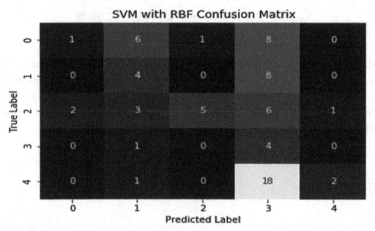

Fig. 4. Heat map representation confusion matrix values using SVM & RBF kernel

Afterward, a comparative analysis was done for various combinations of ML, and statistical techniques results are shown in Table 3.

According to the available literature, the experiments are performed either on local or global features separately. According to the different experiments, it has been suggested that the combination of both features can generate better results to recognize various emotion and speech features. After experiments using LDA and PCA, it can be observed that the different speech samples are scattered in the graph, and most of the samples do not provide an accurate prediction of the emotion. Finally, it is suggested that the use of PCA in place of LDA can generate better results in speech recognition. After experiments, it is observed that dimensional reduction techniques, in combination with

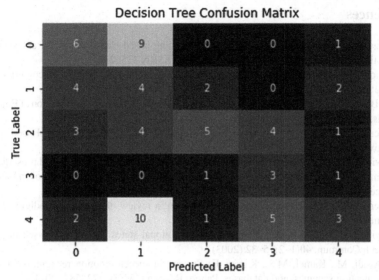

Fig. 5. Heat map representation confusion matrix values of the decision tree

Table 3. Comparative results of prediction of ML techniques (all values are in percentage %)

SVM	SVM + RBF Kernel	SVM with PCA	Decision tree	Decision tree with PCA	KNN With PCA	Naïve Bayes
39	22.38	22.53	29.99	28.14	33.65	72.77

different available machine learning techniques, can not generate satisfactory results. For further improvements of the results, different deep learning and nature-inspired techniques can be applied in place of machine learning techniques.

5   Conclusion and Future work

The performance of the ER can be improved by combining various local and global features. PCA & LDA are applied to the dataset. After applying PCA & LDA to extract meaningful information. Most widely used classification techniques such as KNN, NBC, SVM & DT are applied to minimize the dimensionality of the data to identify the different emotions. Table 3 shows the prediction results of various techniques of ML in which NBC produces better results of defined speech corpora. The local feature & global features can be combined with the Tegor energy feature and qualitative feature, respectively. To further improvement of ER, deep learning and nature-inspired techniques can be applied for getting better quantitative results.

References

1. Agrawal, A., Jain, A., Kumar, B.S.: Deep learning-based classification for assessment of emotion recognition in speech (2019). Available SSRN 3356238
2. Tarnowski Pawełand Kołodziej, M., Majkowski, A., Rak, R.J.: Emotion recognition using facial expressions. Procedia Comput. Sci. **108**, 1175–1184 (2017)
3. van Benzooijen, R.: The Characteristics and Recognizability of Vocal Expression of Emotions. Foris, Drodrecht (1984)
4. Scherer, K.R., Banse, R., Wallboot, H.G., Goldbeck, T.: Vocal clues Emot. Encod. Decod. Motiv Emot. **15**, 123–148 (1991)
5. Cowie, R., Douglas-Cowie, E.: Automatic statistical analysis of the signal and prosodic signs of emotion in speech. In: Proceeding of Fourth International Conference on Spoken Language Processing, ICSLP 1996, vol. 3, pp. 1989–1992 (1996)
6. Scherer, K.R.: Vocal communication of emotion: a review of research paradigms. Speech Commun. **40**(1–2), 227–256 (2003)
7. Cowie, R., Cornelius, R.R.: Describing the emotional states that are expressed in speech. Speech Commun. **40**(1–2), 5–32 (2003)
8. El Ayadi, M., Kamel, M.S., Karray, F.: Survey on speech emotion recognition: features, classification schemes, and databases. Pattern Recognit. **44**(3), 572–587 (2011)
9. Agrawal, S.S., Prakash, N., Jain, A.: Transformation of emotion based on acoustic features of intonation patterns for Hindi speech . IJCSNS Int. J. Comput. Sci. Netw. Secur. **10**(9), 198–205 (2010)
10. Zhao, D.: Design of continuous recognition algorithm for online interactive English speech segment. J. Discret. Math. Sci. Cryptogr. **20**(6–7), 1513–1517 (2017)
11. Hozjan, V., Kačič, Z.: Context-independent multilingual emotion recognition from speech signals. Int. J. Speech Technol. **6**(3), 311–320 (2003)
12. Cahn, J.E.: The generation of affect in synthesized speech. J. Am. Voice I/O Soc. **8**(1), 1 (1990)
13. Palia, N., Kant, S., Dev, A.: Performance evaluation of speaker recognition system. J. Discret. Math. Sci. Cryptogr. **22**(2), 203–218 (2019)
14. Jain, A., Prakash, N., Agrawal, S.S.: Evaluation of MFCC for emotion identification in Hindi speech. In: 2011 IEEE 3rd International Conference on Communication Software and Networks, pp. 189–193 (2011)
15. Dmitrieva, H., Nikitin, K.: Design of automatic speech emotion recognition system. In: Proceedings of the Workshop on Applications in Information Technology, 8–10 October 2015, pp. 47–50 (2015)
16. Chitra, A., Rajkumar, A.: A study on paraphrase recognition using radial basis function neural network. IETE J. Res. **58**(1), 50–56 (2012)
17. Mehndiratta, P., Soni, D.: Identification of sarcasm using word embeddings and hyperparameters tuning. J. Discret. Math. Sci. Cryptogr. **22**(4), 465–489 (2019)
18. Pal, S.K.: Soft computing tools and pattern recognition. IETE J. Res. **44**(1–2), 61–87 (1998)
19. Sun, L., Zou, B., Fu, S., Chen, J., Wang, F.: Speech emotion recognition based on DNN-decision tree SVM model. Speech Commun. (2019)
20. Nwe, T.L., Foo, S.W., De Silva, L.C.: Speech emotion recognition using Hidden Markov models. Speech Commun. **41**(4), 603–623 (2003)
21. Jain, A., Agrawal, S.S., Prakash, N.: An approach for improving quality for emotion transformation for Hindi. CSI J. Comput. **1**(2), 60–66 (2012)
22. Jain, A., Agrawal, S.S., Prakash, N.: Transformation of emotion based on acoustic features of intonation patterns for Hindi speech and their perception. IETE J. Res. **57**(4), 318–324 (2014)

23. Atmaja, B.T., Akagi, M.: Speech emotion recognition based on speech segment using LSTM with attention model. In: Proceedings - 2019 IEEE International Conference on Signals and Systems, ICSigSys 2019, pp. 40–44 (2019)
24. Umamaheswari, J., Akila, A.: An enhanced human speech emotion recognition using hybrid of PRNN and KNN. In: Proceedings of the International Conference on Machine Learning, Big Data, Cloud and Parallel Computing: Trends, Prespectives and Prospects, COMITCon 2019, pp. 177–183 (2019)
25. Shashidhar, G., Koolagudi, K., Sreenivasa, R.: Emotion recognition from speech: a review, vol. 15, pp. 99–117. Springer Science and Business Media (2012)
26. Cowie, R.: Emotional states expressed in speech," ISCA ITRW speech Emot. Dev. a Concept. Framew. Res. pp. 224–231 (2000)
27. Sun, L., Fu, S., Wang, F.: Decision tree SVM model with Fisher feature selection for speech emotion recognition . EURASIP J. Audio, Speech Music Process. **2019**(1), 2 (2019)
28. Maas, R., Huemmer, C., Sehr, A., Kellermann, W.: A Bayesian view on acoustic model-based techniques for robust speech recognition. EURASIP J. Adv. Signal Process. **2015**(1), 1–16 (2015). https://doi.org/10.1186/s13634-015-0287-x
29. Olanrewaju, L., Oyebiyi, O., Misra, S., Maskeliunas, R., Damasevicius, R.: Secure ear biometrics using circular kernel principal component analysis, Chebyshev transform hashing and Bose–Chaudhuri–Hocquenghem error-correcting codes. SIViP **14**(5), 847–855 (2020). https://doi.org/10.1007/s11760-019-01609-y
30. Ramakrishnan, S., El Emary, I.M.M.: Speech emotion recognition approaches in human computer interaction. Telecommun. Syst. **52**(3), 1467–1478 (2013)
31. Nassif, A.B., et al.: Speech recognition using deep neural networks: a systematic review. IEEE Access **7**, 19143–19165 (2019)
32. Sharma, I., Anand, S., Goyal, R., Misra, S.: Representing contexual relations with sanskrit word embeddings. In: International Conference on Computational Science and its Applications, 3 July 2017, pp. 262–273. Springer, Cham (2017)

Application of Supervised Machine Learning Based on Gaussian Process Regression for Extrapolative Cell Availability Evaluation in Cellular Communication Systems

Ojuh O. Divine[1] and Isabona Joseph[2(✉)]

[1] Department of Physical Sciences, Benson Idahosa University, Benin City, Nigeria
[2] Department of Physics, Federal University Lokoja, Lokoja, Kogi State, Nigeria
josabone@yahoo.com

Abstract. Supervised machine learning models and their algorithms play major roles in extrapolative data analysis and getting valuable information of the data. One emerging robust supervised machine learning based model is the Gaussian process regression (GPR) model. A vital strength of the GPR model is its capacity to adaptively model multipath linear/nonlinear functional approximation, dimension reduction and classification problems. Nevertheless, there exist a plethora of approximation (prediction) methods and hyperparameters that systematically impact GPR kernel function for effective modeling and learning capacity. Some of the key approximation methods includes the Exact Gaussian process regression, Fully independent conditional, Subset of data points approximation, and Subset of regressors. Nonetheless, the problem of knowing how to identify or select the best from these approximation methods during data training and learning with GPR model so as to avoid the predictive variance problem is a challenge. In this contribution, we propose a stepwise selection algorithm to tackle the challenge. GPR modelling with stepwise selection algorithm has been tested for extrapolative regression analysis of live cell availability data obtained from an operational telecom service provider. The GPR extrapolative based evaluation results show that the proposed approach is not only tractable, but also yield low errors in terms of accurate service availability quantification and estimation. Also, in terms of mean absolute error, the regression results of the proposed GPR extrapolative based evaluation combined with stepwise kernels selection algorithm were also far better compared with the ones obtained using support vector regression.

Keywords: Supervised learning · Service availability · Kernel · Gaussian process regression · Approximation methods · Stepwise selection algorithm

1 Introduction

The world is progressively tuning into a global village and an essential ingredient to facilitate this process is effective communication wherein robust telecommunication infrastructure availability is a major factor. One of the first major breakthrough in

© Springer Nature Switzerland AG 2021
S. Misra and B. Muhammad-Bello (Eds.): ICTA 2020, CCIS 1350, pp. 130–144, 2021.
https://doi.org/10.1007/978-3-030-69143-1_11

telecommunication industry in the mid-80s was the introduction a digital-based wireless telephone system such as the Global System of Mobile Communications (GSM). One key strength of the GSM technology is its superb voice telephony structure. However, packet-switched communication systems such as the High Speed Packet Access (HSPA), Universal Mobile telecommunication Systems (UMTS) and Long Term Evolution (LTE) have already be introduced to cater for the GSM data communication deficiency.

One key performance parameter to appraise the operational telecommunications systems quality is cell service availability [1–3]. It is always in the heart of any telecom operator to make network service available everywhere for easy access by the subscribers' mobile terminals. This fact has led the network operators, including researchers to unceasingly seek for ways to obtaining and appraising the status and levels of cell service availability of deployed cellular communication networks [4].

Supervised machine learning algorithms and modelling tools play major roles in extrapolative data analysis and getting valuable information of the data [5, 6]. One emerging robust supervised machine learning based model is the Gaussian process regression (GPR) model. A vital strength of the GPR model is its capacity to adaptive model complex linear/nonlinear functional approximation, dimension reduction and classification problems.

However, there exist a number of approximation (prediction) methods that systematically impact GPR kernel function for effective modeling and learning capacity. For example, the choice of a particular approximation method and its hyperparameters defines the inductive biases, inductive learning generalization ability and the hidden function mapping. Therefore, these hyperparameters must carefully be selected or tuned to enhance the GPR learning ability. In some key existing works [7–17], giant strides and efforts have explored by researchers to harness the approximation methods/hyperparameters for different purposes. Particularly, a good exploration of 'BayesOpt' procedure is considered in [16], but it is mainly for kernel function selection.

In this work, a stepwise selection algorithm has been engaged to obtain the best GRP approximation method for tractable cell service availability data extrapolative analysis and estimation. The cell availability data was obtained directly from a commercial GSM/UMTS/LTE telecom network system service provider operating in South Nigeria, between 12th November, 2019 and 18th November, 2019.

The remainder of the research paper is cautiously structured as follows. Section 2 provide the detail materials and methods employed in the paper and these include concept of service availability, service availability targets, Gaussian process regression, methods of approximating the Gaussian regression process and their selection algorithm. In Sect. 3, results and discussion, starting with basic statistical analysis of results, followed by detailed presentation of service availability data estimation using the adopted Gaussian process regression (GPR) model-based learning process. Finally, the conclusion of the research paper is shown in Sect. 4.

2 Materials and Methods

2.1 Concept of Service Availability

According to ITU-T recommendation [18, 19], availability can be described as the period a system is able to carry out to its desired specification, or perform a required function, expressed as percentage. Cell service availability is the percentage ratio of accessible service time to slated service time in a cell. As display in Fig. 1, the key parameters that can be explored to further describe the service availability or service unavailability are Failure rate, Restoration Rate and Mean Time to Restore, all which are related by [19]:

$$SA = 100\left(\frac{M}{M + MTTR}\right) = 100\left(\frac{\mu}{\lambda + \mu}\right) \tag{1}$$

$$SU = 100 - SA_c = 100\left(\frac{MTTR}{M + MTTR}\right) \tag{2}$$

$$= 100\left(\frac{\lambda}{\lambda + \mu}\right) \tag{3}$$

where

μ = Restoration rate
$M = \frac{1}{\lambda}$, λ = Failure Rate
$MTTR = \frac{1}{\mu}$ = Mean Time To Restore
SA = Service Availability
SU = Service Unavailability

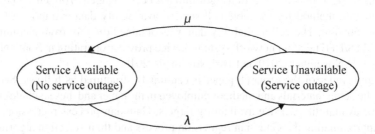

Fig. 1. Cell availability parameters

2.2 The Five-Nine: Service Availability Targets

As mentioned previously, service availability is the percentage ratio of accessible service time to slated service time in a cell. It is period of time that the cellular systems network is available for usage. This definition leads us to the concept of "five-nines (99.999%)", which is a broad view concept that has been adopted in many networks to attain the desired service quality target goal during usage. It is the target value adopted for system networks availability assessment with the sole aim of making sure that agreed level or desire level of operational performance is guaranteed over a period of time [20]. As provided in Table 1, the five nine simply implies 5 min and 26 s (i.e. 326 s) of unplanned cellular network downtime per year.

Table 1. Availability percentage in second (s), minutes (m), milliseconds (ms) and microseconds (μs)

Availability (%)	Downtime per day	Downtime per week	Downtime per month	Downtime per year
99.999 ("5-nines")	864.00 ms	6.05 s	26.30 s	5.26 m
99.9999 ("6-nines")	86.40 ms	604.80 ms	2.63 s	31.56 s
99.99999 ("7-nines")	8.64 ms	60.48 ms	262.98 ms	3.16 s
99.999999 ("8-nines")	864.00 μs	6.05 ms	26.30 ms	315.58 ms
99.9999999 ("9-nines")	86.40 μs	604.80 μs	2.63 ms	31.56 ms

2.3 Gaussian Regression Process

There exist many unknown GMM parameters as shown in Eq. (3). By means of Gaussian processes (GP) is a characteristic stochastic process that possess the capability to provide a high degree nonparametric description of functions. The probabilistic interpretations of the objective functions can be utilized for different purposes, particularly regression or functional approximation and feature classification. In this work, the regression aspect is the focus.

In GP regression, the output response y in correspondence with the input vector x is presumed to be a noisy estimation of the output function, that is:

$$y = f(x) + \epsilon, \text{ where } \epsilon \sim N\left(0, \sigma_\epsilon^2\right) \tag{4}$$

Given a typical dataset $P = \{(x_i, y_i)| i = 1, \ldots, n\}$, the scalar output response $y_t = f(x_t) + \epsilon$ in correspondence with the test input vector x_t can be expressed as:

$$Y_t \sim N\left(\mu(x_t|P), \sigma^2(x_t|P)\right) \tag{5}$$

where $\mu(x_t|P)$ designate the predicted mean and $\sigma^2(x_t|P)$ indicate the variance of y_t, both which can be explicitly defined by:

$$\mu(x_t|P) = k^T\left(K + \sigma_\epsilon^2 I\right)^{-1} y_{1:n} \tag{6}$$

$$\sigma^2(x_t|P) = k(x_t, x_t) - k^T \left(K + \sigma_\in^2 I \right)^{-1} k + \sigma_\in^2 \tag{7}$$

where.

K = kernel matrix.
$k^T = (k(x_1, x_t), \ldots, k(x_n, x_t))$.

2.4 GPR Approximation Methods

There exist a plethora of approximation (prediction) methods and hyperparameters that systematically impact GPR kernel function for effective modeling and learning capacity in literature. Some of the key approximation methods includes the Exact Gaussian process regression, Fully independent conditional, Subset of data points approximation, and Subset of regressors. Choosing from these approximation methods during data training and learning with GPR model so as to avoid the predictive variance problem is a challenge.

2.5 Service Availability Data and GPR Approximation Selection Algorithm

The literature usually recommends a theoretic availability computation (estimation) as a pre-study during cellular network pre-planning, or conducting real availability measurement during post-planning (optimisation stage), that is, when sufficient data would have been accessible in cellular network after deployment to obtain the actual availability data. The daily cell availability data used in this paper were obtained directly from GSM/UMTS/LTE telecom network operator in Port Harcourt City, South-South Nigeria. It is a one week data acquired between 12th–18th, November, 2019.

The adopted GPR-based approximation selection algorithm for cell availability estimation is shown in Fig. 2. First, the cell data is standardize to unity values. This is followed by routing the standardized data through approximation method selection for effective training, estimation and evaluation. To choose the best approximation method, we explore stepwise selection algorithm. As term stepwise selection suggests, this procedure selects the each approximation method in a step-by-step manner, but in iterative process, until the least predictive variance is attained process, until the least predictive variance is attained.

For the purpose of competitive performance benchmarking of the proposed GPR extrapolative based evaluation based on stepwise kernels selection algorithm with any other regression model, we consider the support vector regression (SVR) model.

The SVR model can be approximated in the high-dimensional feature space using [21–23]:

$$y_{SVM} = \langle w, \Phi(x) \rangle + q = \sum_i^k w_i \Phi(x)_i + q, q \in R, x, w \in R^k \tag{8}$$

In matrix form, Eq. (8) turns to:

$$y_{SVM} = \begin{bmatrix} w \\ q \end{bmatrix}^T \begin{bmatrix} x \\ 1 \end{bmatrix} = w^T \Phi(x) + q, x, w \in R^{k+1} \tag{9}$$

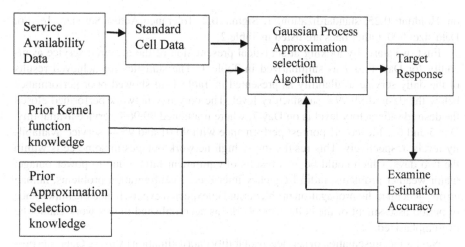

Fig. 2. Adopted GRP algorithm structure for Cell Data Estimation

Table 2. GPR approximation method and matlab implementation codes

GPR approximation method	Abbreviation	Matlab implementation codes
Block Coordinate Descent	'bcd'	fitrgp(X,ytrain,'KernelFunction','matern52',… FitMethod','exact','PredictMethod','bcd','Standardize',1)
Fully independent conditional	'fic'	fitrgp(X,ytrain,'KernelFunction','matern52',… FitMethod','fic','PredictMethod','fic','Standardize',1)
Subset of data points approximation	'sd'	fitrgp(X,ytrain,'KernelFunction','matern52',… FitMethod','sd','PredictMethod','sd','Standardize',1)
Subset of regressors	'sr'	fitrgp(X,ytrain,'KernelFunction','matern52',… FitMethod','bcd','PredictMethod','bcd','Standardize',1)

where, w and q designate the SVR vector of weights, and the modelling coefficient. $\Phi(x)$ expresses the SVR feature function and w, $\Phi(x)$ defines the dot product in the feature space.

3   Results and Discussion

The GPR program scripts used for cell availability data statistical analysis, graphics presentations and computations were performed with Matlab 2018a software and its platform. During the supervised based GPR machine learning, some of the key features employed include Initial Step Size: 100, 'Random Search Set Size: 59, cross validation:

on, Holdout: 0.25; standardization: 1, Sigma: 0.2, Tolerance Active Set size: 1e−06, Data size: 500. Other ones are listed in Table 2.

First, we starts by looking at statistical presentation of the acquired service availability for Day 1 to 7 as summarized in Table 1. The statistics for achieved results of the daily service availability as presented in Table 1 all showed poor performance below the desired 99.99% satisfactory level. The only day network performed closed the desired satisfactory level is on Day 7, where it attained 99.96% service availability. Day 5 and 6 achieved the poorest performance with 96.01 and 95.44 service availability levels, respectively. This results imply high network outages in some cells within the two days, which could be as a results of equipment failure due to power outage, major weather problems, radio frequency interference/configuration problems, human errors, general radio propagation problems and unexpected events; hence the importance of period assessment of the cellular networks as accomplished in this work cannot be overemphasized.

Next is the presentation of service availability data estimation by using Gaussian process regression (GPR) model-based learning. As earlier mentioned, there exist numerous hyperparameters that impact GRP estimation modeling and learning capacity. Figures 3, 4, 5, 6, 7, 8 and 9 display the estimated values using GPR model tuned with subsets of data point approximation method and the daily observed values of cell availability data. The results show a minimal Mean Absolute Error (MAE) values in all the plotted graphs, thus indicating that the GPR model tuned with subsets of data (SD) point approximation method performed very well. The various estimation errors attained in terms of MAE and their interpretations using pareto chart are also displayed in each figure. The highest MAE value of 6.85×10^{-6} is recorded in Day- cell availability data estimation. The lowest MAE value of 4.69×10^{-6} is achieved with the GRP model for Day-4 cell availability data estimation. The pareto chart is provided here to further study the nature of the cell availability data and cumulative percentage distribution of the estimated MAE values with the GPR model. In each figure, the bar with higher pareto values (also call the vital few) reveals the data points where larger errors were recorded during GRP estimation. For example, in Fig. 3, the vital few are located at data points 42, 96, and 143. These are also the cell number where the network availability were poorest. In Fig. 4, the vital few are located at data points 429, 479, 143 (Table 3).

Table 3. Statistical values on acquired cell service availability data for Day 1 to 7

Day	Mean	Mode	Median	Minimum	Maximum
1	99.29	100	100	95.99	100
2	98.83	100	100	84.21	100
3	99.85	100	100	98.40	100
4	99.44	100	100	95.39	100
5	96.01	100	100	68.93	100
6	95.74	100	100	60.45	100
7	99.96	100	100	99.41	100

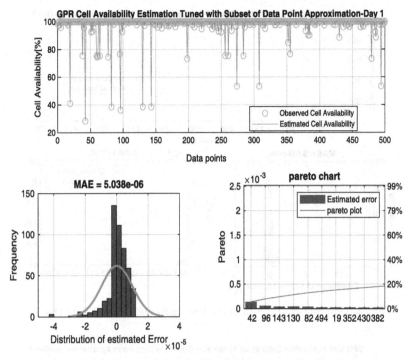

Fig. 3. Observed and Estimated Cell Availability Data with GRP for Day-1

The displayed bar chat in Fig. 10 is plotted to present and compared the estimation accuracy of chosen subsets of data (SD) point approximation method with other three GRP approximation methods, which are Fully Independent Conditional approximation (fic), Block Coordinate Descent BCD) and Subset of Regressors approximation (SR). In terms of Maximum Absolute Percentage Error (MAPE) and Root Mean Square Error (RMSE), the results indicate that the GPR model tuned with SD point approximation method achieve the best cell availability estimation performance.

The SVR graphical results in Figs. 11 and 12 are given to benchmark the performance results of our proposed GPR extrapolative based evaluation combined with stepwise kernels selection algorithm for day 1 and 2. In terms of RMSE (Root Mean Absolute Error), the regression error results of the proposed GPR extrapolative based evaluation combined with stepwise kernels selection algorithm attained 0.000005 and 0.000009, which are quit lower and far better the ones utilizing support vector machines which attained 0.046 and 0.055, for day 1 and 2 observed values of cell availability data. Similar performances were also observed for day 3 to 6.

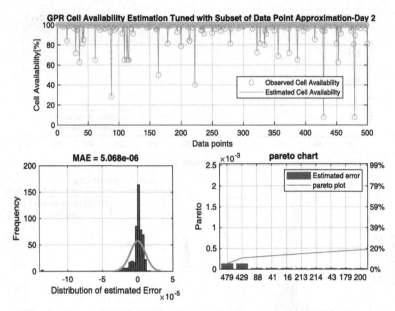

Fig. 4. Observed and Estimated Cell Availability Data with GRP for Day-2

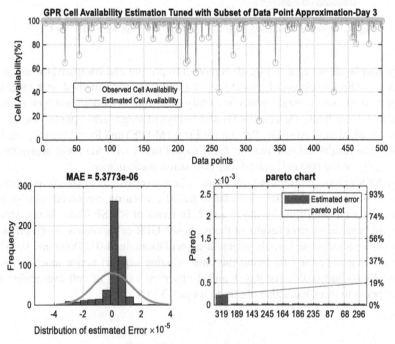

Fig. 5. Observed and Estimated Cell Availability Data with GRP for Day-3

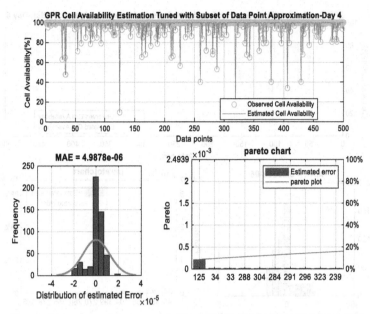

Fig. 6. Observed and Estimated Cell Availability Data with GRP for Day-4

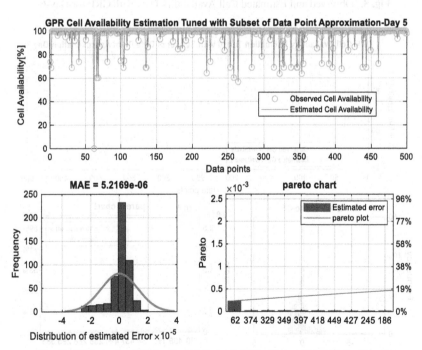

Fig. 7. Observed and Estimated Cell Availability Data with GRP for Day-5

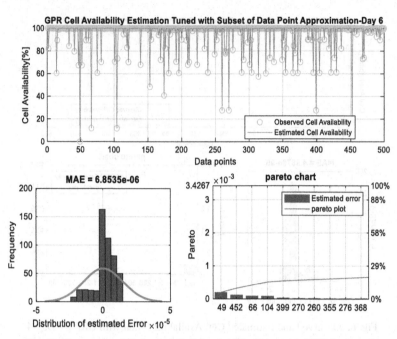

Fig. 8. Observed and Estimated Cell Availability Data with GRP for Day-6

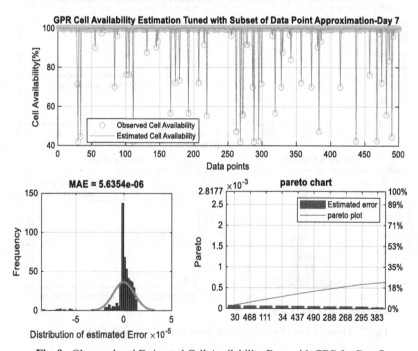

Fig. 9. Observed and Estimated Cell Availability Data with GRP for Day-7

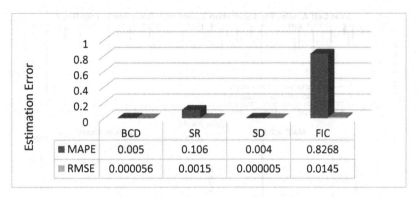

Fig. 10. Estimated MAPE and RMSE with BCD, SR, SD and FIC for Day-1

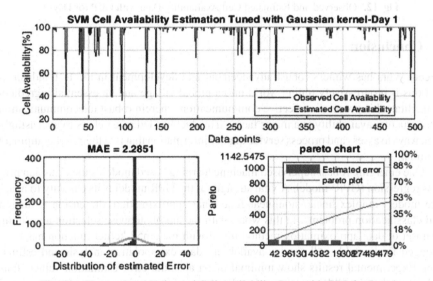

Fig. 11. Observed and Estimated Cell Availability Data with GRP for Day-1

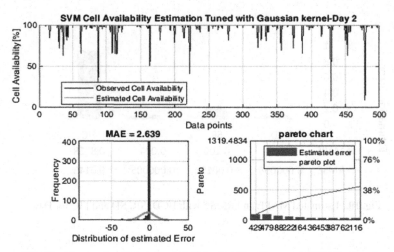

Fig. 12. Observed and Estimated Cell Availability Data with GRP for Day-2

4 Conclusion

Recent years has witness robust advancement and development in the ICT industries and this is progressively tuning world into a global village and an essential ingredient to facilitate this process is effective communication wherein robust telecommunication infrastructure availability is a major factor. This fact has led researchers to unceasingly seek ways to assess and process service quality information that is at their user equipment terminal.

One emerging robust supervised machine learning based model is the Gaussian process regression (GPR) model. A vital strength of the GPR model is its capacity to adaptive model complex linear/ nonlinear functional approximation, dimension reduction and classification problems. In this work, with the aid of stepwise selection algorithm, a subset of data approximation method tuned with metern52 kernel function has been engaged for tractable cell service availability data extrapolative analysis and estimation. Experimental results show minimal mean absolute error estimation values, thus indicating that the GPR model tuned with subsets of data point approximation method performed very well. Apart from the existence of many approximation methods, it is also very imperative to select suitable covariance function to build the prior while performing Gaussian process regression. That is however line up for our immediate future research work.

References

1. Igbinovia, A.O., Isabona, J.: Analytical based calculation approach for radiated electromagnetic energy absorption intensity estimation from fourth generation cellular radio networks base station antennas. Int. J. Res. Stud. Electr. Electron. Eng. (IJRSEEE) **5**(1), 1–10 (2019)
2. Isabona, J., Ojuh, D.O.: Radio link quality measurement survey over HSDPA radio interface: a holistic technique for efficient networks performance monitoring in wireless communication systems. Nigerian J. Phys. **25**(2), 46–54 (2014)

3. Isabona, J., Olayinka, S.A.: Experimental investigation of throughput performance of IEEE 802.11g OFDM based systems in a campus environment. Int. J. Eng. Sci. **2**(8), 427–434 (2013)
4. Oyediran, O., Omoshule, A., Misra, S., Maskeliūnas, R., Damaševičius, R.: Attitude of mobile telecommunication subscribers towards sim card registration in Lagos State, Southwestern Nigeria. Int. J. Syst. Assur. Eng. Manag. **10**(4), 783–791 (2019). https://doi.org/10.1007/s13 198-019-00809-6
5. Isabona, J., Konyeha, C.C.: Site-specific assessment of node b using key service quality indicators over 3G/UMTS networks from outdoor drive-test measurements. J. Inf. Eng. Appl. **3**(9), 48–58 (2013)
6. Isabona, J., Oghu, E.: Modelling based quantitative assessment of operational LTE mobile broadband networks reliability: a case study of university campus environ. IOSR J. Electron. Commun. Eng. (IOSR-JECE) **15**(1), 22–31 (2020). https://doi.org/10.9790/2834-150 1012231
7. Cao, Y., Brubaker, M.A., Fleet, D.J., Hertzmann, A.: Efficient optimization for sparse Gaussian process regression. IEEE Trans. Pattern Anal. Mach. Intell. **37**(12), 2415–2427 (2015)
8. Chalupka, K., Williams, C.K.I., Murray, I.: A framework for evaluating approximation methods for Gaussian process regression. J. Mach. Learn. Res. **14**(1), 333–350 (2013)
9. Chiplunkar, A., Bosco, E., Morlier, J.: Gaussian process for aerodynamic pressures prediction in fast fluid structure interaction simulations. In: Schumacher, A., Vietor, T., Fiebig, S., Bletzinger, K.-U., Maute, K. (eds.) WCSMO 2017, pp. 221–233. Springer, Cham (2018). https://doi.org/10.1007/978-3-319-67988-4_15
10. Cunningham, J.P., Shenoy, K.V., Sahani, M.: Fast Gaussian process methods for point process intensity estimation. In: International Conference on Machine Learning, International Conference on Machine Learning, New York, NY, USA, pp. 192–199. ACM (2008)
11. Wan, H., Ren, W.: A residual-based Gaussian process model framework for finite element model updating. Comput. Struct. **156**, 149–159 (2015). https://doi.org/10.1016/j.compstruc.2015.05.003
12. Dervilis, N., Shi, H., Worden, K., Cross, E.J.: Exploring environmental and operational variations in shm data using heteroscedastic Gaussian processes. In: Pakzad, S., Juan, C. (eds.) Dynamics of Civil Structures, Volume 2. CPSEMS, pp. 145–153. Springer, Cham (2016). https://doi.org/10.1007/978-3-319-29751-4_15
13. Skilling, J.: Nested sampling for general Bayesian computation. Bayesian Anal. **1**, 833–859 (2006). https://doi.org/10.1214/06-BA127
14. Su, G., Peng, L., Hu, L.: A Gaussian process-based dynamic surrogate model for complex engineering structural reliability analysis. Struct. Saf. **68**, 97–109 (2017). https://doi.org/10.1016/j.strusafe.2017.06.003
15. Abdessalem, A.B., Dervilis, N., Wagg, D.J., Worden, K.: Aothomatic Kernel selection for Gaussian Processes Regression with Approximate Bayesian Computation and Sequential Monte Carlo. Front. Built Environ. **3**, 52 (2017). https://doi.org/10.3389/fbuil.2017.00052
16. Kopsiaftis, G., Protopapadakis, E., Voulodimos, A., Doulamis, K., Mantoglou, R.: Gaussian process regression tuned by bayesian optimization for seawater intrusion prediction. Comput. Intell. Neurosci. 1–12 (2019). https://doi.org/10.1155/2019/2859429
17. Abolade, R.O., Famakinde, S.O., Popoola, S.I., Oseni, O.F., Atayero, A.A., Misra, S.: Support vector machine for path loss predictions in urban environment. In: Gervasi, O., et al. (eds.) ICCSA 2020. LNCS, vol. 12255, pp. 995–1006. Springer, Cham (2020). https://doi.org/10.1007/978-3-030-58820-5_71
18. [ITU-T E.802] Recommendation ITU-T E.802. Framework and methodologies for the determination and application of QoS parameters (2007)

19. ITU-T Recommendation G.827. Availability Performance Parameters and Objectives for end-to-end International Constant Bit-rate Digital Paths (2003)
20. Isabona, J., Srivastava, V.M.: Coverage and link quality trends in suburban mobile broadband HSPA network environments. Wirel. Pers. Commun. **95**(4), 3955–3968 (2017). https://doi.org/10.1007/s11277-017-4034-5
21. Yang, C., Liu, J., Zeng, Y., Xie, G.: Prediction of components degradation using support vector regression with optimized parameters. Energy Procedia **127**, 285–293 (2017)
22. Liu, S., Tai, H., Ding, Q., Li, D., Xu, L., Wei, Y.: A hybrid approach of support vector regression with genetic algorithm optimization for aquaculture water quality prediction. Math. Comput. Modell. **58** 458–465 (2013)
23. Popoola, S.I., Misra, S., Atayero, A.A.: Outdoor path loss predictions based on extreme learning machine. Wireless Pers. Commun. **99**(1), 441–460 (2018)

Anomaly Android Malware Detection:
A Comparative Analysis of Six Classifiers

Benjamin A. Gyunka[1]([⊠]), Oluwakemi C. Abikoye[2], and Adekeye S. Adekunle[3]

[1] Central Bank of Nigeria, Abuja, Nigeria
gyunkson@mail.com
[2] University of Ilorin, Ilorin, Kwara State, Nigeria
kemi_adeoye@yahoo.com
[3] Central Bank of Nigeria, Ado-Ekiti, Ekiti Statee, Nigeria
joykeye01@gmail.com

Abstract. The high proliferation rate of Android devices has exposed the platform to wider vulnerabilities of increasing malware attacks. Emerging trends of the malware threats are employing highly sophisticated and dynamic detection avoidance techniques. This has continued to weaken the capacity of existing signature-based detection systems in their protection against new and unknown threats. Thus, the need for effective detection approaches for unknown and novel Android malware has remained a growing challenge in the field of mobile and information security. This study therefore aimed at investigating the best performing machine learning classification algorithm for the anomaly Android malware detection, leveraging on permission-based feature sets, by conduction a performance comparison analysis between six different classification algorithms namely: Naïve Bayes, Simple Logistics, Random Forest, PART, k-Nearest Neighbours (k-NN), and Support Vector Machine (SVM). The Machine learning tool that was used for the pre-processing of the feature sets and the classification processes is WEKA 3.8.2 suite. Findings of the study showed that Random Forest had the best detection result with false alarm rate of 2.2%, accuracy of 97.4%, error rate of 2.6% and ROC Area of 99.6%. The study concluded that, using Android permission features, Random Forest and k-Nearest Neighbours recoded best performances in Android malware detection, followed by Support Vector Machine and Simple Logistics classification algorithms. Partial Decision Tree (PART) performed relatively well, while Naïve Baye recorded the least performance. Consequently, the deployment of Random Forest model and k-NN model are recommended for the development of an anomaly Android malware detection paradigm.

1 Introduction

The concept of learning has received wide adoption in the field of Android security and has been deployed in classifying wide range of applications, dealing particularly with the detection of malware that are generic. The adoption of machine learning methods for Android malware detection has removed the daunting task associated with having to continuously update detection engines with new patterns manually [1]. Learning processes involve the analysis of data using designed algorithms to develop models that

© Springer Nature Switzerland AG 2021
S. Misra and B. Muhammad-Bello (Eds.): ICTA 2020, CCIS 1350, pp. 145–157, 2021.
https://doi.org/10.1007/978-3-030-69143-1_12

can be used to find patterns and regularities in any future set of data [2]. The algorithms are made to learn from data that exist to become intelligent enough to predict future events or instances of data. One of the very important components necessary for effective learning is feature vectors which are normally built for a particular task to be carried out by the learning algorithm. Machine learning is categorized into three; supervised [3–5], Unsupervised [3], and Re-enforcement Learning [6]. For each learning category, there is a method. Classification is the method applied in supervised learning in which the set of data used in the learning process are adequately labelled to indicate their actual nature or class. For unsupervised learning, clustering method is used because the set of data don't gets labelled before the learning is done. Lastly, regression is the method used in re-enforcement learning because it deals with ranking, grading or estimating the end result of the learning. The name given to data when it belongs to a specific class or group is called a label. In learning problems, data are represented by fixed number of features which can be either continuous, nominal, or categorical [7].

The goal of any machine learning algorithms is to search for examples, matches, uniformities, styles, and redundancies in a given dataset in order to create a model that is capable of predicting the correct characteristics of observation in any future similar dataset [8, 9]. A learning method or algorithm or classifier, is a systematic technique that trains on a given data set, usually taken as the input, in order to create a classification model as an output of the process [10, 11]. Furthermore, the aim of a classification model is to be able to both fit the input data well and correctly predict the class labels of data it has never seen before. Hence, the main objective of any learning algorithm is to be able to build a model with good generalization capability (that is, a model that has good accuracy in predicting unknown class labels). Android Operating System (OS) has maintained the largest proportion of mobile market share worldwide compared to all other OS. The proliferation rate of Android devices has given rise to a continuous rapid development and infiltration of dangerous applications in both volume and number of variants, which have toughened their resistance abilities against detection by most standard detection techniques. The complexities of these emerging malwares has opened up a huge loophole and a challenge amongst security experts to continue to seek robust and efficient ways of detecting and overcoming these malicious application threats [12–14]. A study by [15] suggested that machine learning techniques are very powerful tools in recent times for adoption in the fight against complex Android malware. This study thus aims at deploying machine learning concepts, through a comparison analysis of six different classification algorithms, to investigate and evaluate the most effective approach for overcoming the dynamism and sophistication of emerging Android malware.

The remaining part of the study is divided into the following sections: Sect. 2 details related works; Sect. 3 discusses the methodology; Sect. 4 is the result and Discussion. Section 5 is the Conclusion.

2 Related Works

Deep learning technique was employed by [16] and they came up with a system called DL-Droid for the detection of malicious Android applications through dynamic analysis using input generation. The system's performance was compared with the performances of seven classification algorithms: Support Vector Machine (SVM Linear), Support Vector Machine with radial basis function kernel (SVM RBF), Naive Bayes (NB), Simple Logistic (SL), Partial Decision Trees (PART), Random Forest (RF), and J48 Decision Tree. [17] leveraged on the limitation that signature-based and dynamic-based standard malware detection techniques are experiencing due to the level of sophistications of emerging malware. They explored the machine learning detection methods for unknown malware by comparing the performances of binary and multi-classification algorithms. The different classifiers used are KNN, SVM, Bernoulli Naive Baye (Bernoulli NB), J48 Decision Tree (DT), Random Forest (RF), Logistic Regression (LR), and Hard Voting (HV). The findings showed that Decision Tree had the highest accuracy rate of 98.2% for binary classification while Random Forest had 95.8% for multi-class classification. [18] focused their research on generating stronger permission-based feature sets, called Fine-grained Dangerous Permission (FDP), that are mostly unique to malware applications. These set of feature were termed as a better representation of the difference between malicious and benign application and were used to train J48 Decision Tree (DT), KNN, Naive Baye (NB), and SVM. The highest true positive rate of 94.5% was recorded by J48 decision tree on the FDP dataset.

A meticulous survey on machine learning approaches used in Android malware detection was conducted by [19]. The study focused on areas such as sample acquisition, data pre-processing, feature selection, machine learning models, algorithms, and the evaluation of detection effectiveness. An assessment into the future prospects for Android malware detection research based on machine learning was lastly reviewed and shown to provide higher effectiveness. kNN was used by [20] as a scalable and quick machine learning method for the detection of malignant mobile application. The proposed method utilized 5 nearest neighbours and Minkowski as preferred distance metric. A detection accuracy of 94.1% was achieved and an F-score of 92.4% which indicated that the model can successfully detect both malware and benign applications. [21] deployed reverse engineering method and the analysis of Random Forest, kNN, SVM, Naive Bayes and Logistic Regression on java code features in order to study the most effective algorithm for Android malware detection. The study showed that Random Forest had the best detection rate of 80.67% followed by k-NN with 80.33%. [22] focused their study on performance evaluation of classification algorithms with the intention of identifying an algorithm that can produce a more robust malware detection model. The algorithms analyzed included J45, LMT, Naive Bayes, Random Forest, MLT Classifier, Random Tree, REP Tree, Bagging, AdaBoost, Kstar, Simple Logistic, iBK, LWL, SVM, and RBF Network. Their findings showed that Random Forest algorithm produced the best accuracy of 99.2%.

[23] utilized a 17-node Apache Spark cluster to run a performance comparison study on seven machine learning classifiers to identify the most appropriate classification method for the detection of Android malicious applications. The classification algorithms used in the study are Logistic Regression, Decision Tree, Random Forest, Gradient-boosted Tree, Multilayer Perceptron, SVM and Isotonic Regression. Their findings showed that Gradient boosted trees out-performed the other classification mechanisms. [15] made use of five base learners: Random Tree-100, J48, REPTree, Voted Perceptron, and Random Tree-9 to implement a new approach for fussing classifiers

called DroidFusion which depended on a multilevel design that helps in proper combination of learning algorithms that is capable of producing enhanced detection accuracy. [24] proposed a detection framework based on SVM and Active Learning technologies. The made use of features attached with timestamps to have improved detection accuracy. A survey was carried out by [25] in order to find out the relevance and application of machine learning methodologies in malware analysis. The study revealed that machine learning has received great attention in most literatures for complex malware analysis.

PIndroid was proposed by [26] as a novel detection framework for Android malware which was based on intents and permission features. The performances of six distinct classification algorithms were compared. These included: Naïve Bayesian, Decision Tree, Decision Table, Random Forest, Multi Lateral Perceptron (MLP), and SVM. The results showed 99.8% detection accuracy rate through the Product of probability combination method. [27] proposed a practical and effective anomaly based Android malware detection framework that was behavioural in nature. The classification algorithms used for the anomaly analysis were Decision Tree, kNN, Logistic Regression, Multilayer Perceptron Neural Network, Naive Bayes, Random Forest, and SVM. The findings of the study suggested that Random Forest and SVM were best suitable for anomaly detection deployment. [28] designed a composite system for Android malware detection through the parallel joining of distinct classification algorithms based on static features gotten from 6,863 app samples. The classification algorithms used are Naïve Baye (probabilistic), PART (Rule-based), Decision Tree (Tree based), Simple Logistics (function-base), and RIDOR (Rule-based). From the findings, PART performed best as an individual classifier while products of probabilities stood out amongst the composite systems. A meta-ensemble method was proposed by [29]. The study ran a comparative analysis using various classifiers and the best performed algorithms were combined via ensemble precision. SVM, Bayesian Log Regression (BLR), Random Forest (RF), and Random Committee (RC) performed well with RC and RF having more outstanding performance. DynaLog was proposed by [30] to use against malware that deploys obfuscation concealment strategies to escape state-of-the-art static based detection and analysis systems. DynaLog is built upon existing open source tools which gives it an advantage for a wide range scope for dynamic analysis of Android apps. [31] researched on finding malicious URL on twitter using Naïve Bayes classifier.

3 The Methodology

3.1 The Detection Framework

The analysis was done using the same sets of data, the same feature selection algorithm, and all the classification algorithms used were not fine tuned, but were rather used with their default parameter settings. Figure 1 provides the general framework of the study.

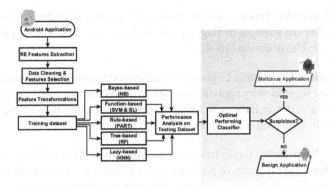

Fig. 1. The detection analysis framework

3.2 Data Collection and Extraction

Android Malware Genome [32] and Contagio Mobile [33] provides an open and free public access to Android malware samples which are used by many research in the analysis and study of Android malware. Therefore, this study collected all the needed Android malware samples from these main public providers. On the other hand, Google Play Store was the primary repository from which the benign Android application samples were collected. Google Play Store is the recognized legal database by Google that stores all legitimate or benign Android applications given the fact that it has an analysis engine called Google Bouncer. Google Bouncer analyzes every single app that comes into the database with the main goal of finding any irregularity in any app and then stops it from getting into the store [34, 35]. Findings has further revealed that, with emerging sophistications in Android malware, Google Bouncer is not longer robust enough to defend the Google Play Store against subtle influx of complex malicious applications [36].

Consequently, in this study, we utilized VirusTotal [37], an online scanner for malicious applications, as a second security check to ensure that all the apps collected from the Google Play Store are truly benign. VirusTotal opens an App (apk) up to series of investigations against malicious contents, by querying URLs, Hash values, IP addresses and domains of the App. A Total of 1000 benign and malicious Android application were reversed engineered using Androguard and Sublime Text and the extracted permission features were further preprocessed into usable features by being transformed into binary vectors, as demonstrated in Fig. 1, before being used for the training and testing phases.

3.3 The Classification Algorithms

Table 1 shows the classification algorithms (methods) analyzed in this study using the extracted and processed feature vector matrix. These classification algorithms were selected and used in this study because research has shown that are very effective for Android malware anomaly detection studies (Ali et al. [27]; Omar, Ngadi, & Jebur [38]; Shabtai, Kanonov, Elovici, Glezer, Weiss [39]).

Random Forest (RF): It belongs to the family of Tree-like algorithms and it works by bringing together the strength of Bagging and Random Decision Tree to produce very high accuracy in classification [40–42].

Simple Logistic (SL): Simple Logistic is an ensemble learning algorithm that deploys additive logistic regression by applying simple regression functions as base learners [43]. It functions in a very similar way to linear regression; its target is to locate a function that can suitably fit the training dataset.

Naive Bayes (NB): Naïve Bayes function based on Bayes' Theorem by relying on the assumption that all the features or predictors are independent of one another [44]. This algorithm makes use of the same principle of posterior probability in Bayes' Theorem to make prediction of the probability of different classes based on various attributes. NB can be expressed by the equation below.

$$P(t_i \backslash c_j) = \prod_{k=1}^{p} P(x_{ik} \backslash c_j) \tag{1}$$

PART: This is a rule-based learning, also known as partial decision tree; it is sometimes refer to as 'separate-and-conquer' learner which is able to produce sets of rules in an orderly structure known as 'decision list'. A C4.5 decision tree is partially builds by PART in every iteration which then converts the best leaf into a rule. This implies that the algorithm creates its rules by a repeated generation of partial decision trees. Unlike C4.5, PART does not need to perform global optimization to creates accurate sets of rules [45]. The algorithm has apparently no full form; it is called PART because it develops a 'partial' C4.5 decision tree in each iteration and makes the "best" leaf into a rule.

Support Vector Machine (SVM): This algorithm is also known as a binary classifier and it is a non-probabilistic supervised learning method which is widely used for anomaly detection problems in Android applications studies [25, 46]. The classifier utilizes a hypothesis space of linear functions in a high dimensional feature space, there it tries to attain linear separability. SVM makes this possible by deploying kernels and margin maximization [47]. SVM is able to work with highly-dimensional and sparse dataset and it can also utilize hyper-planes to split various features into their individual groups and classes.

K-Nearest Neighbours (k-NN) Another name for it is a lazy learner. This is because it does not really train on the given training data set but it rather works by just storing the training dataset and then wait until testing set are introduced before it will then perform the classification by searching for the most closely related instances in stored training set [48]. The prediction is done by looking for the nearest neighbours in the entire training dataset. Thus, k-NN does not have training time. For classification, the kNN algorithm predicted output is computed as the majority class among the k nearest neighbours:

$$\varphi(x) = \operatorname*{argmax}_{c \in y} \sum_{(x_i, y_i) \in NN(x, \tau, k)} 1(y_i = c) \tag{2}$$

Where $NN(x, \tau, k)$ denotes the k nearest neighbours of x in τ.

The basis for determining the neighbourhood is to determine the distance function and in this study, the Euclidean distance, which is a generalization of the distance of points in a two-dimensional space was used.

The Experiment

From inception, the practice and application of machine learning demands, as a matter of pre-requisite, a good knowledge of coding in either Java, R, or python for an effective design and development of different learning algorithms [49]. However, advancement in technology has made available machine learning software repositories which are a collection of various machine learning algorithms, pre-programmed, that enables a complete and effective implementation of learning problems without necessarily involving the technicality of writing any single line of code. These provisions include Waikato Environment for Knowledge Analysis (WEKA) [2, 50], Mallet, MatLab, SciKit-Learn, RapidMiner (formerly known as YALE), R-Programming, Orange, KNIME, NLTK etc. However, for the purpose of this study, WEKA Version 3.8.2, which is one of the leading open source and widely used data mining tool [51, 52] was chosen and deployed for all the experiments conducted. WEKA implements algorithms for data pre-processing, attribute selection, classification, regression, model evaluation, associated rules and visualization tools [50].

Data Pre-processing Phase: A total of 163 attributes (That is, including one class attribute) and a total of 1094 instances (547 each for both Benign and Malicious instances) were used for the experiments. The Class features (attributes) are nominal and have two distinct labels: Benign and Malicious. The Benign label had 453 instances originally but Synthetic Minority Oversampling Technique (SMOTE), which is a supervised filter that enhances over-sampling of a minority class in WEKA, was applied to correct the challenge of imbalances in the dataset by synthetically raising the number of the Benign Instances to equal the number of the Malicious Instances, 547. The SMOTE settings used included a 1-Nearest Neighbours (1-NN), 20.751%, and 1 random seed. Discretize, which is another supervised filter, was applied on the features set in order to turn numeric attributes into discrete ones for a better algorithm training and classification experience [53].

Feature Selection: The application of feature selection was done in order to reduce the dataset size by removing the features or attributes that are not very relevant for the training of the algorithms. When a proper feature selection method is applied on a given dataset, it drastically increases performance by reducing the size of the dataset and the time taken for the classification analysis [54]. Although WEKA provides different feature selection methods, this study made use of principal component analysis (PCA) feature selection method for the selection of key important features, thus reducing dimensionality in the features. PCA has been widely used in machine learning studies and it works by basically selecting features variables according to their magnitude (i.e., from largest to smallest in absolute values) of their coefficients [55].

The Training/Classification Phase: All six learning algorithms deployed are heterogeneous, thus they were trained separately via WEKA by utilizing the same set of data to produce distinct prediction models (classifiers). A total of 1094 instances of applications, after the SMOTE filter was applied, were utilized. The statistics included 547 benign applications features and 547 malicious applications features. The size of the input training matrix used was 1094 by 163 (162 features and 1 column class label – benign and malicious). The classification results of the individual models were further compared and analyzed in order to get the best performing base classifier.

Model Testing and Performance Evaluation Metrics

The developed models were tested and evaluated using 10-fold Cross Validation and performance evaluation metrics. WEKA is inbuilt with 10-fold cross validation as one of its test options and it was used in evaluating all the models developed in this study. It works by partitioning the dataset into 10 disjoint equal blocks (that is, into – 10 partitions or folds), such as $k_1, k_2, k_3, \ldots, k_{10}$ without any overlapping. The system keeps one partition (hold-out) as a test data and uses the remaining nine partitions to generate trained model upon which the test data is applied. This continues until the ten folds cycle is completed, creating ten different models and testing them ten different times before the final performance result for the classifier is provided, which is the average of the results of the performance of all the k models. The results of the experiment are presented using performance metrics such as true positive ratio (TPR) also known as recall or sensitivity, true negative ratio (TNR) also known as Specificity, false positive ratio (FPR) also defined as (1-Specificity), false negative ratio (FNR), F-Measure, precision, error rate, and accuracy as defined below;

$$TPR = \frac{TP}{TP + FN} \tag{3}$$

$$TNR = \frac{TN}{TN + FP} \tag{4}$$

$$FPR = \frac{FP}{TP + FP} \tag{5}$$

$$FNR = \frac{FN}{FN + TN} \tag{6}$$

$$Precision = \frac{TP}{TP + FP} \tag{7}$$

$$F - Measure = \frac{2 * Precision * Recall}{Precision + Recall} \tag{8}$$

$$ACC = \frac{TP + TN}{TP + TN + FP + FN} \tag{9}$$

$$ERR = 1 - ACC \tag{10}$$

4 Results Analysis and Discussion

4.1 Naive Bayes Results Analysis

The predictive output of Naive Bayes has a True Positive detection rate (TPR) for malicious application as 0.879 (i.e., 87.9%) while the true positive detection rate for benign applications as 0.958 (i.e., 95.8%). This implies that the model's detection rate for malicious instances is good given that it has an FPR of 12.1%. The F-score and ROC Area for malware detection are 92.2% and 98.6%. The F-score results revealed that the method correctly classified 98.6% as malware in 10-fold cross-validation.

4.2 Simple Logistic Results Analysis

This Classifier has a true positive predictive rate for malware as 0.984 (i.e., 98.4%) and an F-score and ROC Area of 0.97 (97%) and 0.993 (99.3%). These parameters indicated that the Classifier has very strong predictive strength. The malware detection false alarm rate for this model is 0.044%.

4.3 Random Forest Results Analysis

Random Forest had a TPR of 0.971 (97.1%), ROC Area and F-score of 0.974 (97.4%) and 0.996 (99.6%). The classifier also produced very low FPR of 2.2%. The F-score proves that the classifier correctly classified 97.4% as malware in 10-fold cross-validation.

4.4 PART Results Analysis

The PART classifier has a TPR of 0.958 (95.8%), a ROC Area of 0.979 (97.9%) and an F-Measure of 0.955 (95.5%). The model has low false alarm rate of 4.8%. All these metrics indicates that the detection strength of the Classifier is good.

4.5 Results Analysis for Support Vector Machine (SVM)

The TPR for SVM was 0.969 (i.e., 96.9%). It has an F-score of 0.964 (96.4%) and a ROC Area of 0.963 (96.3%) and FPR of 4.2%. A total of 1054 (96.34%) features were correctly classified by SVM and it took 2.9 s to develop the model. A Kappa statistics of 92.69% was registered.

4.6 Results Analysis for k-Nearest Neighbours (kNN)

The results showed that a TPR of 0.967 (96.7%) was obtained as seen on Table 7. The F-Measure, AUC and Precision for the kNN are 0.972 (97.2%), 0.97.6 (97.6%) and 0.99 (99%) respectively. The classifier has one of the lowest FPR of 2.8% indication an excellent performance.

4.7 Comparison Analysis of the Heterogeneous Predictive Models

The summary of the entire results are shown on Table 1. The Table revealed that, of all the six classifiers, although Simple Logistics (SL) and Random Forest (RF) has the best TPR of 98.4% and 97.1%, RF recorded the best performance amongst all the others. It has the lowest FPR of 2.2%, and an error rate of 2.6%. It also recorded higher Precision of 97.8%, Accuracy of 97.4% and ROC Area of 99.6%. NB recorded the worst prediction results with an error rate of 8.1%, and FPR of 4.2%. The predictive performance of KNN is almost as strong as that of RF. It classified correctly 1063 features while RF correctly classified 1066 instances. SVM recorded the third best TPR of 96.9%.

Table 1. Tabular Results Evaluation for the classification Algorithms

Metrics	The Classification Algorithms					
	NB	SL	RF	PART	SVM	k-NN
TP Rate	0.879	**0.984**	0.971	0.958	0.969	0.967
FP Rate	0.042	0.044	**0.022**	0.048	0.042	0.024
Precision	0.954	0.957	**0.978**	0.953	0.958	0.976
Accuracy	0.919	0.970	**0.974**	0.955	0.963	0.972
F-Measure	0.915	0.970	**0.974**	0.955	0.964	0.972
Error Rate	0.081	0.030	**0.026**	0.045	0.037	0.028
ROC Area	0.986	0.993	**0.996**	0.979	0.963	0.990

4.8 Comparison of Best Developed Models with Existing Works

To be able to point out the importance of the results in this study, a performance evaluation was done with those published in other works as illustrated in Table 2.

Table 2. Performance evaluation of best model with existing models.

Reference	Classifier	Precision	TP rate	FP rate	Acc	Error rate
[28]	PART	0.967	0.958	0.033	0.963	0.037
[56]	Stacking	0.968	0.937	0.018	0.965	0.035
Developed model	RF	**0.978**	0.971	**0.022**	**0.974**	**0.026**

The table above is a comparison between the best performing models obtained in this study with the two other similar studies using the same kind of features. Even though the other studies also introduced other feature elements, permission features, mostly used in this research, proved to produce and excellent model with strong precision and true detection rate for malware. It also has the highest accuracy rate and the lowest error rate.

5 Conclusion

Machine learning classification algorithms behave differently on a given dataset. This was manifested in the results produced by each Classifier on the provided dataset in this study. The model produced by Random Forest classification algorithm turned out to have the best performance amongst the six classifiers. Naive Bayes produced the weakest performance compared to the other five Classifiers. Even though the study has a limitation of fewer sample size for more robust investigation and analysis due to lack of automated reversed engineering tool for apks, the conclusion of the investigation therefore shows that, either a concurrent or individual deployment of the supervised models will produce an effective defence system with high detection accuracy or very low error rates for complex and unknown Android malware.

References

1. Arp, D., Spreitzenbarth, M., Malte, H., Gascon, H., Rieck, K.: Drebin: effective and explainable detection of android malware in your pocket. In: Symposium on Network and Distributed System Security (NDSS), pp. 23–26, February 2014
2. Russell, I., Markov, Z.: An introduction to the weka data mining system. In: Proceedings of the 2017 ACM SIGCSE Technical Symposium on Computer Science Education - SIGCSE 2017, p. 742 (2017)
3. Namratha, M., Prajwala, T.R.: A comprehensive overview of clustering algorithms in pattern recognition. J. Comput. Eng. **4**(6), 23–30 (2012)
4. Garg, B.: Design and Development of Naive Bayes Classifier (Master Thesis). North Dakota State University of Agriculture and Applied Science (2013)
5. Brownlee, J.: Supervised and unsupervised machine learning algorithms. Understand Machine Learning Algorithms (2016). Accessed 13 May 2018
6. Scott, G.: ML 101: Reinforcement Learning (2015). Accessed 23 Nov 2017
7. Guyon, I., Elisseeff, A.: Feature extraction, foundations and applications: an introduction to feature extraction. Stud. Fuzziness Soft Comput. **207**, 1–25 (2006)
8. da Gama, J.M.P.: Combining Classification Algorithms (Doctoral Thesis). Faculdade de Ci^encias da Universidade do Porto (1999)
9. Komal, A.: A Survey on malicious detection technique using data mining and analyzing in web security. In: 2016 IJEDR, vol. 4, no. 2, pp. 319–322 (2016)
10. Duch, W., Grudzinski, K.: Meta-learning: searching in the model space. In: Proceedings of the International Conference on Neural Information Processing (ICONIP), pp. 235–240 (2001)
11. Tan, P.-N., Steinbach, M., Kumar, V.: Classification: basic concepts , decision trees , and model evaluation classification. In: Introduction to Data Mining, vol. 1, pp. 145–205 (2006)
12. Musthaler, L.: Forget signatures for malware detection. SparkCognition says AI is 99% effective. Network World (2017). Accessed 03 Jun 2019
13. Richter, L.: Common weaknesses of android malware analysis frameworks. In: IT Security Conference, University of Erlangen-Nuremberg During Summer Term 2015, pp. 1–10 (2015)
14. Vidas, T., Tan, J., Nahata, J., Tan, C.L., Christin, N., Tague, P.: A5: automated analysis of adversarial android applications. In: SPSM 2014 Proc. 4th ACM Working Security and Privacy Smartphones Mobile Devices, pp. 39–50 (2014)
15. Yerima, S.Y., Sezer, S.: DroidFusion: a novel multilevel classifier fusion approach for android malware detection. IEEE Trans. Cybern. **49**, 453–4566 (2018)
16. Alzaylaee, M.K., Yerima, S.Y., Sezer, S.: DL-droid: deep learning based android malware detection using real devices. Comput. Secur. **89**, 101663 (2020)

17. Shhadat, I., Bataineh, B., Hayajneh, A., Al-Sharif, Z.A.: The use of machine learning techniques to advance the detection and classification of unknown malware. Procedia Comput. Sci. **170**(2019), 917–922 (2020)
18. Jiang, X., Mao, B., Guan, J., Huang, X.: Android malware detection using fine-grained features. Sci. Program. **2020**, 1–3 (2020)
19. Liu, K., Xu, S., Xu, G., Zhang, M., Sun, D., Liu, H.: A review of android malware detection approaches based on machine learning. IEEE Access **8**, 124579–124607 (2020)
20. Arslan, R.S., Yurttakal, A.H.: K-nearest neighbour classifier usage for permission based malware detection in android. Icontech Int. J. **4**(2), 15–27 (2020)
21. Kedziora, M., Gawin, P., Szczepanik, M., Jozwiak, I.: Malware detection using machine learning algorithms and reverse engineering of android java code. Int. J. Netw. Secur. Appl. **11**(01), 01–14 (2019)
22. Dada, E.G., Bassi, J.S., Hurcha, Y.J., Alkali, A.H.: Performance evaluation of machine learning algorithms for detection and prevention of malware attacks. J. Comput. Eng. **21**(3), 18–27 (2019)
23. Memon, L.U., Bawany, N.Z., Shamsi, J.A.: A comparison of machine learning techniques for android malware detection using apache spark. J. Eng. Sci. Technol. **14**(3), 1572–1586 (2019)
24. Rashidi, B., Fung, C., Bertino, E.: Android malicious application detection using support vector machine and active learning. In: 2017 13th International Conference on Network and Service Management, CNSM 2017, vol. 2018 (2018)
25. Ucci, D., Aniello, L., Baldoni, R.: Survey on the usage of machine learning techniques for malware analysis. Comput. Secur. **1**(1), 1–67 (2018)
26. Idrees, F., Rajarajan, M., Conti, M., Chen, T.M., Rahulamathavan, Y.: PIndroid: a novel android malware detection system using ensemble learning methods. Comput. Secur. **68**, 36–46 (2017)
27. Al Ali, M., Svetinovic, D., Aung, Z., Lukman, S.: Malware detection in android mobile platform using machine learning algorithms. In: International Conference on Infocom Technologies and Unmanned Systems (ICTUS 2017), pp. 4–9 (2017)
28. Yerima, S.Y., Sezer, S., Muttik, I.: Android malware detection using parallel machine learning classifiers. In: 2014 Eighth International Conference on Next Generation Mobile Apps, Serving Technology, NGMAST, pp. 37–42 (2016)
29. Coronado-De-Alba, L.D., Rodriguez-Mota, A., Ambrosio, P.J.E.: Feature selection and ensemble of classifiers for Android malware detection. In: 2016 8th IEEE Latin-American Conference on Communications (LATINCOM), pp. 1–6 (2016)
30. Alzaylaee, M.K., Yerima, S.Y., Sezer, S.: DynaLog: an automated dynamic analysis framework for characterizing android applications. In: 2016 International Conference on Cyber Security and Protection of Digital Services, Cyber Security 2016, pp. 1–8 (2016)
31. Azeez, N.A., Atiku, O., Misra, S., Adewumi, A., Ahuja, R., Damasevicius, R.: Detection of malicious URLs on Twitter. In: Sengodan, T., Murugappan, M., Misra, S. (eds.) Advances in Electrical and Computer Technologies. LNEE, vol. 672, pp. 309–318. Springer, Singapore (2020). https://doi.org/10.1007/978-981-15-5558-9_29
32. Yajin, Z., Xuxian, J.: Android Malware Genome Project (2015). Accessed 08 Mar 2017
33. Contagio, M.: Pokemon GO with Droidjack - Android sample. Mobile Malware Mini Dump (2016). Accessed 23 Nov 2017
34. Oberheide, J., Miller, C.: Dissecting the android bouncer. In: Summercon 2012 (2012). Accessed 02 Feb 2016
35. Asghar, M.R.: Dissecting Google Bouncer Lecture 11a, Auckland (2017)
36. Rahman, M., Rahman, M., Carbunar, B., Chau, D.H.: FairPlay: fraud and malware detection in Google play. In: Proceedings of 2016 SIAM International Conference on Data Mining 2016, vol. 29, no. 6, pp. 1329–1342. Society for Industrial Application and Mathematics (2017)

37. VirusTotal. VirusTotal (2017). Accessed 05 Dec 2017
38. Omar, S., Ngadi, A., Jebur, H.H.: Machine learning techniques for anomaly detection: an overview. Int. J. Comput. Appl. **79**(2), 975–8887 (2013)
39. Shabtai, Y., Kanonov, A., Elovici, U., Glezer, Y., Weiss, C.: Andromaly: a behavioral malware detection framework for android devices. J. Intell. Inf. Syst. **38**(1), 161–190 (2012)
40. Breiman, L.: Random forests. Mach. Learn. **45**(1), 5–32 (2001)
41. Witten, I.H., Frank, E.: Data Mining: Practical Machine Learning Tools and Techniques, 2nd edn. Elsevier, Amsterdam (2011)
42. Yerima, S.Y., Sezer, S., Muttik, I.: Android malware detection: an eigenspace analysis approach. In: 2015 Science and Information Conference, no. November, pp. 1236–1242 (2015)
43. Friedman, J., Hastie, T., Tibshirani, R.: Additive logistic regression. Annals Stat. **28**(2), 337–374 (2000)
44. Sunil, R.: 6 Easy Steps to Learn Naive Bayes Algorithm (with code in Python) (2015). Accessed 18 Mar 2017
45. Frank, E., Witten, I.H.: Generating accurate rule sets without global optimization. In: Proceedings of Fifteenth International Conference on Machine Learning, pp. 144–151 (1998)
46. Milosevic, N., Dehghantanha, A., Choo, K.K.R.: Machine learning aided Android malware classification. Comput. Electr. Eng. **61**, 266–274 (2017)
47. Masud, M., Khan, L., Thuraisingham, B.: Data Mining Tools for Malware Detection, 1st edn. Auerbach Publications, Boston (2011)
48. Asiri, S.: Machine Learning Classifiers. In: Towards Data Science (2018). Accessed 04 Jan 2019
49. Team AVC: A Complete Tutorial to learn Data Science in R from Scratch. Data Science (2016). Accessed 12 Apr 2017
50. Waikato, M.L.G.: Waikato Environment for Knowledge Analysis (WEKA). University of Waikato, Waikato (2017)
51. Jagtap, S.B.: Census data mining and data analysis using WEKA. In: ICETSTM – 2013 International Conference in Emerging Trends in Science, Technology and Management-2013, pp. 35–40 (2013)
52. Wahbeh, A.H., Al-Radaideh, Q.A., Al-Kabi, M.N., Al-Shawakfa, E.M.: A comparison study between data mining tools over some classification methods. Int. J. Adv. Comput. Sci. Appl. **1**(3), 18–26 (2011)
53. Liu, H., Setiono, R.: Feature selection via discretization. IEEE Trans. Knowl. Data Eng. **9**(4), 642–645 (1997)
54. Pehlivan, U., Baltaci, N., Acarturk, C., Baykal, N.: The analysis of feature selection methods and classification algorithms in permission based Android malware detection. In: IEEE SSCI 2014: 2014 IEEE Symposium Series on Computational Intelligence - CICS 2014: 2014 IEEE Symposium on Computational Intelligence in Cyber Security, Proceedings, pp. 1–8 (2014)
55. Song, F., Guo, Z., Mei, D.: Feature selection using principal component analysis. In: 2010 International Conference on System Science, Engineering Design and Manufacturing Informatization, pp. 27–30 (2010)
56. Feng, P., Ma, J., Sun, C., Xu, X., Ma, Y.: A novel dynamic android malware detection system with ensemble learning. IEEE Access **6**, 30996–31011 (2018)

Credit Risk Prediction in Commercial Bank Using Chi-Square with SVM-RBF

Kayode Omotosho Alabi[1], Sulaiman Olaniyi Abdulsalam[1],
Roseline Oluwaseun Ogundokun[2]($\boxtimes$) $\textcircled{\scriptsize{iD}}$, and Micheal Olaolu Arowolo[2]

[1] Department of Computer Science, Kwara State University, Malete, Nigeria
[2] Department of Computer Science, Landmark University, Omu-Aran, Nigeria
{ogundokun.roseline,arowolo.olaolu}@lmu.edu.ng

Abstract. Financial credit risk analysis management has been a foremost influence with a lot of challenges, especially for banks reducing their principal loss. In this study, the machine learning technique is a promising area used for credit scoring for analyzing risks in banks. It has become critical to extract beneficial knowledge for a great number of complex datasets. In this study, a machine learning approach using Chi-Square with SVM-RBF classifier was analyzed for Taiwan bank credit data. The model provides important information with enhanced accuracy that will help in predicting loan status. The experiment achieves 93% accuracy compared to the state-of-the-art.

Keywords: Credit risk · Chi-square · SVM · Bank · Machine learning

1 Introduction

Credit risk prediction is a critical issue faced by several sectors such as banks, telecommunications, among others. Nowadays, it helps in evaluating the loyalty of customers and helps the bank in minimizing possible loses and maximize the volume of credits [1]. Credit risk contains the peril taken by the bank, because a customer may fail to meet their loan obligations requiring prediction of the customer by using previous records and information for proper decisions [2]. Divers technology innovations have made it possible for banking sectors to incorporate efficient delivery channels, and deal with several challenges posed by the economy. Banks need to take customers relationships as an important factor that determines their success [3].

Machine learning has proven to be a method that helps in fetching relevant information from huge data with hidden pattern [4–6] that can to solving challenges of whom is worthy of giving loans to and not [7, 8]. A lot of machine methods have been proposed by different researchers, using different algorithms to improve decision-making.

In recent times, several approaches like stochastic optimization technique, evolutionary algorithms and support vector machine (SVM) have revealed capable results in terms of accuracy prediction [9–11].

In this study, a feature selection based on Chi-square algorithm is proposed with SVM classifier for credit scoring tasks, using a Taiwan bank credit dataset, for systemic

© Springer Nature Switzerland AG 2021
S. Misra and B. Muhammad-Bello (Eds.): ICTA 2020, CCIS 1350, pp. 158–169, 2021.
https://doi.org/10.1007/978-3-030-69143-1_13

attributed risks of the banking system, to study and analyzed the design and compare these model on evaluation areas that identify risk customers from a large number of customers and provide an effective procedure for a bank loan agreement.

2 Related Works

Several studies have been carried out in literature by numerous researchers to further enhance prediction of credit risks in banks, as loses encountered in decision making for loan issuance to customers. This section discusses several works done with approaches used to achieve better decision making.

Bank credit default prediction based on a machine learning approach was proposed [7]; it is of the essence to identify the potential risks in giving out bank loans to customers. The objective of their study was to use the classification methods in classifying loans for customers. Random Forest, Logistic Regression, SVM classification algorithms were used to analyze the bank credit data, compared, and identify risk customers from large numbers of customers by providing the solid base for bank loan approvals. Their result showed Random forest outperforming other techniques with 88%. This paper contributed, by providing an efficient experimental basis for bank loan approvals and identifying risks of issuing huge loans to customers using classification techniques, they used a small public bank credit dataset, that suggests the experiment is not well comprehensive enough.

A credit risk analysis and prediction model for bank loans using R was proposed for related risks in bank loans, to reduce the problem of capital loss. The objective of their study is to design a model to identify probable defaulters of bank loan applicants effectively, they used clustering and classification techniques in their methodology, and the class labels were predicted, their experiments achieved high accuracy of 94.3%. In their contribution, they made an effective framework for identifying the probability of customers to defaulting bank loans. Their work was limited to an open-source repository and suggested more efficient data with a better tool for the application of machine learning techniques [1].

There requires the need for the bank industry to predictive modelling issues for credit defaulters accurately. The objective of this paper was to create a credit scoring model using machine learning approach. A prediction loan status for commercial banks using machine learning classifier was proposed [2], by analyzing model for credit data, they used a min-max normalization and KNN classifiers in their method. The model designed provided important information with efficient accuracy of 75%. In their contribution, the proposed loan status model that can help predict validly and defaulting loan customers. The study's limitation suggests further study on the iterations to avoid huge losses in banks.

It is of importance for banking sectors to strategic in their mode of analysis. Data mining has proven to help discover patterns and relationship in data [12–14]. An overview of machine learning techniques and its applications in the banking sector was studied. The objective of this study was to analyze data mining techniques for decision making in banking sectors, several data mining technique methods were analyzed for fraud prevention, detection, retention, marketing and risk management [3]. The result of their study showed several promising approaches, and their contributions were to suggest a combination of various techniques on bank records. Analyzing credit reis is a major problem; the objective of this study was to propose an overview for bank credit risk prediction using systemic reviews where applications of artificial intelligence like ANN were found efficient. In their result, several applications and methods for credit risk research were discussed, and they made a huge contribution by reviewing several works and suggested other approaches for a more accurate prediction approach, and systematic reviews for developing credit risk assessment approaches [15, 16].

A major problem the financial institution faces is credit risks. The objective is to suggest a credit risk prediction model based on SVM method for enterprises [17], using an index approach that considers leading enterprises credit status with neural network for alleviating credit rationing on SMEs, their result was promising, with 94% accuracy. In their contribution, they suggested an approach to help solve the problem of banks incorrect labelling of worthy creditors as a default customer and improve the credit rating status. The limitation of their study evolved around the superiority of predicting default behaviors in customers due to insufficient sample size data. Determination of the probability of defaulters in commercial banks is a big problem; several machine learning approaches have been suggested and requires good suggestions. The objective of this study was to propose a Credit risk assessment using ANN and SVM [18], a comparison was made using performance metrics with the confusion matrix to identify the most efficient model, their results showed RBF-SVM outperformed with 88% accuracy, which is a very efficient model to improve Tunisia credit risk management for monitoring and managing credits in banks. The major contribution of their study was to check through the ability of machine learning models for prediction of credit risks in customers seeking bank loans. The study suggests a hybridize model due to the limitation of the scoring model studied corporate account data.

Analyzing and predicting loan payback is a huge problem in the banking sector. The major objective of this study was to find the customers nature of the application for loans by exploring the analytical techniques of the record for prediction of loans was proposed [19], to find the nature of clients applying for personal loans using an exploratory data analysis technique in dealing with problems. The study used several analytical methods such as the customer income, classification of customers, terms of loan, categories, experience and job. The result analysis showed short term loans. The main contribution of the study is by classifying and analyzing the nature of the applicant's loan. The limitation of the study suggested an extension of the study into a higher level and consideration of other factors for loan prediction.

Credit risk management and its analytical approaches is a major issue in decision making for the financial sector. The objective of this study is to construct a credit scoring model. Credit scoring using feature selection with deep learning method [9], to evaluate applicants credit score from applicants input features on Australian and German credit data, their result showed an efficient prediction rate with comparable performance with 86% overall accuracy. The contribution of this work focused on determining higher acceptable accuracy. The workload for credit evaluation is a limitation as there was less computational intensiveness.

Problems encounter in financial sectors for identifying defaulters and granting credits is alarming. This study proposed model types to address credit scoring. Credit scoring metaheuristic approaches have been proposed [20], with artificial intelligence techniques to address assessment procedures with a compilation of past experiments and results. This study majorly contributed to the formulation of a credit scoring model using SVM and MA approach. Various limitations were observed in the assessment procedure and suggested futuristic directions.

Risks in the banking sector is a problem and require a better analytical approach. The objective of this study is to apply machine learning technique to predict banking risk systems using SVM [21], was suggested to predict bank risks in an attempt to suggest an innovative model with better explanation stability, SVM classifier with Chinese bank data projected an efficient result of 85% accuracy. The major contribution of the study was to validate the prediction performance using SVM classifier and to construct prediction indicators. The empirical analysis of the prediction accuracy can be further enhanced due to the limitation in the prediction model. A problem associated with SVM evaluation of variable predictors requires more work. The objective of this study was to extend an RFE feature selection approach for proposing the visualization of iterations and identification of relevant predictors for non-linear kernel methods. There result proved RFE-pseudo-samples outperformed other methods. The contribution of their study is majorly on the interpretation of variables relevant for classification, with a more computational complexity as a limitation of the study [22].

Business failure prediction is a challenge. Machine learning algorithms [23] were applied to business failure prediction [24]. The objective of the study was to investigate efficient algorithms for commercial bank distress. They proposed a cost-effective prediction variable selected from variable eliminating phases and sensitive attribute evaluators, by considering Naïve Bayes, KNN, ANN, SVM, C4.5, CHAID and CRT methods. Their experiment showed an evaluation performance with enhancement and comparisons of 91% overall accuracy. The major contribution of this study was to efficiently utilize machine learning algorithms for financial distress prediction with a limitation of not assessing financial structure, which can be misleading in prediction methods.

The credit scoring problems in banks requires improvement of predictive approaches that are relevant. The objective of this study is to improve prediction analysis by introducing a credit scoring machine learning technique, using PCA and Binary logistic regression [26] was proposed to improve the predictive power of prediction credit applicant status and compared, with an accuracy of 72%. The major contribution of this study is by using binary logistic regression to predict customers status in the bank. The limitation of the output requires futuristic works to enhance the accuracy and performance of the study.

The problem of predicting factors in the financial institution has drawn the attention of researchers, the objective of this study is to predict microfinance credit defaulter in a Ghana bank [27], by examining factors predicting the bank's credit fault, by using chi-square with classification, the result achieved 83%. This study contributed by predicting loan determinant through customers record and requires further study by consulting other machine learning approach, due to the limitation in the record used.

There is a problem existing in the influencing of banking adoptions. Chi-square approach was used for banking adoption as an approach [28], to investigate factors influencing adoption of bank credits and reveal more insights.

3   Materials and Methods

3.1   Bank Credit Scoring Benefits

A lot of benefits come along with credit scoring, for both lenders, borrowers and the banking industry. It helps in reducing discrimination by providing objective analysis of creditworthiness to customers. It enables credit providers in focusing on the relevant information relating to credit risk and avoiding of personal subjective of an analyst such as; formal loan application, interests, terms and conditions, charges, among others [26].

3.2   Data Mining

Datamining is the discovery of the knowledge of huge amount of data, which helps in discovering interesting patterns within the data for decision making, that can help predicts and classify the behaviour of the model [12, 14, 29]. Converting the information into meaningful form is a needful competitive intelligence. Several techniques have existed in literature, and have been used for creating predictive models. Several dimensionality reduction, clustering and classification approach for datamining have been used to model the prediction of chur customers in the banking sector. Some of these techniques used to achieve these models are the decision trees, SVM, Neural networks, random forest, k-means, PCA, ANOVA [30, 31], among others.

3.3   Dataset

In this study, a customer credits risk prediction was proposed for determining the churn rate of the financial sector. The predictive model uses an open-source Taiwan bank credit dataset with 30,000 instances, and 25 attributes [25], Chi-square and SVM approach is proposed to estimate the credit scoring model.

3.4   Method

In this study a Taiwan credit data is used for the credit risk prediction, Chi-Square algorithm is used as a feature selection algorithm to eliminate unwanted information in the data, the SVM classifier is used to evaluate performance. Figure 1 shows the workflow for the study bypassing the high dimensional data into chi-square, the reduced data is classified, using SVM, and the results of the experiment are evaluated.

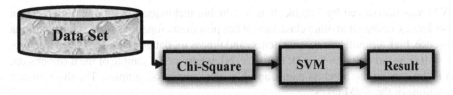

Fig. 1. The framework of the experiment

3.5 Chi-Square Algorithm

Chi-square is a non-parametric algorithm in machine learning used for the testing hypothesis of an association between groups or population, for testing observed distribution [32, 33]. The chi-Square approach consists of specifying the hypothesis, devise an analytical plan, examine the sampling data, and deduce the results [34].

$$\sum X_{i-j}^2 = \frac{(O - E)^2}{E} \tag{1}$$

Chi-square compares obtained values for the frequencies of classes, by splitting predictable frequencies of the class. Samples N_{ij} are the number of samples of C_i classes in the jth intervals. Samples of jth interval is represented by Nij. The predictable frequency of N_{ij} is the $E_{ij} = M_{ij}|C_i|/N$.

Algorithm 1: Chi-Square Algorithm [27]

Chi-squared
Original

```
        /*
            chi_array: two-dimensional array. First column contains feature indexes in DS and
                       second column contains Chi-squared values for the features and class labels.
        */
1:   chi_array ← Ø
2:   For i←1 To N Do
3:       chi_val ← chi.squared(DS[i], CL)   // calculate Chi-squared value between features in DS and CL
4:       Append (i, chi_val) To chi_array
5:   End For
6:   Sort chi_array by the second column (Chi-squaref value) in descending order
7:   Store first column values of chi array To CHOSEN
8:   Return CHOSEN
```

Chi-square is a discrete data hypothesis approach; it evaluates correlations between variables and fixes the independents that are correlated positively or not. Chi-Square hypothetical test methods for counting huge data belongs to the non-parametric test category. Its idea is to majorly compare degrees of frequencies and fitness.

3.6 Support Vector Machine (SVM)

SVM is a supervised machine learning algorithm that solves problems of assigning labels to information where labels are assigned from finite element sets [7, 18, 34].

SVM was introduced by Vapnik. It is a valuable technique for solving classification problems. Compared to other classifiers, it has prominent functions such as local minima absence, high simplification competence, and fitness for dataset samples. Given a dataset $A = \{(x_i, y_i)|x_i \in y_i \in \{-1, +1\}, i = 1, \ldots N\}$, where x_i is a sample of the d-dimension, y_i is the corresponding class name, and N is the number of samples. The discriminant functions of the SVM takes:

$$F(x) = \text{sgn}\left(\sum_{i=1}^{av} \alpha_i y_i C(x, x_i) + b\right) \qquad (2)$$

In Eq. 1, av is the support vector numbers, α_i is the langrange multipliers, b is the optimum bias hyperplane classification, while $C(x, x_i)$ is the kernel functions. SVM-RBF was used as the SVM classification kernel for this study.

$$C(x_i, x_j) = \exp\{-\frac{|x_i - x_j|^2}{2\sigma^2}\} \qquad (3)$$

SVMs uses the feature space hyperplane that is optimal to maximum marginal principles, to make decision boundaries. The kernel functions change the shapes of the hyperplane into non-linear, with two hyperplane parameters which are the parameter regularization C and the kernel width parameter σ. The training vectors are mapped in higher dimensional space function. In predicting the binary classification, the discriminant between objects are one of two groups known as the positive or the or negative. The SVM concepts solves problem by using the huge margin separation and kernel purposes.

An SVM maps input into high-dimensional feature space by finding separating hyperplanes which exploits the margin classes. Lacking somewhat knowledge of mapping, SVM discovers the optimal hyperplane using point product functions in feature space known as the kernels. The optimal hyperplane solution is a grouping of few input points [34]. SVMs are kernel methods of algorithms that are contingent on a given data through dot-products. The dot product is replaced using kernel functions for computing the dot product in high dimensional feature space. SVM comprises of four major kernels known as the; Linear, Quadratic, Polynomial and the Radial Basis Function (RBF).

Selecting suitable kernel function is significant, as kernel function describes the feature space that training set samples are classified. In this study, SVM-RBF is adopted for its high accuracy potentials and its capability to pact with gene expression high-dimensional data.

3.7 Evaluation

Performance evaluation of this experiment, 10-fold cross-validation was used, evaluate the performances. The dataset was reduced using chi-square, a classifier was trained and tested. Measure the performance of the SVM classification algorithm, and evaluation metrics use Accuracy, Precision, and Recall for evaluating the classification [36–39]. This study proposes a Chi-Square feature selection algorithm in selecting relevant features in high-dimensionality customer retention data. An SVM classifier is used as an algorithm to evaluate the performance of the experiment. This study uses a Taiwan bank dataset with 30000 observations and 25 attributes. MATLAB tool is used to analyze and carry out the experiment for this study and achieved a credit scoring investigational results.

In this study the classification confusion matrix is used for the performance evaluation of the model. It comprises of the correctly and incorrectly classified values with the precise test data results. It comprises of the:

True Positive (TP): results that are correctly predicted positively in the class model.
True Negative (TN): results that are correctly predicted negatively in the class model.
False Positive (FP): results that are incorrectly predicted positive in the class model.
False Negative: results that are incorrectly predicted negative in the class model.

There are several measures used in the confusion matrix to determine the performance of the models such as:

Accuracy: this measures the bias, using the formula (TP + TN)/(TP + TN + FP + FN).
Sensitivity: this is called a recall; it is the true positive rate which is the proportion of the actual positives correctly identified as positive. TP/(TP + FN).
Specificity: this is the selectivity of the true negative rate, measuring the proportion of the actual negatives correctly identified as negatives. TN/(FP + TN).
Precision: this is the prositive predictive value. TP/(TP + FP).
F1 Score: this is the measure of the tested accuracy that harmonizes the mean of precision and the recall. 2TP/(2TP + FP + FN).

4 Results and Discussions

In this study Chi-Square was used on the Taiwan Bank Credit data to fetch out relevant information in the data, 11088 features were achieved as a subset and passed into the classification using the SVM-RBF algorithm, a confusion matrix was used as the predictive performance evaluation. Figure 2 shows the confusion matrix used to evaluate the performance of the experiment. It comprises of the true positive and negative, false positive and negative, which is a standard for finding the performance metrics.

The performance evaluation metrics of Chi-Square and SVM-RBF is calculated as follows:

Correctly Classified Instances (accuracy) $= \frac{TP+TN}{TP+TN+FP+FN} = \frac{4+10}{4+10+0+1} * 100 = 93.33\%$

Sensitivity (Recall) $= \frac{TP}{TP+FN} = \frac{4}{4+1} = 0.8 = 80\%$

Specificity $= \frac{TN}{FP+TN} = \frac{10}{0+10} = 1 = 100\%$

Precision $= \frac{TP}{TP+FP} = \frac{4}{4+0} = 1 = 100\%$

F-measure $= \frac{2*Recall*Precision}{Recall+Precision} = \frac{2*0.8*1}{0.8+1} = 0.89 = 89\%$

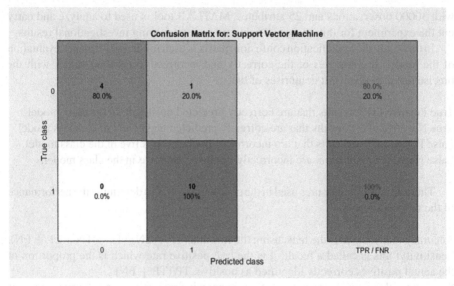

Fig. 2. Confusion matrix for chi-square + RBF-SVM classification TP = 4; TN = 10; FP = 1, FN = 0

In this study, the evaluation of the experiment is calculated using the confusion matrix formulas. Table 1 shows the performance evaluation summary.

Table 1. Predictive performance summary for chi-square with RBF-SVM.

Performance metrics (%)	Experimental results
Accuracy	93.33
Sensitivity	80
Specificity	100
Precision	89
F-measure	89

In this study, a feature selection and classification approaches were carried out on a Taiwan Bank credit dataset, using RFE feature selection algorithms to fetch out relevant information on the given data, for customer credit risk management, SVM was used as a classification, the result shows that RFE outperforms in terms of accuracy, the results are tabulated in Table 1 above. However, this study has shown a relevant output result that can be proposed for banks on loan concerns.

5 Conclusion

From this study, feature selection method using Chi-Square and SVM-RBF classification was used to develop a predictive model in a financial industry using Taiwan dataset to predict and classify loans applicant who is eligible or not eligible for loan collection. The model was implemented using MATLAB application. The result shows that RBF and SVM-RBF accuracy was 93% shown in the predictive performance table. This study confines with the prediction of credit loan. Future research proposes to analyze the retention strategies by choosing fitting variables from the dataset.

References

1. Sudhamathy, G.: Credit risk analysis and prediction modelling of bank loans using R. Int. J. Eng. Technol. **8**(5), 1954–1966 (2016)
2. Arutjothi, G., Senthamarai, C.: Prediction of loan status in commercial bank using machine learning classifier. In: International Conference on Intelligent Sustainable Systems. IEEE (2017)
3. Chitra, K., Subashini, B.: Data mining techniques and its applications in banking sector. Int. J. Emerg. Technol. Adv. Eng. **3**(8), 219–226 (2013)
4. Ogundokun, R.O., Awotunde, J.B.: Machine learning prediction for COVID 19 pandemic in India. medRxiv (2020)
5. Adebiyi, M.O., Ogundokun, R.O., Abokhai, A.A.: Machine learning-based predictive farmland optimization and crop monitoring system. Scientifica **2020**, 9428281 (2020). Article ID 9428281
6. Adegun, A.A., Ogundokun, R.O., Adebiyi, M.O., Asani, E.O.: CAD-based machine learning project for reducing human-factor-related errors in medical image analysis. In: Handbook of Research on the Role of Human Factors in IT Project Management, pp. 164–172. IGI Global (2020)
7. Eweoya, I., Ayodele, A., Azeta, A., Olatunji, O.: Fraud prediction in bank credit administration: a systematic literature review. J. Theor. Appl. Inf. Technol. **97**(11), 3147–3169 (2019)
8. Verma, H., Nandal, R.: A review paper on prediction analysis: acceptance of banking. J. Emerg. Technol. Innov. Res. **5**(1), 746–748 (2018)
9. Ha, V.-S., Nguyen, H.-N.: Credit scoring with a feature selection approach based deep learning. In: MATEC Web of Conferences, vol. 54 (2016)
10. Abolade, R.O., Famakinde, S.O., Popoola, S.I., Oseni, O.F., Atayero, A.A., Misra, S.: Support vector machine for path loss predictions in urban environment. In: Gervasi, O. (ed.) Computational Science and Its Applications – ICCSA 2020: 20th International Conference, Cagliari, Italy, July 1–4, 2020, Proceedings, Part VII, pp. 995–1006. Springer, Cham (2020). https://doi.org/10.1007/978-3-030-58820-5_71
11. Behera, R.K., Rath, S.K., Misra, S., Leon, M., Adewumi, A.: Machine learning approach for reliability assessment of open source software. In: Misra, S. (ed.) Computational Science and Its Applications – ICCSA 2019: 19th International Conference, Saint Petersburg, Russia, July 1–4, 2019, Proceedings, Part IV, pp. 472–482. Springer, Cham (2019). https://doi.org/10.1007/978-3-030-24305-0_35
12. Oladele, T.O., Ogundokun, R.O., Kayode, A.A., Adegun, A.A., Adebiyi, M.O.: Application of data mining algorithms for feature selection and prediction of diabetic retinopathy. In: Misra, S. (ed.) Computational Science and Its Applications – ICCSA 2019: 19th International Conference, Saint Petersburg, Russia, July 1–4, 2019, Proceedings, Part V, pp. 716–730. Springer, Cham (2019). https://doi.org/10.1007/978-3-030-24308-1_56
13. Adebiyi, M.O., Falola, D., Olatunji, O., Ogundokun, R.O., Adeniyi, E.A.: Computational prediction of corynebacterium matruchotii Protein's 3D structure reveals its capacity to bind to DNA domain site in the Malaria Vector, Anopheles. Int. J. Eng. Res. Technol. **12**(11), 1935–1940 (2019)

14. Omolewa, O.T., Oladele, A.T., Adeyinka, A.A., Oluwaseun, O.R.: Prediction of student's academic performance using k-means clustering and multiple linear regressions. J. Eng. Appl. Sci. **14**(22), 8254–8260 (2019)

15. Ogwueleka, F.N., Misra, S., Colomo-Palacios, R., Fernandez, L.: Neural network and classification approach in identifying customer behavior in the banking sector: a case study of an international bank. Hum. Factors Ergon. Manuf. Serv. Ind. **25**(1), 28–42 (2015)

16. Assef, F.M., Steiner, M.T.A.: Ten-year evolution on credit risk research: a systemic literature review approach and discussion. Ing. E Invest. **40**(2), 1–21 (2020)

17. Zhang, L., Hu, H., Zhang, D.: A credit risk assessment model based on SVM for small and medium enterprises in supply chain finance. Financial Innov. **1**(14), 1–21 (2015)

18. Khemakhem, S., Boujelbene, Y.: Artificial intelligence for credit risk assessment: artificial neural network and support vector machines. ACRN Oxford J. Finance Risk Perspect. **6**(2), 1–7 (2017)

19. Jency, X.F., Sumathi, V.P., Janani, S.S.: An exploratory data analysis for loan prediction based on nature of the clients. Int. J. Recent Technol. Eng. **7**(4), 176–179 (2018)

20. Goh, R.Y., Lee, L.S.: Credit scoring: a review on support vector machines and metaheuristic approaches. Adv. Oper. Res. **2019**, 1–30 (2019)

21. Li, S., Wang, M., He, J.: Prediction of banking systemic risk based on support vector machine. Math. Prob. Eng. **2013**, 1–5 (2013)

22. Sanz, H., Valim, C., Vegas, E., Oller, J.M., Reverter, F.: SVM-RFE: selection and visualization of the most relevant features through non-linear kernels. BMC Bioinform. **19**(432), 1–18 (2018)

23. Adebiyi, M.O., Ogundokun, R.O., Abokhai, A.A.: Machine learning–based predictive farmland optimization and crop monitoring system. Scientifica **2020**, 9428281 (2020)

24. Aktan, S.: Application of machine learning algorithms for business failure prediction. Investment Manag. Financ. Innov. **8**(2), 52–65 (2011)

25. https://www.kaggle.com/uciml/default-of-credit-card-clients-dataset

26. Suleiman, S., Burodo, M.S., Suleman, I.: Credit scoring using principal component analysis based binary logistic regression. J. Sci. Eng. Res. **412**, 99–110 (2018)

27. Boateng, E.Y., Oduro, F.T.: Predicting microfinance credit default: a study of Nsoatreman rural bank, Ghana. J. Adv. Math. Comput. Sci. **26**(1), 1–9 (2018)

28. Mavetera, N., Moroke, N.D., Chibonda, C.: A chi-square application on the factors influencing internet banking adoption and usage in Botswana. Mediterr. J. Soc. Sci. **5**(20), 596–606 (2014)

29. Adebiyi, M.O., Adigun, E.B., Ogundokun, R.O., Adeniyi, A.E., Ayegba, P., Oladipupo, O.O.: Semantics-based clustering approach for similar research area detection. Telkomnika **18**(4), 1874–1883 (2020)

30. Ogundokun, R.O., et al.: Evaluation of the scholastic performance of students in 12 programs from a private university in the south-west geopolitical zone in Nigeria. F1000Research **8** 154 (2019)

31. Awotunde, J.B., Ogundokun, R.O., Ayo, F.E., Ajamu, G.J., Adeniyi, E.A., Ogundokun, E.O.: Social media acceptance and use among university students for learning purpose using UTAUT model. In: Borzemski, L., Świątek, J., Wilimowska, Z. (eds.) Information Systems Architecture and Technology: Proceedings of 40th Anniversary International Conference on Information Systems Architecture and Technology – ISAT 2019: Part I, pp. 91–102. Springer, Cham (2020). https://doi.org/10.1007/978-3-030-30440-9_10

32. Rana, R., Singhal, R.: Chi-square test and its application in hypothesis testing. J. Pract. Cardiovasc. Sci. **1**(1), 69–71 (2015)

33. Mashhour, E.M., Houby, E.M.F., Wassif, K.T., Salah, A.I.: Feature selection approach based on firefly algorithm and chi-square. Int. J. Electr. Comput. Eng. **8**(4), 2338–2350 (2018)

34. Ikram, S.T., Cheukuri, A.K.: Intrusion detection model using fusion of chi-square feature selection and multi-class SVM. J. King Saud Univ. Comput. Inf. Sci. **29**(4), 462–472 (2017)

35. A-Harbi, O.: A comparative study of feature selection model methods for dialectal Arabic sentiment classification using support vector machine. Int. J. Comput. Sci. Netw. Secur. **19**(1), 167–176 (2019)

36. Osho, O., Mohammed, U.L., Nimzing, N.N., Uduimoh, A.A., Misra, S.: Forensic analysis of mobile banking apps. In: Misra, S. (ed.) Computational Science and Its Applications – ICCSA 2019: 19th International Conference, Saint Petersburg, Russia, July 1–4, 2019, Proceedings, Part V, pp. 613–626. Springer, Cham (2019). https://doi.org/10.1007/978-3-030-24308-1_49

37. Ogwueleka, F.N., et al.: Neural network and classification approach in identifying customer behavior in the banking sector: a case study of an international bank. Hum. Factors Ergon. Manuf. Serv. Ind. **25**(1), 28–42 (2015)

38. Arogundade, O.T., Abayomi-Alli, A., Misra, S.: An ontology-based security risk management model for information systems. Arab. J. Sci. Eng. **45**(8), 6183–6198 (2020). https://doi.org/10.1007/s13369-020-04524-4

A Conceptual Hybrid Model of Deep Convolutional Neural Network (DCNN) and Long Short-Term Memory (LSTM) for Masquerade Attack Detection

Adam Adenike Azeezat[1]([✉]), Onashoga Sadiat Adebukola[2], Abayomi-Alli Adebayo[2], and Omoyiola Bayo Olushola[3]

[1] Department of Computer Science, Crescent University, Abeokuta, Nigeria
adam.azeezat@crescent-university.edu.ng
[2] Department of Computer Science, Federal University of Agriculture, Abeokuta, Nigeria
{onashogasa,abayomiallia}@funaab.edu.ng
[3] Walden University, Minneapolis, USA
bayo.omoyiola@waldenu.edu, agad1963@yahoo.com

Abstract. Over the years, different issues keep emanating in the area of computer security, ranging from hacking to other security issues such as Ransomware, Distributed Denial of Service (DDoS), Malware, Masquerade attacks and so on. Masquerade attack is one of the most dangerous security attacks, dangerous – because it is can easily go undetected as the damage might have been done before realizing the extent to which it is done. The traditional method of detecting such attack has proven to be ineffective as rate of false positives is always on the high side and True positives are low. This paper presents an automatic deep learning method of Convolutional Neural Network (CNN) with Long Short Term Memory (LSTM) model using the dataset from Greenberg and Schonlau.

Keywords: Computer security · Masquerade attack · Deep learning · Convolutional neural network · Long short term memory · False positives · True positives

1 Introduction

Computer security has become the most significant viewpoint of every organization and individual as technology progresses through the use of computer devices. In trying to protect against data theft, manipulation or obliteration, different identity authentication methods such as Personal Identification Number (PIN) have been used for security management, access and control. These access control schemes are presented to the users before they granted access to their various devices. However, these technique distinguish users just towards the beginning of login and are defenseless against data fraud or deceit.

© Springer Nature Switzerland AG 2021
S. Misra and B. Muhammad-Bello (Eds.): ICTA 2020, CCIS 1350, pp. 170–184, 2021.
https://doi.org/10.1007/978-3-030-69143-1_14

One of the most significant issues in computer security is intrusions detection [1]. In order counter security dangers to computer frameworks and systems, numerous innovations have been created and applied in security activities such as Intrusion Detection System (IDS), firewalls and routers. Each one of those security application gadgets, regardless of whether focused on avoidance or recognition of assaults, usually generate huge volumes of security audit data [2].

Masquerade attack is a type of intrusion that can be detected using a type of IDS where an ill-conceived user expect the character of a genuine user. The user, with illegitimate access is called a masquerader, he/she takes the identity of a legitimate user in a computer system or network with the intent of stealing valuable information, making illegal transaction or damage the system maliciously, the different damages that the masquerade attacks causes makes it one of the most dangerous threats to computer and network infrastructures.

As at the time the assault is occurring it is difficult to identify this kind of security penetrate when started in light of the fact that the assailant gives off an impression of being an ordinary client with legitimate position and benefits [3]. The objective of any masquerade detection systems is to raise an alarm whenever the computer behaviour deviates from its usual or established characteristics to a certain extent [4]. Detecting a masquerade attack involves gathering information about users, developing a profile for each user and then comparing user activities against the established profiles [5].

Data capturing is very essential in masquerade attack detection, there has been difficulty in classifying data using traditional machine learning method as there would be no record of the timestamp when events occurred, the start and end of the attack is unknown. Over the years there are no automatic feature extraction methods in masquerade attacks, these have led to high false positives and low true negatives from the performance of previous IDS [6]. A high false negative rate leaves many attacks uncaught, making detection system useless. A high false positive rate, on the other hand, floods system with a large number of false alarms, eventually causing administrators to ignore true intrusion alarms along with false alarms [7].

This study aims to develop a conceptual hybrid model of Deep Convolutional Neural Network (DCNN) and Long Short Term Memory (LSTM) for masquerade attack detection. The study will employ a fully connected Deep Convolution Neural Network (DCNN) for feature extraction, dimensionality reduction and Long Short Term Memory (LSTM) for capturing time-series data. The rest of the paper is organized as follows; Sect. 2 presents the literature review, Sect. 3 presents the proposed methodology, Sect. 4 will discuss the proposed implementation and evaluation methods.

2 Literature Review

2.1 Computer Security Attacks

An attack is a computer security threat that attempts to obtain, alter, destroy, or remove without authorized access or permission. It happens to both individuals and organizations. There are 2 categories of computer security attack:

Passive Attack: This is a type of attack that does not affect the system nor its resources, even though the information needed is obtained, the information could be a name, password details, e-mail messages but to mention a few. A passive attack is less harmful; the damage in the end can be just as severe if the right type of information is obtained. Information that is assembled in the attack is generally sold in the profit market and dark web for monetary benefit of whoever executed the attack [8].

Active Attack: An active attack is an abuse in which an attacker tries to modify the data on the computer system [9]. The attacker takes charge of the device and pretends to be the legitimate user, thereby making different modification and also conduct illegal transactions on behalf of the legitimate user. In an active attack, the attacker is active and disrupts the operation of the system. Active attacks are generally forceful, deliberate attacks that victims become mindful when they happen. Active attacks are defined by unique characteristics and techniques; it presents unique challenges to victims, system users, system administrators and cyber security professionals [8]. An example of active attack is Masquerade attack.

Masquerade attack detection has been studied in the last couple of years [5]. The future of masquerade attack detection relies on developing an automatic detection rather than using the manual method. To detect this issue of masquerading user, it is essential to note that there are two different approaches in detecting masquerade attack, they are static analysis attack and dynamic analysis attack.

Static Analysis Approach: This is the process of analysing masquerade activities based on data set that had been collected with each data set having static features. It is faster and easier, the data set used in static analysis are collected manually. The static features may include individual command blocks in UNIX commands [6].

Dynamic Analysis Approach: In this approach a ready-made data set is not used [10]. It deals with raw data sources such as texts, images, video etc. and their features are extracted automatically which is one of the objectives of deep learning. Though it requires huge amount of computations which makes it slower.

2.2 Machine Learning, Deep Learning and Deep Neural Network

Machine learning algorithms can take in basic examples from a given prepared set of data, which incorporates both vindictive and benign samples from both an impostor and a genuine user. These allows for clear discrimination between benign and malicious code [11].

Deep learning is an emerging area of Machine Learning (ML) research. It comprises multiple hidden layers of artificial neural networks. The deep learning procedure applies nonlinear changes and model deliberations of significant level in enormous databases [12]. The "Deep" in deep learning refers to the numbers of layers that the data is transformed.

Deep Neural Network is an Artificial Neural Network (ANN) with multiple layers between the input and output layers. As the network travels through various shrouded layers, the likelihood of each output is calculated. They are generally feed forward networks with data flows from input layer to the output layer without a loop back.

2.3 Review of Related Works

Several related works were reviewed in the course of this research and discussed in this section.

Reference [13] presented a hybrid malicious URL detection system using Decision Tree and Naïve Bayes with classification result of 96.6% and 83.7% for benign and malicious URLs, respectively. Reference [14, 15] and [16] made use of traditional machine learning method to detect masquerade attacks, [15] applied 2 different data namely; user based and feature based data, Random forest performed well with both data. The simulated data used in [16] allows for insertion and deletion. In [17], a network intrusion and detection system (NIDS) was developed using deep learning model that is optimized with rule-based hybrid feature selection. The result obtained showed a false alarm rate and accuracy of 1.2% and 98.8%, respectively.

Reference [14] employed the use of Soft computing technique, comprising of fuzzy logic and neural network (Neuro-Fuzzy algorithm) was used to monitor any divergence in the user behaviour, the neural network was utilized to decide designs for user profiling and this is fed as input to the fuzzy system, the fuzzy system was trained by a learning algorithm derived from neural networks.

[18] Proposed the using instance weighted Naive Bayes for adapting concept drift in Masquerade detection. The work was motivated by the need to put users changing instances into consideration as most work done by most researchers focuses more user's behaviour and the masquerade behaviour without considering any update in the user's profile.

Reference [19] used GUI-based Windows systems for masquerade attack detection. The considering factor being that most researches done in the area of masquerade detection had been done so far using UNIX command line, the authors found it imperative to come up with the GUI interface which suitable for Windows system as some users are comfortable with using a GUI interface.

The first study on using deep learning for masquerade attack was done by [6], where they did an empirical study on predictive masquerade detection using DNN, RNN and CNN. Particle Swamp Optimization (PSO) was used for hyper-parameter selection. Static analysis was performed on RNN-LSTM while the dynamic analysis was done using CNN.

Reference [18] did temporal and spatial analysis of file access records. The research work was done putting file paths and file actions into consideration since most file based detection are done with file paths alone. Spatial analysis was used to discuss the file path and the relationship with accessed file within a particular period of time (Table 1).

Table 1. Summary of related works.

S/N	Author(s)	Method	Strength	Weakness
1	[14]	Hybrid neural network and Fuzzy logic	Classification and Degree of maliciousness	Likely situation of concept drift
2	[15]	Different machine learning algorithms were used for two different data set	Random Forest proved comparatively well above others	Limited data set were used
3	[16]	Based on Profile hidden Markov Model	Simulated data generated a good result, it allows for insertion and deletion	No positional information in the data set used
4	[18]	Based on Naïve Bayes with inclusion of IWNB and NBwSU	Users changing instances was put into consideration which worked well with Naïve Bayes	Too slow and much false positives
5	[19]	GUI Windows based	Combination Keystrokes from keyboards and mouse clicks	Data set used in carrying out the experiment is not mostly used (un validated data set)
6	[6]	Static and dynamic analysis using DNN	Dynamic analysis performed better than static with different DNN model	Data set could be swapped to obtain a better result
7	[20]	Based on Temporal and Spatial analysis of file records access	File path and action carried out	No real masquerade data was used
8	[5]	Based om Hidden Markov Model with parallel computing	HMM calculation using parallel computing	No varying dataset

2.4 Research Gap

Existing models of masquerade attack detection are done using the traditional machine learning methods, the problem of automatic feature extraction makes it difficult to know the extent of deviation from the typical genuine use of the system. The complexity of the traditional machine learning is often complex due to high computation which results in high false positive and low true negatives.

Convolutional Neural Network (CNN) has an advantage of feature extraction which is excellent for dynamic analysis and is generally utilized deep learning model for text characterization undertakings [10]. Long Short-Term Memory (LSTM) can store information from past information sources for a long time which makes them more appropriate to model sequential data [21, 22]. The combination of the rich features of both CNN and

LSTM offers an excellent masquerade attack detection by reducing the complexity of the false positives and increasing the true negatives.

3 The Proposed Hybrid Deep Neural Network Masquerade Detection Model

This work seeks to develop a masquerade attack detection technique using dynamic analysis based on; Convolutional Neural Network (CNN) and Long Short Term Memory (LSTM) using the Mini-Batch Gradient Descent Algorithm for training the data set.

3.1 Research Approach

The proposed model will be designed such that the user's commands in form of text files will be tokenized and sent to the vectorization layer, where the tokens are converted to word vectors. Some part of the word vectors is passed as input to the Convolutional Neural Network (CNN) layers reduce the dimensionality and features ae extracted automatically while the same parts are sent as input to the LSTM layer to help map out the previous inputs. The results from the CNN and LSTM layer are concatenated and sent to the softtmax layer for appropriate classification.

3.2 The Tokenization Layer

The process of converting raw data into undecipherable format, so as to remove any sensitive information and noise from the data (Fig. 1).

3.3 The Vectorization Layer

The vectorization layer will convert the tokens to word vector using word embedding. Here, the skip gram variant of word2vec will be employed due to its ability to make use of small amount of training data and also represent rare phrases or words.

3.4 Convolution Layer

Convolution is an important feature of Convolutional network, the primary purpose of a convolution is to extract features from input data, convolution is applied a text like running a filter of particular dimension and sliding it on top of the text and the operation is translated into element-wise multiplication between the two matrices and an addition of multiplication outputs. Here, word vectors will be converted into matrix with different filter size, for onward transfer to the max pooling layer for dimensionality reduction. For a particular CNN layer, there is corresponding max-pooling layer. Algorithm 1 shows the CNN layer algorithm with forward propagation.

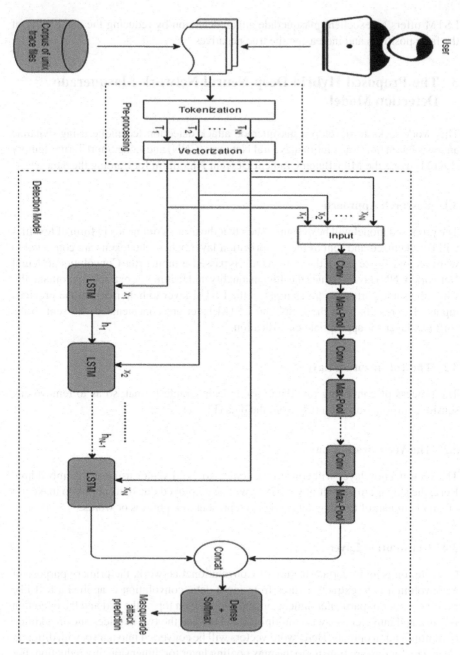

Fig. 1. Architecture of CNN-LSTM hybrid model

The forward propagation involves two steps; first is to figure the initial value of P, which is determined by calculating the information from the past layer with T tensor (containing filters) and a bias b, the second is the using of a non-linear activation function to our intermediate value (our activation is denoted by g).

$$P^{[l]} = T^{[l]} \cdot A^{[l-1]} + b^{[l]} \qquad A^{[l]} = g^{[l]}\left(P^{[l]}\right). \qquad (1)$$

Where

P = Intermediate value
T = Tensor
b = bias
A = Current value

3.5 Max-Pooling Layer

The Max-pooling layer minimizes and down-samples the features in the feature map. There are different types of pooling layer but the *max* operation which select the maximum value is the most commonly used technique for this layer and it will be adopted in the research work.

```
Algorithm 1: CNN LAYER
Input: Word Vectors
Output: Final feature vector C[l]
Process
Step 1: for i = 1 to m do
```
$$\text{Step 2: } A_i^{[l]} \leftarrow g_i^{[l]}\left(T_i^{[l]} A_i^{[l-1]} + b_i^{[l]}\right)$$
$$\text{Step 3: } C_j^{[l]} \leftarrow max(A_j^{[l]})$$
```
Step 4: End for
Step 5: Return C[l]
```

3.6 The LSTM Layer

Algorithm 2 shows how data are passed to the Long Short Term Memory (LSTM) layer, this layer is responsible for capturing sequential data. The LSTM contains several cells where each cell consists of three gates namely; the input gate, the forget gate and the output gate. The internal representation of the LSTM layer makes use of sigmoid function to avoid negative value and to give a clear answer whether to keep a particular feature or to discard it. 0 means the gates are blocking everything while 1 means allowing everything to pass through it.

$$i_t = \sigma\left(w_i[h_{t-1}, x_t] + b_i\right). \qquad (2)$$

$$f_t = \sigma\left(w_f[h_{t-1}, x_t] + b_f\right). \qquad (3)$$

$$o_t = \sigma\left(w_o[h_{t-1}, x_t] + b_o\right). \qquad (4)$$

Where:

i_t — *is the input gate*
f_t — *is the forget gate*
o_t — *is the output gate*
σ — *is the sigmoid function*
w_x — *is the weight of respective gate x neurons*
h_{t-1} — *is the output of the previous lstm block at timestamp $t-1$*
x_t — *is the input at current timestamp*
b_x — *is the biases for each gate respectively*

The input gate accept data from the vectorization layer and it is passed to layers of the LSTM and finally concatenated with the output from the Convolutional Neural Network (CNN) layer. The concatenated result will be sent to the softmax activation function for predicting the probability of the user being a masquerader or not. The softmax function over the logits $z(x)$ is defined as:

$$q_i(z) = \frac{e^{z_i}}{\sum_{j \in \{1, \dots N\}} e^{z_j}} \forall i \in \{1, ..N\}. \tag{5}$$

Algorithm 2: LSTM LAYER

Input: **word vectors**

Output: h_t **last hidden vector**

Process

Step 1: For all LSTM cells do

Step 2: $i_t \leftarrow \sigma(w_i[h_{t-1}, x_t] + b_i)$

Step 3: $f_t \leftarrow \sigma(w_f[h_{t-1}, x_t] + b_f)$

Step 4: $o_t \leftarrow \sigma(w_o[h_{t-1}, x_t] + b_o)$

Step 5: $\tilde{c}_t \leftarrow \tanh(w_c[h_{t-1}, x_t] + b_c)$

Step 6: $c_t \leftarrow f_t * c_{t-1} + i_t * \tilde{c}_t$

Step 7: $h_t \leftarrow o_t * \tanh(c^t)$

end for all

Return h_t

The masquerade classifier algorithm classifies an attack as either legitimate user or a masquerade

```
Algorithm 3: Masquerade Classifier
Input: feature vector f₁ from CNN, feature vector
f₂ from LSTM
Output: Cₘ which is the classifier output
Process
Step 1: f ← Concat(f₁, f₂)
Step 2: For all dense layers do
Step 3: o ← Dense(f)
Step 4: f ← o
end for all
Cₘ= softmax(o)
Return Cₘ
```

3.7 Model Training

Back Propagation Algorithm

The back-propagation algorithm in Algorithm 4 will be used to train the CNN-LSTM model using Mini-batch Gradient Decent (MBGD) to modify the weights of the entire model. The weights are the tunable parameters that determine the performance of the model. MBGD is an iterative minimization method that attempts to obtain the best value for the weights.

MBGD starts by assigning random values to the weights, calculates the change in weight value iteratively by differentiating the error function with respect to the weight and multiplying the value with the learning rate η, the weight values are updated until it gets to the final epoch K. The error function that will be adopted in this research work is the Cross Entropy Loss Function (CELF) shown in Eq. 6:

$$CELF = - \sum_{i=1}^{n} o_i \log(\tilde{o}_i). \tag{6}$$

Where:

o_i - true probability distribution.
$\tilde{o}_i$ - estimated probability distribution
n - Number of training samples

```
Algorithm    4:    Minibatch    Gradient    Descent
Training Algorithm
  Input: Function f(x; w) parameterized with w
  Input: Training set of inputs x₁,....,xₙ and
outputs y₁ ,...., yₙ
  Input: Loss Function L
  Process
  for i = 1 to N do //N is number of epochs
  Sample    a    minibatch    of    m    samples
{(x₁, y₁), ..., (xₘ, yₘ)}
  ĝ ← 0
  for j= 1 to m do
E ← L(f(x; w), y)
  Update gradient ĝ ← ĝ + ∂/dw (E/m)
  end for
  end for
Δw = ηĝ
  Update weight w ← w + Δw
  Return
```

4 Implementation and Evaluation Plan

4.1 Proposed Implementation

The minimum requirement for implementation and evaluation of the proposed CoLong are described as follows in the section.

Hardware Requirements
The proposed system will be implemented on a stand-alone computer using Google Colaboratory (Colab), a cloud based collaborative platform for conducting research in Artificial Intelligence. It offers free Graphical Processing Unit (GPU) needed to speed up training time of deep learning models. The following configurations on the computer are needed for an efficient functionality;

(1) Linux – based operating system.
(2) Tesla K80 GPU
(3) 12.72 GB GDDR5 VRAM
(4) 500 GB hard disk capacity

Software Requirements

(1) Pytorch for model building and training.
(2) Numpy for array processing.

Dataset Description

The proposed model will be trained and evaluated using the:

(1) Greenberg dataset adopted in [6], a UNIX dataset of 168 users has been collected directly from Prof. Saul Greenberg of University of Calgary, Canada.
(2) Schonlau dataset adopted in [32], the dataset corresponds to 50 files per user, each file consists of 15,000 commands.

4.2 Performance Metrics

The proposed model will be benchmarked with [6] since the same dataset will be adopted.

For every classification problem, there are always four possible outcomes True Positive (TP), True Negative (TN), False Positive (FP) and False Negative (FN). A TP whenever a masquerader is correctly classified as one. A TN indicates a legitimate user correctly classified as one. A FP occurs when a good user is misclassified as a masquerader while a FN indicates a masquerader misclassified as a legitimate user.

The evaluation metrics that will be used in this research are as follows: Confusion Matrix Accuracy, Precision, Recall, F1 score, and Matthews Correlation Coefficient (MCC).

(1) Confusion Matrix: It gives us a matrix as output and describes the complete performance of the model.

Actual class	Predicted class	
	Normal user	Masquerader
Normal user	TN	FP
Masquerader	FN	TP

(2) Accuracy: It shows the rate of true detection over all set tests

$$\text{Accuracy} = \frac{\text{TP} + \text{TN}}{\text{TP} + \text{TN} + \text{FP} + \text{FN}} \quad (7)$$

(3) Precision: It shows the rate of correctly classified masqueraders from all blocks in the test set that are classified as masqueraders

$$\text{Precision} = \frac{\text{TP}}{\text{TP} + \text{FP}} \quad (8)$$

(4) Recall: It shows the rate of correctly classified masqueraders over all blocks in the test set.

$$\text{Recall} = \frac{\text{TP}}{\text{TP} + \text{FN}} \quad (9)$$

(5) F1-Score: It gives information about the accuracy of a classifier regarding both Precision (P) and Recall (R) metrics.

$$FI\ Score = \frac{2}{1/P + 1/R} \tag{10}$$

(6) MCC: This performance metric takes into account true and false positives and negatives and it is regarded as a balanced measure which can be used even if there are imbalanced dataset It ranges from -1 to 1, where 1 is correct binary classifier and -1 indicates wrong binary classifier.

$$MCC = \frac{(TP \times TN) - (FP \times Fn)}{\sqrt{(TP + FN) \times (TP + FP) \times (TN + FP) \times (TN + FN)}} \tag{11}$$

Expected Contribution to Knowledge
The proposed hybrid model of Deep Convolutional Neural Network and Long Short Term Memory will contribute to the body knowledge through:

a. The research will also be able to minimize false positives to the barest minimum;
b. It would be deployed on mobile platforms too.

5   Conclusion

In this proposed study, a masquerade attack detection is proposed using a hybrid deep learning method comprising Convolutional Neural Network and Long Short Term Memory. The system will be trained using two data sets; the Schonlau data set and the Greenberg data sets.Parts of the vectorised data are sent to the CNN while the other part is sent to the LSTM layer and their outputs after going through the internal representations of both the deep learning methods are concatenated and sent to the dense layer where softmax activation function is applied and the user is classified as either a masquerader or a legitimate user.The model will be trained using the Mini Batch Gradient Descent (MBGD) while the error function to be adopted will be the Cross Entropy Loss Function (CELF).

References

1. Akarshika, R., Ankita, C.: Ant colony optimization for intrusion detection system based on KNN and KNN-DS with detection of U2R, R2L attack for network probe attack detection. Int. J. Sci. Res. Sci. Eng. Technol. **2**(6), 331–334 (2016). https://doi.org/10.32628/IJSRSE T162650
2. Sodiya, A.S., Folorunso, O., Onashoga, S.A., Ogunderu, O.P.: An improved semi-global alignment algorithm for masquerade detection. Int. J. Netw. Secur. **13**(1), 31–40 (2011)
3. Dash, S.K., Reddy, K.S., Pujari, A.K.: Episode based masquerade detection. In: Jajodia, S., Mazumdar, C. (eds.) ICISS 2005. LNCS, vol. 3803, pp. 251–262. Springer, Heidelberg (2005). https://doi.org/10.1007/11593980_19

4. Gaikwad, K.P.: A survey on object-based masquerade detection system using temporal and spatial locality features. Int. J. Eng. Res. **6**(4), 220–223 (2017). https://doi.org/10.1109/TIFS. 2016.2571679
5. Liu, J., Duan, M., Li, W., Tian, X.: HMMs based masquerade detection for network security on with parallel computing. J. Comput. Commun. **156**, 168–173 (2020)
6. Elmasry, W., Akbulut, A., Zaim, A.H.: Deep learning approaches for predictive masquerade detection. Secur. Commun. Netw. 1–24 (2018). https://doi.org/10.1155/2018/9327215
7. Huang, L.: A study on masquerade detection. SJSU Scholar Works (2010). https://doi.org/ 10.1016/j.comcom.2020.03.048
8. Biswas, S.A., S.: A survey of security attacks, defenses, and security mechanisms in wireless sensor networks. Int. J. Comput. Appl. **131**(17), 28–35 (2015). https://doi.org/10.5120/ijca20 15907654
9. Sobia, A., Saleem, U., Abubakar Siddique, M., Abdul, S.: Active attacks detection mechanism using 3-phase strategy. Int. J. Comput. Sci. Netw. Secur. **1**(17), 131–136 (2017)
10. Martın, A., Fuentes-Hurtado, F., Naranjo, V., Camacho, D.: Evolving deep neural networks architectures for Android malware classification. In: Proceedings of the 2017 IEEE Congress on Evolutionary Computation, CEC 2017, Spain, pp. 1659–1666 (2017). https://doi.org/10. 1109/CEC.2017.7969501
11. Yuxin, D., Siyi, Z.: Malware detection based on deep learning algorithm. Neural Comput. Appl. **31**(2), 461–472 (2017). https://doi.org/10.1007/s00521-017-3077-6
12. Vargas, R., Mosavi, A., Ruiz, L.: Deep learning: a review. Adv. Intell. Syst. Comput. **5**(2), 1–11 (2017)
13. Onashoga, S.A., Abayomi-Alli, A., Idowu, O., Okesola, J.O.: A hybrid approach for detecting malicious web pages using decision tree and Naïve Bayes algorithms. GESJ J. Comput. Sci. Telecommun. **48**(2), 9–17 (2016)
14. D'Silva, C., Mulchandani, D., Pimprikar, R., Nair, S., Priya, R.: User profiling system for detection of masquerading attack on private cloud. Int. J. Tech. Res. Appl. **4**(5), 7–14 (2016). https://doi.org/10.1109/IAW.2006.1652076
15. Kadala Manikoth, S.N., Di Troia, F., Stamp, M.: Masquerade detection on mobile devices. In: Parkinson, S., Crampton, A., Hill, R. (eds.) Guide to Vulnerability Analysis for Computer Networks and Systems. CCN, pp. 301–315. Springer, Cham (2018). https://doi.org/10.1007/ 978-3-319-92624-7_13
16. Huang, L., Stamp, M.: Masquerade detection using profile hidden Markov model. Comput. Secur. **30**, 732–747 (2011). https://doi.org/10.1016/j.cose.2011.08.003
17. Ayo, F.M., Folorunso, S.O., Abayomi-Alli, A.A.A., A.O., Awotunde, J.B.: Network intrusion detection based on deep learning model optimized with rule-based hybrid feature selection. Inf. Secur. J. Glob. Perspect. **29**(6), 267–283 (2020). https://doi.org/10.1080/19393555.2020. 1767240
18. Sen, S.: Using instance-weighted naive Bayes for adapting concept drift in masquerade detection. Int. J. Inf. Secur. **13**(6), 583–590 (2014). https://doi.org/10.1007/s10207-014-0238-9
19. Agrawal, A., Stamp, M.: Masquerade detection on GUI-based Windows systems. Int. J. Netw. Secur. **10**(1), 32–41 (2015). https://doi.org/10.1504/IJSN.2015.068409
20. Wang, J., Cai, L., Yu, A., Zhu, M., Meng, D.: TempatMDS: a masquerade detection system based on temporal and spatial analysis of file access records. In: 2018 17th IEEE International Conference on Trust, Security and Privacy. Computing and Communications/12th IEEE International Conference on Big Data Science and Engineering (TrustCom/BigDataSE), New York, NY, pp. 360–371 (2018). https://doi.org/10.1109/TrustCom/BigDataSE.2018.00061
21. Ruben, Z., Alicia, L.D., Javier, G.D., Doroteo, T.T., Joaquin, G.R.: Language identification in short utterances using long short-term memory recurrent neural networks. PLoS ONE **11**(1), e0146917 (2016). https://doi.org/10.1371/journal.pone.0146917

22. Abayomi-Alli, A., Odusami, M.O., Abayomi-Alli, O.O., Misra, S., Ibeh, G.F.: Long short-term memory model for time series prediction and forecast of solar radiation and other weather parameters. In: Proceedings of the 19th International Conference on Computational Science and Its Applications (ICCSA), Saint Petersburg, Russia, pp. 82–92 (2019). https://doi.org/10.1109/ICCSA.2019.00004

23. Boughorbel, S., Jarray, F., El-Anbari, M.: Optimal classifier for imbalanced data using Matthews Correlation Coefficient metric. PLoS ONE **12**(6), e0177678 (2017). https://doi.org/10.1371/journal.pone.0177678

24. Brownlee, J.: Deep Learning for Natural Language Processing (2019). Ebook. https://machinelearningmastery.com/

25. Chumachenko, K.: Machine learning method for malware detection and classification. B.Sc thesis (2017)

26. Erbacher, R.F., Prakash, S., Claar, C.L., Couraud, J.: Intrusion detection: detecting masquerade attacks using UNIX command lines. In: Proceedings of the 6th Annual Security Conference, 11–12 April 2007 (2007)

27. Hochreiter, S., Schmidhuber, J.: Long short-term memory. Neural Comput. **9**(8), 1735–1780 (1997)

28. Kim, Y.: Convolutional neural networks for sentence classification. In: Proceedings of the 2014 Conference on Empirical Methods in Natural Language Processing (EMNLP), pp. 1746–1751 (2014). https://doi.org/10.3115/v1/D14-1181

29. LeCun, Y., Bengio, Y., Hinton, G.: Deep learning: review. **521**(7553), 436–444 (2015) Macmillan Publishers Limited

30. Maxion, R.A., Townsend, T.N.: Masquerade detection using truncated command lines. In: Proceedings of International Conference on Dependable Systems Networks, Bethesda, Maryland, 23–26 June 2002 (2002). https://doi.org/10.1109/DSN.2002.1028903

31. O'Shea, K., Nash, R.: An introduction to convolutional neural networks (2015). https://white.stanford.edu/teach/index.php/An_Introduction_to_Convolutional_Neural_Networks

32. Schonlau, M., DuMouchel, W., Ju, W., Karr, A.F., Theus, M., Vardi, Y.: Computer intrusion: detecting masquerades. Stat. Sci. **16**(1), 1–17 (2001)

33. Sharfuddin, A.S., Tihami, N., Islam, S.: A deep recurrent neural network with BiLSTM model for sentiment classification. In: International Conference on Bangla Speech and Language Processing (ICBSLP), pp. 1–4 (2018). https://doi.org/10.1109/ICBSLP.2018.8554396

34. Simon, A., Singh, M.D., Venkatesan, S., Ramesh Babu, D.R.: An overview of machine learning and its applications. Int. J. Electr. Sci. Eng. (IJESE) **1**(1), 22–24 (2016)

35. Xing, W., Du, D.: (2019) Dropout prediction in MOOCs: using deep learning for personalized intervention. J. Educ. Comput. Res. **57**(3), 547–570 (2019). https://doi.org/10.1177/0735633118757015

An Automated Framework for Swift Lecture Evaluation Using Speech Recognition and NLP

Ochilbek Rakhmanov[✉] [iD]

Nile University of Nigeria, Plot 681, Cadastral Zone C-OO, Research and Institution Area,
Jabi, Abuja, Nigeria
ochilbek.rakhmanov@nileuniversity.edu.ng

Abstract. Feedback produced by students can give useful insights on lecturer's performance and ability of teaching. Many institutions use the feedbacks from students efficiently to improve the education quality. In this study. A novel framework for collection and swift processing of students' feedbacks about lecture is proposed in this paper, which addresses the shortcomings of traditional scale-rated surveys and open-end comments. The automated framework uses speech recognition and NLP tools to produce frequency graph of mostly used words, which can help to identify the topics need to be revised. An experiment was successfully conducted to test the framework among 3rd year undergraduate students.

Keywords: Lecture evaluation · Speech recognition · NLP · Education

1 Introduction

It is very important for educational institutions and educators to keep track of the quality of the instructional service they offer [1]. The quality of interaction between lecturer and students plays critical role in students' engagement, learning and retention during the educational process [2]. Feedbacks produced by students can give useful insights on lecturer's performance and ability of teaching. There are two commonly used methods of collecting feedback from students, scale rated survey and open-end comments, and both have their pros and cons [3]. Filling scale-rated survey can produce a performance score about the lecturer and the content of the lecture, but this method is very restricted, it cannot not give insight on if the student understood particular topic or not, unless the lecturer must prepare a different survey for each lesson, which is not really feasible from lecturer's aspect. To overcome this issue, open-end comments can be provided [3]. Students can write an evaluation summary text, which can provide more insight on student's response after analyzing it using some natural language processing and machine learning tools [3].

Natural language processing (NLP) can be summarized as application of the tools and algorithms in Artificial Intelligence in linguistics field. NLP is a technique, which is used by computational devices to understand and interpret the natural language [4]. NLP already being widely used in several fields in the education. NLP is helping to automate some writing and reading tasks that traditionally require tremendous effort

© Springer Nature Switzerland AG 2021
S. Misra and B. Muhammad-Bello (Eds.): ICTA 2020, CCIS 1350, pp. 185–195, 2021.
https://doi.org/10.1007/978-3-030-69143-1_15

from educators. For instance, usage of NLP to extract keywords or identifying commonly used terms in discussion forums can be presented as an example to prevent the lecturer from reading every post of crowded forum [4–7]. Moreover, using NLP tools within the classroom showed promising results as well [4]. Figure 1 presents a sample framework on how to use NLP to improve education.

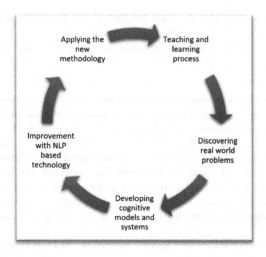

Fig. 1. Sample framework on how to use NLP for better education.

Analyzing open-end comments of the students using NLP can help to solve the shortcomings of the classical scale rated surveys. But the practice shows that students show laziness to submit even a short text to review the lecture. There are several reasons for this; they would not like to spend too much time for it or they are usually postponing it for later and forgetting. To address the shortcomings of the open-end comments, speech recognition can be used as a useful tool. This paper tried to propose a simple but effective framework to develop a method to summarize the lecture using speech recognition and NLP tools.

Automatic speech recognition is commonly used in modern technological application. In brief, one of the goals of the speech recognition is to establish communication between computational device and human via natural speech, where natural implies the common way of oral communications between humans [8]. While they are being used successfully in mobile and some other technologies, the researchers are trying to extend the usage to different fields as well. Most of the powerful technological companies like Google, Microsoft, Amazon and others are investing into speech recognition based technologies, while latest models show promising results with more than 90% of accuracy [8]. But as the nature of the human diverse, the language and dialectic also diverse, even though they are using same language. For instance, the pronunciation of the words in English by Indian and Nigerians can differ, forcing the speech recognition models to do mistakes.

Speech recognition was the subject to many researches in education in recent researches [2, 9–13]. Basically, previous researches can be classified into two categories; researches that used speech recognition as tool to improve the classroom education and researches that used speech recognition as a helpful tool for disabled students. Using speech recognition tools to automatically produce transcript of the lecture was proposed as a useful tool by Ranchal et al., as it can help to students who missed the classes or to compare their own notes with the produced transcript for corrections [9]. It was also proposed as a powerful tool during education of EFL (English as a Foreign Language) as students find it helpful to use speech recognition tools to correct themselves [9, 12].

The existing literature shows that speech recognition was used as lecturer centered, in other words to convert speech of the instructor into text. But the methodology proposed in this paper looks at the issue from student perspective, to extract meaningful insight from the speech of the students. As it was mentioned before, the scale-rated surveys may not give the insightful review of the lecture and expecting students to submit text comments about lecture may create obstacles, as students hold off the process. But sending a short voice message about the lecture can minimize the burden, as almost all students use mobile devices nowadays. As the framework in methodology section proposes, the lesson can be quickly summarized using voice message of the student, speech recognition and NLP tools.

1.1 Purpose of the Study

To present and test a framework which can quickly process and summarize the voice messages of the students after the lecture and present to lecturer the most 'problematic' keywords which students mentioned in their speeches. While this framework can speed up the lecture evaluation process with few steps, it can also give huge opportunity to the students with writing disabilities.

2 Review of Related Literature

During the literature review, the specific importance was given on how the speech recognition was used in classroom and out of classroom in educational institutions, as it was directly related to this study. The existing speech recognition technologies were also reviewed to find out the best performers.

Real-time captioning and post-lecture transcription was compared and evaluated by Ranchal et al. during their studies on conversion of oral lectures into text [9]. They found that post-lecture transcription was superior and usage of speech recognition tools affected students in positive way, most of them improving their grades. Similar to this study, Ahn and Lee tested some mobile devices with speech recognition abilities to observe its effect on students studying EFL [12]. Their students mostly responded well to the experiment and many mentioned that they find it useful using speech recognition tools during their studies as it helps them to compare their text with the transcript produced by the tool.

Wald looked into usage of the speech recognition from different perspective, evaluated the potential benefit of speech recognition systems in the education process of students with disabilities [10]. A disabled student can find it extremely useful to obtain the transcript of the lecture without writing any note. It can also minimize the burden of the deaf students, as they can follow real-time transcripts while lecturer is teaching orally [10]. Azeta et al. used speech of students from different perspective, they investigated the suitability of speech-enabled examination result management system as a tool for checking and managing students' examination results [6].

On the other hand, not all studies support the usage of the speech recognition tools during the classroom education. For instance, Hede conducted a comparative study and found that only few students found screen texts helpful, while many complained that inaccuracies in screen text were distracting [11]. Hede mentioned that the accuracy to text conversion plays important role, as the model which makes many mistakes creates a dissatisfaction in students.

As the speech recognition was major player during this research, it was important to identify the reliable speech recognition tool. Kepuskka et al. and Matarneh et al. were two research groups who conducted and comparative studies on existing speech recognition systems [8, 14]. They compared many existing commonly used state-of-art speech recognition tools; Google API, Siri, Yandex SpeechKit, Microsoft Speech API and some others. While they found that tools may differ with respect to the languages, both groups agreed that Google API was the front runner in this field. Thus, Google API was employed in this research also. As it stands, Google announced that their speech recognition API resulted with only 4.9% error rate in 2017 [14]. Matarneh et al. summarized leading speech recognition tools in their research, which is presented in Fig. 2 [14].

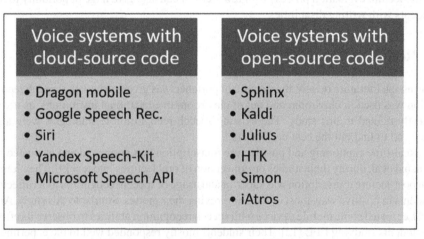

Fig. 2. Summary of speech recognition tools.

3 Instruments

3.1 Programming Tools

Python was used as programming language. During the experiment the mobile communication platform Slack was used to collect the voice records from the students [15], later processed using open source speech recognition tool from Google API [8] and final analyzes were done using NLTK natural language processing library [16].

3.2 NLP Text Processing

During the NLP text processing the data passed through three important preprocessing tools; tokenization, stemming and removal of irrelevant content [13]. Table 1 presents those three main processes and their functions on the given data. It is important to mention that the 3rd process, namely Removal of Irrelevant Content, should be carried out with care. The process may eliminate important words as well, if not programmed well.

Table 1. Preprocessing functions

Process name	Function done by the process
Tokenization	The comments of the students were split into words, tokens
Stemming	To further facilitate word matching, words in student comments are converted to their root word. For example, "rushing" and "rushed" are converted to "rush"
Removal of irrelevant content	Punctuation and stop words are removed to improve the presentation of necessary keywords on the graph

Figure 3 presents a sample process of the NLP text processing the text "Sir you rushed during teaching the pivoting method and simplification".

Once the preprocessing is done, the final stage is to produce a frequency distribution graph. In brief, it is simple operation where total number of each outcome is being counted after each occurrence and turned into graph, to make it easy to analyze. During this experiment, a frequency distribution was used to record the frequency of each word type in a document.

Frequency distributions are generally constructed by running a number of experiments, and incrementing the count for a sample every time it is an outcome of an experiment.

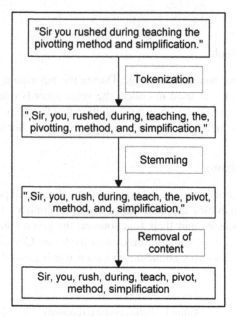

Fig. 3. Sample NLP text processing

4   Methodology

4.1   Overview of the Framework

Figure 4 presents the proposed framework for swift lecture evaluation. The system is automated and the final product is a keyword distribution graph.

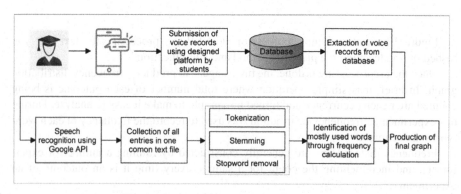

Fig. 4. Framework for swift lecture evaluation

4.2   Process Flow in the Framework

1. First of all, one of the main actors in this process is the platform to be used. Many different types of platforms can be arranged for that since there exist many different open source applications to collect voice records in one common database. For instance, a simple messenger (like Slack, WhatsApp or Telegram) can be used.
2. Immediately after lecture, students should take their 10–15 s to send voice record mentioning the subtopics they could not understand or need revision using designed platform.
3. An automated process using Python language should conduct following operations sequentially: extract the records from the database, convert all voice records to text file, combine all entries into one text files, tokenize the words, stemming the words, remove stop-words, and finally identify mostly used words using frequency distribution. Pseudocode, presented as Algorithm 1 in Fig. 5, is summary of this automation process.

It is important to mention that Google Speech Recognition API can handle only several types of audio files; wav, aiff, aiff-c and flac. So if the audio files produced by students are in different format, a format conversion should be done before feeding the audio file to speech recognition API.

Algorithm 1 Speech to frequency distribution

1: $A \leftarrow$ extract all voice files from database
2: **for** every file in A **do**
3:      $text \leftarrow$ convert voice file to text
4:      $Comb \leftarrow$ combine all $text$ files in one common file
5: **for** every word in Comb **do**
6:      $tokens \leftarrow$ tokenize
7:      $stemmed \leftarrow$ stemming the $tokens$
8:      $final \leftarrow$ remove stopwords from $stemmed$
9: $hist \leftarrow$ calculate the frequency of $final$
10: **return** $hist$

Fig. 5. Pseudocode for automation process mentioned in Sect. 4.2

Figure 6 presents a sample process presented in Algorithm 1 for 3 students' recordings. The recordings are passed through speech-to-text, text processing and graphing processes. Only top 5 frequently appearing words were displayed on graph.

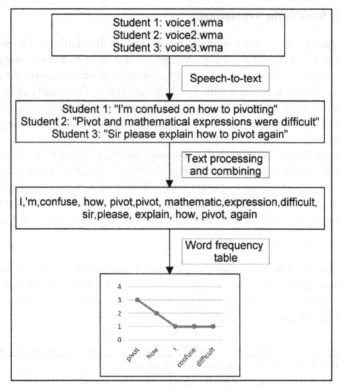

Fig. 6. Sample process of the files as it was described by Algorithm 1.

5 Experiment

To test the proposed framework, an experiment was conducted during 2019/2020 education session. Computer Science students from 300 level (3rd year of education) from Nile University of Nigeria were selected and all students voluntarily participated in this experiment. All ethics and standard of the research were followed and maximum level of privacy were provided for students who voluntarily submitted audio files.

Operation Research class was selected as a target course and for two consecutive weeks students participated in Linear Programming revision class, where topics like forming table, conversion word problems to mathematical equation, conversion to standard form, using simplex method and how to pivot, using LPA software, using Python and dual simplex method were revised. After each lecture, students were requested to send short voice message about subtopics they could not understand well through Slack messenger so the lecturer can identify difficult subtopics to do extra revision. The submission rate was 100%. Totally 30 students participated in the experiment (20 female students, 10 male students).

As it was expected, the class rep reported that all students submitted their voice records within 10–12 min after the lecture, while extraction of the voice messages and processing with codes maximum takes more than 3 min to produce final graph.

6 Results

6.1 Accuracy of Conversion

It was mentioned before that Google claimed that their API error rate is around 5%, which is extremely good. But error rate of conversion was higher in this study. After conversion of all audio files into text, one to one comparison was done and the accuracy was calculated as 82%. As it was summarized by the lecturer, the expected keywords were: word problem, conversion to mathematical equation, summary table, tableau method, pivot and pivoting, simplex method, python programming, LP assistant, dual simplex method. Table 2 shows three mostly mistaken words during speech-to-text conversion.

Table 2. Most frequently mis-converted words

Original word	Conversion
Dual simplex	Dwarf melted, do want me, dual SIM card
Pivot	Paper, private, purport
Python	Bison, by ton

It is clear from Table 2 that the accuracy of the conversion was caused due to specific words which are not used in daily life language. So, the factors affecting the conversion accuracy can be summarized in three points:

1. The dataset collected was relatively small, and the accuracy may get better with larger dataset, as Google Speech Recognition tool was training on large dataset.
2. Using specific words used only in science and technology may affect the speech recognition model's accuracy.
3. As it was mentioned before, the pronunciation of English words by Nigerian or Indian users can differ, which directly affects the speech recognition model.

6.2 Results of the Experiment

Figure 7 presents the result of final frequency distribution of keywords, top 15 words. Comparing to keywords provided by the lecturer, it is clear that 'conversion to mathematical equation' was major complain of the students while 'dual simplex method' also attracted the concerns of the students. So based on this evidence, the lecturer was directed to do quick revision on 'conversion to mathematical equations' and 'dual simplex method' during next lesson.

7 Discussion and Conclusion

The main objective of this study was to present and test the framework, which could evaluate students' lecture review and produce a summary graph of keywords with minimal computation cost. Results presented on Fig. 7 show that the framework worked out successfully. It produced insightful summary from students' voice records.

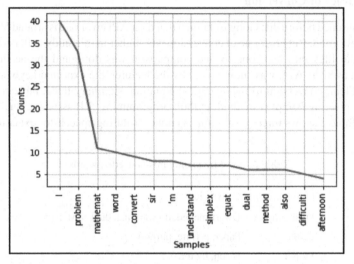

Fig. 7. Frequency distribution of key words

This framework was tested only for student lecture comment submission, but it can be also applied to various different fields in education and out of the education, where a quick feedback is needed based on voice collections.

Results presented in Sect. 6.1 show that the method may get affected from speech recognition inaccuracy. With current speed of technological development, maybe this would not be a problem in the near future. But as for now, scientific terms in English pronounced by different dialects may cause a problem. This issue can be solved manually by requesting from students to pronounce scientific terms clearly during voice record.

8 Future Researches

Clearly the framework needs further researches. Only unigram method was tested during NLP processing, while processing with bigrams may show different results. In the same manner, Google Speech Recognition tool was selected as a best performer. Thus, several speech recognition tools can be tested within this framework and compare the results. All these, the author leaves for the further researches in the future.

As the content of the comments can be different for students from different faculties, the framework should be tested with some students from different faculties and departments, rather than science, to see if the framework responds well.

References

1. Ochilbek, R.: Development of a method for evaluating quality of education in secondary schools using ML algorithms. In: Proceedings of the 2019 11th International Conference on Education Technology and Computers, pp. 23–29 (2019)
2. Fan, X., Luo, W., Menekse, M., Litman, D., Wang, J.: CourseMIRROR: enhancing large classroom instructor-student interactions via mobile interfaces and natural language processing. In: Proceedings of the 33rd Annual ACM Conference Extended Abstracts on Human Factors in Computing Systems, pp. 1473–1478 (2015)
3. Lalata, J.P., Gerardo, B., Medina, R.: A sentiment analysis model for faculty comment evaluation using ensemble machine learning algorithms. In: Proceedings of the 2019 International Conference on Big Data Engineering, pp. 68–73 (2019)
4. Litman, D.: Natural language processing for enhancing teaching and learning. In: Thirtieth AAAI Conference on Artificial Intelligence (2016)
5. Ochilbek, R.: Using data mining techniques to predict and detect important features for book borrowing rate in academic libraries. In: 2019 15th International Conference on Electronics, Computer and Computation (ICECCO), pp. 1–5. IEEE (2019)
6. Azeta, A.A., Misra, S., Azeta, V.I., Osamor, V.C.: Determining suitability of speech-enabled examination result management system. Wireless Netw. 25(6), 3657–3664 (2019). https://doi.org/10.1007/s11276-019-01960-5
7. Azeta, A.A., Azeta, V.I., Misra, S., Ananya, M.: A transition model from web of things to speech of intelligent things in a smart education system. In: Sharma, N., Chakrabarti, A., Balas, V.E. (eds.) Data Management, Analytics and Innovation. AISC, vol. 1042, pp. 673–683. Springer, Singapore (2020). https://doi.org/10.1007/978-981-32-9949-8_47
8. Këpuska, V., Bohouta, G.: Comparing speech recognition systems (Microsoft API, Google API and CMU Sphinx). Int. J. Eng. Res. Appl. 7, 20–24 (2017)
9. Ranchal, R., et al.: Using speech recognition for real-time captioning and lecture transcription in the classroom. IEEE Trans. Learn. Technol. 6, 299–311 (2013)
10. Wald, M.: An exploration of the potential of Automatic Speech Recognition to assist and enable receptive communication in higher education. ALT-J. 14, 9–20 (2006)
11. Hede, A.: Student reaction to speech recognition technology in lectures. In: Untangling the Web: Establishing Learning Links. Proceedings of the Australian Society for Educational Technology (ASET) Conference, Melbourne (2002)
12. Ahn, T.Y., Lee, S.-M.: User experience of a mobile speaking application with automatic speech recognition for EFL learning. Br. J. Edu. Technol. 47, 778–786 (2016)
13. Rakhmanov, O.: On validity of sentiment analysis scores and development of classification model for student-lecturer comments using weight-based approach and deep learning. In: Proceedings of the 21st Annual Conference on Information Technology Education, pp. 174–179 (2020)
14. Matarneh, R., Maksymova, S., Lyashenko, V., Belova, N.: Speech recognition systems: a comparative review (2017)
15. Church, K., De Oliveira, R.: What's up with WhatsApp? Comparing mobile instant messaging behaviors with traditional SMS. In: Proceedings of the 15th International Conference on Human-Computer Interaction with Mobile Devices and Services, pp. 352–361 (2013)
16. Loper, E., Bird, S.: NLTK: the natural language toolkit. arXiv preprint arXiv:cs/0205028 (2002)

DeepFacematch: A Convolutional Neural Network Model for Contactless Attendance on e-SIWES Portal

Emmanuel Adetiba[1,2]([✉]), Amarachi E. Opara[1], Oluwaseun T. Ajayi[1], and Folashade O. Owolabi[3]

[1] Department of Electrical and Information Engineering, Covenant University, Ota, Ogun State, Nigeria
emmanuel.adetiba@covenantuniversity.edu.ng
[2] HRA, Institute for System Science, Durban University of Technology, Durban, South Africa
[3] Department of Accounting, Covenant University, Ota, Ogun State, Nigeria

Abstract. An attendance system has always been a critical instrument that is normally engaged to determine the response of persons to events, programs, or scheduled classes within the educational context. The Student Industrial Work Experience Scheme (SIWES) is a work-integrated learning program developed and made mandatory for all undergraduate students in professional and sciences courses in the Nigerian Higher Education Institutions (HEIs). This is to expose the students to the world of works in the industry before graduation. However, monitoring students and ensuring that they partake fully in the scheme has proven difficult over the years. In this paper, we developed a Convolutional Neural Network (CNN) model named DeepFacematch to realize face recognition based contactless attendance. Given the model's validation accuracy of 92.60%, a contactless attendance app containing the validated model and location tracking support was developed, for incorporation into the e-SIWES web portal. This is to achieve effective monitoring of the students' compliance with the rules of the work experience scheme. Remarkably, the addition of the DeepFacematch feature will be a boost to the viability of e-SIWES portal for improved SIWES coordination across the HEIs in Nigeria. DeepFacematch can also be re-trained and adapted for contactless attendance systems at offices and schools to curb the spread of infectious diseases like coronavirus.

Keywords: Contactless attendance · CNN · e-SIWES · Face recognition · DeepFacematch

1 Introduction

In Higher Education Institutions (HEIs), one major way to ensure that theoretical knowledge is subjected to a pragmatic application is through a work-integrated learning scheme. The Student Industrial Work Experience Scheme (SIWES) was established to allow students to harness industry-relevant skills and on-the-field experience. The

© Springer Nature Switzerland AG 2021
S. Misra and B. Muhammad-Bello (Eds.): ICTA 2020, CCIS 1350, pp. 196–205, 2021.
https://doi.org/10.1007/978-3-030-69143-1_16

Nigerian Industrial Training Fund (ITF) coordinates SIWES nationally and the program is a mandatory requirement for obtaining a degree in Sciences, Engineering, or other professional courses in any Nigerian HEIs. Over the years, universities have experienced a lot of impediments in achieving the aim of SIWES. Also, students have undermined the purpose of the scheme as they play truancy at their respective places of work and give false records in their logbooks and reports. In the past, measures have been taken to mitigate this bad demeanor through – *i) student visitation, ii) call monitoring, and iii) manual attendance marking*. However, these measures have not been optimal in ensuring the realization of the full objectives of the scheme. Therefore, ensuring students are at their workplaces and in time has been a major source of concern for both HEIs and ITF.

e-SIWES portal is a web-based solution developed to enhance all-round coordination of students' activities during SIWES. Specifically, it assists institutions to automate different SIWES activities such as students' registration, dissemination of information, filling of logbook for students' day-to-day activities, and supervision/assessment by lecturers and industry-based supervisors [1, 2]. However, the system does not have any feature for tracking students' attendance at their places of work vis-à-vis their locations. This implies that despite the automation of the SIWES activities (which are major improvements over the traditional approach), students could still play truancy and update their logbooks without being discovered by the institutional and ITF authorities. Thus, there is an apparent need for extending the capability of e-SIWES portal to incorporate electronic attendance and location tracking.

Technologies such as Bluetooth, RFID, GPS/GPRS, and QR code amongst others, have been utilized on the mobile and web platforms for attendance tracking. However, in most recent studies, biometrics traits such as fingerprint, palm print, iris, and face have been employed for attendance tracking and have proved to be more reliable [3–7]. Nevertheless, among the listed biometric traits, face recognition provides a cost-effective edge for the electronic work-integrated learning context since virtually all laptops and smartphones incorporate a webcam as a sensor for capturing of face. In this study, we exploited CNN [8], a deep learning architecture, and face biometrics to develop the DeepFacematch model to achieve contactless attendance on the e-SIWES portal. Location tracking service is also incorporated to ensure that attendance is taken at the right location per time. The rest of this paper comprises of the literature review in Sect. 2, methodology in Sect. 3, experimental results and discussions in Sect. 4, and the conclusion is presented in Sect. 5.

2 Literature Review

Yousaf et al. [9] proposed an attendance system that marks the attendance of students in a class using a camera for face recognition. In the study, students' images are captured, and pre-processed with enhancements and feature extraction before storage into the database. Viola & Jones face detection algorithm [10] was used by the authors to classify each student's image. Sunaryono et al. [6] employed a QR code and face biometrics approach for an android-based attendance system. In the study, two android applications were used, one each for the teacher and the students. The algorithm in [10] was also employed in the study for face detection and recognition as each student's face was captured 10 times with different expressions using a smartphone. Notably, the use of deep learning for biometrics-based recognition has received significant attention over the past few years owing to its reputation for good performance in computer vision and speech recognition tasks. For instance, Albakri and Mokbel [11] proposed a system that uses biometrics to control access to user transactions. The authors utilized Histogram of Oriented Gradients (HOG) algorithm to detect and extract facial features from the sample dataset while a CNN model was trained to identify faces based on the available data. However, the HOG feature descriptor employed in [11] has a pitfall as it is very sensitive and not invariant to image rotation [12]. Therefore, to develop the DeepFacematch model in this study, we inflated the original dataset (students' pictures) using data augmentation technique. Afterwards, we utilized CNN to perform both feature extraction and classification of the augmented face images, which resulted in a model that is invariant to rotation and other major distortions in image dataset.

3   Methodology

This section discusses the design of the CNN architecture to realize the DeepFacematch model as well as the implementation of the location tracking service. The stages involved include; data acquisition and augmentation, model training and evaluation, and development of contactless attendance app. For the experiment, a Personal Computer (PC) with 8 GB RAM, 256 GB SSD, Intel(R) Core(TM) i5-6300U CPU and 2.50 GHz processor was used.

3.1   Data Acquisition and Augmentation

A total of 772 images of SIWES students at Covenant University were collected from 17 different academic programs. Each student's picture was scanned and stored in their respective program folders. The inherent challenge with this dataset is that each class (student) of the dataset has only one sample. To mitigate this challenge, we leveraged data augmentation, which is an established deep learning approach used to artificially expand the size of a training dataset, thereby alleviating the limited data size problem. We artificially inflated the 772 collected images to 3,860 samples by applying five geometric transformation techniques such as rotation, zoom, horizontal flip, width shift, and height shift. The augmented dataset were labeled with the matric number of each of the students and partitioned to 80% for training and 20% for validation in order to build CNN, which is the adopted deep learning architecture.

3.2   DeepFacematch Model Design

As shown in Fig. 1, a CNN architecture is made up of several layers, which includes convolution layers, max pooling layers, a dense/fully connected layer and a softmax layer [13]. *Convolution layer* contains a set of filters whose parameters need to be learned. Convolution is the mathematical process of implementing a filter (or kernel) on an image. A computer interprets an image as a two dimensional array of pixels, with each pixel having a value. A grid of numbers called a kernel is scanned across the image. To do this, the kernel is centered over a pixel, then the corresponding image and kernel value is multiplied together and values are summed up. This value is assigned to the pixel in the convoluted image. After getting all the values from the kernel computation, they are passed through the Rectified Linear Unit (ReLU) activation function. This function converts all the negative values to zero and overcomes the vanishing gradient problems that are often associated with the traditional activation functions. *Max pooling layer* reduces the size of a convoluted image by summarizing regions through downsampling. To perform max pooling, a grid, which is the pool size and a stride need to be selected. In each selected grid, the highest pixel value is selected as the value of the corresponding pixel in the new image. Stride determines the number of pixels to slide the grid across the image. This process is continued until the entire convoluted image is covered. The resulting image will therefore be more compact than the original image. The size of the resulting image after max pooling will vary depending on the choice of the grid size and the stride [14].

A *fully connected or dense layer* in CNN is a stack of layers where each layer is made up of units called neurons. The neurons in each layer are fully connected to neurons in the previous and the following layers. These neurons contain the weights and biases of the model. Weights and biases are values that are tuned during the training process to minimize the cost function [13]. The *softmax layer* is the final output layer in CNN, which performs multi-class classification and object recognition. The number of classes in this layer depends on the number of labels in the dataset used to train the neural network and each prediction is represented as a probability distribution across the classes in this layer.

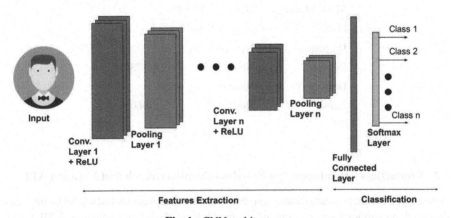

Fig. 1. CNN architecture

The DeepFacematch model, which is based on the CNN architecture and the curated face images, was developed using TensorFlow Python framework in Jupyter Notebook. TensorFlow is an end-to-end open-source framework for building and training machine learning models. We experimentally evolved an 11-layer model with the configurations in Table 1. The dimension of each of the input images is ($150 \times 150 \times 3$). The model has 3 convolution layers with each followed by a max-pooling layer. The last max-pooling layer is followed by a flatten layer. Dropout layers (with 0.2 probabilities) are placed before the fully connected (dense) layers and the output layer in order to prevent the model from overfitting. The output layer consists of 772 output classes corresponding to the total number of students in the dataset. The Rectified Linear Unit (ReLU) activation function was used for all the convolution layers while softmax activation was used for the output layer.

In machine learning, the goal is to reduce the error between the actual and predicted outputs of the model. Thus, we engaged validation accuracy and loss to evaluate the performance of the DeepFacematch model [14, 15]. The numbers of epochs were varied from 1 to 100 with the highest validation accuracy and minimum loss obtained at 80 epochs. The model with the highest accuracy was saved and packaged for deployment on the eSIWES portal. The results are presented in Sect. 4.

Table 1. DeepFacematch model summary.

Layer (type)	Output shape	Parameters
Conv2D	(None, 150, 150, 16)	448
MaxPooling2D	(None, 75, 75, 16)	0
Conv2D_1	(None, 75, 75, 32)	4640
MaxPooling2_1	(None, 37, 37, 32)	0
Conv2D_2	(None, 37, 37, 64)	18496
MaxPooling2_2	(None, 18, 18, 64)	0
Flatten	(None, 20736)	0
Dropout	(None, 20736)	0
Dense	(None, 512)	10617344
Dropout_1	(None, 512)	0
Dense_1	(None, 772)	396036

3.3   Contactless Attendance App Based on DeepFacematch and Location API

A prototype contactless attendance app based on the DeepFacematch model (with location tracking support) was modeled using the Unified Modeling Language (UML). The class diagram of the app is presented in Fig. 2 showing the interaction among the *Image-Data, Attendance, Supervisor* and *Student* classes. Notably, the attributes of the *Supervisor and Student classes* are consumed from the e-SIWES portal for uniformity of attributes. The sequence and activity diagrams for the contactless attendance app are presented in Fig. 3 and Fig. 4 respectively, showing the flow of actions/activities, order of the interactions and operations between the user and the different components of the system. The DeepFacematch model was converted to TensorFlow.js format (.json file) and saved as.*h5* file so that it can run on the web browser. The app was implemented

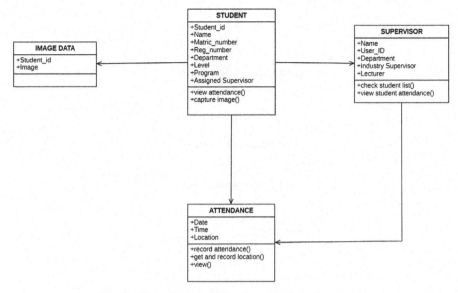

Fig. 2. Class diagram of the contactless attendance app

with front-end and back-end tools such as HTML/CSS, PHP, JavaScript, MySQL and Geolocation Web Application Programming Interface (API). A menu that links to the

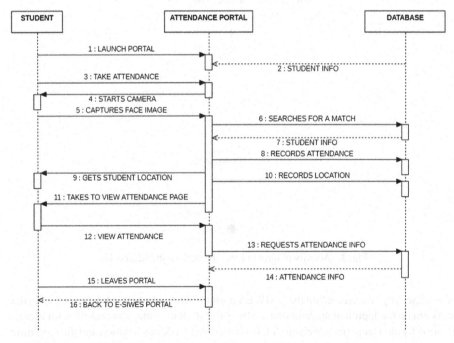

Fig. 3. Sequence diagram of the contactless attendance app

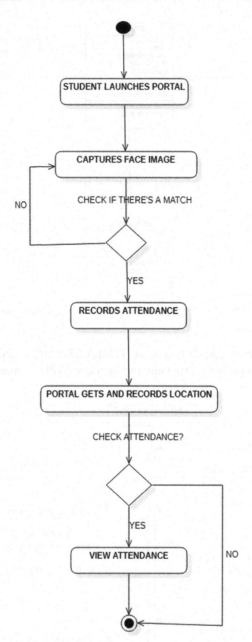

Fig. 4. Activity diagram of the contactless attendance app

attendance app was created on the e-SIWES portal and for a student to take attendance, the webcam on the laptop or smartphone captures the student's image in real-time for identification by the DeepFacematch model. If verified, the student's location and the date/time on the webserver are logged on the *Attendance database* in the MySQL database to mark his/her attendance for the day. Supervisors and other relevant institutional stakeholders of SIWES can then view the cumulative attendance information stored in the database and generate reports for further decision making.

4   Experimental Results and Discussion

The adoption of data augmentation techniques allows a single image to serve as a seed for inflating the dataset size that is appropriate for building a CNN model. Results from the experiment carried out in Jupyter Notebook using the augmented dataset and the CNN configurations in Table 1, yielded the best training and validation accuracies of 71.5% and 92.60% respectively with 80 epochs. The plots of the training and validation accuracies with their respective losses (accuracy/loss on the y-axis and number of epochs on the x-axis) are shown in Fig. 5, confirming that the augmented dataset improved the overall generalization of the model. To track and log students' location for attendance on the e-SIWES portal, we engaged a student in Okpanam, Delta State, South-South, Nigeria to test the app; the Geolocation API was used to retrieve the latitude, longitude, and timestamp, and save it in the database, as shown in Fig. 6. To further test the app, the same student took the attendance several times and was logged in the database. Figure 7 shows the attendance information (address, date, time, and status) of the student for each of the attempts. Past works in [4, 6, 7, 16–18] have reported the use of RFID cards for class attendance and face recognition for image retrieval and annotation [7]. However, most classical methods pose some challenges like impersonation for automated attendance capturing and management in schools and workplaces. Hence, this study leverages

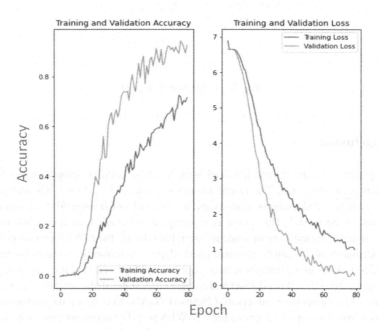

Fig. 5. DeepFacematch model accuracy and loss

the mathematical strength and the state-of-the-art breakthroughs in deep learning to mitigate impersonation and truancy in the highly critical student industrial work experience scheme.

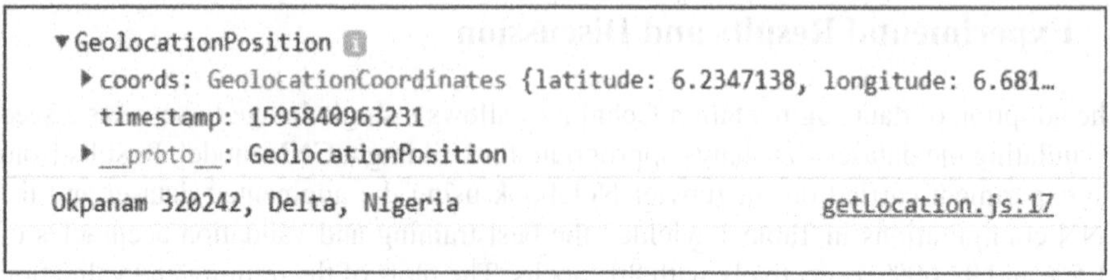

```
▼ GeolocationPosition 🛈
  ▶ coords: GeolocationCoordinates {latitude: 6.2347138, longitude: 6.681...
    timestamp: 1595840963231
  ▶ __proto__: GeolocationPosition
  Okpanam 320242, Delta, Nigeria                          getLocation.js:17
```

Fig. 6. Output of the geolocation API

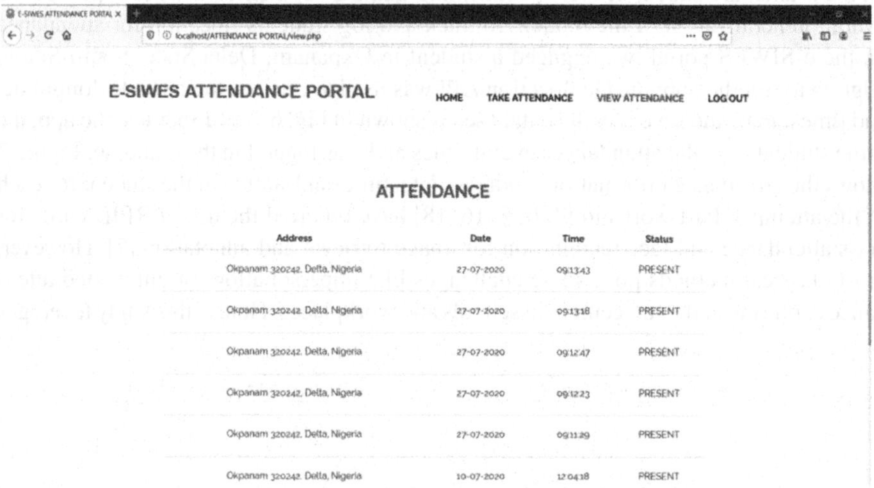

Fig. 7. Attendance view page

5 Conclusion

In this paper, a DeepFacematch model with location tracking support for e-SIWES portal has been presented. The DeepFacematch model is based on CNN architecture, using data augmented students' images and the TensorFlow framework for training, and validation of the model. This effort is to mitigate the challenges associated with the coordination and monitoring of students' activities during the SIWES programme. The DeepFacematch model can be re-trained and adapted continuously to cater for new sets of SIWES students using transfer learning approach. However, for future adaptation, we hope to extend the size of the dataset and engage other state-of-the-art data augmentation techniques like Generative Adversarial Network (GAN) to enhance the performance of the model. We also hope to improve the e-SIWES portal to accommodate more features beyond the contactless attendance and location tracking features.

Acknowledgments. This work was carried out at the Advanced Signal Processing and Machine Intelligence Research (ASPMIR) Group laboratory, IoT Enabled Smart and Connected Community Research Cluster, Covenant University. The High Performance Computing node of the Covenant Applied Informatics and Communication African Centre of Excellence (CApIC-ACE) FEDGEN Testbed was utilized for experimentations. The Covenant University Centre for Research, Innovation and Development (CUCRID), Covenant University, Ota, Nigeria provided full sponsorship for the publication of this work.

References

1. Adetiba, E., Matthews, V., Egunjobi, V., Olajide, A.: Development of e-SIWES portal: a web based platform for student industrial work experience scheme (SIWES) management. Int. J. Bus. Inf. Syst. **3**, 10–17 (2012)
2. Adetiba, E., Iortim, O., Olajide, A.T., Awoseyin, R.: OBCAMS: an online biometrics-based class attendance management system. Afr. J. Comput. ICT **6**(3), 25–38 (2013)
3. Lodha, R., Gupta, S., Jain, H., Narula, H.: Bluetooth smart based attendance management system. Procedia Comput. Sci. **45**, 524–527 (2015)
4. Pireva, K.R., Siqeca, J., Berisha, S.: RFID: management system for students' attendance. IFAC Proc. Volumes **46**, 137–140 (2013)
5. Nagothu, S.K., Kumar, O.P., Anitha, G.: GPS Aided Auton. Monit. Attendance Syst. Procedia Comput. Sci. **87**, 99–104 (2016)
6. Sunaryono, D., Siswantoro, J., Anggoro, R.: An android based course attendance system using face recognition. J. King Saud Univ. Comput. Inf. Sci, 1–9 (2019)
7. Ahmed, A., Olaniyi, O.M., Kolo, J.G., Durugo, C.: A multifactor student attendance management system using fingerprint biometrics and RFID techniques. In: International Conference on Information and Communication Technology and Its Applications (2016)
8. Krizhevsky, A., Sutskever, I., Hinton, G.E.: Imagenet classification with deep convolutional neural networks. Commun. ACM **60**(6), 84–90 (2017)
9. Yousaf, M.H., Baloch, N.K., Ahmad, W., Baig, M.: Algorithm efficient attendance management face recognition based approach. Int. J. Comput. Sci. Issues **9**(4), 146 (2012)
10. P. Viola and M. J. Jones, "Robust Real-Time Face Detection," *International Journal of Computer Vision,* vol. 57, pp. 137–154, 2004/05/01 2004.
11. Albakri, A., Mokbel, C.: Convolutional neural network biometric cryptosystem for the protection of the blockchain's private key. Procedia Comput. Sci. **160**, 235–240 (2019)
12. Cheon, M.-K., Lee, W.-J., Hyun, C.-H., Park, M.: Rotation invariant histogram of oriented gradients. Int. J. Fuzzy Logic Intell. Syst. **11**(4), 293298 (2011)
13. Li, X.K., Zhang, G., Zheng, W.: Deep learning and its parallelization. Big Data (12, 2016)
14. Fang, Z., Feng, H., Huang, S., Zhou, D.X.: Theory of deep convolutional neural networks II: spherical analysis. Neural Netw. **131**, 154–162 (2020)
15. Abadi, M., et al.: Tensorflow: A system for large-scale machine learning. In: 12th {USENIX} symposium on operating systems design and implementation, {OSDI} 2016, pp. 265–283 (2016)
16. Srivastava, N., Hinton, G.E., Krizhevsky, A., Sutskever, I., Salakhutdinov, R.: Dropout: A simple way to prevent neural networks from overfitting. J. Mach. Learn. Res. **15**(1), 1929–1958 (2014)
17. Borovikov, E., Vajda, S.: FaceMatch: real-world face image retrieval. In: Santosh, K.C., Hangarge, M., Bevilacqua, V., Negi, A. (eds.) RTIP2R 2016. CCIS, vol. 709, pp. 405–419. Springer, Singapore (2017)
18. Mohammed, K., Tolba, A.S., Elmogy, M.: Multimodal student attendance management system (MSAMS). Ain Shams Eng. J. **9**, 2917–2929 (2018)

Hausa Intelligence Chatbot System

Usman Haruna[1]([✉]), Umar Sunusi Maitalata[1], Murtala Mohammed[1],
and Jaafar Zubairu Maitama[2]

[1] Department of Computer Science, Faculty of Science, Yusuf Maitama Sule University,
Kano, Nigeria
Usmancyz01@gmail.com
[2] Department of Information Technology, Faculty of Computer Science and Information
Technology, Bayero University, Kano 3011, Nigeria

Abstract. Chatbot is an AI based application that stimulates human conversations. In this research, we proposed a noble approach to the design of Chatbot that interacts with people in Hausa Language, which is the second most famous languages in Africa. Numerous chatbots have been created and continue to be created. To the best of our knowledge, there is very limited or no Chatbot that target Hausa Language, hence the catalyst of this research. The proposed Chatbot is capable of communicating with users in Hausa Language, tell some funny stories and above all has the ability of learning from users. It was designed as a web-based application that can feature in any platform with internet access and a web browser, where PHP was used as programming Language in conjunction with MySQL database. The interface was designed using HTML and CSS with JavaScript for interactivity. Developing this Chatbot system would bring the Hausa language into the Artificial intelligence stage and it would serve as a reference material for future research and development. The result shows that the system is capable of communicating in simple Hausa words and will be able to learn simple words in Hausa. Developing system whose ability is to learn, adapt and perform autonomously can be a major field of competition between technology inventors and Hausa-based language processing over the next few years.

Keywords: Chatbot · Hausa · Intelligent system · Human-Computer Interaction

1 Introduction

Computers have greatly affected or changed the way we conduct our normal activities in this contemporary world. Many researchers and practitioners in the area of human-computer interaction (HCI) have been improving their skills in designing graphical user interfaces of computer system. Presently, things may take an unexpected view toward Natural-language user interfaces, whereby the interaction with digital systems take place not only via scrolling, button clicks, or swiping, but through set of strings of texts in natural language (NLP). This particularly exists in recent developments associated with designing chatbots. Generally, chatbots are computer agents that serve as natural-language user interfaces to data and service providers [1]. The notion of chatbots is as

© Springer Nature Switzerland AG 2021
S. Misra and B. Muhammad-Bello (Eds.): ICTA 2020, CCIS 1350, pp. 206–219, 2021.
https://doi.org/10.1007/978-3-030-69143-1_17

old as a computer itself. The Chatbot was first time invented by Alan Turing, who was considered to be a founder of theoretical computer science in 1950. Alan Turing introduced the concept of Turing Test, which is conducted to determine whether a computer can act indistinguishably from the way a human acts.

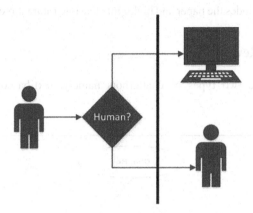

Fig. 1. Interpretation of Turing Test [2]

The interpretation of the Turing Test is best depicted in the Fig. 1. The test contains three participants: a human, a machine and a judge. The judge is the one who decide whether the discussion is taking place with either human or a machine. The judge would interrogate both the human and machine with a series of questions and make a decision based on their reactions, tone, and how they reply to the questions being asked [3].

ELIZA was the first program to pass the Turing Test, and was created in 1966 by Joseph Weizenbaum at the Massachusetts Institute of Technology (MIT) Artificial Intelligence Laboratory in United State of America. In the Eliza program, text was read and check for the presence of a keyword. If a keyword is found, then the answer is transformed based on the rule associating with the word. In simplicity, program was recognizing words or phrases in the input, and producing the output with corresponding pre-programmed sentences. The same trend is being used by Chatbot programmers ever since. Although true artificial intelligence remains years or even decades out of reach, Artificial Intelligence-based messaging tools are available today which are capable of solving real-world problems. The chatbots are not only restrictly designed to solve problems for corporations. There are chatbots that are solely designed for entertainment and targeted at some group of people.

After a critical review of the text-based and voice-based Chatbot agents, currently it is apparent that there is limited or no Chatbot in Hausa Language despite Hausa language being a language that is widely spoken in West Africa with estimated speakers of 52 million. Hausa language is a very popular language in many African countries like Cameroon, Nigeria, Niger, Benin, Togo, Ghana among others, where Nigeria happened to be the most populous among the entire other African countries [4]. With respect to the mother' tongue, Hausa happens to be the first among all the language in Africa, or even in any of the Nigerian Languages [5]. Therefore, this study aimed at filling the gap left by other researchers.

This paper is structured as follows. Section 1 contains an introductory part of the paper. Section 2 reports the existing literature. In Sect. 3, our proposed Chatbot methodology was described. Section 4 contains description of the system testing and validation. Finally, Sect. 5 concludes the paper and highlights feasible future directions for the work.

2   Literature Review

Basically, there are two types of chatterbots namely, text-based and voice-based chatterbots (Fig. 2).

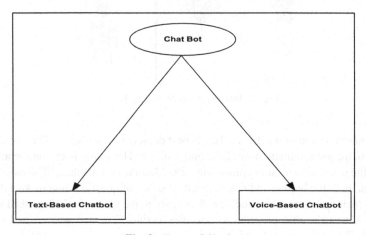

Fig. 2. Types of Chatbot

2.1   Text Based Chatbots

The earliest Natural language processing (NLP) program is ELIZA, which was designed at the MIT Artificial Intelligence Laboratory to present the superficiality of communication between humans and computers [2]. The pattern matching' and substitution methodology is used to simulate conversation. This gave users an illusion of understanding on the part of the program, but it had no or lacks built in framework for contextualizing events. Eliza is the first Chatbot, as such it paves way for further research and development of the field of Natural Language Processing. It also provides an efficient means of communication with humans. However, the Eliza has a crude nature, and it was not a true intelligent system, since it is just echoing the user's input.

Another text-based Chatbot system is ALICE (acronym for Artificial Linguistic Internet Computer Entity), which is often referred to as an Alicebot was proposed in [6]. The system is one of the natural language processing chatterbots which has a program that converse with a human through applying some heuristical pattern matching rules to the human's input. It was motivated by Joseph Weizenbaum's classical ELIZA program, which was one of the strongest programs of its kind. It has won the Loebner Prize, awarded to accomplished talking robots (humanoid), three times (in 2000, 2001 as well as in 2004). Despite all these successes, the program was unable to pass the Turing test, as even the casual user will often expose its mechanistic aspects in short conversations.

Similarly, a text-based Chatbot called SmarterChild Chatbot was proposed in [7] which resides on AOL Instant Messenger and Windows Live Messenger (formally MSN Messenger) networks. The system was designed for the ActiveBuddy Software Company and it was one of the first chatbots to be featured in Instant Messaging Platform [7]. The system was very user friendly interface which allows communication to take place easily. However, the SmarterChild is not widely popular.

Another text-based Chatbot called PARRY was proposed by a Psychiatrist and designed at the Stanford University [8]. This Chatbot was attempted to simulate a person with paranoid schizophrenia. The program PARRY implemented a crude model of the behavior of a person with paranoid schizophrenia based on concepts, conceptualizations, and beliefs. It also includes a conversational strategy, which was a much more serious and advanced program than ELIZA. The PARRY Chatbot is best described as "ELIZA with attitude".

A Spanish football Chatterbot called a Chatbol was proposed in [9] for the Laliga Football league to provide information to users on the Spanish domestic league. The bot was designed using features of a classical Eliza, and is very fast despite the fact that everything is in Spanish.

A multilingual chatterbot was proposed which leverages the Google Translate platform to provide interactive chat in different languages [10]. This Chatbot is one of the first chatbots that interface with Google Translate and has multilingual capability. However, the user interface of the system was not very catchy and user friendly. It also favoured some developed languages like English and Arabic among others than the developing ones like Hausa, Swahili, Yoruba among many others.

A recommender Chatbot for the programming community on Discord forum was proposed in [11]. The Chatbot helps organization recruit developers by giving them the best recommendations and suggestions. The bot however, suffered from the restricted domain, and hence, it has a limited intelligence. Additionally, the DiscordSt library used while designing the bot was not well standardized, and as such, the bot may suffer from broken parts.

A banking system Chatbot which was also based on the text-based bots was proposed in [12]. This Chatbot provides customer service 24/7 in an accurate and efficient manner for financial institutions. The bot however suffered from every drawback associated with ALICE, since it is based on the Chatbot.

2.2 Voice Based Chatbots

Any software agent who has the ability to interpret a human speech and response through synthesized voice is referred to as Voice assistant [13]. Many voice chatbots are being developed to help human converse with computer.

Siri is among the voice-based chatbots systems, and it was proposed in the research of [14]. This Chatbot is a virtual assistant which was first released in October, 2011 as part of Apple Inc.'s iOS, iPadOS, watchOS, macOS, and tvOS operating systems. The bot developers were originally part of a company called Siri Inc before Apple bought the company and made the product part of its array of services [15]. It uses voice queries and a natural-language user interface to respond to questions been posed by the human, suggest recommendations, and execute actions by delegating requests to a set of Internet services. The program agent adapts to users' individual language usages, searches, and preferences, with continuing use. The results obtained are individualized. One major problem associated with the Siri is the difficulty associated with recognizing some words.

The voice Chatbot for Microsoft Windows is Cortana, which uses the Bing Search engine technique to do tasks such as setting reminders and answering questions posed by the user [16]. The Chatbot has a good user graphical interface and it is also easy to use. However, the system is only available in English, French, Chinese, German, Italian, Japanese and Spanish Languages.

Another voice based intelligent Chatbot was proposed in [17] to allow users have a dialog with the system via their voices. The system was designed using Java Programming Language that is distributed in nature. However, the Chatbot suffers from lack of speed associated with Java applications.

LiSA is another voice-based Chatbot, and it was designed to assist students in their campus daily activities via information and services [18]. The focus here was on how the bot influences the user experience and the interaction, and which level of intelligence should be designed and implemented. One good thing about the system is that while using the tool, it allows understanding of both the user's need and their behaviour. However, this system is limited to be use only in the university campus.

Amazon Alexa which is often called Alexa is a voice-based Chatbot which was developed by Rohit Prasad and some employees of Amazon in 2014 [19]. This Chatbot has the ability of voice interaction, music playback, making to-do lists, setting alarms, streaming podcasts, playing audiobooks, and weather information, traffic, sports, and other activities that requires real-time information, such as news. Alexa can also be used to control several smart devices using itself as a home automation system. There is an ongoing security issues associated with Amazon Alexa, which allow third party attackers access the device and eavesdrop on users.

After a careful and critical review of the text-based and voice-based Chatbot agents, it is apparent that there is no Chatbot created in Hausa Language or even in any of the Nigerian Languages, hence the catalyst of this research and development is filling the gap left by other researches and developments.

3 Methodology

3.1 System Analysis

The purpose of system analysis is to study a system or part of it so as to make the identification of its objectives easier. It contains steps that are to be followed in order to gather requirements and determine the best way a system shall be developed and to determine the overall possibility of the system [20, 21].

Requirement Analysis Techniques
Techniques used in requirement gathering have become more structured over time. In this research project, the traditional methods of requirements (i.e. Interview and analyzing documents) were used.

Analyzing Procedures and Other Documents
Analyzing documented works and literature is the best way to understand a concept and make a proper analysis on it [22]. This system being the first of its kind has led to consultations of a vast number of works, literature, thesaurus and other important documents from different domains and areas of study, such as Kamus (Hausa Dictionary), Hausa novels, Chatbot documentations of other languages.

The process of analyzing the procedures and other documents during the course of the fact-finding process has been a great success, as it paves way for more understanding of the topic of discussion.

Interview
Open ended questions were employed to interview scholars in the field of study (Hausa) about overall Language, what they consider to be a proper Hausa chat, and if chatter bot will be implemented in Hausa, how it should be.

Feasibility Analysis
This analysis is use to determine whether a given project can be started and completed successfully. A project is a unique endeavor. This means that, every project has a unique challenge that affects it is feasibility.

Technical Feasibility
Technical feasibility answers the questions of whether a project is technically feasibility, e.g. there is a technology that can be used to implement it, and there are technical experts to implement it. A project could not be possible if it fail pass any of the questions. The Hausa Intelligent Chatbot is technically feasible, as there are the technology available and the professional to implement the project.

Legal/Ethical Feasibility
The legal question of any project is whether it is legal or it may encourage illegal activities. There have been numerous illegal activities associated with Artificial Intelligence, like botnets [23]. This project however is perfectly legal and critical analysis has not found a way it can be used for illegal activities. Hence it is legally feasible.

Operational Feasibility

A system is useless if it cannot be operated by its intended users. Hence, operational feasibility of a system is a very important analysis phase of any project. The Hausa Intelligent Chatbot is operationally feasible as its interface is very user friendly, and there is not any complex operation that requires heads to roll.

Economic Feasibility

The Economic Feasibility of a system ensures that a system is economically feasible (there a fund to design and implement it). The System is economically feasible as it does not require much fund for the implementation. As the hardware cost is insignificant and it does not need to be hosted online.

Description of the Current System

Currently, there are numerous chatbots as can be seen from the Sect. 2 of this paper, it range from general purpose chatbots that can interact with users for general conversations to specific Chatbots that are developed for a particular domain or purpose, example is the Bank Chatbot that provide customers support to bank customers and bots for ordering food.

Two categories of chatbots exist: text-based and voice-based. There is however a third category of hybrid chatbots, which combine both voice and text. All the categories of chatbots use one technique or another in understanding user input and providing an appropriate response. One of these techniques is pattern matching, which was used in designing the classical Eliza.

Shortcomings of the Current System

All the current chatbots have one shortcoming or another, the one shortcoming that is general to all the chatbots is their lack of support for African Languages like Hausa Language.

Description of the Proposed System

The proposed system is a web based application which uses pattern matching algorithm to interact with users in the Hausa Language. The Hausa Chatbot also has the ability to learn some Hausa words from users.

The system has this refined algorithm:

1. *Get users input.*
2. *Determine what the input is, as the system has category of input, some for general matching and others for learning.*
3. *If input matched to what the system know, then return appropriate response.*
4. *If the category of input is for learning, then system shall attempt to learn the new word.*
   End Program.

3.2   System Design

System Flowchart

A flowchart is used diagrammatically to represent an algorithm. Flowcharts are also used both as aids in showing the way a proposed program will work and as a means of understanding the operations of an existing program.

The Hausa Intelligent Chatbot has a quite complex flow. However, Fig. 3 best depicts the system.

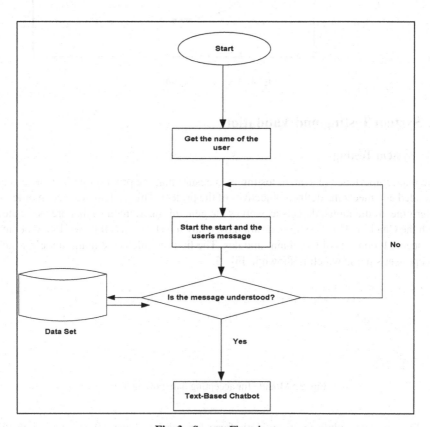

Fig. 3. System Flowchart

Use Case Diagram

This diagram is used to show how a system interacts with different system modules, and what category of user has access to what module. The Hausa Intelligent Chatbot is quite peculiar in the sense that it has only one category of user which could be any person who intends to chat with the Chatbot. The user is restricted to only two actions, which are providing name and chatting with the bot, the chatting process is however unrestricted and unbounded. Figure 4 represents the use case diagram for the Hausa Intelligent Chatbot.

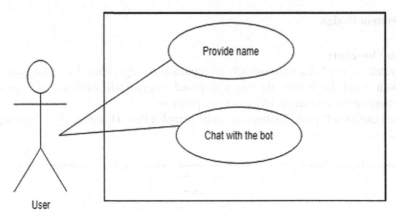

Fig. 4. Use case diagram

4 System Testing and Validation

4.1 System Testing

The main importance of system testing is to ensure that the program performance is as intended and meets the defined objectives of the project. This system is tested in order to determine all the faults, defects as well as the general functionalities that are associated with the Chatbot. This system does not have many interfaces, as all its works are behind the scene. It consists of two main modules. The first module is the main module which accept user's name which is shown in Fig. 5.

Yusuf Maitama Sule University University, Kano

Chatbot

Enter Your Name To Start

Your name eg. Muhd

Start

Fig. 5. Module for accepting name of the user

The second module provides a platform for users to have conversation with the system as demonstrated on Fig. 6 to Fig. 8 with different interactions. As the Chatbot uses pattern matching to provide appropriate response to users and also learn from users. The Chatbot cannot learn complete sentences, rather it learn new words and add them to its vocabulary periodically.

In the Fig. 6, a simple Hausa greeting is exchanged between user and the bot, where the bot is able to recognize the word and reply with an appropriate messages. Figure 7 shows a Bot telling a time, a day, as well as response to the word that it did not understand.

Figure 8 presents a Bot given short interesting story and test for non-recognized chat, in which the system is fed with a words that includes what it does not recognized.

Fig. 6. General greetings

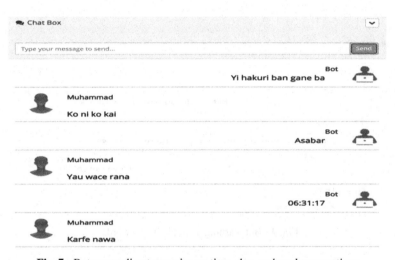

Fig. 7. Bot responding to queries on time, day, and unclear questions

Figure 9 shows how the system can recognize and learn a new word or phrase parsed on to it. It simply returns a response that inform the user that the input is not been recognized, but it has leaned and captured to its vocabulary based on the explanation given by the user.

4.2 Validation

Validation is use to examine whether the proposed system satisfies the user requirements, and conducted at the end of the SDLC. This Chatbot is validated with Hausa language chats, short sentences or phrases as input. The system processes and returns an appropriate response once the input patterns are duly understood as seen in the test section.

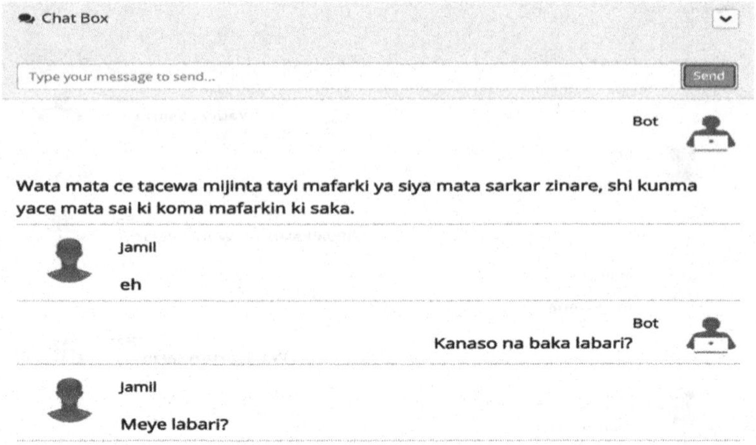

Fig. 8. Bot telling a short story

Fig. 9. Bot learning a simple hausa words

The main system validation was conducted using 55 final year Computer Science undergraduate students as participants. These students have already undergone an Artificial Intelligence CSC4305 which exposed them to the concept of Chatbots and how they operate. The second group of the participants involves 5 computer science lecturers denoted as experts. The testing was not conducted concurrently. Both the students and the experts participated in this study were selected from the Department of Computer Science, Faculty of Science, Yusuf Maitama Sule University, Kano. Each of the participants is asked to chat with the system and provide a feedback. After chatting with the system, each participant was asked to determine whether they are conversing with human or computers. 90.9% of the students' response were "non-differentiate" whether they are chatting with human or computer systems, while the remaining said it is "differentiable" as shown in Fig. 9. As for the experts, 78.0% revealed that it is "non-differentiate" whether they are chatting with human or computer systems, while the remaining said it is "differentiable" as presented in Fig. 10. These results shows that our proposed system has passed the Turing Test, thus could ultimately be considered as intelligent system in its own right (Fig. 11).

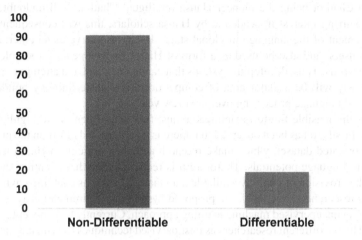

Fig. 10. Students response

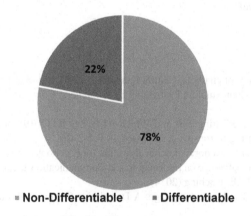

Fig. 11. Experts response

5 Conclusion

This paper proposed a novel approach to the design of Chatbot that interacts with people in Hausa Language. To the best of our knowledge, there is very limited or no Chatbot that target Hausa Language which is capable of communicating with users, tell some interesting stories and above all has the ability of learning from users. The system was designed as a web-based application that can feature in any platform with internet access and a web browser, where PHP was used as programming Language in conjunction with MySQL database. The interface was designed using HTML and CSS with JavaScript for interactivity. The result shows that the system is capable of communicating in simple Hausa words and able to learn simple words in Hausa.

Hausa Chatbot being the pioneer Hausa intelligent Chatbot, will undoubtedly go a long in stirring interest in academia by Hausa scholars, this will consequently lead to advancement of the language in global stage. It can also serve as an entertainment tool to its users, and also be used as a form of Hausa Encyclopedia for simple Hausa Language words. Thus, developing systems that can learn, adapt and attempt to perform autonomously will be a major area of competition between technology builders and Hausa-based language processing over next few years.

As for the feasible future recommendations, two major areas were highlighted in this study. Firstly, it has been observed that there is a very limited effort on the provision of Hausa oriented dataset, which make research activities difficult in Hausa language in spite the language potentials. Therefore it is recommended that attention should be given to the provision of publicly available data that will serve as enabling environment to various researchers. Secondly, the proposed system can be tremendously improved by deploying unsupervised machine learning approach. Currently this concept is widely employed by the different researchers as unsupervised techniques uses unannotated data in another word, it does not require data training. This could make the approach more suitable for data constraint languages like Hausa, thus reduce the cost of the language processing at all levels.

References

1. Dale, R.: The return of chatbots. Natural Lang. Eng. **22**(5), 811–817 (2016)
2. Weizenbaum, J.: Contextual understanding by computers. Commun. ACM **10**(8), 474–480 (1966)
3. Irwin, P.: What's the Turing Test and Which AI Passes It? (2019). https://www.knowmail.me/blog/whats-turing-test-ai-pass/. Accessed 20 Feb 2020
4. Maitama, J.Z., et al.: Text normalization algorithm for Facebook chats in Hausa language. In: 5th International Conference on Information and Communication Technology for the Muslim World, pp. 1–4. IEEE, Kuching (2014)
5. Smirnova, M.K.: The Hausa Language: A Descriptive Grammar. Routledge Kegan & Paul, London (1982)
6. Wallace, R.S.: The anatomy of A.L.I.C.E. In: Epstein, R., Roberts, G., Beber, G. (eds.) Parsing the Turing Test, pp. 181–210. Springer, Dordrecht (2009). https://doi.org/10.1007/978-1-4020-6710-5_13
7. Hoffer, R.: SmarterChild Bot (2001). https://www.chatbots.org/chatterbot/smarterchild/. Accessed 20 Dec 2020
8. Colby, A.K.: Artificial paranoia. Artif. Intell. **2**, 1–26 (1972)
9. Segura, C., Palau, À., Luque, J., Costa-Jussà, M.R., Banchs, R.E.: Chatbol, a Chatbot for the Spanish "La Liga." In: D'Haro, L.F., Banchs, R.E., Li, H. (eds.) 9th International Workshop on Spoken Dialogue System Technology. LNEE, vol. 579, pp. 319–330. Springer, Singapore (2019). https://doi.org/10.1007/978-981-13-9443-0_28
10. Vanjani, M., Aiken, M., Park, M.: Chatbots for multilingual conversations. J. Manage. Sci. Bus. Intell. **4**(1), 19–24 (2019)

11. Cerezo, J., Kubelka, J., Robbes, R., Bergel, A.: Building an expert recommender chatbot. In: 1st IEEE/ACM International Workshop on bots in Software Engineering (BotSE), pp. 59–63. IEEE, Montreal (2019)

12. Dole, A., Sansara, H., Harekar, R., Athalye, S.: Intelligent chat bot banking system. Int. J. Emerg. Trends Technol. Comput. Sci. (IJETTCS) **4**(5), 49–51 (2015)

13. Hoy, M.B.: Alexa, Siri, Cortana, and more: an introduction to voice assistants. Med. Ref. Serv. Q. **37**(1), 81–88 (2018)

14. Cheyer, A., Kittlaus, D., Gruber, T.: Adam Cheyer (2017). https://www.bigspeak.com 29 Oct 2020

15. Quora.: How was Siri Created? (2017). https://www.quora.com/How-was-Siri-created 27 Dec 2019

16. Bhat, H.R., Lone, T.A., Paul, Z.M.: Cortana-intelligent personal digital assistant: a review. Int. J. Adv. Res. Comput. Sci. **8**(7), 55–57 (2017)

17. du Preez, S.J., Lall, M., Sinha, S.: An inteligent web-based voice chat bot. In: 2009 IEEE EUROCON, pp. 386–391. IEEE, St. Petersburg (2009)

18. Dibitonto, M., Leszczynska, K., Tazzi, F., Medaglia, C.M.: Chatbot in a campus environment: design of LiSA, a virtual assistant to help students in their university life. In: Kurosu, M. (ed.) HCI 2018. LNCS, vol. 10903, pp. 103–116. Springer, Cham (2018). https://doi.org/10.1007/978-3-319-91250-9_9

19. Lopatovska, I., et al.: Talk to me: exploring user interactions with the Amazon Alexa. J. Librarianship Inf. Sci. **51**(4), 984–997 (2018)

20. Kennedy, D.: Literature Reviews (2019). https://www.rlf.org.uk/resources/what-is-a-literature-review/. Accessed 15 June 2020

21. Adewumi, A., et al.: A Unified framework for outfit design and advice. In: Sharma, N., Chakrabarti, A., Balas, V.E. (eds.) Data Management, Analytics and Innovation. AISC, vol. 1016, pp. 31–41. Springer, Singapore (2020). https://doi.org/10.1007/978-981-13-9364-8_3

22. Adewumi, A., Olatunde, G., Misra, S., Maskeli, R., Damaševi, R.: Developing a calorie counter fitness app for smartphones. In: Antipova, T., Rocha, Á. (eds.) Information Technology Science, pp. 23–33. Springer International Publishing, Cham (2018). https://doi.org/10.1007/978-3-319-74980-8_3

23. Oyesiku, D., Adewumi, A., Misra, S., Ahuja, R., Damasevicius, R., Maskeliunas, R.: An educational math game for high school students in Sub-Saharan Africa. In: Florez, H., Diaz, C., Chavarriaga, J. (eds.) Applied Informatics: First International Conference, ICAI 2018, Bogotá, Colombia, November 1-3, 2018, Proceedings, pp. 228–238. Springer International Publishing, Cham (2018). https://doi.org/10.1007/978-3-030-01535-0_17

An Empirical Study to Investigate Data Sampling Techniques for Improving Code-Smell Prediction Using Imbalanced Data

Himanshu Gupta[1(✉)], Sanjay Misra[2(✉)], Lov Kumar[1(✉)],
and N. L. Bhanu Murthy[1(✉)]

[1] BITS Pilani, Hyderabad Campus, Hyderabad, India
{f20150339,lovkumar,bhanu}@hyderabad.bits-pilani.ac.in
[2] Covenant University, Ota, Nigeria
sanjay.misra@covenantuniversity.edu.ng

Abstract. A code smell refers to a surface indication that usually indicates a deeper problem within a system. Usually it is associated with an easily traceable issue that often indicates a deeper inherent problem in the code. It has been observed that codes containing code smells are more susceptible to a higher probability of change during the software development process. Refactoring the code at an early stage during the development process saves a lot of time and prevents any kind of hassles at later stages. This paper aims at finding eight different types of code smells using feature engineering and sampling techniques with the purpose of handling imbalanced data. Three naive Bayes classifier are used to find code smells over 629 different packages. The results of this research indicate that the Gaussian Naive Bayes classifier performed the best out of all three classifiers in all samples of data. The results also indicate that the original data was the best data to use in which all three classifiers performed better than other two data sets.

Keywords: LSSVM Kernels Refactoring · Source code metrics · SMOTE

1 Introduction

A code smell indicates sub-par programming practices and problems present in the basic design and structure of the software [1,2]. A programmatic error within the software may not be reflected by a code smell. However, it can lead to problems during the maintenance or updating of the code for the purpose of adding functionalities in the future [3]. A code smell may not be an indicator of an programming error but can lead to problems during maintenance or updating of the code for further development. The method in which programmers search through thousands of lines of code and spend hundreds of hours combing through

© Springer Nature Switzerland AG 2021
S. Misra and B. Muhammad-Bello (Eds.): ICTA 2020, CCIS 1350, pp. 220–233, 2021.
https://doi.org/10.1007/978-3-030-69143-1_18

the code is highly inefficient. The efficiency of this process can be significantly improved by developing models based on the software's internal structure to predict code smell [4,5]. In our work, a set of source code metrics have been used as an input, which was extracted from source code of the software to help with the development of a model for predicting code smell present in software modules. The ability to investigate these problems at the time of development can lead to reduction of the time required for the purpose of testing as well as maintenance.

In this paper, we used three flavors of Naive Bayesian Classifiers: Boolean Naive Bayes, Multinomial Naive Bayes [6,7] and Gaussian Naive Bayes Algorithm. We applied these algorithms on the following code smells - Blob Class (BLOB), Complex Class (CC), Internal Getter/Setter (IGS), Leaking Inner Class (LIC), Long Method (LM), No Low Memory Resolver (NLMR), Member Ignoring Method (MIM), and Swiss Army Knife (SAK). However, as they make use of different metrics, which may not be statistically relevant for the task at hand, we conducted this study using the Wilcoxon sign rank test as well as Cross-Correlation Analysis to select the relevant metrics to predict code smells [8]. In this paper, we attempted to answer the following Research Questions:

- **RQ1: Discussing the efficiency of selected features as compared to the original features in detecting Code Smell.** Our aim was to distinguish between the related and the unrelated features using the Cross-Correlation Analysis and the Wilcoxon Rank test. Then we verified the statistical significance difference of each using techniques like the Statistical Significance Tests and Area Under the Curve (AUC) Analysis.
- **RQ2: Discussing Data Sampling Techniques' ability to detect Code Smell.** We have used three sample sets: the original dataset, Synthetic Minority Over-sampling (SMOTE), Adaptive Synthetic Sampling Method (ADASYN). Our purpose was to balance the considered imbalanced data. We then compared the performance of the three sampling techniques using Area Under the Curve Analysis and statistical significance tests.
- **RQ3: Discussing the ability of Classification Techniques to detect Code Smell.** We used three Naive Bayes Classifiers: Bernoulli Naive Bayes, Multinomial Naive Bayes and Gaussian Naive Bayes Classifiers. We obtained a comparison of the performance of these techniques with the help of statistical significance tests and Area Under the Curve Analysis.

2 Related Work

In his work, Van Emden et al. [1] discussed a method for creation of an application inspection tool that provides functionalities like automatic detection and code visualization. The feasibility of this approach is demonstrated by the development of a mock-up code smell browser, jCOSMO, that assisted in the detection and visualization of code smells in a JAVA code. Yamashita et al. [2] has discussed about the various factors that were considered significant for maintainability. The result is derived from the analysis of an industrial case study performed by the author. Khomh et al. [3] in his paper has elaborated on how code smells are linked to code changes. Author has conducted intensive research to determine whether or not classes with code smells are more susceptible to change in comparison to other classes and vice-versa. The conclusion is indicative of the fact that specific code smells have adverse effects on classes.

Coleman et al. [9] demonstrated how automated software maintainability analysis can improve software-related decision making. The analysis helped with the decisions related to controlling the software quality, targeting the sub components for the purpose of essential maintenance and others. Wang et al. [6] has demonstrated defect prediction by the use of the Naive Bayes method. The author analyzed the prediction models and their construction. Turhan et al. [10] has attempted to develop a technique that facilitate the use of software metrics for assistance in prediction of defects. According to the statistics, the methodology proposed yielded better results.

3   Research Methods

Our paper used the following fundamental analysis: Firstly, we created two more data sets apart from the original data set using sampling techniques. Then we captured the variables that count with the help of correlation analysis and then performed Normalization on the data on which we finally run the Naive Bayes Classifiers.

3.1   Experimental Dataset

In our research, the codebases of 629 open source projects present on GitHub were analyzed. The dataset comprised of a list of packages and the corresponding code smells. Table 1 consists of the Anti-Patterns observed over the repositories. In the table, it can be observed that code-smell typically lie in the range from 75.2% to 26.4%. Apart from this, it is also evident that the lowest code smell was found for the Swiss Army Knife metric, whereas the maximum was observed for the Long Method metric.

3.2   Software Metrics

There are four Primary Software Metric Categories which were captured in our study. These four categories gave us 22 metrics which were used to capture code smells. The broad description of the categories and 22 metrics' description is given below:

- **Dimensional Metrics.** These metrics are aimed towards providing a quantitative metric for understanding code sizes and making it flexible. It makes the code difficult to handle in the long run because the code eventually has more features [11]. The following Dimensional Metrics were identified and used in our study :

- **Number of Byte Code Instructions:** It counts the number of executable instructions.
- **Number of Classes:** It finds the number of classes within a package.
- **Number of Methods:** It finds the number of methods within a package.
- **Instructions per Method:** It gives the ration between total number of instructions and total number of methods.

– **Complexity Metrics.** These metrics help us gauge the complexity of applications as an increase in complexity makes it difficult to understand and thus, difficult to test and maintain due to a larger number of paths of execution [12]. The following Metrics were used and identified in our study:

- **Cyclomatic Complexity:** This metric finds the number of linearly independent paths contained in the control flow of a program.
- **Weighted Methods per Class:** This metric is the sum of the complexities of all class methods. It is found by multiplying Number of Paths to the Ratio of Number of Methods to Number of Classes.

– **Object Oriented Metrics.** These metrics are used to find the complexity and coupling between the software modules. The following Metrics are used and identified in our study:

- **Number of Children:** This metric refers to the number of immediate subclasses to a class in hierarchy. This leads to more code reuse, but also requires more rigorous testing for accounting greater number of methods.
- **Depth of the Inheritance Tree:** This metric refers to length of maximal path from node representing root of tree of class in inheritance tree. Deeper trees can be associated with greater design complexity.
- **Lack of Cohesion in Methods:** This metric indicates the level of cohesion between methods and the attributes in a class.
- **Coupling Between Objects:** It is a metric that gives count of number of classes that are coupled to a particular class, where coupling refers to method of class referring to method or attribute of another class.
- **Percent Public Instance Variables:** This metric is the ratio of variables introduced by a public modifier. A large number of public variables breaks the principle of encapsulation as changes in the variable value can be safely handled by methods as they mask the internal workings.
- **Access to Pubic Data:** This metric counts the number of access to public or protected attributes of each class.

– **Android Oriented Metrics.** These metrics help us find how Android specific dependencies and operations affect execution speed and User Experience. The following Metrics are used and identified in our study:

- **Bad Smell Method Calls:** It consists of methods which have not accounted for exceptions that will be raised in course of program execution.
- **WakeLocks with no Timeout:** Wakelocks keep the device in an active state, which stops the display from switching off.
- **Number of Location Listeners:** This is used to keep track of the user location. But repeated use can cause an increase in battery consumption.

• **Number of GPS Uses:** GPS uses give a more accurate picture of the user locations. However, this comes at a price as repeated use of GPS leads to increased battery consumption.

• **XML Parsers:** Event based parsers are preferred as they tend to save battery power over the other. In addition, we look at the size of the files, element count, depth and width of the tree hierarchy.

• **Network Timeouts.** This metric investigates the timeouts in the network connections, small timeouts tend to improve the respnsiveness of applications, but struggle when the network connection is bad.

• **Networking:** This finds number of network operations in a program. A large number of network dependencies can cause application to slow down as it has to wait to get all requisite data, before it can respond.

• **File I/O:** This finds number of disk operations in program whose large number can reduce the responsiveness of the program.

• **SQLite:** This metric finds the number of Database Invocations whose large number can also reduce the responsiveness of the program.

• **Bitmaps:** This metric finds the number of invocations of methods that render bit maps. Processing of large bitmaps can be computationally expensive and can cause Application Not Responding processes.

Table 1. Statistical measures on AUC: sets of metrics.

Code smell type	No smell number	No smell percentage	Smelly number	Smelly percent
BLOB	236	37.59%	393	62.48%
LM	156	24.80%	475	75.20%
SAK	463	73.60%	166	26.40%
CC	188	29.88%	441	70.12%
IGS	277	44.03%	352	55.97%
MIM	261	41.49%	368	58.51%
NLMR	158	25.11%	471	74.89%
LIC	227	36.08%	402	63.92%

3.3 Data Sampling Techniques to Handle Imbalanced Data

From the 22 Metrics described in Sect. 3.2, we captured the 8 code smells whose distribution is shown in Table 1. It can clearly seen from the table that this data is not uniformly spread across all the 629 projects. In order to make it uniform we used SMOTE and ADASYN sampling techniques. SMOTE over samples the minority class in each data set to make it equal to the majority class and uses uniform density distribution of the data points. ADASYN on the other hand uses predefined density distribution to create additional data points.

3.4   Feature Selection Techniques

Since not all of the 22 metrics were relevant to find the 8 code smells associated with the packages, we used Wilcoxon Sign Rank Test [13] and Cross-Correlation analysis [14] for finding the relevant ones. After finding the relevant features, we used cross-correlation analysis to find unrelated features. This premise is based on the fact that relevant variables to be strongly correlated to the output variable and unrelated to each other. The null hypothesis is the fact that the code metric is incapable of finding out a particular code smell. In this study, we have made use of a p-value of 0.05; that is, we could reject the hypothesis if the probability of the null hypothesis is below 0.05.

3.5   Classification Algorithms

In this paper, we used three variants of the Naive Bayes Algorithm.

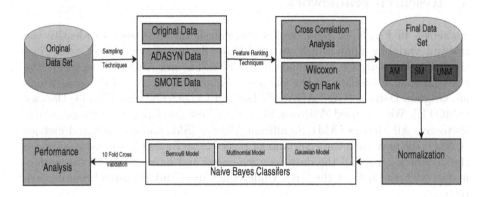

Fig. 1. Flowchart of the research framework

The first approach is to model them as independent boolean variables and make use of the Bernoulli Naive Bayes Algorithm [15]. If x_i is a boolean expressing the occurrence of the ith code smell metric, then the likelihood of a Code smell C_k is given by :

$$p(x|C_k) = \prod_{i=1}^{n} p_{ki}^{x_i}(1 - p_{ki})^{1-x_i}$$

where p_{ki} is the probability of class C_k generating the term x_i. It has the benefit of modelling the absence of terms.

The second approach is to make use of a multinomial event model [16], in which the feature vectors represent the frequencies with which the events have been generated by a multinomial distribution where p_i is the probability that the event i occurs. We make use of a feature vector $x = (x_1, x_2, ..., x_n)$ is a histogram, with x_i counting the number of times the event i was an observed instance. The event represents the occurrence of a code smell metric in a single file. The likelihood of observing a histogram x and it is given by the following expression:

$$p(x|C_k) = \frac{(\sum_i x_i)!}{\prod_i x_i!} \prod_i p_{ki}^{x_i}$$

The final approach is to make use of Gaussian Naive Bayes. It assumes that the continuous values associated with each class are distributed according to Gaussian distribution. Let μ_k be the mean values of a code smell metric x associated with the class C_k and let σ_k^2 be the variance of the values in x associated with class C_k. For an observation v, it can be described by the following distribution.

$$p(x = v|C_k) = \frac{1}{\sqrt{2\pi\sigma_k^2}} e^{-\frac{(v-\mu_k)*2}{2\sigma_k^2}}$$

4   Research Framework

As shown in Fig. 1, we have used statistical significance tests to identify the relevant variables upon which we used three flavors of the Naive Bayes Classifier. Furthermore, we have made use of SMOTE and ADASYN to tackle the class imbalance problem in the dataset to obtain three sets of datasets which are Original Dataset (OD), ADASYN Dataset (ADASYN) and SMOTE Dataset (SMOTE). We also used Wilcoxon Sign Rank Test and Cross-Correlation analysis to give All Metrics (AM), Significant Metrics (SM) and uncorrelated metrics (UNM). We have used three variants of three Naive Bayes Classifiers to compare the accuracy across all the data sets generated and have compared the performance with the help of the Area Under the Curve and Statistical Significance tests.

5   Experiment Results

The experimental results in terms of accuracy and AUC values are shown in Tables 2A and 2B for eight different types of code smells. From the information given in Tables 2A and 2B, it has been observed that the value of AUC parameters of the models trained using Gaussian naive Bayes classifiers (GNB) were higher than those in case of Bernoulli naive Bayes classifiers (BNB), and multinomial naive Bayes classifiers (MNB). The high value of these performance parameters showed the goodness of code smell developed prediction models. This information also suggested that the models provided good performance value in case of the metrics selected after uncorrelated analysis as an input. Finally, we have also observed that the performance was not changed after applying data imbalance techniques.

Table 2. Accuracy and AUC values for 3 sampled data sets

Table A: Accuracy Value

	OD								
	AM			**SM**			**UNM**		
	BNB	**MNB**	**GNB**	**BNB**	**MNB**	**GNB**	**BNB**	**MNB**	**GNB**
CS1	69.84	65.08	84.13	73.02	65.08	82.54	73.02	66.67	82.54
CS2	84.13	73.02	98.41	88.89	58.73	98.41	82.54	73.02	98.41
CS3	79.37	65.08	52.38	69.84	66.67	73.02	85.71	60.32	52.38
CS4	82.54	69.84	96.83	82.54	60.32	96.83	79.37	69.84	96.83
CS5	69.84	61.91	80.95	71.43	65.08	77.78	65.08	61.91	80.95
CS6	71.43	64.52	79.37	71.43	61.29	77.78	71.43	66.13	82.54
CS7	88.89	71.43	92.06	85.71	68.25	92.06	85.71	71.43	95.24
CS8	77.78	76.19	85.71	76.19	76.19	85.71	69.84	76.19	85.71
	SMOTE								
CS1	70.89	55.13	83.54	70.89	70.51	83.54	43.59	55.13	84.81
CS2	78.95	70.21	94.74	80.00	69.15	94.74	80.00	70.21	91.58
CS3	80.44	63.04	70.97	38.04	59.78	40.86	59.14	61.96	72.04
CS4	87.50	59.09	70.46	87.50	70.46	70.46	57.96	59.09	70.46
CS5	71.43	62.86	75.71	57.14	65.71	71.43	24.29	61.97	81.43
CS6	58.90	43.84	82.43	58.90	53.43	79.73	66.22	43.84	85.14
CS7	81.05	72.34	94.68	78.95	72.34	94.68	79.79	72.34	95.79
CS8	72.50	53.75	88.75	71.61	53.75	88.75	87.50	53.75	88.75
	ADASYN								
CS1	53.25	35.07	85.71	49.35	47.37	83.12	64.94	37.66	85.71
CS2	100.00	74.47	94.68	100.00	52.13	95.75	100.00	77.66	90.43
CS3	71.43	40.66	67.03	42.39	65.22	40.86	57.61	41.76	69.23
CS4	69.23	70.33	91.21	67.03	58.24	91.21	61.54	36.67	90.11
CS5	73.53	73.53	75.00	44.12	60.87	76.47	62.32	64.71	76.47
CS6	65.28	30.99	79.17	70.83	35.21	75.00	68.06	30.99	84.72
CS7	94.68	57.45	92.63	77.90	57.45	92.63	71.28	57.45	90.53
CS8	75.61	81.71	89.02	70.73	81.71	89.02	59.76	81.71	89.02

(*continued*)

Table 2. (*continued*)

Table B: AUC Values

	OD								
	AM			SM			UNM		
	BNB	MNB	GNB	BNB	MNB	GNB	BNB	MNB	GNB
CS1	0.67	0.66	0.82	0.70	0.66	0.81	0.61	0.67	0.82
CS2	0.87	0.76	0.94	0.88	0.65	0.94	0.54	0.76	0.94
CS3	0.64	0.66	0.72	0.59	0.64	0.64	0.55	0.66	0.72
CS4	0.76	0.72	0.90	0.76	0.64	0.90	0.54	0.72	0.90
CS5	0.68	0.62	0.81	0.72	0.65	0.78	0.64	0.63	0.81
CS6	0.70	0.67	0.76	0.70	0.64	0.78	0.64	0.69	0.79
CS7	0.93	0.75	0.93	0.91	0.70	0.93	0.55	0.75	0.95
CS8	0.77	0.77	0.84	0.78	0.77	0.84	0.53	0.77	0.84
	SMOTE								
CS1	0.73	0.77	0.80	0.73	0.85	0.80	0.57	0.77	0.80
CS2	0.85	0.85	0.94	0.86	0.84	0.94	0.74	0.85	0.92
CS3	0.90	0.81	0.74	0.69	0.80	0.59	0.67	0.81	0.74
CS4	0.94	0.79	0.85	0.94	0.85	0.85	0.68	0.79	0.85
CS5	0.72	0.63	0.77	0.78	0.66	0.73	0.62	0.63	0.83
CS6	0.79	0.72	0.79	0.79	0.76	0.77	0.66	0.72	0.81
CS7	0.84	0.86	0.92	0.83	0.86	0.92	0.78	0.86	0.93
CS8	0.73	0.77	0.85	0.71	0.77	0.85	0.94	0.77	0.85
	ADASYN								
CS1	0.75	0.67	0.82	0.73	0.73	0.80	0.58	0.68	0.81
CS2	1.00	0.78	0.94	1.00	0.76	0.95	1.00	0.78	0.92
CS3	0.86	0.70	0.70	0.71	0.82	0.59	0.65	0.71	0.72
CS4	0.77	0.72	0.83	0.75	0.66	0.83	0.67	0.68	0.83
CS5	0.74	0.68	0.74	0.70	0.62	0.76	0.62	0.64	0.78
CS6	0.69	0.65	0.77	0.71	0.67	0.75	0.65	0.65	0.81
CS7	0.97	0.79	0.93	0.82	0.79	0.93	0.86	0.79	0.92
CS8	0.76	0.77	0.83	0.72	0.77	0.83	0.64	0.77	0.83

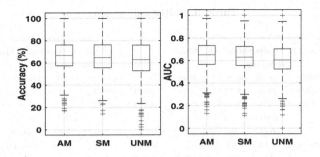

Fig. 2. Boxplots for AUC for different combinations of features

6   Comparison

RQ1: Discussing the Efficiency of Selected Features as Compared to the Original Features in Detecting Code Smell.
In this section, we attempted to analyze the performance of the features used within the model, obtained with the help of the significance test and cross-correlation analysis. The box plots give us an easy way to visualize the accuracy of the model on the dataset. The accuracy is further validated by the rank-sum test, which is used to show the statistical significance to the combination of features used to predict code smell. The results have been elaborated in the following section.

Comparison of Different Combinations of Features Using Descriptive Statistics and Box-Plot Diagram: From Fig. 2 and Table 3A, we observe both accuracy and AUC values for three different combinations of features, namely: All Metrics [AM], significant metrics obtained from the Ranksum Test [SM], and features obtained from the Cross-Correlation Analysis [CCF]. The upper and lower edges of the box plot refer to the first and the third quartile value. Also, the top and the bottom line refer to the maximum and minimum value, respectively. The red line refers to the average value of the data. In a nutshell, this diagram tells us about distribution for maximum, minimum, percentiles, and dispersion of data. From Fig. 2 and Table 3A, it is evident that the model which used all the features instead selected features, performs better than the other models.

Comparison of Different Combinations of Features Using Ranksum Test: The null hypothesis for the Ranksum test is the following: "The model developed with the help of selected features shows no improvement as compared to the model, which makes use of all features." The results of the Ranksum test have been tabulated in Table 4A. All values having a value smaller than 0.05% were considered to be statistically significant.

Table 3. Statistical measure

Table A: Different Feature Combination

	Max	Q3	Median	Mean	Q1	Min
Accuracy						
AM	100.00	76.19	66.84	66.26	57.34	16.90
SM	100.00	76.19	64.90	65.12	55.56	14.08
UNM	100.00	76.00	62.90	63.53	52.73	0.00
AUC						
AM	1.00	0.73	0.65	0.64	0.56	0.13
SM	1.00	0.72	0.63	0.63	0.55	0.11
UNM	1.00	0.70	0.61	0.61	0.52	0.00

Table B: Different Sampling Techniques

	Max	Q3	Median	Mean	Q1	Min
Accuracy						
OD	98.41	77.78	69.35	68.41	59.68	34.92
SMOTE	95.79	75.79	63.63	65.12	55.62	4.55
ADASYN	100	73.61	61.72	61.38	50	0
AUC						
OD	0.95	0.72	0.63	0.64	0.55	0.36
SMOTE	0.94	0.73	0.63	0.62	0.53	0.17
ADASYN	1	0.72	0.63	0.62	0.55	0

Table 4. Ranksum test

Table A: Different Feature Combination

	AM	SM	UNM
AM	1.000	0.046	0.000
SM	0.046	1.000	0.001
UNM	0.000	0.001	1.000

Table B: Different Sampling Techniques

	OD	SMOTE	ADASYN
OD	1.00	0.32	0.63
SMOTE	0.32	1.00	0.90
ADASYN	0.63	0.90	1.00

RQ2: Discussing Data Sampling Techniques' Ability to Detect Code Smell.

In this regard, we attempted to analyze the difference in performance for the datasets generated by the class imbalance techniques. As in the previous section, we used the same tools: box-plots denoting the Accuracy and the Area Under the Curve for the models under consideration. Also, we have made use of the Ranksum test to compare the performance of the data between the different sample sets.

Comparison of Different Samples using Descriptive Statistics and Box-Plot Diagram: From Fig. 3 and Table 3B, we compared the difference in performance between the original sample and the unbiased samples obtained from SMOTE and ADASYN, respectively. Like the previous section, the box represents the first and the third quartile, and the red line represents the mean.

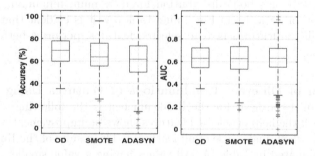

Fig. 3. Boxplots for AUC for different sampling techniques

We observed that the original dataset performed better than other generated datasets. However, we should take note of the fact that the decision boundary in the other two cases are likely to generalize better as the original dataset was biased towards the majority classes.

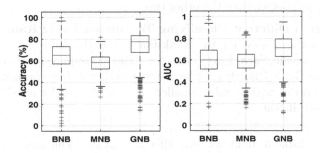

Fig. 4. Boxplots for AUC for different forms of naive bayes classifiers

Comparison of Different Sampling Techniques Using Ranksum Test:
The null hypothesis used for the Ranksum is the following: "The model trained on the balanced datasets show no improvement compared to the original." The result of the corresponding test has been tabulated in Table 4B. All entries with a value smaller than 0.05% can be considered to be statistically significant.

RQ3: Discuss the ability of Classification Techniques to Detect Code Smell.
In this section, we tried to compare the performance of the three Naive Bayes Classifiers: Bernoulli, Multinomial, and Gaussian Naive Bayes Classifier. We performed graphical analysis with the help of box-plots on Accuracy and Area Under Curve Metrics for each classifier. The Ranksum Test helps us get a grip on the level up to which it can improve predictions for the other classifier.

Comparison of Different Classifiers Using Descriptive Statistics and Box-Plot Diagram: From Fig. 4 and Table 5, we compared the performance

Table 5. Statistical measure: different forms of naive bayes classifiers

	Max	Q3	Median	Mean	Q1	Min
Accuracy						
BNB	100.00	73.02	65.08	64.33	57.14	0.00
MNB	81.71	63.49	58.38	57.86	52.38	26.67
GNB	98.41	83.16	77.66	72.73	67.63	14.08
AUC						
BNB	1.00	0.69	0.60	0.60	0.52	0.00
MNB	0.86	0.65	0.58	0.58	0.52	0.16
GNB	0.95	0.79	0.71	0.70	0.63	0.11

between the three classifiers. We graphically represented this with the help of box-plots to reflect the accuracy and the Area Under the Curve. The box in the figure refers to the first quartile and the third quartile of the dataset. The red line represents the average of the data, and the remaining two represent the maxima and the minima. In the figure, we observed that the Gaussian Naive Bayes performed better than the other two.

Comparison of Different Classifying Techniques Using Ranksum Test:
The null hypothesis used for the Ranksum test is the following: "The model trained on a specific Naive Bayes classifier shows no improvement compared to another Naive Bayes Classifier:" The results of this test have been tabulated in Table 6. All entries with a value smaller than 0.05% can be considered to be statistically significant.

Table 6. Ranksum test: different sampling techniques

	BNB	MNB	GNB
BNB	1.00	0.03	0.00
MNB	0.03	1.00	0.00
GNB	0.00	0.00	1.00

7 Conclusion

The primary goal of this paper was to determine the Code Smell present in a software project with the help of features that reflect the code smell and we answered the questions listed below:

- Selection of significant metrics from considered sets of metrics.
- Investigating the effects of sampling techniques such as SMOTE and ADASYN.
- Predict code smell with the help of three different Naive Bayes Classifiers.

The results of the work are as follows:

- The models developed using all metrics showed little better performance as compared to models developed using SM and UNM.
- The models developed using different sets of features were significantly different.
- The models developed using original data showed better performance as compared to models developed using sample data.
- The models developed using original data and sampled data were not significantly different.
- The models developed using Gaussian naive Bayes classifiers (GNB) showed little better performance as compared to models developed using Bernoulli naive Bayes classifiers (BNB), and multinomial naive Bayes classifiers (MNB)
- The models developed using different naive Bayes classifiers were significantly different.

References

1. van Emden, E., Moonen, L.: Java quality assurance by detecting code smells. In: Proceedings of Ninth Working Conference on Reverse Engineering, 2002, pp. 97–106 (2002)
2. Yamashita, A., Moonen, L.: Do code smells reflect important maintainability aspects? In 2012 28th IEEE International Conference on Software Maintenance (ICSM), pp. 306–315. IEEE (2012)
3. Khomh, F., Di Penta, M., Gueheneuc, Y.G.: An exploratory study of the impact of code smells on software change-proneness. In: 2009 16th Working Conference on Reverse Engineering, pp. 75–84. IEEE (2009)
4. Gupta, A., Suri, B., Kumar, V., Misra, S., Blažauskas, T., Damaševičius, R.: Software code smell prediction model using shannon, rényi and tsallis entropies. Entropy **20**(5), 372 (2018)
5. Gupta, A., Suri, B., Misra, S.: A systematic literature review: code bad smells in Java source code. In: Gervasi, O. (ed.) ICCSA 2017. LNCS, vol. 10408, pp. 665–682. Springer, Cham (2017). https://doi.org/10.1007/978-3-319-62404-4_49
6. Wang, T., Li, W.H.: Naive bayes software defect prediction model. In: 2010 International Conference on Computational Intelligence and Software Engineering, pp. 1–4. IEEE (2010)
7. Turhan, B., Bener, A.: Analysis of naive bayes' assumptions on software fault data: an empirical study. Data Knowl. Eng. **68**(2), 278–290 (2009)
8. Chaturvedi, K.K., Bedi, P., Misra, S., Singh, V.B.: An empirical validation of the complexity of code changes and bugs in predicting the release time of open source software. In: 2013 IEEE 16th International Conference on Computational Science and Engineering, pp. 1201–1206. IEEE (2013)
9. Coleman, D., Ash, D., Lowther, B., Oman, P.: Using metrics to evaluate software system maintainability. Computer **27**(8), 44–49 (1994)
10. Turhan, B., Bener, A.B.: Software defect prediction: Heuristics for weighted naïve bayes. In: ICSOFT (SE), pp. 244–249 (2007)
11. Abd-El-Hafiz, S.K.: A metrics-based data mining approach for software clone detection. In: 2012 IEEE 36th Annual Computer Software and Applications Conference, pp. 35–41. IEEE (2012)
12. Fenton, N.E., Neil, M.: Software metrics: roadmap. In: Proceedings of the Conference on the Future of Software Engineering, pp. 357–370 (2000)
13. Wilcoxon, F., Katti, S.K., Wilcox, R.A.: Critical values and probability levels for the Wilcoxon rank sum test and the Wilcoxon signed rank test. Selected tables in mathematical statistics 1, 171–259 (1970)
14. Podobnik, B., Stanley, H.E.: Detrended cross-correlation analysis: a new method for analyzing two nonstationary time series. Phys. Rev. Lett. **100**(8), 084102 (2008)
15. Singh, G., Kumar, B., Gaur, L., Tyagi, A.: Comparison between multinomial and bernoulli naïve bayes for text classification. In: 2019 International Conference on Automation, Computational and Technology Management (ICACTM), pp. 593–596. IEEE (2019)
16. Kibriya, A.M., Frank, E., Pfahringer, B., Holmes, G.: Multinomial Naive Bayes for text categorization revisited. In: Webb, G.I., Yu, X. (eds.) AI 2004. LNCS (LNAI), vol. 3339, pp. 488–499. Springer, Heidelberg (2004). https://doi.org/10.1007/978-3-540-30549-1_43

A Statistical Linguistic Terms Interrelationship Approach to Query Expansion Based on Terms Selection Value

Nuhu Yusuf[1,2], Mohd Amin Mohd Yunus[1(✉)], Norfaradilla Wahid[1],
and Mohd Najib Mohd Salleh[1]

[1] Faculty of Computer Science and Information Technology, Universiti Tun Hussein Onn Malaysia, Parit Raja, Malaysia
ynuhu@atbu.edu.ng, {aminy,faradila,najib}@uthm.edu.my
[2] Management and Information Technology Department, Abubakar Tafawa Balewa University, Bauchi, Nigeria

Abstract. Query expansion has changed the information retrieval process to improve search performance. It aimed at improving the performance of information retrieval system to retrieve user information need. However, the term selection process still lacks precision results due to lexical ambiguity challenge. Many researchers have focused on pseudo-relevance feedback to select terms from the top-retrieved documents using some statistical linguistic techniques. However, their methods have limitations. This paper proposed a statistical linguistic terms interrelationship that exploits term selection in query expansion and retrieved relevance results. The proposed approach was tested on Malay, Hausa and Urdu Quran translated datasets and the results indicate that the proposed approach outperforms the previous method in retrieving relevance results. Future work should focus on the weighting score based on terms interrelationship to improve the query expansion performance.

Keywords: Term selection · Term selection value · Query expansion · Terms interrelationship · Pseudo-relevance feedbacks · Statistical linguistic techniques

1 Introduction

With the advances in query expansion research, term selection value is now possible to expand query and improve retrieval performance. This provides a new way for query expansion to select expansion terms based on term frequency with a ranking score [1]. Query expansion adds additional terms to query for better search results [2].

Query expansion is important to information retrieval systems in retrieving relevant user information needs. Different query expansion techniques are now available. Previous works emphasized the importance of using query log [3], syllable [4], stemming [5, 6] and Wikipedia [7] in selecting terms for query expansion. Recently, the relevant feedbacks have been given much attention to retrieving relevant results from query expansion [8]. However, all these mentioned techniques found it difficult to select

S. Misra and B. Muhammad-Bello (Eds.): ICTA 2020, CCIS 1350, pp. 234–244, 2021.
https://doi.org/10.1007/978-3-030-69143-1_19

terms for query expansion [9]. To address this challenge, recent studies proposed the use of pseudo-relevant feedback technique to select terms from top-retrieved documents [10–12]. Though, the term frequency and ranked documents provide better query expansion results, there is still room for improvement. This study aims to enhance the query expansion based on terms interrelationship in term selection value taking into account the shortcomings of previous studies.

Synonyms of terms in a query are usually influenced by the relationship. This is because a query term in one WordNet may be different from another WordNet but contain the same meaning. For example, a WordNet 1 may contain no synonym of a particular query term but WordNet 2 contains the synonym of that terms. Thus, when expanding a query, it is necessary to consider the relationship of terms that are closely related with other terms from more than one semantic dictionaries or WordNet. Yusuf et al. [13] proposed terms interrelationship approach where three WordNet are used as a semantic dictionary to obtained synonyms in term selection value. However, this study doesn't consider word context for term selection in query expansion. This motivated the present study to define a new statistical linguistic query expansion and named it statistical linguistic terms interrelationship term selection value (slTI-TSV) that aims to expand the query by selecting terms based on term context within the top-ranked documents with multiple synonyms.

Considering this challenge, this study proposed slTI-TSV, a terms interrelationship query expansion approach. This approach considers the terms interrelationship in selecting query expansion terms based on statistic linguistic technique. The contribution of this paper is to study the terms interrelationship in query expansion problem and develop a new approach to solve this problem. The new approach is named slTI-TSV.

The rest of this paper is organized as follows: Sect. 2 reviews of related works. Section 3 presents the proposed approach. The experiments are presented in Sect. 4. Finally, Sect. 5 presents the conclusion.

2   Review of Related Work

Term selection in query expansion is used to choose additional terms for expanding the query to improve the performance of information retrieval systems. Majority of the previous studies do not consider the set of candidate terms for expansion but rather directly expand each query term with synonyms [14–16]. Subsequently, Gupta and Saini [12] examine how term selection challenge to query expansion can be addressed using pseudo-relevant feedbacks technique. Saleh and Pecina [16] introduced term selection methods to predict retrieval performance for candidate terms. Nasir et al. [17] introduced the new query expansion technique that integrates knowledge-based and relevant feedback to select terms for query expansion. Esposito et al. [18] discussed how the efficient term selection query expansion can present higher performance results utilizing lexical resources and word embedding. When comparing these mentioned studies with the proposed slTI-TSV, it was found that the proposed slTI-TSV has the capability of expanding query with more synonyms for selecting terms.

Relationship of query term is important in selecting query expansion terms. Majority of previous studies use synonyms relations of terms. Subsequent studies used synonyms and hypernym [7, 19]. However, all these studies found it difficult to capture the relationship of abstract words, specifically for synonyms. Recently, word2vec based on pseudo-relevance feedbacks have been proposed in Khennak and Drias [10], El Mahdaouy et al. [19] and Almarwani et al. [20]. Khennak and Drias [10] examine query expansion utilizing particle swarm optimization based on pseudo-relevance feedback. For instance, Yusuf et al. [13, 21–23] select the synonyms of query terms based on pseudo-relevance feedback. In Yusuf et al. [13], the paper adopts the TSV [1] approach by introducing a new set of synonyms variable $ti_j \in Synsets$ for terms interrelationship. This idea combined with TSV and lead to the Eq. (1):

$$TSV_t = \left(\frac{f_t}{N}\right)^{r_t} \left(\frac{R}{r_t}\right) \sum\nolimits_{j \in (synsets \cap q)} ti_j \qquad (1)$$

Where R is the number of top-ranked document examine, r_t represent the number of documents that contain term t and N is the total number of documents. The frequency of term t is represented as f_t while ti_j represents the terms interrelationship of term j. The q represent the query terms as $q = \{t_i, \ldots, t_m\}$ and $synsets$ represent the set of synonyms from different semantic dictionaries as $synset = \{t_1, t_2, \ldots, t_s\}$. The use of terms interrelationship has improved term selection over TSV. This paper doesn't take into account the context of the query terms as appear in a sentence. Therefore, there is a need to consider the context of query terms to provide more relevant search results.

The statistical linguistic technique (SLT) proposed by the Kadir et al. [24] involves examining likelihood estimation towards the identification of concept and detecting relevant predicate as in Eq. (2):

$$P(W_n/W_{n-1}) = \frac{C(W_{n-1}, W_n)}{C(W_{n-1})} \qquad (2)$$

Where W_n and W_{n-1} represent word n and its previous word respectively. However, there is a limitation in expanding the query terms with synonyms from WordNet and doesn't capture the proper context of terms. Their algorithm is limited to only one WordNet as a source of the semantic dictionary to obtain query term synonyms. Their approach does not support terms interrelationship for pseudo-relevance feedback or top-retrieved documents from multiple semantic dictionaries. For instance, in some semantic dictionaries, a single or group of words contained many definitions.

3 Methodology

The proposed approach consists of several components and these components are illustrated in Fig. 1. Firstly, the user issues input statements and then translate these statements to form query. The proposed approached was evaluated using three Quran translation datasets each from Malay, Hausa and Urdu languages. These datasets were collected from Tazil [25]. Two WordNets from three different languages have been used for this study making a total of fifteen. Wordnet Bahasa [26] from Open Multilingual Word-Net in Indonesia and standard Malay is used for the Malay Language and Malay word synonyms from Cambridge dictionary [27]. For Urdu WordNet, the Urdu wordnet 1.0

[28], Urdu word synonyms from Ijunoon [29] and Urdu All-words WSD (UAW-WSD-18-Corpus) [31] is used for the Urdu language. Lastly, Kamus [31], and Hausa word synonyms from English Hausa dictionary [29] and Hausa dictionary [31] which was translated based on Princeton Wordnet are also used for the Hausa Language.

A total of seventy queries translated from the English language to other languages were used to test the performance of the proposed approach and was evaluated using average precision, average recall, MRR, nDCG, f-measure and MAP.

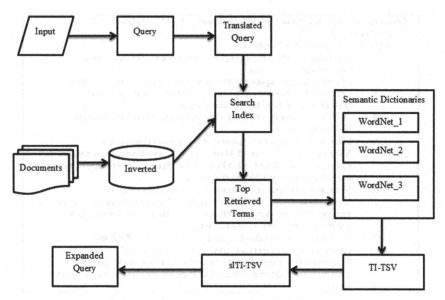

Fig. 1. A proposed slTI-TSV.

3.1 Proposed Approach

Statistical linguistic TI-TSV (slTI-TSV) adapts the TI-TSV algorithm presented in Yusuf et al. [13] based on Chandra and Dwivedi [1] to address lexical ambiguity. Here, the paper introduced additional new variable D, w_t based on the Kadir et al. [24] that enrich the term t and better capture relationship of the query term. Specifically, the paper computes the term context based on the previous terms and lead to the Eq. (3):

$$TSV_t = \left(\frac{f_t}{N}\right)^{r_t} \binom{R}{r_t} P(w_t/w_{t-1}) \sum_{j \in (synsets \cap q)} ti_j \tag{3}$$

Where:

$$P(w_n/w_{n-1}) = \frac{C(D, w_{n-1}w_n)}{C(D, w_{n-1})}$$

$$C(D, w_n) = \left\{ a/a, \left(w_n \in \sum_{j \in (synsets \cap q)} ti_j \right) \wedge a \neq w_n \wedge D \in R \wedge a \in D \right\}$$

w_t is the word t and w_{t-1} is the previous word before word t. R is the number of top-ranked document examine, r_t represent the number of documents that contain term t and N is the total number of documents. The frequency of term t is represented as f_t while ti_j represents the terms interrelationship of term j. The q represent the query terms as $q = \{t_i, \ldots, t_m\}$ and *synsets* represent the set of synonyms from different semantic dictionaries as $synset = \{t_1, t_2, \ldots, t_s\}$. The use of term context improves the TI-TSV of term selection. Figure 2 present the proposed slTI-TSV algorithm.

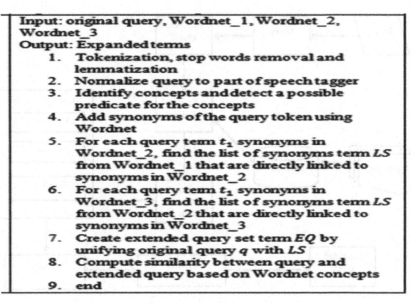

Input: original query, Wordnet_1, Wordnet_2, Wordnet_3
Output: Expanded terms
1. Tokenization, stop words removal and lemmatization
2. Normalize query to part of speech tagger
3. Identify concepts and detect a possible predicate for the concepts
4. Add synonyms of the query token using Wordnet
5. For each query term t_1 synonyms in Wordnet_2, find the list of synonyms term *LS* from Wordnet_1 that are directly linked to synonyms in Wordnet_2
6. For each query term t_1 synonyms in Wordnet_3, find the list of synonyms term *LS* from Wordnet_2 that are directly linked to synonyms in Wordnet_3
7. Create extended query set term *EQ* by unifying original query q with *LS*
8. Compute similarity between query and extended query based on Wordnet concepts
9. end

Fig. 2. A proposed slTI-TSV Algorithm.

4 Experiments Results and Discussion

This section summarizes the experimental results and provides detail discussion on the performance of both the SLT and proposed slTI-TSV.

4.1 Experiments Results

Figure 3 shows the performance of both the SLT and proposed slTI-TSV on Malay dataset. In the Fig. 3, the proposed slTI-TSV achieved better performance on average precision while the SLT obtained highest results on average recall.

As seen from Fig. 4, the proposed slTI-TSV achieved better performance in MAP, f-measure and MRR on Malay dataset while performed inferior compared to SLT in nDCG.

Figure 5 shows the performance of both the SLT and proposed slTI-TSV on Hausa dataset. In the Fig. 5, the proposed slTI-TSV achieved better performance on both average precision and average recall.

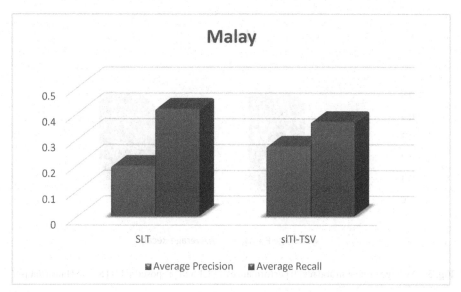

Fig. 3. Average precision and recall performance of SLT and proposed slTI-TSV on Malay dataset.

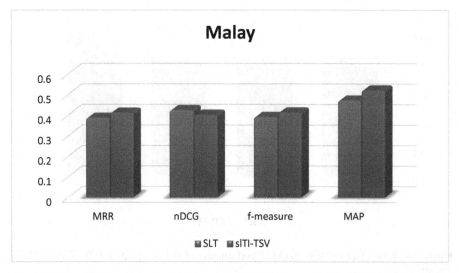

Fig. 4. MRR, nDCG, and recall performance of SLT and proposed slTI-TSV on Malay dataset.

As it is shown by Fig. 6, the MAP, f-measure and MRR for proposed slTI-TSV achieved better performance compared to SLT which obtained highest results in nDCG.

Figure 7 shows the performance of both the SLT and proposed slTI-TSV on Urdu dataset. In the Fig. 7, the proposed slTI-TSV achieved better performance on average precision while the SLT and proposed slTI-TSV obtained similar results on average recall.

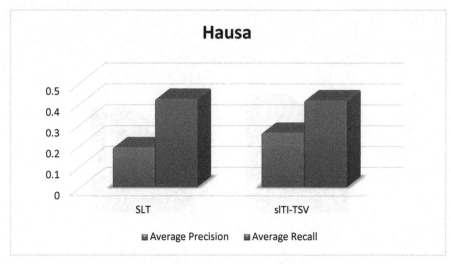

Fig. 5. Average precision and recall performance of SLT and proposed slTI-TSV on Hausa dataset.

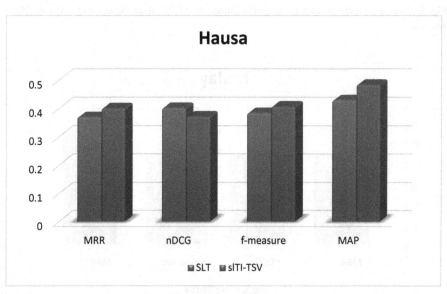

Fig. 6. MRR, nDCG, f-measure and MAP performance of SLT and proposed slTI-TSV on Hausa dataset.

In Fig. 8, it can be seen that proposed slTI-TSV approach present very good compared to the SLT method on Urdu dataset. However, the SLT achieved best results in nDCG.

4.2 Discussion

This paper studies the term selection problem by proposing a statistical linguistic terms interrelationship query expansion to address lexical ambiguity. The proposed slTI-TSV

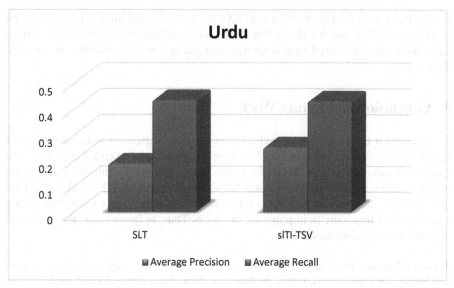

Fig. 7. Average precision and recall performance of SLT and proposed slTI-TSV on Urdu dataset.

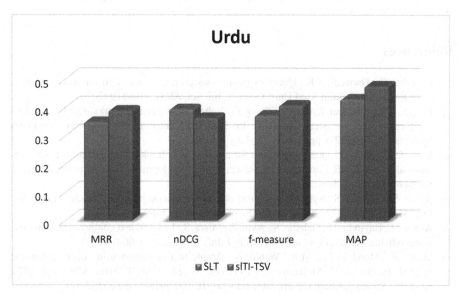

Fig. 8. MRR, nDCG, f-measure and MAP performance of SLT and proposed slTI-TSV on Urdu dataset.

uses synonyms from different semantic dictionaries to expand the query. The slTI-TSV employs the use of word context, where the n-gram probability of word from the top-ranked document and that of the previous word. The proposed slTI-TSV performed better compared to SLT method in average precision, MAP, MRR and f-measure. This indicates that the proposed slTI-TSV can effectively expand query and retrieve relevant results. In terms of average recall and nDCG, the SLT obtained highest results than the proposed slTI-TSV which indicate that more results can be retrieved based on selecting terms within the top-ranked documents with multiple synonyms from different semantic dictionaries.

5   Conclusion and Future Work

Term selection is one of the most challenges in query expansion to retrieve relevant search results. Since term selection based on top-ranked documents often show low precision results. To address this problem, the papers propose a terms interrelationship based context with term selection value (TSV) which named slTI-TSV. The slTI-TSV improves precision values. There is a limitation of this paper experiments that do not consider weighting score to improve the precision. Thus, in future work, the paper will improve the weighting score.

Acknowledgment. The authors would like to thank the Center for Graduate Studies Universiti Tun Hussein Onn Malaysia (UTHM), the Research Management Centre UTHM, the Faculty of Computer Science & Information Technology UTHM and indeed the faculty of Management Science, Abubakar Tafawa Balewa University Bauchi for their support during this research paper.

References

1. Chandra, G., Dwivedi, S.K.: Query expansion based on term selection for Hindi - English cross lingual IR. J. King Saud Univ. Comput. Inf. Sci. **32**(3), 310–319 (2020)
2. Liu, Q., Huang, H., Lut, J., Gao, Y., Zhang, G.: Enhanced word embedding similarity measures using fuzzy rules for query expansion. In: 2017 IEEE International Conference on Fuzzy Systems (FUZZ-IEEE), pp. 1–6. IEEE, Italy (2017)
3. Kuzi, S., Carmel, D.: Query expansion for email search. In: 40th Proceedings of the International ACM SIGIR Conference on Research and Development in Information Retrieval, pp. 849–852. ACM, Japan (2017)
4. Adubi, S.A., Misra, S.: Syllable-based text compression: a language case study. Arab. J. Sci. Eng. **41**(8), 3089–3097 (2016). https://doi.org/10.1007/s13369-016-2070-1
5. Akman, I., Bayindir, H., Ozleme, S., Akin, Z., Misra, S.: Lossless text compression technique using syllable based morphology. Int. Arab J. Inf. Technol. **8**(1), 66–74 (2011)
6. Yusuf, N., Mohd Yunus, M.A., Wahid, N.: Arabic text stemming using query expansion method. In: Saeed, F., Mohammed, F., Gazem, N. (eds.) IRICT 2019. AISC, vol. 1073, pp. 3–11. Springer, Cham (2020). https://doi.org/10.1007/978-3-030-33582-3_1
7. Azad, H.K., Deepak, A.: A new approach for query expansion using Wikipedia and WordNet. Inf. Sci. **492**, 147–163 (2019). https://doi.org/10.1016/j.ins.2019.04.019
8. Sankhavara, J.: Feature weighting in finding feedback documents for query expansion in biomedical document retrieval. SN Comput. Sci. **1**(2), 1–7 (2020). https://doi.org/10.1007/s42979-020-0069-x
9. Singh, J., Sharan, A.: A new fuzzy logic-based query expansion model for efficient information retrieval using relevance feedback approach. Neural Comput. Appl. **28**(9), 2557–2580 (2016). https://doi.org/10.1007/s00521-016-2207-x

10. Khennak, I., Drias, H.: An accelerated PSO for query expansion in web information retrieval: application to medical dataset. Appl. Intell. **47**(3), 793–808 (2017). https://doi.org/10.1007/s10489-017-0924-1

11. Gupta, Y., Saini, A.: A novel fuzzy-PSO term weighting automatic query expansion approach using combined semantic filtering. Knowl. Based Syst. **136**(15), 97–120 (2017)

12. Gupta, Y., Saini, A.: A novel term selection based automatic query expansion approach using PRF and semantic filtering. Int. J. Adv. Comput. Res. **8**, 130–137 (2019)

13. Yusuf, N., Mohd Yunus, M.A., Wahid, N., Mustapha, A., Mohd Najib, M.S.: A terms interrelationship approach to query expansion based on terms selection value. In: 5th International Conference of Reliable Information and Communication Technology, Springer (2020)

14. Abbache, A., Meziane, F., Belalem, G., Belkredim, F.Z.: Arabic query expansion using wordnet and association rules. Inf. Retr. Manag. Concepts, Methodol. Tools, Appl. **3**, 1239–1254 (2018)

15. Yusuf, N., Mohd Yunus, M.A., Wahid, N.: Query expansion based on explicit-relevant feedback and synonyms for english quran translation information retrieval. Int. J. Adv. Comput. Sci. Appl. **10**(5), 227–234 (2019)

16. Saleh, S., Pecina, P.: Term selection for query expansion in medical cross-lingual information retrieval. In: Azzopardi, L., Stein, B., Fuhr, N., Mayr, P., Hauff, C., Hiemstra, D. (eds.) ECIR 2019. LNCS, vol. 11437, pp. 507–522. Springer, Cham (2019). https://doi.org/10.1007/978-3-030-15712-8_33

17. Abdul, J., Varlamis, I.: A knowledge-based semantic framework for query expansion. Inf. Process. Manag. **56**(5), 1605–1617 (2019)

18. Esposito, M., Damiano, E., Minutolo, A., De Pietro, G., Fujita, H.: Hybrid query expansion using lexical resources and word embeddings for sentence retrieval in question answering. Inf. Sci. (Ny) **514**, 88–105 (2020)

19. El Mahdaouy, A., El Alaoui, A.S.O., Gaussier, E.: Word-embedding-based pseudo-relevance feedback for Arabic information retrieval. J. Inf. Sci. **45**(4), 429–442 (2019)

20. ALMarwi, H., Ghurab, M., Al-Baltah, I.: A hybrid semantic query expansion approach for Arabic information retrieval. J. Big Data. **7**(1), 1–19 (2020). https://doi.org/10.1186/s40537-020-00310-z

21. Yusuf, N., Mohd Yunus, M.A., Wahid, N., Nawi, N.M., Samsudin, N.A., Arbaiy, N.: Query expansion method for quran search using semantic search and lucene ranking. J. Eng. Sci. Technol. **15**(1), 675–692 (2020)

22. Yusuf, N., Mohd Yunus, M.A., Wahid, N., Nawi, N.M., Samsudin, N.A.: Enhancing query expansion method using word embedding. In: 9th International Conference System Engineering Technololgy ICSET 2019 - Proceeding, pp. 232–235. IEEE (2019)

23. Yusuf, N., Mohd Yunus, M.A., Wahid, N., Mustapha, A., Nawi, N.M., Samsudin, N.A.: Arabic text semantic-based query expansion. Int. J. Data Mining Model. Manag. (2020, in press)

24. Kadir, R.A., Yauri, R.A., Azman, A.: Semantic ambiguous query formulation using statistical Linguistics technique. Malaysian J. Comput. Sci. **31**(5), 48–56 (2018)

25. Hamid, Z.Z.: Quran Translations. Tanzil Documents. https://tanzil.net/trans/. Accessed 29 July 2019

26. Noor, N.H.M., Sapuan, S., Bond, F.: Creating the open wordnet Bahasa. In: 25th Pacific Asia Conference on Language, Information and Computation, pp. 255–264 (2011)

27. Dictionary, C.: Cambridge dictionary. Cambridge University Press. https://dictionary.cambridge.org/dictionary/english-malaysian/. Accessed 24 Dec 2018

28. CLE.: Urdu Wordnet 1.0. www.cle.org.pk/software/ling-resources/UrduWordNetWordlist.html. Accessed 03 Apr 2020

29. Ijunoon, English to Urdu Text Translation, Ijunoon. https://www.ijunoon.com/urdudic/. Accessed 24 Dec 2018

30. Saeed, A., Nawab, R.M.A, Stevenson, M., Rayson, P.: A sense annotated corpus for all-words Urdu word sense disambiguation. ACM Trans. Asian Low-Resource Lang. Inf. Process. **18**(4), 1–9 (2019)
31. Shamsuddeen, K. https://kamus.com.ng/index.php. Accessed 30 Apr 2020

Validation of Student Psychological Player Types for Game-Based Learning in University Math Lectures

Tatjana Sidekerskienė[1]($\boxtimes$), Robertas Damaševičius[2], and Rytis Maskeliūnas[3]

[1] Department of Applied Mathematics, Kaunas University of Technology, Kaunas, Lithuania
`tatjana.sidekerskiene@ktu.lt`
[2] Faculty of Applied Mathematics, Silesian University of Technology, Gliwice, Poland
[3] Department of Applied Informatics, Vytautas Magnus University, Kaunas, Lithuania

Abstract. Game-based learning can make educational activities more manageable and planned, and therefore contribute to the achievement of a more productive educational result. To enable adaptive and personalized learning process, the knowledge of learning game player psychological types is required. Player type can be established using a questionnaire such as HEXAD. We present the analysis of the student survey results using statistical analysis, correlation analysis, Principal Component Analysis (PCA) and Exploratory Factor Analysis (EFA). The simplification of the questionnaire is suggested. We shortened the 30-item HEXAD survey to a 12-item survey (named sHEXAD) using a factor analysis on responses from university course students. Testing demonstrated that the items of the sHEXAD survey correlated and well agreed with the original HEXAD survey items and could be used to derive the same outcomes.

Keywords: Game-based learning · Gamification · Player psychology · HEXAD questionnaire

1 Introduction

The emergence of a generation of "digital natives" [1] (as the children who grew up in the Internet era began to be called), which stimulated, among other factors, "the transition to an educational paradigm for post-industrial society and a novel type of education (technological or project-based technological) [2], makes you take a fresh look at the role of games, including computer, in educational activities. We believe that the phenomenon of human activity, called gamification [3], can make educational activities more manageable and planned, and therefore contribute to the achievement of a more productive educational result.

The scope of gamification can be any complex and rather routine activity (such as business project management [4]), non-game context, that is causing the user, student, individual to be depressed and reduce motivation. Gamification is designed to make the necessary routine fascinating, whether it is the study of a large amount of information, but at the same time leaving the person in his reality, by himself, allowing him to

© Springer Nature Switzerland AG 2021
S. Misra and B. Muhammad-Bello (Eds.): ICTA 2020, CCIS 1350, pp. 245–258, 2021.
https://doi.org/10.1007/978-3-030-69143-1_20

improve the skills necessary for this particular subject. The game and game technologies in pedagogical practice are the creation of certain conditions for achieving goals, the modeling of a special game reality with its own internal laws [5].

Certain qualities of educational games can help increase student interest [6]: a challenge that encourages children to explore a specific topic and bring knowledge and skill to perfection, because only in this case can one go to the next level. Achieving affective involvement, full immersion in the process, which can make you forget about time, can help to improve the outcomes of training.

In this case, we are talking about the state of the psychological flow [7], when there is a relative balance between the task that needs to be solved - the challenge, and the abilities of the player. If the difficulty of the task exceeds the ability of the player, this leads to anxiety and may cause rejection, if the goal is easily achievable, boredom occurs. The state between boredom and anxiety, supporting the development of productivity, requiring the formulation of tasks that correspond to existing skills, is the state of flow, when a person is maximally immersed in his occupation [8]. For students (especially, elementary courses), the fear of the complexity of the discipline blocks the ability to perceive information, minimizing them. It is necessary to create an environment that will allow students to relieve emotional stress and show their abilities to the maximum. Gaming technology can solve this problem, which was demonstrated by several serious games applied for preschool children [9], high school student [10] and adult vocational education [11].

The performance of personalization has been shown in the context of persuasive technology [12], learning content design [13] and also in gamification [14]. As a result, we believe that gamified systems are better performing when personally customized to fit personality and needs of each user.

The goal and expected result of gamification becomes a change in the usual behavior of the audience, involvement in activities. At the same time, the content of the selected activity remains the same, but is structured in a certain way, thereby increasing motivation [15]. The gameplay involves interaction with other participants in the game. Any human-human interaction can be defined as communication. This is especially true in case of teacher-learner communication [16]. Often, in the game, communication is a means of achieving gaming goals. That is, the success of communication largely determines the gain/ loss, which motivates participants to improve their communication skills. However, the player reaction to game mechanics and reward system greatly depends on the player psychological types [17] and personality [18].

A number of survey questionnaires were developed to address the problem of establishing player typology. For example, BrainHex player typology [19], which provides a model based on 7 different types of players: 'Achievers' are very goal-oriented and well motivated by achieving long-term aims. 'Conquerors' enjoy and overcome difficult challenges. 'Daredevils' like taking risks. 'Masterminds' are entertained by solving puzzles. Seekers like exploring and discovering new ideas. 'Socialisers' enjoy communicating with others. 'Survivors' cherish and strive for new experiences. Player Experience of Need Satisfaction Scale (PENS) is a proprietary questionnaire investigating the 'motivational pull' of digital games [20]. It is based on self-determination theory and focuses on the three basic human needs: autonomy (volitional aspects of an activity), competence (experience of control and mastery), and relatedness (connection to others). Immersive Experience Questionnaire (IEQ) [21] and measures the player-related factors cognitive and emotional involvement, and dissociation from real-world, as well as the game-related factors challenge and control. Player Experience Inventory (PXI) aims to measure the player experience broadly. The PXI measures functional consequences (dynamics) and psychosocial consequences (aesthetics) with various subscales as well as overall enjoyment from playing the game [22]. Game Experience Questionnaire (GEQ) measures player experience during playing of digital games [23].

Although several models of player type models were proposed and are currently used for developing new games and gamified systems, the research on their validity is often missing [24]. The aim of this paper is to explore the results of student survey using the 30-item HEXAD [25, 26] questionnaire using statistical analysis, correlation analysis, Principal Component Analysis (PCA) and Exploratory Factor Analysis (EFA). The main novelty and the results of our study is a shortened 12-item HEXAD questionnaire, called sHEXAD, which is well correlated with the original HEXAD questionnaire and could potentially be used to derive the same outcomes.

The structure of the remaining parts of the paper is as follows. Section 2 describes the methods used. Section 3 presents and analyses the results of the student survey. Finally, the conclusions presented in Sect. 4.

2 Methodology

2.1 Outline

We apply the concepts of game-based learning [27] during the university course of applied mathematics. The process is based on four main elements: 1) learning context, i.e., the content of the course and pedagogical aims focus on transfer of knowledge from a teacher to students; 2) adaptive learning, i.e., the use of computer algorithms to orchestrate the interaction with the learner. In our case we use the educational quiz game as a tool to engage students and motivate for learning. As the student behavior with regards to the game and reward mechanisms differ, we study the third element, i.e. 3) psychology types, which can be refined using the HEXAD questionnaire. The answers to the HEXAD questionnaire are analyzed using correlation analysis, PCA and Factor Analysis. Once the psychological type of a student as a player is established, the fourth element, 4) game mechanics can be adjusted to best fit the serious pedagogical aims in order to improve knowledge transfer and maximize learning outcomes. The outline of our methodology is summarized in Fig. 1.

2.2 Game-Based Learning

In our lectures after theoretical lecture material is presented, the quiz-type game is arranged using the Mentimeter platform. Below, the game process is described. The students join to the www.menti.com system and enter their game names. The students are asked to answer 6 quiz questions as fast as possible. The students see the question and provides answers using their smartphone (see Fig. 2). The questions are not so difficult from the topic of lecture, they just focus on the retention of essential facts.

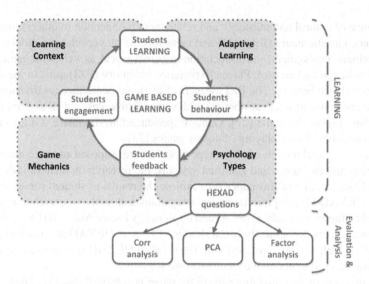

Fig. 1. Summary of methodology

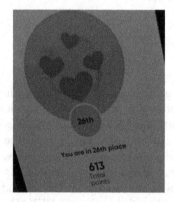

Fig. 2. Students play the game during in-class lectures and game results are presented in their smartphones

For each question, the time limit is set, for example, 30 s. The sooner a student answers, the more the points he/she will get. If a student does not answer correctly, he receives zero points for the corresponding question. After the time has expired or all students have answered, the results are shown on the screen (see Fig. 3). The leaderboard shows ten leading students. After all questions have been answered, the final results are presented and the winners are acknowledged by presenting a leaderboard for supporting student motivation for competition.

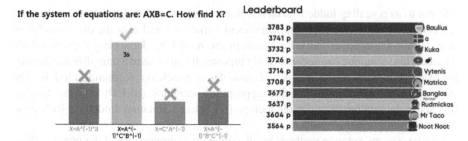

Fig. 3. Example of quiz game results. Feedback loop provides a teacher with crucial knowledge for adaptation of learning content and process.

2.3 HEXAD Questionnaire and the Psychological Player Types

The HEXAD player type questioner allows to retrieve player motivations in user interactions with games using a self-report questionnaire [25, 26]. Below, we describe the game player typology introduced by HEXAD: Philanthropists are driven by purpose and do not expect a reward. Socializers like to reach out and built new social links. Achievers seek to progress by completing tasks and solving hard challenges. Free Spirits are inspired by self-autonomy, meaning freedom to assert themselves and perform without outside control. They like to create and explore. Players are galvanized by external remunerations. They will perform to get a reward, regardless of the type of the activity. Disruptors are incited by change. They like to disrupt the system to cause some changes. They enjoy to explore the system boundaries and try to step beyond them.

2.4 Correlation Analysis

Correlation analysis is a test about relationships between dependent variables, which is a quantitative measure of the relationship (joint variability) of two variables. Thus, this is a set of methods for detecting the correlation dependence between random variables or features. Correlation analysis for two random variables includes: building a correlation field and compiling a correlation table; calculation of sample correlation coefficients and correlation ratios; testing the statistical hypothesis of the significance of the relationship.

2.5 PCA Analysis

Principal Component Analysis (PCA) is the simplest linear method of dimensionality reduction in data. The idea of the method is to search in the source space of a hyperplane of a given dimension d with subsequent projection on a given hyperplane. The first two principal components with largest variance are used for visualization and analysis of the relationship between analyzed features of data.

2.6 Factor Analysis

Factor analysis (FA) is an exploratory technique that is similar to PCA. Similar to cluster analysis, FA groups similar variables into the same factor [25]. This process is commonly referred to as revealing hidden variables. Because of its exploratory nature, it does not separate between independent and dependent variations; and uses the data correlation matrix only. FA reduces the information in the model by decreasing the size of the dataset. This technique can serve several purposes. It can be used to simplify the dataset, for example, to reduce the number of variables in predictive regression models. The steps of FA are as follows: (i) Select appropriate variables. (ii) Extract initial factors. (iii) Select the number of retainable factors. (iv) Select estimation model. (v) Rotate the matrix and interpret the results.

FA has several rotation methods to guarantee the orthogonality of the factors. Thus, the correlation between the two factors is zero. This eliminates multicollinearity problems in regression analysis. We follow Thurstone [28], who suggested five guidelines for factor rotation applied on a matrix of factor loadings as follows:

1. Each row of the matrix must contain at least one close to zero loading.
2. Each column should include several near-zero loadings.
3. Each column pair should include several pairs of loadings, which differ in that one is close to zero and the other is large.
4. If four or more factors are extracted, each column pair should include many pairs of near-zero loadings.
5. Each column pair should contain only a few pairs of large loadings.

3   Results

3.1   Data Collection

39 students (mean age: 20.2 years) of Applied Mathematics course delivered at Kaunas University of Technology (Lithuania) have participated in the survey. The survey was anonymous. The students were informed about the aims of the survey and agreed to participate voluntarily. The principles of the Helsinki declaration were adhered. After the students have played the quiz game described in Sect. 2, the standard HEXAD questionnaire was given to fill in the electronic form (Google Forms). The results of the survey were analysed using MATLAB 2019a.

3.2   Statistical Analysis

The paired t-test was employed to analyse the difference between the responses of students attributed to different player types (socializer, philantrop, free spirit, disruptor, achiever, player) according to the HEXAD methodology. The results presented in Fig. 4 show significant ($p < 0.001$) difference between socializers and free spirits, free spirits and disruptors, disruptors and achievers, disruptors and players, and socializers and players. Differences between other pairs of types were not significant.

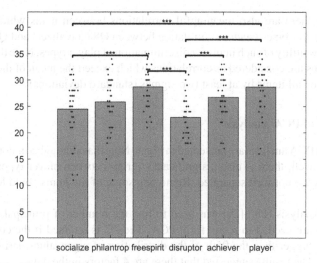

Fig. 4. Significance of differences between player types. Here *** means $p < 0.001$.

3.3 Results of Correlation Analysis

The Pearson correlation coefficients were calculated between the responses to the HEXAD questions (Q1...Q30). The results (only meaningful correlations are shown), presented in Fig. 5, show that although the questions assigned to the same player type group show good correspondence (for example, Q4, Q8, Q12, and Q19 correlate well as items which contribute to the socializer score, which suggests some redundancy).

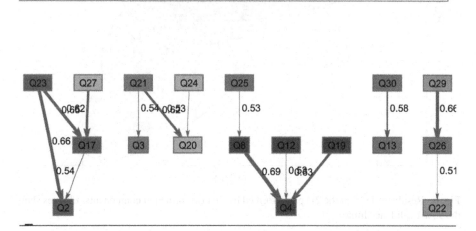

Fig. 5. Meaningful correlations between questions in the HEXAD questionnaire. Questions (Q) are grouped by player types.

However, there are also meaningful correlations between items which contribute to different player types (such as correlation between Q8 (socializer) and Q25 (player)) suggesting low utility of such items for discrimination of player types. Note that meaningful correlations are considered as correlations which exceed the mean of the correlation matrix between all items by at least two sigmas (standard deviations).

3.4   Results of PCA Analysis

The results of PCA analysis are presented in Fig. 6. Note that although a majority HEXAD items cluster well, there is also a significant overlap between player types suggesting that the types are not well separated. Removing some of the items could lead to better separation.

Parallel Analysis (PA) [29] was used to find the number of principal components (PCs), which are needed to retain from PCA. The PC is retained if the corresponding eigenvalue is bigger than the 95th of the distribution of eigenvalues derived from the random data. The results suggested that there are 4 factors in the data.

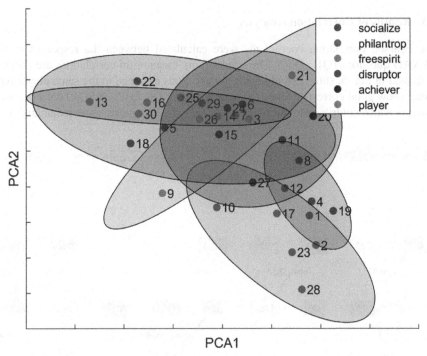

Fig. 6. Results of PCA in the 2D plane formed by first two principal components. Ellipses show the 95% confidence limits

3.5 Results of Factor Analysis

Bartlett's test of sphericity was executed to evaluate the factorability of data. The significance of Bartlett's test of sphericity was less than 0.001, which means that EFA can be applied to the obtained dataset. First, we perform factor analysis of data using a single common factor. From the estimated loadings (Fig. 7), you can see that the one common factor in this model puts large positive weights on questions 20 and 21. The $p = 2.512 \cdot 10^{-12}$ rejects the null hypothesis of a single common factor, suggesting that a factoring can be performed.

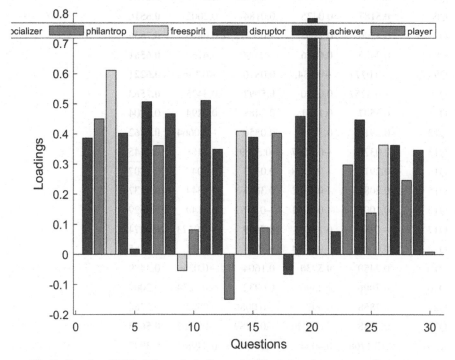

Fig. 7. Results of EFA using a single factor. Loadings show importance of questions.

The Promax rotation was employed with parallel analysis to determine the number of factors. Next, less significant questions (having a maximum factor loading less than 0.4) were removed factor analysis repeated. The results are presented in Table 1. Here Cronbach's α shows the internal consistency, the corresponding question (item) was removed. Cronbach's α can have values from 0 to 1, where $\alpha = 0$ shows no internal consistency, while $\alpha = 1$ indicates perfect internal consistency. In practice, Cronbach's $\alpha \geq 0.70$ is used as a threshold of adequate internal consistency. Low Cronbach's α value shows bad inter-relatedness between items. Therefore, the items with low correlations with target score should be discarded. High Cronbach's α value ($\alpha \geq 0.90$) indicates that some items may be redundant and may be removed as well.

Table 1. Loadings for Promax rotated matrix of four-factor model explaining about 50% of the total data variance (absolute values greater than 0.5 are shown in bold).

Question	F1	F2	F3	F4	Cronbach's α if item is deleted
Q1	0.4012	**0.5046**	−0.0058	−0.2441	**0.7753**
Q2	0.0117	**0.5180**	0.6722	−0.0682	**0.6099**
Q3	**0.6500**	0.0543	0.0539	0.0491	**0.7193**
Q4	0.1838	**0.6866**	0.0169	0.3318	**0.7652**
Q5	0.0894	−0.1985	−0.0481	0.1893	**0.6984**
Q6	**0.5187**	0.0425	0.0184	0.2002	**0.6516**
Q7	0.4200	0.1103	−0.1972	0.0896	**0.7836**
Q8	0.2485	**0.6456**	−0.0802	0.6139	**0.6561**
Q9	−0.0774	−0.0343	0.0816	−0.1362	**0.6221**
Q10	−0.3257	0.0050	**0.5097**	0.3425	**0.7563**
Q11	0.3507	0.1291	0.2488	0.0294	0.3904
Q12	0.2916	0.3278	0.0550	−0.0664	**0.6762**
Q13	0.0378	−0.3597	-0.3069	0.2468	0.4145
Q14	0.2913	−0.0678	0.0753	0.4047	0.1807
Q15	0.2082	−0.1102	0.3653	0.1344	0.4137
Q15	0.1001	−0.2951	−0.0792	0.4149	0.4629
Q17	−0.0437	0.1797	**0.7649**	−0.0573	0.4274
Q18	0.0008	−0.3714	0.1054	0.0221	0.3465
Q19	0.2450	**0.5930**	0.1604	−0.0260	0.3489
Q20	**0.7006**	0.2396	0.0932	−0.0234	0.2000
Q21	**0.7858**	0.0976	−0.0086	0.0583	**0.5766**
Q22	0.3788	−0.3049	−0.1289	−0.2767	**0.5643**
Q23	−0.1768	0.4024	**0.6669**	0.0498	0.3992
Q24	0.7351	−0.0060	−0.2878	−0.1946	**0.5727**
Q25	−0.0971	−0.0056	−0.0736	1.0189	**0.6456**
Q26	0.4050	−0.4148	0.4122	−0.1850	**0.7212**
Q27	0.0083	−0.0561	**0.7509**	−0.0903	**0.5236**
Q28	−0.0119	**0.5615**	0.1866	−0.0468	**0.5106**
Q29	0.3317	−0.4939	**0.5069**	−0.1355	**0.5405**
Q30	0.0885	−0.4506	0.0483	0.1839	**0.5242**

3.6 Evaluation of Reliability

Survey results can be distorted by measurement error or differences across raters. The reliability of a survey can be evaluated as the consistency of the survey results using the test-retest method, which shows an extent to which individuals' responses remain relatively consistent with the final score. The Pearson's correlation coefficient (Pearson's r) is used to evaluate consistency. A larger Pearson's r coefficient means stronger test-retest reliability, i.e. measurement error of the survey is less likely to be assigned to the changes in the subjects' responses.

In our case, we have performed test-retest by randomly splitting all subjects into two groups and calculating the correlation between the responses to items of subjects attributed to the same player type. The results presented in Fig. 8 show good reliability (the largest achieved by Q22, while the smallest one was by Q9), while mean reliability across all items reached 0.92.

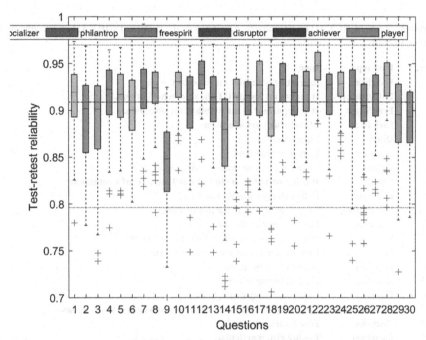

Fig. 8. Results of test-retest reliability analysis of HEXAD questionnaire. The results show mean reliability of 0.92

4 Conclusion

The game can act in several roles: the learning role - the evolution of general educational skills, such as attention, memory, assimilation of information of various modality; entertaining role - creating a favorable atmosphere in the classroom, turning them from boredom state to excitation state; communicative role - the unification of student groups, the establishment of emotional contacts; relaxation role - relieving emotional stress caused by strain on the nervous system with intensive training; psychotechnical role - the formation of skills to prepare their physiological state for more effective activities, the restructuring of the psyche for the assimilation of large amounts of information [30].

In this paper we presented the analysis of the results of student survey performed with the HEXAD questionnaire using statistical analysis, correlation analysis, Principal Component Analysis (PCA) and Exploratory Factor Analysis (EFA).

The results of analysis allowed us to shorten the 30-item HEXAD survey to a shorter 12-item survey (sHEXAD) obtained using a factor analysis on responses from the university mathematics course students. Testing demonstrated that the proposed sHEXAD survey (Table 2) correlated and agreed with the original survey and could potentially be used to derive the same outcomes. Moreover, a shorter survey is more likely to be used as it is more convenient for subjects and takes less time to complete.

Table 2. Items of HEXAD questionnaire. The items of the proposed sHEXAD questionnaire are shown in bold.

Nr.	User type	Item
1	Socializer	Interacting with others is important to me.
2	**Philanthropist**	**It makes me happy if I am able to help others.**
3	**Free Spirit**	**It is important to me to follow my own path.**
4	**Socializer**	**I like being part of a team.**
5	Disruptor	I like to provoke.
6	Achiever	I am very ambitious.
7	Player	I like competitions where a prize can be won.
8	**Socializer**	**It is important to me to feel like I am part of a community.**
9	Free Spirit	I often let my curiosity guide me.
10	Philanthropist	I feel good taking on the role of a mentor.
11	Disruptor	I like to question the status quo.
12	Socializer	It is more fun to be with others than by myself.
13	Player	Rewards are a great way to motivate me.
14	Free Spirit	I like to try new things.
15	Achiever	I like defeating obstacles.
16	Player	I look out for my own interests.
17	**Philanthropist**	**I like helping others to orient themselves in new situations.**
18	Disruptor	I see myself as a rebel.
19	**Socializer**	**I enjoy group activities.**
20	**Achiever**	**It is important to me to always carry out my tasks completely.**
21	**Free Spirit**	**I prefer setting my own goals.**
22	Disruptor	I dislike following rules.
23	**Philanthropist**	**I like sharing my knowledge.**
24	**Achiever**	**It is difficult for me to let go of a problem before I have found a solution.**
25	**Player**	**Return of investment is important to me.**
26	Free Spirit	Being independent is important to me.
27	**Achiever**	**I like mastering difficult tasks.**
28	Philanthropist	The well-being of others is important to me.
29	Disruptor	I like to take changing things into my own hands.
30	Player	If the reward is sufficient I will put in the effort.

Future work will involve the analysis of other questionnaires used for evaluating the effect of serious games on the learning process.

References

1. Margaryan, A., Littlejohn, A., Vojt, G.: Are digital natives a myth or reality? University students' use of digital technologies. Comput. Educ. **56**(2), 429–440 (2011). https://doi.org/10.1016/j.compedu.2010.09.004
2. Levin, I., Kojukhov, A.: Personalizing education in post-industrial society. In: 2009 Third International Conference on Digital Society (ICDS), Cancun, Mexico, 1–6 February 2009, pp. 20–21 (2009). https://doi.org/10.1109/icds.2009.13
3. Seaborn, K., Fels, D.I.: Gamification in theory and action: a survey. Int. J. Hum. Comput. Stud. **74**, 14–31 (2015). https://doi.org/10.1016/j.ijhcs.2014.09.006
4. Ašeriškis, D., Damaševičius, R.: Gamification of a project management system. In: 7th International Conference on Advances in Computer-Human Interactions, ACHI 2014, 23–27 March 2014, Barcelona, Spain, pp. 200-207 (2014)
5. Knutas, A., van Roy, R., Hynninen, T., Granato, M., Kasurinen, J., Ikonen, J.: A process for designing algorithm-based personalized gamification. Multimedia Tools Appl. **78**(10), 13593–13612 (2018). https://doi.org/10.1007/s11042-018-6913-5
6. Domínguez, A., Saenz-De-Navarrete, J., De-Marcos, L., Fernández-Sanz, L., Pagés, C., Martínez-Herráiz, J.: Gamifying learning experiences: practical implications and outcomes. Comput. Educ. **63**, 380–392 (2013)
7. Darzi, A., Wondra, T., McCrea, S., Novak, D.: Classification of different cognitive and affective states in computer game players using physiology, performance and intrinsic factors. In: Karwowski, W., Ahram, T. (eds.) IHSI 2019. AISC, vol. 903, pp. 23–29. Springer, Cham (2019). https://doi.org/10.1007/978-3-030-11051-2_4
8. Hamari, J., Shernoff, D.J., Rowe, E., Coller, B., Asbell-Clarke, J., Edwards, T.: Challenging games help students learn: An empirical study on engagement, flow and immersion in game-based learning. Comput. Hum. Behav. **54**, 170–179 (2016). https://doi.org/10.1016/j.chb.2015.07.045
9. Raziunaite, P., Miliunaite, A., Maskeliunas, R., Damasevicius, R., Sidekerskiene, T., Narkeviciene, B.: Designing an educational music game for digital game based learning: a lithuanian case study. In: 2018 41st International Convention on Information and Communication Technology, Electronics and Microelectronics, MIPRO 2018, pp. 800–805 (2018). https://doi.org/10.23919/MIPRO.2018.8400148
10. Oyesiku, D., Adewumi, A., Misra, S., Ahuja, R., Damasevicius, R., Maskeliunas, R.: An educational math game for high school students in sub-saharan Africa. In: Florez, H., Diaz, C., Chavarriaga, J. (eds.) ICAI 2018. CCIS, vol. 942, pp. 228–238. Springer, Cham (2018). https://doi.org/10.1007/978-3-030-01535-0_17
11. Maskeliunas, R., et al.: Serious game iDO: Towards better education in dementia care. Information **10**(11), 355 (2019). https://doi.org/10.3390/info10110355
12. Kaptein, M., Markopoulos, P., de Ruyter, B., Aarts, E.: Personalizing persuasive technologies: explicit and implicit personalization using persuasion profiles. Int. J. Hum Comput Stud. **77**, 38–51 (2015). https://doi.org/10.1016/j.ijhcs.2015.01.004
13. Mora, A., Tondello, G.F., Nacke, L.E., Arnedo-Moreno, J.: Effect of personalized gameful design on student engagement. In: IEEE Global Engineering Education Conference, EDUCON, 2018 April, pp. 1925–1933 (2018). https://doi.org/10.1109/EDUCON.2018.8363471

14. Orji, R., Tondello, G.F., Nacke, L.E.: Personalizing persuasive strategies in gameful systems to gamification user types. In: Proceedings of the 2018 CHI Conference on Human Factors in Computing Systems, CHI 2018, Montreal, QC, Canada, 21–26 April 2018, p. 435 (2018). https://doi.org/10.1145/3173574.3174009

15. Ašeriškis, D., Damaševičius, R.: Computational evaluation of effects of motivation reinforcement on player retention. J. Univ. Comput. Sci. **23**(5), 432–453 (2017)

16. Damaševičius, R.: Towards empirical modelling of knowledge transfer in teaching/learning process. In: Dregvaite, G., Damasevicius, R. (eds.) ICIST 2014. CCIS, vol. 465, pp. 359–372. Springer, Cham (2014). https://doi.org/10.1007/978-3-319-11958-8_29

17. Lopez, C.E., Tucker, C.S.: The effects of player type on performance: a gamification case study. Comput. Hum. Behav. **91**, 333–345 (2019)

18. Bourke, P., Murphy, D., O'Mullane, J., Marshall, K., Howell, S.: Review of player personality classifications to inform game design. In: IEEE Games, Entertainment, Media Conference, GEM 2018, Galway, Ireland, 15–17 August 2018, pp. 271–274 (2018)

19. Nacke, L.E., Bateman, C., Mandryk, R.L.: BrainHex: a neurobiological gamer typology survey. Entertain. Comput. **5**(1), 55–62 (2014)

20. Ryan, R.M., Rigby, C., Przybylski, A.: The motivational pull of video games: a self-determination theory approach. Motiv. Emot. **30**(4), 344–360 (2006). https://doi.org/10.1007/s11031-006-9051-8

21. Jennett, C., Cox, A.L., Cairns, P., Dhoparee, S., Epps, A., Tijs, T., Walton, A.: Measuring and defining the experience of immersion in games. Int. J. Hum Comput Stud. **66**(9), 641–661 (2008)

22. Abeele, V.V, Nacke, L.E., Mekler, E.D., Johnson, D.: Design and preliminary validation of the player experience inventory. In: 2016 Annual Symposium on Computer-Human Interaction in Play Companion Extended Abstracts, pp. 335–341. ACM, New York (2016)

23. Law, E.L., Brühlmann, F., Mekler, E.D.: Systematic review and validation of the game experience questionnaire (GEQ) – implications for citation and reporting practice. In: 2018 Annual Symposium on Computer-Human Interaction in Play, CHI PLAY 2018, Melbourne, Australia, 28–31 October 2018, pp. 271–283 (2018). https://doi.org/10.1145/3242671.3242683

24. Busch, M., Mattheiss, E., Orji, R., Fröhlich, P., Lankes, M., Tscheligi, M.: Player type models: towards empirical validation. In: 2016 CHI Conference Extended Abstracts on Human Factors in Computing Systems, CHI EA 2016, San Jose, CA, USA, 7–12 May 2016, pp. 1835–1841. ACM Press (2016). https://doi.org/10.1145/2851581.2892399

25. Tondello, G.F., Wehbe, R.R., Diamond, L., Busch, M., Marczewski, A., Nacke, L.E.: The gamification user types hexad scale. In: Proceedings of the 2016 Annual Symposium on Computer-Human Interaction in Play, CHI PLAY 2016, Austin, TX, USA, 16–19 October 2016, pp. 229–243 (2016). https://doi.org/10.1145/2967934.2968082

26. Tondello, G.F., Mora, A., Marczewski, A., Nacke, L.E.: Empirical validation of the gamification user types hexad scale in English and Spanish. Int. J. Hum Comput Stud. **127**, 95–111 (2018). https://doi.org/10.1016/j.ijhcs.2018.10.002

27. Plass, J.L., Homer, B.D., Kinzer, C.K.: Foundations of game-based learning. Educ. Psychol. **50**(4), 258–283 (2015). https://doi.org/10.1080/00461520.2015.1122533

28. Thurstone, L.L.: Multiple-Factor Analysis. University of Chicago Press, Chicago (1947)

29. Franklin, S.B., Gibson, D.J., Robertson, P.A., Pohlmann, J.T., Fralish, J.S.: Parallel analysis: a method for determining significant principal components. J. Veg. Sci. **6**(1), 99–106 (1995). https://doi.org/10.2307/3236261

30. Zamyatina, O.M., Yurutkina, T.Y. Mozgaleva, P.I., Gulyaeva, K.V.: Implementation of games in mathematics and physics modules. In: The 8th European Conference on Games Based Learning, ECGBL 2014, Berlin, Germany, vol. 2, no. C, pp. 652–661 (2014)

Outlier Detection in Multivariate Time Series Data Using a Fusion of K-Medoid, Standardized Euclidean Distance and Z-Score

Nwodo Benita Chikodili$^{(\boxtimes)}$ ⓘ, Mohammed D. Abdulmalik ⓘ,
Opeyemi A. Abisoye ⓘ, and Sulaimon A. Bashir ⓘ

Department of Computer Science, Federal University of Technology, Minna, Nigeria
bennychika2@gmail.com, {drmalik,o.a.abisoye,
bashirsulaimon}@futminna.edu.ng

Abstract. Data mining technique has been used to extract potentially useful knowledge from big data. However, data mining sometimes faces the issue of incorrect results which could be due to the presence of an outlier in the analyzed data. In the literature, it has been identified that the detection of this outlier could enhance the quality of the dataset. An important type of data that requires outlier detection for accurate prediction and enhanced decision making is time series data. Time series data are valuable as it helps to understand the past behavior which is helpful for future predictions hence, it is important to detect the presence of outliers in time series dataset. This paper proposes an algorithm for outlier detection in Multivariate Time Series (MTS) data based on a fusion of K-medoid, Standard Euclidean Distance (SED), and Z-score. Apart from SED, experiments were also performed on two other distance metrics which are City Block and Euclidean Distance. Z-score performance was compared to that of inter-quartile. However, the result obtained showed that the Z-score technique produced a better outlier detection result of 0.9978 F-measure as compared to inter-quartile of 0.8571 F-measure. Furthermore, SED performed better when combined with both Z-score and inter-quartile than City Block and Euclidean Distance.

Keywords: Outlier detection · Time series data · Multivariate · Outliers · K-Medoid · Euclidean distance · Z-scores · City block

1 Introduction

Currently, the volume of data is significantly increasing with each passing day in various application fields, hence, it is essential to use more effective technology to examine and manage these volumes of data to discover the integral, previously unknown, and potentially useful knowledge. One key data processing technology that is used to examine and manage data is data mining. Data mining is a method of obtaining valuable information from unprocessed-data [1]. With data mining, a search engine can be used to analyze massive quantities of data and detect interesting trends automatically without needing human involvement [2]. Data mining is generally about finding non-trivial, concealed,

© Springer Nature Switzerland AG 2021
S. Misra and B. Muhammad-Bello (Eds.): ICTA 2020, CCIS 1350, pp. 259–271, 2021.
https://doi.org/10.1007/978-3-030-69143-1_21

and important information from different data types. There are many fields in which data mining is commonly used: retail, network security, financial data processing, biochemical data analysis, telecommunications industry, and other research applications [1].

One of the fundamental issues of data mining is to achieve a profound and accurate conclusion of the study. And outlier detection is a crucial step in solving this basic problem [3, 4]. An outlier is a data point that does not fit into the usual data set classification points. Outlier detection has major applications in data preprocessing and the elimination of abnormal points for stock price prediction, credit scoring, advertisement, intrusion detection, system evaluation, and e-mail spam identification among others [5]. Outlier detection is also known in some researches as anomaly detection and is a critical longstanding research concern in the fields of data mining and statistics. The principal principle behind finding an outlier is to locate unusual points in the data points. Outlier detection points out artifacts that often deviate from a given set of data [6] and Outliers may potentially contain some valuable information [7]. For example, the identification of unusual trends in patient databases can be helpful for disease identification in clinical applications [5, 8].

Time series data is an essential form of data that needs outlier detection for accurate prediction and effective decision making. Data from time series are valuable because it helps to explain the past actions that would be useful for future predictions [9, 10]. Time series data can be used for business forecasting which in turn can improve business decision making. These data are applicable in various fields such as mathematics, sensor processing, pattern recognition, economics, mathematical finance, weather monitoring, earthquake prediction, electromyography, industrial engineering, astronomy, telecommunications and, in large part, any field of applied engineering and science [11]. The identification of outliers in time series data is therefore critical for better decision making and prediction. Considering the importance of outlier detection in time series data, numerous researches have been carried out using various types of algorithms in the success of an outlier detection function in time series data. Algorithms that have been proposed in the literature for outlier detection in multivariate time series dataset include genetic algorithm, Mahalanobis distance, Euclidean distance, autoregressive integrated moving average with exogenous inputs (ARIMAX) model and k-means algorithm while z-score and inter-quartile (box plot) algorithm have been used for univariate time series dataset. This paper proposes a method that combines K-Medoid which is a cluster-based algorithm, Standard Euclidean Distance which is a distance-based, and Z-Score algorithm for outlier detection in multivariate time series (MTS) data. This study's principal contributions are as follows:

1. A fusion of cluster-based and distance-based algorithms for improved outlier detection.
2. Comparative experimentation of different distance-based algorithm on the data cluster obtained from the clustering algorithm.
3. Extension of Z-score and Box plot algorithms for effective outlier detection in MTS dataset.

The organization of these studies is as follows: section two presents the relevant work, section three presents the methods used, section four describes the findings and discussion and finally, in section five and section six conclusions were drawn and recommendations for future works were presented.

2   Related Work

The presence of outliers in time series and non-time series data could provide important information that can be used by an analyst in drawing conclusions. Also, an outlier presence could alter the result produced during analysis. Hence several types of research have been carried to detect these outliers and even remove them when necessary.

Jones et al. [12] performed outlier detection in physical activity using the k-means clustering algorithm. In this work, a FilterK technique was introduced to boost the quality of clusters of k-means based on physical activity. The FilterK algorithm uses an outlier score function that allocates a level of abnormality based mostly on the standardized score obtained from each of its 3 tests which are average distance to neighbors, distance to the closest centroid, and density of the neighborhood. This allows the setting of a standard outlier threshold score as an exclusion criterion when searching the data for abnormalities on the accelerometer. However, the robustness, strength, and weakness of this proposed method were not tested as the method was tested on a small range of accelerometer dataset.

Souza, Aquino and Gomes [13] integrated tensor decomposition with data categorization to outliers in urban spaces detect applications and provide useful information for urban planning and operation. This method consists of three stages which are dimensionality reduction stage in which several latent variables are derived from the contraction, classification of latent variables stage in which the latent variables produced are being used for classification to obtain high-quality groups from the factorization stage, and finally, the production of a polished environmental sequence identification phase that deals with the design of a monitoring process statistics to detect events outside the regularity trends of the measured dataset. A drawback of this proposed approach is that it needs a large sample size to classify the outliers and this necessity has an effect on applications in real-time.

Erkus and Purutc [4] proposed a non-parametric method for quasi-periodic outliers detection in time series data based on a combination of frequency-domain and Fourier transform definition. The result of the algorithm was compared to four existing algorithms namely: Grubbs, box-plot, autonomous anomaly detection, and z-score method, and it was proven that the developed approach worked even better if the data had quasi-periodic structures from start to finish. However, this method did not consider outlier detection for high dimensional datasets as only outliers in univariate dimensions were considered.

Wang et al. [14] considered outliers detection based on its importance in air pollution forecasting. It was found that the identification and correction of the outlier point of the original time series affect air pollution prediction. To improve their air quality index forecasting, a novel hybrid approach based on outlier detection, corrective algorithm, and a heuristic intelligent optimizing algorithm was developed. To achieve outlier identification and correction, the Hampel recognition system was based on measured local median and standard deviation was adopted. Only the air quality index time series was considered while other influencing factors were not considered in this work.

Borah and Nath [15] proposed a method for solving the problem of outlier detection for incremental medical data, as most of the current outlier recognition algorithms are capable of controlling just static data, and must therefore perform incremental data from scratch. Rare pattern-based outlier detection (RPOD) technique was used to carry out this task. The RPOD consists of two stages: the full info on the database is stored in a compact prefix-tree structure at the first stage. So then the desired set of uncommon patterns is extracted progressively from the prefix-tree by skimming down the index only once. While the second phase includes the identification of outliers based on the unusual patterns obtained during the first stage. The outliers were identified using 3 techniques of outlier detection: Rare Pattern Support Deviation Factor (RPSDF), Transaction Outlier Factor (TOF), and Rare Pattern Outlier Factor (RPOF), respectively. The drawback of this approach is that by setting a minimum support level, RPOD creates outliers based upon the notion of uncommon patterns. And the number of uncommon patterns produced is basically too large and it can be very cumbersome to assign an acceptable support value for outlier detection

Ghallab, Fahmy and Nasr [16] model called NRDD-DBSCAN focused on density-dependent spatial clustering of noise-based applications (DBSCAN) algorithms and using resilient distributed data sets (RDDs) to identify anomalies that affect Internet of Things (IoT) technology data quality. The NRDD-DBSCAN has been used to solve the RDD-DBSCAN system's low-dimensionality problem and also to solve the DBSCAN algorithm issue not being able to handle IoT data. And NRDD-DBSCAN can also be used to boost the efficiency of the present data in IoT devices and applications. The primary drawback of this proposed system is that the data reduction and distribution process uses principal component analysis (PCA) to reduce the dimensionality of the datasets, however, PCA works well by reducing the dimensionality of a strongly correlated linear n-dimension data that prevents the system from processing non-linear data.

3 Methodology

This section discusses the techniques that were used to carry out this research work. Figure 1 shows the processes and techniques that were used to achieve the research goal. Each of the steps shown in the diagram in Fig. 1 is discussed in the sub-sections below.

3.1 Data Acquisition

The time series dataset used in this study was gotten from the Time series section in the UCI repository. Two labeled multivariate time series datasets were used which are the occupancy dataset and the MHEALTH dataset. The MHEALTH which is a multivariate time series dataset consists of observations of body movement and vital signs for 10 individuals of different personalities while undertaking 12 physical activities, and it consists of 23 feature vectors. The occupancy data set defines the dimensions of a room and is intended to determine whether space is occupied or not and it has 20,560 one minute observations taken over a period of few weeks.

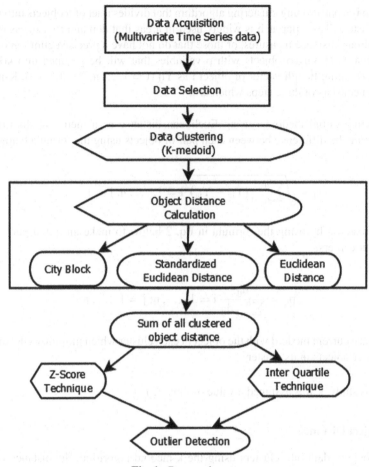

Fig. 1. Proposed system

3.2 Data Selection

In this work, not all instances in the dataset were used and this was done in order to make the dataset suitable for the outlier detection task. For the MHealth dataset 2000 instances were used out of 161280 instances contained in the MHealth dataset. Out of the 2000 instances used, 1975 instances are labeled as a normal class while 25 instances were inserted as outliers. For the occupancy dataset, 1500 observations were taken out of 9753 observations contained in the dataset and the 1500 observations used consist of 1485 occupied rooms observations labeled as a normal class and 15 empty room observations identified as outliers.

3.3 Data Clustering (K-Medoid)

In the literature, the clustering result of the k-medoid clustering method cannot be influenced by the presence of outliers as data points are selected to be the medoids. K-medoid algorithm is a partitioning clustering algorithm that divides a set of n objects into k number of clusters. This approach is widely used in areas that demand robustness to outer data, arbitrary distance measures, or those that do not have a precise definition of mean and median [17]. Given objects with p variables that will be grouped into $k(k < n)$ clusters. Defining the jth vector of object i as Yij ($i = 1, ...,n; j = 1, ...,p$). K-medoid algorithm consists of three steps which are:

1. Selecting initial medoids: using Euclidean distance as a metric of dissimilarity, compute the difference between each pair of objects using the formula below:

$$D_{ij} = \sqrt{\sum_{a=1}^{p} (Y_{ia} - Y_{ja})^2} \, i = 1, \ldots, n; j = 1, \ldots, n \tag{1}$$

2. Calculate p_{ij} by using the formula in Eq. 2 below to make an initial guess at the cluster centers.

$$p_{ij} = \frac{d_{ij}}{\sum_{i=1}^{n} d_{ij}} \, i = 1, \ldots, n; j = 1, \ldots, n \tag{2}$$

3. Replace current medoid with the object in each cluster which minimizes the distance to other objects in its cluster.

In this study, k was assigned a value of three (3).

3.4   Object Distance

After grouping data into clusters using the k-medoid algorithm, the distance of each object from the medoid of each cluster was calculated using three distance-based algorithms which are: the SED, City Block, and the Euclidean distance. Considering the m-by-n data matrix X, which will be handled as m (1-by-n) row vectors x1, x2,...xm, the different distances between both the xs and xt vectors are stated as follows:

1. **Euclidean Distance:** A linear distance in Euclidean space between two points [18].

$$D_{st}^2 = (x_s - x_t)(x_s - x_t)' \tag{3}$$

2. **Standardized Euclidean Distance (SED):**

$$D_{st}^2 = (x_s - x_t) U^{-1} (x_s - x_t)' \tag{4}$$

Where U is the n-by-n diagonal matrix with diagonal elements given by s_j^2, which signifies the variance of the variable x_j over the m objects.

3. **City Block Distance**: the city block distance between two vectors x_s and x_t in an n-dimensional vector space with static Cartesian coordinate is the addition of the lengths of the projections of the line section between the points onto the coordinate axes. The formula is as follows:

$$D_{st} = \sum_{j=1}^{n} |x_{sj} - x_{tj}| \tag{5}$$

3.5 Distance Summation

After using the above distance metrics to calculate the distance of objects from each cluster medoid, this calculated distances for all clusters are summed together for each object. Hence a single distance gotten from the summation of all an object distance from each cluster medoid is used as an input for the inter-quartile and z-score technique. Given that there are i ($i = 1,\ldots,n$) instances grouped into 3 clusters with various calculated distance (Ci1, Ci2, Ci3). This distance summation is given as:

$$d_s = C_{i1} + C_{i2} + C_{i3} \tag{6}$$

3.6 Outlier Detection Techniques

Two techniques were considered for outlier detection and these techniques are the z-core and inter-quartile techniques.

1. **Z-core technique:** This is a statistical measurement of a score's correlation to the mean in a collection of scores [19]. A Z-score of zero indicates that the score is the same as the average. It can also be a negative/positive value, signifying if it is below or above the average and by how many standard deviations [20]. Z-score makes use of average and standard deviation values to detect outliers in a dataset. Z-score is calculated as follows:

$$Z_{score}(i) = \frac{x_i - \mu}{sd} \tag{7}$$

Where μ = distribution mean, sd = standard deviation and x_i = each object in the distribution. The standard deviation can be calculated using:

$$sd = \sqrt{\frac{1}{n-1} \sum_{i=1}^{n} (x_i - \mu)^2} \tag{8}$$

To detect outliers based on z-score a cut-off value of 3 was used. That is any distance value with an integer value greater than 3 are detected as outliers.

2. **Inter-quartile technique:** this technique is also known as box plot method. It is called the box plot technique because it forms a box chart, which shows information such as the upper and lower outliers of the univariate data set, lower and upper quartiles, and the median. This method has only been used to detect outliers in a univariate dataset but this study extends its usage to a multivariate dataset. This extension is possible as the sum of the distances was used as a single univariate input to the box-plot and based on input the technique was able to detect outliers in a multivariate dataset. The rule for this method is as follows.

a. Calculate the interquartile range (IQR)

$$IQR = Q_3 - Q_1 \tag{9}$$

b. Calculate the lower and upper internal boundaries using the formulas:

$$LIB = Q_1 - 1.5IQR \tag{10}$$

$$UIB = Q_3 - 1.5IQR \tag{11}$$

c. Calculate the lower and upper external boundaries using the formulas.

$$LEB = Q_1 - 3IQR \; Q\_1 - 3IQR \tag{12}$$

$$UEB = Q_3 - 3IQR \tag{13}$$

d. Observation values between internal and external boundaries are defined as possible outliers.
e. Observation values outside the external boundaries are determined as outliers.

3.7 Performance Metrics

Four performance measures were used to evaluate the proposed method. These measures are explained below.

- **Precision:** is a measure that evaluates the number of accurate predictions made correctly. It is determined as the ratio of correctly predicted positive examples, divided by the total number of predicted positive examples.

$$Precision = True\_Positives/(True\_Positives + False\_Positives) \tag{14}$$

- **Recall:** is a statistic that evaluates the amount of accurate positive predictions that could have been made from all the positive predictions.

$$Recall = True\_Positives/(True\_Positives + False\_Negatives) \quad (SEQ\ "equation"\ \backslash n\ \backslash * \ MERGEFORMAT\ 15) \tag{15}$$

- **F-measure:** It is the harmonious measure of precision and the recall

$$F - measure = 2 * \frac{precision * recall}{precision + recall} \quad (SEQ\ "equation"\ \backslash n\ \backslash * \ MERGEFORMAT\ 16) \tag{16}$$

- **Accuracy:** Accuracy is basically defined as the rate of correct classifications. And it is calculated as follows:

$$Accuracy = \frac{True\ Positive + True\ negative}{True\ Positive + True\ negative + False\ Positive + False\ negative} \quad (SEQ\ "equation"\ \backslash n\ \backslash * \ MERGEFORMAT\ 17) \tag{17}$$

This study deals with imbalanced classification problems where the number of examples in the dataset for each class label is not balanced, that is the distribution of examples across the known class is skewed. For example, in the occupancy dataset, only 15 examples are of class 1 (outliers) while the remaining 904 examples are class 0 (normal). Hence the most important performance metrics considered for evaluation are precision, recall, and f-measure which evaluates imbalanced classification problems effectively.

3.8 Algorithm Fusion

After performing the data acquisition and data selection process. The K-medoid, Standard Euclidean Distance (SED), and Z-score were combined as follows: The data were then grouped into 3 clusters using the k-medoid algorithm. After clustering the distance of each object from the medoid of each cluster was calculated using Standard Euclidean Distance. Given that there are 3 clusters 3 different SED distances were obtained for each object from each cluster. In order to utilize the 3 SED distances obtained for each object a single distance for each object was generated by summing all of the 3 cluster distances. This generated single distance was used as input data to the z-score technique. The z–score of the SED distances was computed and based on a threshold value of the z-score a data was identified as an outlier.

4 Results and Discussion

In this study, outlier detection was performed using K-Medoid, SED, and Z-Score. The performance of SED was compared to that of Euclidean Distance and City clock. And the performance of z-score was compared to that of inter-quartile. The algorithms were tested using the MHealth and Occupancy multivariate time series dataset. The results obtained are presented in Tables 1, 2, 3, and 4 below. Table 1 and Table 2 shows the results obtained for MHealth multivariate time series dataset.

Table 1. Results of inter-quartile outlier detection technique for the three different distance metric for MHealth dataset

Outlier detection algorithm	Precision	Recall	F-measure	Accuracy
K-Medoid + SED + inter-quartile	0.2778	1.0000	0.4348	0.9133
K-Medoid + Euclidean + inter-quartile	0.2400	0.933	0.3889	0.9022
K-Medoid + City Block + inter-quartile	0.2727	1.0000	0.4286	0.9111

The results obtained for inter-quartile outlier detection technique based on the three different distance metric is shown in Table 1 above. Table 1 shows that standardized Euclidean distance performed better with an f-measure of 0.4348 as compared to Euclidean and City block distance with f-measure of 0.3889 and 0.4286 respectively.

Table 2. Results of Z-score outlier detection technique for the three different distance metric for MHealth dataset

Outlier detection algorithm	Precision	Recall	F-measure	Accuracy
K-Medoid + SED + Z-score (Proposed System)	0.9704	0.9793	0.9748	0.9511
K-Medoid + Euclidean + Z-score	0.9748	0.9770	0.9759	0.9533
K-Medoid + City Block + Z-score	0.9725	0.9747	0.9736	0.9489

Table 2 shows the results obtained for the z-score detection technique based on the three different distance metrics for the MHealth dataset. Based on the precision, recall, and f-measure obtained in Table 2 it can be seen that the z-score technique performs better with f-measures of 0.9748, 0.9759, and 0.9736 for Standardized Euclidean, Euclidean, and city block respectively than the inter-quartile technique with f-measure of 0.4348, 0.3889 and 0.4286 for Standardized Euclidean, Euclidean and city block respectively. Table 3 and Table 4 shows the results obtained for Occupancy multivariate time series dataset.

Table 3. Results of inter-quartile outlier detection technique for the three different distance metric for Occupancy dataset

Outlier detection algorithm	Precision	Recall	F-Measure	Accuracy
K-Medoid + SED + inter-quartile	0.7500	1.0000	0.8571	**0.9946**
K-Medoid + Euclidean + inter-quartile	0.4286	1.0000	0.6000	0.9782
K-Medoid + City Block + inter-quartile	0.7500	1.000	0.8571	0.9946

Table 3 shows the results obtained for the inter-quartile outlier detection technique based on the three different distance metrics for the occupancy dataset. From Table 3 it can be seen that standardized Euclidean distance and city block distance performed better with an f-measure of 0. 8571 as compared to Euclidean with an f-measure of 0. 6000.

Table 4. Results of Z-score outlier detection technique for the three different distance metric for Occupancy dataset

Outlier detection algorithm	Precision	Recall	F-Measure	Accuracy
K-Medoid + SED + Z-score (Proposed System)	1.000	0.9956	0.9978	0.9956
K-Medoid + Euclidean + Z-score	1.000	0.9934	0.9967	0.9935
K-Medoid + City Block + Z-score	1.000	0.9956	0.9978	0.9956

Table 4 shows the results obtained for z-score detection technique based on the three different distance metrics for the Occupancy dataset. Based on the precision, recall, and f-measure obtained in Table 4 it can be seen that the z-score technique still performs better with f-measures of 0.9978, 0.9967, and 0.9978 for Standardized Euclidean, Euclidean and city block respectively than the inter-quartile technique with f-measure of 0.8571, 0.6000, and 0.8571 for Standardized Euclidean, Euclidean, and city block respectively.

From the results obtained for the inter-quartile technique for both occupancy and MHealth dataset as shown in Table 3 and Table 1 respectively, it can be seen that squared Euclidean distance performs better than Euclidean and city block distance. Hence it can be concluded that the inter-quartile technique performs better when combined with squared Euclidean distance. Also from Table 2 and Table 4, it can be seen from the precision, recall, and f-measure that all three distance metrics produce good and satisfactory results when combined with z-score. However, in both Mhealth and occupancy dataset z-score produces a better result as compared to inter-quartile technique. With high precision, recall, f-measure, and accuracy it can be deduced that outliers can be detected effectively with z-score when combined with any of the distance metric especially with the Standardized Euclidean distance. Hence a system which combines k-medoid, SED and z-score is proposed for effective outlier detection in multivariate time series dataset.

5 Conclusion

This study was able to extend the inter-quartile and z-score technique for outlier detection on multivariate time series dataset as compared to existing works which used these techniques for outlier detection on only univariate datasets. This is due to the ability of the algorithm to combine the multivariate features into a univariate feature. Also, this study was able to detect outliers more effectively as compared to existing works on outlier detection. From the study, it can be concluded that the z-score technique performs better than the inter-quartile technique for outlier detection.

6 Future Works

In this study, only the extreme outlier values generated by the inter-quartile techniques were identified as outliers while the mild identified outlier values were ignored and assigned to the normal class because the data used are skewed it caused a large number of observations to be determined as outliers in the data. This is due to the use of the interquartile distances and lower and upper quadrants measured without considering the skewness of the data set. Hence is it recommended that the skewness of the dataset should be considered to improve the performance of the inter-quartile technique. Three distance metric was used in this work, for future work other distance metrics can be used. This work can be extended for outlier detection for other non-time series datasets.

References

1. Jain, S., Sahib, F., Kaur, A., Sahib, F.: A review paper on comparison of clustering algorithms based on outliers, vol. 3, no. 05, pp. 178–182 (2016)
2. Rajagopal, S.: Customer data clustering using data mining technique, vol. 3, no. 4 (2011). https://doi.org/10.5121/ijdms.2011.3401
3. Ramesh, K.B., Aljinu, K.K.V.: A survey on outlier detection techniques in dynamic data stream. Int. J. Latest Eng. Manag. Res. IJLEMR **02**(08), 23–30 (2017)
4. Erkus, E.C., Purutc, V.: Journal Pre-proof. Eur. J. Oper. Res. (2020). https://doi.org/10.1016/j.ejor.2020.01.014
5. Pamula, R., Deka, J.K., Nandi, S.: An outlier detection method based on clustering. In: Proceedings - 2nd International Conference on Emerging Applications of Information Technology, EAIT 2011, pp. 253–256, February 2011. https://doi.org/10.1109/eait.2011.25
6. Akouemo, H.N., Povinelli, R.J.: Time series outlier detection and imputation, pp. 1–5 (2014)
7. Jiadong, R., Hongna, L., Changzhen, H., Haitao, H.: ODMC: outlier detection on multivariate time series data based on clustering. J. Converg. Inf. Technol. **6**(2), 70–77 (2011). https://doi.org/10.4156/jcit.vol6.issue2.8
8. Ren, J., Li, H., Hu, C., He, H.: ODMC: outlier detection on multivariate time series data based on clustering. J. Converg. Inf. Technol. **6**(2), 70–77 (2011). https://doi.org/10.4156/jcit.vol6
9. Liu, S., Wright, A., Hauskrecht, M.: Online conditional outlier detection in nonstationary time series. In: Association Advance Artificial Intelligence (2017)
10. Abayomi-Alli, A., Odusami, M.O., Abayomi-Alli, O., Misra, S., Ibeh, G.F.: Long short-term memory model for time series prediction and forecast of solar radiation and other weather parameters. In: 2019 19th International Conference on Computational Science and Its Applications (ICCSA), Saint Petersburg, Russia, pp. 82–92, July 2019. https://doi.org/10.1109/iccsa.2019.00004

11. Hasan, E.A.: A method for detection of outliers in time series data. Int. J. Chem. Math. Phys. IJCMP **3**(3), 56–66 (2019). https://doi.org/10.22161/ijcmp.3.3.2
12. Jones, P.J., et al.: FilterK : a new outlier detection method for k-means clustering of physical activity. J. Biomed. Inform. **104**, 103397 (2020). https://doi.org/10.1016/j.jbi.2020.103397
13. Souza, T.I.A., Aquino, A.L.L., Gomes, D.G.: A method to detect data outliers from smart urban spaces via multiway analysis. Future Gener. Comput. Syst. (2018). https://doi.org/10.1016/j.future.2018.09.062
14. Wang, J., Du, P., Hao, Y., Ma, X., Niu, T., Yang, W.: An innovative hybrid model based on outlier detection and correction algorithm and heuristic intelligent optimization algorithm for daily air quality index forecasting. J. Environ. Manage. **255**, 109855 (2020). https://doi.org/10.1016/j.jenvman.2019.109855
15. Borah, A., Nath, B.: Journal pre-proof. Appl. Soft Comput. J. 1–51 (2019). https://doi.org/10.1016/j.asoc.2019.105824
16. Ghallab, H., Fahmy, H., Nasr, M.: Detection outliers on Internet of Things using big data technology. Egypt. Inform. J. **21**, 1–8 (2019). https://doi.org/10.1016/j.eij.2019.12.001
17. Hudaib, A., Khanafseh, M., Surakhi, O.: An improved version of K-medoid algorithm using CRO. Mod. Appl. Sci. **12**(2), 116–127 (2018). https://doi.org/10.5539/mas.v12n2p116
18. Dokmani, I., Parhizkar, R., Ranieri, J., Vetterli, M.: Essential theory, algorithms and applications. IEEE Signal Process. Mag. **32**, 1–17 (2015)
19. Kolbaşi, A., Ünsal, P.A.: A comparison of the outlier detecting methods: an application on Turkish foreign trade data. J. Math. Stat. Sci. **5**, 213–234 (2015)
20. Anuradha, C., Murty, P.S.R.C., Kiran, C.S.: Detecting outliers in high dimensional data sets using Z-score methodology. Int. J. Innov. Technol. Explor. Eng. IJITEE **9**(1), 48–53 (2019). https://doi.org/10.35940/ijitee.a3910.119119

An Improved Hybridization in the Diagnosis of Diabetes Mellitus Using Selected Computational Intelligence

Idowu Dauda Oladipo ⓘ, Abdulrauph Olarewaju Babatunde,
Joseph Bamidele Awotunde(✉) ⓘ, and Muyideen Abdulraheem ⓘ

Department of Computer Science, University of Ilorin, Ilorin, Nigeria
{odidowu,babatunde.ao,awotunde.jb,muyideen}@unilorin.edu

Abstract. Artificial Intelligence (AI) in medicine has provided numerous advantages in diagnosis, management, and prediction of highly complicated and uncertain diseases like diabetes. Despite the high rate of complexity and uncertainty in this area, computational intelligent systems such as the Artificial Neural Network (ANN), Fuzzy Logic (FL) and Genetic Algorithm (GA) have been used to enhance healthcare services, reduce medical costs and improve quality of life. Hence, Computational Intelligence Techniques (CIT) has been successfully employed in diabetes disease diagnosis, risk evaluation, patient monitoring, and prediction in the medical field. Using single technique in the diagnosis of diabetes has been comprehensively investigated showing some level of accuracy, but the use of hybridized can still perform better. Diabetes Mellitus (DM) is one of contemporary society's most chronic and crippling diseases and poses not just a medical issue but also a socio-economic issue. Therefore, the paper develops an improved hybrid system for the diagnosis of diabetes mellitus using FL, ANN, and Genetic Algorithm (GA). FL and ANN was combined for the diagnosis of diabetes mellitus and GA is used for features selection and optimization. The result performed better during the diagnosis process for diabetes mellitus. Hence the results of the comparison showed that Genetic-Neuro-Fuzzy Inferential System (GNFIS) had a better performance with 99.34% accuracy on the whole dataset used when compared with FL and ANN with 96.14% and 95.14% respectively. The proposed system can be used in assisting medical practitioners in diagnose diabetes mellitus and increase its accuracy

Keywords: Diabetes mellitus · Fuzzy logic · Artificial neural network · Genetic algorithm · Computational intelligence technique

1 Introduction

Diabetes is increasing rapidly in developed countries; the increase is widespread because over 246 million people worldwide were treated from this chronic disease according to data from the International Diabetes Foundation in 2005. It was also reported that by 2025 at least 300 million people worldwide may develop diabetes disease [1]. The exact

© Springer Nature Switzerland AG 2021
S. Misra and B. Muhammad-Bello (Eds.): ICTA 2020, CCIS 1350, pp. 272–285, 2021.
https://doi.org/10.1007/978-3-030-69143-1_22

number of people with diabetes mellitus is higher since, by a definite epidemiological study on each diagnosed patient, there is one non-diagnosed patient. [2]. A large number of patients with diabetes belong to the group of the working population.

According to the International Diabetes Foundation, 2010 Nigeria is one of Africa's most populous countries with the largest number of people with diabetes, with 3.0 million, 1.9 million South Africans, 1.4 million Ethiopians, and 769,000 Kenyans. Providing a remedy for insufficient medical care using human resource education involves long and high costs which can result in an improved patient morbidity rate.

Meanwhile, emphasis on the need for preventive methods has been the interest of health care, researchers, and medical personnel around the world [3–5]. The preventive method that would support the well-planned assessment that could moderate or lower the risk of transitioning from pre-diabetes to diabetes. Diabetes mellitus is graded as "type 1," "type 2," "gestational diabetes" and other different forms of [6].

Diabetes Mellitus represents both the medical and socio-economic problems in modern society [7–10]. In developed and developing countries the disease is widespread. It was estimated that 175 million people having diabetes in 2004, worldwide and it was projected that an estimate of 354 million will have diabetes by 2030 [11]. According to the International Diabetes Foundation, 2010, Nigeria is one of the most known countries in Africa that records the huge figure of DM, three million in South Africa, one million and nine hundred thousand in Ethiopia, and one million and four hundred thousand in Kenya 769,000 [12]. Providing a solution for inadequate medical services using the education of human resources requires a long time and high expenses that may result in an increased morbidity rate in patients [13, 27].

Artificial Intelligence (AI) in medicine has provided numerous advantages in diagnosis, management, and prediction of highly complicated and uncertain diseases [14, 15]. Despite the high rate of complexity and uncertainty in this field, computational intelligent systems like NN, FL, and genetic algorithm (GA) have been used to improve health care, minimize treatment expenses and improve the quality of life [16–18]. A new system category is the hybrid intelligent system focused on artificial intelligence techniques such as fuzzy logic, neural network, expert system, and genetic algorithms [19, 20].

Using single technique in the diagnosis of diabetes has been comprehensively investigated showing some level of accuracy [12, 21]. Researchers have investigated the effect of hybridizing more than one techniques to show better results in the diagnosis of diabetes [22] but to the best of our knowledge none use GA for features selection. Therefore, the work developed an improved neuro-fuzzy inferential system that combines NN and FL and used GA for the optimization of parameters before the classification of DM.

2 Related Work

Different types of intelligent system techniques have been applied to detect, classify, and diagnose diabetes and its complications. Expert System (ES) is built using one or combination of these techniques: Artificial Neural Networks (ANN), Genetic Algorithm (GA), Fuzzy Logic (FL) [23] used fuzzy logic to build an expert diabetes diagnostics program with judgment mechanism for instance. Triangular membership functions with

Mamdani's inference are used in a fuzzy verdict mechanism. The conversion of fuzzy values into crisp values was done with the Defuzzification method. The judgment process was used to enforce rules to make a decision about the probability of diabetes sufferers and to present the information with descriptions. The experimental result shows that the expert system can pass the information acquired into the expertise to replicate the human thought process and can analyze data from the database [24].

[25] used an adaptive neuro-fuzzy inference system (ANFIS) and principal component analysis (PCA) for diabetes diagnosis to improve the diagnostic accuracy of diabetes. He divided the system into two stages, the first stage of 8 features dataset is reduced to 4 features by PCA and in stage two the reduced dataset was used to diagnose patients with diabetes disease using the designed system classifier (adaptive neuro-fuzzy inference system). The proposed system recorded 89.47% classification accuracy.

[26] proposed a fuzzy logic expert system to improve on Pima diabetes dataset classification accuracy. Artificial neural network (ANN) with two neural networks were combined to form a hybrid system, a back propagation algorithm was used to train the proposed system. Fuzzy like age, blood pressure, and the rest were used as crisp data after dividing the inputs into two groups. The standardized crisp input values are fed to the first ANN in the first stage (ANN1) and the result of the defuzzyfied from fuzzing fuzzy data and their values are presented to FNN. To calculate the final output, the results from ANN1 and FNN were fed to the second ANN (ANN2). If the output value is different from the actual value, the weights of these networks will change, and the process was repeated until reasonable results are reached. The developed system was tested using K-fold cross-validation and achieved an accuracy of 84.24%.

The hybridized intelligent system used the fuzzy expert system in addition to the neural network base. The inputs have been separated into a couple of groups: fuzzy such as blood pressure and medical tests and rest are deemed to be crisp data. A fuzzy system is applied to integrate the fuzzy inputs then feeding them to ANN together with the crisp inputs. ANN has been used for the prediction of DM. This paper tends to add GA for features selection before applying ANN and FL.

3   An Overview of the Techniques

3.1   Brief Description of Some Computational Intelligence Techniques Used

Neural Network (NN)
Neural networks can easily handle both continuous and discrete data and can gather data from available indicators. A neural network has been used to train and test the designed Fuzzy system, as well as to develop the per-for-mance of the overall system. This consists of 8 features, namely: diastolic blood pressure, 2 h of oral glucose tolerance test (plasma glucose concentration), some pregnant days, skin folding thickness of Triceps, 2-h serum insulin (INS), body mass index (BMI), diabetes pedigree function (DPF), and sex. Wi has been used to show that that attribute has a weight that contributes to the process of diagnosis. The attributes of patient diagnosis were fed into the neural network as input

layer and contribution was calculated at the hidden layer of each group of variables. The equation used is as follows:

$$CAT_i = \sum_{i}^{n} A_i * W_{Ai} \tag{1}$$

Fuzzy logic has the power of handling imprecise and imperfect data which is one of the characteristics of medical records, and it is a superset of traditional Boolean. This seeks a definite solution to a given problem and often parallels human decision-making in its ability to function from indirect reasoning. The steps involved in diagnosing and controlling diabetes through fuzzy logic are the following process:

$$Output_{NeuralNetwork} = \sum_{i}^{n} CAT_i * W_{CATi} \tag{2}$$

Where WCATi is the connection weight of CATi

Fuzzy Logic
Fuzzy logic has the strength of handling imprecise and incomplete data that is one of the characteristics of medical records, and it is a superset of the conventional Boolean. It finds a precise solution to a given problem and its ability to work from approximate reasoning also resembles human decision making. The following process is the stages involves in diagnosis and management of diabetes by fuzzy logic:

1. Fuzzification of the attributes input by the patient
2. Formation of a fuzzy rule base system.
3. Inference engine: the building of decision making for the fuzzy logic component.
4. Defuzzification of the output results from the inference engine into crisp values.

Algorithm for Fuzzy Logic
Phase 1: Glucose, INS, BMI, DPF, and age were used as crisp values for the data.
Phase 2: Set the Fuzzy Number triangular membership function.
Phase 3: Construct the Fuzzy numbers for the input set & output set of the five (5) attributes
Phase 4: Mamdani was used for executing a fuzzy inference process.
Phase 5: Enter the rules and measure the corresponding degree of law for the fuzzy input collection "OR" disjunction (Glucoselow, Glucosemedium, Glucosehigh, INSlow, INS-medium, INShigh, BMIlow, BMImedium, BMIhigh, DPFlow, DPFmedium, DPFhigh, Ageyoung, Age-old).
Phase 6: Calculate the aggregation of the fuzzy output set DM fired rules (DMverylow, DMlow, DMmedium, DMhigh, DMveryhigh).
Phase 7: Defuzzify into the crisp values by:

$$z^* = \frac{\int \mu A(z) \cdot zdz}{\int \mu A(z)dz} \tag{3}$$

Where $\int$ is the algebraic integration, $\mu A(z)$ is the number of fuzzy numbers of the fuzzy DM output variable and z is the weight of $\mu A(z)$. Step 8: Reflect the type of information in the human language.

Fuzzification

Fuzzification is the first step in the Fuzzy Inference method. It's a domain transformation that transforms crisp inputs into fuzzy inputs. In fuzzification, the fuzzy sets for the indicators, and the performance of diagnosis and diabetes management along with membership function were established.

Table 1. Ranges of the output fuzzy set for diabetes mellitus application

Output fields	Range	Fuzzy set
Result	<0.4	Low
	0.4–0.6	Medium
	0.61–1	High

The Fuzzy Sets for the Indicators and the Output of Diabetes Mellitus is as follow;

Number of Pregnancy: {Absent, Normal, Risk}.
Diastolic Blood Pressure: {Low, Medium, High, Very High}.
Triceps Skin Thickness: {Good, Average, Below Average}.
Glucose: {Low, Medium, High}.
Insulin: {Low, Medium, High}.
Body Mass Index (BMI): {Low, Medium, High}.
Diabetes Pedigree Function (DPF): {Low, Medium, High}.
Age: {Young, Medium, Old}.
Output: {Low, Medium, High}.

For the output fuzzy set, the system used 0 = Low, 1 = Medium, and 2 = High. The following:

For the final result, this study considered low as No Diabetes, medium, and high as Diabetes. After identifying the indicators and their fuzzy sets, the range values for each indicator's fuzzy sets were prepared, and the evaluation for the data used for the model was performed by the doctors. Once the range values for the fuzzy sets were ready, the equations were built to produce the membership function using the range values. Triangular, trapezoidal, and bell-shaped membership functions are some of the types of membership functions that have been proposed. In this work, triangular membership function was used because calculations with triangular membership are easy, and shapes are simpler and more versatile and have fewer complexes when comparing other membership functions when dividing values (low, mid, and high MF). In Eq. 3.4 the triangular component function is seen.

$$0 \begin{cases} 0, & x < a \\ \frac{x-a}{x-b} & a < x \leq b \\ \frac{c-x}{c-b} & b < x < c \\ 0, & x > a \end{cases} \text{Triangular membership functions} \quad (4)$$

After generating the membership functions of the fuzzy sets, to get the most appropriate membership from the fuzzy set of each indicator, the maximum was taken from the generated membership function of the fuzzy set in each indicator. The maximum was considered because this study followed the Mamdani method to develop the FIS. In Mamdani, the maximum is taken from the generated membership function of the fuzzy sets to choose the appropriate membership function.

3.2 Genetic Algorithm

Genetic algorithms have been used to select optimal attributes (values) from the diagnostic parameters that serve as input, as well as device optimization. Indian diabetes dataset PIMA has eight attributes. In Neural Network, a genetic algorithm was used to choose which attributes to be used as input to reduce the complexity of computation.

3.3 Genetic-Neuro-Fuzzy Inference System (GNFIS)

The proposed approach incorporates ANN, Fuzzy logic, and Genetic Algorithm to construct an inferential system called the Genetic-Neuro-Fuzzy Inference System (GNFIS), designed to handle ambiguous and imprecise diabetes diagnostic data, self-learning, and adaptive system. To construct the inference method, the feed-forward propagation learning technique composed of nine layers of neurons was employed. Both secret and output layers consist of active nodes, which are inactive nodes at the input layer where computations occur. The reasoning algorithm based inference engine used Mamdani's Inference Mechanism which is a law of development. The active nodes represent inputs from computers and are one of seven layers. Numeric values are used as variables for the diagnosis to reflect how bad a patient is feeling. For every input tag, the output layer is the corresponding linguistic labels.

Using the formula below, the second layer composed of adaptive nodes was used to obtain the output of the preceding layer as input and generated their corresponding membership grade:

$$L_2(x_i) = \mu_{Ai}(X_i) \quad (5)$$

Increasing variable's Fuzzy value is calculated using triangular MF, given as:

$$(X_i) = \frac{x_i - b}{a - b} \quad (6)$$

4   Methodology

4.1   Model Diagram

A Block diagram of the theoretical model for diabetes diagnosis is shown in Fig. 1 below; it demonstrates the flow of a diabetic Mellitus diagnostic model.

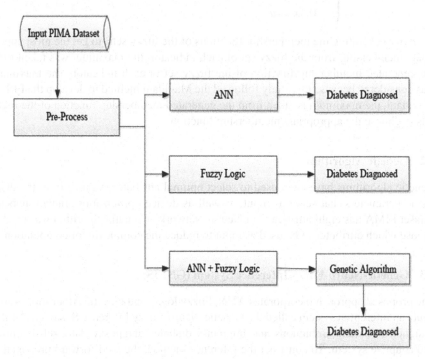

Fig. 1. Block diagram for the proposed system model

4.2   Data Used for the System

In this work, the direct rating method was used for acquiring data, which is an effective way of constructing a membership function and direct means of collecting data. Also, to rate the membership function, all the rating indicators (subject) in sequences of data were presented (objects) to the domain experts. To construct a membership function, the responses of several physicians were collected. Both lowest and highest values were used finally to form the ranges for membership function calculation. Minimum values are the lowest and highest as the maximum values. The data used fell within the range, removing any chance of losing data. Table 2 shows the ratings of the data for the proposed system for diagnoses of diabetes mellitus.

Table 2. Results of rating for the indicators of the diabetes mellitus by physicians

Input field	Range				Fuzzy set
	1st Physician	2nd Physician	3rd Physician	4th Physician	
1. Glucose	≤71–110	≤90	≤120	≤121	Low
	94–120	95–130	97–138	96–145	Medium
	≥121	≥122	≥124	≥125	High
2. INS	≤15–80	≤15–78	≤20–86	≤17–87	Low
	15–100	20–150	17–90	15–100	Medium
	≥89–194	≥95–193	≥192	≥194	High
3. BMI	≤24	≤27	≤33	≤30	Low
	24	35	39	40	Medium
	≥33	≥35	≥37	≥40	High
4. DPF	≤0	≤0.2	≤0.3	≤0.4	Low
	0.2	0.3	0.4	0.6	Medium
	≥0.4	≥0.6	≥0.7	≥0.4	High
5. Age	≤30	≤29	≤38	≤35	Young
	33	40	42	43	Mid
	≥45–55	≥47–54	≥50	≥58	Old

Indicators of Diabetes Mellitus

i.   **Pregnancy number:** This is graded as absent, weak, and risky. If a person is male then there will be no pregnancy number.
ii. **Diastolic blood pressure:** This field has four fuzzy sets low, medium, high, and very high.
iii. **Triceps skinfold thickness:** It a measurement factor used for body fat.
iv. **Glucose:** Glucose or blood sugar is the principal source of energy in the blood. It is measured by a 2-h glucose concentration after 2 h of having breakfast (American Diabetes Association, 2014). Glucose has three low, medium, and high Fuzzy sets.
v.   **Insulin (INS):** Insulin is the hormone that the pancreas excretes to help transfer glucose from the blood into the cells that are used for energy. It is measured by 2-h serum insulin (INS) after 2 h of having breakfast (American Diabetes Association, 2014). If insulin is not responded well by the cells, then glucose cannot enter the cells. As a result, the cells lack the fuel they need, and glucose builds up in the bloodstream. INS has three low, medium, and high Fuzzy sets.

vi. **Body Mass Index (BMI):** BMI is used as a measure of the body's weight to a person's height. This area consists of three small, medium, and high Fuzzy sets in the developed system.

vii. **Diabetes Pedigree Function (DPF):** DPF is the statistical classification of a certain data category (American Diabetes Association 2014). For example, of the age group 40–45, data are analyzed and calculated when determining statistical values for the age group. DPF consists of three fuzzy sets low, medium, and high.

viii. **Age:** Age is considered a further diabetes predictor. Age has three new, medium, and old Fuzzy collections.

5 Result and Discussion

The program has been developed to diagnose Mellitus Diabetes. The program was developed and using the Pima Indian Diabetes Database (PIDD) dataset to test the performance of the proposed system. The database has 8 input attributes, and the third as goal variable. The following are the attributes of PIDD database namely: Triceps skinfold thickness (mm), number of times pregnant, 2-H serum insulin (mu U/ml), diastolic blood pressure (mm Hg), diabetes pedigree size, body mass index (weight in kg/(height in m) ^2), 2-h oral glucose tolerance test plasma glucose concentration, and age (years). The attributes were used to test if a patient is tested-positive or tested-negative. The totals of 768 patients are available in PIDD.

100 patients were used for training test from the Pima database diabetes dataset and stored as rules in the database (patient medical records) to assess the efficiency of the built program. To get a simple estimate 100 patients were used to check the proposed program from the dataset. Human respiratory disease experts assess the production value of each rule from the documents that were obtained for the program. Human knowledge is used to determine the sensitivity of the input variables. The severity of each variable reflects their contribution to the disease of diabetes.

Java programming language was chosen to build the system this is because it is a high-level programming language and object-oriented based program with functions and class which could be used to develop and link a graphic user interface for user interaction and responsiveness. The diagnostic system employed several components in JavaScript to achieve the implementation of this system.

5.1 Performance Evaluation Metrics

Basic assessment criteria and evaluation focused based on classification accuracy using True Negative (TN), True Positive (TP), False Negative (FN), and False Positive (FP). Table 3 displayed the performance evaluation metrics used in the paper.

Where:

TN = the number of healthy people among those diagnosed with diabetes
TP = means the number of people who currently have diabetes among those who have been diagnosed as diabetic
FN = number of people who were diagnosed as diabetic found to be stable
FP = depicts the number of unhealthy individuals, i.e. diabetic, but diagnosed as well.

Table 3. Performance evaluation metrics

Measures	Definition	Formula
Sensitivity test	Measure the ability to correctly detect diabetes disease	$TP/(TP + FN)$
Specificity test	Measure the ability to avoid calling normal things as diabetes disease in medical tests	$TN/(TN + FP)$
PPV	Positively predicated value	$TP/(TP + FP)$
NPV	Negatively predicated value	$TN/(TN + FN)$
Accuracy	Measure the percentage of correctly detect diabetes disease	$\frac{TN+TP}{TN+FP+FN+TP} \times 100$

5.2 Genetic Neuro-Fuzzy Inference Diagnostic System Experimental Results

The results gathered from the developed GNFIS diagnostics system for Diabetes Mellitus are shown in the following sections.

The Experimental Results of the GNFIS

Fifty (50) specimens were chosen for test runs from the sample. To evaluate the different output metrics the one trail/run closer to the average classification accuracy value was selected. The overall accuracy of the results rating was 97.79%. The GNFIS system performance assessment metrics for classifying the reduced dataset are shown in Table 2 and Table 3; this demonstrates that the developed system's classification accuracy is better than the current research.

Genetic algorithm (GA) was used to delete samples and cases that were outliers, noisy, and inconsistent, with missing values being replaced by mean. Using a 10-fold cross-validation technique for classification, the algorithm was used as a feature selection method, and its output was fed to NFIS. During each run, GA was used to select different features from the original collection of attributes, and their classification accuracy for each run was registered. To obtain the satisfactory result the experiment was replicated 50 times. Table 4 and Fig. 2 shown the evaluation metrics obtained from the proposed system.

Table 4. Evaluation metrics obtained from GNFIS diagnosis

Performance measures	Reduced dataset
No. of attributes used	**5**
Sensitivity (%)	96.00
Specificity (%)	99.00
Positively predicted value (%)	99.00
Negatively predicted value (%)	98.00
GNFIS accuracy (%)	98.00

Table 5. The accuracy obtained from the three systems for diagnosis

Performance measures	Reduced dataset
No. of attributes used	5
Fuzzy logic accuracy (%)	97.00
ANN accuracy (%)	96.00
GNFIS accuracy (%)	99.00

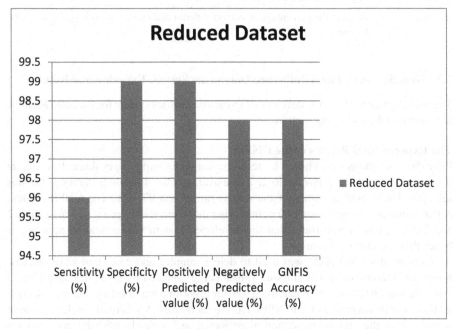

Fig. 2. Graphical representation of evaluation metrics for GNFIS

The accuracy obtained from the system for diabetes mellitus diagnosis is displayed in Table 5 and Fig. 3. The results show that the hybridized system performed better compared with the single technique.

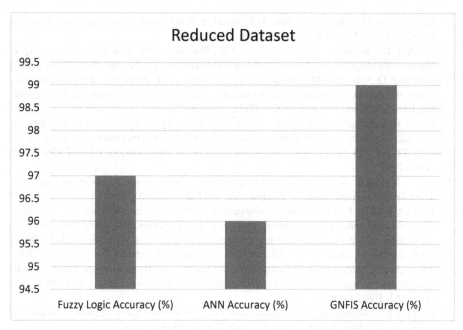

Fig. 3. The accuracy (%) for the three system for diabetes diagnosis

6 Conclusion and Recommendation

Test findings showed that the GNFIS works best, with 96% accuracy over the entire dataset being used. The Fuzzy logic model provided 94% accuracy. With 92% accuracy of the three models, the ANNs model registered the least accuracy. From the sensitivity study, as shown in Table 3, age, diabetes family history, BMI, and salty food preference played a significant role in the occurrence of the diabetes dataset, and the findings provide proof of diabetes prevention through community interventions. This research introduced Genetic Algorithms for dimensionality reduction, as well as Neural Network and Fuzzy Logic for diagnosing the data set for diabetes. The GNFIS analysis of the proposed system's accuracy is 2.08% higher than the neural network and the fuzzy logic. However, the accuracy of the system can be increased using other combinations of other machine learning algorithms. Besides, this application runs on a standalone system. In future work, the system can be applied on high-performance client-server and mobile applications, thus client-server application installed can request and receive information over the network which will be easier to access by all users.

References

1. Alade, O.M., Sowunmi, O.Y., Misra, S., Maskeliūnas, R., Damaševičius, R.: A neural network based expert system for the diagnosis of diabetes mellitus. In: Antipova, T., Rocha, A. (eds.) MOSITS 2017. AISC, vol. 724, pp. 14–22. Springer, Cham (2018). https://doi.org/10.1007/978-3-319-74980-8_2

2. International Diabetes Federation. IDF Member Association Consultation on Diabetes Priorities for the UN Summit on NCDs. Brussels (2010)
3. Jimoh, R.G., Afolayan, A.A., Awotunde, J.B., Matiluko, O.E.: Fuzzy logic based expert system in the diagnosis of ebola virus. Ilorin J. Comput. Sci. Inf. Technol. 2(1), 73–94 (2017)
4. Ameen, A.O., Olagunju, M., Awotunde, J.B., Adebakin, T.O., Alabi, I.O.: Performance evaluation of breast cancer diagnosis using radial basis function, C4. 5 and adaboost. Univ. Pitesti Sci. Bull. Ser. Electron. Comput. Sci. 17(2), 1–12 (2017)
5. Iheme, P., Omoregbe, N., Misra, S., Ayeni, F., Adeloye, D.: A decision support system for pediatric diagnosis. In: M. F. Kebe, C., Gueye, A., Ndiaye, A. (eds.) InterSol/CNRIA -2017. LNICST, vol. 204, pp. 177–185. Springer, Cham (2018). https://doi.org/10.1007/978-3-319-72965-7_17
6. Nonso, N., Farath, A., David, E., Jiten, V., James, N.: Model for type 2 diabetes management: a tool for regimen alterations. J. Comput. Sci. Appl. 3(3), 40–45 (2015)
7. Lindner, L.M.E., Rathmann, W., Rosenbauer, J.: Inequalities in glycaemic control, hypoglycemia, and diabetic ketoacidosis according to socio-economic status and area-level deprivation in type 1 diabetes mellitus: a systematic review. Diab. Med. 35(1), 12–32 (2018)
8. Abdulrahman, M., Husain, Z.S., Abdouli, K.A., Kazim, M.N., Ahmad, F.S.M., Carrick, F.R.: Association between knowledge, awareness, and practice of patients with type 2 diabetes with socio-economic status, adherence to medication, and disease complications. Diab. Res. Clin. Pract. 163, 108124 (2020)
9. Oladipo, I.D., Babatunde, A.O.: Framework for genetic-neuro-fuzzy inferential system for diagnosis of diabetes mellitus. Ann. Comput. Sci. Ser. 16(1) (2018)
10. Oladipo, I.D., Babatunde, A.O., Aro, T.O., Awotunde, J.B.: Enhanced neuro-fuzzy inferential system for diagnosis of diabetes mellitus (DM). Int. J. Inf. Process. Commun. (IJIPC) 8(1), 17–25 (2020)
11. Persson, M., et al.: The better diabetes diagnosis (BDD) study – a review of a nationwide prospective cohort study in Sweden. Diab. Res. Clin. Pract. 140, 236–244 (2018). https://doi.org/10.1016/j.diabres.2018.03.057
12. Kaur, C., Omisakin, O.M.: Data mining methods to improve clinical trials in diabetic patients. Ann. Clin. Lab. Res. 06(04), 1–9 (2018). https://doi.org/10.21767/2386-5180.100266
13. Rinsho, N., Sugihara, S.: Diagnosis and treatment of type 1 diabetes mellitus in children. Jpn. J. Clin. Med. 74, 501–505 (2016)
14. Pandey, S., Tripathi, M.M.: Diagnosis of diabetes using artificial intelligence techniques by using biomedical signal data. Int. J. Res. Dev. Appl. Sci. Eng. 13(2), 1–6 (2017)
15. Ayo, F.E., Awotunde, J.B., Ogundokun, R.O., Folorunso, S.O., Adekunle, A.O.: A decision support system for multi-target disease diagnosis: a bioinformatics approach. Heliyon 6(3), e03657 (2020)
16. Thirugnanam, M., Kumar, P., Vignesh, S., Nerlesh, C.R.: Improving, the prediction rate of diabetes diagnosis using fuzzy, neural network, case-based (FNC) approach. Proc. Eng. 38, 1709–1718 (2012). https://doi.org/10.1016/j.proeng.2012.06.208
17. Awotunde, J.B., Matiluko, O.E., Fatai, O.W.: Medical diagnosis system using fuzzy logic. Afr. J. Comput. ICT 7(2), 99–106 (2014)
18. Azeez, N.A., et al.: A Fuzzy expert system for diagnosing and analyzing human diseases. In: Abraham, A., Gandhi, N., Pant, M. (eds.) IBICA 2018. AISC, vol. 939, pp. 474–484. Springer, Cham (2019). https://doi.org/10.1007/978-3-030-16681-6_47
19. Durairaj, M., Kalaiselvi, G.: Prediction of diabetes using the backpropagation algorithm. International Journal of Emerging Technology and Innovative Eng. 1(8), 21–25 (2015)
20. Abdullah, A.A., Fadil, N.S., Khairunizam, W.: Development of a fuzzy expert system for the diagnosis of diabetes. In: 2018 International Conference on Computational Approach in Smart Systems Design and Applications (ICASSDA), pp. 1–8. IEEE August 2018

21. Nilashi, M., Ibrahim, O., Dalvi, M., Ahmadi, H., Shahmoradi, L.: Accuracy improvement for diabetes disease classification: a case on a public medical dataset. Fuzzy Inf. Eng. 9(3), 345–357 (2017). https://doi.org/10.1016/j.fiae.2017.09.006
22. Qureshi, I., Ma, J., Abbas, Q.: A recent development in detection methods for the diagnosis of diabetic retinopathy. Symmetry 11(6), 1–34 (2019). https://doi.org/10.3390/sym11060749
23. Thompson, T., Sowunmi, O., Misra, S., Fernandez-Sanz, L., Crawford, B., Soto, R.: An expert system for the diagnosis of sexually transmitted diseases–ESSTD. J. Intell. Fuzzy Syst. 33(4), 2007–2017 (2017)
24. Omisore, M.O., Samuel, O.W., Atajeromavwo, E.J.: A genetic-neuro-fuzzy inferential model for diagnosis of tuberculosis. Saudi Comput. Soc. King Saud Univ. Appl. Comput. Inform. 13, 27–37 (2017)
25. Uğuz, H.: A biomedical system based on artificial neural network and principal component analysis for diagnosis of the heart valve diseases. J. Med. Syst. 36(1), 61–72 (2012)
26. Tejashri, N.G., Satish, R.T.: Prognosis of Diabetes using Neural Network, Fuzzy Logic, Gaussian Kernel Method. Int. J. Comput. Appl. 0975–8887, 124(10), 21–34 (2015)
27. Iheme, P., Omoregbe, N.A., Misra, S., Adeloye, D., Adewumi, A.: Mobile-Bayesian diagnostic system for childhood infectious diseases. In: ICADIWT, pp. 109–118 July 2017

Optimizing the Classification of Network Intrusion Detection Using Ensembles of Decision Trees Algorithm

Olamatanmi J. Mebawondu[1]([⊠]) [iD], Olufunso D. Alowolodu[2] [iD],
Adebayo O. Adetunmbi[3] [iD], and Jacob O. Mebawondu[1] [iD]

[1] Department of Computer Science, Federal Polytechnic, Nasarawa, Nigeria
jpmebawondu@gmail.com, mebawondu1010@gmail.com
[2] Department of Computer Science, Federal University of Technology, Akure, Nigeria
odalowolodu@futa.edu.ng
[3] Department of Cyber Security, Federal University of Technology, Akure, Nigeria
aoadetunmbi@futa.edu.ng

Abstract. Over the years, the vulnerability of the network system has completely revolutionized the security system. Attackers simply exploit these exposures to gain undue access to network resources. It is essential to safeguard network resources with the Intrusion Prevention System (IPS) and Intrusion Detection System (IDS). Hence, to develop an optimized IDS model using ensemble modeling of machine learning technique is paramount. Therefore, this research attempts to build a network IDS using an ensemble of Decision Trees (DT) algorithms to optimize an IDS model. Furthermore, the C4.5 DT classifier used on the University of New South Wales Network-Based 2015 (UNSW-NB15) network data set. Then the ensemble techniques of bagging and AdaBoost are compared during the performance evaluation. The results of this work depict that performance increase as training size increases. Consequently, the results showed that adopting the ensemble model for the C4.5 decision tree classified improved network intrusion classification compared to using the machine learning algorithm in isolation. Moreover, the result also showed an improved classification model for network IDS model. The AdaBoost ensemble model of the C4.5 DT algorithm using partitions of 90% of training and 10% of testing data sets performs the best with 98% accuracy and precision.

Keywords: Decision trees · Ensemble learning · Network intrusion detection · Boosting · Bagging

1 Introduction

The Internet application has helped the socio-economic ways of human endeavour as entertainment, education, commerce, and communication; it has transformed people's daily lives [1]. However, the security of the Internet has turn vulnerable because of the innumerable developments of networks and the fast emergence of hacking instruments

© Springer Nature Switzerland AG 2021
S. Misra and B. Muhammad-Bello (Eds.): ICTA 2020, CCIS 1350, pp. 286–300, 2021.
https://doi.org/10.1007/978-3-030-69143-1_23

and intrusion technologies [2]. Therefore, the importance of developing adequate security has drawn appreciable notice from the academia and industry around the universe. Therefore, various security programs, user authentication, data encryption, firewalls, and malware prevention are entrenched, many enterprises and establishments still fall victim to cyber-attacks [3].

Bhattacharyya, and Kalita [4] reported an increase in the risk and sophistication of hackers' attacks to Internet users as linked systems turn out to be, to a greater extent, pervasive, and businesses stay to move new sensitive data online [4]. Consequently, companies who understand the risks of exposure try to identify flaws in their networks while others simply ignore the risk and remain vulnerable to cyber-attacks by hackers [5]. Therefore, an intrusion is action that attempts to bypass computer systems' security mechanisms within a private or public network. Intrusions may take numerous forms: attackers using the Internet to access a system; authorized (official) users' effort to gain and abuse non-authorized privileges [6]. Hence, network intrusions are any set of activities that endanger a network resource's confidentiality, availability, or integrity.

The uncovering of intrusion along the network can be achieved by monitoring the events on a system and analyzing them for intrusion signs but Network IDS (NIDS) raises the alert whenever possible occurrence of intrusion. For companies to protect possessions, organizations are increasingly dependent on NIDS to automatically detect abnormal or suspicious behavior [7, 8]. Therefore, in reality, NIDS is a hardware or software application used for monitoring network activities with a significant goal of discovering and reporting malicious activities to the network administrator [9]. Nevertheless, in any NIDS development, the classification and selection of features are the two prominent essential issues to be resolved. The algorithm is carried out to provide a value for a set of features from the chance of network intrusion to be determined. On the other hand, the inputs of the features selected and fed to the NIDS algorithm include network packets, protocols, and much more [10, 11].

Machine learning, described as a branch of artificial intelligence, allows computers to learn from past examples of data records [12, 13]. The ML does not rely on prior hypotheses like traditional explanatory statistical modeling techniques do [14]. Machine learning techniques are classified into supervised and unsupervised techniques. Hence, the classification model is a supervised approach aimed at allocating the values of a set of input features to one of the values of a discrete target class [8, 15].

Over the past decades, the ensemble approaches have been very effective since various classifiers have unique inductive biases [16]. A collection of sets of models is used by ensemble classifier, in which each of the original task is solved to produce the global composite classifier with more reliable and accurate decisions than using a single classifier [17, 18]. According to [16, 19], bagging and boosting are techniques that could improve the precision and accuracy of weak classifiers. Boosting theory is a foundation for AdaBoost algorithms, which extends its concepts to regression and multiple class problems [20].

Since ensemble techniques have successfully curbed all machine learning problems, such as error correction, class imbalanced data, feature selection, and others [21–23], hence, this study aims to apply the ensemble modeling approach to improve network intrusion classification via the use of a network intrusion data set. Furthermore, analysis of the performance of various ensembles of a machine learning algorithm utilized for the binary class of network intrusion detection is considered.

This paper is arranged as follows: In Sect. 1, the introduction is presented, a review of related works is explained in Sect. 2, while the methods and materials are presented in Sect. 3. In Sect. 4, the results and discussion is presented, followed by the conclusion in Sect. 5.

2 Related Works

[24], worked on developing a classification model for network intrusion using ensemble modeling. The study collected records from the "Network Socket Layer – Knowledge Discovery in Databases" (NSL-KDD). It features information alongside identification as either attacks or Non Attacks. Hence, the study adopted an ensemble model called the extreme gradient boosting (XGBoost) to develop a network intrusion detection model required for identifying records based on information about the input features extracted from the NSL-KDD data set. The study adopted 125973 and 22544 records for training and testing the XGBoost-based classification model respectively, with an accuracy of 98.7%.

Also [18] developed an optimized intrusion model to detect layer seven distributed denial of service intrusion on the web server using deep learning algorithm approach. The results reveal a high detection accuracy rate. But [17] presented an updated review of prevention and detection of intrusion system, giving most recent review discovered as at 2016. The review was able to identify vulnerabilities in the network as prevention against further intrusion.

[25] developed a classification model for the "severity of sickle cell disorders" (SCD) pediatrics using ensemble modeling. The study collated data from pediatric patients aged 15 years and below who had varying SCD severity degrees. The study developed a voting-based ensemble model of "support vector machines" (SVM), "decision trees" (DT), and "naïve Bayes" (NB) in varying combinations of 2 and 3 algorithms. The results showed that SCD severity classification had a maximum accuracy of 96.96% of an ensemble of NB and DT alone techniques.

[26] worked on an evaluation of the performance of intrusion detection using machine learning. The study collected the UNSW-NB15 data set from the online repository and performed a comparative analysis of network intrusion classification using machine learning algorithms. The study results showed that decision trees showed better performance than naïve Bayes for the classification of network intrusion using the UNSW-NB15 data set. In [8], presented a lightweight IDS using Neural Network classification on selected ranked features. The ranked features on the UNSW-NB15 benchmark dataset produces better results. But [21], it opined the use of apriori algorithm on MapReduce framework for network intrusion detection. The KDD dataset was used with evaluation of high detection accuracy for attack.

[27], applied discriminative feature selection for the classification of network intrusion detection. The study collected the KDD Cup 1999 data set, which consisted of 43 features and a target class with five labels. Relevant features extracted from the initially identified features, following which the logistic regression technique applied for NIDS.

Therefore, the results showed that the adoption of extraction of features improved the model's accuracy compared to using identified initial features.

[2], in their study, applied feature selection and ensemble modeling for effective intrusion detection from network-related data. The study collected data from 3 different sources: NSL-KDD, AWID, and CIC-IDS 2017 data sets. Therefore, the study identified relevant features for network intrusion using correlation-based measures. Hence, the classification model was formulated from a majority voting-based ensemble of 3 DT classifiers, namely: "Forest Penalizing Attributes" (Forest PA), "Random Forest" (RF), and C4.5 algorithms. Consequently, the results showed that the ensemble provided the best results using the NSL-KDD data set among collected data with 99.1% accuracy.

[28], developed a spam classification model for the detection of unsolicited mails using an ensemble of evolutionary algorithms. The study collected classified e-mail data from the Enron e-mail and SpamAssassin data sets. The total data collected consisted of 2350 ham and 2350 spam e-mail files. The study adopted the use of a genetic algorithm (GA) for the identification of the most relevant features required for improving the spam detection rate. Hence, the study adopted an ensemble of genetic programming (GP) algorithms with 50 generations as weak learners for the classification of unsolicited (spam) e-mails based on the AdaBoost ensemble algorithm. Therefore, results showed that GP achieved the highest accuracy of 94.1% and 98.2% using Enron and SpamAssassin, respectively, at the 40th generation for both algorithms.

3   The Methods and Materials

3.1   Network Intrusion Detection System Data Set

The data set adopted is a secondary data set, also called the University of New South Wales Network-Based 2015 (UNSW-NB15) network data set was created in 2015 at the "Cyber range" Laboratory, Australian Center for Cyber Security. The data set consists of a total of 82332 records such that 37000 (44.94%) were normal, while 45332 (55.06%) were network attacks in a stored using ".csv" file format. The UNSW-NB15 network data set considered in this study contains 42 attributes, which are further classified within five features classes: basic, flow, content-based, time, and generated features. The dataset has two target features – binary and multi-class of ten attributes [8, 22, 26].

3.2   C4.5 Decision Trees Classifier

The method adopted for the classification model to detect network intrusion. The problem required the identification of the relationship that exists between the features X and the analysis of the normal or malicious invasion of network activities [20, 22, 25]. Therefore, the classification model identified as relationship f, which mapped a set of i features X selected from a data set to a target variable Y, as shown in Eq. (1).

$$f : X_i \rightarrow Y \tag{1}$$

Equation (2) shows the problem identified as a binary class in which an activity is considered either an attack or normal activity.

$$f(X_1, X_2, X_3.....X_i) = \begin{cases} Normal\ Activity \\ Network\ Attack \end{cases} \tag{2}$$

The classification model is a function f representing a set of possible mappings that maps a set of input features to a target class describing the type of activity observed based on the input features.

The DT classifier is a hierarchical set of nodes representing the features with their respective values pointed out towards child nodes. Moreover, the child nodes represent the conditional features on the values of their respective parent node, which are connected to successive child nodes to the terminal node (leaf). The terminal nodes are used to describe the target class. The branches called edges connecting subsequent parent nodes to child nodes and terminate at a leaf. A root node represents the starting point of the tree.

Let a set X_{ij} of j of web hosts' records; the DT algorithm was used to develop a tree of a "divide-and-conquer" algorithm. According to "Hunt's algorithm," the program for the DT that was adopted is stated as follows:

i.   If all the values of the class targets in X_{ij}, $X_{ij} \epsilon\ C_i$ or X_{ij} is few, then X_{ij} is a leaf labeled with the dominant class X_{ij}
ii. else, select the attribute with the highest merit based on a test conducted on all attributes.
a.   Then this attribute becomes the root tree, then a branch is created for each value attribute then make a partition in the data set into its corresponding subsets of each value;
b.   For each subset of data set, repeat (i) and (ii); and
c.   Move to next subset subsequent child nodes of the tree until all possible partitions of data set only fulfill condition (i)
iii. end DT algorithm

The C4.5 DT algorithm is considered here due to its popularity and effectiveness among all other DT algorithms. C4.5 DT is based on gain ratio attribute evaluator and select the successive nodes of the decision tree using the divide-and-conquer approach.

The IG of each feature evaluated an assessment of the difference between the mutual entropy of the feature X with respect to the class Y denoted by H(Y|X) and the entropy of the attribute X denoted by H(X). Given a data set with a feature set having b values and target class with values, the IG can be computed, using in Eq. (3).

$$IG(X) = H(Y|X) - H(X) \tag{3}$$

where:

$$H(Y|X) = -\sum_{m=1}^{a}\sum_{n=1}^{b} p(Y_m|X_n)\log_2 p(Y_m|X_n)\ H(X) = -\sum_{n=1}^{b} p(X_n)\log_2 p(X_n)$$

The Gain Ratio (GR) of each attribute is a standardization of the information gain of the data set's features. The GR calculation is done by dividing the IG via the split information of each feature's values. Hence, the essence of the gain ratio is to use the number of values of features as a basis for assessing the relevance of the feature such that features with lesser values tend to have a higher GR compared to numeric attributes and nominal attributes with a higher number of values [25]. Therefore, the higher the GR of a feature, the higher the relevance and rank. The split information of an attribute X with T values is estimated as shown in Eq. (4), while the GR is estimated as a function of the IG, as shown in Eq. (5).

$$Split\ information(X) = -\sum\nolimits_{n=1}^{b} \frac{T_n}{|X|} \log_2 \frac{T_n}{|X|} \tag{4}$$

$$Gain\ Ratio(X) = \frac{information\ Gain(X)}{Split\ Information(X)} \tag{5}$$

3.3 Ensemble Models

The two ensembles algorithms for improving network intrusion classification are boosting and bagging (bootstrap aggregation) are adopted in this study [19, 28].

Bagging NIDS Input: Training data P; algorithm = baseClassifier; ensemble size = integer T; train size = R
    START:
        Do $t = 1,2,3,4,5,\ldots\ldots, T$
            i.   Take a bootstrapped replica P_t by randomly drawing $R\%$ of P.
            ii. Fetch baseClassifier with P_t and receive the hypothesis (classi
                  fier) h_t.
            iii. Add h_t to the ensemble, $\mathcal{E} \longleftarrow \mathcal{E} \cup h_t$.
    End Do
Ensemble Combination: "Simple Majority Voting" – *Given x of unlabeled instance*
            i.   Evaluate the ensemble $\mathcal{E} = \{h_1,\ldots,h_t\}$ on x.
            ii. Let $v_{t,c} = 1$, and if h_t chooses class w_c, 0, or else.
            iii. Fetch total vote collected by each class

$$V_c = \sum\nolimits_{t=1}^{T} v_{t,c}, c = 1,\ldots., C$$

Output: Class with the highest V_c.
STOP

Fig. 1. Bagging algorithm

Bagging Algorithm. The bootstrap aggregation algorithm for NIDS improved the performance by creating a composite classifier through amalgamating the outputs of trained classifiers, collected from T independent classifiers trained by random sampling into a single prediction. The independent classifier results were collected, and a majority voting scheme was used to estimate the final output of the ensemble model. The bagging for NIDS pseudo-code as presented in depicted Fig. 1 [16]:

Boosting Algorithm. Boosting algorithm is adopted as a repetitive approach for producing a robust classifier, achieving randomly small training error, from weak classifiers ensembled only from random guessing. Nevertheless, each subsequent classifier's training data set increasingly focused on wrongly classified instances by the previously generated classifiers.

The AdaBoost (short for Adaptive Boosting). Ensemble is used to draw training records by iteratively updating the sample distribution of the data that have been trained. The "weighted majority voting" mechanism is used to combine the classifiers through "voting weights," which is based on training errors of the classifiers weighted according to the distribution of the sample, thus ensuring records wrongly classified previously were included in the following classifiers data.

3.4 Ensemble Model Simulation

The UNSW-NB15 data set collected subjected to the ensembles of the C4.5 DT algorithms selected for the NIDS process. Moreover, the ensemble model simulated using the percentage split technique, requiring a higher proportion of the data set used for training and a lower proportion of the data set used for testing in comparison. Nevertheless, the use of 4 sets of training which consisted of 60%, 70%, 80%, and 90% of the data sets and the use of 4 sets for testing which consisted of 40%, 30%, 20%, and 10% adopted to test each ensemble model respectively based on several performance evaluation metrics [23]. The ensemble model simulation is done using the WEKA simulation software based on the selected algorithms, namely: Bagging and AdaBoostM1, listed under the meta-classifiers section of the WEKA Explorer interface.

3.5 Validation of the Classification Model

Following the adoption of the testing proportion of the data set for assessing the ensemble model performance for network IDS, the validation results are presented using the confusion matrix in Fig. 2.

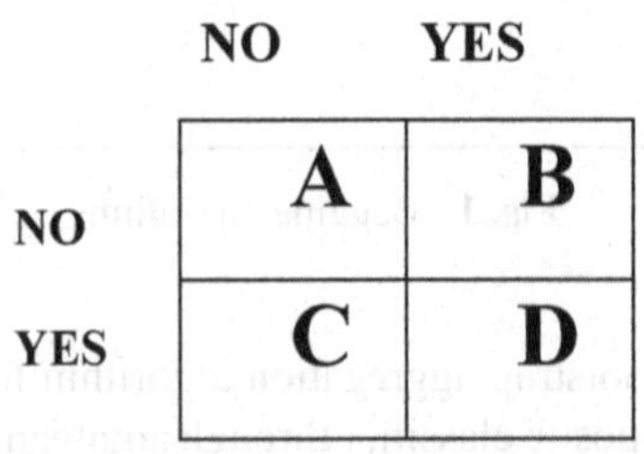

	NO	YES
NO	**A**	**B**
YES	**C**	**D**

Fig. 2. Confusion matrix of simulation results

Furthermore, the confusion matrix contained several cells that stated the total number of correctly and incorrectly classified records by the ensemble model, as shown in Fig. 2. The simulation results were interpreted using a two by two confusion matrix with four-cell.

Therefore, the ensemble model's correct classifications presented along the diagonals at the top-left corner (A for the number of correctly classified No attacks records) and the bottom-right corner (D for the number of correctly classified Yes attacks records). At the same time, the remaining cells B and C described the number of incorrect classifications of No and Yes attacks respectively by the ensemble model based on the UNSW-NB15 data set. Therefore, C + D and A + B were the total number of actual No and Yes attack records, respectively, while A + C and B + D were the numbers of predicted No and Yes attack records, respectively. The classification models evaluated using the values in the blocks of the confusion matrix as follows.

a. **Accuracy** –

$$Accuracy = \frac{A+D}{A+B+C+D} \times 100\% \tag{7}$$

b. **TP (True Positive) rate/Sensitivity** –

$$TP\ rate_{No\ Attack} = \frac{A}{A+B} \tag{8a}$$

$$TP\ rate_{Yes\ Attack} = \frac{D}{C+D} \tag{8b}$$

c. **FP (False Positive)/FAR (False Alarm rate)** –

$$FP\ rate_{No\ Attack} = \frac{C}{C+D} \tag{9a}$$

$$FP\ rate_{Yes\ Attack} = \frac{B}{A+B} \tag{9b}$$

d. **Precision** –

$$Precision_{No\ Attack} = \frac{A}{A+C} \tag{10a}$$

$$Precision_{Yes\ Attack} = \frac{D}{B+D} \tag{10b}$$

4   Results and Discussion

The results of the NIDS development methods using the UNSW-NB15 data set provide peculiar optimized results. The simulation was carried out on WEKA Dumpy platform.

4.1 Data Identification and Collection Results

The results showed that most of the data set collected consisted of attacks records, as shown in Table 1, displaying the target class labels' distribution within the 2 class data set. Furthermore, the Table results shows that a total of 82332 records made up of 37000 (44.94%) Non Attacks records and 45332 (55.06%) attack records.

Table 1. Distribution of the classes within the data set

Target class	Frequency	Percentage (%)
Non attacks	37000	44.94
Attacks	45332	55.06
Total	**82332**	**100.00**

The description of the nominal features as integer attributes in the UNSW-NB15 data set, their corresponding data type and the total number of unique attribute values in each are shown in Table 2.

Table 2. Distribution of the nominal and integer attributes in data set

Attribute name	Data type	Number of unique labels *(distinct values/protocols/services)*
Proto	Nominal	131
Service	Nominal	13
State	Nominal	7
Sttl	Integer	11
Dttl	Integer	8
Swin	Integer	11
Dwin	Integer	14
is_ftp_login	Binary	2
ct_ftp_cmd	Integer	3
is_sm_ips_ports	Binary	2

4.2 Simulation of Ensemble NIDS Results

The ensemble model simulation results show network intrusion detection using two ensembles of the C4.5 DT classifier: bagging and boosting algorithms via the WEKA simulation software. The data set generated from the UNSW-NB15 data set divided into

Table 3. Records distribution in testing and training data set

Simulation (Proportion, %)	Training data set	Testing data set
Simulation I (60% - 40%)	49399	32933
Simulation II (70% - 30%)	57632	24700
Simulation III (80% - 20%)	65866	16466
Simulation IV (90% - 10%)	74099	8233

proportions of testing and training. Table 3 shows a number of records distributions that constituted the testing and training proportions for varying percentage split.

Table 4 displayed the number of records distributed for each class in the 2 class data set. Consequently, it shows that the respective proportion within each simulation is 45% off Non attack and 55% of attacks records.

Table 4. Number of testing and training records in simulations distribution

Simulation name	Number of testing records	Number of records		Proportion of test data	
		Non attack	Attack	Non attack	Attack
Simulation I	32933	14812	18121	44.98	55.02
Simulation II	24700	11092	13608	44.91	55.09
Simulation III	16466	7395	9071	44.91	55.09
Simulation IV	8233	3712	4571	45.08	54.91

The ensemble model simulation for detecting NIDS using the two algorithms presented in terms of the correct and incorrect classifications alongside the accuracy (measured in percentage) generated. Consequently, Table 5 shows the ensemble model results for NIDS based on the UNSW-NB15 data set considered for this study.

Using the C4.5 DT in Isolation. The simulation results revealed that there was 14390 correct classification of the 14812 Non Attacks records and 17568 correct classifications out of the 18121 owing for 31958 correct classifications and 975 misclassifications with an accuracy of 97.04%. Notwithstanding, Simulation II's results revealed that there was 10767 correct classification of the 11092 Non Attacks records and 13208 correct classifications out of the 13608 owing for 23975 correct classifications and 725 misclassifications with an accuracy of 97.06%. Moreover, the results of Simulation IV revealed that there was 3615 correct classification of the 3712 Non Attacks records and 4392 correct classifications out of the 4521 owing for 8007 correct classifications and 226 misclassifications with an accuracy of 97.25%.

Using the Bagging Ensemble. The simulation results revealed that there was 14425 correct classification of the 14812 Non Attacks records and 17640 correct classifications

Table 5. Results of simulation of ensemble model using the UNSW-NB15 data set

Simulation	Machine learning	Total correct classification	Total incorrect classification	Accuracy (%)
Simulation I	Without Ensemble	31958	925	97.04
	Bagging	32065	868	97.36
	AdaBoost	32135	798	97.58
Simulation II	Without Ensemble	23975	725	97.06
	Bagging	24065	635	97.43
	AdaBoost	24129	571	97.69
Simulation III	Without Ensemble	16022	444	97.30
	Bagging	16088	378	97.70
	AdaBoost	16095	371	97.75
Simulation IV	Without Ensemble	8007	226	97.25
	Bagging	8046	187	97.73
	AdaBoost	**8066**	**167**	**97.97**

out of the 18121 due for 32065 correct classifications and 868 misclassifications with an accuracy of 97.36%. Nevertheless, Simulation II results revealed a 10833 correct classification of the 11092 Non Attacks records and 13232 correct classifications out of the 13608 owing for 24065 correct classifications and 635 misclassifications with an accuracy of 97.43%. Furthermore, results of Simulation III revealed that there was 7247 correct classification of the 7395 Non Attacks records and 8841 correct classifications out of the 9071 owing for 16088 correct classifications and 378 misclassifications with an accuracy of 97.70%.

Using the Boosting Ensemble. The ensemble model simulation showed that among the various classification models developed for NIDS, the ensemble system improved classification of testing data set compared to using the C4.5 DT algorithm alone. The study also showed that among the ensemble adopted, the C4.5 DT algorithm's boosting ensemble showed the highest performance among network intrusion detection classification, followed by the bagging ensemble model. Furthermore, the study showed that among the simulations performed, the model performance improved as the training data increased, and the testing data set decreased. Thus, more knowledge about network intrusion was extracted from the ensemble model's data as the training data set size increased.

The simulation I result revealed 14451 correct classifications of the 14812 Non Attacks records and 17684 correct classifications out of the 18121 due for 32135 correct classifications and 798 misclassifications with an accuracy of 97.56%. Simulation II results revealed that there was 10839 correct classification of the 11092 Non Attacks records and 13290 correct classifications out of the 13608 owing for 24129 correct classifications and 571 misclassifications with an accuracy of 97.69%. The results of Simulation III revealed that there was 7241 correct classification of the 7395 Non Attacks records and 8854 correct classifications out of the 9071 owing for 16095 correct classifications and 371 misclassifications with an accuracy of 97.75%.

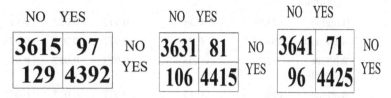

Fig. 4. Confusion matrices of simulation IV output

The confusion matrices in Fig. 4 displays the output of Simulation IV for C4.5 DT in isolation (left), using the bagging (center) and boosting (right) ensemble algorithms.

Therefore, the results of Simulation IV revealed that there was 3641 correct classification of the 3712 Non Attacks records and 4425 correct classifications out of the 4521 owing for 8066 correct classifications and 167 misclassifications with an accuracy of 97.97%.

4.3 Results of Validation of Ensemble NIDS

The validation of NIDS for the discovery of network intrusion was implemented based on the assessment of test and build time (both recorded in seconds) alongside the TP rate, FP rate, and the precision. Table 6 shows a synopsis of the validation of ensemble NIDS for the network intrusion classification.

Table 6. Results of the validation of ensemble models

Simulation	Machine learning algorithm	Build time (s)	Test time (s)	TP rate	FP rate	Precision
I	Without ensemble	38.39	0.15	0.970	0.029	0.970
	Bagging	197.67	0.99	0.974	0.026	0.974
	AdaBoost	*471.65*	*1.16*	*0.976*	*0.024*	*0.976*
II	Without Ensemble	34.16	0.38	0.971	0.029	0.971
	Bagging	202.37	0.45	0.974	0.025	0.974
	AdaBoost	*643.53*	*1.13*	*0.977*	*0.023*	*0.977*
III	Without Ensemble	32.81	0.15	0.973	0.026	0.973

(continued)

Table 6. (*continued*)

Simulation	Machine learning algorithm	Build time (s)	Test time (s)	TP rate	FP rate	Precision
	Bagging	193.04	0.34	0.977	0.022	0.977
	AdaBoost	*606.15*	*0.73*	*0.977*	*0.022*	*0.978*
IV	Without ensemble	32.24	0.05	0.973	0.027	0.973
	Bagging	194.55	0.17	0.977	0.023	0.977
	AdaBoost	*596.58*	*0.82*	*0.980*	*0.020*	*0.980*
	Minimum	32.24	0.05	0.970	**0.020**	0.970
	Maximum	643.53	1.16	**0.980**	0.089	**0.980**
	Mean	**235.75**	**0.59**	0.949	0.047	0.952
	Standard deviation	223.52	0.43	0.035	0.031	0.032

The validation of the classification model based on the TP and FP rate alongside the precision also further supports these observations. Meanwhile, the TP rate results regarding the proportion of correctly classified records showed that using the AdaBoost ensemble of C4.5 DT was higher than that of the bagging ensemble, followed by using the C4.5 DT algorithm in isolation for all simulations performed. The results of the precision regarding the proportion of classification made by the correct ensemble showed that using the AdaBoost ensemble of C4.5 DT was higher than that of the bagging ensemble followed by that of using the C4.5 DT algorithm in isolation for all simulations performed. Consequently, the AdaBoost ensemble of C4.5 DT is recommended used for an improved classification for this research.

Furthermore, results showed that an improved classification model for network intrusion detection was developed based on the UNSW-NB15 data sets via the AdaBoost ensemble model of the C4.5 DT algorithm using 90% the data set for training and 10% of the data set for testing (Simulation IV). The graphical plot of the TP rate, FP rate, and precision of all the simulations are presented in Fig. 5.

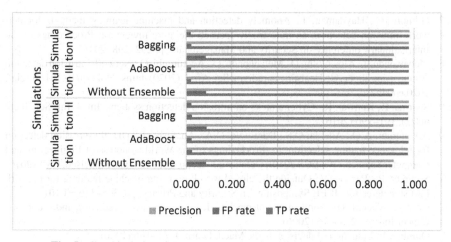

Fig. 5. Graphical plot of TP rate, FP rate and precision of ensemble models

5   Conclusion

This study aimed at an improved NIDS for the classification of network traffics using a network UNSW-NB15 intrusion detection data set. The data set consists of 42 input features and two target classes describing the records, which are attack (Yes) and non_ attack (No). The study concluded from the simulation results for network intrusion that as the training data set increases, the performance of the classification of network intrusion also increased. Therefore, the more the information available about classified records for network intrusion, the more knowledge can be extracted for network intrusion classification. The study also shows that the adoption of ensemble modeling for network intrusion classification improved the classification accuracy compared to base learners' algorithms in isolation. However, with drawbacks on increased build and testing time of the ensemble model.

References

1. Mebawondu, J., Mebawondu, O., Atsanan, A., Suleiman, N.: The Impact of Information Technology on Poverty Alleviation in Nigeria. Cont. J. Inf. Technol. **6**, 1–5 (2012)
2. Zhou, Y., Cheng, G., Jiang, S., Dai, M.: Building an efficient intrusion detection system based on feature selection and ensemble classifier. Comput. Netw. **174**, 107247 (2020)
3. Al-Jarrah, O., Alhussein, O., Yoo, P., Muhaidat, S., Taha, K., Kim, K.: Data randomization and cluster-based partitioning for botnet intrusion detection. IEEE Trans. Cybern. **46**(8), 1796–1806 (2016)
4. Bhattacharyya, D.K., Kalita, J.K.: Network anomaly detection: a machine learning perspective. Crc Press, Boca Raton (2013)
5. Chandola, V., Banerjee, A., Kumar, V.: Anomaly detection: a survey. ACM Comput. Surv. J. **9**, 1–72 (2009)
6. Fares, A., Sharawy, M.: Intrusion detection: supervised machine learning. J. Comput. Sci. Eng. **5**(4), 305–313 (2011)

7. Gilmore, C., Haydaman, J.: Anomaly detection and machine learning methods for network intrusion detection: an industrially focused literature review. In: Proceedings of the International Conference on Security and Management, pp. 292–298 (2016)
8. Mebawondu, J., Alowolodu, D., Mebawondu, O., Adetunmbi, O.: Network intrusion detection system using supervised learning paradigm. Sci. Afr. J. (2020). https://doi.org/10.1016/j.sciaf.2020.e00497
9. Sharma, P., Kunwar, R.: Cyber attacks on intrusion detection systems. Int. J. Inf. Sci. Tech. **6**(1/2), 191–196 (2016)
10. Adetunmbi, A.O., Adeola, O.S., Daramola, O.A.: Analysis of KDD '99 intrusion detection for relevance feature selection. In: Proceedings of the World Congress of Engineering and Computer Science, (WCECS 2010), October 20–22, pp. 162–168, San Francisco, USA (2010)
11. Sommer, R., Paxson, V.: Outside the closed world: on using machine learning for network intrusion detection. IEEE Symposium on Security and Privacy, pp. 305–316 (2010)
12. Cruz, J., Wishart, D.: Applications of machine learning in cancer prediction and prognosis. Cancer Inform. **2**, 59–75 (2006)
13. Quinlan, J.: Induction of decision trees. Mach. Learn. **1**, 81–106 (1986)
14. Waljee, K., Higgings, R., Singal, G.: A primer on predictive models. Clin. Trans. Gastroenterol. **4**(44), 1–4 (2013)
15. Mitchell, T.: Machine Learning. McGraw Hill, New York (1997)
16. Adetunmbi, A.: A bagging approach to network intrusions detection. J. Niger. Assoc. Math. Phys. **15**, 379–390 (2009)
17. Azeez, N.A., Bada, T.M., Misra, S., Adewumi, A., Van der Vyver, C., Ahuja, R.: Intrusion detection and prevention systems: an updated review. In: Sharma, N., Chakrabarti, A., Balas, V.E. (eds.) Data Management, Analytics and Innovation. AISC, vol. 1042, pp. 685–696. Springer, Singapore (2020). https://doi.org/10.1007/978-981-32-9949-8_48
18. Odusami, M., Misra, S., Adetiba, E., Abayomi-Alli, O., Damasevicius, R., Ahuja, R.: An improved model for alleviating layer seven distributed denial of service intrusion on webserver. J. Phys. Conf. Ser. IOP Publishing **1235**(1), 1–13 (2020)
19. Schapire, E.: The boosting approach to machine learning: an overview. In Nonlinear estimation and classification Springer, New York, NY, 149–171 (2003). https://doi.org/10.1007/978-0-387-21579-2_9
20. Freund, Y., Schapire, E.: Decision-theoretic generalization of on-line learning and an application to boosting. J. Comput. Syst. Sci. **55**(1), 119–139 (1997)
21. Azeez, N.A., Ayemobola, T.J., Misra, S., Maskeliūnas, R., Damaševičius, R.: Network intrusion detection with a hashing based apriori algorithm using Hadoop MapReduce. Computers **8**(4), 86–97 (2019)
22. Joshi, N., Srivastava, S.: Improving classification accuracy using ensemble learning technique (using different decision trees). Int. J. Comput. Sci. Mob. Comput. **3**(5), 727–732 (2014)
23. King, M., Ensemble learning techniques for Structured and Unstructured Data. Unpublished PhD Thesis of the Department of Business Information Technology (2015)
24. Dhaliwal, S., Nahid, A., Abbas, R.: Effective intrusion detection using XGBoost. J. Inf. **9**(149), 1–24 (2018)
25. Balogun, J.A., Aderounmu, T., Egejuru, N., Idowu, P.: An ensemble model of machine learning algorithms for the severity of sickle cell disorder (SCD) among pediatrics. Comput. Rev. J. **2**, 331–338 (2018)
26. Belouch, M., El Hadaj, S., Idhammad, M.: Performance evaluation of intrusion detection based on machine learning using Apache spark. Proc. Comput. Sci. **127**, 1–6 (2018)
27. Shah, R., Qian, Y., Kumar, D., Ali, M., Alvi, M.: Network intrusion detection through discriminative feature selection by using sparse logistic regression. Future Internet **9**(4), 81 (2017)
28. Trivedi, K., Dey, S.: Interplay between probabilistic classifiers and boosting algorithms for detecting complex unsolicited emails. J. Adv. Comput. Netw. **1**(2), 132–136 (2013)

Identification of Bacterial Leaf Blight and Powdery Mildew Diseases Based on a Combination of Histogram of Oriented Gradient and Local Binary Pattern Features

Zakari Hassan Mohammed[1](✉) (iD), Oyefolahan I. O[2] (iD),
Mohammed D. Abdulmalik[1] (iD), and Sulaimon A. Bashir[1] (iD)

[1] Department of Computer Science, Federal University of Technology, Minna, Nigeria
hassan_bagu@yahoo.com, {drmalik,bashirsulaimon}@futminna.edu.ng
[2] School of Information and Communication Technology, Federal University of Technology,
Minna, Nigeria
o.ishaq@futminna.edu.ng

Abstract. Quantity and quality of agricultural products are significantly reduced by diseases. Identification and classification of these plant diseases using plant leaf images is one of the important agricultural areas of research for which machine-learning models can be employed. The Powdery Mildew and Bacterial Leaf Blight diseases are two common diseases that can have a severe effect on crop production. To minimize the loss incurred by Powdery Mildew and Bacterial Leaf Blight diseases and to ensure more accurate automatic detection of these pathogens, this paper proposes an approach for identifying these diseases, based on a combination of Histogram of Oriented Gradient (HOG) and Local Binary Pattern (LBP) features (HOG + LBP) using Naïve Bayes (NB) Classifier. The NB classifier was also trained with only the HOG features and also trained with only the LBP features. However the NB classifier trained with the HOG + LBP features obtained a higher performance accuracy of 95.45% as compared to NB classifier trained with only HOG features and NB classifier trained only with LBP features with accuracy of 90.91% and 86.36% respectively.

Keywords: Plant disease · Bacterial leaf blight · Powdery mildew · Plant disease detection

1 Introduction

Detection and classification of plant diseases is one of the most important trending topics in agricultural literature [1]. Identification and classification of plant diseases has drawn increasing attention given the significance of automating this process in many agricultural crops such as strawberry, rice, cucumber, tomatoes, potatoes, corn, soya beans, yam, vegetables etc.

Digital image processing and examination is a significant technology generally used to monitor, recognize, and analyze these diseases that influence plant development [2].

© Springer Nature Switzerland AG 2021
S. Misra and B. Muhammad-Bello (Eds.): ICTA 2020, CCIS 1350, pp. 301–314, 2021.
https://doi.org/10.1007/978-3-030-69143-1_24

Through the improvement of computer handling capabilities and the ongoing growth of digital image acquisition systems, digital image processing and examination technology have become an imperative method for plant disease discovery and recognition [2, 3].

In every aspect of human life, agriculture plays a crucial role, such as clothing, food, medicines, and jobs [4]. Rural people in Nigeria rely on crop production as their main source of revenue, and a large part of Nigeria's economy also depends on agricultural products. The revenue and satisfaction from agricultural commodities relies on the quality and quantity of the harvest. Diseases have been described as one of the key factors for the deterioration of the quality and quantity of agricultural products which can contribute to food insecurity and reduction in the farmer sales revenue and thus affect the country's GDP [5]. Since these plant diseases are inevitable, the identification and recognition of these plant diseases is imperative for better production. And one of the best ways to identify a plant infected by a disease is by testing its leaf condition [6].

This paper is centered on recognizing two regular plant diseases which are the Bacterial Leaf Blight (BLB) and the Powdery Mildew (PM) disease. PM is brought about by pathogens producing specificity parasitic on the surface of plants which develop pathogenic fungi with white powder disease signs [2]. Powdery mildew can affect many different plants, like vegetable, fruit, and agronomic crops, as well as ornamental woody and herbaceous. In commercial and residential plantings, this common and widespread disease may occur [7]. Powdery mildew can damage fruit production, flowering, plant strength, and yields. It has been recognized that this disease causes a yield reduction of up to 40%–80% and this makes its identification important [8].

Rice is one of Nigeria's main food crops and BLB infection is a typical rice disease in Nigeria caused by Xanthomonas oryzae pv. oryzae [9]. It is a vascular ailment that causes a systemic infection along the veins that produces tannish-grey to white lesions. Side effects are seen at the tillering stage and the illness rate increases with plant development, peaking at the flowering stage [10]. Rice yield loss can be as high as 50% when the crop is seriously infected with this disease [10, 11]. The intensity and effect of the harm caused by this disease has prompted the creation of strategies for detecting, controlling and managing this disease, in order to minimize crop loss and avoid a widespread outbreak.

The seriousness of the harm caused by BLB and PM disease has made it early discovery significant, so as to control and deal with their widespread. Despite, years of plant disease identification and classification research, the identification accuracy has not been satisfactory especially for diseases like bacteria leaf blight and powdery mildew with an accuracy below 92%. Also most researches on powdery mildew diseases focuses on a single crop type while powdery mildew affect many types of crops.

Several efforts have been made to overcome this limitations by implementing various working machine learning algorithms. However, these methods has not produced considerable achievement as evident in numerous research such as Prajapati, Shah and Dabhi [12], Maniyath et al. [13] and Mahmud, Chang and Esau [14]. This is due to the fact that the amount of dataset used for experimentation is quite small or due to the fact that the feature vectors extracted are not sufficient enough to describe the diseases efficiently.

Based on this identified limitations, this study considers detection of powdery mildew disease for various crop types for improved robustness of the proposed system. The

LBP and HOG as texture descriptors and gradient descriptor respectively are combined together to create a more robust feature vector that describes the diseases efficiently for improved detection rate. This study's principal contributions are as follows:

1. Fusion of HOG and LBP features for improved disease identification using Naïve Bayes Classifier.
2. Comparative experimentation of different feature descriptors used for plant disease classification.
3. Presentation of a method for detecting BLB and PM diseases.

2   Related Work

Food is an essential survival requirement for humans. And as the global population rises daily, it has become imperative to grow enough crops to feed the growing population. Nevertheless, these crops are threatened by various diseases, which cause serious harm to the crop quantity and quality. Because plant disease is inevitable, disease detection plays a crucial role in the domain of agriculture [15].

Maniyath et al. [13] conducted crop diseases detection by leveraging on HOG to accomplish feature extraction, and these extracted features were feed to a random forest classifier to categorize the images into disease or healthy images. The proposed system was trained using pictures of papaya leaves. Nevertheless the model performance accuracy of 70% was low as compared to related works with 96.6% accuracy [16] and 85% accuracy [4]. It is suggested that by training with an increased number of images the accuracy of the system could be improved.

Prajapati, Shah and Dabhi [12] suggested a system for the identification and classification of rice plant disease based on the segmentation and Support Vector Machine (SVM). The three rice diseases that have been identified are bacterial leaf blight, brown spot, and leaf smut. This study attained a training accuracy of 93.33% while achieving a test accuracy of 73.3%. However the size of dataset used was small with a total of 120 images, 40 images for each identified diseases. This shows that the model accuracy could be improved by increasing the dataset size.

Mahmud, Chang and Esau [14] used Color Co-occurrence Matrix (CCM) which is an image processing based texture analysis technique with SVM and K-Nearest Neighbor (KNN) classifier to discover PM disease of strawberry plant. The experimental result indicated that SVM could effectively detect PM disease of strawberry with an accuracy of 95.5% as compared to KNN which obtained an accuracy of 89.78%. But conducting classification with SVM was found to have some limitation on the speed of training and testing. The model, however, focused on detecting only powdery mildew without considering other common diseases that could affect strawberry plants.

Durga and Anuradha [4] have proposed the identification of 4 common maize and tomato diseases, namely tomato mosaic virus, common rust, northern blight, and bacterial spot, using SVM and Artificial Neural Network (ANN). 200 tomatoes and maize leaf images were used, 160 of the images were used for training whereas 40 images were used for testing. HOG feature descriptor was used for extraction of features. SVM achieved an accuracy of 60–70% for tomato crops and 70–75% for maize crops while

ANN achieved an accuracy of 80–85% for tomato crops and 55–65% for maize crops. It can be seen from the obtained results that more improved algorithms, such as deep neural networks, are recommended to improve the detection rate of maize crops diseases.

Al-qarallah et al. [1] proposed an image processing method for detection of cucumber powdery mildew infection. In this work several classifiers have been tested on the extracted features, and these classifiers are Random Forest (RF), SVM, Instance Based k-nearest neighbor (IBk), and Multilayer Perceptron (MLP). Results obtained suggested that IBk and RF performed better than MLP and SVM. Nevertheless, this study did not discuss the feature extraction process used or explain how the extracted features were obtained or what features were used for classification, such as textural, color or shape features [17].

3 Methodology

This section describes the techniques used to attain this study's objective. Figure 1 describes the techniques used, such as image acquisition, color segmentation, pre-processing of images, extraction of features, normalization of features, combination of features and classification of diseases. These steps are discussed below.

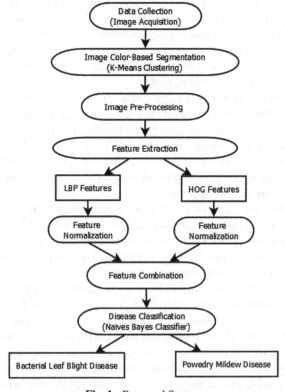

Fig. 1. Proposed System

3.1 Data Collection (Image Acquisition)

Appropriate datasets are needed at all phases of object recognition study, starting with the training phase to testing the efficiency of the recognition algorithms. The leaf image datasets were collected from UCI repository and the Embrapa Repositório Digipathos plant database. A total of 200 images were collected which consist of 106 leaf images infected with powdery mildew disease and 94 leaf images infected with bacterial leaf blight.

Figure 2 shows a rice leaf infected with bacterial leaf blight disease and Fig. 3 shows a cucumber leaf infected with powdery mildew disease.

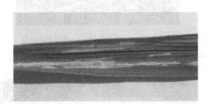   

Fig. 2. Rice leaf infected with Bacterial Leaf Blight Disease

Fig. 3. Cucumber Leaf Infected with Powdery Mildew Disease

3.2 Image Color-Based Segmentation (K-Means Clustering)

Image segmentation is a process of splitting a digital image into multiple distinctive regions, containing each pixel having similar traits [18]. K-means algorithm was used for clustering the existing spectral groupings embedded in the datasets. The goal of color-based segmentation is to separate colors using the L*a*b * color space and K-means clustering in an automated manner. The method of segmentation is summarized as follows:

1. Read image, and convert image from color space RGB to color space L*a*b *. The color space L*a*b * helps one to calculate the subtle variations in colour. The L*a*b* space consists of 'L*' layer of luminosity, 'a*' layer of chromaticity showing where color falls across the red-green axis, and 'b*' layer of chromaticity indicating where color occurs along the blue-yellow axis. All of the color information is in the 'a*' and 'b*' layers [19].
2. Categorize the colors in 'a*b*' space via K-means clustering.
3. Tag every pixel in the Image using the results from K-means.
4. Generate images that segment the image by color.
5. Segment the disease into a separate image.
6. Eradicate noise from separated disease image, mask original image with separated disease image and store the image.

Figure 4 shows the original leaf image infected with powdery mildew while Fig. 5 demonstrates a segmented PM disease after the color segmentation was done using k-means clustering. Figure 6 shows the original image of the leaf infected with BLB disease while Fig. 7 shows the segmented BLB disease after the color segmentation was done using k-means clustering.

 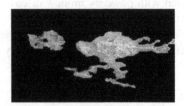

Fig. 4. Powdery Mildew infected leaf   **Fig. 5.** K-means clustering color-based segmented image for Powdery Mildew

Fig. 6. Bacterial Leaf Blight Infected Leaf   **Fig. 7.** K-means clustering color-based segmented image for Bacterial Leaf Blight

3.3 Image Pre-processing

The following image pre-processing procedures were used: The image of the segmented disease was translated to gray scale format after which the gray scale image was enhanced using the histogram equalization technique [20]. The improved gray scale image was transformed to binary form, holes of the objects were filled and unwanted noise were eliminated in order to make the image better, clearer and easier to interpret.

3.4 Feature Extraction

Feature extraction is performed on the pre-processed images for both PM and BLB images. Two feature extraction techniques were used to extract the disease features and these techniques are:

- **Local Binary Pattern (LBP):** LBP was selected for feature retrieval, as it has demonstrated to extract relatively high quality features that improves the efficiency of classification [21]. LBP is a type of gray level that supports the local contrast function of an image within the reach of the texture function. LBP is an effective image texture identifier that thresholds the neighboring pixels based on the value of the present pixels. Given a neighborhood of S sampling points on an R radius circle. And a pixel given at (x_p, y_p). LBP can be stated as presented in Eq. 1 below:

$$LBP_{S,R(x_p,y_p)} = \sum_{S=0}^{S-1} C(i_S - i_P)2^S \tag{1}$$

Where i_S and i_p are, individually, gray-level values of the focal pixel and P surrounding pixels in the circle neighborhood with R radius, and function $c(x)$ is defined in Eq. 2 as:

$$c(x) = \begin{cases} 1 \text{ if } x \geq 0 \\ 0 \text{ if } x < 0 \end{cases} \tag{2}$$

- **Histogram of Oriented Gradient (HOG):** HOG is a feature descriptor centered on the gradient approximation used in computer vision and image processing for object recognition purposes. HOG descriptor technique counts gradient orientation incidents in located portions of an image detection window [22]. HOG has been used for extraction of features, as it demonstrates invariance to geometric and photometric changes [22]. The HOG features can be created as follows: firstly the image is preprocessed and resized, then the gradient in the x and y direction for every pixel in the image is calculated, after which the magnitude and orientation is calculated using the formulas in Eq. 3 and Eq. 4 respectively.

$$\text{Total Gradient Magnitude} = \sqrt{(G_x)^2 + (G_y)^2} \tag{3}$$

Where G_y is the gradient in the y direction, and G_x is the gradient in the x direction.

$$\text{Orientation} = tan(\theta) = G_y/G_x \tag{4}$$

The value of the angle (θ) is presented in Eq. 5

$$\theta = atan(G_y/G_x) \tag{5}$$

3.5 Feature Normalization

After Extracting the HOG and LBP features from the disease images, the LBP and the HOG features were normalized using Z-Score. This was done in order to scale the features within a specific range as the HOG and LBP features can greatly be of different scale which can have a great effect on the ability of the classifier to learn. Therefore normalization was done to ensure feature values of both HOG and LBP weights on the same scale. Z-Score is a statistical calculation of a score's correlation to the mean in a group of scores [23]. Z-Score can be determined using the formula in Eq. 6.

$$Z_{score}(i) = \frac{x_i - \mu}{s} \tag{6}$$

Where s = standard deviation, μ = distribution mean and x_i = each object in the distribution. The standard deviation can be determined using the formula in Eq. 7:

$$s = \sqrt{\frac{1}{n-1} \sum_{i=1}^{n} (x_i - \mu)^2} \tag{7}$$

3.6 Feature Combination

In this step the normalized HOG and LBP features were concatenated to form new features. HOG consists of 10 features as only the features of the ten (10) strongest points in the disease images were extracted and the LBP consist of 59 features. The 10 HOG features and 59 LBP features were concatenated to form new dataset consisting of 69 features. And this 69 features were used to train and test the Naïve Bayes classifier.

3.7 Disease Classification

The concatenated features were feed to a Naïve Bayes (NB) classifier to perform classification task. NB model is a family of simple probabilistic classifier based on the implementation of the Bayes theorem with clear assumptions of independence between the features. NB classifiers are vastly scalable, and allow a number of linear parameters in the number of learning problem features. Naïve Bayes (NB) classifier classifies the leaf images into two categories which are BLB or PM diseases.

3.8 Performance Metrics

The five performance metric used to evaluate the proposed method is discussed below and shown in Eq. 8, 9, 10 and 11 respectively.

1. **Accuracy:** Accuracy is measured in terms of the rate of correct classifications. That is the number of accurate predictions made divided by the total number of predictions made. The exact formula is illustrated in Eq. 5 below:

$$Accuracy = \frac{True\ Positive\ +\ True\ negative}{True\ Positive\ +\ True\ negative\ +\ False\ Positive\ +\ False\ negative}$$

(8)

2. **F-Score:** is a proportion of the validity of the test. This is the weighted harmonic mean of a test precision and recall. The formula for F-score is given in Eq. 6 below:

$$F - Score = 2 * \frac{precision * recall}{precision + recall}$$

(9)

3. **Recall:** it is also known as sensitivity and it is a statistic that calculates the amount of accurate positive predictions that could have been made from all positive predictions. Recall is determined based on the formula in Eq. 7.

$$Recall = \frac{True\ Positives}{True\ Positives\ +\ False\ Negatives}$$

(10)

4. **Precision:** is a measure which calculates the amount of positive predictions which are correct. It is defined as the number of true positives divided by the total amount of true positives and false positives. Precision is determined according to the formula in Eq. 8.

$$Precision = \frac{True\ Positives}{True\ Positives\ +\ False\ Positives} \qquad (11)$$

5. **Area under the Curve (AUC):** the Area under ROC Curve is used to rate the performance of a model for classification. This measures all of the entire 2-dimensional field below the ROC curve. AUC provides an aggregate output metric over all possible classification thresholds.

4   Result and Discussion

To evaluate this proposed system the examples were randomly selected and split into training and testing dataset. The dataset was split into training and testing based on a ratio of 75% for training and 25% for testing. In this study BLB and PM plant diseases were identified using three algorithms which are:

1. Feature extraction using HOG algorithm and classification using NB based on HOG Features.
2. Feature extraction using LBP algorithm and classification using NB based on LBP Features.
3. Merging HOG and LBP features to generate new features and classification using NB based on concatenated features.

Table 1 presents results obtained after running the three algorithms described above.

Table 1. Performance of Proposed Algorithm (Combined HOG and LBP Features) as compared to use of LBP Features only and HOG Features Only

Algorithm	Accuracy (%)	Precision (%)	Recall (%)	F-Score (%)	AUC
HOG + NB	90.91	100	77.78	87.50	0.9813
LBP +NB	86.36	87.50	77.78	82.35	0.9938
HOG + LBP + NB (Proposed system)	95.45	100	88.89	94.12	0.9948

From Table 1 it can be seen on the accuracy column that the proposed method (HOG + LBP +NB) performs better with an accuracy of 95.45% as compared to HOG + NB with an accuracy of 90.91% and LBP +NB with an accuracy of 86.36%. From the Precision column it can be seen that LBP + NB has a lower precision of 87.50% as compared to HOG +NB and HOG + LBP +NB with a precision of 100%.

Under the Recall column HOG + LBP +NB is able to achieve a true positive rate of 88.89% which is higher than the true positive rate of 77.78% achieved by HOG + NB and LBP +NB. Based on the F-Score of 94.12% achieved by HOG + LBP +NB is can be seen that HOG + LBP +NB performs better than HOG +NB and LBP +NB with and F-Score of 87.50% and 82.35% respectively. Also by comparing the values of the AUC for each algorithm it can be seen that HOG + LBP +NB has a higher value of 0.9948 as compared to HOG +NB and LBP +NB with values of 0.9813 and 0.9938 respectively.

Table 2 presents the confusion matrix for LBP + NB model with 21 predicted positives and 29 predicated negatives whereas the actual positive is 18 examples and the actual negative is 32 examples.

Table 2. Confusion Matrix for LBP + NB

n = 50	Actual Positive (1)	Actual Negative (0)	
Predicted Positive (1)	16 (32%)	5 (10%)	**21**
Predicted Negative (0)	2 (4%)	27 (54%)	**29**
	18	**32**	

Table 3 presents the confusion matrix for HOG + NB model with 20 predicted positives and 30 predicated negatives whereas the actual positive is 16 examples and the actual negative is 34 examples.

Table 3. Confusion Matrix for HOG + NB

n = 50	Actual Positive (1)	Actual Negative (0)	
Predicted Positive (1)	16 (32%)	4 (8%)	**20**
Predicted Negative (0)	0 (0%)	30 (60%)	**30**
	16	**34**	

Table 4 presents the confusion matrix for HOG + LBP + NB model with 20 predicted positives and 30 predicated negatives whereas the actual positive is 18 examples and the actual negative is 32 examples.

With the proposed system (HOG + LBP + NB) achieving a higher Accuracy, Precision, Recall and AUC as compared to HOG + NB and LBP + NB, it can be deduced that bacterial leaf blight and powdery mildew plant disease can effectively be detection using the proposed system.

From the accuracy results in Table 5 it can be seen that the proposed system produced 95.45% accuracy which is the highest accuracy when compared to existing works such as Maniyath et al. [13] with 70.14% accuracy, Prajapati, Shah and Dabhi [12] with 88.57% accuracy and Mahmud, Chang and Esau [14] with 91.86% accuracy. This shows that the proposed system can detects plant diseases effectively.

Table 4. Confusion Matrix for HOG + LBP + NB

n = 50	Actual Positive (1)	Actual Negative (0)	
Predicted Positive (1)	18 (36%)	2 (4%)	**20**
Predicted Negative (0)	0 (0%)	30 (60%)	**30**
	18	**32**	

Table 5. Comparison of Proposed System with Existing Methods

Algorithm	Accuracy (%)
SVM (trained with color, texture and shape feature) [12]	88.57%
Color Co-occurrence Matrices + SVM [14]	91.86%
HOG + Random forest [13]	70.14%
HOG + LBP + NB (Proposed System)	**95.45%**

Figure 8 shows the ROC curve of Naive Bayes (NB) classifier trained using only HOG extracted Features for bacterial leaf blight and powdery mildew plant disease identification. Figure 9 shows the ROC curve of Naive Bayes (NB) classifier trained using only LBP extracted Features for bacterial leaf blight and powdery mildew plant disease detection and Fig. 10 shows the ROC curve of Naive Bayes (NB) classifier trained using the concatenated HOG + LBP extracted Features for bacterial leaf blight and powdery mildew plant disease identification.

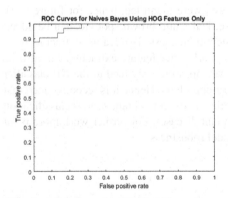

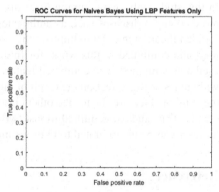

Fig. 8. ROC Curve for NB Classifier using HOG features only

Fig. 9. ROC Curve for NB Classifier Using LBP Features only

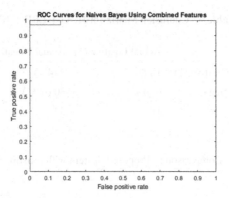

Fig. 10. ROC Curve for NB Classifier using combined LBP and HOG features

5 Conclusion

In this paper, we were able to detect BLB and PM disease effectively as compared to existing researches on disease identification due to the combination of features extracted using two powerful feature extractors namely LBP and HOG. From this study it can be established that feeding a Naïve Bayes classifier with concatenated feature vectors (HOG +LBP) can improve the classification accuracy as compared to use of features extracted using a single feature extractor. In conclusion a system was developed which can perform BLB and PM disease detection based on LBP + HOG + NB algorithm.

6 Future Work

In this study only two common plant diseases were identified, hence for future work more common diseases such as anthracnose, leaf smut, brown spot etc. can be added for identification in order to improve the system robustness. Two feature extractors were used and combined in this work, for future work other feature extractors can also be used and combined. The combined feature vectors were only feed to the NB classifier without testing its effect on the result of other classifiers. Hence it is recommended that the combined features be feed to other classifiers in order to obtain various classification results. This study was limited to just two plant diseases. For further work more plant diseases can be incorporated to improve model robustness.

References

1. Al-qarallah, B., Al-shboul, B., Hiary, H., Aljawawdeh, A.: An image processing approach for cucumber powdery mildew infection an image processing approach for cucumber powdery mildew infection detection. In: Proceedings New Trends Information Technology, April 2017
2. Wu, C., Wang, X.: Preliminary research on the identification system for anthracnose and powdery mildew of sandalwood leaf based on image processing. PLoS ONE **12**(7), 1–12 (2017). https://doi.org/10.1371/journal.pone.0811537

3. Pujari, J.D., Yakkundimath, R., Byadgi, A.: www.sciencedirect.com. In: International Conference Information Communication Technology, vol. 46, no. Icict 2014, pp. 1802–1808, 2015. https://doi.org/10.1016/j.procs.2015.02.137
4. Durga, N.K., Anuradha, G.: Plant disease identification using SVM and ANN algorithms. Int. J. Recent Technol. Eng. IJRTE 7(5), 471–473 (2019)
5. Vamsidhar, E., Rani, P.J., Babu, K.R.: Plant Disease Identification and Classification using Image Processing, no. 3, pp. 442–446 (2019)
6. Sharma, P., Paul, Y., Berwal, S., Ghai, W.: Performance analysis of deep learning CNN models for disease detection in plants using image segmentation. In: Information Processing Agriculture, pp. 1–9 (2019). https://doi.org/10.1016/j.inpa.2019.11.001
7. Pfeufer, E., Gauthier, N.W., Bradley, C.A.: Powdery Mildew, University of Kentucky (2017)
8. Bem, A.A., Igbawundu, J.T., Bem, S.L., Akesa, M., Fadimu, O.Y.: Preliminary evaluation of incidence and severity of powdery mildews of some crop plants in Makurdi, Benue State, Nigeria. Int. J. Adv. Biol. Res. 3(4), 519–523 (2013)
9. Sundaram, R.M., Chatterjee, S., Oliva, R., Laha, G.S., Cruz, C.V., Leach, J.E., Sonti, R.V.: Update on bacterial blight of rice: fourth international conference on bacterial blight. Rice 7(1), 1–3 (2014). https://doi.org/10.1186/s12284-014-0012-7
10. Gnanamanickam, S.S., Priyadarisini, V.B., Narayanan, N.N.: An overview of bacterial blight disease of rice and strategies for its management, vol. 77, no. 11 (2014)
11. Krishnan, N., Muthurajan, R.: Management of bacterial leaf blight disease in rice with endophytic bacteria management of bacterial leaf blight disease in rice with endophytic bacteria. World Appl. Sci. J. 28(12), 2229–2241 (2013). https://doi.org/10.5829/idosi.wasj.2013.28.12.2009
12. Prajapati, H.B., Shah, J.P., Dabhi, V.K.: Detection and classification of rice plant diseases, vol. 11, pp. 357–373 (2017). https://doi.org/10.3233/idt-170301
13. Maniyath, S.R., et al.: Plant disease detection using machine learning. In: 2018 International Conference Des. Innovation 3Cs Computer Communication Control ICDI3C, July 2019, pp. 41–45 (2018). https://doi.org/10.1109/icdi3c.2018.00017
14. Mahmud, S.M., Chang, Y.K., Esau, T.: Detection of strawberry powdery mildew disease in leaf using image texture and supervised classifiers detection of strawberry powdery mildew disease in leaf using image texture and supervised classifiers, In: Canadian Social Engineering Agriculture Food Environment Biology System (2018)
15. Halder, M., Sarkar, A., Bahar, H.: Plant disease detction by image processing: a literature review. In: SDRP Journal Food Science Technology, vol. 3, no. 6, pp. 534–538 (2018). https://doi.org/10.25177/jfst.3.6.6
16. Hossain, E., Rahaman, M.: A color and texture based approach for the detection and classification of plant leaf disease using KNN classifier. In: International Conference on Electrical, Computer and Communication Engineering (ECCE) (2019). https://doi.org/10.1109/ecace.2019.8679247
17. Patil, M.Y., Dhawale, C.A., Misra, S.: Analytical study of combined approaches to content based image retrieval systems. Int. J. Pharm. Technol. 8(4), 14 (2016)
18. Dhawale, C.A., Misra, S., Thakur, S., Dattatraya Jambhekar, N.: Analysis of nutritional deficiency in citrus species tree leaf using image processing. In: 2016 International Conference on Advances in Computing, Communications and Informatics (ICACCI), Jaipur, India, September 2016, pp. 2248–2252 (2016). https://doi.org/10.1109/icacci.2016.7732386
19. Chitade, A.Z.: Colour based image segmentation using K-means clustering. Int. J. Eng. Sci. Technol. 2, 7 (2010)
20. Temiatse, O.S., Misra, S., Dhawale, C., Ahuja, R., Matthews, V.: Image enhancement of lemon grasses using image processing techniques (Histogram Equalization). In: Panda, B., Sharma, S., Roy, N.R. (eds.) REDSET 2017. CCIS, vol. 799, pp. 298–308. Springer, Singapore (2018). https://doi.org/10.1007/978-981-10-8527-7_24

21. Huang, D., Shan, C., Ardabilian, M.: Local binary patterns and its application to facial image analysis : a survey. In: IEEE Transaction System MAN Cybernatics, November, 2011. https://doi.org/10.1109/tsmcc.2011.2118750

22. Surasak, T., Takahiro, I., Cheng, C.H., Wang, C.E., Sheng, P.Y.: Histogram of oriented gradients for human detection in video. In: Proceedings 2018 5th International Conference Business Industrial Res. Smart Technology Generation Information Engineering Business Social Science ICBIR 2018, pp. 172–176 (2018). https://doi.org/10.1109/icbir.2018.8391187

23. Kolbaşi, A., Ünsal, P.A.: A comparison of the outlier detecting methods : an application on turkish foreign trade data. J. Math. Stat. Sci. **5**, 213–234 (2015)

Feature Weighting and Classification Modeling for Network Intrusion Detection Using Machine Learning Algorithms

Olamatanmi J. Mebawondu[1]([✉]) [iD], Adebayo O. Adetunmbi[1] [iD],
Jacob O. Mebawondu[2] [iD], and Olufunso D. Alowolodu[3] [iD]

[1] Department of Computer Science, Federal University of Technology, Akure, Nigeria
jpmebawondu@gmail.com, aoadetunmbi@futa.edu.ng
[2] Department of Computer Science, Federal Polytechnic, Nasarawa, Nigeria
mebawondu1010@gmail.com
[3] Department of Cyber Security, Federal University of Technology, Akure, Nigeria
odalowolodu@futa.edu.ng

Abstract. Globally, as the upsurge in dependencies on computer network services, so are the activities of attackers that gain undue access to network resources for selfish interest at the expense of the stakeholders. Attackers threaten integrity, availability, and confidentiality of network resources despite various preventive security measures, hence the need to study ways to detect and minimize attackers' activities. This paper develops a Network-Based Intrusion Detection System (NBIDS) using the machine learning algorithms capable of detecting and preventing anomaly (attack) network traffic from the Internet, thereby reducing cases of successful network attacks. Gain Ratio and Information Gain are used for features ranking on the UNSW-NB15 benchmark network intrusion dataset. The first fifteen highly ranked features are selected for developing classification models using C4.5 and Naïve Bayes (NB), coincidentally the two feature ranking approaches to select the same features but in a different ordering. Empirical results show that the C4.5 algorithm outperformed NB for all simulations based on a different spilled ratio of testing and training sets as it returns the highest accuracy of 90.44% against 75.09% for NB for two-class models on simulation IV. For all the experimental setup, both DT and NB have a constant precision of 91% to 75%, the True Positive value of 90%:75%, and False Positive value of 8.6%:22.8%, respectively. The experiments revealed that accuracy increases as the training ratio increases. The results show that the approach is practicable for real-time network intrusion detection.

Keywords: Naïve Bayes (NB) · Decision Tree (DT) · Feature Selection (FS) · Classification · Attribute evaluators · Feature weighting

1 Introduction

In this current dispensation of the information age, it is crucial to maintain high-level security due to the enormous contribution of the Internet to business transactions, which

© Springer Nature Switzerland AG 2021
S. Misra and B. Muhammad-Bello (Eds.): ICTA 2020, CCIS 1350, pp. 315–327, 2021.
https://doi.org/10.1007/978-3-030-69143-1_25

has effect in an increasing number of hackers and internet users. However, attackers simply take advantage of the network system's weakness to access network resources, thereby compromising the system's integrity. These intruders may be unauthorized or authorized (masquerader) users attempting to misuse and gain non-authorized access [1]. Hence, intrusions are any set of actions that threaten confidentiality, integrity, or availability of network resources [2–4]. Furthermore, an IDS analyzes the system's actions in a network for intrusions' signs. the alarm is raised by IDS when there is possible occurrence of intrusions. The three (3) significant categories are Stack Based Intrusion Detection System (SIDS), Host based Intrusion Detection System (HIDS), NIDS. However, for companies to protect their infrastructure and data, organizations are increasingly relying on NIDS to monitor their network traffic automatically and report suspicious or anomalous behavior [5]. NIDS is a hardware or software application used to monitor the network activities and report malicious activities to the network administrator [6]. However, the widening attack surface area brings a limit to signature-based NIDS that can easily be bypassed by an intruder by little variations in the known signatures; hence, anomaly-based NIDS (ABNIDS) comes to play. Consequently, this is why artificial intelligence AI techniques are employed to learn non-normal and normal packets from network traffic. The model learned is then used to detect intrusion without signatures [7].

In recent times, this branch of Artificial Intelligence AI - Data Mining or its subset machine learning (ML) techniques have been compelled to wider application in IDS development with the utmost aim of improving classification accuracy. Thus, data mining is a technique used in extracting hidden patterns from data. Simultaneously, ML is a branch of AI that made computers learn from previous examples of data records [8, 9]. ML does not depend on a prior hypothesis, unlike traditional explanatory statistical modeling techniques [10]. However, the ML techniques are classified into two: supervised and unsupervised methods. The supervised approach matches a set of input records to one out of two or more target classes. The unsupervised system is used to create clusters or attribute relationships from raw, unlabeled, or unclassified datasets [11].

In any IDS development using machine learning techniques, there are two notable challenges - feature selection and classification. Features are inputs such as the Internet Protocol (IP) addresses (source and destination, service, duration, among others [12, 13]. Furthermore, the Feature selection (FS) approach is crucial in identifying irrelevant and redundant attributes within a dataset, which may increase computational complexity. [12, 14, 15] opined that selecting features which are relevant leads to accurate and faster detection rate. However, there are two effective approaches to FS - Individual and Subset Evaluations. The Individual evaluation uses a ranking method on the features that use a weight to measure the degree of relevance of a feature. The subset evaluation method is when the candidate subset of features is constructed using a search strategy.

This paper employs an individual evaluation approach because of its ability to use weight to mark the degree of relevance of a feature before building classification models using NB and C4.5. The efficacy of the proposed techniques will be carried out on the recent benchmark UNSW-NB15 dataset, which show current movement in network traffic of today [17]. The other parts of the work are as follow: review of related literature, experimental setup, results, and discussion, followed by a conclusion in Sects. 2, 3, 4, and 5 respectively.

2 Review of Related Literature

The effectiveness of feature weighting and classification for NIDS using a Machine Learning Algorithms (MLA) is evaluated based on the literature review. However, researchers have made frantic efforts in using the MLA to develop classification models for network intrusion detection. In [16], an algorithm for real time intrusion detection documented. The performance analysis was carried on the KDD99 intrusion detection dataset, and the paper reported high detection accuracy for all attack types.

In [18, 19], the MLA were used in developing classification models for network intrusion detection. The efficacy of different algorithms was examined on the KDDCUP '99 intrusion detection dataset, and both works reported that the techniques used were viable for anomaly detection on computer networks. [20] presented a data pre-processing technique for a small dataset, improving the classifier's performance for both binary and multi-class datasets. However, it did not consider weighting the features for better results.

[21] The paper employed feature selection approach for distributed denial of service detection reported. The paper reported that filter methods such as Gain Ratio and chi-square for FS have proven crucial when designing a lightweight IDS. Nevertheless, their work's efficacy was demonstrated on the NSL-KDD dataset. [7] worked on evaluating network anomaly detection by performing a statistical analysis of two different datasets. Subsequently, the study made use of five MLA for the simulation of the classification model. The study results showed that the Naïve Bayes (NB) classifier outperformed decision trees (DTs) to classify network anomaly. However, the study also revealed that the first data set was very reliable than using the second dataset to detect network anomaly [17].

[5] surveyed the application of MLA to anomaly detection, also reported the impossibility to select the algorithm with the best performance due to a large number of algorithms considered. Moreover, the paper did not explain the effect of FS on the performance of MLA. The study was limited to review of an existing MLA for anomaly detection. [22] applied discriminative feature selection for the classification of network intrusion detection. The study collected the intrusion detection KDD99 dataset, which consisted of 41 features and a target class with five labels. Nevertheless, relevant features extracted from initially identified features, following which logistic regression was applied as the classification model for network intrusion detection. The paper reported that the extraction of relevant features improved the model's accuracy compared to using identified initial features. [12] analyzed the KDD99 intrusion detection dataset for relevant FS and reported that five features do not contribute to detecting any attack types and normal. Consequently, this shows FS's relevance, and in this work, relevant features are extracted to improve accuracy.

In [23], presented university web server log files pre-processing for intrusion detection. The pre-processing analysis of data from a University domain web server was carried out, and then applied NB to detect anomalies. Nevertheless, a published standard dataset was not used, and the weighting features not considered as well. [24] evaluated the performance of the four ML techniques: Support Vector Machine (SVM), NB, DTs, and Random Forests (RT) on the UNSW-NB15 data set. Moreover, the results showed that DTs outperformed others in terms of classification accuracy. However, the limitation of this work was that no FS technique was applied.

[25] developed a network violation detection using ML techniques. Therefore, the work investigated the relevance of correlated patterns of the dataset features, which alters the distinct classes. However, the work did not cover specific feature reduction, which can enhance classification results. [29] employed deep learning algorithm to detect intruders on the web server. Data collected from the center for applied internet Data Analysis (CAIDA) DDoS attack dataset was used to evaluate the proposed study. Experimental results reveal a high detection rate. [30] developed new model for wireless networks. The performance adjudged is very accurate at a higher attack frequencies.

Hence, this paper adopts FS for ranking available features and selecting relevant features before network intrusion detection models and evaluations.

3   Materials and Methods

The methodology adopted in developing NIDS using NB and DT algorithms is presented. Evaluation is based on Precision, False Positive Rate, and accuracy on class labels.

3.1   NIDS System Architecture

Figure 1 displays the NIDS architecture, where the training and testing of data set are implemented. Furthermore, Feature ranking is carried out using information gain and gain ratio prior to machine learning classifications on two sets of datasets, and the result evaluated using the performance evaluation metrics of accuracy, among others.

3.2   Data Identification and Collection

The dataset adopted for this study is the UNSW-NB15 network dataset. However, the dataset was created in 2015. Therefore, the dataset was retrieved online from Kaggle. Moreover, the data consists of 82335 records such that 37000 (44.94%) were healthy, while 45332 (55.06%) were network attacks. This study generated a dataset that consists of 42 input features, and a target class of 2 features [17, 26–28].

3.3   The Weighting of Feature Relevance

This sub-section describes the technique to determine relevant features of network intrusion detection based on information in the UNSW-NB15 dataset. Thus, the FS process adopted in our study is information gain and gain ratio algorithms.

Information Gain (IG) of each attribute is the difference between the mutual entropy of the attribute X to the class Y denoted by $H(Y|X)$ and the entropy of the attribute X denoted by $H(X)$. However, the higher the difference, the higher the IG of the attribute

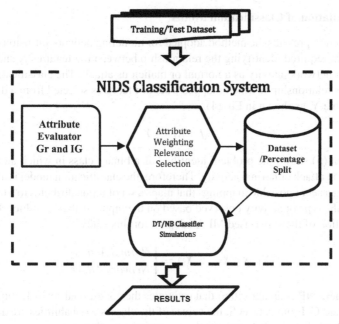

Fig. 1. NIDS system architecture

X. Given a dataset with a feature set having b values and target class with values, IG can be computed, as shown in the Eq. (1).

$$IG(Xi) = H(Yi|X) - H(Xi) \tag{1}$$

given:

$$H(Yi|Xi) = -\sum_{m=1}^{a} \sum_{n=1}^{b} p(Y_m|X_n) \log_2 p(Y_m|X_n)$$

$$H(Xi) = -\sum_{n=1}^{b} p(X_n) \log_2 p(X_n), \text{ where } m = 1, \ldots, a \text{ and } n = 1, \ldots, b$$

The Gain Ratio (GR) of each attribute is a standardization of the data set's features' information gain. Furthermore, the GR computed by dividing the IG by the Split Information (SI) of each feature's values.

$$SI(X) = -\sum_{n=1}^{b} \frac{T_n}{|X|} \log_2 \frac{T_n}{|X|} \tag{2}$$

However, the split information of an attribute X with T values is estimated, and the GR is calculated as a function of the IG.

$$GR(X) = \frac{IG(X)}{SI(X)} \tag{3}$$

The gain ratio's essence is to overcome the bias of information gain to attribute having more attribute values than others. Therefore, the higher the GR of a feature, the higher the relevance and rank.

3.4 Formulation of Classification Model

This sub-section presents the method adopted for modeling network intrusion detection. The problem required identifying the relationship between the features X and the classification of network activity as a normal or malicious attack. The classification model identified as relationship f, which mapped a set of i features selected from a dataset to a target variable Y, as shown in Eq. (4).

$$f : X_i \rightarrow Y \tag{4}$$

Equation (5) shows the problem identified as a binary class in which an activity is considered an attack or normal activity. Therefore, the classification model is a function f representing a set of possible mappings that maps a set of input attributes to a target class describing the type of activity observed based on the input attributes' values. Following is a description of the supervised MLA adopted for this study.

$$f(X_1, X_2, X_3, \ldots X_i) = \begin{cases} Normal\ Activity \\ Network\ Attack \end{cases} \tag{5}$$

NB Classifier. NB is an algorithm that estimates the conditional set of features X, X is subset of class C. From dataset S, the values of the classes' probabilities are determined as the number of class labels ratio to the aggregate records number in set according to Eq. (6) for n class labels. Moreover, the attributes' probability values are determined as the number of feature values to sum number of records in the set according to Eq. (7), where the total number of variables adopted is n. Meanwhile, class label values of conditional probabilities is the ratio of several features with values that belong to a class of class labels in the set according to Eq. (8).

$$P(C_j) = \frac{n(C_k)}{|S|} for\ k = 1, \ldots, m \tag{6}$$

$$P(X_i) = \frac{n(X_c)}{|S|} for\ c = 1, 2, \ldots m \tag{7}$$

$$P(X_i|C_j) = \frac{m(X_i \cap C_j)}{m(C_j)} for\ each\ c = 1, 2, \ldots, m\ for\ k = 1, .., n \tag{8}$$

Therefore, given a query Q containing the values of r attributes required for monitoring network intrusion. The probability that an attribute belongs to a class label is determined using Eq. (9), while the class with maximum probability is allocated to each query item Q according to Eq. (10). Therefore, the class with the maximum probability is returned as the class label C for the query Q.

$$P(C_j|X_i) = \prod_{i=1}^{r} \frac{P(X_i|C_j) * P(C_j)}{P(X_i)} for\ j = 1, \ldots, n \tag{9}$$

$$Class(Q) = max[P(C_1|Q)*, \ldots, *P(C_n|Q)] \tag{10}$$

C4.5 DT Classifier. The DTs classifier is a hierarchical set of nodes representing the attributes and their respective values pointed out towards child nodes below. The C4.5 DT algorithm was considered for this study, to develop the DTs. The effectiveness and popularity of the C4.5 among all other DT algorithms, such as CART, CHAID, and ID3, justified the C4.5 algorithm's choice. C4.5 DT algorithm is used based on the Gain Ratio discussed in Sect. 3.3. Consequently, highest GR is selected for a node. It is used to evaluate the features and select the successive nodes of the DT until all the tuples are exhausted.

3.5 Classification Model Evaluation metrics

Following the adoption of the testing proportion of the dataset for assessing the classification model's performance for NID, the results of the validation presented using the confusion matrix. Therefore, the simulation-based on the dataset containing classes was interpreted using a two by two confusion matrix with four cells.

Furthermore, each confusion matrix consisted of many cells of numerical value such that a sum of the horizontal cells as actual records. In contrast, the sum of vertical cells as predicted records. Also, correct predictions made by the classification model were presented along the diagonals from the top-left corner to the bottom-right corner. At the same time, other cells used to describe incorrect predictions (misclassifications) of the classification model based on data set, as shown in Fig. 2.

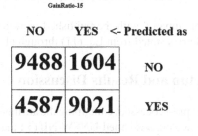

Fig. 2. Two by two confusion matrix

For illustration, the confusion matrix in Fig. 2 depicts 9,488 and 9,021 are correctly classified, others not correctly classified.

Using values in the confusion matrix cells, the evaluation of classification models was determined as follows:

a. **Accuracy:**

$$Accuracy = \frac{total\ value\ in\ diagonal\ cells}{total\ value\ in\ all\ cells} \times 100\% \tag{11}$$

b. **True Positive (TP) rate/Sensitivity:**

$$TPrate = \frac{value\ of\ respective\ target\ class\ cell\ in\ diagonal}{sum\ of\ horizontal\ cells\ of\ respecive\ target\ class} \tag{12}$$

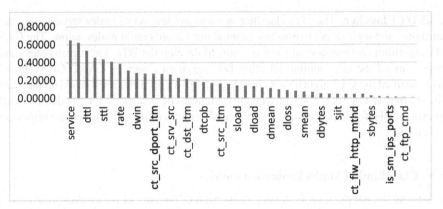

Fig. 3. Results of the evaluation of features using information gain

c. **False Positive (FP)/False Alarm rate**

$$FPrate = \frac{sum\ of\ values\ in\ incorrect\ cells\ along\ vertical}{total\ records\ -\ number\ of\ class\ records} \quad (13)$$

d. **Precision**:

$$Precision = \frac{value\ of\ respective\ target\ class\ cell\ in\ diagonal}{sum\ of\ vertical\ cells\ of\ respective\ target\ class} \quad (14)$$

This work's result is compared with the published work of Moustafa and Slay [7] using the performance metrics stated from Eq. (11) through (14).

4 Experimental Setup and Results Discussion

The UNSW-NB15 dataset pre-processed, containing the attributes. However, one dataset had a target feature with two classes called UNSW-NB15 binary dataset, saved as .csv files. Following this, the dataset pre-processed.

Meanwhile, the dataset subjected to the two supervised MLA earlier discussed. The classification model simulated using the percentage split technique, which required a higher proportion of the dataset to be used for training, while the lower proportion was used to test the classification model. Furthermore, four sets of training were carried out, which consisted of 60%, 70%, 80%, and 90% of the datasets, while corresponding test of 40%, 30%, 20%, and 10%.

Table 1 shows the distribution of the target class labels within the two class dataset. It shows 82332 records within the dataset made up of 37000 (44.94%) non-attacks records and 45332 (55.06%) attack records. The 45332 attack records comprise of nine attack groups, generic (22.92%), exploits (13.5%), fuzers (7.36%), DoS (4.96%), reconnaissance (4.25%), analysis (0.82%), backdoors (0.71%), Shellcode (0.46%) and worms (0.01%).

Table 2 depicts the description of the nominal features in the collected UNSW-NB15 dataset. The transaction protocol (proto) has the highest number of unique labels with

Table 1. The distribution of classes within the dataset

Target class	Frequency	Percentage (%)
Non_Attacks	37000	44.94
Attacks	45332	55.06
Total	**82332**	**100.00**

131, followed by destination TCP window advertisement with 14, type of service with 13, a command in ftp session (ct_ftp) with 3. The ftp session accessed by user and password (is_ftp_log) and Boolean status when the source and destination port are the same (is_ports) with 2 each.

Table 2. The nominal and integer attributes distribution in the dataset

Attribute name	Data type	Number of unique labels (distinct)
Proto	Nominal	131 protocols
Service	Nominal	13 services
State	Nominal	7 states
Sttl	Integer	11 values
Dttl	Integer	8 values
Swin	Integer	11 values
Dwin_1	Integer	14 values
is_ftp_log	Binary	2 values
ct_ftp	Integer	3 values
is_ ports	Binary	2 values

4.1   Results of Feature Selection

This section, features weighted/ranked results using IG and GR. The evaluation of each feature by these metrics is used to rank them in decreasing order of metrics scores.

Therefore, the results of the ranking of feature relevance of the 42 features using the GR metric revealed a maximum metric score of 0.5472 for the ct_dst_sport_ltm and a minimum metric score of 0.0779 for the bytes. The ranking of the relevance features using the IG metric returned a maximum metric score of 0.6483 for the service and a minimum metric score of 0.00698 for the is_ftp_log. The first 15 ranked features out of the 42 features for both metrics contained the same set of features; however, with varying positions between the two metrics used. Hence, the top 15 most relevant features are visible can be drawn out.

4.2 Results of Classification Models

This segment presents the two classification models- NB and DT results, for NIDS. The data sets obtained were divided into training and testing tests. Table 3 shows the distribution for iteration for varying training percentage and testing percentage.

Table 3. The number of varying test and train records

Simulation (Proportion, %)	Training dataset	Testing dataset
Simulation I (60–40)	49399	32933
Simulation II (70–30)	57632	24700
Simulation III (80–20)	65866	16466
Simulation IV (90–10)	74099	8233

Table 4 shows the distribution of the number of instances of attacks and normal in the test set for varying percentage split. It reveals the respective proportion within each simulation to be an average of 45% of Non_attack (normal) and 55% of attacks records.

Table 4. The number of different test and train records (Simulations)

Simulation name	Number of testing records	Number of records		Proportion of test data	
		Non Attack	Attack	Non_Attack	Attack
I	32933	14812	18121	44.98	55.02
II	24700	11092	13608	44.91	55.09
III	16466	7395	9071	44.91	55.09
IV	8233	3712	4521	45.08	54.91

Using 2 Class Dataset. Table 5 shows the confusion matrix obtained on test data for both Attack and Non_attack for each experimental setup and their corresponding accuracies while, Table 6 shows the evaluation results of the two classifiers.

The build time results revealed that the NB classifier spent a minimum of 1.28 s and a maximum time of 1.69 s while the DT spent a minimum and maximum time of 19.24 and 21.63 s. The outputs of the model validation showed that although the DT spends a long time building the model, the time spent in testing is lesser than that of the NB classifier. Empirical results show that the DT C4.5 algorithms outperformed NB for all simulations based on the different spilled ratio of training and testing as the highest for C4.5 returns an accuracy of 90.44% and 75.09% for NB for two-class models. Meanwhile, Moustafa and Slay's IDS model using all the forty-two features returns an accuracy of 85.14%, which shows that the remaining twenty-seven attributes are not used to make a minimal contribution. In order to justify the impact of the FS, the model of complete 42 features is developed using the same classification model of DT and NB. Table 7 shows the result which indicates lower rates than the split ratio simulations.

Table 5. Results of simulation of classification model using 2-class dataset

Simulation/ (Instances)	Classifiers	Non_attack/ Non_attack	Non_attack/ Attack	Attack/ Attack	Attack/ Non_attack	Correct classification	Incorrect classification
I (32933)	NB	18569	6162	6160	2042	24729	8204
	DT	26833	2912	2912	312	29745	3188
II (24700)	NB	13908	4626	4627	1539	18535	6165
	DT	20110	2176	2178	236	22288	2412
III (16466)	NB	9292	3085	3064	1025	12356	4110
	DT	13429	1445	1440	155	14870	1596
IV(8233)	NB	4642	1540	1540	511	6182	2051
	DT	6734	710	712	77	7446	787

Table 6. Results of the validation of classification model for NIDS

Simulation (Instances)	MLA	Build time(s)	Test time(s)	TP rate	FP rate	Precision	Accuracy%
I	NB	1.69	3.55	0.751	0.228	0.775	75.09
	DT	21.28	0.22	0.903	0.087	0.910	90.21
II	NB	1.22	2.35	0.750	0.229	0.774	75.04
	DT	20.52	1.13	0.902	0.089	0.908	90.23
III	NB	1.33	1.45	0.750	0.229	0.773	75.04
	DT	20.88	0.06	0.903	0.087	0.910	90.31
IV	NB	1.29	0.55	0.751	0.228	0.775	75.09
	DT	21.63	0.06	0.904	0.086	0.911	90.44

Table 7. Complete 42 features valuation result

Simulation (Proportion, %)	MLA	Non_attack/ Non_attack FP	Non_attack/ Attack FN	Attack/Attack TP	Attack/ Non_attack TN	Accuracy%
I	NB	1937	2317	6732	5481	74.17
(80%–20%)	DT	478	1239	7810	6940	89.57
II	NB	943	1146	3411	2738	74.63
(90%–10%)	DT	230	591	3966	3447	90.03

5 Conclusion

This paper has successfully developed NIDS models using NB and DT based on the UNSW-NB15 dataset that contained a target variable with two classes. Filter-based FS techniques - IG and GR were used in ranking the forty-two features available in the dataset to reveal the importance of each feature to build the NIDS model.

The study revealed that the first 15 ranked features observed contained the same set of features using the two methods selected as the most informative for intrusions detection. Meanwhile, the DT classifier performed better than the NB irrespective of the training and testing proportion adopted.

Future studies will employ more sophisticated FS approaches on different classifiers to establish the most relevant intrusion detection features in "UNSW-NB15" data set suitable for accurate detection in computer networks.

References

1. Fares, A., Sharawy, I.: Intrusion detection: supervised machine learning. J. Comput. Sci. Eng. 5(4), 305–313 (2011)
2. Hoffmann, R., Napiórkowski, J., Protasowicki, T., Stanik, J.: Risk based approach in scope of cybersecurity threats and requirements. Procedia Manuf. 44, 655–662 (2020)
3. Mebawondu, J.: Development of a Network Intrusion Detection System Using Neural Network. M.Tech Dissertation submitted to the Department of Computer Science Federal University of Technology. Akure Nigeria (2018)
4. Alowolodu, D., Alese, K., Adetunmbi, O., Adewale, S., Ogundele, S.: Elliptic curve cryptography for securing cloud computing applications. Int. J. Comput. Appl. 66(23), 10–17 (2013)
5. Gilmore, C., Haydaman, J.: Anomaly detection and machine learning methods for network intrusion detection: an industrially focused literature review. In: International Conference on Security and Management, pp. 292–298 (2016)
6. Sharma, P., Kunwar, R.: Cyber attacks on intrusion detection systems. Int. J. Inf. Sci. Techn. 6(1/2), 191–196 (2016)
7. Moustafa, N., Slay, J.: The evaluation of network anomaly detection systems: statistical analysis of the UNSW-NB15 data set and the with the KDD99 dataset. Inf. Secur. J. A Global Perspective 25(1–3), 18–31 (2016)
8. Oguntimilehin, A., Adetunmbi, A.O., Osho, I.B.: Towards achieving optimal performance using stacked generalization algorithm: a case study of clinical diagnosis of malaria fever. Int. Arab J. Inf. Technol. (IAJIT) Elsevier 16(6), 1074–1081 (2019)
9. Adetunmbi, A.O., Alese, B.K., Ogundele, O.S., Falaki, S.O.: A data mining approach to network intrusion detection. J. Comput. Sci. Appl. 14(2), 24–37 (2007)
10. Waljee, A., Higgings, P., Singal, A.: A primer on predictive models. Clin. Translational Gastroenterol. 4(44), 1–4 (2013)
11. Mitchell, T.: Machine Learning. McGraw Hill, New York (1997)
12. Adetunmbi, A.O., Adeola, O.S., Daramola, O.A.: Analysis of KDD 1999 intrusion detection for relevance feature selection. I: Proceedings of the World Congress of Engineering and Computer Science, (WCECS 2010), October 20–22, pp. 162–168, San Francisco, USA (2010)
13. Sommer, R., Paxson, V.: Outside the closed world: On using machine learning for network intrusion detection. In: IEEE Symposium on Security and Privacy, pp. 305–316 (2010)

14. Hall, M.: Correlation-based Feature Selection for Machine learning. PhD Thesis of the University of Waikato, Hamilton, New Zealand (1999)
15. Yildirim, P.: Filter-based feature selection methods for prediction of risks in hepatitis disease. Int. J. Machine Learn. Comput. **5**(4), 258–263 (2015)
16. Azeez, N.A., Ayemobola, T.J., Misra, S., Maskeliūnas, R., Damaševičius, R.: Network intrusion detection with a hashing based apriori algorithm using Hadoop MapReduce. Computers **8**(4), 86–97 (2019)
17. Mebawondu, J., Alowolodu, D., Mebawondu, O., Adetunmbi, O.: Network Intrusion Detection System using supervised Learning Paradigm. Elsevier publication, Scientific African Journal, https://doi.org/10.1016/j.sciaf.2020.e00497 (2020)
18. Neethu, B.: Classification of intrusion detection dataset using machine learning approaches. Int. J. Electron. Comput. Sci. Eng. **1**(3), 1044–1051 (2015)
19. Das, V., Pathak, V., Sharma, S., Srikanth, M., Kumar, G., Nadu, T.: Network Intrusion Detection System Based on Machine Learning Algorithms, pp. 235–239 (2010)
20. Dixit, S., Navjot, G.: An implementation of data pre-processing for small dataset. Int. J. Comput. Appl. **103**(6), 123–126 (2014)
21. Osanaiye, O., Cai, H., Choo, K., Dehghantanha, A., Xu, Z., Dlodlo, M.:Ensemble-based multi-filter feature selection method for DDoS detection in cloud computing. EURASIP J. Wireless Commun. Network., **1**, 130 (2016)
22. Shah, R., Qian, Y., Kumar, D., Ali, M., Alvi, M.: Network intrusion detection through discriminative feature selection by using sparse logistic regression. Future Internet **9**(4), 81 (2017)
23. Onyekwelu, A.B., Adetunmbi, A.O.: Bayesian approach to network intrusion detection on web server log data. FUTA J. Res. Sci. **13**(2), 364–370 (2017). International Journal of Computer Network and Information Security **9**(1), 20–30 (2017)
24. Belouch, M., El Hadaj, S., Idhammad, M.: Performance evaluation of intrusion detection based on machine learning using apache spark. In: 1st International Conference on Intelligent Computing in Data Sciences, **127**, 1–6 (2018)
25. Peketi, S., Varma, S., Mutukuri, R.: Classification of network violation detection using machine learning. Int. J. Adv. Res. Comput. Sci. **9**(1), 10–18 (2018)
26. Guo, F., Zhao, Q., Li, X., Kuang, X., Zhang, J., Han, Y., Tan, Y.: Detecting adversarial examples via prediction difference for deep. Inf. Sci. Elsevier Ltd. **501**, 182–192 (2019)
27. Grosse, K., Manoharan, P., Papernot, N., Backes, M., McDaniel, P.: On the (statistical) detection of adversarial examples. arXiv preprint arXiv, 1702.06280 (2017)
28. Akhtar, N., Mian, A.: Threat of adversarial attacks on deep learning in computer vision: a survey. IEEE Access **6**, 14410–14430 (2018)
29. Odusami, M., Misra, S., Adetiba, E., Abayomi-Alli, O., Damasevicius, R., Ahuja, R.: An improved model for alleviating layer seven distributed denial of service intrusion on webserver. J. Phys.: Conf. Ser. IOP Publishing **1235**(1), 1–13 (2020)
30. Shamshirband, S., et al.: Co-FAIS: cooperative fuzzy artificial immune system for detecting intrusion in wireless sensor networks. J. Network Comput. Appl. **42**, 102–117 (2014)

Spoof Detection in a Zigbee Network Using Forge-Resistant Network Characteristics (RSSI and LQI)

Christopher Bahago Martins[✉] ⓘ, Emmanuel Adedokun Adewale, Ime Umoh Jarlath, and Muhammed Bashir Mu'azu

Department of Computer Engineering, Faculty of Engineering, Ahmadu Bello University, Samaru, Zaria, Kaduna, Nigeria
xkrsnor@gmail.com, wale@abu.edu.ng, ime.umoh@gmail.com, muazumb1@yahoo.com

Abstract. The development of a spoof detection framework in a ZigBee network using forge-resistant network characteristics is presented. ZigBee has become ubiquitous in application areas such as Wireless Sensor Networks (WSNs), Home Area Networks (HANs), Smart Metering, Smart Grid, Internet of Things (IoT) and smart devices. Its pervasiveness and suitability for vast applications makes it a tempting target for attackers. Due to the open nature of the wireless medium, ZigBee networks are susceptible to spoofing attacks; where an illegitimate/Sybil node impersonates or disguises as one or multiple legitimate nodes with malicious intentions. A testbed consisting of two ZU10 ZigBee modules was setup to create a real ZigBee network environment. Received Signal Strength Indicator (RSSI) and the corresponding Link Quality Indicator (LQI) data were collected. The Dynamic Time Warping (DTW) algorithm was used for time series classification and similarity measurement of these dataset over variable physical distances. The framework was able to differentiate ZigBee signals that are at least 1 m apart.

Keywords: ZigBee · Spoofing · Received Signal Strength Indicator (RSSI) · Link Quality Indicator (LQI)

1 Introduction

ZigBee[TM] is an implementation of (IEEE) 802.15.4. It is a standard radio technology designed for low data rate, low power applications [1, 2]. It builds on the Physical (PHY) and Media Access Control (MAC) layers of the IEEE 802.15.4 protocol stack [3]. In recent times, ZigBee devices have become ubiquitous, especially in application areas such as Wireless Sensor Networks (WSNs) [4, 5], HANs within the Smart Grid [6]. This has made ZigBee devices vulnerable [4, 7–12]. Due to the open nature of the wireless medium, wireless networks are susceptible to spoofing attacks [4, 13]. In a spoofing attack, an illegitimate or Sybil node masquerades as one or multiple legitimate nodes [4, 5, 14] with malicious intentions. During passive monitoring by an adversary, important identity information can be acquired and used to launch spoofing attacks using cheap

© Springer Nature Switzerland AG 2021
S. Misra and B. Muhammad-Bello (Eds.): ICTA 2020, CCIS 1350, pp. 328–339, 2021.
https://doi.org/10.1007/978-3-030-69143-1_26

commercial off-the-shelf wireless devices that utilize broadcast-based paradigm for communication [4, 8, 15]. These spoofed identities could be used by the adversaries to disrupt network/resource(s) access such as for Denial of Service (DoS) attacks [4, 8, 15, 16] or to advertise false services to nearby hosts such as man-in-the-middle-attacks [4, 8, 10], de-authentication/de-association attacks [4, 7, 8, 15, 17]. It is imperative and crucial that these attacks that lead to identity compromise or service disruption are curtailed [18]. Cryptographic and authentication techniques have traditionally been employed to check against such attacks [4, 19] with little or no success especially in resource constrained networks where nodes usually run on battery power such as ZigBee devices [13]; where power management is key in successful deployment. Moreover, additional overhead is accrued with authentication for deployment and management of authentication keys [8]. In wireless networks, only data frames are authenticated, hence, management and control frames are easily compromised [4].

It becomes desirable to use properties of wireless signals that do not accrue additional overhead due to deploying additional traffic measuring and monitoring devices or even when nodes are compromised [4]. These properties are difficult to manipulate or mimic and are highly correlated to a devices' location [8, 11, 13]. Received Signal Strength Indicator (RSSI) and Link Quality Indicator (LQI) are properties of wireless signals that are not easily compromised. Received Signal Strength Indicator (RSSI) is an open research area [13] and has been widely used as a physical network attribute of wireless signals to formulate spoofing detection schemes [8, 13, 15, 19], but the unreliability and variation overtime of RSSI infers that other physical network attributes be considered alongside RSSI to improve reliability and consistency [11]. LQI is one such physical network attribute that has been used as a substitute to RSSI [20].

[21] proposed using RSSI signalprint as the basis for spoofing detection in a WSN. Battery discharge (power constraint), the unreliability of RSSI and decentralized nature of WSNs was considered in formulating the detection mechanism.

However, accuracy was largely dependent on increasing number of receivers since fewer receivers are unable to generate enough RSSI to form a signalprint vector for a sending node. [22] developed Reciprocal Channel Variation-based Identification (RCVI) to detect Identity Based Attacks (IBAs) in mobile wireless networks. The technique utilizes location decorrelation, randomness and reciprocity of the wireless fading channel and is used to determine if all packets are from a single or multiple source(s). Results shows that the developed technique (RCVI) is able to detect IBAs with high probability but with additional overhead. Additional overhead introduces a performance bottleneck. Further, their scheme is only effective as long as there are bi-directional frames exchanged between the communicating nodes within a time interval shorter than the channel coherence time. [23] analyzed RSSI and LQI data in order to distinguish good links from weak ones and particularly, be able to derive a metric that best estimates the Packet Reception Rate (PRR). It was found that estimations based on RSSI resulted in wrong PRR values, hence, not a good in differentiating link categories. A fermi-dirac function was plotted. A fit to the scattered diagram of the average and standard variation of LQI was used to obtain an estimator for PRR for a given level of LQI. The estimator was evaluated by computing PRR over a varying window size of transmissions and comparing with the estimator of PRR. It was deduced that good LQI entails good Packet

Reception Rate (PRR). The result shows LQI as a reliable metric for signal strength/good link estimation and RSSI alone is not a good link estimator since it incorrectly estimates PRR. [11] Introduced a novel concept of similarity measurement for time-series of a devices' physical network characteristic (RSSI) and measure any marked change(s) in such measurements to be able to detect spoofing. A framework that analyzes the variation of RSSI values of ZigBee packets over varying distances in a ZigBee network environment was proposed. Euclidean Distance and Dynamic Time Warping (DTW) distance was used for time-series classification and similarity measurements. If the similarity between subsequent packet sequences exceeds a pre-computed threshold, τ, spoofing is suspected. meaningful RSSI measurements occurred when devices distance was 6 m onwards i.e. distance from which ZigBee devices could be differentiated was at more than 4 m. The reliability of the scheme cannot be consistent over time since RSSI is known to be affected by environmental factors.

In this paper, RSSI based on good LQI of ZigBee packets were used to classify ZigBee signals and formulate a spoof detection scheme using Dynamic Time Warping (DTW) algorithm for similarity measurement in a real network environment.

2 Fundamental Concepts

IEEE 802.15.4/ZigBee

IEEE 802.15.4 is a standard designed for low-power, low-data-rate applications [1]. Figure 1 depicts ZigBee Protocol stack.

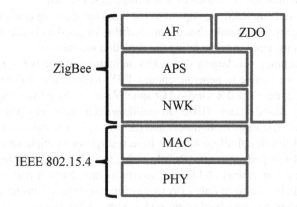

Fig. 1. ZigBee Protocol Stack Architecture

Spoofing

Spoofing is a type of identity compromise achieved by passively listening on a communication channel or capturing and manipulating legitimate packets [4, 8, 9, 19] which consequently allows a series of traffic injection attacks such as spoof based DoS [4] and evil twin Access Points attacks [19]. In a spoofing scenario, an attacker disguises as another device, node or Access Point (AP) or creates multiple fake identities for malicious intentions.

Another form of a spoofing attack is the Sybil attack, in which malicious nodes are able to impersonate multiple identities by maintaining false credentials [4, 13, 24]. The malicious node can then generate fake recommendations about trustworthiness of a node(s) to redirect more network traffic to it. This offers the attacker an ideal starting point for subsequent attacks [13, 14].

In a typical spoofing attack scenario, at least 3 nodes are involved: a sender (legitimate) node, a receiver (victim) node and an attacker (adversary) node. The sender (legitimate) node exchanges important information with the receiver ('would-be' victim). The receiver uses the identity of the legitimate node to determine if the traffic is from a genuine source. On a ZigBee network, IEEE Address (MAC) and node IDs usually are the identities [6, 25]. The attacker listens on the communication channel with the aim of learning identities of the sender (legitimate node) and receiver (victim); by forging its identity, it modifies and sends malicious messages to the victim. To effectively carryout spoofing attacks, an adversary must possess these capabilities:

– be at the appropriate communication range of the nodes to initiate any spoofing attempts;
– ability to monitor traffic by listening on the communication channel to be able to identify users' identity;
– ability to decipher sent/received packets in an encrypted communication; and
– ability to modify frames and inject packets into the network.

Received Signal Strength Indicator (RSSI)
Received Signal Strength Indicator (RSSI) is a measured value of the power present in a received radio signal [21]. RSSI at the receiver is an indicator of the amount of residual battery life in the transmitter [26]. RSSI measures the overall energy of the received signal expressed in dBm [27]. RSSI is estimated when a packet is received, it is affected by environmental factors, distance between sender and receiver, variation of transceiver and antenna orientation [20, 28]. During signal transmission from the sender to receiver, several environmental factors (such as absorption and multipath effect) modify the transmitted signal strength. This reflected signal interferes with the original signal leading to modifications in signal intensity.

The power of the received signal is inversely proportional to the square of the distance between the receiver and the transmitter.

$$RSSI = 10 n \log PwrX \; Pref \tag{1}$$

Where PwrX is the senders' transmission power, Pref is the reference power usually taken as 1 mW.

RSSI is a negative dBm value, the closer the values are to 0 dBm, the stronger the signals [29];

$$P_{out} = 10 \char`\^ (dBm/10) \tag{2}$$

$$dBm = 10 \log_{10} P_{out} P_{ref}\char`\^(-1) \tag{3}$$

Where Pout is the output power of the sending node and 1 mW is taken as the reference power.

Link Quality Indicator (LQI)
LQI defines the reliability of a link from information at packet delivery. The LQI metric characterizes the strength and quality of a received packet, it estimates the error in the incoming modulation of the successfully received packets and the resulting integer ranges from 0×00 to $0 \times ff$ (0–255), depicting the lowest and highest quality signals sensed by the receiver (between $-100\,dBm$ and $0\,dBm$) [30]. LQI generally describes the quality of the received Radio Frequency (RF) signal. This measurement could be carried out using receiver Energy Detection (ED), Signal-to-Noise Ratio (SNR) estimation, or a combination of both methods.

The LQI parameter depends on the distance between the transmitter and the receiver [26]. LQI can complement/substitute for RSSI because it represents the quality of the received packet, therefore, it is not adversely affected by environmental factors [26]. A combination of RSSI and correlation values generate the LQI value as follows:

$$LQI = -0.33d + 110 \qquad (4)$$

where d represent distance between the sending and receiving node and 0.33 is the correlation value (raw LQI value usually obtained from the last byte of the received message).

A high LQI value corresponds to high Packet Reception Rate (PRR). The estimation of LQI is based on the first eight symbols of the received physical header. Each symbol represents the sequence of bytes that are compared against known symbols stored in the embedded table. The correlation of these two values defines the average of the properly received bits [27].

3 Materials and Method

A pair of ProBee ZU10 ZigBee modules of Senna Technologies were used for setting up the testbed. The software used in the work includes ProBee Configuration Manager, Termite RS-232 terminal and Python software.

Method
The testbed consists of two ZU10 USB-emulated ZigBee modules of SENA Technologies. The testbed area measures 22×6 m. The testbed's setup covered the third floor of the Department of Computer and Control Engineering, Ahmadu Bello University Zaria. The 3rd floor was the preferred location for this setup because several 802.11 based Access Points (APs) and rogue APs known to interfere with ZigBee signals exist, hence, this serves to demonstrate the effectiveness of the our scheme even in noisy environments.

The two ZU10 modules were configured as ZigBee Coordinator and ZigBee End device based on mesh topology. Both nodes are configured to exchange unicast messages at specified intervals.

Dataset collection
Data collection was carried out by varying distances di for i = 3,4,5,6,7,8,9,10,12 and 15, between communicating devices on the ZigBee network. For each d meters between a parent and child node, RSSI measurements were collected every 1500 ms and the recorded data are logged and saved in a repository defined at setup.

Feature (RSSI/LQI Vectors) Extraction
RSSI/LQI feature are extracted from the ZigBee communication log based on strong and consistent RSSI/LQI pair to form feature vectors of the form:

$$\text{RSSIi} = [\text{RSSI}_1, \text{RSSI}_2, \text{RSSI}_3 \ldots \text{RSSI}_n] \text{ for } i = 1, 2, 3 \ldots n \tag{5}$$

$$\text{LQIi} = \left[\text{LQI}_1, \text{LQI}_2, \text{LQI}_3 \ldots \text{LQI}_n\right] \text{ for } i = 1, 2, 3 \ldots n \tag{6}$$

For data collected at every d meters, a reference time series, T_{ref}, and three different test series T_1, T_2, T_3 and T_{spoof} (spoofed time series) were defined. T_{ref} represents the vectors of time series assumed to be uncompromised and taken as a reference to be compared against other series taken at another time instance. T_1, T_2, T_3 and T_{spoof} represent test time series taken from subsequent communication between supposed genuine nodes. These series defined are all samples taken from a population (36,000 samples collected).

Framework for Spoof Detection
The framework for spoof detection consists of three stages/processes:

1. Using Dynamic Time Warping algorithm for RSSI time series classification and similarity measurement of reference, tests and spoofed series.
2. Dynamically computing threshold values of the recorded time series. The threshold used in this framework is the Variance (σ) of the RSSI time series (based on good link indicator); and
3. Making decision whether or not the change between subsequent DTW_{dist} exceeds the predefined threshold which determines if a spoof is detected for a time series and at a certain distance or the recursion restarts.

Figure 2 depicts the flowchart showing the method and developed spoof detection framework (Fig. 3).

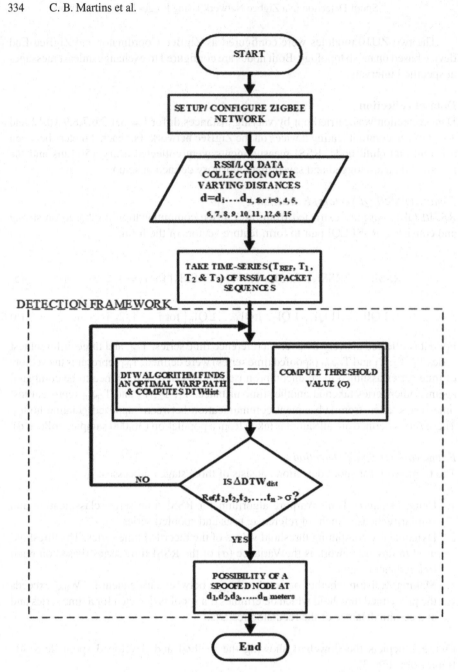

Fig. 2. method and the developed Framework for spoof detection

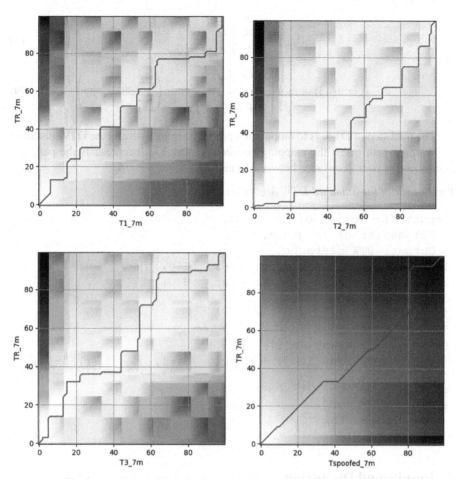

Fig. 3. Warping path between T_{ref}, tests and spoofed time series at 7 m

Threshold of Measured Data

For every d meter of RSSI data collected, a threshold value σ, is computed. The threshold is dynamically updated to enable the system adjust to changes in network condition.

RSSI Similarity Measure Using DTW Algorithm

Similarity measurement was based on DTW implemented in Python.

The 1st stage is to fill a local distance matrix, d, with n x m elements which represents the Euclidean distance between every two points in the time series.

Secondly, it fills the warping matrix, d. Equations (7), (8) and (9) respectively describe the initial condition and the recursion that governs every stage of the computations.

$$d(i, j) = \left| a_i - b_j \right| \tag{7}$$

$$d\,(i, j) = \begin{cases} \infty \ if\ i = 0\ or\ j = 0 \\ 0, \ if\ i = j = 0 \end{cases} \tag{8}$$

$$d(i, j) = d(i, j) + \min \begin{cases} d(i-1, j) \\ d(i, j-1) \\ d(i-1, j-1) \end{cases} \min_{P} \left(\sum_{s=1}^{k} \mathrm{dist}(i_s, j_s) \right) \tag{9}$$

The final step of DTW is to output the optimal warping path and the DTW distance.

Warping path traces the mapping between Xi and Yk. It represents the path that minimizes the overall distance between Xi and Yk.

Pseudocode of the Standard DTW Algorithm

```
Input: Xi: series of length n,
   Yk: series of length m,
   Output: DTW distance
1:   start d (i, 0) = ∞ for every i∈[0, n]
2:   start d (0, j) = ∞ for every j∈[0, m]
3:   d [0, 0] = 0;
4:   for i = 1 to n
5:   for j = 1 to m
6:   d [i, j] = abs (a[i] - b[j]);
7:   d [i, j] = d [i, j] + min (d ([i-1, j], d [i, j-1], d
[i-1, j-1]);
8:   end for
9:   end for
10:    return d (n, m)
```

4 Results and Discussion

Similarity Measurement

The outputs of the DTW algorithm for the RSSI dataset measured for 7 m are presented here. These outputs, for each experimental distance include a plot of the warping path and a DTW_{dist}, for each of the tests and suspected spoofed series. The DTW_{dist} for all distances are summarized in Table 1.

The DTW_{dist} for all distances are summarized in Table 1.

The rate of change of the Dynamic Time Warping distance (DTW_{dist}) between the tests and the spoofed plots compared to the threshold values shall be used to determine whether or not the time series is spoofed.

Table 1 shows a summary of the computed parameters such as thresholds, DTW_{dist} for all warping path plot at varying physical distances. It can be observed from the table that ΔDTW_{dist} for T_{ref}, T_1, T_2 and T_3, is within the computed threshold values between 3 to 15 meters signifying that there is no spoofed RSSI time series suspected therefore, these time series are from the same source. In contrast, the change (ΔDTW_{dist}) for each suspected spoofed distance is significantly greater than the pre-defined threshold

Table 1. Summary of DTW_{dist} similarity measurement results

Phy dist (m)	Threshold (σ)	DTW_{dist} T_{REF}/T_1	DTW_{dist} T_{REF}/T_2	DTW_{dist} T_{REF}/T_3	DTW_{dist} $T_{REF}/T_{spoofed}$	$\Delta DTW_{dist\_}$ T_1/T_2	$\Delta DTW_{dist\_}$ T_2/T_3	$\Delta DTW_{dist\_}$ $T_3/T_{spoofed}$
3	10.17	74	74	86	1193	0	10.1	1107
4	11.41	37	37	35	1054	0	2	1019
5	12.30	7	10	7	1155	3	3	1544
6	10.14	56	56	54	1793	0	2	739
7	10.10	48	45	47	1089	3	2	1042
8	9.55	46	39	49	1156	7	8.4	1507
9	10.86	115	16	81	1569	9.9	6.5	1488
12	9.80	12	38	37	1446	8.6	1	1409
15	10.43	6	25	75	1252	9.1	8.5	1077

culminating in suspicion of spoofed RSSI time series; hence, those time series at the particular time window are not from the legitimate sender/source at those distances.

Based on the inferences deduced from Table 1, it can be concluded that the developed detection scheme is able to detect spoofed time-series when the malicious node is at least 1 m away from the communicating devices.

5 Summary and Conclusion

In this paper, a framework for spoof detection in a real ZigBee network utilizing physical network attributes inherent in wireless communications was presented. DTW algorithm was used for time-series similarities measurement of these attributes. Feature RSSI vectors were extracted from ZigBee packets based on strong and consistent LQI vectors to form a time series. These time series of different time intervals were compared using the DTW algorithm to test for the possibility of a spoofed time series by comparing the rate of change of the output (ΔDTW_{Dist}) for the sample tests and spoofed time series from the algorithm with a pre-computed threshold value (variance of the dataset). With reference to Table 1, the time series from the test series are from a legitimate source and therefore not spoofed since the rate of change did not exceed the pre-computed threshold values. Similarly, the time series from the spoofed series are undoubtedly from a spoofed source since the rate of change greatly exceed the pre-computed threshold value. Utilizing these attributes was aimed at addressing existing issues associated with other methods of spoof detection mostly reliant on cryptography and authentication. The developed system was able to differentiate signals that are at least 1 m apart.

References

1. Vasseur, J.-P., Dunkels, A.: Interconnecting smart objects with ip: The next internet, in Inter-connecting Smart Objects with IP: The Next Internet. Morgan Kaufmann Publishers, Elsevier Science (2010)

2. Xiao, Y., et al.: Security services and enhancements in the IEEE 802.15. 4 wireless sensor networks. In: GLOBECOM 2005 IEEE Global Telecommunications Conference, 2005, St. Louis, MO, USA: IEEE. https://doi.org/10.1109/GLOCOM.2005.1577958
3. Tennina, S., et al.: IEEE 802.15. 4 and ZigBee as enabling technologies for low-power wireless systems with quality-of-service constraints, Springer, Cham (2013). https://doi.org/10.1007/978-3-642-37368-8
4. Yang, J.: Pervasive Wireless Environments: Detecting and Localizing User Spoofing. SCS. Springer, Cham (2014). https://doi.org/10.1007/978-3-319-07356-9
5. Eronu, E., Misra, S., Aibinu, M.: Reconfiguration approaches in wireless sensor network: issues and challenges. In: 2013 IEEE International Conference on Emerging & Sustainable Technologies for Power & ICT in a Developing Society (NIGERCON), IEEE (2013). https://doi.org/10.1109/NIGERCON.2013.6715648
6. Jokar, P., Arianpoo, N., Leung, V.C.: Spoofing prevention using received signal strength for ZigBee-based home area networks. In: Smart Grid Communications (SmartGridComm) Symposium, 2013 IEEE International Conference on Smart Grid, Cyber Security and Privacy, IEEE, Vancouver, BC, Canada (2013). https://doi.org/10.1109/SmartGridComm.2013.6687997
7. Vaidya, A., Jaiswal, S., Motghare, M.: A review paper on spoofing detection methods in wireless LAN. In: 2016 10th International Conference on Intelligent Systems and Control (ISCO), 2016. IEEE, Coimbatore, India. https://doi.org/10.1109/ISCO.2016.7727054
8. Sheng, Y., et al.: Detecting 802.11 MAC layer spoofing using received signal strength. In: IEEE INFOCOM 2008 - The 27th Conference on Computer Communications, IEEE, Phoenix, AZ, USA (2008). https://doi.org/10.1109/INFOCOM.2008.239
9. Chen, Y., et al.: Detecting and localizing identity-based attacks in wireless and sensor networks. IEEE Trans. Veh. Technol. **59**(5), 2418–2434 (2010). https://doi.org/10.1109/TVT.2010.2044904
10. Meena, T., Nishanthy, M., Kamalanaban, E.: Cluster-based mechanism for multiple spoofing attackers in WSN. In: International Conference on Information Communication and Embedded Systems (ICICES), IEEE, Chennai, India (2014). https://doi.org/10.1109/ICICES.2014.7034164
11. Yu, J., et al.: A framework for detecting MAC and IP spoofing attacks with network characteristics. In: 2016 International Conference on Software Security and Assurance (ICSSA), IEEE, St. Polten, Austria (2016). https://doi.org/10.1109/ICSSA.2016.16
12. Gupta, D., Dhawale, C., Misra, S.: A cooperative approach for malicious node detection in impromptu wireless networks. In: 2016 International Conference on Computational Techniques in Information and Communication Technologies (ICCTICT), IEEE (2016). https://doi.org/10.1109/ICCTICT.2016.7514654
13. Jokar, P., Arianpoo, N., Leung, V.C.: Spoofing detection in IEEE 802.15. 4 networks based on received signal strength. Ad Hoc Networks, **11**(8), pp. 2648–2660 (2013). https://doi.org/10.1016/j.adhoc.2013.04.015
14. Das, S.K., Kant, K., Zhang, N.: Handbook on securing cyber-physical critical infrastructure, Elsevier. p. 191–203 (2012). https://doi.org/10.1016/C2011-0-04434-4
15. Faria, D.B., Cheriton, D.R.: Detecting identity-based attacks in wireless networks using signalprints. In: Proceedings of the 5th ACM workshop on Wireless security, ACM, Hangzhou, China (2006). https://doi.org/10.1109/GreenCom-CPSCom.2010.61
16. Odusami, M., Misra, S., Abayomi Alli, O., Abayomi Alli, A., Fernandez Sanz, L.: A survey and meta analysis of application layer distributed denial of service attack, **33**(18), p. e4603 (2020). https://doi.org/10.1002/dac.4603
17. Guo, F., Chiueh, T.: Sequence number-based MAC address spoof detection. In: Valdes, A., Zamboni, D. (eds.) RAID 2005. LNCS, vol. 3858, pp. 309–329. Springer, Heidelberg (2006). https://doi.org/10.1007/11663812_16

18. Maivizhi, R., Matilda, S.: Distance based Detection and Localization of multiple spoofing attackers for wireless networks. In: International Conference on Computation of Power, Energy, Information and Communication (ICCPEIC), IEEE, Chennai, India (2014). https://doi.org/10.1109/ICCPEIC.2014.6915341

19. Chen, Y., Trappe, W., Martin, R.P.: Detecting and localizing wireless spoofing attacks. In: 2007 4th Annual IEEE Communications Society Conference on Sensor, Mesh and Ad Hoc Communications and Networks, IEEE, San Diego, CA (2007). https://doi.org/10.1109/SAHCN.2007.4292831

20. Wang, Y., Guardiola, I.G., Wu, X.: RSSI and LQI data clustering techniques to determine the number of nodes in wireless sensor networks. Int. J. Distrib. Sens. Netw. **10**(5), 380526 (2014). https://doi.org/10.1155/2014/380526

21. Misra, S., Ghosh, A., Obaidat, M.S.: Detection of identity-based attacks in wireless sensor networks using signalprints. In: IEEE/ACM International Conference on Green Computing and Communications (GreenCom)-Cyber, Physical and Social Computing (CPSCom), 2010, IEEE, Hangzhou, China (2010). https://doi.org/10.1109/GreenCom-CPSCom.2010.61

22. Zeng, K., et al.: Identity-based attack detection in mobile wireless networks. In: 2011 Proceedings IEEE INFOCOM. 2011, IEEE, Shanghai, China. https://doi.org/10.1109/INFCOM.2011.5934990

23. Bildea, A., et al.: Link quality metrics in large scale indoor wireless sensor networks. In: 2013 IEEE 24th Annual International Symposium on Personal, Indoor, and Mobile Radio Communications (PIMRC), IEEE, London, UK (2013). https://doi.org/10.1109/PIMRC.2013.6666451

24. Yang, J., et al.: Detection and localization of multiple spoofing attackers in wireless networks. IEEE Trans. Parallel Distrib. Syst. **24**(1), 44–58 (2013). https://doi.org/10.1109/TPDS.2012.104

25. Thakur, P., Patel, R., Patel, N.: A proposed framework for protection of identity based attack in ZigBee. In: 2015 Fifth International Conference on Communication Systems and Network Technologies (CSNT), IEEE, Gwalior, India (2015). https://doi.org/10.1109/CSNT.2015.243

26. Roy, S., Nene, M.J.: Prevention of node replication in wireless sensor network using received signal strength indicator, link quality indicator and packet sequence number. In: Online International Conference on Green Engineering and Technologies (IC-GET), IEEE, Coimbatore, India (2016). https://doi.org/10.1109/GET.2016.7916613

27. Wolosz, K., Bodin, U., Riliskis, L.: A measurement study for predicting throughput from LQI and RSSI. In: Bellalta, B., Vinel, A., Jonsson, M., Barcelo, J., Maslennikov, R., Chatzimisios, P., Malone, D. (eds.) MACOM 2012. LNCS, vol. 7642, pp. 89–92. Springer, Heidelberg (2012). https://doi.org/10.1007/978-3-642-34976-8_10

28. Zhang, Z., et al.: Item-level indoor localization with passive UHF RFID based on tag interaction analysis. IEEE Trans. Ind. Electron. **61**(4), 2122–2135 (2014). https://doi.org/10.1109/TIE.2013.2264785

29. Barai, S., Biswas, D., Sau, B.: Estimate distance measurement using NodeMCU ESP8266 based on RSSI technique. In: IEEE Conference on Antenna Measurements & Applications (CAMA), 2017, IEEE (2017). https://doi.org/10.1109/CAMA.2017.8273392

30. Nnebe, S., et al.: Performance evaluation of link quality indicator of a wireless sensor network in an outdoor environment. Int. J. Electron. Commun. Comput. Eng. (IJECCE) **4**(4), 1190–1193 (2013)

Face Morphing Attack Detection in the Presence of Post-processed Image Sources Using Neighborhood Component Analysis and Decision Tree Classifier

Ogbuka Mary Kenneth$^{(\boxtimes)}$ ⑩, Sulaimon Adebayo Bashir⑩,
Opeyemi Aderiike Abisoye⑩, and Abdulmalik Danlami Mohammed⑩

Department of Computer Science, Federal University of Technology, Minna, Nigeria
kenneth.pg918157@st.futminna.edu.ng, {bashirsulaimon,
o.a.abisoye,drmalik}@futminna.edu.ng

Abstract. Recently, Face Morphing Attack Detection (MAD) has gained a great deal of attention as criminals have started to use freely and easily available digital manipulation techniques to combine two or more subject facial images to create a new facial image that can be viewed as an accurate image of any of the individual images that constitute it. Some of these morphing tools create morphed images of high quality which pose a serious threat to existing Face Recognition Systems (FRS). In the literatures, it has been identified that FRS is vulnerable to multiform morphing attacks. Based on this vulnerability, several types of research on the detection of this morph attack was conducted using several techniques. Despite the remarkable levels of MAD reported in various literature, so far no suitable solution has been found to handle post-processed images such as images modified after morphing with sharpening operation that can dramatically reduce visible artifacts of morphed photos. In this work, an approach is proposed for MAD before image post-processing and after image post-processing built on a combination of Local Binary Pattern (LBP) for extraction of feature, Neighborhood Component Analysis (NCA) for selection of features and classification using K-Nearest Neighbor (KNN), Decision Tree Classifier (DTC) and Naïve Bayes (NB) classifier. The outcome gotten by training the different classifiers with feature vectors selected using the NCA algorithm improved the classification accuracy from 90% to 94%, consequently improving the general performance of the MAD.

Keywords: Face morphing · Morphing Attack Detection · Post-processing · Sharpening · Bona fide images · Machine learning

1 Introduction

Biometric features are unique characteristics of an individual that can be used for authentication, identification, and access control across a series of contexts including driving license, smartphone unlocking, border control, forensic identification, national identity card, voter's card, and several other identifications [1]. Authentication and recognition

© Springer Nature Switzerland AG 2021
S. Misra and B. Muhammad-Bello (Eds.): ICTA 2020, CCIS 1350, pp. 340–354, 2021.
https://doi.org/10.1007/978-3-030-69143-1_27

are based on biometric characteristics such as fingerprint, iris, speech, and facial features. Face features are commonly used among these different characteristics because of the uninterrupted idea of the capture procedure and the client comfort involved [2]. Photographs of the face are provided in different types of documentation universally, with driving licenses and passports included. However facial identification systems have recently been identified as defenseless against attacks based on morphed facial images [3]. Studies by Scherhag et al. [4] and Ferrara, Franco and Maltoni [5] showed that electronic passports are particularly sensitive to morphing attacks, especially when the face photograph published on paper and presented by an individual has been manipulated. Face morphing is defined as a technique of image manipulation, where two or more faces of subjects are blended to form a single face in the image [6, 7]. Morphed images may look exactly like all the contributing subjects that make up the image. As a result, a morphed image can be used as an identity credential by multiple, if not all of the individual facial images comprising the morphed image [5, 8]. For a morph attack to be effective, the morphed face image has to be identical to any of the multiple subjects particularly the person requesting the electronic passport, this is important to fool the officials in the issuing process, however, the morphed image must at the same time comprise sufficient characteristics of the concealed subject to allow optimistic authentication at the ABC gate for both/multiple individuals [5].

Morph images may be used to mislead human beings [9], and existing facial recognition systems [10]. This has made the latest identity verification processes insecure, such as those used in automatic border control gates (ABC) [6]. In a typical situation of face morphing attack (MA), if the partner applies for an electronic passport with the transformed face image, a criminal on the run could morph his/her passport with one of the lookalike partners, he/she will get a legal e-passport incorporated with matching security features of the document. With this, the companion as well as the suspect could be checked against the warped picture held in the e-passport with success. This scenario shows that the suspect can use the e-passport to successfully cross the ABC gates [8].

Different researches have been carried out for MAD. Research conducted by Ramachandra [2], Seibold et al. [11], Wandzik, Kaeding and Garcia [12], and Jassim and Asaad [13] have achieved remarkable detection rates, but these results are barely applicable to post-processed images such as image compression [14] and post-morphing image sharpening, which can significantly reduce noticeable artifacts from the morphing process, making the previous algorithms less effective. However some existing research works on MAD considered MAD on post-processed images. The post-processing operations considered in existing research works are print-scan [5], image resizing, and image compression [7], but image sharpening as a post-processing operation have not been considered. Image sharpening is a very common post-processing image operation. It is important to automatically detect this face morphing attack even after the morphed images are post-processed using the image sharpening operation.

Along these lines, we propose an approach to detect face morphing attacks even after image post-processing using a combination of Local Binary Pattern (LBP) technique for extraction of features, NCA for feature selection, and DTC, KNN, and NB for classification. Hence, the fundamental contributions of this paper include:

1. Presentation of a method for detecting post-processed morphed images which are more hardened to detection compared to ordinary morphed images.
2. Introduction of a post-processed morphed image dataset that is created from our generated ordinary morphed images. The dataset is composed in a way to eliminate bias.
3. Comparative experimentation of different classifiers on the features obtained from the proposed approach.

The rest of this paper is organized as follows: Sect. 2 offers a summary of recent MAD works. The methodology used for conducting the study is outlined in Sect. 3. Section 4 describes the findings obtained during the experiment and addresses the results presented. Conclusions were drawn in Sect. 5, and Sect. 6 presents future works.

2 Related Work

A variety of methods suggested in recent years for detecting MAD is loosely categorized into two major classes [15]: the single image-based (given a single image identity, it is either categorized as bona-fide or morph) and the differential image-based (manages the correlation between a live picture and that stored on the e-archive). The vast majority of the literature belong to the single category of images.

Ramachandra et al. [2] proposed another methodology of recognizing face morphing attack dependent on removing scale-space highlights utilizing the Steerable pyramid, which is generally a set of oriented filters that are produced as a linear grouping of an elementary function. These separated features were sorted utilizing a collaborative representation classifier. The proposed algorithm achieved a Bona fide Presentation Classification Error (BPCER) of 13:12% at an Attack Presentation Classification Error Rate (APCER) of 10%. Furthermore, the suggested strategy was utilized to detect MA even after the print-scan procedure has been performed. However, this proposed algorithm did not consider other image post-processing tasks such as image sharpening, compression, contrast enhancement, and blurring.

Scherhag et al. [3] developed a MAD method founded on the Non-Uniformity Photo Response (PRNU) analysis. The spectral and spatial features mined from the PRNU designs across picture cells were inspected. In the threshold selection point, the dissimilarities between the features of morphed images and bona fide were measured via the Dresden image database, which is precisely constructed for the PRNU examination in digital image forensics. The algorithm proposed was robust as MAD was performed on morphed images created using various morphing tools that represent a typical real-life scenario. However picture post-processing tasks, for example, contrast enhancement, sharpening, or blurring, can seriously influence the PRNU features which can thoroughly lessen the proficiency of a PRNU-based MAD system [16].

The profound neural system as viable feature extraction and classification procedure in machine learning was embraced by Raghavendra et al. [17] for MAD. The proposed method exploited transferrable features acquired from a pre-trained Convolutional Neural Network (CNN) to execute MAD for both print-scan and digital morphed pictures. Two CNN strategies which are VGG19 and AlexNet were utilized to carry out the feature mining task. The image features were extracted separately from the first fully connected layers of both the AlexNet and VGG19 model and these features were joined to produce a single feature vector using the feature level fusion method. Anyway, the proposed method accomplish a superior exhibition result for digital images with an equal error rate of 8.223% when contrasted with the print-scan pictures with an equal error rate of 12.47%.

Topology data analysis (TDA) as an advancing structure for investigation of big data was adopted by Jassim and Asaad [13] for MAD. For each image, a series of simplex complexes were fabricated, whose vertices are the assigned set of landmarks, for a series of distance thresholds. The assorted variety of topological invariants was utilized to separate the regular face pictures from the morphed ones. The proposed method achieved high accuracy for MAD on digital images but performed poorly on print and scan images. After performing feature concatenation the single feature vector was feed to a collaborative representation classifier for final classification.

Singh et al. [18] performed MAD using the decomposed 3d shape and diffuse reflectance. This method was proposed as it can detect MA in the incidence of posture, print-scan, and lighting artifacts. In this technique, the genuine image taken at the ABC gate and the face image mined from the electronic Machine Readable Travel Document (eMTRD) are disintegrated into a quantized ordinary guide and diffuse remake image. These extracted structures are then used for training linear SVM for MAD founded on the evaluation of the dissimilarities between the bona fide image taken at the ABC gate and the face image mined from the eMTRD. The impediment of this paper is that the proposed algorithm did not consider picture post-processing tasks, for example, the print-scan operation, image compression, contrast enhancement, sharpening, and blurring.

Wandzik, Kaeding and Garcia [12] addresses the issue of MAD utilizing facial recognition techniques dependent on Convolutional Neural Networks (CNN) and hand-crafted features. Four feature extraction algorithms were used to mine the facial features and these algorithms include faceNet, Dlib, and VGG-Face and one shallow learning approach dependent on High- Dim Local binary pattern. After performing feature extraction using any of the feature extraction algorithms, the output feature vectors were used to calculate the Euclidean distance for the face verification task. The reference image vectors were supplied to the support vector machine (SVM) to perform binary classification for MAD. This work can be utilized to perform both face verification and MAD. However, this work only considered MAD of digital images without considering the print and scanned images which are used for verification in some countries.

3 Methodology

This section includes an overview of the techniques used in performing this study. The proposed solution is shown in Fig. 1, and this solution is discussed in detail in this section. These methods include data collection, post-processing, pre-processing, extraction of features, selection of features, classification, and finally the decision (bona fide or morphed).

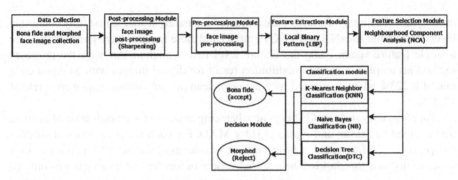

Fig. 1. Proposed approach

3.1 Data Collection

In this study, a new morphed face database comprising of 300 morphed images was produced using different facial images from 100 subjects. To diversify the database, the face pictures utilized contains male and female of both white and dark skin people. The subject pictures were gathered from different online databases, for example, the Yale face database, surveillance cameras face database, and also some arbitrarily looked through online face pictures were utilized.

The morphed face pictures were produced utilizing two morphing apparatuses which are:

1. **Magic morph tool:** This is an elite transforming and wrapping software. It is anything but difficult to utilize, and it delivers top-notch transformed pictures. It utilizes a multithread pyramid calculation.
2. **FantaMorph tool:** This is a transforming software utilized for making a photograph transform and modern transform activity impacts. It helps users to consequently find facial highlights, for example, the nose, eye, and mouth. And consolidates these highlights of various genuine countenances to create a virtual face.

The face pictures were manually adjusted and merged to shroud the transformed antique. The morphing software creates a progression of picture outlines showing the transition of one subject to another. The last transformed image is picked manually by underwriting its similarity to the faces of the contributing subjects to the transforming procedure. Henceforth the made transforms are of high caliber and are low to no recognizable artifacts.

3.2 Post-processing (Image Sharpening)

The images used in identity credentials can go through several processing operations before been embedded into e-visa. A post-processed morphed image loses some of its artifacts which makes MAD of such images troublesome. A typical image post-processing technique is picture sharpening and compression. Image sharpening activity is usually utilized as an image post-processing activity since human perception is incredibly touchy to edges and fine subtleties of a picture and since pictures are made up predominantly of high-frequency segments, the graphic quality can be decreased if the high frequencies are distorted. Improvement of the high-frequency segments of a picture leads to an upgrade in the image graphic quality. Hence sharpening of morphed images can highlight edges and adjust subtleties in the picture which can likewise modify the morph highlights making such a picture hard to detect. Image sharpening operation was identified by Scherhag [8] as one challenge faced in MAD. Hence image sharpening was performed on the morphed images to hardened their detection and elicit the effectiveness of the proposed MAD method even after performing post-processing operation for enhancement of the morphed images.

3.3 Face Pre-processing

In the image pre-processing phase facial landmarks detection was carried out. Facial landmarks are used to confine and signify noticeable areas of the face, for example, nose, eyes, mouth, eyebrows, and jawline [19]. Identification of facial landmarks involves the following steps:

- **Step 1:** Localize the object of interest (face in the image).
- **Step 2:** Recognize the principle facial characteristics on the face region of interest.

In this work, the Viola-Jones algorithm was embraced for face feature discovery. Viola-Jones algorithm was applied because of its exceptionally high discovery rate, and its functional application. The Viola-Jones calculation utilizes the Haar-basis filters, which is a scalar item amid the picture and some Haar-like layouts [20]. This algorithm has four phases for face recognition which are: Haar feature selection, an indispensable image selection, Adaboost training, and cascading classifier. The indispensable image is a method for the operational generation of the sum of pixel concentrations in a stated rectangle in an image.

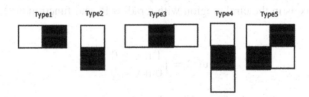

Fig. 2. Haar features in Viola Jones

The Haar features in Fig. 2 have various width and height. In Fig. 2 it can be seen that the image is represented with either black or white pixels and the summation of white pixel and summation of the black pixel are gotten and then deducted to get a lone value. If this calculated value is more in that region, then it signifies a part of the face and is recognized as nose, eyes, mouth, etc. Ada boost diminishes redundant features by determining the significant features and insignificant features. Subsequently, after the identification of the significant features and the insignificant features the Ada boost allocates weight to all of them. And hence generate robust classifiers as a linear grouping of feeble classifiers. Nearly 2500 features are calculated [21]. Hence cascading is used to reduce the number of computations. The features are retained in an additional set of classifiers in a cascading format, to aid it to discover if it is a face or not in a faster time.

After the facial landmarks were detected the face images were cropped to a size of 130 by 130 pixels based on the detected landmarks to ensure that the MAD algorithm is only used on the facial region. Lastly, the cropped face image is transformed into a gray-scale image.

3.4 Feature Extraction

Image features, like edges and points of interest, contain rich data about the content of an image. In an image, features correspond to local regions and are vital in several image analysis application domains such as identification, matching, and reconstruction. These image features can be extracted using several feature extraction techniques. Feature extraction defines the specific shape details found in an image such that a structured procedure makes the task of classifying the image simple.

In this study, feature extraction was performed on the pre-processed images (bona fide and morphed) using the Local Binary Pattern (LBP) technique. The LBP was used as a feature extractor as it has proved to extract very high-quality features that improve the accuracy of classification [22]. Texture features are responsible for the measure of properties such as regularity, coarseness, and smoothness [23]. LBP is an active texture feature descriptor for images that threshold the surrounding pixels based on the current pixel value. The histogram of LBP labels summed over an image is used as a descriptor of that image's texture [27]. Given a neighborhood of Q sample points on a circle of radius of R. And given a pixel at (x_c, y_c). LBP is expressed in Eq. 1 below:

$$LBP_{Q,R(x_c,y_c)} = \sum_{Q=0}^{Q-1} u(i_Q - i_c)2^Q \tag{1}$$

where i_c and i_Q are, correspondingly, gray-level values of the dominant pixel and Q neighboring pixels in the circle region with a radius R, and function u(x) is defined in Eq. 2 as:

$$u(x) = \begin{cases} 1 \text{ if } x \geq 0 \\ 0 \text{ if } x < 0 \end{cases} \tag{2}$$

The LBP was used as the feature descriptor because it is anticipated that the image morphing process will lead to a change in the textual properties of morphed images which will make it a useful function for differentiating between morph and bona fide images.

3.5 Feature Selection

Feature selection was performed on the extracted LBP image features. The NCA was utilized to perform the feature selection operation. The NCA is a non-parametric algorithm for choosing features with the point of augmenting forecast accuracy of classification systems. NCA learns a component weighting vector by augmenting the likely leave one out classification accuracy with a regularization term. A key advantage of NCA as distinguished by Yang, Wang and Zuo [25], is that it is commonly unaffected by the rise in the number of insignificant features and it does superior to most feature selection approaches in most cases. Hence feature selection was performed to improve the classification accuracy. The working of NCA is described below.

Given that $A = \{(x1,y1),...,(xi,yi),...,(xN,yN)\}$ is a collection of training examples, where xi is a feature vector, yi is the matching label and N is a number of examples. The weighting vector w that chooses the feature subset is given in Eq. 3:

$$V_w(x_i, x_j) = \sum_{l=1}^{d} w_l^2 |x_{il} - x_{jl}| \tag{3}$$

Where $V_w(x_i, x_j)$ is the weighted distance between two examples x_j and x_i. To succeed in nearest neighbor classification, an inherent and active approach is to make the most of its leave-one-out CA on the training examples A. hence the likelihood of x_i selecting x_j as its reference point is given in Eq. 4.

$$p_{ij} = \begin{cases} \dfrac{B(V(x_i, x_j))}{\sum_{B \neq 1} B(V_w(x_i, x_B))}, & \text{if } i \neq j \\ 0, & \text{if } i = j \end{cases} \tag{4}$$

Where $B(z) = \exp(-z/\sigma)$ is a kernel function and the kernel width σ is an input parameter that impacts the likelihood of the respective points being chosen as the reference point. From the formula above the likelihood of the query point xi being properly grouped is presented in Eq. 5:

$$p_i = \sum_j y_{ij} p_{ij} \tag{5}$$

Where $y_{ij} = 1$ if and only if $y_i = y_j$ and $y_{ij} = 0$ otherwise. Hence, the estimated leave-one-out accuracy is presented in Eq. 6:

$$\xi(v) = \frac{1}{N} \sum_i p_i = \frac{1}{N} \sum_i \sum_j y_{ij} p_{ij} \tag{6}$$

Where $\xi(v)$ is the true leave-one-out CA. To implement feature selection and ease over-fitting, regularization is introduced which is given in Eq. 7:

$$\xi(v) = \sum_i p_i - \lambda \sum_{i=1}^{d} w_l^2 \tag{7}$$

Where $\lambda > 0$ is a regularization parameter that is tuned through cross-validation. Since $\xi(v)$ is differentiable the resultant derivative is given in Eq. 8:

$$\frac{\partial \xi(v)}{\partial v_l} = 2\left(\frac{1}{\sigma}\sum_i \left(p_i \sum_{j \neq i} p_{ij}|x_{il} - x_{jl}| - \sum_j y_{ij}p_{ij}|x_{il} - x_{jl}|\right) - \lambda\right)v_l \tag{8}$$

Hence the formula in Eq. 8 represents the NCA for feature selection.

3.6 Image Classification

The last phase of the proposed system is the classification stage. The selected features generated from the feature selection stage were feed to three classifiers namely DTC, KNN, and NB. These classifiers were used for the classification of the Images into either bona fide or morphed images.

1. **Decision Tree Classifier (DTC):** A decision tree is a simple and commonly used predictive modeling technique. This is a type of supervised learning where the data is continuously divided according to a certain parameter. The decision tree is represented in a tree-like structure, in this tree structure leaves denote labels and branches signify combinations of features that produce the class labels. DTC is easy to understand and interpret, does not require normalization or scaling of data and it involves less work for data preparation.
2. **K-Nearest Neighbor (KNN):** KNN is a non-parametric algorithm applied to solve regression and classification problems. In KNN an object is grouped by the majority vote of its neighbors, with an object being distributed to a class most common among its k-nearest neighbor. KNN requires no training step, it is easy to understand and implement and can be used for both regression and classification problems. However KNN suffers from the curse of dimensionality, it requires homogeneous features and KNN is sensitive to outliers.
3. **Naïve Bayes (NB):** NB classifier is a probabilistic machine learning model centered on using Bayes theorem with high independence assumptions between the features and it is used for the classification task. NB is also easy to implement and the training period is less as it requires a small amount of data to estimate the test data. However, the main limitation of NB is the assumption of independent predictors.

3.7 Performance Metrics

The proposed technique performance was estimated utilizing the following assessment measurements.

1. **False Acceptance Rate (FAR):** is identical to the APCER. It is described as a relative amount of MA classified as genuine images [2]. The formula is given in Eq. 9:

$$FAR = \text{False positive}/(\text{True Positive} + \text{False Positive}) \tag{9}$$

2. **False Rejection Rate (FRR):** this is identical to the BPCER. FRR is described as the ratio of bona fide presentations inaccurately categorized as presentation attacks in a particular situation or as the comparative quantity of genuine images categorized as MA [13]. The FRR formula is given in Eq. 10 as:

$$FRR = \text{False Negative}/(\text{True Positive} + \text{False Negative}) \tag{10}$$

3. **Accuracy (ACC):** is a metric used for the evaluation of classification models. Accuracy can simply be defined as the degree of accurate classifications either for an independent test set or using some deviation of the cross-validation idea. The formula is given in Eq. 11 as:

$$ACC = \frac{True\ Positive\ +\ True\ negative}{True\ Positive\ +\ True\ negative\ +\ False\ Positive\ +\ False\ negative}$$

(11)

4 Results and Discussion

In this work, experiments were conducted on three algorithms which are DTC, KNN, and NB classifiers for post-processed images (image sharpening) and NCA feature selection algorithm. Four types of experiments were carried out which are:

1. Classification of non-post-processed images (bona fide and morphed) using feature vectors selected based on the NCA algorithm.
2. Classification of non-post-processed images (bona fide and morphed) without application of the NCA feature selection algorithm.
3. Classification of post-processed images (bona fide and morphed) without application of the NCA feature selection algorithm.
4. Classification of post-processed images (bona fide and morphed) using feature vectors selected based on the NCA algorithm.

The results of the four experiments conducted using the three aforementioned classification techniques are shown in Table 1.

Table 1. MAD classification result

Algorithm	Non-post-processed images			Post-processed images (Sharpening)		
	Accuracy (%)	FAR (%)	FRR (%)	Accuracy (%)	FAR (%)	FRR (%)
LBP + NCA + DTC	94	4.8	7.7	85	15.8	14.3
LBP + DTC	90	11.8	7.7	82	10.5	25.0
LBP + NCA + NB	82	23.8	7.7	80	36.8	4.8
LBP + NB	80	29.4	7.7	72	47.4	10.0
LBP + NCA + KNN	77	41.2	0.0	83	21.1	14.3
LBP + KNN	74	28.6	23.1	79	31.6	10.0

From Table 1 above it can be deduced that for the non-post-processed images the decision tree classifier (DTC) trained with NCA selected feature vectors produced the highest accuracy with a value of 94% as compared to KNN and NB that were also trained with the NCA selected feature vector which produced an accuracy of 77% and 80% respectively. Also for the post-processed images using the NCA selected feature vectors DTC performed better with an accuracy of 85% as compared to NB and KNN with an accuracy of 80% and 83%. Based on the FAR (4.8%) and FRR (7.7%) metric it can be seen that DTC trained with NCA selected feature vector has a very low percentage which is below 10%. This shows that DTC performed better with NCA selected feature vectors as compared to KNN and NB. The accuracy rate is high in LBP + NCA + DTC and low in LBP + NCA + KNN for non-post processed images because the features used in this experimentation were not normalized and KNN is sensitive to the scale of the data while DTC is insensitive to the scale of data [26]. The number of neighbors used can also affect KNN classification accuracy.

From Table 1 is can be seen that DTC gave a higher accuracy when trained with all the extracted feature vectors (i.e. is without performing feature selection with NCA) for both non-post-processed images (bona fide and morphed) and the post-processed images. As compared with the post-processed images it can be deduced that the proposed system was able to perform MAD better on images that were not post-processed as it got an accuracy of 94% while the experiment on post-processed images gave an accuracy of 85%. It can also be seen that LBP + KNN got the least accuracy for non-post-processed images and LBP + NB got the least accuracy rate for post-processed images (sharpening), this is because post-processing reduces the morphing artifact. That is, after applying post-processing operation on the image, the features of the image is been altered to a different set of features, which makes NB and KNN react differently to the non-post processed and the post-processed image features.

From the conducted experiment it can be inferred that training a classifier for MAD using NCA selected feature vectors improves the performance accuracy of the system. With low FAR and FRR and high prediction accuracy, it can be seen that the LBP + NCA + DTC algorithm is suitable for a reliable MAD.

Table 2. MAD classification results for non-post-processed images

Non post-processed images			
Algorithm	Accuracy (%)	FRR (%) @	
		FAR = 5%	FAR = 10%
Proposed method (LBP + NCA + DTC)	94	7.39	3.69
Steerable textures [2]	-	45.76	13.12

Based on the values of FRR and FAR presented in Table 2 it can be seen that LBP + NCA + DTC has indicated the best performance with FRR of 7.39% at FAR = 5% and FRR of 3.69% at FAR = 10%. While the method proposed by Ramachandra et al. [2] has FRR of 45.76% at APCER = 5% and FRR of 13.12% at APCER = 10%.

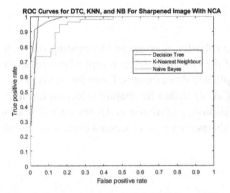

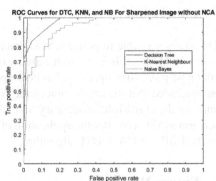

Fig. 3. ROC Curves for DTC, KNN, and NB classifiers trained with NCA selected features of post-processed images.

Fig. 4. ROC Curves for DTC, KNN, and NB classifiers trained without NCA selected features of post-processed images.

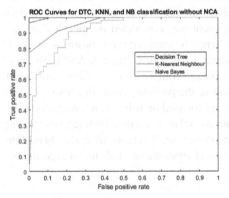

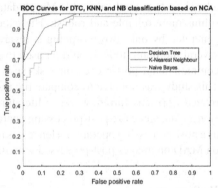

Fig. 5. ROC Curves for DTC, KNN, and NB classifiers trained without NCA selected features of non-post-processed images.

Fig. 6. ROC Curves for DTC, KNN, and NB classifiers trained with NCA selected features of non-post-processed images.

In Fig. 3 the ROC curves of the three classifiers for the post-processed images based on NCA selected feature vectors are shown. Figure 4 shows the ROC curve for the KNN, NB, and DTC classifiers for the post-processed images trained with extracted features without application of the NCA algorithm. Figure 5 presents the ROC curves for the NB, KNN, and DTC classifiers for the images which were not post-processed and trained with the normal features without application NCA algorithm. Figure 6 presents the ROC curve for the three classifiers for the images which were not post-processed based on NCA selected feature vectors. From the ROC curves, it can be seen that the DTC classifier has a higher area under a curve (AUC) value as compared to the other two classifiers KNN and NB which shows that DTC generally has a high performance as compared to KNN and NB.

5 Conclusion

This study was able to perform MAD more robustly as compared to existing research works on MAD. This is due to the ability of the system to detect morphed images even after post-processing operation has been applied to those images. From this study, it can be concluded that the application of the NCA algorithm for feature selection can also improve the classification accuracy. In conclusion, a system was developed which can perform MAD even after the application of sharpening post-processed operations based on the LBP + NCA + DTC algorithm.

6 Future Works

The morphed dataset used for this work was generated using available morphing software as there was no publicly available large-scale database for MAD and most researches have been conducted using different in-house databases. Hence it is recommended that a large-scale publicly available Morph database should be created to make MAD algorithms more reliable and robust. The experiment was conducted on morphed images generated by only two morphing software hence to improve the robustness of MAD several morphing tools should be used to generate morphed datasets. And lastly more common image post-processing tasks such as image compression should be considered. This study was not able to compare the result of the post-processed images with other related works, as current works of literature are focused on print-scan, image compression and image resize post-processing operations and none focused on image sharpening as a post-processing operation. Hence it is recommended that more work should be done on MAD on images post-processed with image sharpening using different algorithms.

References

1. Kramer, R.S.S., Mireku, M.O., Flack, T.R., Ritchie, K.L.: Face morphing attacks: investigating detection with humans and computers. Cogn. Res. Principles Implications **4**(1), 1–15 (2019). https://doi.org/10.1186/s41235-019-0181-4
2. Ramachandra, R., Venkatesh, S., Raja, K., Busch, C.: Detecting face morphing attacks with collaborative representation of steerable features. In: Chaudhuri, B.B., Nakagawa, M., Khanna, P., Kumar, S. (eds.) Proceedings of 3rd International Conference on Computer Vision and Image Processing. AISC, vol. 1022, pp. 255–265. Springer, Singapore (2020). https://doi.org/10.1007/978-981-32-9088-4_22
3. Scherhag, U., Debiasi, L., Rathgeb, C., Busch, C., Uhl, A.: Detection of face morphing attacks based on PRNU analysis. IEEE Trans. Biom. Behav. Identity Sci. **1**(4), 302–317 (2019). https://doi.org/10.1109/TBIOM.2019.2942395
4. Scherhag, U., Budhrani, D., Gomez-Barrero, M., Busch, C.: Detecting morphed face images using facial landmarks. In: Mansouri, A., El Moataz, A., Nouboud, F., Mammass, D. (eds.) ICISP 2018. LNCS, vol. 10884, pp. 444–452. Springer, Cham (2018). https://doi.org/10.1007/978-3-319-94211-7_48
5. Ferrara, M., Franco, A., Maltoni, D.: Face morphing detection in the presence of printing/scanning and heterogeneous image sources, p. 23 (2019)

6. Ngan, M., Grother, P., Hanaoka, K., Kuo, J.: Face Recognition Vendor Test (FRVT) part 4:: MORPH - performance of automated face morph detection, National Institute of Standards and Technology, Gaithersburg, MD, NIST IR 8292, March 2020. https://doi.org/10.6028/NIST.IR.8292

7. Scherhag, U., Rathgeb, C., Merkle, J., Busch, C.: Deep Face Representations for Differential Morphing Attack Detection, April 2020. arXiv200101202. https://arxiv.org/abs/2001.01202. Accessed 01 Sept 2020

8. Scherhag, U., Rathgeb, C., Merkle, J., Breithaupt, R., Busch, C.: Face recognition systems under morphing attacks: a survey. IEEE Access **7**, 23012–23026 (2019). https://doi.org/10.1109/ACCESS.2019.2899367

9. Robertson, D.J., Mungall, A., Watson, D.G., Wade, K.A., Nightingale, S.J., Butler, S.: Detecting morphed passport photos: a training and individual differences approach. Cogn. Res. Principles Implications **3**(1), 1–11 (2018). https://doi.org/10.1186/s41235-018-0113-8

10. Ferrara, M., Franco, A., Maltoni, D.: The magic passport. In: IEEE International Joint Conference on Biometrics, Clearwater, FL, USA, pp. 1–7, September 2014. https://doi.org/10.1109/BTAS.2014.6996240

11. Seibold, C., Samek, W., Hilsmann, A., Eisert, P.: Accurate and Robust Neural Networks for Security Related Applications Exampled by Face Morphing Attacks, June 2018. arXiv180604265. https://arxiv.org/abs/1806.04265. Accessed 01 Sept 2020

12. Wandzik, L., Kaeding, G., Garcia, R.V.: Morphing detection using a general-purpose face recognition system. In: 2018 26th European Signal Processing Conference (EUSIPCO), Rome, pp. 1012–1016, September 2018. https://doi.org/10.23919/EUSIPCO.2018.8553375

13. Jassim, S., Asaad, A.: Automatic detection of image morphing by topology-based analysis. In: 2018 26th European Signal Processing Conference (EUSIPCO), Rome, pp. 1007–1011, September 2018. https://doi.org/10.23919/EUSIPCO.2018.8553317

14. Alfa, A.A., Ahmed, K.B., Misra, S., Adewumi, A., Ahuja, R., Ayeni, F., Damasevicius, R.: A comparative study of methods for hiding large size audio file in smaller image carriers. In: Somani, A.K., Ramakrishna, S., Chaudhary, A., Choudhary, C., Agarwal, B. (eds.) ICETCE 2019. CCIS, vol. 985, pp. 179–191. Springer, Singapore (2019). https://doi.org/10.1007/978-981-13-8300-7_15

15. Makrushin, A., Wolf, A.: An overview of recent advances in assessing and mitigating the face morphing attack. In: 2018 26th European Signal Processing Conference (EUSIPCO), Rome, pp. 1017–1021, September 2018. https://doi.org/10.23919/EUSIPCO.2018.8553599

16. Debiasi, L., Scherhag, U., Rathgeb, C., Uhl, A., Busch, C.: PRNU-based detection of morphed face images. In: 2018 International Workshop on Biometrics and Forensics (IWBF), Sassari, pp. 1–7, June 2018. https://doi.org/10.1109/IWBF.2018.8401555

17. Raghavendra, R., Raja, K.B., Venkatesh, S., Busch, C.: Transferable Deep-CNN features for detecting digital and print-scanned morphed face images. In: 2017 IEEE Conference on Computer Vision and Pattern Recognition Workshops (CVPRW), Honolulu, HI, USA, pp. 1822–1830, July 2017. https://doi.org/10.1109/CVPRW.2017.228

18. Singh, J.M., Ramachandra, R., Raja, K.B., Busch, C.: Robust Morph-Detection at Automated Border Control Gate using Deep Decomposed 3D Shape and Diffuse Reflectance, December 2019. arXiv191201372. https://arxiv.org/abs/1912.01372. Accessed 01 Sept 2020

19. Seibold, C., Samek, W., Hilsmann, A., Eisert, P.: Detection of face morphing attacks by deep learning. In: Kraetzer, C., Shi, Y.-Q., Dittmann, J., Kim, H.J. (eds.) IWDW 2017. LNCS, vol. 10431, pp. 107–120. Springer, Cham (2017). https://doi.org/10.1007/978-3-319-64185-0_9

20. Wang, Y.-Q.: An analysis of the Viola-Jones face detection algorithm. Image Process. Line **4**, 128–148 (2014). https://doi.org/10.5201/ipol.2014.104

21. Deshpande, N.T., Ravishankar, S.: Face detection and recognition using Viola-Jones algorithm and Fusion of PCA and ANN. Adv. Comput. Sci. Technol. **10**(5), 18 (2017). ISSN 0973-6107

22. Huang, D., Shan, C., Ardabilian, M., Wang, Y., Chen, L.: Local binary patterns and its application to facial image analysis: a survey. IEEE Trans. Syst. Man Cybern. Part C Appl. Rev. **41**(6), 765–781, November 2011. https://doi.org/10.1109/TSMCC.2011.2118750

23. Patil, M.Y., Dhawale, C.A., Misra, S.: Analytical study of combined approaches to content based image retrieval systems. Int. J. Pharm. Technol. **8**(4), 14 (2016)

24. Oloyede, M.O., Hancke, G.P., Myburgh, H.C.: A review on face recognition systems: recent approaches and challenges. Multimedia Tools Appl. **79**(37–38), 27891–27922 (2020). https://doi.org/10.1007/s11042-020-09261-2

25. Yang, W., Wang, K., Zuo, W.: Neighborhood component feature selection for high-dimensional data. J. Comput. **7**(1), 161–168 (2012). https://doi.org/10.4304/jcp.7.1.161-168

26. Comparative study of K-NN, Naive Bayes and decision tree classification techniques. Int. J. Sci. Res. IJSR **5**(1), 1842–1845, January 2016. https://doi.org/10.21275/v5i1.NOV153131

Enhanced Back-Translation for Low Resource Neural Machine Translation Using Self-training

Idris Abdulmumin[1,2(✉)] ⓘ, Bashir Shehu Galadanci[2], and Abubakar Isa[1]

[1] Ahmadu Bello University, Samaru Campus, Zaria, Kaduna State, Nigeria
{iabdulmumin,abubakarisa}@abu.edu.ng
[2] Bayero University, Kano, Kano State, Nigeria
bsgaladanci.se@buk.edu.ng

Abstract. Improving neural machine translation (NMT) models using the back-translations of the monolingual target data (synthetic parallel data) is currently the state-of-the-art approach for training improved translation systems. The quality of the backward system – which is trained on the available parallel data and used for the back-translation – has been shown in many studies to affect the performance of the final NMT model. In low resource conditions, the available parallel data is usually not enough to train a backward model that can produce the qualitative synthetic data needed to train a standard translation model. This work proposes a self-training strategy where the output of the backward model is used to improve the model itself through the forward translation technique. The technique was shown to improve baseline low resource IWSLT'14 English-German and IWSLT'15 English-Vietnamese backward translation models by 11.06 and 1.5 BLEUs respectively. The synthetic data generated by the improved English-German backward model was used to train a forward model which out-performed another forward model trained using standard back-translation by 2.7 BLEU.

Keywords: Forward translation · Self-training · Self-learning · Back-translation · Neural Machine Translation

1 Introduction

The neural machine translation (NMT) [1–3] is currently the simplest and yet the state-of-the-art approach for training improved translation systems [4,5]. They out-perform other statistical machine translation approaches if there exists a large amount of parallel data between the languages [6,7]. Given the "right" amount of qualitative parallel data only, the models can learn the probability of mapping sentences in the source language to their equivalents in another language – the target language [8]. This "right" amount of qualitative parallel

Supported by NITDEF PhD Scholarship Scheme 2018.

data is usually very large and, therefore, expensive to compile because it requires manual translation. The absence of large amounts of high-quality parallel data in many languages has led to various proposals for leveraging the abundant monolingual data that exists in either or both of the languages. These approaches include the self-training [9], forward translation [10], back-translation [4,11–13], dual learning [15] and transfer learning [7,16–18].

The back-translation has been used in current state-of-the-art neural machine translation systems [4,19,20], outperforming other approaches in high resource languages and improving performance in low resource conditions [4,21,22]. The approach involves training a target-to-source (backward) model on the available parallel data and using that model to generate synthetic translations of a large number of monolingual sentences in the target language. The available authentic parallel data is then mixed with the generated synthetic parallel data without differentiating between the two [11] to train a final source-to-target (forward) model. The quality of the forward translation model depends on the NMT architecture used in building the models [11], the quality of the backward model [21,23,24], the suitability of the synthetic data generation method used [4,25] and the ratio of the authentic data to the synthetic data [26,27]. In low resource NMT, the authentic parallel data available is not sufficient to train a backward model that will generate qualitative synthetic data. Thus, various methods have been proposed to improve the quality of the backward model despite the lack of sufficient parallel data.

Hoang et al. [21] and Zhang et al. [23] used an iterative approach to enable the forward model to generate synthetic data that will be used to improve the backward model. Imamura et al. [12] suggest generating multiple synthetic sources through sampling given a target sentence. Niu et al. [22] trained a bilingual model for both the backward and forward translations and they reported improvement in low resource translations. Graca et al. [25] proposed that selecting the most suitable synthetic data generation method will help reduce the inadequacies of the backward model. Dabre et al. [17] and Kocmi and Bojar [18] proposed the use of a high-resource parent language pair through transfer learning to improve the backward model.

This work proposes the use of self-training – also referred within the document as self-learning and forward translation – [9,10,28] approach to improve the backward model. The output of the backward model – which is ideally used with the authentic data to train the forward model in back-translation – is used to improve the backward model itself. The self-training approach used is similar to that in [9,10,28] where a synthetic target-side data is used to improve the performance of the translation model instead of the synthetic source-side data in back-translation. But instead of using the approach to enhance the final model, we aim to enhance the backward model which then generates improved synthetic data for enhancing the final model. We also simplify the approach by removing the need for synthetic data quality estimation [9] or freezing of training parameters [10].

The work is similar to the iterative back-translation of Hoang et al. [21] and Zhang et al. [23]. The iterative back-translation requires the use of the monolingual source and target data to improve the backward and forward models respectively. The backward model generates synthetic sources to improve the forward model while the forward does the same for the backward model. This process is repeated iteratively until the required quality of translations are obtained. Instead, this work relies only on the monolingual target data to improve both models. Whereas the approaches above perform iterative back-translation to improve both models, our work uses forward translation (self-learning) to improve the backward model and back-translation to improve the forward model.

It was shown by Specia and Shah [9] and Zhang and Zong [10] that using the monolingual source – or the synthetic target – data will potentially reduce the performance of the decoder. To mitigate this, Ueffing [28] and Specia and Shah [9] used quality estimation [29] to determine the best-translated sentences to be used to retraining, while Zhang and Zong [10] proposed freezing the parameters of the decoder when training the model on the synthetic data. In this work, we showed that the self-learning approach is capable of improving a translation model even without synthetic data cleaning or freezing any learned parameters. We hypothesize that the amount of parallel data used in retraining the model is sufficient to improve the quality of the model if the model can differentiate between and learn effectively from the synthetic and natural data.

1.1 Summary of Contributions

We make the following contributions in this paper:

- instead of requiring the source and target data for improving the backward and forward models respectively, as in previous works, we investigated utilizing only the target-side monolingual data to improve both the backward and forward models in back-translation. Whereas the monolingual target data is used as the source data to improve the backward model (forward translation), we use the same data as the target data in the forward model training (back-translation). The work investigates different approaches for using the all of the synthetic data to improve the models.
- we showed that even without data cleaning and/or freezing learned parameters, self-training improves the backward model; and that a forward model trained using the synthetic data generated from the improved backward model performs better than a forward model trained using the standard back-translation.
- we showed that when a model – backward or forward – can differentiate between the authentic and synthetic data, it is able to utilize the quality in the authentic data and also, efficiently benefits from the increase in quantity resulted from adding the synthetic data.
- we showed that the technique improves baseline low resource IWSLT'14 English-German and IWSLT'15 English-Vietnamese backward NMT models by 11.06 and 1.5 BLEUs respectively; and the synthetic data generated by

the improved English-German backward model was used to train a forward model whose performance bettered that of a forward model trained using the standard back-translation technique by 2.7 BLEU.

2   Related Works

This section presents prior work on back-translation, forward translation and self-training.

2.1   Back-Translation

The use of monolingual data of target and/or source language has been studied extensively to improve the performance of translation models, especially in low resource settings. Gulcehre et al. [36] explored the infusion of language models trained on monolingual data into the translation models. Currey et al. [37] and Burlot and Yvon [24] proposed augmenting a copy or slightly modified copy of the target data as source respectively. Sennrich et al. [38] and Zhang and Zong [10] proposed the back-translation and forward translation approaches respectively and He et al. [15] used both source and target-side monolingual data to improve the translation models.

The back-translation approach has been shown to outperform other approaches in low and high resource languages [4,21]. The quality of the models trained using back-translation depends on the quality of the backward model [4,8,18,21,24–26]. In low resource NMT, the authentic parallel data available is not sufficient to train a backward model that will generate qualitative synthetic data. To improve the quality of the synthetic parallel data, Hoang et al. [21], Zhang et al. [23] and Caswell et al. [13] proposed the iterative back-translation – iteratively using the back-translations of the source and target data to improve the backward and forward models respectively. Kocmi and Bojar [18] and Dabre et al. [17] pre-trained a model using high resource languages and initialize the training of the low resource languages with the learned pre-trained weights – transfer learning. Niu et al. [22] trained a bilingual system based on Johnson et al. [39] to do both forward and backward translations, eliminating the need for separate backward model. They reported improvement in low resource NMT.

2.2   Forward Translation and Self-training

Forward translation (reverse back-translation, self-training or self-learning) was used to improve NMT [10] and other forms of statistical machine translation systems [9,28]. Instead of the target-side monolingual data, forward translation uses the source-side monolingual data to improve the performance of a translation model. The available authentic data is used to train a source-to-target model. This model is then used to generate synthetic translations of the available (usually huge) source-side monolingual sentences. This data (synthetic target) is paired with the source-side data to create the synthetic parallel dataset.

The resulting huge data is used to train a better source-to-target translation model. The synthetic data might contain mistakes that will likely reduce the performance of the models. Various works that used the forward translation (self-learning) approach proposed the use of other techniques to mitigate the effects of the noise present in the data, e.g. using quality estimation to automatically remove the sentences that are considered to be badly translated. Specia and Shah [9] utilized an iterative approach to select the top n translations to retrain the generating model. Automatic quality estimation was used to determine sentences that are considered to be translated better than the others.

Ueffing [28] explained self-training as an approach that takes the output of the machine translation model to improve the model itself. The work proposed the translation of monolingual source data, estimating the quality of the translated sentences, discarding those sentences whose quality is below a set threshold and subsequently training a new improved model on the mixed authentic and synthetic bilingual data. Zhang and Zong [10] proposed the forward translation (self-learning) to improve the encoder side of the NMT model. The authors suggested that back-translation improved the decoder by training it authentic target data and that when the NMT model is trained on authentic source data, the encoder will be improved. The use of synthetic data in back-translation may reduce the performance of the encoder because it is trained on the synthetic data. When using the synthetic target data in their approach, the authors tried to mitigate this problem by freezing the parameters of the decoder for the synthetic data during training.

3   Methodology

3.1   Neural Machine Translation (NMT)

This work is based on a unidirectional LSTM encoder-decoder architecture with Luong attention [2]. This is a recurrent neural network RNMT architecture and it is summarized below. Our approach can be applied to other architectures such as the convolutional neural network NMT (CNMT) [30,31] and the Transformer [3,32].

Neural Machine Translation (NMT) is based on a sequence-to-sequence encoder-decoder system made of neural networks that models the conditional probability of a source sentence to a target sentence [1,2,33]. The encoder converts the input in the source language into a set of vectors while the decoder converts the set of vectors into the target language, word by word, through an attention mechanism – introduced to keep track of context in longer sentences [1]. The NMT model produces the translated sentence by generating one target word at every time step. Given the "right" amount of qualitative parallel data only, the NMT model can learn the probability of mapping sentences in the source language to their equivalents in another language – the target language – word by word [8].

Given an input sequence $X = (x_1, ..., x_{T_x})$, the encoder – made up of a bidirectional or unidirectional neural network with Long Short-Term Memory (LSTM) [34] or gated recurrent units (GRU) [35] – computes the annotation

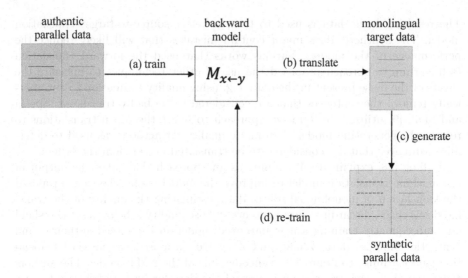

authentic   backward   monolingual
parallel data   model   target data

(a) train $M_{x \leftarrow y}$ (b) translate

(c) generate

(d) re-train

synthetic
parallel data

Fig. 1. Self-Learning for Improving the Backward Model: enabling the backward model to learn from the target language monolingual data

vector h_j, which is a concatenation of the forward and backward hidden states $\overrightarrow{h_j}$ and $\overleftarrow{h_j}$ respectively. The decoder is made up of a recurrent neural network that takes a recurrent hidden state s_i, the previously translated words $(y_1, ..., y_{i-1})$ and a context vector c_i to predict the probability of the next word y_i as the weighted summation of the annotations h_j. An alignment model – a single layer feed-forward network which is learned jointly with the rest of the network through back-propagation – which models the probability that y_i is aligned to x_i is used to compute the weight of each annotation h_j.

All of the parameters in the NMT model, θ, are optimized to maximize the following conditional log-likelihood of the M sentence aligned bilingual samples

$$L(\theta) = \frac{1}{M} \sum_{m=1}^{M} \sum_{i=1}^{T_y} \log(p(y_i^m | y_{<i}^m, X^m, \theta))$$

3.2 Overview of the Method

As shown in Algorithm 1, given a set of parallel data and monolingual target sentences: $D^P = \{(x^{(u)}, y^{(u)})\}_{u=1}^{U}$ and $Y = \{(y^{(v)})\}_{v=1}^{V}$ respectively, we used the authentic parallel data: D^P to train a target-to-source model, $M_{x \leftarrow y}$. This model – the backward model – is then used to translate the monolingual target data, Y, to generate the synthetic parallel data: $D' = \{(x^{(v)}, y^{(v)})\}_{v=1}^{V}$. The resulting synthetic data is then used to improve the model either through fine-tuning it on the synthetic data, standard forward translation, tagged forward translation (similar to the tagged back-translation [13]) or through pre-training and fine-tuning [40]. This technique is illustrated in Fig. 1.

ALGORITHM 1: SELF-TRAINING

Input: Parallel data $D^P = \{(x^{(u)}, y^{(u)})\}_{u=1}^U$ and Monolingual
      target data $Y = \{(y^{(v)})\}_{v=1}^V$

1: **procedure** SELF-TRAINING
2:    Train backward model $M_{x \leftarrow y}$ on bilingual data D^P
3:    Let $D' = $ synthetic parallel corpora generated for Y using $M_{x \leftarrow y}$;
4:    Train improved backward model $M_{x \leftarrow y}^+$ on bilingual data $D^P \cup D'$;
5: **end procedure**
6: **procedure** BACK-TRANSLATION
7:    Let $D^* = $ synthetic parallel corpora generated for Y using $M_{x \leftarrow y}^+$;
8:    Train forward model $M_{x \rightarrow y}$ on bilingual data $D^P \cup D^*$;
9: **end procedure**

Output: improved $M_{x \leftarrow y}$ and $M_{x \rightarrow y}$ models

---

Previous works that used self-training to improve machine translation models (e.g. [9,28]) proposed an extra step of data cleaning or freezing parameters (not updating the parameters of the decoder when training on the synthetic target data) to achieve the required performance. Our approach does not require any specialized approach of data cleaning or training regime. We showed that the simple act of joining the synthetic and authentic data can improve the model. We went further to show that when the backward model can differentiate between the synthetic data and authentic data, the performance increases even further. We investigated pre-training and fine-tuning, and tagging as methods that will help the model differentiate between the data. Also, we used self-training in this work only to enhance the backward model in the back-translation approach rather than training a final translation model.

3.3 Data

In this work, we used the data from the IWSLT 2014 German-English shared translation task [41]. For pre-processing, we used the data cleanup and train, dev and test split in Ranzato et al. [42], resulting in 153,348, 6,970 and 6,750 parallel sentences for training, development and testing respectively. For the second low resource dataset, we used the pre-processed low resource English-Vietnamese parallel data [2] of the IWSLT 2015 Translation task [43]. We then utilized the 2012 and 2013 test sets for development and testing respectively. Table 1 shows the data statistics. We used 400,000 English monolingual sentences of the pre-processed [2] WMT 2014 English-German translation task [44] for the monolingual data. We learned byte pair encoding (BPE) [45] with 10,000 merge operations on the training dataset, applied it on the train, development and test datasets and, afterwards, build the vocabulary on the training dataset.

Table 1. Data statistics

Data	Train			Dev	Test
	Sentences	Words (vocab)			
IWSLT'14 En-De	153, 348	En	De	6, 970	6, 750
		2,837,240 (50,045)	2,688,387 (103,796)		
IWSLT'15 En-Vi	133, 317	En	Vi	1, 553	1, 268
		2,706,255 (54,169)	3,311,508 (25,615)		
WMT'14 En-De – Monolingual English	400, 000	9,918,380 (266,640)		–	–

3.4 Set-Up

We used the NMTSmallV1 configuration of the OpenNMT-tf [46], the Tensor-Flow [47] implementation, a framework for training NMT models. The configuration is a 2-layer unidirectional LSTM encoder-decoder model with Luong attention [2] with 512 hidden units and a vocabulary size of 50,000 for both source and target languages. The optimizer we used is Adam [48], a batch size of 64, a dropout probability of 0.3 and a static learning rate of 0.0002. The models are evaluated on the development set after every 5,000 training steps. For evaluation, we used the bi-lingual evaluation understudy (BLEU) [14].

Training is stopped when the models reach a total of 200,000 training steps or when there is no improvement of over 0.2 BLEU after the evaluation of four consecutive training steps. We used this set-up to train all the models and unless stated otherwise: (1) there was no extra training for any model after either of the stopping criteria were met; (2) we average the last 8 checkpoints of every model trained to obtain a better performance and; (3) we update the vocabulary of every checkpoint with the that of the new training data before fine-tuning.

4 Experiments and Results

First, we train a backward model (En-De) – *baseline* – for 80,000 training steps, achieving the best score of 10.03 BLEU after 65,000 training steps. Averaging the last 8 checkpoints results in a better performance of 10.25 BLEU and we used this average checkpoint as our backward model for generating the synthetic data. The resulting parallel data is labelled as *synth-A*. We then used the authentic parallel data and *synth-A* to train an improved backward model. Apart from the standard forward translation (self-learning) technique of mixing the data and training from the scratch, we followed other training strategies to enable the model to differentiate between the authentic and synthetic parallel data. The results obtained by using these various strategies are shown in Table 2.

Table 2. Scores for best checkpoints and checkpoint averaging of backward models trained using different techniques.

	Baseline [2, 38]	Self-training (this work)				
		Backward_ft	Tagged_ft	Pre-train & fine-tune A	Pre-train & fine-tune B	Pre-train & fine-tune C
Best score	10.03	20.48	20.72	8.94	20.72	20.77
(training step)	(65k)	(150k)	(150k)	(80k)	(135k)	(115k)
Average	10.25	20.98	21.02	8.08	21.22	20.35

4.1 Forward Translation

We mixed the authentic parallel data and *synth-A* without differentiating between the two and trained the backward model from scratch. The model trained for 180,000 steps before stopping. The best score obtained was more than double the performance of *baseline* with an improvement of 10.45 BLEU. The averaged checkpoint – *backward_ft* – gained an improvement of 10.73 BLEU over *baseline*. This huge improvement supports the hypothesis that even without data cleaning and/or freezing of decoder parameters, the model is able to learn from the synthetic data generated by itself. After a few training steps, the performance of *backward_ft* started to improve significantly over *baseline* (see Fig. 2).

4.2 Tagged Forward Translation

To enable the backward model to differentiate between the two data, we experimented the 'tagged forward translation' – coined from the tagged back-translation of [13]. While they used the '$<BT>$' tag to indicate if a source was synthetic, we instead utilized the '$<SYN>$' tag to differentiate between authentic and synthetic target sentences. We named the model that was trained using this approach as *tagged_ft*. Although the tagged approach outperforms the standard approach, the difference observed in the performances of the *tagged_ft* and *backward_ft* models was not significant.

4.3 Pre-training and Fine-Tuning

Following the work of Abdulmumin et al. [40], we trained the models using the following approache: pre-training on the synthetic data and fine-tuning on the authentic data. We experimented mixing the authentic data and *synth-A* to learn joint BPE and build a vocabulary of the mixed data. Afterwards, we pre-trained the backward model on *synth-A* and fine-tuned it on the authentic data. The performance of the average checkpoints was a little bit lower (−0.87 BLEU) than that of the previous pre-train and fine-tune strategy, but the best checkpoints in each strategy have similar BLEU scores.

We realized that averaging the last 8 checkpoints hurts the performance because continuing to train the model after 145,000 training steps produced poor checkpoints (see Fig. 2). We, instead, took the average of the previous 8

Table 3. Improvements observed after re-training the backward model on the synthetic target data for English Vietnamese machine translation.

	Baseline	Self-training	
		Forward translation	Pre-training & fine-tuning
Best score (training step)	24.78 (50k)	25.97 (105k)	26.22 (125k)
Average	25.79	26.38	27.29

checkpoints starting from the checkpoint at 145,000 training steps. This resulted in an increased performance of the model to 21.31 BLEU (+0.96), an increase of 0.1 BLEU over the previous approach. This appears to have the best performance among the models trained so far. We, therefore, used this model to generate *synth-B* – a synthetic parallel data generated for the monolingual sentences.

4.4 English Vietnamese (En-Vi)

We used the En-Vi dataset to test the results obtained on the En-De dataset. A backward model was trained using the English-Vietnamese parallel data for 55,000 training steps. The model (En-Vi) achieved a BLEU score of 24.78 after 50,000 training steps. An average of the last 8 checkpoints resulted in an improved performance of 25.79 BLEU and the checkpoint was labelled *envi_baseline*. The model, *envi_baseline*, was used to translate the monolingual English data to generate the synthetic parallel data – *synth-C*. The authentic data was mixed with *synth-C* to train a backward model – *envi_backward* – from the scratch. The model gained a +1.19 BLEU (see Table 3) on the best checkpoint and 0.59 BLEU on the average checkpoint over *envi_baseline*. The results are shown in Table 3.

We then used the pre-training and fine-tuning approach to train the backward model. Even during the pre-train stage of this approach, the average checkpoint achieved a performance that is close to that of *envi_baseline* – a score of 24.82 (−0.97) BLEU. This supports the claim by [4] that training a translation model on the synthetic parallel data only can reach a performance similar to the model that is trained on authentic data only. We observed that although the quality of the synthetic data determines the feasibility of the claim, it is true for either synthetic target or source data. The performance of the backward model that was pre-trained on the synthetic data generated by *baseline* (Sect. 4) – which was in itself poor (10.25 BLEU) – was significantly less than the that of the baseline (−2.83 BLEU). After fine-tuning, the performance of the model improved to 27.29 (+1.5). Although some gain in performance was realized, the difference was not as significant as it was observed on the En-De dataset – +1.5 on En-Vi compared to +9.1 on En-De. This may have been because the backward model, *envi_baseline*, was already good compared to *baseline*.

Table 4. Forward models (De-En) trained using different quality of synthetic data.

	Baseline forward model [2]	Baseline backward model [38] (10.25 BLEU)		Self-trained backward model (this work; 21.22 BLEU)	
		Standard back-translation	Pre-training & fine-tuning	Standard back-translation	Pre-training & fine-tuning
Best score	20.30	25.11	25.32	27.41	28.38
(training step)	(75k)	(150k)	(115k)	(110k)	(135k)
Average	20.95	25.87	26.03	27.87	28.73

4.5 Back-Translation

It is expected, as shown in many studies (e.g. [4,27]), that a better synthetic data generated using a good backward model will result in an improved forward model. We used the outputs of the backward models – *synth-A* and *synth-B* – to train final forward models. We expected the quality of *synth-B* to be better since it was generated using the best backward model among those trained in the experiments above. Both of the models trained using the standard back-translation and the pre-training and fine-tuning approaches performed better than the models trained using the same approaches but with *synth-A* (see Fig. 3).

Table 4 shows the performance of the models trained: without synthetic data; with *synth-A* and; with *synth-B*. The best model was obtained through pre-training and fine-tuning using authentic data and *synth-B*. The model outperformed the baseline forward model by a BLEU score of 7.78 (28.73 BLEU). Although using *synth-A* improved the performance of the forward model over the baseline (+4.92 and +5.08 BLEUs using standard back-translation and pre-training and fine-tuning respectively), the effect of the backward model self-training ensured that the quality of *synth-B* was superior and the model trained using this data improved the forward model further by over +2 BLEU.

5   Discussion

Neural machine translation systems suffer when trained on scanty data - low resource languages. Back-translation is an approach that was introduced to improve the performance of these and other category of languages. But various studies have shown that in low resource set-ups, the performance require other special approaches to reach an acceptable standard for translation quality. This work, therefore, proposes a new method of using the target-side monolingual data more effectively to improve the performance of the back-translation approach. Whereas the back-translation was used to specifically improve the forward model, we used the self-training approach through forward translation to improve, also, the performance of the backward model. The method performed

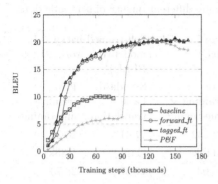
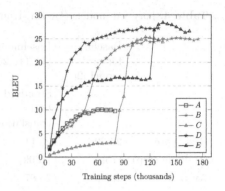

Fig. 2. Performance of *baseline* backward model compared to self-trained backward models using tagging, standard forward translation and the pre-train and fine-tune approaches. NOTE: P&F means Pre-train and Fine-tune

Fig. 3. Forward models (De-En) trained using different quality of synthetic data. KEY: A = *baseline*, B = *back-translation*, C = *pre-train & fine-tune*, D = *improved back-translation*, E = *improved pre-train & fine-tune*

very well on low resource English-German and English-Vietnamese languages and can be applied to any other low resource neural machine translation. The method can be investigated also in high resource languages.

We investigated various approaches such as the forward translation, tagged forward translation and various pre-training and fine-tuning strategies with the later two implemented to enable the model differentiate between synthetic and authentic parallel data during training. We observed that the proposed method out-performed the backward model in standard back-translation. It was claimed in [9] and [10] that the model's performance may be affected when using self-training because of the noise in the synthetic data. Instead, we found that providing a means for the model to differentiate between synthetic and authentic parallel data is just sufficient for the self-training method to perform as desired. Even though the self-training is by itself successful at improving the model, using tags or pre-training and fine-tuning have shown to improve the model's performance.

The work was evaluated on the low resource IWSLT 14 English-German translation. We also used the IWSLT 15 English-Vietnamese parallel data to confirm the positive results obtained using the approach. In Table 5, we showed a sample translation from English to German. Our improved model was able to produce exact translation to most of the referenced translation: "... wir 3 milliarden stunden pro woche mit online-spielen" and the other part where the translation generated was different, the meaning was the same: "derzeit verbringen" 'vs' "im moment geben". The self-trained model was also able to generate exact translation to most of the referenced text but the model could only specify the adverb "now" instead of the referenced "right now". The improved

Table 5. A German-to-English translation example in the IWSLT-DE 14 test set.

Source	und es funktionierte. wieder hatten wir etwas magisches geschaffen. und die wirkung im publikum war dieselbe. allerdings haben wir mit dem film schon ein bisschen mehr geld eingespielt
Reference	and it did, and we created magic again, and we had the same result with an audience – although we did make a little more money on that one
Baseline	and it worked. again. we had something magical, and the effect in the audience was the same thing, but we had a little more compound with a little more money
Standard BT	and it worked. again, we created something magical, and the effect in the audience was the same, but we had a little bit more money on the film
Pre-train & fine-tune	and it worked. again, we created something magical, and the effect in the audience was the same thing, but we had a little bit more money in the movie
Improved standard BT	and it worked. again, we created something magical, and the effect in the audience was the same. but we have a little bit more money
Improved pre-train & fine-tune	and it worked. again, we had created something magical, and the effect in the audience was the same. but we did a little bit more with the movie

model (trained using the best pre-train and fine-tune approach) generated "at the moment" which was a better equivalent to the next best translation system. Though the rest of the models could not perform better than the two discussed, the quality superiority of our approach can be seen on the models trained. For the forward model, the effects of the improved models were observed in their performances. In Table 5, we also translated a given German source text to English. The performances of the last two models (trained on the synthetic sentences generated by the backward model improved using our approach), and especially the last model, were superior than the rest of the other models.

The pre-training and fine-tuning approach has shown to be the better approach when applying the method we proposed in this work. Unlike in [40], we investigated different approaches that will suit better for our approach. We found that pre-training first on the synthetic data and thereafter fine-tuning the model on the authentic data is the best strategy. Fine-tuning on the synthetic data was found to hurt the model. This can be attributed to the lack of quality in the synthetic data used for fine-tuning compared to the authentic data used during pre-training, supporting the same claim in the work of [40] that fine-tuning on the synthetic data does not improve performance, it only hurts it.

6   Conclusion and Future Work

To the best of our knowledge, this is the first work that investigated an all-round utilization of the synthetic data to improve neural machine translation especially on low resource languages. These category of languages lag their high resource counterparts even if the same methods for improving their performance are applied. The back-translation has been shown to improve translation performance across board but in low resource languages, the performance is still less than desirable. We applied joint backward and forward translation to utilize the target-side monolingual data in improving the performance of neural machine translation systems in low resource languages. Experimental results obtained on English-German and English-Vietnamese have shown that the approach is superior to that of the widely successful back-translation approach. The approach is straightforward and can be applied on any low resource language translation to achieve a better and more acceptable translation performance. It could also be applied on high resource languages to improve the performance.

We showed that the approach is capable of improving the performance of the model even without using specialized data cleaning methods such as quality estimation. We also showed that the quality of the backward model is improved when the model can differentiate between the two data. This is also true for all models trained on synthetic and authentic data as shown in the training of the forward models. The work can be extended by comparing the performance of the proposed method with the other implementations of the self-learning approach when improving the backward model. Repeated retraining of the backward model – iterative self-training – can be explored in future works to determine the extent to which the backward model's output can be used to improve itself. We also intend to investigate the efficacy of the approach on high resource languages.

References

1. Bahdanau, D., Cho, K., Bengio, Y.: Neural Machine Translation by Jointly Learning to Align and Translate. arXiv preprint arXiv:14090473 (2014)
2. Luong, M.T., Pham, H., Manning, C.D.: Effective Approaches to Attention-based Neural Machine Translation. arXiv:150804025v5 (2015)
3. Vaswani, A., et al.: Attention is all you need. In: 31st Conference on Neural Information Processing Systems, Long Beach, CA, USA (2017)
4. Edunov, S., Ott, M., Auli, M., Grangier, D.: Understanding Back-Translation at Scale. arXiv:180809381v2 (2018)
5. Ott, M., Edunov, S., Grangier, D., Auli, M.: Scaling Neural Machine Translation. arXiv:180600187v3 (2018)
6. Koehn, P.: Statistical Machine Translation. arXiv:170907809v1 (2017)
7. Zoph, B., Yuret, D., May, J., Knight, K.: Transfer Learning for Low-Resource Neural Machine Translation. arXiv:160402201v1 (2016)
8. Yang, Z., Chen, W., Wang, F., Xu, B.: Effectively training neural machine translation models with monolingual data. Neurocomputing **333**, 240–247 (2019). https://doi.org/10.1016/j.neucom.2018.12.032

9. Specia, L., Shah, K.: Machine translation quality estimation: applications and future perspectives. In: Moorkens, J., Castilho, S., Gaspari, F., Doherty, S. (eds.) Translation Quality Assessment. MTTA, vol. 1, pp. 201–235. Springer, Cham (2018). https://doi.org/10.1007/978-3-319-91241-7_10

10. Zhang, J., Zong, C.: Exploiting source-side monolingual data in neural machine translation. In: Proceedings of the 2016 Conference on Empirical Methods in Natural Language Processing, pp. 1535–1545, Austin, Texas: Association for Computational Linguistics (2016)

11. Sennrich, R., Haddow, B., Birch, A.: Improving neural machine translation models with monolingual data. In: Proceedings of the 54th Annual Meeting of the Association for Computational Linguistics, pp. 86–96, Berlin, Germany: Association for Computational Linguistics (2016)

12. Imamura, K., Fujita, A., Sumita, E.: Enhancement of encoder and attention using target monolingual corpora in neural machine translation. In: Proceedings of the 2nd Workshop on Neural Machine Translation and Generation, pp. 55–63, Melbourne, Australia: Association for Computational Linguistics (2018)

13. Caswell, I., Chelba, C., Grangier, D.: Tagged Back-Translation. arXiv:190606442v1 (2019)

14. Papineni, K., Roukos, S., Ward, T., Zhu, W.J.: BLEU: a method for automatic evaluation of machine translation. In: Proceedings of the 40th Annual Meeting on Association for Computational Linguistics, pp. 311–318, Stroudsburg, PA, USA (2002). https://doi.org/10.3115/1073083.1073135

15. He, D., et al.: Dual learning for machine translation. In: Proceedings of the 30th International Conference on Neural Information Processing Systems. NIPS 2016. USA: Curran Associates Inc., pp. 820–828 (2016). http://dl.acm.org/citation.cfm?id=3157096.3157188

16. Nguyen, T.Q., Chiang, D.: Transfer learning across low-resource, related languages for neural machine translation. In: Proceedings of the Eighth International Joint Conference on Natural Language Processing, vol. 2, pp. 296–301. Asian Federation of Natural Language Processing (2017)

17. Dabre, R., et al.: NICT's supervised neural machine translation systems for the WMT19 news translation task. In: Proceedings of the Fourth Conference on Machine Translation (WMT), vol. 2, pp. 168–174, Florence, Italy (2019)

18. Kocmi, T., Bojar, O.: CUNI submission for low-resource languages in WMT news 2019. In: Proceedings of the Fourth Conference on Machine Translation (WMT), vol. 2, pp. 234–240, Florence, Italy (2019)

19. Lample, G., Conneau, A.: Cross-lingual Language Model Pretraining. arXiv:190107291v1 (2019)

20. Lioutas, V., Guo, Y.: Time-aware Large Kernel Convolutions. arXiv:200203184v1 (2020)

21. Hoang, V.C.D., Koehn, P., Haffari, G., Cohn, T.: Iterative back-translation for neural machine translation. In: Proceedings of the 2nd Workshop on Neural Machine Translation and Generation, pp. 18–24, Melbourne, Australia: Association for Computational Linguistics (2018)

22. Niu, X., Denkowski, M., Carpuat, M.: Bi-Directional Neural Machine Translation with Synthetic Parallel Data. arXiv:180511213v2 (2018)

23. Zhang, Z., Liu, S., Li, M., Zhou, M., Chen, E.: Joint Training for Neural Machine Translation Models. arXiv:180300353v1 (2018)

24. Burlot, F., Yvon, F.: Using Monolingual Data in Neural Machine Translation: a Systematic Study. arXiv:190311437v1 (2019)

25. Graca, M., Kim, Y., Schamper, J., Khadivi, S., Ney, H.: Generalizing Back-Translation in Neural Machine Translation. arXiv:190607286v1 (2019)
26. Fadaee, M., Monz, C.: Back-Translation Sampling by Targeting Difficult Words in Neural Machine Translation. arXiv:180809006v2 (2018)
27. Poncelas, A., Shterionov, D., Way, A., Maillette de Buy, G.W., Passban, P.: Investigating Backtranslation in Neural Machine Translation. arXiv:180406189v1 (2018)
28. Ueffing, N.: Using monolingual source-language data to improve MT performance. In: International Workshop on Spoken Language Translation, pp. 174–181, Kyoto, Japan (2006)
29. Specia, L., Shah, K., de Souza, J.G.C., Cohn, T.: QuEst - A translation quality estimation framework. In: Proceedings of the 51st ACL: System Demonstrations, pp. 79–84, Sofia, Bulgaria: Association for Computational Linguistics (2013). http://staffwww.dcs.shef.ac.uk/people/K.Shah/papers/Quest.pdf
30. Gehring, J., Michael, A., Grangier, D., Yarats, D., Dauphin, Y.N.: Convolutional Sequence to Sequence Learning. arXiv:170503122v3 (2017)
31. Wu, F., Fan, A., Baevski, A., Dauphin, Y.N., Auli, M.: Pay Less Attention with Lightweight and Dynamic Convolutions, pp. 1–14. arXiv:190110430v2 (2019)
32. Dehghani, M., Gouws, S., Vinyals, O., Uszkoreit, J., Kaiser, L.: Universal transformers. In: ICLR, pp. 1–23 (2019)
33. Sutskever, I., Vinyals, O., Le, Q.V.: Sequence to sequence learning with neural networks. In: NIPS (2014)
34. Hochreiter, S., Schmidhuber, J.: Long short-term memory. Neural Comput. 9(8), 1735–1780 (1997)
35. Cho, K., van Merrienboer, B., Gülçehre, Ç., Bougares, F., Schwenk, H., Bengio, Y.: Learning Phrase Representations using RNN Encoder-Decoder for Statistical Machine Translation. CoRR.abs/1406.1 (2014)
36. Gulcehre, C., Firat, O., Xu, K., Cho, K., Bengio, Y.: On integrating a language model into neural machine translation. Comput. Speech Lang. 2017(45), 137–148 (2017). https://doi.org/10.1016/j.csl.2017.01.014
37. Currey, A., Miceli Barone, A.V., Heafield, K.: Copied monolingual data improves low-resource neural machine translation. In: Proceedings of the Second Conference on Machine Translation, vol. 1, pp. 148–156, Copenhagen, Denmark: Association for Computational Linguistics (2017)
38. Sennrich, R., Haddow, B., Birch, A.: Edinburgh Neural Machine Translation Systems for WMT 16. arXiv:160602891v2 (2016)
39. Johnson, M., Schuster, M., Le, Q.V., Krikun, M., Wu, Y., Chen, Z., et al.: Google's multilingual neural machine translation system: enabling zero-shot translation. Trans. Assoc. Comput. Linguist. 5, 339–351 (2017)
40. Abdulmumin, I., Galadanci, B.S., Garba, A.: Tag-less Back-Translation. http://arxiv.org/abs/191210514 (2019)
41. Cettolo, M., Niehues, J., Stüker, S., Bentivogli, L., Federico, M.: Report on the 11th IWSLT Evaluation Campaign, IWSLT 2014. In: Proceedings of the 11th Workshop on Spoken Language Translation, pp. 2–16. Lake Tahoe, CA, USA (2014)
42. Ranzato, M., Chopra, S., Auli, M., Zaremba, W.: Sequence level training with recurrent neural networks. In: International Conference on Learning Representations (2016)
43. Cettolo, M., Christian, G., Federico, M.: WIT3: web inventory of transcribed and translated talks. In: Conference of European Association for Machine Translation, pp. 261–268, Trento, Italy (2012)

44. Bojar, O., et al.: Findings of the 2017 conference on machine translation (WMT17). In: Proceedings of the Second Conference on Machine Translation: Shared Task Papers, vol. 2, pp. 169–214, Copenhagen, Denmark: Association for Computational Linguistics (2017). http://www.aclweb.org/anthology/W17-4717

45. Sennrich, R., Haddow, B., Birch, A.: Neural Machine Translation of Rare Words with Subword Units. arXiv:150807909v5 (2016)

46. Klein, G., Kim, Y., Deng, Y., Senellart, J., Rush, A.M.: OpenNMT: Open-Source Toolkit for Neural Machine Translation. arXiv e-prints arXiv:1701.02810 (2017)

47. Abadi, M., et al.: TensorFlow: a system for large-scale machine learning. In: Proceedings of the 12th USENIX Conference on Operating Systems Design and Implementation. OSDI 2016, pp. 265–283, Berkeley, CA, USA: USENIX Association (2016). http://dl.acm.org/citation.cfm?id=3026877.3026899

48. Kingma, D.P., Ba, J.: Adam: A method for stochastic optimization. arXiv preprint arXiv:14126980 (2014)

Information Security Privacy and Trust

SIMP-REAUTH: A Simple Multilevel Real User Remote Authentication Scheme for Mobile Cloud Computing

Omoniyi Wale Salami[1](✉) ⓘ, Yuri Demchenko[1], Emmanuel Adewale Adedokun[2] ⓘ,
and Muhammed Bashir Mu'azu[2]

[1] University of Liverpool, Liverpool L69 3BX, UK
{salami.omoniyiwale,yuri.demchenko}@online.liverpool.ac.uk
[2] Ahmadu Bello University, Zaria, Nigeria
wale@abu.edu.ng, muazumb1@yahoo.com

Abstract. Remote authentication is commonly required for online transactions. Many computing activities are now done online through Cloud computing. Most of devices used to access data in the Cloud are low capacity mobile devices. The advancement of computing technology is also accompanied with increased cybercrimes. Thus, security system for securing user data online must meet up with the new wave of attacks. Many solutions for improved remote authentication have been proposed but the security of remote authentication with mobile devices is still facing challenges. This research proposes a Simple Multilevel Real User Remote Authentication Scheme (SIMP-REAUTH) for Mobile Cloud Computing to prevent misuse of authentication token. SIMP-REAUTH is designed to enable implementation of advance authentication on low memory, low capacity mobile devices for a more accurate real user identification. SIMP-REAUTH consists of three stages comprising the facial, voice, and password authentications. The authentication processes are carried out by separate modules. Failure of any of the stages will cause the system to deny the user access to data. The high capacity and memory consuming biometric processes were outsourced to the Cloud. Misuse of authentication information was prevented with liveness test challenges. The reports obtained from the test users and results of simulated attacks carried out using the testbench show that SIMP-REAUTH is well suited for mitigating authentication token misuse by identity thieves. The test results recorded 94% and 92% resistance against the facial and voice attacks tests, respectively.

Keywords: Attacks · Remote authentication · Mobile devices

1 Introduction

Mobile phones and tablet PCs with low capacities are common devices used for online transactions. Their low memory, limited computing capacity [1] and limited power [2] make them not suitable for rigorous computations involved in advanced authentication systems [3] like Iris scan [4]. Cloud Computing has a promising future for connecting

© Springer Nature Switzerland AG 2021
S. Misra and B. Muhammad-Bello (Eds.): ICTA 2020, CCIS 1350, pp. 375–388, 2021.
https://doi.org/10.1007/978-3-030-69143-1_29

and managing Internet of Things (IoT) [3] which will increase the volume of online transactions considerably. Mobile Cloud Computing (MCC) is enabled by the computation capability and storage capacity augmentation services provided by the Cloud through its resource-on-demand services [5]. Thus, it provides cost-effective access to computing assets and optimized unbounded heterogeneous computation resources that can be exploited for business opportunities [6]. Remote authentication through mobile devices is frequently employed to authenticate users for accessing MCC services.

Remote authentication is an essential security service [7] for protecting data and users privacy. Personal identification information (PII) is a key player in remote authentication process that should be well protected [8]. PII includes password and other set of information that user normally supplies to a digital system for verification and authentication in order to be granted access to their protected data. It may include one or a combination of bio data (e.g. name, passport photograph, etc.), biometric samples (e.g. fingerprint, retina scan, etc.), and personal information like physical location or network address, etc. Identity thief can use this information for identity fraud to implicate, harm, rob or deprive the PII owners of their valuables [9]. Different tricks like phishing emails or calls, dumpster diving, malicious software [10], side-channel analysis, power analysis [11], Man-in-the-middle (MITM) and key logging attacks may be used to retrieve the PII from the owner.

Many solutions have been proffered for preventing loss of PII to wrong hands including the enlightenment trainings on attackers tricks [12–14], emphasis on using strong password, and encryption mechanisms [15, 16] for preventing stealing PII from the transmission channels. These methods have not been able to eradicate the loss of password to identity thieves. Evolution of new technology and introduction of new applications are making it easier for the attackers to gain access to the PII [17]. Technology like mobile cloud computing needs enhanced remote authentication security to protect online data. More so, the dispersive nature of the humongous data in the Cloud pose challenges to implementation of adequate security requirements on the servers, [18].

Mordor Intelligence reported that mobile cloud market registered $30.71 billion in 2019 and projected $118.70 billion market for it by the end of 2025 with compound annual growth rate (CAGR) of 25.28% [19]. The Corona Virus (COVID-19) pandemic outbreak also caused increased use of MCC for teleworking, shopping, online meeting, etc. [20] by users including grassroot people. With the increased inexpert online users who can easily fall prey to identity thief the possible vulnerability from these users should be technically mitigated.

The contribution of this work is addressing the challenges of loss of authentication parameters by preventing its misuse. The proposed scheme emulates human mode of identification with physical sighting and hearing in real time for authenticating users. It is called Simple Multilevel Remote Authentication Scheme for Mobile Cloud Computing (SIMP-REAUTH). The scheme is not complex because it uses the resources available on the mobile devices that users are familiar with and can easily. SIMP-REAUTH will secure users who may not be able to properly keep their log-in tokens by making it difficult for a wrong user to be authenticated with stolen authentication parameters.

The rest of this paper is arranged thus; relevant research works are reviewed in Sect. 2, the materials and the method are discussed in Sect. 3, Sect. 4 contains the performance evaluation of this research and the conclusion is in Sect. 5.

2 Related Works

MobiCloud [21] was proposed to secure mobile ad hoc network (MANET) using Extended Semi-Shadow Images of the MANET nodes. It provides a trust model with identity management, key management, and security data access policy enforcement for use to develop future mobile applications. A solution for preserving privacy of data owner was proposed in [15] using Ciphertext Policy Attribute-Based Encryption (CP-ABE) scheme that allows multiple users to use the same attribute was used for privacy protection. A fully homomorphic encryption technique was proposed in [18] to mitigate the difficulty of been able to effectively implement security framework for the big data of the Cloud computing. Privacy protection inherently conflicts efficient authentication because it constraints the disclosure of personal identification information [8] required for authentication. The solution proposed in [8] used user attributes shared among multiple identity providers to provide "identification of pseudonyms" of a user by collecting attributes of the user from proxies without disclosing the user as a workaround. Mo et al. [2] proposed an elliptical curve cryptography (ECC) key agreement based anonymous two-factor user authentication scheme to secure data in the wireless channel and prevents dictionary attack with Fuzzy verifier. Cao et al. [22] proposed a solution to mitigate some challenges found with existing remote authentication schemes. The problems include privacy protection with anonymity, vulnerability to slow wrong password detection, masquerading attack and password guessing attack. The Advanced lightweight multi-factor remote user authentication scheme developed in [3] for cloud-IoT applications uses current timestamp to prevent replay attacks and smart card to identify a valid registered user. Secure remote anonymous user authentication scheme was also developed for smart home environment [23]. The authentication process involves generation of a nonce and calculating a unique identity token using the nonce and another unique number generated for the session. The location parameters were then used to generate a hash value using present location and location history of the device. Eliza Mik [24] analyzed different modes of communication that are used for carrying out transactions with focus on technological mistakes of identifying users in computer-based transactions. Eliza reported that mistake of identity basically voids a transaction while mistake of attribute can only make the transaction in which it occurred voidable [24]. Attribute based security systems cannot be adequate to mitigate misuse of authentication information unless unique irrefutable identity attributes are used. Therefore, the problem of unauthorized use of a compromised authentication information is not a mistaken attribute problem but that of identity. It should be mitigated on the frontend devices. The method used for identifying other parties in a transaction can also influence the efficacy of the identification system. A Face-to-face communication that involves seeing and hearing enables better identification of a claimant than descriptive attributes [24]. Thus, a system that can mimic human face-to-face identification method will increase the efficacy of authentication security and generates better evidence for claims against identity fraud. The solutions reviewed did not solved the problems of using compromised parameters for misrepresentation of authentication information. The solutions that use smart card and the encryption-based solutions lost their security when the card or the encryption key is compromised. Others involved higher computations beyond the capability of a mobile device. Besides, none of them employed such a simple method easily imple-mentable on mobile devices as the one SIMP-REAUTH uses to test for freshness and liveness of the samples. SIMP-REAUTH used existing technologies to develop a solu-tion that can imitate real-life human face-to-face method of authentication to mitigate misappropriation of authentication to misrepresentation of authentication information. In physical face-to-face communication fresh samples are collected every time which makes the system formidable. SIMP-REAUTH incorporates processes that dynamically define and randomize specifications for the expected samples for authentication for dif-ferent transactions. This ensures that fresh samples from the original user is collected for every authentication request.

3   Materials and Methods

SIMP-REAUTH consists of the user device, cloud server and the authentication station (AS). The flow of authentication request and its processing is explained in the block diagram in Fig. 1.

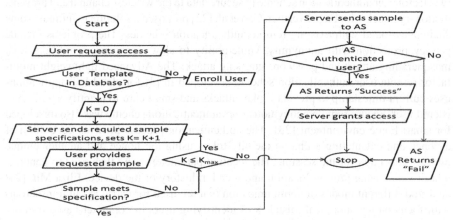

Fig. 1. Sequence of the authentication process by the mechanism

A portal, project.sowinfocomtech.com, was created on GoDaddy web host-ing platform for the users to create online accounts as Cloud users. The project.sowinfocomtech.com serves as the AS which users are log-in into. The identifica-tion was implemented using online biometric face authentication and speech recognition servers. The face authentication service was provided by Animetrics face recognition server, Face™R, [25]. This was the cloud provider's biometric facial User Identification Server (UIS) for this project. The google chrome x-webkit-speech was used as speech recognition interface for this prototype. The features of the services provided by the UIS that were useful to this project were utilized as provided by the providers.

3.1   User Account

Each of the users creates an account at project.sowinfocomtech.com by registering on the registration page. A username and a password were chosen during registration to be used for initiating consequent authentication requests.

3.2 Password Interface

This is the first step in the authentication process. At this stage the Cloud server only authenticates the requestor as a registered user on the cloud server. The portal, project.sowinfocomtech.com, was built on WordPress web applications. The registration and login pages for this project are modified from WordPress registration and login pages. The default page to the portal is the login page which has links to registration page for new user and password reset for returning users that forgotten their passwords. After successful log-in the user is redirected to authentication page where the biometric samples are taken and confirmed against the templates in the database.

3.3 Voice Authentication Module

This is the second stage in the authentication process. Here the voice authenticator validates the authentication requestor as a human being. The voice randomizer picks a word or a phrase or short statement at random from the database. The text list in the database is updated periodically to avoid compromising. The text is displayed as an altered image to the user to prevent screen reader attack. There is an instruction asking the user to click the microphone icon to activates the google x-webkit-speech. The camera snaps the user face while the user reads the text. The recorded user's speech was then sent to the speech-to-text in the voice authenticator to be transcribed to text and return the text contained in the speech. The randomizer receives returned text validates it against the one sent to the user. Successful validation prompts the user to progress to the next stage, otherwise the process stops. If randomizer did not send a text for a user recognition before receiving a voice, Intrusion Detection System, IDS, on the server will raise alarm.

3.4 Face Image Authentication

This is the third and the final stage of the authentication process. The face capturing interface was developed with a PHP (Hypertext Preprocessing) script. The image container for capturing face image is displayed together below the text image on the client screen. The face sample was taken on the same HTML GUI with the voice. The user face sample was sent by ajax to the PHP script residing on project.sowinfocomtech.com. The PHP script saves the captured image on the server and forwards a copy to the UIS. This PHP script receives the response from the facial UIS and presents it to the Cloud authentication server. The number of face images taken and the image upload status are shown on the client screen after uploading the images. The steps in the facial recognition are explained in the following.

Image Position Randomizer. The UIS facial recognition system calculates the location of the face organs like eyes, nose, upper lip, lower lip etc. of the user from the template in the database. An example of the parameters values is shown in Fig. 2.

```
{
    "images": [
        {
            "time": 4.05193,
            "status": "Complete",
            "url":
"http://project.sowinfocomtech.com/images/20131030203349.jpg",
            "width": 250,
            "height": 250,
            "setpose_image":
"http://api.animetrics.com/img/setpose/afc6a85f0c56ec64c5ebdb80f
8e88466.jpg",
            "faces": [
                {
                    "topLeftX": 92,
                    "topLeftY": 87,
                    "width": 98,
                    "height": 98,
                    "leftEyeCenterX": 119.66,
                    "leftEyeCenterY": 107.903,
                    "rightEyeCenterX": 153.483,
                    "rightEyeCenterY": 113.224,
                    "noseTipX": 142.82,
                    "noseTipY": 133.373,
                    "noseBtwEyesX": 139.212,
                    "noseBtwEyesY": 107.477,
                    "chinTipX": -1,
                    "chinTipY": -1,
                    "leftEyeCornerLeftX": 112.624,
                    "leftEyeCornerLeftY": 107.88,
                    "leftEyeCornerRightX": 126.198,
                    "leftEyeCornerRightY": 111.098,
                    "rightEyeCornerLeftX": 145.306,
                    "rightEyeCornerLeftY": 113.562,
                    "rightEyeCornerRightX": 159.13,
                    "rightEyeCornerRightY": 115.195,
                    "rightEarTragusX": -1,
                    "rightEarTragusY": -1,
                    "leftEarTragusX": -1,
                    "leftEarTragusY": -1,
                    "leftEyeBrowLeftX": 106.046,
                    "leftEyeBrowLeftY": 95.7276,
                    "leftEyeBrowMiddleX": 121.89,
                    "leftEyeBrowMiddleY": 92.9425,
                    "leftEyeBrowRightX": 133.979,
                    "leftEyeBrowRightY": 97.3697,
                    "rightEyeBrowLeftX": 148.067,
                    "rightEyeBrowLeftY": 99.3118,
                    "rightEyeBrowMiddleX": 160.063,
                    "rightEyeBrowMiddleY": 100.413,
                    "rightEyeBrowRightX": 164.267,
                    "rightEyeBrowRightY": 105.962,
                    "nostrilLeftHoleBottomX": 131.086,
                    "nostrilLeftHoleBottomY": 138.382,
                    "nostrilRightHoleBottomX": 144.632,
                    "nostrilRightHoleBottomY": 140.249,
                    "nostrilLeftSideX": 125.256,
```

Fig. 2. The detected face organs data returned by the face recognizer

```
"nostrilLeftSideY": 132.609,
"nostrilRightSideX": 149.49,
"nostrilRightSideY": 137.054,
"lipCornerLeftX": 125.594,
"lipCornerLeftY": 154.189,
"lipLineMiddleX": 138.748,
"lipLineMiddleY": 154.898,
"lipCornerRightX": 145.792,
"lipCornerRightY": 155.869,
"pitch": 4.63151,
"yaw": -28.4365,
"roll": 7.99711
} ]   } ]   }
```

Fig. 2. (*continued*)

The Face Randomizer use the organs location parameter values to generate the position of the image container where the user face is expected to appear for capturing as depicted in Fig. 3a. In Fig. 3b, the dotted lines indicate the detected face organs before capturing.

The randomizer randomly generates different position for the image container. This causes a transformation to the expected values of the organs' locations. This is equivalent to shifting of the image container of the original template by r pixels in both horizontal and vertical directions, as shown in Fig. 3c, which will add r value to the original template values as may be appropriate. Apart from shifting face in the image, some facial emotion and postures, e.g. closing an eye or opening mouth or doing both, were also requested randomly. Other options include shifting the container horizontally only or vertically only. In this case only one coordinate, either X or Y as may be desired, will be increased or decreased by the generated random value. The values in the returned sample may not be exactly the same with the calculated values in the above. A small margin, possibly 1/3 r, may be allowed to avoid high number of rejections of the users by the system. But values that are exact equivalent of those in the template or outside the margin were not acceptable.

Face Image Capturing. The face sample is taken automatically when the required conditions are met. There is a static green circle (Static point in Fig. 4a) which user will be required to align the centre of their face image with. The centre of the face image is indicated with a smaller green circle on the recognized face image as shown in Fig. 4a indicated as "point to align". The "point to align" moves in the image container as the user moves the head. Also, the required face image size in the picture is determined by the specified face width which the user can match by moving the head towards the camera to enlarge the face image, or move the head away from the camera to reduce the face image size.

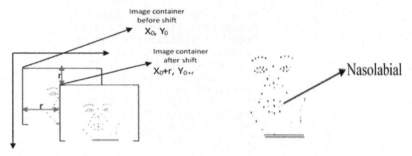

a. Image container location shift   **b.** Face organs detection by UIS

```
Position of the left eye in the template in pixels = Xle, Yle
Position of the right eye in the template in pixels = Xre, Yre
Distance between left eye and the right eye = Xre -Xle, Yre-Yle
= Xd, Yd
Position of the left Nasolabial Sulcus in the template in pixels
= Xln, Yln
Position of the right Nasolabial Sulcus in the template in pix-
els = Xrn, Yrn
Distance between the left and the right Nasolabial Sulcus = Xrn
-Xln, Yrn-Yln = Xdn, Ydn
Randomizer generated value = r
Then, expected positions of the organs in the sample will be
calculated thus,
Position of the left eye in the sample in pixels = Xlpe, Ylpe
Xlpe = Xle + r
Ylpe = Yle + r
Position of the right eye in the sample in pixels = Xrpe, Yrpe
Xrpe = Xlpe + Xd
Yrpe = Ylpe + Yd
Position of the left Nasolabial Sulcus in the sample in pixels =
Xlpn, Ylpn
Xlpn = Xln + r
Ylpn = Yln + r
Position of the right Nasolabial Sulcus in the sample in pixels
= Xrpn, Yrpn
Xrpn = Xlpn + Xdn
Yrpn = Ylpn + Ydn
```

c. Using positions of face organs in the template to specify image position

Fig. 3. Face image positioning and detection for capturing

As soon as the face image size is equal to the specified value and the face image center aligns with the indicated point a number of the face images is automatically captured. Figure 4b shows captured face sample that matched required specifications. The number captured is randomly determined. The captured images are saved on the server and one of them was randomly selected and sent to the facial UIS for recognition.

Only x-coordinate was varied in this project. A value withing ±5-pixel margin was accepted for the matching of the face center with the static point to make it easier for the user to align. Y-coordinate is not considered because it could be very difficult for some users to match x and y values at the same time.

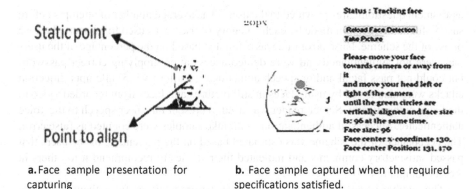

a. Face sample presentation for capturing

b. Face sample captured when the required specifications satisfied.

Fig. 4. Face image capturing (Color figure online)

Facial Recognition Validation. The PHP 'Imagick::getImageProperties' method was used in the PHP script by the cloud server to check the properties of the face image samples. For validation, the creation date and modification date on the images were checked to be recent and the same on the samples taken. These dates on one image are compared to those on the other images captured together and ensured that they did not differ by a value greater than a predetermined acceptable range, 2 s used here. The face size and the face center are returned by the UIS together with recognition results. The values returned were compared with the estimated values specified for capturing the image sample. Images with differences greater than ±5 pixels between returned values from UIS and the specified values sent to the user were rejected. The presence of facial expression specified was also checked in the captured image. Absence of the expression also invalidates the image sample.

All the user samples presented for the authentication, i.e. password, voice and face image, must pass their individual tests. Failure of one sample caused rejection of all others. The user samples that pass all the tests above was used to grant the user access.

4 Performance Evaluation

A total of one hundred and two (102) users located in different parts of Nigeria participated in test running the prototype of this solution. The test users consisted of people with different levels of IT skills. Users with vast experience on computing devices usage and operations and possibly have degree or certification in IT were considered expert users. Medium users were those with good experience on mobile device usage and operations. Low experience users consisted of those that were only able to use basic functions of mobile devices, e.g. make calls and use short message services (SMS). The number of users that participated in the test consisted of twenty-nine (29) expert users, thirty (30) medium users, and forty-three (43) low experience users. Metrics used to assess this scheme are ease of use, false error rate (including false acceptance and false rejection), and the users' assessment of the scheme. The metrics were extracted from the records of the log-in attempts by the users and the responses of the users to assessment questionnaires provided to the users. The average number of attempts before successful authentication made by each category of users was used to measure the ease of use of the scheme. False error rate was estimated based on the percentage of the users that were not authenticated and were denied access after supplying correct password but could not pass facial and/or speech authentication after five (5) attempts. Injection attacks were also tested by using faces in still pictures and faces from recorded video to the facial authenticator. Screen reader was used to present fake user speech to the voice authenticator. Successful authentications with fake samples were counted as false error. The acceptance of the scheme was estimated based on the percentage of the users that passed satisfactory comments and indicated their wishes to recommend it to others in the questionnaires.

The number of attempts made by each user before a successful authentication are plotted in Fig. 5a. The comparative average ease-of-use by different categories of the users is depicted in Fig. 5b pie chart. The ratio was 42:35:23% for expert, medium and low experience users respectively.

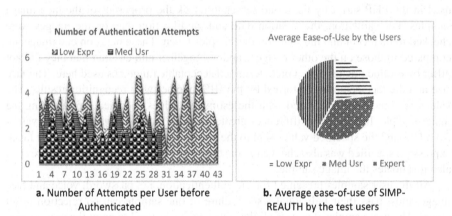

a. Number of Attempts per User before Authenticated

b. Average ease-of-use of SIMP-REAUTH by the test users

Fig. 5. Test Users usage report of SIMP-REAUTH

The users' acceptance of the scheme based on the users' ratings on the scale of 1 to 10 is plotted in Fig. 6. It can be seen in the figure that the rating corresponds to the ease-of-use of the scheme for different categories of the users. Out of the 43 low experience users 26 gave the scheme from 5 to 9 ratings. Among the 30 of medium users 26 rated it between 5 and 8 inclusive, while the ratings given by 26 out of the 29 expert users range between 6 and 8 inclusive, as can be seen in Fig. 6. The ratings show that the scheme would be readily acceptable to users.

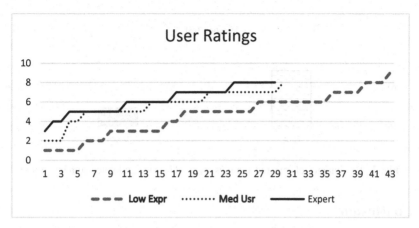

Fig. 6. User ratings of SIMP-REAUTH

5   Results and Discussion

The major usage challenge encountered reported by users was caused by the speech-to-text unable to recognize the words pronounced by the user. It shows that the scheme is easier for expert users and they had least difficulty with it. Majority of expert users were able to get through with one or two attempts. Most Medium users succeeded in one to three attempts. But majority of low experience users made three to five attempts before been authenticated. Difficulties in getting face images captured were less for each group than passing the speech-to-text challenge. Different intonations of the speakers caused problem of recognition of their pronounced words by the system. The ease-of-use of the system was hampered by the voice authentication more than the facial authentication module. An efficient machine learning algorithm could be used for the speech-to-text application for a faster recognition of different users' intonations.

Fake authentications were tested with still face images of registered users presented to the system. Good samples of registered users still face images were correctly positioned to match the specified size and position within the allowed time for the authentication requests. They could not pass for authentication because facial emotional postures were requested at random in different specifications and could not be met. Most of the face samples of the registered users injected into the system did not scaled through authentication.

Video injection also failed because they could not match emotion postures, sizes and positions randomly stipulated for different authentication requests within required time. Screen reader failed to read challenge phrases presented correctly when they were presented as deformed text images. Figure 7 shows the percentage rejections of the injected samples by the voice and face authentication modules.

Majority of expert users and medium users passed good comment on the scheme and indicated interest to recommend it to other users. The low experienced users that pass comments are fewer than the other categories.

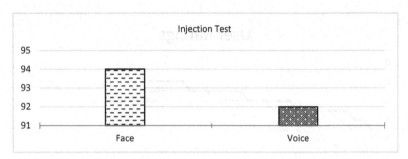

Fig. 7. Percentages of injected samples rejected by face and voice authentication

6 Conclusion

The SIMP-REAUTH remote authentication mechanism proposed by this work for securing mobile cloud computing users was able to minimize the successful use of compromised account information by attackers. The face image authenticator and voice sample authenticator modules together largely prevented brute-force attacks and injection of fake biometric samples. Also, replay attacks whereby used biometric samples of the original owner of the account could be reused for authentication is prevented by randomly defined specifications for every new sample to be presented for the authentication. SIMP-REAUTH makes it possible to implement advanced multilevel security process on resource limited mobile devices like mobile phones. It makes possible the authentication of genuine remote user of highly confidential data. This solution can be improved by adding more challenges and it can be adapted for use in different applications.

SIMP-REAUTH as presented here may not prevent attacks that hijacks transactions from an authenticated user. Those attacks can be more effectively prevented by incorporating other security measures like using dynamic transaction ID or data encryption. Future works will explore improvement of SIMP-REAUTH by incorporating more security measures.

References

1. Jegadeesan, S., et al.: An efficient anonymous mutual authentication technique for providing secure communication in mobile cloud computing for smart city applications. Sustain. Cities Soc. **49**, 101522 (2019). https://doi.org/10.1016/j.scs.2019.101522
2. Mo, J., Hu, Z., Chen, H., Shen, W.: An efficient and provably secure anonymous user authentication and key agreement for mobile cloud computing. Wirel. Commun. Mob. Comput. **2019**, Article ID 4520685, 1–12 (2019). https://doi.org/10.1155/2019/4520685
3. Sharma, G., Kalra, S.: Advanced lightweight multi-factor remote user authentication scheme for cloud-IoT applications. J. Ambient Intell. Humaniz. Comput. **11**(4), 1771–1794 (2020). https://doi.org/10.1007/s12652-019-01225-1
4. Mohammed, A.F., Qyser, A.A.M.: A hybrid approach for secure iris-based authentication in IoT. In: ICICCT 2019 – System Reliability, Quality Control, Safety, Maintenance and Management, pp. 159–167, January 2020. https://doi.org/10.1007/978-981-13-8461-5_18

5. Saeid, A., Zohreh, S., Abdullah, G., Shiraz, M.: MOMCC: market-oriented architecture for mobile cloud computing based on service oriented architecture. In: 2012 1st IEEE International Conference on Communications in China Workshops, pp. 8–13 (2012)
6. Celesti, A., Tusa, F., Villari, M., Puliafito, A.: Three-phase cross-cloud federation model: the cloud sso authentication. In: 2010 Second International Conference on Advances in Future Internet (AFIN), pp. 94–101 (2010)
7. Munivel, E., Kannammal, A.: New authentication scheme to secure against the phishing attack in the mobile cloud computing. Secur. Commun. Netw. **2019** (2019). https://doi.org/10.1155/2019/5141395
8. Sato, H., Okabe, Y., Nakamura, M.: User Identification of pseudonyms without identity information exposure in access federations. In: Proceedings - International Computer Software and Applications Conference, vol. 1, pp. 487–492, August 2016. https://doi.org/10.1109/compsac.2016.215
9. Sullivan, C.: Is identity theft really theft? Int. Rev. Law, Comput. Technol. **23**(1), 77 (2009)
10. Dwan, B.: Identity theft. Comput. Fraud Secur. **2004**(4), 14–17 (2004)
11. Hospodar, G., Gierlichs, B., De Mulder, E., Verbauwhede, I., Vandewalle, J.: Machine learning in side-channel analysis: a first study. J. Cryptogr. Eng. **1**(4), 293–302 (2011). https://doi.org/10.1007/s13389-011-0023-x
12. Tsai, H.S., Jiang, M., Alhabash, S., LaRose, R., Rifon, N.J., Cotten, S.R.: Understanding online safety behaviors a protection motivation theory perspective. Comput. Secur. **59**, 138–150 (2016)
13. Fujun, L., Dahui, L., Chang-Tseh, H.: Fighting identity theft: the coping perspective. Decis. Support Syst. **52**(2), 353–363 (2012)
14. Shillair, R., Cotten, S.R., Tsai, H.-Y.S., Alhabash, S., LaRose, R., Rifon, N.J.: Online safety begins with you and me: convincing Internet users to protect themselves. Comput. Human Behav. **48**, 199–207 (2015)
15. Zhou, Z., Huang, D.: Efficient and secure data storage operations for mobile cloud computing. In: Proceedings of the 8th International Conference on Network and Service Management, pp. 37–45 (2012)
16. Khan, A.N., Kiah, M.L.M., Madani, S.A., ur Khan, A.R., Ali, M.: Enhanced dynamic credential generation. J. Supercomput. 1–20 (2013)
17. Irshad, S., Soomro, T.R.: Identity theft and social media. Int. J. Comput. Sci. Netw. Secur. **18**(1), 43–55 (2018)
18. Jambhekar, N.D., Misra, S., Dhawale, C.A.: Cloud computing security with collaborating encryption. Indian J. Sci. Technol. **9**(21), 1–7 (2016). https://doi.org/10.17485/ijst/2016/v9i21/95239
19. Intelligence, M.: Mobile Cloud Market Size, Share, Trends, Forecast (2020-25) (2020). https://www.mordorintelligence.com/industry-reports/global-mobile-cloud-market-industry. Accessed 22 Aug 2020
20. Kellerman, A.: The post-Corona city: virus imprints and precautions. Environ. Plan. B Urban Anal. City Sci. **47**(7), 1124–1127 (2020). https://doi.org/10.1177/2399808320949296
21. Huang, D., Zhang, X., Kang, M., Luo, J.: MobiCloud: building secure cloud framework for mobile computing and communication. In: Fifth IEEE International Symposium on Service Oriented System Engineering, pp. 27–34 (2010)
22. Cao, S.-Q., Sun, Q., Cao, L.-L.: Security analysis and enhancements of a remote user authentication scheme. Int. J. Netw. Secur. **21**(4), 15 (2019). https://doi.org/10.6633/ijns.201907
23. Fakroon, M., Alshahrani, M., Gebali, F., Traore, I.: Secure remote anonymous user authentication scheme for smart home environment. Internet of Things **9**(100158), 1–20 (2020). https://doi.org/10.1016/j.iot.2020.100158

24. Mik, E.: Mistaken identity, identity theft and problems of remote authentication in e-commerce. Comput. Law Secur. Rev. **28**(4), 396–402 (2012)
25. FaceR API. http://api.animetrics.com/. Accessed 01 Sep 2020

Formulation and Optimization of Overcurrent Relay Coordination in Distribution Networks Using Metaheuristic Algorithms

Ahmed Tijani Salawudeen[1](✉) ⓘ, Abdulrahman Adebayo Olaniyan[2] ⓘ,
Gbenga Abidemi Olarinoye[2], and Tajudeen Humble Sikiru[2]

[1] Faculty of Engineering, University of Jos, Jos, Nigeria
atsalawudeen@unijos.edu.ng
[2] Faculty of Engineering, Ahmadu Bello University, Zaria, Nigeria

Abstract. This paper implements an optimized solution to Over Current Relay Coordination (OCR) using a new metaheuristics algorithm called Smell Agent Optimization (SAO). We first formulate the relay coordination as a single objective multi-variable optimization problem. The main objective of the optimization is to optimize the time required for operation of the protective relays. We employed the IEEE standard 15-bus and IEEE standard 30-bus test networks to implement the OCR methods. Simulations were carried using Matlab R2019b and results were compared with Particle Swarm Optimization (PSO). Experimental analysis of results showed that both SAO and PSO algorithms are effective in solving the relay coordination problem. The SAO obtained a better solution when compared with the PSO, however, the PSO convergence was faster than SAO.

Keywords: Smell agent optimization · Overcurrent relay coordination · Time multiplier settings · Plug settings · IEEE test systems

1 Introduction

The continuous growth in population is an indication of increase in demand for electrical energy which in turn, has pushed suppliers of electrical energy to search for new means of meeting load demand. This birthed the introduction of distributed generation to ensure increased security and reliability of the power system network [1]. The introduction of renewable energy sources such as Wind generation system would help achieve the required reliability at distribution voltage level, however, this will also cause an increase in the level of short circuit current during fault basically because of large size of power generation infrastructure [2]. Infrastructure protection in power system is one of the most pertinent aspects which require adequate attention and full concentration [3]. This is because occurrence of major disturbances can only be mitigated through adequate coordinated protection and control actions which will halt system degradation, minimize the impact of faults and restore system normalcy [4]. During fault conditions, interruption and damage to equipment can occur. This is undesired and as such, the fault section must

© Springer Nature Switzerland AG 2021
S. Misra and B. Muhammad-Bello (Eds.): ICTA 2020, CCIS 1350, pp. 389–402, 2021.
https://doi.org/10.1007/978-3-030-69143-1_30

be swiftly identified and isolated so as to continue normal system operation by supplying other aspects of the network (where there is no fault) and maintaining system reliability and stability [5].

Protection relays ensure that abnormities and undesired conditions are detected as fast as possible while immediately isolating those faulted parts selectively and as fast possible. Different relays have their unique principle of operation with regards to system protection, fault detection and isolation. However, these relays must be coordinated in their design such that they are able to detect abnormality, undesired conditions and irregularities within their zones i.e., a protective relay must be able to differentiate between healthy and unhealthy operating condition. The design of protection relays should make sure that relays must perfectly detect abnormalities, and timely trip the circuit breaker where the fault is located without affecting other healthy areas [6]. The relay coordination concept deals with isolation discrimination, selectivity and backup protection for the relay located closest to the fault or point of disturbance/abnormality to operate and avoid severe problems or total outage [7]. Then primary relay can then be backed up by a secondary relay which is also coordinated to ensure that there is sufficient delay to permit the primary relay and its circuit breakers clear the fault [8].

The primary relay which is supposed to be the first protective device to sense faults first within its closest zone has a backup secondary relay. The relay must have appropriate chance to protect the precinct within its primary responsibility before the backup can initiate tripping if the primary relay does not clear the fault. Each relay needs to be adequately coordinated, as a typical power system network consist of more than hundreds of relays [9]. Coordination problem in overcurrent relays is a complex problem in power system planning and operation because these directional relays need to be strategically placed as standalone devices in the entire network for protection and isolation [10]. The problem of optimal coordination of relays evolved to become a popular power system problem of which selectivity, sensitivity, reliability and speed became fundamental performance metrics. These yardsticks are categorized as desired quantities which indicates the level of acceptability of any relay coordination solution [8, 11]. Investigations have shown that an appreciable number of false tripping in relays are due to improper coordination and poor settings. The optimal coordination of overcurrent relay has been investigated by several researchers and the main challenge has always been designing an optimal relay coordination system which is free from false tripping and satisfies all performance indices. This problem however involves degrees of uncertainties as it is complex and nonstandard in nature and thus, it is quite hard in obtaining a global optimum [12].

Numerous publications have tried to solve the optimal relay coordination problem in recent times. The methods adopted include guessing method, topological analysis method, heuristics and metaheuristics optimization methods. The complexity of the guessing method and topological method have automatically made most researchers opt for the heuristic and metaheuristics solution methods [6, 10, 13]. A solution technique employing the use of Particle Swarm Optimization technique for optimizing the pickup current and time dial setting of relays was proposed by [14] while [15] used a hybrid Differential Evolution, DE and PSO for the same purpose. Ref. [16] and [17] used different variants of Particle Swarm Optimization techniques for optimal selection of Time Multiplier Settings and Plug Settings in relay coordination. Other techniques have also been used in this problem area such as Cuckoo Search Optimization algorithm in [18], Time-Varying Acceleration based particle Swarm Optimization algorithm by [5], the use of hybrid Biogeography-Based Optimization and Differential Evolution Algorithm by [19] as well as [20] which used Electromagnetic Field Optimization algorithm. More recently, [21] developed a unique Genetic Algorithm based optimization solution for overcurrent relay coordination thereby showing that the application of artificial intelligence cannot be over-emphasized. It is obvious that this research area has proven its relevance over time, to be an active area despite several efforts from researchers. The relay coordination problem is still very much valid and persistent in power system planning and operation thus more effort is still required.

In view of this, we present a novel solution technique called the Smell Agent Optimization (SAO) technique for coordination of Overcurrent relays. This method will minimize the time taken to obtain optimal solution while considering the Coordination Time Interval and improving the efficiency of the relay coordination solution. The efficiency of the solution method was implemented on the standard IEEE 15-Bus and 30-Bus networks.

2 Materials

2.1 Directional Overcurrent Relay Coordination

The optimization of relay coordination is based on calculation of current and time dial settings. The current setting which is determined by minimizing the fault current and maximum load current is highly instrumental in obtaining the TDS (Time Dial Setting) and Time Multiplier Setting (TMS) [22]. There are standard relay characteristics as provided by the IEC and IEEE as well as non-standard characteristic which are used as a guide by researchers and industrial experts in the overcurrent relays coordination in sub-transmission and distribution networks. The IEC characteristics shows that the relay operation time is directly proportional to the TMS where some constant values are the determinants. These values have been presented after laboratory experiments to ensure proper representation of relay characteristics.

For the IEC standard, the value of relay operating time is computed from Eq. (1):

$$t = TMS \times \frac{A}{\left(\frac{I_f}{I_p}\right)^B - 1} \tag{1}$$

Where; A and B are constants, I_f is the fault current in the relay, Ip is the fault current in the line.

On the other hand, the IEEE characteristics has included one more constant which is as a result of the nonstandard connection between current at the input and electromagnetic flux in the relay core. Thus, the value of the operating time of the relay which reflects the fixed tripping time can be obtained as:

$$t = TMS \times \left[\frac{A}{\left(\frac{I_f}{I_p}\right)^B - 1} + C \right] \qquad (2)$$

Where; C is the third characteristic which accounts for the fixed tripping time. The values of A, B, and C can be obtained from Table 1. depending on the scenario which the designer wishes to consider.

Table 1. Coefficient of IEC 60255-3 and IEEE C37.112 1996 standards

	Extreme inverse		Very inverse		Normal inverse	
	IEC 60255-3	IEEE C37.112 1996	IEC 60255-3	IEEE C37.112 ₭6	IEC 60255-3	IEEE C37.112 1996
A	80	28.2	3.5	19.61	0.14	0.0515
B	2	2	1	2	0.02	0.02
C	–	0.1217	–	0.491	–	0.0114

Furthermore, there are nonstandard characteristics that can be used for relay coordination built on electric magnitudes which are popularly voltage and current. The current based characteristic is peculiarized with a different constant which is a fault current function and is obtained using (3). However, there is a third nonstandard characteristic which using value of fault admittance but disregards the use of Time Multiplier Settings [23].

$$A(I_f) = A e^{\frac{-I_f}{C}} \qquad (3)$$

$$t = \left[\frac{A(I_f)}{\left(\frac{I_f}{I_p}\right)^B - 1} \right] \times TMS \qquad (4)$$

The relay operating time of the nonstandard current characteristic is expressed in (4) where it is obvious that the special constant, A is still of essence and it's is a major function in determining the operating time. The voltage based nonstandard characteristics method is especially appreciated when there is a Distributed Generator (DG) on the network and it is obvious that this DG contributes to the value of fault current. Thus, for the voltage based characteristics, the relay operating time can be obtained using [24];

$$t = TMS \times \left(\frac{A}{\left(\frac{I_f}{I_p}\right)^B - 1} \right) \times \left(\frac{1}{e^{(1-V_f)}} \right)^k \qquad (5)$$

Where; V_f is the fault voltage and k is a constant parameter based on choice or individual setting.

2.2 The IEEE Standard 15-Bus Radial Network

The IEEE 15-Bus is a radial distribution network having fifteen (15) buses with thirteen (13) connected loads having twenty-eight (28) digital overcurrent protection relays for optimal values settings as adopted from [17]. The Figure of the network highlighting the position of the relays on the system, Fig. 1. The network is employed to investigate the performance of the developed Smell Agent Optimization Algorithm for finding the optimal values of Coordination Time Interval (CTI).

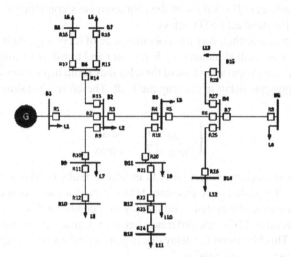

Fig. 1. The IEEE 15-bus network

3 Methods

3.1 OCR Problem Formulation

In optimization problem formulation, significant attention should be on identifying the decision variables appropriately. Here, the Time Multiplier Setting (TMS) and Plug Setting (PS) are considered as the decision variables of the overcurrent relay optimization problem. The PS gives the minimum relay operating value of current whereas the TMS defined time operation of the relays for each current value. Thus, minimize the overall time of relays operation is the optimization objective formulated as:

$$f(O_{t_i}) = \min \sum_{i=1}^{m} w \times O_{t_i} \tag{6}$$

The number of relays in the network is given by m, w is a weighted coefficient whose value is selected as 1, indicating the probability of fault occurrence, O_{ti} is the relay operating time $R_i = 1, 2, ..., m$.

Relays are presumed identical and with normal IDMT which is define as the Inverse Definite Minimum Time characteristic. The operating time O_{ti} is;

$$O_{t_i} = \sum_{i=1}^{m} \frac{\lambda \times \delta_i}{\left(\frac{I_f}{\alpha_i \times \beta_i}\right)^{\eta} - 1} + L \tag{7}$$

where; PS is Plug Setting, δ is the Time Multiplier Setting (TMS), I_f is fault current, β_i is plug setting (PS), α is the current transformer ratio CTR, λ, η and L are relays characteristics constant. The values of the characteristic's constant are $\lambda = 0.14$, $\eta = 0.02$ and L = 0 for standard IDMT relays.

It is important to note that, very low operating time of relay may result to an unwanted stimulation under no-fault situations, such as motor and transformer inrush currents. In the same vain, very high operating time of the relay may result in power system equipment damage due to possible delay in clearing the fault. Therefore, operating time objective is constrained as:

$$\begin{cases} \delta_{min} \leq \delta_i \leq \delta_{max} \\ \beta_{min} \leq \beta_i \leq \beta_{max} \end{cases} \tag{8}$$

The essence of backup protection is to eliminate faults occurrence due to failure of primary relay. To evade any interference between primary and secondary relays, it's essential to supplement the system with a delay in secondary relay activation. Coordination Time Interval (CTI) is time difference between primary and secondary relays in a particular fault. This hinges on the delay due to primary relays, instrument transformers and operating time of circuit breakers.

$$T_b - T_p \geq CTI \tag{9}$$

A predefined time interval should be maintained between the operating times of Primary-Backup relay pairs for sequential operation. The coordination time interval between the primary and the secondary relays must not be violated to avoid false tripping of protective relays in the system. Thus, we choose 0.3 and 0.4 as the range of CTI for this work is 0.3 to 0.4 s.

3.2 Smell Agent Optimization (SAO)

The SAO is one of the most recent metaheuristics algorithm a new metaheuristics algorithm inspired from the concept of smell perception [25, 26]. The operating principles of the algorithm revolved around three distinct modes describes as follows:

Sniffing Mode. This mode implements the aptitude of a smell agent sniff the presence of a smell molecules within its surrounding. For instance, the molecules smell constantly diffused from a smell source towards the agent. A smell agent sniffs these molecules and classify the smell as pleasant or harmful. Assuming N is the total number of smell molecules (number of optimization sample) diffusing from a source, if D is the dimension of search space (number of optimization variable), then, the smell molecules is generated as Eq. (10).

$$x_i^t = [x_{N,1}^t, \; x_{N,2}^t, \ldots, \; x_{N,D}^t] \tag{10}$$

Since the smell molecules diffuse like gas molecules, each molecule in Eq. (10) is given a velocity with which they diffuse using Eq. (11)

$$v_i^t = [v_{N,1}^t, \; v_{N,2}^t, \ldots, \; v_{N,D}^t] \tag{11}$$

From Eq. (10) and Eq. (12), the diffusion of smell molecules is then, represented as:

$$x_i^{t+1} = x_i^t + v_i^t \tag{12}$$

The velocity of smell molecules is updated using Eq. (13)

$$v_i^{t+1} = v_i^t + r_1 \times \sqrt{\frac{3kT}{m}} \tag{13}$$

where, k is a smell constant given by $1.38 \times 10^{-23} JK^{-1}$, r_1 is a random number in the interval of $(0,1]$, m and T are mass and Temperature of smell respectively.

The implementation of the sniffing mode is consequently represented as Eq. (14):

$$x_i^{t+1} = x_i^t + v_i^{t+1} \tag{14}$$

Trailing Mode. In this mode, the agent evaluates the fitness of the sniffing mode and then determine its own position and the position of the worst smell molecules. The agent can then search for the object generating smell molecule by sprawling the path of smell with maximum concentration. This behavior is modeled into sniffing mode as in Eq. (15).

$$x_i^{t+1} = x_i^t + r_2 \times olc \times (x_i^t - x_{agent}^t) - r_3 \times olf \times (x_i^t - x_{worst}^t) \tag{15}$$

where, olc is agent olfaction capacity, r_2 and r_3 are random number in the range of 0 and 1, x_{agent}^t is the sniffing position of the agent (which is the molecules with the best fitness) and x_{worst}^t is the molecules with the worst fitness.

Random Mode. The random mode is a tactics the agent adopts to avoid loss of trail. This mode can be implemented as follows Eq. (16):

$$x_i^{t+1} = x_i^t + r_4 \times \phi \tag{16}$$

where r_4 is a random number generated in the interval of $(0,1]$, ϕ is a constant step size. The pseudo code implementation of SAO is given in Algorithm 1.

Algorithm 1: SAO Description

Input: $X : n \times m$ matrix of smell molecules, other algorithm parameters:

Output: $Y : n \times 1$, position of best smell molecules

$n \leftarrow$ size(X)

best $\leftarrow$ an empty dictionary

for $k = 1$ to n do

    Sniffing

    Trailing

    Random

y: #return solution of best mode

end for

$best_{sorted} \leftarrow$ **sort**(y)

$y \leftarrow$ key $(best_{sorted}[0])$

---

4 Results and Discussion

This section discusses the result of relay coordination obtained using both SAO and PSO algorithms on two IEEE test system. We computing the optimized values for the TMS, PS and relays operating time (Objective Function-OF). The results obtained for IEEE standard 15 bus test systems and IEEE standard 30 bus test systems are presented in Subsect. 4.1 and 4.2 respectively.

4.1 Results Analysis on IEEE 15-Bus System

The results showing the optimized values of TMS and PS on IEEE 15 bus standard test system is given in Table 1. The table also presents the optimized values obtained for relays operating time. These results were obtained using a fixed current transformer ratio of 500:1 in the simulation. To ensure stability of the results, the simulation was run 20 times and the average of these runs were presented.

It is observed that, the cost function value which are the sum of the individual operating time of the relays obtained by PSO and SAO are 23.2221 s and 16.2065 s respectively. These results showed that the SAO performed better than PSO by 31.78%. The convergence analysis of both algorithms on the IEEE 15 bus test system is shown in Fig. 2.

The convergence analysis showed that PSO converges to it optimum operating time faster than the SAO. From Fig. 2, it took PSO 11th iteration to converge, while the SAO convergences after 32nd iteration.

4.2 Results Analysis on IEEE 30-Bus Test

Experimental results obtained on IEEE standard 30-bus relay coordination test system are presented in this subsection. Table 2 shows the optimized values obtained for the time multiliyer settings, plug settings and the relays operating.

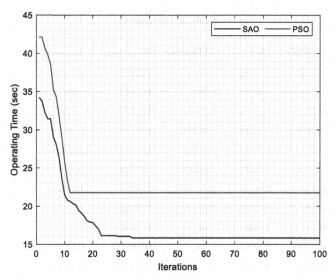

Fig. 2. Operarting time convergence for IEEE 15 bus-test system.

Table 2. Results for IEEE 15 bus test systems

Relay No.	PS-PSO	PS-SAO	TMS-PSO	TMS-SAO	$T_{op\text{-}PSO}$	$T_{op\text{-}SAO}$
1	0.8136	0.5678	0.3126	0.2182	0.522	0.3643
2	0.6609	0.4612	0.4307	0.3006	0.8189	0.5715
3	0.7812	0.5452	0.6612	0.4614	1.3223	0.9228
4	0.5686	0.3968	0.3987	0.2782	0.8181	0.5709
5	0.7974	0.5565	0.2053	0.1433	0.4712	0.3288
6	0.7596	0.5301	0.1948	0.1359	0.496	0.3462
7	0.7318	0.5107	0.2042	0.1425	0.5036	0.3515
8	0.5375	0.3751	0.4567	0.3187	1.0909	0.7613
9	0.7927	0.5532	0.2263	0.1579	0.4546	0.3173
10	0.6592	0.4600	0.235	0.1640	0.5055	0.3528
11	0.7277	0.5079	0.3409	0.2379	0.7582	0.5291
12	0.8165	0.5698	0.2103	0.1468	0.5405	0.3772
13	0.6887	0.4806	0.7773	0.5425	1.4967	1.0445
14	0.7113	0.4964	0.4189	0.2923	0.9242	0.6450
15	0.5057	0.3529	0.4749	0.3314	0.9402	0.6562
16	0.5319	0.3712	0.3462	0.2416	0.7627	0.5323

(*continued*)

Table 2. (*continued*)

Relay No.	PS-PSO	PS-SAO	TMS-PSO	TMS-SAO	$T_{op\text{-}PSO}$	$T_{op\text{-}SAO}$
17	0.817	0.5702	0.4087	0.2852	0.9459	0.6601
18	0.6917	0.4827	0.2597	0.1812	0.6271	0.4376
19	0.7255	0.5063	0.2512	0.1753	0.5581	0.3895
20	0.5826	0.4066	0.1709	0.1193	0.3883	0.2710
21	0.7172	0.5005	0.5222	0.3644	1.2783	0.8921
22	0.5276	0.3682	0.2441	0.1704	0.5792	0.4042
23	0.726	0.5067	0.5544	0.3869	1.4856	1.0368
24	0.5617	0.3920	0.5566	0.3884	1.4473	1.0101
25	0.7166	0.5001	0.4069	0.2840	0.9957	0.6949
26	0.8396	0.5859	0.242	0.1689	0.6885	0.4805
27	0.7342	0.5124	0.3541	0.2471	0.8744	0.6102
28	0.6161	0.4300	0.3694	0.2578	0.9281	0.6477
					$\sum OF$ 23.2221	15.8421

From Table 2, we noticed that, the optimized objective function values obtained by SAO and PSO for 30-bus IEEE test system are 20.1414 and 27.9588 respectively. This also indicate a 29.96% improvement of SAO over PSO algorithm. However, the convergence plot given in Fig. 3 show that, the PSO converged faster than the SAO algorithm. From the figure, the PSO converged to its optimum operating time after the 12th iteration, while the SAO took up to 21st iteration to converge to its optimum results (Table 3).

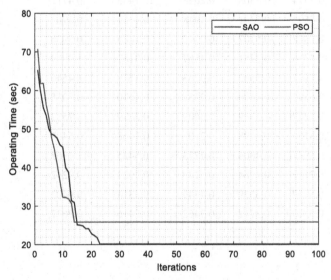

Fig. 3. Operarting time convergence for IEEE 30 bus-test system.

Table 3. Results for IEEE 30 bus test systems

Relay No.	PS-PSO	PS-SAO	TMS-PSO	TMS-SAO	Top-PSO	Top-SAO
1	0.6240	0.4495	0.2292	0.1651	0.4022	0.2897
2	0.6082	0.4381	0.2075	0.1495	0.3548	0.2556
3	0.5995	0.4319	0.5998	0.4321	1.2491	0.8998
4	0.6341	0.4568	0.162	0.1167	0.3031	0.2184
5	0.6369	0.4588	0.1846	0.1330	0.3543	0.2552
6	0.7782	0.5606	0.5572	0.4014	1.4213	1.0239
7	0.7788	0.5610	0.3888	0.2801	0.7817	0.5631
8	0.5143	0.3705	0.1153	0.0831	1.2055	0.8684
9	0.5399	0.3889	0.2069	0.1490	0.3492	0.2516
10	0.6586	0.4745	0.2616	0.1885	0.4602	0.3315
11	0.5371	0.3869	0.1684	0.1213	1.3410	0.9661
12	0.7308	0.5265	0.5730	0.4128	1.1520	0.8299
13	0.7644	0.5507	0.1407	0.1014	0.3239	0.2333
14	0.7372	0.5311	0.114	0.0821	1.2718	0.9162
15	0.7509	0.5409	0.3318	0.2390	0.8509	0.6130
16	0.6369	0.4588	0.1846	0.1330	0.2181	0.1571
17	0.5761	0.4150	0.3179	0.2290	0.5437	0.3917
18	0.6970	0.5021	0.3036	0.2187	0.6066	0.4370
19	0.4338	0.3125	0.1434	0.1033	1.2487	0.8996
20	0.7152	0.5152	0.1352	0.0974	0.2914	0.2099
21	0.7105	0.5118	0.1425	0.1027	0.2171	0.1564
22	0.6424	0.4628	0.3741	0.2695	0.7320	0.5273
23	0.4937	0.3557	0.194	0.1398	0.3817	0.2750
24	0.7983	0.5751	0.1926	0.1387	0.5138	0.3701
25	0.5354	0.3857	0.3353	0.2415	0.6975	0.5025
26	0.5938	0.4278	0.5531	0.3985	1.8273	1.3164
27	0.5044	0.3634	0.1576	0.1135	0.4194	0.3021
28	0.6549	0.4718	0.1612	0.1161	0.4343	0.3129
29	0.5507	0.3967	0.327	0.2356	0.7815	0.5630
30	0.5157	0.3715	0.1887	0.1359	0.4162	0.2998
31	0.6152	0.4432	0.2949	0.2124	0.6507	0.4688
32	0.6234	0.4491	0.4461	0.3214	1.0092	0.7270

(continued)

Table 3. (*continued*)

Relay No.	PS-PSO	PS-SAO	TMS-PSO	TMS-SAO	Top-PSO	Top-SAO
33	0.7152	0.5152	0.158	0.1138	0.3027	0.2181
34	0.6568	0.4732	0.4919	0.3544	0.9289	0.6692
35	0.5181	0.3732	0.1382	0.0996	1.2659	0.9119
36	0.6963	0.5016	0.4643	0.3345	0.8619	0.6209
37	0.5991	0.4316	0.5267	0.3794	1.097	0.7903
38	0.5064	0.3648	0.3351	0.2414	0.6922	0.4987
				$\sum OF$	27.9588	20.1414

5 Conclusion and Recommendation

In this paper, we present an optimized solution to directional overcurrent relay coordination using SAO and PSO. First, we expressed the relay coordination problem as a single objective multi-parameter optimization problem where the main focus is to obtain the minimum operating time of the over current relays. We implemented the formulated problem on IEEE standard 15-bus systems and IEEE standard 30-bus system as a practical means of validating our developed model. All simulation was carried in Matlab R2019b simulation environment. Comparative results showed that the SAO obtained best operating time in both the IEEE 15 and 30 bus test system which 15.8421 s and 20.1414 s respectively as against 23.2221 s and 27.9588 s obtained by PSO. However, the PSO converges faster than SAO in both test systems.

In our next research, we will consider various system compensation and implement the compensated OCR system using SAO. The performance of SAO will be compared with other optimization algorithms such as those present [27, 28]. The SAO will be applied to other engineering problems such HRES, MPPT, intelligent control systems etc.

References

1. El-Khattam, W., Salama, M.: Distributed generation technologies, definitions and benefits. Electric Power Syst. Res. **71**(2), 119–128 (2004)
2. Zellagui, M., et al.: Mixed integer optimization of IDMT overcurrent relays in the resence of wind energy farms using PSO algorithm. Periodica Polytech. Electr. Eng. Comput. Sci. **59**(1), 9–17 (2015)
3. Mousavi Motlagh, S.H., Mazlumi, K.: Optimal overcurrent relay coordination using optimized objective function. ISRN Power Eng. **2014** (2014)
4. Razavi, F., et al.: A new comprehensive genetic algorithm method for optimal overcurrent relays coordination. Electric Power Syst. Res. **78**(4), 713–720 (2008)
5. Mancer, N., Mahdad, B., Srairi, K.: Optimal coordination of directional overcurrent relays using PSO-TVAC considering series compensation. Adv. Electr. Electron. Eng. **13**(2), 96–106 (2015)

6. Hussain, M.H., Rahim, S.R.A., Musirin, I.: Optimal overcurrent relay coordination: a review. Procedia Eng. **53**(1), 332–336 (2013)
7. Patel, A., Mathur, H., Bhanot, S.: An improved control method for unified power quality conditioner with unbalanced load. Int. J. Electr. Power Energy Syst. **100**, 129–138 (2018)
8. Singh, M., Panigrahi, B., Abhyankar, A.: Optimal overcurrent relay coordination in distribution system. In: 2011 International Conference on Energy, Automation and Signal. IEEE (2011)
9. Bedekar, P.P., Bhide, S.R., Kale, V.S.: Optimum coordination of overcurrent relays in distribution system using genetic algorithm. In: 2009 International Conference on Power Systems. IEEE (2009)
10. Vijayakumar, D., Nema, R.: A novel optimal setting for directional over current relay coordination using particle swarm optimization. Int. J. Electr. Power Energy Syst. Eng. **1**(4) (2008)
11. Najy, W.K., Zeineldin, H.H., Woon, W.L.: Optimal protection coordination for microgrids with grid-connected and islanded capability. IEEE Trans. Ind. Electron. **60**(4), 1668–1677 (2012)
12. Shih, M.Y., et al.: Enhanced differential evolution algorithm for coordination of directional overcurrent relays. Electric Power Syst. Res. **143**, 365–375 (2017)
13. Raza, S., Mahmood, T., Bukhari, S.: Optimum overcurrent relay coordination: a review. Nucleus **51**(1), 37–49 (2014)
14. Zeineldin, H., El-Saadany, E., Salama, M.: Optimal coordination of overcurrent relays using a modified particle swarm optimization. Electric Power Syst. Res. **76**(11), 988–995 (2006)
15. Zellagui, M., Abdelaziz, A.Y.: Optimal coordination of directional overcurrent relays using hybrid PSO-DE algorithm. Int. Electr. Eng. J. (IEEJ) **6**(4), 1841–1849 (2015)
16. Farzinfar, M., Jazaeri, M., Razavi, F.: A new approach for optimal coordination of distance and directional over-current relays using multiple embedded crossover PSO. Int. J. Electr. Power Energy Syst. **61**, 620–628 (2014)
17. Kheshti, M., Tekpeti, B.S., Kang, X.: The optimal coordination of over-current relay protection in radial network based on particle swarm optimization. In: 2016 IEEE PES Asia-Pacific Power and Energy Engineering Conference (APPEEC). IEEE (2016)
18. Darji, G., et al.: A tuned cuckoo search algorithm for optimal coordination of directional overcurrent relays. In: 2015 International Conference on Power and Advanced Control Engineering (ICPACE). IEEE (2015)
19. Al-Roomi, A.R., El-Hawary, M.E.: Optimal coordination of directional overcurrent relays using hybrid BBO/DE algorithm and considering double primary relays strategy. In: 2016 IEEE Electrical Power and Energy Conference (EPEC). IEEE (2016)
20. Bouchekara, H., Zellagui, M., Abido, M.A.: Optimal coordination of directional overcurrent relays using a modified electromagnetic field optimization algorithm. Appl. Soft Comput. **54**, 267–283 (2017)
21. Rezaei, N., et al.: Genetic algorithm-based optimization of overcurrent relay coordination for improved protection of DFIG operated wind farms. IEEE Trans. Ind. Appl. **55**(6), 5727–5736 (2019)
22. Karegar, H.K., et al.: Pre-processing of the optimal coordination of overcurrent relays. Electric Power Syst. Res. **75**(2–3), 134–141 (2005)
23. Godwal, S.D., Pandya, K.S., Rajput, V.N., Vora, S.C.: A review on approaches employed for solving directional overcurrent relays' coordination problem. In: Mehta, A., Rawat, A., Chauhan, P. (eds.) Advances in Electric Power and Energy Infrastructure. LNEE, vol. 608, pp. 35–51. Springer, Singapore (2020). https://doi.org/10.1007/978-981-15-0206-4_4
24. Saleh, K.A., et al.: Optimal coordination of directional overcurrent relays using a new time–current–voltage characteristic. IEEE Trans. Power Deliv. **30**(2), 537–544 (2014)

25. Salawudeen, A.T., et al.: On the development of a novel smell agent optimization (SAO) for optimization problems. i-managers J. Pattern Recogn. **5**(4), 287–297 (2018)
26. Salawudeen, A.T., et al.: From smell phenomenon to smell agent optimization (SAO): a feasibility study. Proc. Int. Conf. Global Emerg. Trends ICGET **2**(5), 99–110 (2016)
27. Adubi, S.A., Misra, S.: A comparative study on the ant colony optimization algorithms. In: Proceedings 11th International Conference on Electronics, Computer and Computation (ICECCO), Abuja, pp. 1–4. IEEE (2014)
28. Crawford, B., et al.: A teaching-learning-based optimization algorithm for the weighted set-covering problem. Tehnički vjesnik **27**(5), 1678–1684 (2020)

A Gamified Technique to Improve Users' Phishing and Typosquatting Awareness

Adebayo Omotosho[1]([⊠]) [iD], Divine Awazie[2], Peace Ayegba[1] [iD],
and Justice Emuoyibofarhe[1] [iD]

[1] Mobile and e-Computing Research Group, Department of Computer Science and Engineering,
Ladoke Akintola University of Technology, Ogbomoso, Nigeria
bayotosho@gmail.com
[2] Department of Computer Science, Landmark University, Omu-Aran, Kwara, Nigeria

Abstract. Security is an important aspect of technology and it requires continuous attention, but the user agent plays a crucial role in cyber risks that sensitive data are exposed to. Users' mistakes and nonchalant behavior have been found to be responsible for various breaches resulting in the increase of identity theft, extortion, loss of information and possibilities of intrusion. This paper explores the use of web-based gamification application to motivate users of the web to be cyber conscious through a fun approach designed to improve their online behavior. Results of the study shows the potentials of a gamified technique in enhancing security awareness and building more secure behaviours in users.

Keywords: Gamification · Phishing · Typosquatting · User-engagement · Web-based app

1 Introduction

In computing, security is the combination of cybersecurity and physical security to prevent unauthorized access to virtual information and physical systems where sensitive information resides [1–4]. Cybersecurity includes all measures taken to protect networks, interconnected systems including hardware and software devices and data from attacks, damages, unauthorized access and other cyber threats [5]. In recent years, cyber-attacks have outgrown exploiting vulnerabilities in computer infrastructure but now focus on human weaknesses which are now more evident with the increase of social engineering attacks thus making cyberattacks more complicated and difficult to combat [6, 7]. End-users are often lured into breaking security protocols and giving out sensitive information and this is often done through internet fraud, phishing attacks, spams and so on [8]. Many studies have focused on technological interventions in solving cyber-attacks and neglected human weaknesses and vulnerabilities [9], but human errors have been reported to be responsible for 37% of cyberattack incidents that occurred in 2015 particularly in healthcare [10, 11]. In 2016, the top causes of cyber-attacks were phishing emails, hacking and malware incidents all of which were also attributed to human errors [10]. An investigation by Sophos Security Company showed that, of the 45% phishing

© Springer Nature Switzerland AG 2021
S. Misra and B. Muhammad-Bello (Eds.): ICTA 2020, CCIS 1350, pp. 403–414, 2021.
https://doi.org/10.1007/978-3-030-69143-1_31

attacks that occurred in the United Kingdom between 2016 and 2018, 54% were caused by employees clicking on spam links or replying to fake emails [12]. Typo-squatters are also cybercriminals who buy URLs of famous brands with the intent of deceiving internet users or selling the URLs eventually to the real brand owners [13]. Many of the fake domains also instigate phishing attacks, steal sensitive information and add malware to the user's computer systems. In 2017, the Identity Theft Resource Center (ITRC) recorded a total of 1579 device breaches which is a 44.7% increase from that of 2016 with a total of 14.2 million credit card numbers exposed [14]. With sensitive information such as the user's social security number, credit card information, home, and email addresses, legal notices and health information leaked, customers can be easily blackmailed or terrorized. The neglect of cybersecurity re-education could result in an increase of identity theft, extortion, loss of information and possibilities of intrusion [3, 15].

Interestingly, some studies have shown that lack of adequate information on cyber-security, inadaptability of secure approaches, and lack of social motivation are some of the reason's users break security protocols [16, 17]. In order to deal with the attacks that result from human errors, increasing awareness and building security-oriented cultures have been recommended through end-user training, education, and other human-centric safeguards [7, 9, 17, 18]. Various advances in learning technologies have given rise to online delivery, game-based, simulation-based and video-based methods for teaching or training users on cybersecurity [19–23]. This paper will focus on a game-based app-roach; gamification is the utilization of technology to animate diversion attributes with the possibility to propel players [24, 25]. Gamification can be used as a training method to motivate learners, with the use of components such as leaderboards, points, badges, and difficulties which enables users to perform certain tasks or assignments and upgrade their profile [26, 27].

Whereas gamification focuses on increasing users' engagement and motivation, seri-ous games follow a typical game structure but include a learning strategy or objective [28]. Serious games often follow a story narrative and instigate behavioral changes over time. Although several serious game-based applications for cybersecurity such as Cyber-ciege, Antiphishing Phil, InternetHero, and PICOCTF, have been developed, very few have been evaluated and proven effective [29]. Lean, shallow and deep gamification are other popular gamification approaches. Lean gamification focuses on gamifying abstract learning activities rather than core contents, it teaches the real behaviours and outcomes of diverse events that imitate an overall system allowing for a positive, competitive and cooperative environment [30, 31]. Deep gamification introduces game elements that alter the core steps in learning while in shallow gamification, the core learning process is not altered. Shallow gamification techniques include the use of stars and badges and though have been criticized for excessive motivation [32]. The use of game-based strategies has been recommended in cybersecurity education; the use of game-theory for cybersecurity education has great potentials in promoting cybersecurity knowledge, engaging young minds and instilling in them adequate expertise required for cyber-secure behavior even while learning new and existing advancements in cybersecurity [20, 21, 33].

The following sections have been ordered as follows. Section two gives a detailed description of the methodology used in developing the proposed system as well as the system architecture, Section three details the implementation phase, Section four gives the results and discussion of findings and Sect. 5 is the concluding chapter of the study.

2 Methodology

A web-based gamified system was developed to improve the cybersecurity behavior of users by training them to identify some common web spoofing attacks. These attacks may make a forged website look similar to a legitimate website, or user typing wrong uniform resource locator (typosquatting) which also takes them to a genuinely faked website. Our review of users most visited websites showed that google.com, youtube.com, facebook.com, baidu.com, and insta-gram.com remains the top 5 most visited website [34, 35]. Therefore, our framework in Fig. 1 is built around some of these frequently visited websites by using snapshots of the real sites and their pharmed or phished counterpart which are then arranged in a four-picture grid where users were asked to identify or distinguish a real page. The game also included a timer in order to make the app more competitive and enjoyable.

2.1 Components of the Proposed System

Users: These are individuals who use the app and they are the most important entity in the entire system because they are the learners whose cybersecurity psychology the app is trying to re-train.

Devices: These are the platforms through which users can access the gamified system and participate in the learning process. Gamified application server: This is a localhost server where the gamified application is hosted. This research makes use of xampp as a localhost server.

Picture Database: This is the database in the gamified application that contains all the snapshots of some selected real websites' home pages and their pharmed counterparts used for this study.

Administrator: This is the person who will be in charge of the entire system and will be making a regular update to the database.

Leaderboard: This is a feature that allows players to be ranked according to their performance in the game. The leaderboard recognizes the players who have acquired the most points and puts them at the top of the list and at the same time lets other players know who they have to surpass and how far ahead they are. It is a great way to preview the top-ranked players regularly.

Score Sheet: This shows the real-time performance of the player toward achieving the set goals. The human-centered design approach based on [36] was adopted in the development model for this research. It is an approach to interactive framework development that aims to make a system usable and useful by focusing on the users, their needs and requirements, by applying human factor and usability knowledge and techniques.

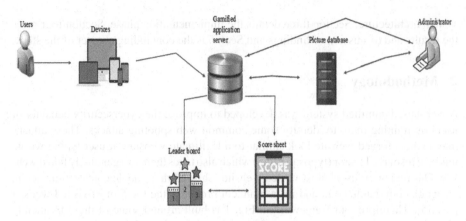

Fig. 1. System architecture

The web-based gamified app aims at mitigating typosquatting and phishing threats that arise from users' mistakes or carelessness. For instance, typosquatting depends on internet users' mistakes when they type an incorrect web address in their browsers e.g. (instgram.com instead of instagram.com). The learning goal of this research is derived based on the topic of cyber threats and their mitigation in our computer security course curriculum.

3 Implementation

Some functional screenshots that described the different components of the application are compiled in this section to give a better understanding of how the application works. Figure 2 shows the login page of the system. A user must enter their login details before they will be able to access the system and if the user is not registered, the system will require them to register first before they can access the system. Figure 3 shows the registration page. There are three options on the landing page, a play game button that takes the user to the gaming environment, the leaderboard option and the logout option.

The game screen is the core of the application, where users accumulate points overtime from the gameplay. This interface is the interactive page between the user and the application, users are expected to pick the correct web page from the pictures displayed. The correct option must be picked within the time allocated to the stage; the point is then assigned based on the time taken to get the right option. Users can also check their present score and also view the leaderboard. The game screen has multiple views; the game grid and the success screen notification that pops up after a stage is completed, the 'try again' notification pops up when a question is failed. Additional features include on the game screen include three icons at the bottom of the screen, the extreme left is the timer for the stage, the middle icon keeps track of question number been answered, the right icon is the next button that moves the user to the next question on click. Figure 4, 5 and Fig. 6 show samples of the game interfaces for Facebook, Instagram and Google tests. The leaderboard in Fig. 7 is a visual representation of the performance history of participants based on heights attained in order of hierarchy. In this study, the game points awarded per question is 10 points and players are ranked based on the number of points in descending order.

4   Results and Discussion

4.1   Testing and Rating

Users were asked to rate the application based on how the system influenced their phishing and typosquatting awareness. 105 users tested and rated the application on a scale of 1 to 5 where 1,2,3,4,5 was coded as very low, low, neutral, high and very high respectively in the application. The different statistical distribution of the scores and ratings, such as the mean, mode, and standard deviation are shown in Fig. 8 and Table 1. The students participated in the testing over a period of 3 weeks, the most frequent score was 400 marks which were obtained by 20% of the students. 40% of the students

Fig. 2. User login page

Fig. 3. Registration page

Fig. 4. Gaming screen (a)

Fig. 5. Gaming screen (b)

Fig. 6. Gaming screen (c)

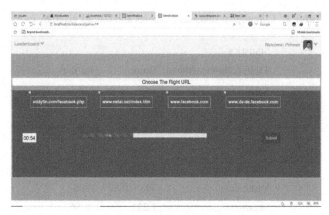

Fig. 7. Gaming screen (d)

rated the application high and 33% rated the application very high, and only 6.7% of the students rated the application low. Based on the score and rating crosstabulation in Table 2, out of the 35 students who gave the highest ratings, only 7 students scored 900 and 1000 marks respectively but they do not have the highest scores. The 14 students with the highest scores of 2000 rated the influence high but also did not give the highest ratings. This means that a student with the highest score might not necessarily give the highest rating.

Fig. 8. Gaming screen and leaderboard

However, from a deeper look using the Pearson chi-square tests in Table 3, it shows a p-value less than 0.05 which indicates the scores and ratings are significantly dependent on each other. In Table 4, Pearson's R-value in the symmetric measures is greater than 0.5 (indicating that the correlation is a "strong positive"). A strong positive value shows that as the scores are directly proportional to the ratings meaning students with high scores would possibly give high ratings. This means that our participants are likely to benefit from the developed app through more practice. (Fig 9)

Table 1. Cumulative statistics of scores and ratings given by users

Statistics		
Table column subhead	Score	Rating
Valid	105	105
Missing	0	0
Mean	696.67	4.00
Median	500.00	4.00
Std. Deviation	590.602	.899
Variance	348810.897	.808
Skewness	1.221	−.567
Std. Error of skewness	.236	.236
Kurtosis	.589	−.465
Std. Error of kurtosis	.467	.467
Range	2000	3

Table 2. Crosstabulation of users' scores and ratings

Score * Rating crosstabulation						
	Rating					Total
Score		2	3	4	5	
	0	7	0	0	0	7
	50	0	0	7	0	7
	300	0	0	7	7	14
	400	0	7	7	7	21
	500	0	0	7	7	14
	700	0	7	0	0	7
	900	0	0	0	7	7
	1000	0	0	7	7	14
	2000	0	7	7	0	14
Total		7	21	42	35	105

Table 3. Chi-square test for Users' scores against ratings

	Chi-square tests		
	Value	df	Asymp. Sig. (2-sided)
Pearson Chi-square	182.000	24	.000
Likelihood ratio	135.606	24	.000
Linear-by-Linear association	.000	1	1.000

Table 4. Pearson's R and Spearman correlation of users' scores against the rating

	Symmetric measures				
		Value	Asymp. Std. Error	Approx. T	Approx. Sig.
Interval by interval	Pearson's R	.000	.098	.000	1.000
Ordinal by Ordinal	Spearman Correlation	.093	.105	.950	.344
N of valid cases			105		

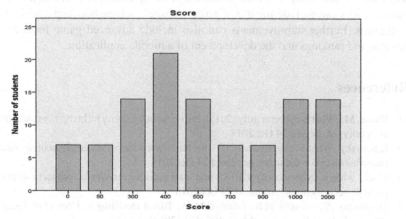

Fig. 9. Students' vs Scores chart

4.2 Discussion of Findings

A study carried out by [36, 37] showed that there are several cases of cybersecurity negligence particularly in developing countries, and proposed the need for web-based techniques for improving user side awareness of such threats. In a bid to reduce phishing attacks, existing studies have made use of machine learning techniques [38] and analyzing address-bar based features [39]. Several studies have shown significant improvements in the use of gamification methods for improving learning outcomes. However, these studies either made use of a small sample set and only a few evaluated their proposed system [21]. In this study, a gamified method of improving awareness has been developed and evaluated by 105 users. The overall testing phase of the application showed that users found the app easy to use and submitted high ratings after testing the application. We can also infer from the score and ratings cross tabulation, that the users of the application are likely to benefit more from the application with continuous practice and higher scores. The results have also shown the effectiveness of a gamified training approach in improving phishing and typosquatting awareness.

5 Conclusion

Typosquatting and phishing threats thrive off the user's ignorance and negligence which is the leading cause of cyber insecurity. As typosquatting and phishing threats cannot be eradicated completely, users can always use a trainer system to gain awareness. In this paper, gamification was used in a web-based system to train against typosquatting and phishing threats, by using some game elements such as points, leaderboards, and badges to encourage users' participation. The application was evaluated by 105 users using a star rating ranging from 1 through 5. The ratings and scores per user were recorded accordingly, and 33.3% of the test participant gave the application a 5-star rating, 40% gave 4 stars, 20% rated the application 3 stars, 6.7% rated the application 2 stars and no user gave a 1-star rating; this is an indication of the system's performance and influence. Future works can include the use of more website's screenshots and a wider range of challenges. Further improvements can also include advanced game features such as rewards and rankings and the development of a mobile application.

References

1. Rouse, M.: What is cybersecurity (2018). https://searchsecurity.techtarget.com/definition/cyb ersecurity/. Accessed 24 Oct 2018
2. Kaspersky: What is cybersecurity (2018). http://www.kaspersky.com/resource-center/defini tion/what-is-cyber-security/. Accessed 24 Oct 2018
3. Cisco: what is cybersecurity (2018). http://www.cisco.com/c/en/us/products/security/what-is-cyber-security.html/. Accessed 24 Oct 2018
4. Omotosho, A., Ayemlo, H.B., Olaniyi, M.O.: Threat modeling of Internet of Things health devices. J. Appl. Secur. Res. **14**(1), 106–121 (2019)
5. Yan, Z., et al.: Finding the weakest links in the weakest link: How well do undergraduate students make cybersecurity judgments? Comput. Hum. Behav. **84**, 375–382 (2018)

6. Tsohou, A., Karyda, M., Kokolakis, S.: Analyzing the role of cognitive and cultural biases in the internalization of information security policies: recommendations for information security awareness programs. Comput. Secur. **52**, 128–141 (2015)
7. Aldawood, H., Skinner, G.: Educating and raising awareness on cybersecurity social engineering: a literature review. In: 2018 IEEE International Conference on Teaching, Assessment, and Learning for Engineering (TALE), pp. 62–68. IEEE December 2018
8. Omotosho, A., Emuoyibofarhe, J., Meinel, C.: Securing e-prescription from medical identity theft using steganography and antiphishing techniques. J. Appl. Secur. Res. **12**(3), 447–461 (2017)
9. Coffey, J.W.: Ameliorating sources of human error in cybersecurity: technological and human-centered approaches. In: The 8th International Multi-Conference on Complexity, Informatics, and Cybernetics, Pensacola, pp. 85–88 (2017)
10. Daugherty, W.: Human errors is to blame for most breaches, June 2016. http://www.cyb ersecuritytrend.com/topics/cyber-security/articles/421821-human-error-to-blame-most-bre aches.htm. Accessed 16 June 2019
11. Omotosho, A., Emuoyibofarhe, J., Oke, A.: Securing private keys in electronic health records using session-based hierarchical key encryption. J. Appl. Secur. Res. **12**(4), 463–477 (2017)
12. Palmer, D.: Phishing attacks: Half of organisations have fallen victim in last two years, 13 March 2019. https://www.zdnet.com/article/half-of-organisations-have-fallen-victim-to-phi shing-attacks-in-last-two-years/. Accessed 16 June 2019
13. Upcounsel: Cyberlaw: Everything you need to know (2019). https://www.upcounsel.com/cyb er-law. Accessed 16 June 2019
14. ITRC: 2014 Data breaches (2019). https://www.idtheftcenter.org/data-breaches-up-nearly-45-percent-according-to-annual-review-by-identity-theft-resource-center-and-cyberscout/. Accessed 16 June 2019
15. Joyce, A.L., Evans, N., Tanzman, E.A., Israeli, D.: International cyber incident repository system: information sharing on a global scale. In: 2016 International Conference on Cyber Conflict (CyCon US), pp. 1–6. IEEE, October 2016
16. Fagan, M., Khan, M.M.H.: Why do they do what they do?: a study of what motivates users to (not) follow computer security advice. In: 12th Symposium on Usable Privacy and Security (SOUPS 2016), pp. 59–75 (2016)
17. Stewart, G., Lacey, D.: Death by a thousand facts: criticising the technocratic approach to information security awareness. Inf. Manage. Comput. Secur. **20**(1), 29–38 (2012)
18. Mittal, S.: Understanding the human dimension of cyber security. Indian J. Criminol. Criminalistics (ISSN 0970–4345), **34**(1), 141–152 (2015)
19. Holdsworth, J., Apeh, E.: An effective immersive cyber security awareness learning platform for businesses in the hospitality sector. In: 2017 IEEE 25th International Requirements Engineering Conference Workshops (REW), pp. 111–117. IEEE, September 2017
20. Awojana, T., Chou, T.S.: Overview of learning cybersecurity through game based systems. In: Proceedings of the 2019 Conference for Industry and Education Collaboration, pp. 1–9. ASEE, January 2019
21. Hendrix, M., Al-Sherbaz, A., Victoria, B.: Game based cyber security training: are serious games suitable for cyber security training? Int. J. Serious Game. **3**(1), 53–61 (2016)
22. Pastor, V., Díaz, G., Castro, M.: State-of-the-art simulation systems for information security education, training and awareness. In: IEEE EDUCON 2010 Conference, pp. 1907–1916. IEEE April 2010
23. Miranda, M.J.: Enhancing cybersecurity awareness training: a comprehensive phishing exercise approach. Int. Manage. Rev. **14**(2), 5–56 (2018)
24. Hamari, J., Koivisto, J.: Why do people use gamification services? Int. J. Inf. Manage. **35**(4), 419–431 (2015)

25. Omotosho, A., Tyoden, T., Ayegba, P., Ayoola, J.: A gamified approach to improving students participation in farm practice – a case study of Landmark university. Int. J. Interact. Mob. Technol. **13**(5), 94–109 (2019)
26. Koivisto, J., Hamari, J.: Demographic differences in perceived benefits from gamification. Comput. Hum. Behav. **35**, 179–188 (2014)
27. Kapp, K.M., Blair, L., Mesch, R.: The Gamification of Learning and Instruction Fieldbook: Ideas into Practice. John Wiley & Sons, San Fransisco (2014)
28. Boughzala, I., Michel, H.: Introduction to the serious games, gamification and innovation minitrack. In: 2016 49th Hawaii International Conference on System Sciences (HICSS), pp. 817–817. IEEE, January 2016
29. Tioh, J.N., Mina, M., Jacobson, D. W.: Cyber security training a survey of serious games in cyber security. In: 2017 IEEE Frontiers in Education Conference (FIE), pp. 1–5. IEEE, October 2017
30. Santos, P.A.: Deep gamification of a university course. In proceedings of sciences and technologies of interaction (SciTecIN 2015). Departamento de Engenharia Electrotécnica Polo II da Universidade de Coimbra, pp. 1 –5, November 2015
31. Deif, A.: Insights on lean gamification for higher education. Int. J. Lean Six Sigma **8**(3), 359–376 (2017)
32. Bogost, I.: Why Gamification is Bullshit: The Gameful World Approaches, Issues, Applications, pp. 65–80. MIT Press, Cambridge (2015)
33. Alotaibi, F., Furnell, S., Stengel, I., Papadaki, M.: Enhancing cybersecurity awareness with mobile games. In: 2017 12th International Conference for Internet Technology and Secured Transactions (ICITST), pp. 129–134. IEEE December 2017
34. Similarweb: Top Websites Ranking (2019). https://www.similarweb.com/
35. Trackalytics: Free social media and website statistics/analytics (2019). https://www.trackalytics.com/
36. Oyelere, S.S., Sajoh, D.I., Malgwi, Y.M., Oyelere, L.S.: Cybersecurity issues on web-based systems in Nigeria: M-learning case study. In: 2015 International Conference on Cyberspace (CYBER-Abuja), pp. 259–264. IEEE, November 2015
37. Azeez, N.A., Salaudeen, B.B., Misra, S., Damaševičius, R., Maskeliūnas, R.: Identifying phishing attacks in communication networks using URL consistency features. Int. J. Electron. Secur. Digit. Forensics **12**(2), 200–213 (2020)
38. Azeez, N.A., Ade, J., Misra, S., Adewumi, A., Van derVyver, C., Ahuja, R.: Identifying phishing through web content and addressed bar-based features. In: Sharma, N., Chakrabarti, A., Balas, V.E. (eds.) Data Management, Analytics and Innovation. AISC, vol. 1016, pp. 19–29. Springer, Singapore (2020). https://doi.org/10.1007/978-981-13-9364-8_2
39. Osho, O., Oluyomi, A., Misra, S., Ahuja, R., Damasevicius, R., Maskeliunas, R.: Comparative evaluation of techniques for detection of phishing URLs. In: Florez, H., Leon, M., Diaz-Nafria, J.M., Belli, S. (eds.) ICAI 2019. CCIS, vol. 1051, pp. 385–394. Springer, Cham (2019). https://doi.org/10.1007/978-3-030-32475-9_28

Sooner Lightweight Cryptosystem: Towards Privacy Preservation of Resource-Constrained Devices

Abraham Ayegba Alfa(✉) ⓘ, John Kolo Alhassanⓘ, Olayemi Mikail Olaniyiⓘ,
and Morufu Olalereⓘ

Federal University of Technology, Minna, Nigeria
abraham.alfa@st.futminna.edu.ng, {jkalhassan,mikail.olaniyi,
lerejide}@futminna.edu.ng

Abstract. The use of cryptosystem became popular because of the increased need for exchanges across untrusted medium especially Internet-enabled networks. On the basis of application several forms of cryptosystems have been developed for purpose of authentication, confidentiality, integrity, and non-repudiation. Cryptosystems make use of encryption schemes that convert plaintext to ciphertext in diverse areas of applications. The vast progressions in the Internet of Things (IoT) technology and resource-constrained devices have given rise to massive deployment of sensor devices and growth of services targeted at lightweight devices. Though, these devices support a number of services, they require strong lightweight encryption approaches for privacy protection of data. Existing lightweight cryptosystems fall short on the expected privacy levels and applicability in emerging resource-constrained environment. This paper develops a mathematical model for a Sooner lightweight cryptographic scheme based on reduced and hardened ciphertext block sizes, hash sizes and key sizes of traditional cryptosystems and Public Blockchain technology for ubiquitous systems. Thereafter, the hardening procedure offered by the RSA homomorphic encryption was applied for the purpose of generating stronger, secure and lightweight AES, RSA and SHA-3 in order to deal with untrusted channels exchanges. The proposed Sooner is recommended for adoption in public Blockchain-based smart systems and applications for the purpose of data privacy.

Keywords: Lightweight cryptosystem · Block size · Key size · Resource-constrained devices · Hashes · Hardening

1 Introduction

There is need to address the various problems faced by users when generating, storing and transmitting data across the cloud-based services [1]. There are high demands to secure cloud infrastructure stack at network, host, application and data levels. A number of data security problems have been reported in [2] including: data privacy, confidentiality and authentication. In cloud services such as traditional smart rice farming that is built on

© Springer Nature Switzerland AG 2021
S. Misra and B. Muhammad-Bello (Eds.): ICTA 2020, CCIS 1350, pp. 415–429, 2021.
https://doi.org/10.1007/978-3-030-69143-1_32

cloud utilizes plaintext data format for generation, transmission and storage. Recently, users are capable of applying encryption and decryption algorithms for the purpose of providing protection for data for varying processing operations [2]. According to studies in [3, 4], encryption approaches are most effective means of preserving privacy of all kinds of sensitive data or information. The process of many old generation encryption systems relies on secret keys sharing (such as private or public keys) within users' nodes for communicating encrypted messages, which are susceptible to privacy breaches [3].

Recently, it was possible for content of encrypted data to be shared with third party having no need for it; and especially on untrusted servers, providers and operators that are required to carry out diverse computation and maintenance of users' encrypted data relationships such as DynamoDB deployed on Amazon Web Service public cloud [5].

In effect, lightweight cryptosystems are most desirable in bringing reprieve to IoT and ubiquitous settings [4]. Several lightweight cryptosystems are available with substantial protection guarantees, better speed of execution, real-time, energy dissipation and memory specifications. Nevertheless, these schemes have enormous key sizes and take up internal memory spaces and with large authentication processes. Also, information collection and processing on real-time bases could be impacted, and diminishes resources of IoT.

This paper presents a mathematical derivation and preliminary evaluation of the Sooner cryptographic scheme using lightweight cryptosystems, hashing algorithms and homomorphic encryption hardening procedure for ubiquitous systems. The remaining parts of the paper are structured as follows: Sect. 2 is the literature review. Section 3 is the methodology. Section 4 is the results. The conclusion is in Sect. 5.

2 Literature Review

2.1 Ubiquitous Data Protection Issues

One major drawback for deploying ubiquitous is organizing the multifaceted networks into a complete IP system, in addition to ensuring that resulting systems enjoy high quality services, availability, reliability and flexibility. In everyday life of peoples, IoT have played huge roles in workplaces, families, social facilities, enterprises and lifestyles. Consequently, they are capable of harvesting, storing and broadcasting enormous personal details about their owners; thereby throwing up security and privacy issues in cloud communication [1]. Wireless Ad-hoc networks continue to evolve serve moving objects especially with birth of IoT [6]. Regardless of the huge benefits of wireless exchanges, several issues abound such as disconnection, interference of transmission, sparse availability, low power, low computation, attacks and fading of signals [7].

IoT is renowned for facilitating remote communication and transmission of media. The main idea of IoT is to facilitate the interconnections of things, data, processes, and persons into simple networks with increased benefits and pertinence. Traditionally, IoT is composed of consistent computing objects (including sensors, RFID tags, mobile phones and actuators), digital machines and persons, which make data transfer across a network feasible needless of human-to-human or human-to-computer interfaces [8].

Conversely, IoT devices have evolved into vast and multifaceted network owing to the huge quantity of data communicated across it. These growths could face enormous challenges and risks including management of huge data generations, energy inefficiencies, low processing capabilities, security threats, and large data encryption/decryption operations [1]. More problematic is the dealing with these issues in connected IoT settings for the smart devices. Hence, the quest for development and usage of suitable cryptographic solutions for embedded applications. As a result, the traditional cryptographic schemes (such as 1204-bit RSA algorithm) became unfit for smart devices (such as RFID tags) [9].

2.2 Hardening of Data Encryption Schemes

Homomorphic encryption is described as an encryption approach with allowable operations on ciphertext by means of public key algorithms for secured data storage and broadcast operations [10]. The idea is to generate outcomes on plaintext upon appropriate calculations done by the users of big data for the purpose of security. It has been applied to wireless sensor networks and cloud computing in order to provide privacy preservation, private retrieval of information and aggregation of data.

The traditional cryptosystems utilize varying sizes of public keys infrastructure (PKI), which form the bases of their classification (that is, symmetric and asymmetric). There are high risks of attacks and threats to traditional cryptosystems. There are no data privacy protection assurances. Consequently, homomorphic encryption is being considered to overcome the identified challenges in traditional cryptosystems (such as data privacy). However, they require ample amount of time to complete encryption and decryption operations on data due to its complexity [11].

Another kind of cryptosystem was introduced with regards to protection of multimedia data is selective encryption. The goal is to minimize the complexities of data securing processes though the speedups of available encryption standards such as AES and DES. This generates two information partitions: firstly, private subsection deserving strong security, and public subsection requiring weak cryptographic scheme. But, few issues were observed including optimal size of private subsection, and the leakage of valuable information arising from weak protection for public subsections as well as its suitability for multimedia content only [12].

The concept of homomorphism in abstract algebra is a map preserving all the algebraic structures between the range and domain of an algebraic set. The map is a function or operation taking an input from the set of domains to produce an item in the range of addition and multiplication as an output [3]. In the context of cryptography, homomorphic encryption functions enable two distinct operations to be applied to the ciphertext on the bases of its two attributes including: additive and multiplicative homomorphism [3, 11]. In case of the additive homomorphism, addition operation is to be carried out on the ciphertext whenever the decrypt text has analogous operation as the plaintext obtainable by Paillier algorithm as shown in Eq. 1.

$$S(t_1 + t_2) = S(t_1) + S(t_2) \tag{1}$$

In the same vein, the multiplicative operation is to be carried out on the ciphertext whenever the decrypt text has similar operation carried out on the plaintext by Rivest-Shamir-Adelman (RSA) algorithm as shown in Eq. 2.

$$S(t_1 * t_2) = S(t_1) * S(t_2) \tag{2}$$

where, S is encryption function, t_1 and t_2 is the message samples.

The benefits accruable from homomorphic encryption over the traditional cryptosystems (that is, symmetric and asymmetric) include: improved privacy and confidentiality: Homomorphic encryption enforces optimal confidentiality of encryption and decryption keys as well as required operations to be carried out on the ciphertext. This minimizes the frequency of attacks when compared to the traditional cryptosystems.

The forms of homomorphic encryptions [13] are: the partially homomorphic encryption (PHE), somewhat homomorphic encryption (SWHE), and the fully homomorphic encryption (FHE). The PHE utilizes one of the additive or multiplicative functions to carry operations on the ciphertext such as RSA, Paillier and ElGamal (asymmetric) cryptosystems. The SWHE uses additive functions whereas the FHE combines the distinct operations on the cyphertext with addition and multiplication such as Graig Gentry schema (lattice-based cryptosystem). SWHE enables certain kinds of operations and a limited amount of usage. FHE enables all kinds of operations and unlimited usages as against PHE and SWHE [3]. They are applied to domain of sensitive data storage and secure communication by means of hop-to-hop and end-to-end encryptions.

2.3 Privacy Preservation Approaches

The main philosophy of Blockchain relies on the use of private key in order to unlock the digital assets protected with cryptographic schemes [14]. Nevertheless, the private keys become greatly susceptible to injections attacks in Blockchain system. The usual practice for safeguarding private keys is achieved the use of hardware or software digital wallets (such as Keepkey or Trezor). Recently, hardware security modules (HSMs) approaches allowed the use of a crypto-processor to securely creates, protects and stores keys. Accordingly, the complete cryptographic key lifecycle takes place inside the HSM, which is a standalone device operating offline or embedded in a server. The HSM can be hardened to counter damage or tampering situated in a secure location to check unapproved access. Presently, the ultra-secure Personal Computers (PCs) come with an in-built HSM that requires two-factor authentication [15] in tamper-proof casing for the purpose of automatic deletion of the private key to forestall breaches of logical and physical security controls [16].

Theorem 1. The length of encryption keys is relational to the brute-force attacks successes rates. It implies that longer encryption keys provide most protection for data against brute-force related threats. Given that the encryption key size is a 256-bit, a brute-force attacker may take up decades to break. This is unsuitable for IoT devices because of their shortfalls in terms of computational and memory capabilities. Nevertheless, the AES schemes are widespread, and most effective for preventing brute-force risks in WiFi, SSH, Skype and other network-based applications [17] such as resource-constrained devices.

Proof. The encryption key of 128-bit is appropriate. Even more challenging is to utilize the lightweight AES on portable 8-bit processor based IoT devices, which involves lesser than a 128-bit encryption key sizes and matching decryption key sizes. This diminishes the level of protection available to the data leading to susceptibility of cyphertext.

Theorem 2. In cloud-based services, information outsourcing is commonplace for the purpose of processing or storage due to perceived security, privacy and resilience. The hardening of data protection is a concept that enables several techniques aside encryption alone to be utilized to counter continuous attacks capable of altering, destroying or spying on sensitive information [12, 18]. Though, encryption techniques are evolving to include lightweight encryption schemes; high complexity in terms of computation, low cipher block sizes or PKIs continue to limit their performances.

Proof. To strengthen the security level offered by the encryption schemes, a hardening information security is proposed in this paper. Therefore, the paper introduces a second layer of encryption that enables usage of encrypted data with need to decrypt the original cyphertext through the concept of Homomorphism.

Theorem 3. Whenever an encryption scheme is known FHE, then it is must enable unbounded amount of evaluation functions on the ciphertext (or encrypted message) in which the output is the range of ciphertext set. The work on privacy homomorphism by Rivest et al. [19] is the bedrock of several present-day FHE techniques such as Gentry [18]. In fact, Gentry [20] version of the FHE reinforces the data privacy preservation and security through advanced mathematical theories (that is, ideal lattice) in order to derive its hardening bases. The ideal lattice operation comprises of distinct or unique vectors (commonly referred to as basis vectors) that is linearly super-imposed as represented by Eq. 3.

$$C = \sum_{r=1}^{m} \vec{d}_r * u_r, u_r \in \Psi, \tag{3}$$

where, C is the lattice notion, d_r is the basis vectors of the lattice C, u_r is item in the Lagrange coefficients Ψ, and r is set from of vectors $\{1, 2, 3, \ldots, m\}$.

Proof. According to the findings in [3], there are prospects with ideal lattice-based FHE approaches including post-quantum cryptology-compliant, security proofs, easy implementations and simplicity; not without complexity, implementation difficulty, and high cost of computation for real-life applications. It was proposed that, further optimizations (such as generating shorter lattice bases) are required to evolve fresh designs to secure diverse applications and systems. The ideal lattice-based FHS in 2009 by Gentry [20], over integers [21], Lightweight encryption based FHS [22], and NTRU-like [23] are considered primitive schemes. RSA is homomorphic in terms of multiplicative property [12], which is a top-choice for performing protection hardening operations on ciphertext. Nevertheless, large sizes of resulting ciphertext are to be reduced in subsequent versions [2]. RSA performance is better than the primitive FHS cryptosystems regardless of its slow speed [10].

2.4 Related Studies

The lightweight cryptographic scheme is proposed to ensure: end-to-end communications efficiency, and seamless integration into resources-constrained and smart devices.

Sybil attacks of peer-to-peer network. A number of identity-based attacks have been reported for Blockchain by [24] such as Key attack, Replay attack, Impersonation attack, and Sybil attack. In the context of Blockchain networks, a network of computers is attacked by inserting fake or malicious nodes. Public Blockchains (PBC) are considered the best but susceptible to Sybil attacks whose solution is to protect transactions by means of Proof of Work (PoW) and cryptographic schemes. In particular, hash algorithms are used to operate PoW including SHA-256, Black-256, and Scrypt [25].

PBC enables any node to join on the network and used hash values of users' addresses. Other features include:

1. Public keys are utilized for authentications in which every node has powers to audit, edit, mine and transactions.
2. PBC are composed of unknown users/participants.
3. PBC are decentralized in architecture.
4. PBC are open and permission-less.
5. PBC are a class of the truly decentralized because participating nodes are capable of creating new blocks and accessing contents of the Blockchain.

The permission-less character enables nodes to maintain a copy of the Blockchain and the block header hold all the consensus algorithm information as need in the Block network [11]. Smart contracts were developed for Blockchain networks in order to carry out several transactions in specified ways on the basis of agreement (or contract) entered by participants. Smart contracts are self-regulated agents having distinct accounts and addresses on Blockchain for the purpose of holding tokenized assets for parties to work under different conditions set.

Recently, lightweight cryptosystems were introduced as consisting of lightweight cryptographic algorithms and lightweight hash functions. Firstly, the lightweight cryptographic algorithms (LCA) offer different level of security and effectiveness as mention by [26]. The details of recent LCA are presented in Table 1.

In Table 1, the study in [26] revealed that the Speck is best for minimal storage space, the Rectangle is desirable for speed of processing, and the Present is most secured for resource-constraint or IoT devices especially Arduino UNO and Raspberry Pi model B. The asymmetric lightweight algorithms (such as Elliptic Curve Cryptography (ECC)) utilize a smaller key size, which could be applicable in IoT (nodes in 6LoWPAN) for fast speed, lesser memory space and real-time processing. The memory limitation and time constraint of IoT device make use of 128-bit key size for cyphertext [17].

Secondly, the lightweight hash functions were proposed by Feldhofer and Rechberger in year 2006 in order to reduce the larger internal state size and computation complexities of traditional hash functions before deploying them in resource-constrained devices or IoT. There are number of lightweight hash functions (LHF) including PHOTO, Quark, Lesamnta-LW, and SPONGENT. The main idea behind the two concepts of lightweight cryptosystems (that is, LCA and LHF) are summarized in Table 2.

Shortfalls. There are needs to extended them to multimedia data other than binary and text data-based design of present-day lightweight cryptosystems. Again, there is need to factor-in cryptanalysis of linear and differential operations for exigency of security.

Table 1. Existing lightweight cryptosystems [8, 26].

Cryptosystem	Data block size	Key size	No. of rounds	Operations	Standard	Target
Prince	64-bit	128-bit	11	Addition	Substitution-permutation network (SPN) structure	Symmetric structure
Speck	Unspecified	Unspecified	Unspecified	XOR	Unspecified	High performance software and hardware
Simon	64-bit	128-bit	Unspecified	XOR	Feistel structure	Asymmetric structure
Rectangle	64-bit	64-bit or 128-bits	25	Mixing and substitution	SPN structure	Symmetric structure for hardware
Pride	64-bit	128-bit	20	Addition and substitution	SPN structure	Symmetric structure
LBlock	64-bit	80-bit	32	Substitution	Feistel structure	Asymmetric structure
Present	64-bit	80-bit, 128-bit	31	XOR	SPN structure	Symmetric structure
AES - Cipher Block Chaining (CBC)	128-bit, 192-bit, 256-bit	128-bit	1	XOR		Symmetric structure
Twine	64-bit	80-bit, 128-bit	32	Unspecified	Feistel	Symmetric structure
Seed	128-bit	128-bit	16	Unspecified	Feistel	Symmetric structure
Iceberg	64-bit	128-bit	16	Unspecified	SPN	Symmetric structure
Hummingbird	16-bit	256-bit	4	Unspecified	SPN	Symmetric structure

(continued)

Table 1. (*continued*)

Cryptosystem	Data block size	Key size	No. of rounds	Operations	Standard	Target
Hummingbird2	16-bit	256-bit	4	Unspecified	SPN	Symmetric structure
DES	64-bit	54-bit	16	Unspecified	Feistel	Symmetric structure
LEA	128-bit	128-bit, 192-bit, 256-bit	24, 28, 32	Unspecified	Feistel	Symmetric structure
XTEA	64-bit	128-bit	64	Unspecified	Feistel	Symmetric structure
TEA	64-bit	128-bit	64	Unspecified	Feistel	Symmetric structure
AES	128-bit	128-bit, 192-bit, 256-bit	10, 12, 14	Unspecified	SPN	Symmetric structure
HEIGHT	64-bits	128-bit	32	Unspecified	GFS	Symmetric structure
RC5	32-bit, 64-bit, 128-bit	0-2040-bit	1-255	Unspecified	Feistel	Symmetric structure
3DES	64-bit	56-bit, 112-bit, 168-bit	48	Unspecified	Feistel	Symmetric structure

Table 2. Summary of lightweight cryptosystems targets and purposes.

S/N	LCA	LHF
1.	Smaller block size – reduced block cipher for original plaintext	Smaller output size – generate hash with fewer block size
2.	Smaller key size – public keys and private keys for encryption and decryption at reduced lengths respectively	Smaller message size – to create hash from larger hash of 264-bit to 256-bit or lower
3.	Simple rounds – to enable lesser computational operations on block ciphers	High speed, lesser memory and energy consumption for low-cost 8-bit or 16-bit micro-controllers

More so, RSA is unsuitable for IoT environment because of long key size built from two large prime numbers based on modulo operations. RSA is most secure, and offers better privacy preservations regardless of the fact that it cannot be categorized as asymmetric lightweight algorithm [8]. The AES larger key sizes (such as 192-bit, 128-bit) take up many rounds, and increased time of processing. In case of key size altered from 128-bit to 256-bit, this influences negatively on the time taken for decryption by double folds. The most secure key size is 256-bit for cyphertext, but could be broken within a few days of brute force hacking activity on AES 128-bit cyphertext key size.

3   Methodology

3.1   Mathematical Model of the Proposed Sooner Cryptosystem

The Sooner cryptosystem is composed of the plaintext, encryption function, homomorphic encryption function, the hash function and the linear and differential term for cryptanalysis.

Definition 1. *The Edge Network Nodes* are the IoT devices available on the public network, which are synchronized into Blockchain to collect and transmit sensor data from external environment such as temperature, Nitrogen, pH and moisture content. Thereafter, data is packaged and encrypted with 32-bit AES and transmitted across the gateway device built on an 8-bit processor. The data type depends on the sensor type (or nature), which is textual, numerical, or multimedia. The plaintext collected from the sensors is made up of an arbitrary length of string characters, numerical or alphabetical, as illustrated in Eq. 4:

$$R(y_n) = \begin{cases} \gamma, \gamma = [0, 1, 2, \ldots, 9] \\ \beta, \beta = [a, b, c, , z] \end{cases} \tag{4}$$

where, R = Plaintext representation function, γ, β = Numerical, string data type for plaintext.

The varying sizes of plaintext are encrypted from the field sensors; and the ciphertext blocks and keys are generated with lightweight AES algorithm represented in Eq. 5.

$$\vartheta(R(y_n))_j^t = \frac{V^{-rt}}{\eta(R(y_n))} + \{\mu\} \otimes \{D^{j*n}\} \tag{5}$$

where, ϑ = Original lightweight encryption function, V^{-rt} = Hash block-cipher, j = Number of rounds, t = Time of encryption, r = Size of computational blocks, $\{\mu\}$ = Public key for encryption, $\{D^{j*n}\}$ = Private key for decryption, η = Hashing function.

Definition 2. *Residence Network* enables the cloud transmission of data and subsequent transactions performed on data between the Edge Network Node and the PBC network. In IoT based system fewer than 128-bits key sizes are required for generating cyphertext due to resource constraints, which could reduce protection capability. Despite decentralized and transparency attributes of BCs, encrypted data or cyphertext is susceptible to privacy compromises during the transmission from the edge sensors. Therefore, homomorphism (FHE) is introduced to disallow unauthorized reconstruction of original plaintext using pieces of cypher keys and message cypher blocks at the edge things prior to further processing by nodes on BCs with smart contracts.

In case of FHE, two group sets (A and B) belonging to the same set are generates from Eq. 6 by computing A * B to obtain for the corresponding homomorphic string (original ciphertext) as $\psi(A)$ and $\psi(B)$. This operation hardens the previous data protection at the Edge Network Node as given by Eq. 6:

$$h(\vartheta(R(y_n))_j^t) = \psi(A) * \psi(B) \in \vartheta(R(y_n))_j^t + \epsilon \tag{6}$$

where, ϵ = Linear or differential term for cryptanalysis.

The final ciphertext (that is hardened with FHE procedure) is generated and transmitted to communicating parties in network edge to all participating devices/nodes in decentralized setup. The privacy of data is further enforced as represented in Eq. 7.

$$D = h\left(\vartheta(R(y_n))_j^t\right) \tag{7}$$

where, D = Data sent from IoT device on field, h = Homomorphic encryption function.

The original ciphertext is pushed into various blocks in the BC's smart contracts. These blocks hold smaller sizes public keys generated to protect transactions on cyphertext by limiting capability of an attacker or intruder in the residence network (PBC network). The cryptanalysis term is included to check the complexity of attacks or security level provided throughout the network (both at the first layer (IoT component) or second layer (PBC component).

Definition 3. *Protected data transactions* - Assume that one IoT device wants to send data (D) from the field to the data center (or another IoT device) with unique address (A)

of the sender broadcast (I_S), which is the data encrypted using the public key of receiver (I_R). Then, the resulting block cipher is transmitted through the BC's second-level public key (K_R). This entire procedure of the transformation of the ciphertext within prior the BC's smart contracts block computation is depicted in Eq. 8.

$$K_S(z_0, K_R(z_1, D), I_S) \rightarrow -(K_R(z_1, D), I_R) \tag{8}$$

where, $\rightarrow$ =Transformation function of initial ciphertext (from field) to BC's smart contract, I_S = IoT device of sender of data, I_R = IoT device of receiver of data, D = Data sent from field, K_R = Private key of receiver, K_S = Public key for encryption, and z_0, z_1 = BC's smart contracts.

In Eq. 8, the right-hand side illustrates the restructured transformation operations which is the decryption of the initial cyphertext (D) on the left-hand side using the private key. The sub-cyphertext is delivered to the receiver of data (D), who performs decryption operation using private key (K_R). This way, the privacy and confidentiality of transactions and data are preserved using smart contracts, z_0 and z_1 alongside the hardening function.

3.2 Performance Evaluation Parameters

This paper adopted the standard evaluation parameter defined for cryptosystem including [17, 26, 27]:

Speed. This is used to determine the execution time and quantity of clock cycles needed for running the cryptosystem in which lower value is desirous. This includes encryption time and decryption time.

Memory. This is used to calculate the required RAM and ROM of memory space used to store temporary data and running the code respectively.

Security Level. This is measured by the diffusion state, confusion state, and linear/differential cryptanalysis. The *diffusion state* checks that an input inversion bit in the key or plaintext produces 50% alteration in the corresponding output bits. The *confusion state* fosters complex and tougher interrelationships among the ciphertext, plaintext and the key infrastructure, which is determined with Hamming distance between plaintext and ciphertext as illustrated by Eq. 9:

$$Q = \sum_{j=1}^{t_x} (F_j \oplus G_j). \tag{9}$$

where, t_x represent the plaintext size of block, Q represents the difference quantity between ciphertext and plaintext, F_j represents the bits in the plaintext, G_j represents the bits in the ciphertext, and j represents the vector from $\{1, 2, 3, ..., t_x\}$.

The *linear and differential cryptanalysis* offer symmetric attack vectors for cryptosystems. It determines attacks penetration and complexity as well as the resistant to linear and differential attacks [27]. Effective cryptosystems must be less than the entire search operation greater than 2^{M_J}, where, M_J represent the bits of the key length.

Number of Rounds. The larger key sizes (such as 192-bit, 128-bit) take up many rounds, and increased time of processing. In particular, key size altered from 128-bit to 256-bit negatively impacts twice on the time required for decryption [17].

3.3 Experimental Parameters

In this paper, the minimal system configurations for the preliminary evaluation and validation of the proposed Sooner cryptosystem are shown in Table 3.

Table 3. Experimental configurations.

Parameter	Value
Hardware	
Processor	AMD E1-1200 APU, Radeon™ HD Graphics 1.40 GHz
RAM	4.00 GB
Hard Disk Drive (HDD)	282 GB
Software	
System Type	64-bit Operating System, x64-based processor
Operating System	Windows 8 Single Language
Application programming Interface	Java JDK 1.8.0_65/JRE8/NetBeans 8.1 Version
Traditional Cryptosystems	AES-256, RSA-256, SHA-3

4 Results

This paper validated the proposed Sooner cryptosystem using the preliminary implementation outputs against the conventional cryptosystems and benchmark lightweight cryptosystem are shown in Table 4.

From Table 4, the encryption and decryption time of the traditional cryptosystem trailed the proposed Sooner Cryptosystem using the same experimental settings. When the size of data block is considered, the Sooner has the smallest (32-bits) as against 256-bits, 64-bits, 64-bits for the traditional cryptosystem, Prince and Simon lightweight schemes.

Similarly, the proposed Sooner cryptosystem offered the best number of rounds of 10 as against 14 and 11 number of rounds for traditional cryptosystem and Prince respectively. The most important metric is the Security level provided by cryptosystem

Table 4. Performance of cryptosystems compared.

Metric	Traditional cryptosystem	Prince	Simon	Sonner (Proposed)
Encryption time (s)	1025	Unspecified	Unspecified	425
Decryption time (s)	1011	Unspecified	Unspecified	421
Data block size (bits)	256	64	64	32
Key size (bits)	2048	128	128	32, 128
Number of rounds	14	11	Unspecified	10
Security level $>= (2^{128})$	2^{256}	2^{128}	2^{128}	2^{196}

which is expected to exceed (2^{128}) in order to withstand computational techniques needed to break the private/public keys used for protecting data [27].

Consequently, the cryptosystems (that is, the traditional and the lightweight) schemes considered are largely secured against attacks (such as brute force attacks), and out of reach of the present-day computing approaches. The Sooner performed better because of the lightweight encryption, hashing, and hardening procedures introduced for data security of resource-constrained devices in this paper. This agrees with the findings of two-level factors or more layers of protection for cloud data in work of [16].

5 Conclusion

This paper found that, the concept of lightweight cryptosystem depends on the quantity of bits in the ciphertext (block cipher and keys). It follows that, the sizes of cipher block and cipher key depend largely on the underlying computational and memory capabilities of IoT devices connected to the wireless sensor networks and smart environments. The preliminary outcomes of the Sooner cryptosystem hold promise for data privacy preservation in IoT-based systems through its reduced block ciphers sizes, keys ciphers and hashes needed for protection. The proposed Sooner cryptosystem target the peculiarity of the resource-constrained devices, and seamless integration of IoT in PBC.

Consequent upon the traditional roles of IoT and PBC in enormous data generation, transmission, and storage which make shorter sizes of keys and block ciphers in appropriate. Therefore, the FHE was introduced to serve as a second layer protection by enforcing anonymity of the block cipher and key ciphers in untrusted edge IoT network, and then, across public networks (PBC). The hardening procedure of FHE enables data computation and aggregation in protected mode for privacy.

The next phase of this work is to consider the full adoption of the Sooner Cryptosystem in PBC based smart systems and applications such as smart rice farming, smart Health, and smart homes, in order to determine its effectiveness for resource-constrained devices in real-life scenarios.

References

1. Olowu, M., Yinka-Banjo, C., Misra, S., Florez, H.: A secured private-cloud computing system. In: Florez, H., Leon, M., Diaz-Nafria, J.M., Belli, S. (eds.) ICAI 2019. CCIS, vol. 1051, pp. 373–384. Springer, Cham (2019). https://doi.org/10.1007/978-3-030-32475-9_27
2. Potey, M.M., Dhote, C.A., Sharma, D.H.: Homomorphic encryption for security of cloud data. Procedia Comput. Sci. **79**, 175–181 (2016)
3. Acar, A., Aksu, H., Uluagac, A.S., Conti, M.: A survey on homomorphic encryption schemes. ACM Comput. Surv. **51**(4), 1–35 (2018)
4. Hassan, M.U., Rehmani, M.H., Chen, J.: Privacy preservation in blockchain based IoT systems: Integration issues, prospects, challenges, and future research directions. Future Gener. Comput. Syst. **97**, 512–529 (2019)
5. Das, A., Patterson, S., Wittie, M. P.: EdgeBench: benchmarking edge computing platforms. In: IEEE/ACM International Conference on Utility and Cloud Computing Companion, pp. 175–180 (2018)
6. Olowu, M., Yinka-Banjo, C., Misra, S., Oluranti, J., Ahuja, R.: Internet of things: demystifying smart cities and communities. In: Chillarige, R., Distefano, S., Rawat, S.S. (eds.) ICACII 2019. LNNS, vol. 119, pp. 363–371. Springer, Singapore (2020). https://doi.org/10.1007/978-981-15-3338-9_41
7. Lee, H., et al.: A stochastic process based routing algorithm for wireless Ad Hoc networks. In: IEEE 2019 International Conference on Computing, Networking and Communications, pp. 1018–1023 (2019)
8. Singh, S., Sharma, P.K., Moon, S.Y., Park, J.H.: Advanced lightweight encryption algorithms for IoT devices: survey, challenges and solutions. J. Ambient Intell. Human. Comput. 1-8 (2017). https://doi.org/10.1007/s12652-017-0494-4
9. Padmavathi, B., Kumari, S.R.: A survey on performance analysis of DES, AES and RSA algorithm along with LSB substitution. Int. J. Sci Res. **2**(4), 170–174 (2013)
10. Patel, N., Oza, P., Agrawal, S.: Homomorphic cryptography and its applications in various domains. In: Bhattacharyya, S., Hassanien, A.E., Gupta, D., Khanna, A., Pan, I. (eds.) International Conference on Innovative Computing and Communications. LNNS, vol. 55, pp. 269–278. Springer, Singapore (2019). https://doi.org/10.1007/978-981-13-2324-9_27
11. Ali, M.S., Vecchio, M., Pincheira, M., Dolui, K., Antonelli, F., Rehmani, M.H., Member, S.: Applications of blockchains in the internet of things: a comprehensive survey. IEEE Commun. Surv. Tutorials **21**(2), 1676–1717 (2019)
12. Qui, H.: An efficient data protection architecture based on fragmentation and encryption. PhD Thesis, Paris Institute of Technology (ParisTech), Paris, France (2017)
13. Mekki, N., Hamdi, M., Aguili, T., Kin, T.-H.: A privacy-preserving scheme using chaos theory for wireless body area network. In: 2018 14th International Wireless Communications & Mobile Computing Conference, IEEE, pp. 774–779 (2018)
14. Gill, S.S., et al.: Transformative effects of IoT, Blockchain and artificial intelligence on cloud computing: evolution, vision, trends and open challenges. Internet of Things, **8**, p. 100118 (2019)
15. Abayomi-Zannu, T.P., Odun-Ayo, I., Tatama, B.F., Misra, S.: Implementing a mobile voting system utilizing blockchain technology and two-factor authentication in Nigeria. In: 1st International Conference on Computing, Communication, and Cyber-Security, pp. 857–872 (2020)
16. Venkateswara Rao, P.V., Mohan Krishna Varma, N., Sudhakar, R.: A systematic survey on software-defined networks, routing protocols and security infrastructure for underwater wireless sensor networks (UWSNs). In: Venkata Krishna, P., Obaidat, M.S. (eds.) Emerging Research in Data Engineering Systems and Computer Communications. AISC, vol. 1054, pp. 551–559. Springer, Singapore (2020). https://doi.org/10.1007/978-981-15-0135-7_50

17. Richards, D., Abdelgawad, A., Yelamarthi, K.: How does encryption influence timing in IoT? In: 2018 IEEE Global Conference on Internet of Things, GCIoT 2018 (2019). https://doi.org/10.1109/GCIoT.2018.8620133

18. Adrian, D., et al.: Imperfect forward secrecy: How diffie-hellman fails in practice. In: The 22nd ACM SIGSAC Conference on Computer and Communications Security, pp. 5–17 (2015)

19. Rivest, R.L., Adelman, L., Dertouzos, M.L.: On data banks and privacy homomorphisms. Found. Secure Comput. 4(11), 169–180 (1978)

20. Gentry, C.: A fully homomorphic encryption scheme. Ph.D. Dissertation. Stanford University (2009)

21. van Dijk, M., Gentry, C., Halevi, S., Vaikuntanathan, V.: Fully homomorphic encryption over the integers. In: Gilbert, H. (ed.) EUROCRYPT 2010. LNCS, vol. 6110, pp. 24–43. Springer, Heidelberg (2010). https://doi.org/10.1007/978-3-642-13190-5_2

22. Brakerski, Z., Vaikuntanathan, V.: Fully homomorphic encryption from ring-LWE and security for key dependent messages. In: 31st Annual Cryptology Conference, Advances in Cryptology (CRYPTO 2011), pp. 505–524 (2011)

23. López-Alt, A., Tromer, E., Vaikuntanathan, V.: On-the-fly multiparty computation on the cloud via multikey fully homomorphic encryption. In: The 44th Annual ACM Symposium on Theory of Computing, pp. 1219–1234 (2012)

24. Ferrag, M.A., Derdour, M., Mukherjee, M., Derhab, A., Maglaras, L., Janicke, H.: Blockchain technologies for the internet of things: research issues and challenges. IEEE Internet Things J. 6(2), 2044–2188 (2018)

25. Christidis, K., Devetsikiotis, M.: Blockchains and smart contracts for the internet of things. IEEE Access 4, 2292–2303 (2016)

26. Omrani, T., Rhouma, R., Sliman, L.: Lightweight cryptography for resource-constrained devices: a comparative study and rectangle cryptanalysis. In: Bach Tobji, M.A., Jallouli, R., Koubaa, Y., Nijholt, A. (eds.) ICDEc 2018. LNBIP, vol. 325, pp. 107–118. Springer, Cham (2018). https://doi.org/10.1007/978-3-319-97749-2_8

27. Liu, Z., Han, S., Wang, Q., Li, W., Liu, Y., Gu, D.: New insights on linear cryptanalysis. Sci. Chin. Inf. Sci. 63(1), 1–11 (2020)

Comparative Performance Analysis
of Anti-virus Software

Noel Moses Dogonyaro[(✉)], Waziri Onomza Victor, Abdulhamid Muhammad Shafii,
and Salisu Lukman Obada

Cyber Security Science Department, School of Information and Communication Technology,
Federal University of Technology, Minna, Nigeria
{moses.noel,victor.waziri,shafii.abdulhamid,
salisu.obada}@futminna.edu.ng

Abstract. The threats and damages posed by malwares these days are alarming as Anti-virus vendors tend to combat the menace of malwares by the design of Anti-Virus software. This software also has tremendous impact on the performance of the computer system which in turn can become vulnerability for malware attacks. Anti-Virus (anti-malware) software is a computer program used to detects, prevents and deletes files infected by malwares from communicating devices by scanning. A virus is a malware which replicates itself by copying its code into other computer programs or software. It can perform harmful task on affected host computer such as processors time, accessing private information, corrupting and deleting files. This research carry out malware evasion and detection techniques and then focuses on the comparative performance analysis of some selected Anti-Virus software (Avast, Kaspersky, Bitdefender and Norton) using a VMware. Quick, full and custom scans and other parameters were used. Based on the analysis of the selected anti-virus software, the parameters that offers the utmost performance considering malware detection, removal rate, memory usage of the installed antivirus, and the interface launch time is considered the best.

Keywords: Anti-virus; malware · Evasion · Computer scan

1 Introduction

A computer virus can be defined as a software program that is capable of replicating itself to produce a new file that can harm the computer files. The replication by the virus but it requires a host system or somebody to assist in its spread [1]. Computer virus can destroy or hampered the working processes of a computer and hence always result to negative impact to the computer. Software programmes that are used to work against the computer virus are known as antivirus. The antivirus has the capability of scanning all file programmes on the hard drive and comparing the signature with the one found in the database [2]. The antivirus program can identify, avert and erase computer viruses.

© Springer Nature Switzerland AG 2021
S. Misra and B. Muhammad-Bello (Eds.): ICTA 2020, CCIS 1350, pp. 430–443, 2021.
https://doi.org/10.1007/978-3-030-69143-1_33

The impact, behavior and damage on a computer system, network system or data varies. Companies developing antivirus have developed detecting techniques that this antivirus software can apply. These techniques detection include: behavioral, heuristic and the static methods. Malicious software developers use different dodging principles to avoid been detected. The task for antivirus developers appears to be more on a daily because malware are advancing in developing codes that the antivirus find it difficult to detect.

In recent times, there is an increase threats to data that these malware have caused to computer or network systems. Even with the constant threats to the security of data, antivirus companies still claim that their software products are efficient and reliable to handle all forms of malware. Despite all these assurances many organizations, individuals, and corporation systems or network are been attack and infected with virus with the antivirus installed on their systems [3]. To determine the efficiency and effectiveness of these promising antivirus against malware is of great concern. The question that may be ask is, what are the parameters that a user need to use when testing for the performance of any selected antivirus software? To actualize a better test analysis of an antivirus, the user need to know the following: the negative impact of the antivirus software on its host, and the effectiveness of the scanning process. This research work analyze the performance of Anti-virus software and their individual impact on their hosting computer system.

The research is structure this way: Sect. 2 is the review of related literatures, Sect. 3 describes malware detection and evasion techniques, Sect. 4 briefly explain materials and methods used in the experiment, while section is discussion of results.

2 Review of Related Literatures

The study of anti-virus software has attracted many researchers due to the increase cases in cybercrime globally. The research work of [4] analyzed the effectiveness and the defense obtain by Anti-Virus software. In this work, the author used diverse antivirus software to test Uniform Resource Locator (URL) that is infected with a malware. Forty antivirus software were used to test for the infected URL to ascertain for the strength of all the antivirus software.

In the same line of research, [5] carried out the study on the performance and comparative analysis of different antivirus software. The authors used 193 malicious URL pointed to a malware through download. The results showed that many infected URL were unable to compromise some selected computer system and applications just because the system is patched regularly. This suggest that weaknesses that exist in third-party software applications may have been patched and hence unable to upload any malicious payload on the system.

The research work of [6] takes a different approach. The authors carried out performance study of some selected antivirus software which include: McAFee, Avast, Avira, Bitdefender and Norton. The performance investigation was centered on the scanning period. The performance metrics adopted were, full scan, custom scan and quick scan. Bitdefender outperformed the other antivirus. In order to identify the best antivirus software in 2019, [7] performed comparative study on14 anti-virus programs by using

452 live malware samples. The result obtained showed that Bitdefender was the best after 700 h of the test. The parameters used were, the effects of the antivirus on a computer system, protection capability of the malware protection, security of the browsing, and how spam are filtered.

In this research work, four anti-virus software products commonly used in Federal University of Technology, Minna was selected. The selection was based on the results obtained during survey of antivirus software in some selected higher institutions in Niger state including the Federal University of technology, Minna. These include: Avast, Bitdefender, Kaspersky, and Norton. Unlike the work of [7], this research would consider using the following performance metrics for the analysis: quick scan, full scan, custom scan, size of the installed anti-virus, how the processor is used when idle and when performing a scan, memory used when idle state, and the time taken for the antivirus to launch.

3   Malware Detection and Evasion Techniques

Malware (malicious software) as defined by [8] are program codes that can harm a computer system or network. The malicious codes have the tendency of infecting computer files or installed software programmes. The research work of [9] classify malware into the following categories based of their behavioral pattern. These include: Virus, and Worm. Those that their spread does not require human intervention are the Trojan or Trojan horse, Spyware, and the Ransomware. Malware detection techniques can be classify into three basic group: signature based, behavioral based, and the heuristic based [10]. In the signature based technique, searching of different bytes sequences is done so as to recognize particular portion of the malware. While the behavioral-based method, the technique observes the behavior of the computer software to ascertain whether it is harmful or not [10]. The heuristic-based technique try to examine system abnormality behavior. In this technique, constant software update is not necessary [11]. However, it is good to acknowledge that each detection techniques has its weaknesses and strength on the computer resources in which it is implemented.

With the recent proliferation of malware which are used in most cybercrime, Antivirus companies are also writing antivirus codes that could detect and neutralize malware [12]. As the antivirus software companies are making efforts to detect and neutralize these malware, hackers in turn are deploying malware programs that can go undetected, hide or bypass the antivirus programs. Some of the techniques adopted by the malware writers to execute their nefarious acts include: Polymorphism, Oligomorphism, and Metamorphic malware evasion techniques [13].

4   Materials and Methods

Materials: The following materials were used during the experiment: Windows 10 Pro O.S; 4 GB installed memory card, Core i5 CPU with 2.5 GHz processor speed; 64-bit O.S; VMware workstation 12 pro.

Methodology: To start the experiment, the authors first installed the VMware software on the host computer. Thereafter, the windows 10 O.S was also installed on the virtual machine and configured before installing the anti-virus software. Individual performance of each anti-virus software was done using some selected parameters. The parameters selected include: quick scan, full scan, custom scan, installation size of the antivirus, normal processor usage when it is idle, average processor usage during scanning, average memory usage during idle, and anti-virus interface launch time.

The experiment was conducted in a virtual environment. The selected anti-virus software were installed on the windows 10 pro operating system. Each of the antivirus software was used to scan for malware to test for the efficiency. The block diagram for the analysis is shown in Fig. 1.

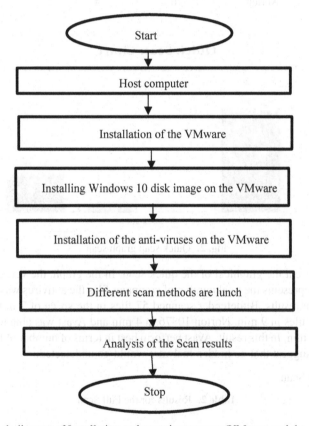

Fig. 1. Block diagram of Installation and scanning process (VMware and the anti-viruses)

5 Discussion of Results

5.1 Performance Measures

Metric 1: Quick Scan

Table 1. Results for the Quick Scan

Anti-virus type	Total files scanned	Time (minutes)
Avast	28887	13
Bitdefender	57	2
Kaspersky	3571	9
Norton	10876	4

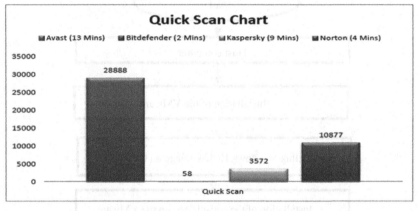

Fig. 2. Quick scan graph scan

Figure 2 represent the graphical of the quick scan. In the graph, the vertical line is the y-axis and it represents the total number of computer files the antivirus was able to scan. Looking at the results, Bitdefender scanned 57 files in the space of 2 min, Kaspersky scanned 3571 files in 9 min, Norton 10876 in 4 min and Avast was able to scan 28887 files in just 13 min. In this result, Avast perform best in terms of number of files scanned. Avast results suggest that no hidden malware would go undetected.

Metric 2. Full Scan

Table 2. Results for the Full Scan

Anti-virus type	All files scanned	Time (minutes)
Avast	260661	43
Bitdefender	333118	49
Kaspersky	129871	14
Norton	159117	44

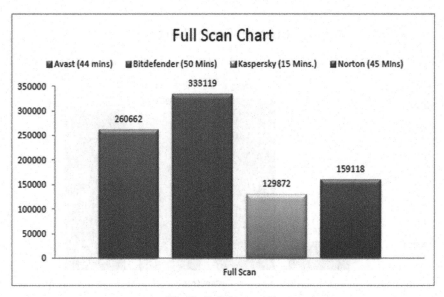

Fig. 3. Full Scan graph

In Fig. 3, it can be seen from the result that Kaspersky scanned 129872 of all files in the system in just fifteen minutes. Norton and Avast scanned 159118 and 260662 files in just 45 and 44 min. Bitdefender was able to scanned 333119 files in fifty minutes. This showed that Kaspersky scanned lesser documents in fewer time when comparing this to Norton anti-virus in which more files where scanned with longer time taken. Avast on the other side scanned more documents taken much time when you are making comparison to Norton. Bitdefender scanned much files with much time than Avast and Norton. Based on the analysis, Bitdefender performs better because of the total number of documents scanned. The scan can reveal hidden malware no matter its location in the computer system.

Metric 3. Custom Scan

Table 3. Results for the Custom Scan

Anti-virus type	Total files scanned	Time (minutes)
Avast	23561	10
Bitdefender	147652	10
Kaspersky	135961	57
Norton	141332	13

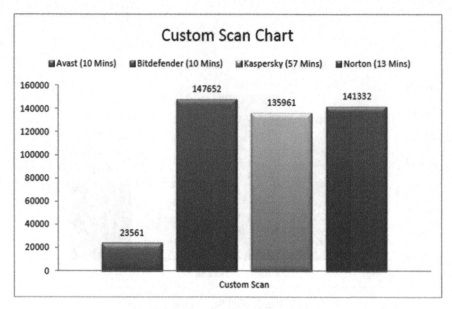

Fig. 4. Chart of the Custom Scan

Figure 4 represents the chart of the custom scan. In the chart, Avast anti-virus software scanned 23562 documents in just 10 min. A total of 135961 documents in 57 min were scanned by Kaspersky. Norton used 13 min to scan 141332 files, and 147652 files were scanned by Bitdefender in 10 min. In this result, Kaspersky scanned few files although the time taken was higher as compare to Norton. Avast total number of files scanned were less and the time was also short as compare to Kaspersky. More documents were scanned by Bitdefender than Avast within the same time frame. Lastly, Bitdefender and Avast scanned more files at the same time interval.

Metric 4. Installation size

Table 4. Custom scan results

Anti-virus type	Size in bytes	Size in (MB)
Avast	1035387855	987
Bitdefender	645437870	615
Kaspersky	284127515	270
Norton	675759587	644

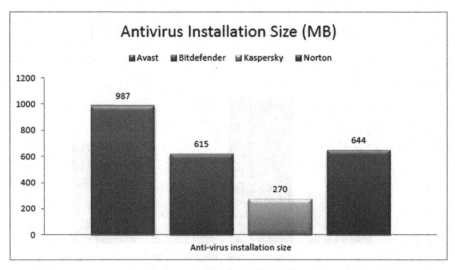

Fig. 5. Anti-virus installation size

Figure 5 is the chart that represent the size of the antivirus when installed on the computer and it is in gigabytes. From the results, Avast has 987 MB on disk, Bitdefender used 615 MB size on disk after installation, Kaspersky used 270 MB and Norton used 644 MB respectively. In this results, Kaspersky occupies less memory space after installation followed by Bitdefender. The memory space any antivirus occupies has a negative or positive impact on the host computer system. The size of the antivirus may slow down the computer system especially during updates installation.

Metric 5. Idle state of the processor usage

Table 5. Custom scan results

Serial No	Type of anti-virus	Ave. Processor usage (%)
1	Avast	0.38
2	Bitdefender	1.07
3	Kaspersky	0.45
4	Norton	0.74

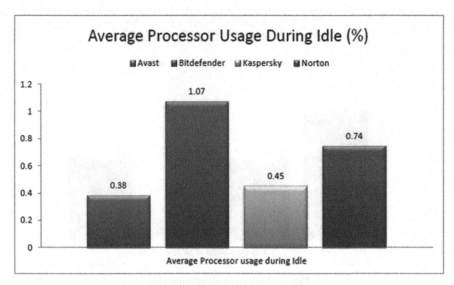

Fig. 6. During idle time average processor usage

Figure 6 is the bar chart representing the idle state of the processor usage. It is recorded in percentage form. From the result, with a 2 GB processor, Avast uses 0.38% of the processing space. Also, 1.07% space was used by Bitdefender, 0.45% processing space by Kaspersky, while 0.74% of the processing space was used by Norton. From the results, it showed that Avast uses less processor when it is in the idle state when compare to the other anti-virus software products. The system performance is impacted negatively or positively. The result also indicates how slowly or fast a system could be. If a system is too slow in executing some basic commands, hackers could take advantage of this limitation to hack into the system or cause Denial of Service attacks.

Metric 6. Result of scanning of Processor Usage

Table 6. Custom scan results (%)

S/N	Anti-virus type	Ave. Processor usage (%)
1	Avast	11.19
2	Bitdefender	16.04
3	Kaspersky	23.58
4	Norton	31.75

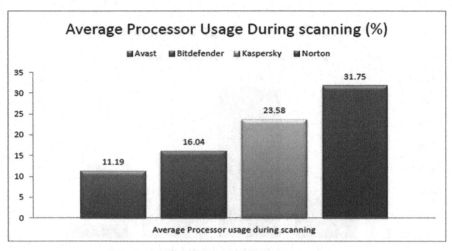

Fig. 7. Average processor usage during scanning

During scanning state, the average processor usage is represented in Fig. 7. From the chart, 11.19% of scanning was used by Avast, while Bitdefender requires 11.06% of the scanning. Kaspersky used 23.58% for scanning while 31.75% of the scanning the computer system was used by Norton. It is proven when an anti-virus software utilize more of the processor memory during scanning, there is this tendency that the system may slow down the system processor thereby affecting other processes. Norton anti-virus software consumes more processor memory than the other anti-virus software. In summary of the result, Avast uses less memory compared to the other anti-virus software. This showed that in terms of average processor usage and memory consumption during scanning, Avast is the best.

Metric 7. Average Memory Usage (Idle state)

Table 7. Custom scan results

S/N	Anti-virus type	Ave. Memory usage KB
1	Avast	41317
2	Bitdefender	131893
3	Kaspersky	47704
4	Norton	11425

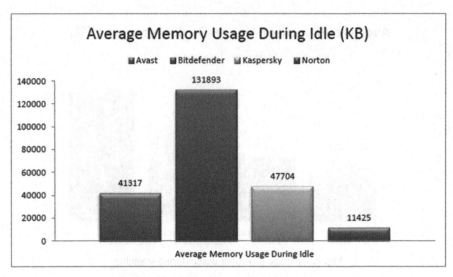

Fig. 8. During idle state memory usage

Figure 8 is the chart of the all the anti-virus software average memory usage while on idle state. The memory usage is measured in kilobytes. The results showed that Bitdefender consumes an average of 131893 KB per minute when the system is in the idle state. Average consumed by Kaspersky is 47704 KB, Avast takes 41317 KB, while on an average of 11425 KB was used by Norton. The analysis of the results showed that more memory usage was required by Bitdefender in idle state while Norton uses less memory when on idle state. When the memory consumption is less, it implies better performance by the system.

Metric 8. Memory Usage during Scanning

Table 8. During scanning average memory usage

S/N	Anti-virus type	Ave. Memory usage in KB
1	Avast	107879
2	Bitdefender	223142
3	Kaspersky	109593
4	Norton	107027

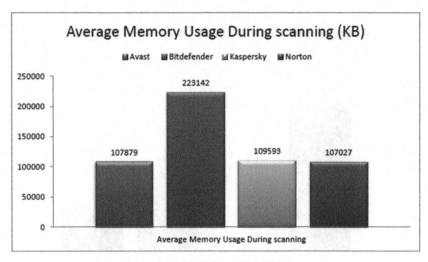

Fig. 9. During scanning- (average memory usage)

During scanning, the average memory usage by all the antivirus software is represented in Fig. 9 and it is measured in kilobytes. From the scanning results, an average of 2231 KB was used by Bitdefender, while 109593 KB of memory was used by Kaspersky. Avast uses an average of 107879 KB, while on average, 107027 KB of memory was used by Norton. It could be concluded that from the result more memory space was used by Bitdefender during scanning of files than Norton antivirus. Using this parameter, it helps in determining the performance of the system and also its efficiency.

Metric 9. The interface launch time.

Table 9. Custom scan results

S/N	Anti-virus type	Ave. Launch Time (milliseconds)
1	Avast	0.4387
2	Bitdefender	–
3	Kaspersky	0.2398
4	Norton	0.1296

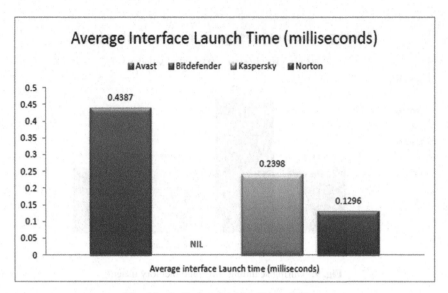

Fig. 10. Anti-virus Interface Launch Time

The average interface launch time of all the antivirus software are represented in Fig. 10. This is measured in milliseconds. In Table 9, The user interface launch time for Avast is in the average of 0.4387 ms, Kaspersky used 0.2398 ms, while 0.1296 ms was taken by Norton for the user interface to be fully launched. There was denial access of interface by the 'apptimer' on Bitdefender. When the time taken to launch the interface is less, it implies better performance by the selected antivirus software. The User Interface response time by any antivirus determines the operability and user friendly the antivirus should be. Using this parameter indicates that Norton anti-virus User interface launched time is faster as compared to Kaspersky and the other two antivirus software.

6   Conclusion

This research used three (3) basic parameters: quick scan, full scan, and custom scan. To know the time and the total files scanned, the authors used the quick scan method. In order to obtain the time and the total number of scanned documents, the authors applied the full scan method. The effectiveness of an anti-virus was determine by sing the custom scan method. The research also considered the following parameters to determine the performance and effectiveness of the chosen antivirus: the installation size of the antivirus on disk, size of the memory it occupy on the C: drive, the processor usage during scanning and when the system is in its idle state, the average memory usage during scanning and while on ide state, the interface launched time for all the selected antivirus software was calculated. The recommendation that could be made on any antivirus software is based on the parameters that gives the utmost performance as regards to malware detection and removal rate, memory usage of the installed antivirus, and the interface launch time should be consider.

The authors therefore recommend future research of other antivirus software and applying other malware detection techniques. Antivirus vendors should be up to date with the recent trends and techniques used by malware writers to evade detection.

References

1. Gandotra, E., Bansal, D., Sofat, S.: Malware analysis and classification: a survey. J. Inf. Secur. (2014)
2. Barriga, J.J., Yoo, S.G.: Malware detection and evasion with machine learning techniques: a survey. Int. J. Appl. Eng. Res. **12**(18), 7207–7214 (2017)
3. Al-Asli, M., Ghaleb, T.A.: Review of signature-based techniques in antivirus products. In: 2019 International Conference on Computer and Information Science (ICCIS), pp. 1–6. IEEE, Saudi Arabia (2019)
4. Willems, E.: The antivirus companies. In: Cyberdanger, pp. 65–83. Springer, Cham (2019). https://doi.org/10.1007/978-3-030-04531-9_5
5. Johar, A.H., Gerard, A., Athar, N., Asgher, U.: Feature based comparative analysis of online malware scanners (OMS). In: Ayaz, H., Asgher, U. (eds.) AHFE 2020. AISC, vol. 1201, pp. 385–392. Springer, Cham (2021). https://doi.org/10.1007/978-3-030-51041-1_51
6. Alqurashi, S., Batarfi, O.: A comparison of malware detection techniques based on hidden markov model. J. Inf. Secur. **7**(3), 215–223 (2016)
7. Johnston, N.: The best antivirus software for 2018, 25 August 2018. https://www.toptenreviews.com/software/security/best-antivirus-software/. Accessed 28 April 2020
8. Deylami, H.M., Muniyandi, R.C., Ardekani, I.T., Sarrafzadeh, A.: Taxonomy of malware detection techniques: a systematic literature review. In: 2016 14th Annual Conference on Privacy, Security and Trust (PST), pp. 629–636. IEEE, New Zealand (2016)
9. Bai, L., Rao, Y., Lu, S., Liu, X., Hu, Y.: The software gene-based test set automatic generation framework for antivirus software. JSW **14**(10), 449–456 (2019)
10. Al Amro, S., Alkhalifah, A.: A comparative study of virus detection techniques. Int. J. Comput. Inf. Eng. **9**(6), 1566–1573 (2015)
11. Euh, S., Lee, H., Kim, D., Hwang, D.: Comparative analysis of low-dimensional features and tree-based ensembles for malware detection systems. IEEE Access **8**, 76796–76808 (2020)
12. Garba, F.A., Kunya, K.I., Ibrahim, S.A., Isa, A.B., Muhammad, K.M., Wali, N.N.: Evaluating the state of the art antivirus evasion tools on windows and android platform. In: 2019 2nd International Conference of the IEEE Nigeria Computer Chapter (NigeriaComputConf). IEEE, Zaria, Nigeria, pp. 1–4 (2019).
13. Chakkaravarthy, S.S., Sangeetha, D., Vaidehi, V.: A survey on malware analysis and mitigation techniques. Comput. Sci. Rev. **32**, 1–23 (2019)

An Efficient Lightweight Cryptographic Algorithm for IoT Security

Muyideen Abdulraheem◉, Joseph Bamidele Awotunde(✉)◉,
Rasheed Gbenga Jimoh◉, and Idowu Dauda Oladipo◉

Department of Computer Science, University of Ilorin, Ilorin, Nigeria
{muyideen,awotunde.jb,jimoh_rasheed,odidowu}@unilorin.edu.ng

Abstract. To perform various tasks, different devices are interconnected and interact in several emerging areas. The emergence of the Internet of Things (IoT) and its applications makes it possible in the network for many constrained and low-resource devices to communicate, compute processes, and making a decision within themselves. But IoT has many challenges and problems, such as system power consumption, limited battery capacity, memory space, performance cost, resource constraints due to their small size and protection of the communication network. The traditional algorithms have been slow for data protection point of view, and cannot be used for data encryption on an IoT platform given the resource constraints. Therefore, this paper proposes lightweight cryptography based on the Tiny Encryption Algorithm (TEA) for an IoT driven setup to enhance speed benefit from software perspective rather than hardware implementation. The proposed algorithm was used to reduce the time for encryption in the IoT platform and to preserve the trade-off between security and efficiency. In terms of memory use, execution time, and precision, the proposed work is compared with recent works on lightweight start-ups. Results show that in an IoT driven setup, the algorithm is more secure and efficient, and more suitable for data securing.

Keywords: Tiny encryption algorithm · Cryptography · Communication network · Internet of things · Lightweight cryptographic algorithm · IoT security

1 Introduction

In remote media communication, the Internet of Things (IoT) has been a new technology that is cutting-edge and it is progressing globally [1, 2]. IoT creates network connections that are efficient and very important in uniting data, processes, and people more ever before [2, 3]. Without communicating with the devices, computer hardware, and software, and interrelated artifacts can transfer data over the network, such artifacts are digital machines, sensors, cell phones, RFID tags, and people. IoT consists of millions of embedded devices capable of data identification, analysis, and transmission [1, 2, 4–7].

By the year 2020, it was estimated that almost 50 billion devices will be connected via the Internet [8, 9] and the number will continue to rise exponentially. Considering this volume of devices, privacy, and security of the devices as well as security the data

© Springer Nature Switzerland AG 2021
S. Misra and B. Muhammad-Bello (Eds.): ICTA 2020, CCIS 1350, pp. 444–456, 2021.
https://doi.org/10.1007/978-3-030-69143-1_34

transmitted is a source of concern to researchers. The operations of IoT are susceptible to insecurity which if compromised threat the security and privacy of its users. IoT security and protection of data need to provide standard and basic principles of security requirements of integrity, confidentiality, authorization, authentication, and availability of users' data. Large volumes of data are transferred every second between those devices. The information transmitted remained a major concern in IoT applications due it network vulnerability [10, 11].

IoT provides different services for different users which can be accessed through users' small devices such as a smartphone. Controlling access is paramount. [12] Proposed the use of Lightweight Biometric Access Control for Remote Authentication Users and Key Access Agreement Scheme for IoT Services. IoT deserves an efficient and effective authentication and key agreement to secure its environment because of its resource constraint. [13] propose lightweight authentication and key agreement protocol to secure WiFi Sensor Network (WSN) of IoT. In their effort to secure IoT devices, [14] proposed Elliptic Curve Cryptography based Authentication Protocol to secure IoT. But to make the mission very difficult, the number of hackers and intruders have been increased recently.

To ensure data transmitted are very secure and keep away from intruders and hackers, different cryptographic algorithms have been employed. The techniques used handling of cryptographic algorithms will determine its effectiveness over handling, defining, and transmitting the secret keys. The algorithm may be technically and functionally working well, but poor handling and maintenance of secret keys make the cryptographic algorithm useless [15, 16]. In the IoT network, two prominent cryptographic algorithms are used namely symmetric and asymmetric algorithms. The same key is used for both encryption and decryption in the symmetric algorithm, while the asymmetric algorithm makes use of two distinct keys called private and public keys. The exchanged of keys within sender and receivers determines the efficiency of any algorithm. The asymmetric algorithm has a better advantage over the symmetric algorithms due to different keys used for the sender and receiver since the private key is protected and not transmitted through the network.

The network is used to forward the public key that will be used to encrypts sender plaintext by the receiver, thus sends ciphertext results to the recipient through the network. Since the hidden key cannot be received by the hacker, even if the public key is received, he/she will not be able to read the massage. The receiver will use their private key to decrypt ciphertext. The symmetric is very easy to use and deploy when compare with asymmetric algorithms [17–19]. Therefore, symmetric algorithms are always employed in IoT network implementation to protect information transmission. The algorithm is very easy to implement, reliable as long as the key remains secret and useless overhead resources. This paper, therefore, proposes a tiny efficiency encryption algorithm for IoT-based devices for more effective use. Similar to several other encryption algorithms, the proposed algorithm requires less time to encrypt and decrypt, resulting in increased security and efficiency for all modern IoT network applications. Figure 1 revealed various Internet of Things devices.

The remaining sections of the paper are arranged as follows: Sect. 2 details the design of IoT. Section 3 looks at the framework for Cryptography Tiny Algorithms. Section 4

Fig. 1. Internet of Things with different devices

deals with IoT protection and privacy, while Sect. 5 and Sect. 6 deals with experimental results and discussion, and conclusion.

2   Security and Privacy of Internet of Things

Different attacks are the target of this layer with diverse techniques employ by attackers. One of the attacks of this layer is node capture in which an attacker gets access to control important node and obtain communication details of the sender and receiver nodes. The information stored in the memory could be altered or changed completely. An attacker can intercept secret communication in real-time in an unauthorized manner and steal information transmitted over the network. Such an attack is an eavesdropping attack common in the perception layer. In the replay attack, an attacker can playback communication that occurred in a network to access authentication information on the network. The attacker spy to obtain authentication details from the sender and later use it to communicate with other authentic users in the network. Since the authentication information is genuine, other users will accept the message as authentic.

The Internet of Things (IoT) is an emerging global Internet-based information architecture that facilitates the exchange of goods and services in global supply chain networks. For example, the lack of certain goods would be reported to the provider automatically, which in turn causes electronic or physical delivery immediately. The architecture is based, from a technical point of view, on data communication devices, mainly RFID-tagged items (Radio-Frequency Identification) [20]. The IoT aims to provide a stable and reliable IT-infrastructure to enable the exchange of "things" [21].

The identified technological architecture of the IoT affects the protection and privacy of the concerned stakeholders. Privacy involves the concealment of sensitive information and the right to monitor what happens to it [22]. The right to privacy can be treated either as a human right, fundamental and inalienable or as a personal right of possession [23];

Consumers may not be aware of the attribution of tags to objects, and there may not be an auditory or visual cue to draw the user's attention. Individuals can also be tracked without even thinking about it, leaving their data or at least signs of it in cyberspace [24, 25]. Further aggravating the problem, it is no longer only the State that is interested in collecting the data, but also private actors like marketing companies [26].

Peer-to-Peer (P2P) networks are another tool for improving security and privacy, which usually demonstrate strong scalability and efficiency in apps. These P2P systems may be based on DHT (Distributed Hash Tables). How-ever access control must be executed at the actual EPCIS itself, not on the data stored in the DHT, as none of these two prototypes provide encryption [27, 28]. Insofar, it is fair to believe that encryption of the EPCIS link and customer authentication could be enforced without significant difficulties, using the security mechanisms for the Web and the web service [24]. In particular, customer authentication can be done through the issuance of shared secrets or the use of public-key cryptography [29, 30].

Man-in-the-middle (MiTM) and denial of service (DoS) attacks are major assaults in the network layer. In MiTM attack, an attacker intercept modifies or removes a communication between authentic sender and receiver and then forwards it to the receiver as sources. However, in DoS attack, authentic sender and receiver are denied access to the network and network resources by persistently making an unnecessary request and therefore keeping the network constantly busy. This would make it impossible for authentic users to access the network.

Instead, the framework layer isn't spare. One of the attacks on the application layer is cross-site scripting, in which the attacker inserts malicious script into a message from the sender to the receiver. By so doing attackers can alter the message or replace the message to the receiver and later use the original message for an illegal action. Malicious code is another attack in the application layer where self-activation code is inserted and it automatically requests the user for some information. Such information is subsequently forwarded to the attacker.

[31] proposed a Machine Learning approach in securing the IoT network and discussed a comprehensive account of IoT architecture, as well as different approaches of an attack on the IoT network. [32] proposes the use of elliptic curve cryptography ECC to provide security of IoT devices at the Network layer of the IoT architecture. The conventional security algorithms in existence cannot carter for the security of IoT devices as a result of their small size, low battery capacity, and speed. [33] propose a modified lightweight cipher to address the security issue in IoT devices.

3 Methodology

Wheeler and Needham, in 1994, developed the Tiny Encryption Algorithm (TEA) as a lightweight block cipher solution for securing wireless communication. TEA is based on a Feistel structure. It encrypts 64 bits of data using a 128-bit key schedule. To provide non-linearity, it employs XOR, ADD and SHIFT operations for secured communication rather than using P-boxes and S-boxes to achieve diffusion and confusion respectively. It uses the mixed algebraic technique used for IDEA but in a simple way making it faster to implement and take less memory space. It is considered resistant to differential cryptanalysis and in about six rounds, it achieves complete diffusion.

The basic process of TEA is extremely simple and easy to understand. The main inputs of TEA are essentially a plaintext block P and a transfer key K. The plaintext P is split into two halves: left[0] and right[0] while left[64] is ciphertext C. Every half of plaintext P is used to encrypt the other half over 64 processing rounds, and combined to create ciphertext block.

The TEA structure criteria involve splitting a 128-bit key into four 32-bit keywords and splitting the block size of each encryption into two 32-bit terms as well. In encryption rounds, TEA uses a Feistel scheme known as F, where two Feistel operations and many variations, bitwise XOR and SHIFT, are used in one round of Tea.

3.1 TEA Encryption Process

In the encryption method, the 64-bit plaintext P is divided into two input halves of 32-bit each LP and RP, respectively as left plaintext and right plaintext. The 128-bit key to the encryption process is divided into four K0, K1, K2, and K3 subkey parts. Every subkey in each round is used as an input to TEA encryption.

The original 32-bit half RP is left-shifted 4-bit, and then the output is added to the first subkey K0. From memory, the result is stored as RP1. The original 32-bit half RP is again added to a decimal value of the Golden Ratio constant 2654435769, and the output is stored as RP2 in the memory. The 32-bit half R is the next 5-bit right-shifted, adding the result to the K1 subkey and saving the result as RP3.

XOR operation is then performed on RP1, RP2, and RP3 and the final result is then recorded as RP4. Furthermore, the value stored in RP4 is added to the initial 32-bit half LP and the result is hence stored as RP5. This process completes the first round of the half-cycle of TEA.

The second round of half-cycle of TEA starts with the initial stored result RP5 being 4-bit left-shifted and the result is then added up with the first subkey K2. The results are stored as an LP1 in the memory. The stored result R5 is again applied in decimal value to a constant of the Golden Ratio 2654435769 and the result is stored as LP2 in the memory. The stored result R5 is the next 5-bit right-shifted and the result added to K3 and saved as LP3.

XOR operation is then performed on LP1, LP2, and LP3 and the final result is then recorded as LP4. Furthermore, the value stored in RP4 is added to the initial 32-bit half RP and the result is hence stored as LP5. This process completes the second round of half-cycle of TEA.

That process completes the entire TEA cycle. Thirty-two complete process of TEA encryption is repeated to satisfy the requirement of a full TEA.

$$RP1 = RP \ll 4 + K0$$

$$RP2 = RP + delta$$

$$RP3 = RP \gg 5 + K1$$

$$RP4 = RP1 \oplus RP2 \oplus RP3$$

$$RP5 = RP4 + LP$$

Equations of first-round encryption

$$LP1 = RP5 \ll 4 + K2$$

$$LP2 = RP5 + delta$$

$$LP3 = RP5 \gg 5 + K3$$

$$LP4 = LP1 \oplus LP2 \oplus LP3$$

$$LP5 = LP4 + RP$$

Equations of second-round encryption.

3.2 TEA Decryption Process

TEA being a Feistel structure, TEA decryption is nearly the same as TEA encryption with reversed function operation. The encrypted text of RP5 and LP5 starts the decryption process as the input that is now known as right ciphertext RC and left ciphertext LC respectively.

The original 32-bit half RC is left-shifted 4-bit, and the output is then added to the third K2 subkey. The result is stored as RC1 in your memory. The original 32-bit half RC is again applied to a decimal value of 2654435769 that represents the Golden Ratio constant, thus output is stored in the memory as RC2. The 32-bit half RC is the next 5-bit right-shifted, applying the result to the fourth K3 subkey and saving the result as RC3.

XOR operation is then performed on RC1, RC2, and RC3 and the final result is then recorded as RC4. Furthermore, the value stored in RC4 is added to the initial 32-bit half LC and the result is hence stored as RC5. This process completes the first round of the half-cycle of TEA.

TEA 's second half-loop round begins with the initial stored result RC5 being left-shifted 4-bit, and the result is then added with the first subkey K0. The result shall be stored as LC1 in the memory. The stored result RC5 is again added in decimal value to 2654435769 as constant of Golden Ratio and stored the result in a memory called LC2. The stored value RC5 is right-shifted next 5-bit and the value is added to K1 and saved as LC3.

XOR operation is then performed on LC1, LC2, and LC3 and the final result is then recorded as LC4. Furthermore, the value stored in LC4 is added to the initial 32-bit half RC and the result is hence stored as LC5. This process ends TEA's second half cycle round.

This process completes the full cycle of TEA. Thirty-two complete process of TEA encryption is repeated to satisfy the requirement of a full TEA. The decrypted ciphertext is then compared with the encryption process's input plaintext to prove both are the same value or message.

$$RC1 = RC \ll 4 + K2$$

$$RC2 = RC + delta$$

$$RC3 = RC \gg 5 + K3$$

$$RC4 = RC1 \oplus RC2 \oplus RC3$$

$$RC5 = RC4\,LC$$

Equations of the first-round decryption

$$LC1 = RC5 \ll 4 + K0$$

$$LC2 = RC5 + delta$$

$$LC3 = RC5 \gg 5 + K1$$

$$LC4 = LC1 \oplus LC2 \oplus LC3$$

$$LC5 = LC4 + RC$$

Equations of second-round decryption.

Figure 2 displayed the encryption and decryption of the TEA algorithm framework.

The source data can be any form data including structure, semi-structured and structure data and the data can contain text, video, or audio, and both. To access the cipher code data can be sent straight to the TEA encryption algorithm. This data are converted to binaries apart from text data and streams of the ones and the zeros. To access the ciphertext the binary stream is sent to the TEA encryption algorithm using the secret key

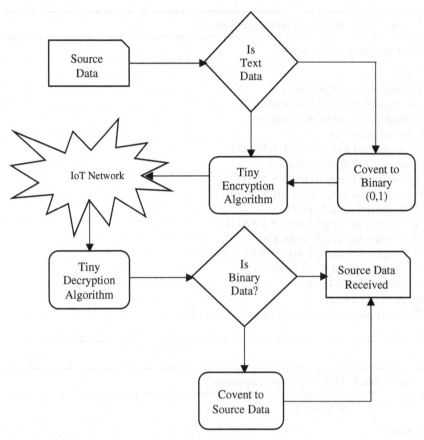

Fig. 2. Framework for TEA symmetric encryption algorithm encryption and decryption

certain by the sender and the receiver. The TEA transforms the ciphertext into plaintext after receiving ciphertext from the sender. The file must be translated to the source file after converted file to zeros and other streams (binary), otherwise, the plaintext will be provided by the sender. Both encryption and decryption of the TEA algorithm are presented in Algorithm 1 and Algorithm 2.

Algorithm 1 TEA Encryption Algorithm

Encrypt (plaintext p, key k):

1: Start
2: Assign delta = 9E3779B9
3: Compute k0, k1, k2, k3 from k
4: slip p into 32-bit bock rp and lp
5: Assign cycle = 0
6: compute rp1 as rp LSHIFT 4 AND k0
7: compute rp2 as rp AND delta
8: compute rp3 as rp RSHIFT 5 AND k1
9: compute rp4 as rp1 XOR rp2 XOR rp3
10: assign rp4 AND lp to rp5
11: compute lp1 as rp5 LSHIFT 4 AND k2
12: compute lp2 as rp5 AND delta
13: compute lp3 as rp5 RSHIFT 5 AND k3
14: compute lp1 XOR lp2 XOR lp3
15: assign lp4 AND rp to lp5
16: Increment cycle by 1
17: Repeat step 6 through step 16 until cycle = 32

Algorithm 2. TEA Decryption Algorithm

Decrypt (cipher c, key k):

1: Start
2: Assign delta = 9E3779B9
3: Compute k0, k1, k2, k3 from k
4: slip c into 32-bit bock rc and lc
5: Assign cycle = 0
6: compute rc1 as rc LSHIFT 4 AND k2
7: compute rc2 as rc AND delta
8: compute rc3 as rc RSHIFT 5 AND k3
9: compute rc4 as rc1 XOR rc2 XOR rc3
10: assign rc4 AND lc to rc5
11: compute lc1 as rc5 LSHIFT 4 AND k0
12: compute lc2 as rc5 AND delta
13: compute lc3 as rc5 RSHIFT 5 AND k1
14: compute lc1 XOR lc2 XOR lc3
15: assign lc4 AND rc to lc5
16: Increment cycle by 1
17: Repeat step 6 through step 16 until cycle = 32

---

4 Experimental Results and Discussion

TEA's output is evaluated and compared with the latest start-of-the-art methods. A network Low-power Wide Area Networks (LPWAN) was used to test the performance of the algorithm with Sigfox and IoT infrastructures. LPWAN was specifically designed for M2M and IoT devices to enable low power consumption and wireless connectivity over long distances. Sigfox offers a very advantageous battery life, power, and cost. In embedded devices, the TEA algorithm was implemented. The experimental setup used system architecture close to [1, 34, 35]. For the experiment, the text files contained in a cloud service database were used. The text files are then encrypted separately in four different situations using the TEA algorithm, and the algorithm's encryption and decryption times for various file sizes and key sizes were calculated (Table 1).

Table 1. Encryption time for a key size of 48 bits

FILE SIZE (Kilobytes)	Encryption time (MM)
0.82	0.121
1.65	0.216
12.32	0.893
36.50	2.014
50.2	3.142
100.7	5.461

Table 2 shown the results of encryption time in mm, the TEA achieved a lower time for various sizes used and the following results were obtained 0.121, 0.216, 0.893, 2.014, 3.142, and 5.461, the encryption time of the files is increasing as the size of the files keep on increasing and the is the normal time in IoT platform when compared with other algorithms.

Table 2. Decryption time for a key size of 48 bits

FILE SIZE (Kilobytes)	Encryption time (MM)
0.82	0.120
1.65	0.215
12.32	0.891
36.50	2.012
50.2	3.138
100.7	5.459

From the results obtained in Table 3, the TEA achieved a lower decryption time for various text file sizes of 0.120, 0.215, 0.891, 2.012, 3.138, and 5.459, the encryption time of the files is increasing as the size of the files keep on increasing and the is the normal time in IoT platform when compared with other algorithms.

Table 3. Comparison of the proposed system with an existing method

Algorithm	Execution time		ROM	
	Clock cycles	Time gain (%)	(bytes)	ROM gain %
[3] SIMON	108901089	28%	1752	2.9%
[3] Optimized SIMON	86293887		1712	
TEA	62,546,057		1683	

For each encryption code, an MSP-cycle-watcher was used to count the CPU cycles, and serve as a quality-checking tool for measuring the CPU cycles. The encryption part is calculated by subtracting the cycle number within the code from the entire cycle code. The comparison of the encryption cycles by approximation is assumed that it will lead to a reasonable study of the power consumption. Also, adding a checkpoint to decide the start and endpoint of executing encryption cycles was achieved for counting the encryption cycles in this stage.

The results of the comparison of execution time and, ROM consumption are shown in Table 3. The TEA (48/72) absorbs by around 28 percent fewer clock cycles than SIMON (32/64) and SIMON (48/72). Also, the number of TEA execution cycles (48/72) is lower than SIMON (48/72) and SIMON (48/72) is optimized by 2.9%. The SIMON is versatile and appealing to IoT and multimedia applications. It provides a variety of block and key sizes and TEA also has almost the same characteristics as it offers a different set of key sizes and thus TEA algorithm was used for lightweight IoT security cryptographic.

5   Conclusion

In a lightweight block cipher, both the design part and implementation part go simultaneously which has revealed some significant limits and inherent conditions. Efficiency is a critical part of the Internet of Things but in an IoT architecture edge node devices also have resource constraints such as memory and power. This paper presented an IoT protection Implementation TEA algorithm. The development continued from interesting features found in the TEA algorithm and attractive results were obtained. The result indicates improved efficiency as compared to SIMON and modified SIMON with a minor reordering within the process based on execution time and memory usage. The TEA with 48/72 block models reveals an improvement percentage of 28% and 2.9% respectively in execution time and memory computation. Thus, TEA showed great efficiency both in terms of execution times for encryption and decryption. An improved TEA algorithm can also be used to boost IoT protection to increase the encryption of compressed files by further. Future work may also include and implement the data transfer algorithm in sensor, for and ad hoc networks.

References

1. Rajesh, S., Paul, V., Menon, V.G., Khosravi, M.R.: A secure and efficient lightweight symmetric encryption scheme for the transfer of text files between embedded IoT devices. Symmetry **11**(2), 293 (2019)
2. Singh, S., Sharma, P.K., Moon, S.Y., Park, J.H.: Advanced lightweight encryption algorithms for IoT devices: survey, challenges and solutions. J. Ambient Intell. Human. Comput. 1–18 (2017). https://doi.org/10.1007/s12652-017-0494-4
3. Alassaf, N., Gutub, A., Parah, S.A., Al Ghamdi, M.: Enhancing the speed of SIMON: A light-weight-cryptographic algorithm for IoT applications. Multimedia Tools Appl. **78**(23), 32633–32657 (2019)
4. Porambage, P., Okwuibe, J., Liyanage, M., Ylianttila, M., Taleb, T.: Survey on multi-access edge computing for the internet of things realization. IEEE Commun. Surv. Tutorials **20**(4), 2961–2991 (2018)
5. Ploennigs, J., Cohn, J., Stanford-Clark, A.: The future of IoT. IEEE Internet Things Mag. **1**(1), 28–33 (2018)
6. Philip, V., Suman, V.K., Menon, V.G., Dhanya, K.A.: A review on the latest internet of things based on healthcare applications. Int. J. Comput. Sci. Inf. Secur. **15**(1), 248 (2017)
7. Deshkar, S., Thanseeh, R.A., Menon, V.G.: A review of IoT based m-Health systems for diabetes. Int. J. Comput. Sci. Telecommun. **8**(1), 13–18 (2017)
8. Fink, G.A., Zarzhitsky, D.V., Carroll, T.E., Farquhar, E.D.: Security and privacy grand challenges for the Internet of Things. In: 2015 International Conference on Collaboration Technologies and Systems (CTS), pp. 27–34. IEEE, June 2015.
9. Mahdavinejad, M.S., Rezvan, M., Barekatain, M., Adibi, P., Barnaghi, P., Sheth, A.P.: Machine learning for Internet of Things data analysis: a survey. Digital Commun. Netw. **4**(3), 161–175 (2018)
10. Bordel, B., Alcarria, R., De Andrés, D.M., You, I.: Securing Internet-of-Things systems through implicit and explicit reputation models. IEEE Access **6**, 47472–47488 (2018)
11. Frustaci, M., Pace, P., Aloi, G., Fortino, G.: Evaluating critical security issues of the IoT world: present and future challenges. IEEE Internet Things J. **5**(4), 2483–2495 (2017)
12. Dhillon, P.K., Kalra, S.: A lightweight biometrics-based remote user authentication scheme for IoT services. J. Inf. Secur. Appl. **34**, 255–270 (2017)
13. Ostad-Sharif, A., Arshad, H., Nikooghadam, M., Abbasinezhad-Mood, D.: Three party secure data transmission in IoT networks through the design of a lightweight authenticated key agreement scheme. Future Generation Comput. Syst. **100**, 882–892 (2019)
14. Rostampour, S., Safkhani, M., Bendavid, Y., Bagheri, N.: ECCbAP: A secure ECC-based authentication protocol for IoT edge devices. Pervasive Mob. Comput. **67**, 101194 (2020)
15. Wang, B., Zhan, Y., Zhang, Z.: Cryptanalysis of the asymmetric fully homomorphic encryption scheme. IEEE Trans. Inf. Forensics Secur. **13**(6), 1460–1467 (2018)
16. Jambhekar, N.D., Misra, S., Dhawale, C.A.: Cloud computing security with collaborating encryption. Indian J. Sci. Technol **9**(21), 1–7 (2016)
17. Yassein, M.B., Aljawarneh, S., Qawasmeh, E., Mardini, W., Khamayseh, Y.: A comprehensive study of symmetric key and asymmetric key encryption algorithms. In: 2017 International Conference on Engineering and Technology (ICET), pp. 1–7. IEEE, August 2017
18. Ahmad, S., Alam, K.M.R., Rahman, H., Tamura, S.: A comparison between symmetric and asymmetric key encryption algorithm based decryption mixnets. In: 2015 International Conference on Networking Systems and Security (NSysS), pp. 1–5. IEEE, January 2015.
19. Arogundade, O.T., Abayomi-Alli, A., Misra, S.: An ontology-based security risk management model for information systems. Arabian J. Sci. Eng. **45**(8), 6183–6198 (2020). https://doi.org/10.1007/s13369-020-04524-4

20. Osho, O., Musa, F.A., Misra, S., Uduimoh, A.A., Adewunmi, A., Ahuja, R.: AbsoluteSecure: a tri-layered data security system. In: Damaševičius, R., Vasiljevienė, G. (eds.) ICIST 2019. CCIS, vol. 1078, pp. 243–255. Springer, Cham (2019). https://doi.org/10.1007/978-3-030-30275-7_19
21. Tripathy, B.K., Anuradha, J. (Eds.) Internet of Things (IoT): Technologies, Applications, Challenges, and Solutions. CRC Press, Boca Raton (2017).
22. Gürses, S., Berendt, B., Santen, T.: Multilateral security requirements analysis for preserving privacy in ubiquitous environments. In: Proceedings of the UKDU Workshop, pp. 51–64 (2006).
23. Campbell, J.: The origins and development of the right to privacy. Edward Elgar Publishing, In Comparative Privacy and Defamation (2020)
24. Weber, R.H.: Internet of Things-New security and privacy challenges. Computer law security review 26(1), 23–30 (2010)
25. Ben-Daya, M., Hassini, E., Bahroun, Z.: Internet of things and supply chain management: a literature review. Int. J. Prod. Res. 57(15–16), 4719–4742 (2019)
26. Grubbauer, M.: Assisted self-help housing in mexico: advocacy, (micro) finance, and the making of markets. Int. J. Urban Reg. Res. 44(6), 947–966 (2020)
27. Fabian, B., Gunther, O.: Distributed ONS and its privacy impact. In: 2007 IEEE International Conference on Communications, pp. 1223–1228. IEEE, June 2007
28. Čolaković, A., Hadžialić, M.: Internet of Things (IoT): a review of enabling technologies, challenges, and open research issues. Comput. Netw. 144, 17–39 (2018)
29. Malik, M., Dutta, M., Granjal, J.: A survey of key bootstrapping protocols based on public-key cryptography in the Internet of Things. IEEE Access 7, 27443–27464 (2019)
30. Jiang, W., Li, H., Xu, G., Wen, M., Dong, G., Lin, X.: PTAS: privacy-preserving thin-client authentication scheme in blockchain-based PKI. Future Generation Comput. Syst. 96, 185–195 (2019)
31. Tahsien, S.M., Karimipour, H., Spachos, P.: Machine learning-based solutions for the security of the Internet of Things (IoT): a survey. J. Netw. Comput. Appl. 161, 102630 (2020)
32. De Rango, F., Potrino, G., Tropea, M., Fazio, P.: Energy-aware dynamic Internet of a Things security system based on Elliptic Curve Cryptography and Message Queue Telemetry Transport protocol for mitigating Replay attacks. Pervasive Mob. Comput. 61, 101105 (2020)
33. Chatterjee, R., Chakraborty, R.: A modified lightweight PRESENT cipher For IoT security. In: 2020 International Conference on Computer Science, Engineering and Applications (ICCSEA), pp. 1–6. IEEE, March 2020
34. Wu, F., Wu, T., Yuce, M.R.: An internet-of-things (IoT) network system for connected efficiency and health monitoring applications. Sensors 19(1), 21 (2019)
35. Odun-Ayo, I., Misra, S., Omoregbe, N.A., Onibere, E., Bulama, Y., Damasevicius, R.: Cloud-based security driven human resource management system. In: ICADIWT, pp. 96–106, March 2017

Analysis and Classification of Some Selected Media Apps Vulnerability

Olawale Surajudeen Adebayo[1](✉), Joel Sokoyebom Anyam[1], Shefiu Ganiyu[1], and Sule Ajiboye Salawu[2]

[1] Federal University of Technology Minna, Minna, Niger, Nigeria
{waleadebayo,shefiu.ganiyu}@futminna.edu.ng,
anyamjoel01@gmail.com
[2] Aminu Saleh College of Education, Azare, Bauchi, Nigeria
salawu_sul@yahoo.com

Abstract. This research investigates popular messaging applications' traffic in other to assess the security or vulnerability of communication on those applications. The experiment was carried out in a Local Area Network. Wireshark, NetworkMiner and Netwitness Investigators were used to capture and analyse the traffic. Ten (10) instant messaging applications were installed on Android platforms and used for the experiment. Different types of sensitive media files were recovered from the network traffic, including images, documents/texts and audio. The Internet Service Provider (ISP) of the sender was also recovered along with the resident city of the third party. The research classifies the mobile applications into vulnerable and nonvulnerable applications using the gathered data. Thus, it was discovered that out of ten mobile applications investigated, only Viber application was non-vulnerable to tested attacks. The classification result also shows random forest as the best classifier using this research data.

Keywords: Social media · Vulnerability · Social media vulnerability · Instant messaging applications · Mobile applications · Vulnerability classification

1 Introduction

Instant messaging applications, running on portable devices such as smartphones and tablets, have become increasingly popular around the world [1]. As new messaging applications started to emerge and tried to replace traditional SMS, developing them with security and privacy in mind was not a top priority for the developers. Popular messaging tools used in recent years do not support end-to-end encryption, only standard client to server encryption, this gives the service providers access to more private information than required. The use of mobile applications for communication has experienced accelerated growth and has fast become the standard method of communication. Based on recent revelations of the widespread state surveillance of personal communication, many products now claim to offer secure and private messaging. However, these messaging applications have been proven over time to be vulnerable notwithstanding

© Springer Nature Switzerland AG 2021
S. Misra and B. Muhammad-Bello (Eds.): ICTA 2020, CCIS 1350, pp. 457–469, 2021.
https://doi.org/10.1007/978-3-030-69143-1_35

improvements. The leakage communication on instant messaging applications poses a serious risk especially in sensitive conversations like organizational matters, where sensitive data like a customer list or sales report may be revealed on the internet.

The efficiency and effectiveness of the information systems, in many ways, depend on its architecture and how data are transmitted among different parties. Similarly, a very crucial aspect of the software development is the security of data that flows through open communication channels. One of the most popular architecture is client/server architecture that makes the centralization of data storage and processing enable and provide flexibility for applying authentication methods and encryption algorithms within information systems. The increase in the number of clients necessitated the increase in the authentication and encryption level as high as possible. Client/server is a technology that allows opening an interactive session between the user's browser and the server [2]. One of the biggest potential security flaws for most authentication schemes in the client/server architecture is the ability of the users to ensure their secrecy [3]. In this work, authors perform an experimental analysis on ten instant messaging applications for the Android mobile phone operating system. The study reveals that despite the claim by instant messaging applications about providing end-to-end security, unencrypted data could still be retrieved from the traffic of these applications. The remainder of this paper is organized as follows: the related works on the analysis of instant messaging vulnerability was discussed in section two; the research methodology and experimental setup were discussed in section three. In section four, the research experiment and implementation were highlighted. The overview of the experimental results was discussed in section five while the conclusion and further research were provided in sections six and seven.

2 Related Works

Dickson and Messenger [4] carried out experiments to mimic the reality of an investigation linking one party to another, including 'pre-determined' text conversations and the exchange of data files. Monitoring software was used at all times on the suspect's system to record the changes being effected to it. The results show that conversation content and transferred files, evidence of contact, display picture, transmitted files, connection logging, unallocated clusters and swap file, network passwords and data on the RAM were retrieved. Meghanathan, Allam, and Moore [5] discusses different tools and techniques available to conduct network forensics. The tools discussed include: eMailTrackerPro to identify the physical location of an email sender; Web Historian to find the duration of each visit and the files uploaded and downloaded from the visited website; packet sniffers like Ethereal to capture and analyze the data exchanged among the different computers in the network. Default iPhone web browser Safari (customized for iPhone presented) was used by Husain and Sridhar [6] to test for three Volatile Instant Messaging (VIM) applications where participants can enjoy instant messaging by just using a web browser without installing any application on the user's local system. In their results, unique Phrases, timestamps, screen names and buddy list for Aim and Yahoo were recovered while Plain text passwords for AIM were retrieved.

Chin, Felt, Greenwood, and Wagner [7] while analysing inter-application communication on Android platforms conducted an Intent-Based Attack using ComDroid for vulnerability and bug detection. They analysed 20 applications and found 34 exploitable vulnerabilities; 12 of the 20 applications had at the least one vulnerability. Vidas et al. [8] after exploring special device boot modes and Android's partitioning schema, detail the composition of an Android bootable image and discuss the creation of such an image designed for forensic collection. Their major contribution is a general process for data collection of Android devices. Their results show that the use of the recovery booting provides a consistent, repeatable method of collecting numerous Android devices without "rooting" the device in normal operating mode. Zhang, He, Liu, and Bridges [9] investigated users' online activities including web browsing, chatting, online gaming, downloading, uploading and video watching, etc. through traffic analysis. A hierarchical classification system based on machine learning algorithms was implemented to discover what a user is doing on his/her computer. Results show that their system can differentiate online applications on the accuracy of about 80% in 5 s and over 90% accuracy if the eavesdropping lasts for 1 min. Appelman, Bosma, and Veerman [10] investigated how Viber performs security wise in comparison to other services. A definitive conclusion was not found but most details of the protocol used to transfer the voice data were documented. The application code was analysed but no real weaknesses were found. Results show that in the Local Storage everything is unencrypted and can be viewed fairly easily, although your phone needs to be rooted or jailbreaked while for the Transferred Data, Manual Reverse Engineering is possible but is a long process which requires a lot of experience.

Schrittwieser et al. [11] analysed nine popular mobile messaging and VoIP applications and evaluated their security models with a focus on authentication mechanisms. They found out that most of the examined applications use the user's phone number as a unique token to identify accounts, which further restricts the implementation of security measures. Results show that major security flaws exist in most of the tested applications, allowing attackers to hijack accounts, spoofsender-IDs or enumerate subscribers. Adami, Callegari, Giordano, Pagano, and Pepe [12] proposed a real-time algorithm (named Skype-Hunter) to detect and classify Skype traffic. By means of both signature-based and statistical procedures, they were able to correctly reveal and classify the signalling traffic as well as the data traffic (calls and file transfers). Thakur [13] conducted a Forensic Analysis of WhatsApp on Android Smartphones in which they carry out a live analysis of an Android smartphone to extract user interaction information from the whatsApp application's volatile and non-volatile memory. The results for the volatile memory show that critical application data is present in the RAM and can be extracted for further analysis, while for the Non-volatile memory, all similar applications that load data from a SQLite database can be tested for data recovery using non-volatile memory forensics. Mahajan and Sanghvi [14] used Cellebrite UFED (Universal Forensic Extraction Device) Classic Ultimate (V 1.8.0.0), to extract files and folders from five (5) android devices. Rafique, and Khan [15] present a critical review of static and live analysis approaches and evaluate the reliability of different tools and techniques used in static and live digital forensic analysis.

Coull and Dyer [16] show that it is possible for an eavesdropper to learn information about user actions, the language of messages, and even the length of those messages with greater than 96% accuracy despite the use of state-of-the-art encryption technologies simply by observing the sizes of encrypted packets. Anglano [17] used a set of YouWave virtual machines, namely one for each device involved in the experiments, running Android v. 4.0.4. On each one of these machines WhatsApp Messenger v. 2.11 was installed and used. SqliteMan was used to examine the databases maintained by WhatsApp Messenger and notepad++ to examine textual files. The results indicate that list of contacts, inference also of when a specific contact has been added, recovery of deleted contacts, time of deletion, deleted messages, time of deletion and users that exchanged them. Karpisek, Baggili, and Breitinger, [18] were able to decrypt the network traffic and obtain forensic artifacts that relate to this new calling feature on WhatsApp, which included the WhatsApp phone numbers, server IPs, audio codec (Opus), call duration, and call termination using Wireshark v1.12.5, 32-bit, with the WhatsApp dissector and Pidgin v2.12.115, 32-bit, with the WhatsApp plugin. [11] Abdul Aziz, Mokhti, Nadhar, and Nozri [19] studied and experimented several techniques on the extraction and analysis of smartphones' data using Sleuth Kit Autopsy. Authors' aim was to identify methods of extracting and analysing data on android based smartphone. Authors were able to extract email and contact artefacts. Walnycky, Baggili, Marrington, Moore, and Breitinger [20] acquired the traffic capture files and conducted examination using Wireshark, NetworkMiner, and NetWitness Investigator, to extract Text chat, Audio, video, image, sketch, and location sharing. This research follows this methodology given its high level of efficiency in exposing vulnerabilities as shown in past material. We worked on a wide range of updated applications with a focus on text/documents, audio, ISP, image, and location sharing.

Adebayo, Sulaiman, Osho, Abdulhamid, and Alhassan [21] in their seminar paper focus on the forensic analysis of Kik messenger which is a multi-platform instant messaging application on android devices. Authors captured and examined data related Kik and forensic images of three android devices with android versions 4.4 (KitKat), and 5.0 (Lollipop) and different android manufacturers. The artefacts of forensic values were identified and analyzed. The result was to help digital forensic investigators and academia in locating and acquiring digital evidence from Kik messenger on android platforms. One of the applications considered in this research; Viber, offers a difficult paradigm of traffic analysis. Hence, Sudozai and Saleem [22] presented a novel methodology for identification of Viber traffic over the network and established a model which can classify its services of audio and audio/video calls, message chats including text and voice chats, group messages and file/media sharing. In an attempt to retrieve correct traffic path, protocols, visible data, certificates and credentials, Network Traffic Forensics on Firefox Mobile OS using facebook, twitter and telegram as case studies were conducted by Yusoff and Dehghantanha [23] using Network Miner 1.0 and Wireshark Portable 1.6.5 to capture the network traffic. The result was the retrieval of Image files, communication texts and authentication credentials. A Comparison of Secure Messaging Protocols and Implementations was conducted by Mujaj [24] where experiments were conducted on real-world implementations of six (6) secure messaging applications to check for Security Properties, Usability and Adoption. All of the applications tested required contact list Upload, five required verification by phone call, phone registration and verification by SMS, four had access to SMS Inbox, could delete devices from account and contained details about transmission of message, three required notification about end-to-end encryption, notification about key changes, QR-code and verified check, two required e-mail Registration, enabled trust-on-first-use, shared keys through 3rd party, passphrase/code, two-step verification and had screen security, one enabled blocking messages, clear trusted contacts and re-encrypt and send message.

Abdul Aziz, Yusof, and AbdRahman [25] use PenDua and Kloner to extract digital evidence from electronic application while FTK and Autopsy with other tools were used for analysis of the extracted evidences. Authors compiled the forensics exercise as a learning package to serve as an eye opener to expose the beginners of Digital Evidence Forensics learners to the tasks. The learning package was tested with 120 students of a Digital Evidence Forensic class for 3 semesters. Majority of the students found the system interesting and best proper procedure of acquiring and analyzing digital evidence. The Saputra, and Riadi [26] research generates information in the form of alerts from attacks displayed by IDS Snort that are already installed on the web server. Authors analyzed the log file using Wireshark for exploration of digital forensics evidence in the form of an IP Address attacks. The results of the analysis using Snort are digital forensics evidence in the form of IP Address and port used by attackers to access the web server. Authors suggested the blocking of IP address and port used by the attacker to access the web server in order to mitigate the attacks. Kumar et al. propose a distributed computing approach for the calculation of network centrality value for each user using the MapReduce approach [27]. Azeez et al. [28] locate phishing sites in order to prevent the users of internet from forms of phishing attacks. It examines the conceptual and literal consistency between the uses uniform resource locator (URL) and the web content.

2.1 Justification of the Study

The justification for this study is to examine the security and privacy of human daily communication using the messaging applications by determining how much information can be reconstructed from the network traffic using traffic capture and analysis tools. The results from this research will be of great importance and significance to developers of both future and existing applications. Measures can be implemented to tighten up the privacy of communication and these measures can be taken note of by future developers. The study can also help in letting users know the extent their communication is secured on different instant messengers; hence they can know what instant messengers should be adopted for confidential communications.

In addition, the tests which were conducted on a wide range of applications in the past were found to have failed at encrypting their data in one way or another. Therefore, there is more need to work in this area. Another reason is the constant changing of these communication applications; the features are added and securities are updated frequently. Facebook Messenger's new in-app downloads are an instance of this. Applications, whether or not they are present in Facebook Messenger, can store data differently depending on user settings, OS version, and manufacturer. Hence, testing needs to be carried out on new versions of these applications/OSs continually as they are released to ascertain what has changed and how much of the prior knowledge of these applications is still valid. Another importance of this research is to encourage both developers and users to care more about security and privacy of their data. It is also needful to mention that new security patches and updates in the communication protocol of any social media application called for re-verification of previous results of the analysis.

3 Methodology

The technique adopts in this research involves data gathering of applications' vulnerabilities from the vulnerabilities analysis and data classification using gathered data to carry out classification of application into malicious or benign. The flow chart in Fig. 1 depicts the process used in carrying out this experiment. In data gathering, the data related to vulnerabilities of application were gathered using the packet capture tools on a Local Area Network, where each of these tools were installed and tested to verify if they are functioning properly as required. If this is true, the tool is used for the packet capture. In addition to using instant messengers to send and receive traffic, each of these messaging applications, was downloaded and installed from the Google Play Store and accounts created or logged into. One of the two smart phones and the host system are connected to the same network while the other smart phone is connected to a different network. Both smart phones then communicate using each instant messenger, while the host system is used for traffic capture and analysis. This analysis reveals the data requires to perform the classification experiment. The second phase was the classification of data gathered from the analysis. This classification was done using the three selected classification algorithms namely Naïve Bayes, Neural network, and Random forest algorithms. The data gathering process and data classification algorithms were discussed in the section below.

The problem is to identify the vulnerability associated with some selected social media communication applications and use these variables to classify the applications into either vulnerable or non-vulnerable. In order to achieve these, selected applications were tested using two selected vulnerability tools namely wireshark and NetworkMiner Capture. The captured vulnerability data were displayed in the Tables 2 and 3. The data were "Yes" or "No" which signify whether an application is susceptible a certain attack or not. The attack could be an application can reveal "text document sent by a sender", "Image", "ISP of sender", "Location of sender", and "Audio". If any of these information can be detected or captured by the vulnerability tools, then the data is "Yes" while "No" is used to represent the scenario where the tools cannot detect the information across the application. After the successful gathering of these data, the data was represented in a binary n by m dimensional vector using "1" for yes and "0" for no data. In this case, 1 was used to represent the presence of vulnerability while 0 was used to represent the absence of vulnerability. The final data was presented for three classification algorithms namely Naïve Bayes, random forest, and neural network. These machine learning algorithms classify the vulnerability data into classification model for identifying vulnerable or non-vulnerable application.

3.1 Experiment Setting

In order to gather data through analysis of application, a TP-LINK wireless router was used to create a Local Area Network (LAN) and to provide internet access for the network. Wireshark, NetworkMiner and Netwitness Investigator were installed on the host system which had a windows10 operating system installed on it. Also, ten (10) instant messaging applications on the Android platform were installed and used for the experiment; the applications were Whatsapp, Viber, Facebook Messenger, Telegram, Imo, Snapchat, BBM, Tango, Skype and Wickr. The applications were randomly chosen with emphasis on popularity and usage. An Ethernet cable was used to connect the router to the internet while the host system was connected to the router's wireless access point. The host system was used in providing mobile hotspot for one smart phone while the other smart phone was connected to the internet through a wireless access point outside the network. Figure 2 displayed the experimental setup for the data gathering process using LAN and combination of tools.

Data Gathering. The data gathered and used were the presence or absence of a particular vulnerability in each of the application. If an application contains a vulnerability or vulnerable to an attack, then "Yes" is used to denote the presence of vulnerability, while "No" is used to denote the absence of vulnerability or an application is not vulnerable to attack. This data was depicted and presented using Table 2 and Table 3. The data was represented using n × m binary dimensional vector with yes represents presence and no represents absence. The yes and no in the Table 2 and 3 were converted to binary 1 and 0 respectively for effective training and testing of classification model.

3.2 Materials

Data Gathering Materials. The materials used for the data gathering are listed as follows:

I.   HOST SYSTEM: HP 2000 running windows 10 operating system, Intel(R) Core (TM) I3-3110M CPU @ 2.40 GHz, 2.40 GHz, installed memory RAM is 6.00 GB.
II.   TP-LINK wireless router (Model: TL-MR3420, S/N: 215B439005103, build 150319 Rel.60489n, running firmware version 3.16.9 and hardware version MR3420 V2 00000000, SSID – TP-LINK_4B98)
III. Wireshark-2.6.1 installed on host system
IV.   NetworkMiner_2–3-2 installed on host system
V.   NetwitnessInvestigator-10.6.1.1.696 installed on host system
VI.   A TECNO Camon CX Air (build number - H3713A-N-170618V105, running android version 7.0), along with a gionee m5 mini (build number – [SW VERSION] M5 mini_0301_V8334 [HW VERSION] M5 mini_Mainboard_P3, Android version 6.0)
VII. 9. Instant messaging applications (Whatsapp, Viber, Facebook Messenger, Telegram, Imo, Snapchat, Tango, Skype, Wickr) installed on both smart phones.

3.3 Classification Algorithms

Three classification algorithms used are random forest, neural network, and Naïve Bayes algorithms. These algorithms classify the input data into either malicious or benign application based on the specified classification parameters. The classification forms the model for the new classifier to be used for the identification of application. In the classification process, data were initially converted to numeric binary form and presented in an n by m binary dimensional, where "yes" or "1" represents the presence of vulnerability and "No" or "0" represents the absence of vulnerability. Data was normalized by removing redundant and duplicate. The normalized data were used to feed the classification algorithms to acquire appropriate models. two levels of headings should be numbered. Lower level headings remain unnumbered; they are formatted as run-in headings.

4 Results and Discussion

4.1 Performance Metrics

Statistical tests were used to measure the performance of the proposed model. The metrics like true positive rate, false positive, accuracy, recall, precision and F – measure are used.

TP (True positive) was defined as the vulnerable mobile application that was actually classified as vulnerable i.e. TPR is the proportion of positive instances classified correctly.

TN: non-vulnerable mobile application that was actually classified as non-vulnerable i.e. TNR is the proportion of non-vulnerable instances classified correctly.

FP: Non-vulnerable mobile application that was classified as vulnerable i.e. FPR is the proportion of non-vulnerable instances classified wrongly as positive (vulnerable).

FN: vulnerable mobile application that was classified as non-vulnerable i.e. FNR is the proportion of positive instances wrongly classified as negative (non-vulnerable mobile application.

Therefore:

$$TPR = TP/(TP + FN) \quad 4.1$$
$$TNR = TN/(TN + FP) \quad 4.2$$
$$FPR = FP/(FP + TN) \quad 4.3$$
$$FNR = TN/(TN + FN) \quad 4.4$$

The accuracy actually measures the proportion of correctly classified instances (features).

$$ACC = (TP + TN)/(TP + TN + FP + FN) \quad 4.5$$

Accuracy.

The accuracy of an algorithm is calculated as the percentage of the dataset correctly classified by the algorithm. It looks at positives or negatives dependently and therefore other measures for performance evaluation apart from the accuracy were used.

$$A = (TP + TN)/(TP + TN + FP + FN) * 100\% \quad 4.6$$

Where.

$TP = True\ Positive$
$FP = False\ Positive$
$TN = True\ Negative$

FN = False Negative

Positive and negative represents the classifier's prediction, true and false signify the classifier's expectation.

Precision *Precision = TP/(TP + FP) 4.7*

It indicates the number of instances which are positively classified and are relevant. A high precision shows high relevance in detecting positives.

4.2 Results Presentation

4.3 Result Discussion

The result of the data analysis and classification are presented in Tables 1, 2, and 3. Tables 1 and 2 presented the classification results of the vulnerabilities. This research was able to recover different traffic, including images, documents, and audio. The internet service provider of the sender was also recovered and the resident city of the third party. However, no text/document, image, audio, ISP, Location (Destination City) was recovered from only Viber application. Images were recovered from Facebook messenger, Imo, BBM, Tango and Skype. Texts/documents in different formats like octet-stream, .html, .docx, hexadecimal and plain text were recovered for all applications excluding Viber. The internet service provider of the sender was recovered when testing for WhatsApp, Facebook Messenger, Imo, Snapchat, BBM, Tango and Skype. The location of the receiver was recovered when testing for WhatsApp, Facebook Messenger, Imo, Snapchat, BBM, Tango and Skype. Tango was the only application from which an audio file was recovered. It is also very clear that only Viber messaging application is non-vulnerable while others namely Tango, Facebook Messenger, Imo, BBM, Skype, WhatsApp, Snapchat, Telegram and Wickr are vulnerable to one or more attacks. The Table 1 and 2 shown the classification accuracy, false positive and true positive rates of the models form through classification algorithms earlier mentioned. These results show random forest has better accuracy and false rate prediction than others neural network and naïve bayes, with this research data.

According to the chart in Fig. 3, it can be seen that WhatsApp has 60% vulnerability and 40% security, Facebook Messenger has 80% vulnerability with 20% security, Telegram has 20% vulnerability with 80% security, Imo has 80% vulnerability with 20% security, Snapchat has 60% vulnerability with 40% security, BBM has 80% vulnerability with 20% security, Skype has 80% vulnerability with 20% security and Wickr has 20% vulnerability with 80% security.

Table 1. Classification result of data from NetworkMiner Capture.

Models	TPR	FPR	ACC
Naïve Bayes	0.871921	0.132743	0.938095
Neural Network	0.936585	0.061364	0.938967
Random Forest	0.975432	0.031395	0.969267

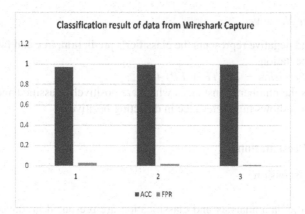

Fig. 1. Classification Accuracy and FPR from Wireshark Capture

Table 2. Classification result of data from NetworkMiner Capture

Models	TPR	FPR	ACC
Naïve Bayes	0.975432	0.031395	0.969267
Neural Network	0.981232	0.020188	0.991125
Random Forest	0.986804	0.014178	0.99381

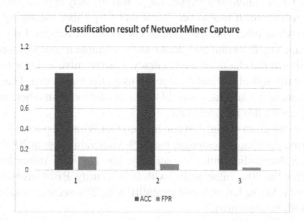

Fig. 2. Classification Accuracy and FPR from NetworkMiner Capture

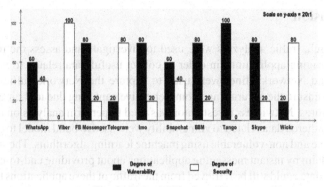

Fig. 3. Vulnerability bar chart

Table 3. Related works Applications vs. Applications used for Experiment

S/N	Applications used in previous Researches	Vulnerability Status before	Applications used in this Research	Vulnerability Status in new Experiment
1	WhatsApp Messenger v.2.11	Non-Vulnerable	WhatsApp – v2.18.267	Vulnerable
2	Audio/Video calls	Non-Vulnerable	Viber – v9.6.5	Non-Vulnerable
3	Facebook	Non-Vulnerable	Facebook Messenger – v3.2.1	Vulnerable
4	Telegram	Non-Vulnerable	Telegram – v1.4.0	Vulnerable
5	Group messages and file/media sharing	Vulnerable	Imo – v9.8.000000010451	Vulnerable
6	Message chats including text and voice chats	Non-Vulnerable	Snapchat – v10.41.5.0	Vulnerable
7	Twitter	Non-Vulnerable	BBM – v3.3.8.73	Vulnerable
8			Tango – v4.9.227627	Most-Vulnerable
9			Skype – Version 8	Vulnerable
10			Wickr Me – v4.55.1	Vulnerable

5 Conclusion

In this research, traffic analyzers were used to investigate and assess the traffic of ten popular messaging applications in order to collect useful data related to vulnerability. Wireshark and Network Miner were used to capture the Network traffic. Both tools were used to ensure the accurate and comprehensive capturing due to their emphasis on different features. Netwitness investigator was used to perform analysis on the captured traffic. The gathered data related to vulnerability were used to build model to classify data into vulnerable and non-vulnerable using machine learning algorithms. The study reveals despite the claim by instant messaging applications about providing end-to-end security, unencrypted data could still be retrieved from the traffic of these applications based on the metrics considered. Viber was shown to be the most secure for private communications while Tango was shown to be the most vulnerable for private communications.

Consequently, sensitive information should be transmitted only through channels that have been proven to be secure and insecure instant messengers should learn from secured ones in other to enhance their security.

6 Recommendation

In view of the overwhelming usage of social media applications, and consider the results of this research which found many of these applications vulnerable it is highly recommended users ensure the adequate privacy setting of the applications. In addition, users must reduce the rate of private or personal data being kept on or sent using these applications. It is also recommended the authors of these applications ensure regular and adequate update of their applications by building patches on the outdated apps.

References

1. Zhou, X., Zhao, Z., Li, R., Zhou, Y., Palicot, J., Zhang, H.: Understanding the Nature of Social Mobile Instant Messaging in Cellular Networks. 18(3), 389–392 (2014)
2. Andersson, F.: Designing a Secure Client-Server System, September 2009
3. Joshi, M., Hadi, T.H.: A review of network traffic analysis and prediction techniques. *ArXiv Preprint* ArXiv:1507.05722 (2015)
4. Dickson, M., Messenger, M.S.N.: An examination into Trillian basic 3. x contact. Digit. Investig. 4(1), 36–45 (2007). https://doi.org/10.1016/j.diin.2007.01.003
5. Meghanathan, N., Allam, S.R., Moore, L.A.: Tools and techniques for network forensics. Int. J. Netw. Secur. Appl. (IJNSA), 1(1). https://arxiv.org/ftp/arxiv/papers/1004/1004.0570.pdf
6. Husain, M.I., Sridhar, R.: iForensics : Forensic Analysis of Instant Messaging on, no. Vim, pp. 9–18 (2010.
7. Chin, E., Felt, A.P., Wagner, D.: Analyzing Inter-Application Communication in Android (2011).
8. Vidas, T., Zhang, C., Christin, N., Vidas, T., Zhang, C., Christin, N.: Towards a general collection methodology for android devices by (2011). https://doi.org/10.1016/j.diin.2011.05.003
9. Zhang, F., He, W., Liu, X., Bridges, P.G.: Inferring Users ' Online Activities Through Traffic Analysis, 59–69 (2011)

10. Appelman, M., Bosma, J., Veerman, G.: Viber communication security. Syst. Netw. Eng. Univ, Amsterdam, Netherlands (2011)
11. Schrittwieser, S., et al.: "Guess Who's Texting You? Evaluating the Security of Smartphone Messaging Applications (2012)
12. Adami, D., Callegari, C., Giordano, S., Pagano, M., Pepe, T.: Skype-hunter: a real-time system for the detection and classification of Skype traffic, no. February 2011, pp. 386–403 (2012). https://doi.org/10.1002/dac.
13. Thakur, N.S.: Forensic Analysis of WhatsApp on Android Smartphones (University Of New Orleans) (2013). https://scholarworks.uno.edu/td/1706
14. Mahajan, A., Dahiya, M., Sanghvi, H.: Forensic Analysis of Instant Messenger Applications on Android Devices. Int. J. Comput. Appl. **68**(8), 38–44 (2013). https://doi.org/10.5120/11602-6965
15. Rafique, M., Khan, M.N.A.: Exploring static and live digital forensics: methods, practices and tools. Int. J. Sci. Eng. Res. **4**(10), 1048–1056 (2013). ISSN 2229–5518
16. Coull, S.E., Dyer, K.P.: Traffic analysis of encrypted messaging services: Apple imessage and beyond. ACM SIGCOMM Comput. Commun. Rev. **44**(5), 5–11 (2014)
17. Anglano, C.: Forensic analysis of WhatsApp messenger on android smartphones arXiv : 1507 . 07739v1 [cs . CR] 28 July 2015, pp. 1–32 (2014). https://doi.org/10.1016/j.diin.2014.04.003.
18. Karpisek, F., Baggili, I., Breitinger, F.: WhatsApp network forensics: decrypting and understanding the WhatsApp call signaling messages, vol. 15, no. October, pp. 110–118 (2015)
19. Abdul Aziz, N., Mokhti, F., Nadhar, M., Nozri, M.: Mobile device forensics: extracting and analysing data from an android-based smartphone. In: 2015 Fourth International Conference on Cyber Security, Cyber Warfare, and Digital Forensic (CyberSec), pp. 123–128. IEEE Publisher (2015).
20. Walnycky, D., Baggili, I., Marrington, A., Moore, J., Breitinger, F.: Network and device forensic analysis of Android social-messaging applications. Digit. Investig. **14**, S77–S84 (2015). https://doi.org/10.1016/j.diin.2015.05.009
21. O. S. Adebayo, S. A. Sulaiman, O. Osho, S. M. Abdulhamid, J. K. Alhassan (2017). Forensics Analysis of KIK Messengers on Android Devices. 2nd International Engineering Conference (IEC: Federal University of Technology. Minna, Nigeria (2017)
22. Sudozai, M.A.K., Saleem, S.: Signatures of Viber Security Traffic Signatures of Viber Secure Traffic, vol. 12, no. 2 (2017)
23. Yusoff, M.N., Dehghantanha, A.: Network Traffic Forensics on Firefox Mobile OS : Facebook , Twitter and Telegram as Case Studies, pp. 63–78 (2017)
24. Mujaj, A.: A comparison of secure messaging protocols and implementations. University of Oslo (2017)
25. Abdul Aziz, N., Yusof, M.S.M., AbdRahman, L.H.: Acquiring and Analysing Digital Evidence - a Teaching and Learning Experience in Class. Cyber Resilience Conference (2018)
26. Riadi, D.S.: Network forensics analysis of man in the middle attack using live forensics method. Int. J. Cyber-Secur. Digit. Forensics (IJCSDF) **8**(1), 66–73 (2019). The Society of Digital Information and Wireless Communications (SDIWC). ISSN: 2305–001
27. Behera, R.K., Rath, S.K., Misra, S., Damaševičius, R., Maskeliūnas, R.: Distributed centrality analysis of social network data using MapReduce. Algorithms **12**(8), 161 (2019)
28. Azeez, N.A., Salaudeen, B.B., Misra, S., Damaševičius, R., Maskeliūnas, R.: Identifying phishing attacks in communication networks using URL consistency features. Int. J. Electron. Secur. Digit. Forensics **12**(2), 200–213 (2020)

Appraisal of Electronic Banking Acceptance in Nigeria Amidst Cyber Attacks Using Unified Theory of Acceptance and Use of Technology

Ali Usman Abdullahi[1]([✉]) [ORCID], Stephany Adamu[2], Ali Muhammad Usman[1], Munir Adewoye[1], Mustapha Abubakar Yusuf[3], Enem Theophlus Aniemeka[4], and Haruna Chiroma[1]

[1] Computer Science Education Department, Federal College of Education (Tech), Gombe, Nigeria
{usmanali,chiromaharuna}@fcetgombe.edu.ng, mayormunir0071@gmail.com, mygawuna@gmail.com
[2] Stanbic Bank Abuja, Abuja, Nigeria
adamustephanie@gmail.com
[3] Computer Sciences Department Kano State Polytechnic Kano, Kano, Nigeria
aliakko2000@gmail.com
[4] Department of Computer Science, Air Force Institute of Technology, Kaduna, Nigeria
enemtheophilus@gmail.com
http://www.fcetgombe.edu.ng

Abstract. The rolling out of different technological advancement in the day to day human endeavors are enormous. These advancements have both positive and negative effects. The positive effects are the intended ones and the most recognized. The Negative ones though not intended, but provide opportunity for criminals to thrive on them. Cyber Attack on computers and Internet technology is one of the most prominent negative effects of Information and Communication Technology. Hence, there is need for systemic study of how these negative effects affect the acceptability of these technological advancement. This paper, attempts using the Unified Theory of Acceptance and Use of Technology (UTAUT) to appraise the acceptance of Electronic banking in Nigeria despite prevalence of cyber attacks. The study used a 7 Likert scale rating questionnaire to collect data from 286 respondents from across Nigerian Commercial bankings resident in Gombe State. The study uses the Cronbach' Alhpa and Spearman's Rho Correlation to test factors of the adopted theory. The result of the work showed that there is significant correlation amongst all the UTAUT factors, implying that e-banking is accepted and used in Nigeria even with re-occurrence of cyber attacks on such system.

Keywords: Information technology · Cyber attack · Cyber crime · Unified theory of acceptance and usage of technology

© Springer Nature Switzerland AG 2021
S. Misra and B. Muhammad-Bello (Eds.): ICTA 2020, CCIS 1350, pp. 470–481, 2021.
https://doi.org/10.1007/978-3-030-69143-1_36

1   Introduction

Information Technology (IT) plays a very integral role in the development of banking industry. IT has transformed the traditional banking system making it possible for transactions to be performed conveniently without being present in the banking Hall. Electronic banking (E-banking) has led to a reasonable progress in terms of growth in the banking sector. The E-banking enables its users to carry out financial transactions with a variety of options to banking services such as opening of account, checking of balance, inter-account transfers, payment of utility bills etc. through a telecommunication networks at the users' comfort [12].

The transformation from traditional way of banking to E-Banking has brought about a significant change and development in different aspects of human life. The rapid growth in IT has led to a considerable growth and progress in the banking sector that one cannot recommend a non-electronic banking system [3,16].

The day-to-day activities of Businesses and individuals relied on information and communications technologies (ICT) in many countries. Convenience of customers and efficiency of services have become the order of the day through e-banking. Since customers are able to access their account information and perform transactions at their fingertips [4].

The definite changes brought about by rapid technological advancement covers areas of communication, education, business and entertainment. More so, this technological advancements are accompanied by greater vulnerabilities and loopholes. The Information technology has also provided new criminal opportunities of which the old criminals would not have dreamed [1,17].

Despite the positive impact of technology on our society, it has on the other hand led to unintended criminal activities in form of cyber-attacks. The fear of attackers gaining access to customers' data for fraudulent activities, have affects the acceptance of the electronic banking platform. This has make it easier the attackers to for example, steal a Kobo from millions of bank accounts through what is called Internet bank robbery [13].

The cyber-fraud as a phenomena has become more complex due to fact that the world moves closer to becoming a cashless society. Recently, not only have cyber-attacks caused financial loss but also leaked other very sensitive information. The attackers spent lot of their time in developing new means for cyber crime. Also the criminals simultaneously work on finding the solutions to bridge these defense measures [8,19].

It is reported that Cyber-attacks have been heightened by several developments. These developments include social networking and constant online communication, investing/online banking, retail and wholesale trade, foreign rogue governments [18].

In order to maintain the trust of customers and the financial institutions' integrity in-check, the Internet banking services have to be at the top-most level of security. With the advent of lots of technologies, the banks need to evaluate their security policies to ensure acceptability and patronage [6].

This study focuses on the appraising the effects of cyber-attacks on electronic banking platforms. This was done through the use of one of the IT developed and test models - the Unified Theory of the Acceptance and Use of Technology. The model was used to test the way and manner criminal attacks on the E-banking platform affect or otherwise the acceptance and usage of the E-banking platforms. The factors of the UTAUT are aligned with the measures, perceptions, technology and environment for conducting the E-banking system. This can be done by making attempt to provide answers to the following questions:

i. What are the factors that contributed to the re-occurrence of cyber-attacks on E-banking in Nigeria?
ii. To what extent do cyber-attacks affect E-banking platforms usage in Nigeria?
iii. What are the security measures put in place to prevent cyber-attacks on E-banking platforms?

Also, this study aligns the types of Cyber-attacks that affect e-banking system in Nigeria; The sensitization of users on how to detect and avoid these attacks; The security measures put in place by the banks to prevent re-occurrence of such attacks.

The remaining sections of the chapter are as follows: Sect. 2 presents the review of the literatures, Sect. 3 discusses the methodology used in the study and Sect. 4 presents the experimental setup and the results of the experiments conducted. The conclusion and future work are discussed in Sect. 5.

2   Literature Review

In this section the review of the concepts of cyber crimes, their types and security measures taken are presented.

2.1   Cyber Attacks

A cyber-attack is defined as a deliberate exploitation of computer systems, networks or technology-dependent enterprises. The Cyber-attacks are also referred to as a computer network attack (CNA). The attacker uses malicious code to alter computer logic, code or data which may result in disruptive consequences such as data compromise and theft of information and identity [9].

According to crime-research.org [9], as early as 2003 the United States was leading the world with 35.4% of cyber-attacks, followed by South Korea having 12.8% [10].

The list of Cyber-attacks includes but not limited to the following: identity theft, denial of service, fraud extortion, phishing, malware, pharming, spyware, breach of access, Trojans, viruses and Spams.

According to Javelin Strategy and Research, about US16 billion was stolen from 12.7 million consumers in the US alone in 2014 through identity theft [17].

Also, the identity theft is not used for than just financial fraud, but is a central pillar for all manner of cyber-crimes. Once individual's identity is impersonated, then access can gained to their accounts; and multiple frauds can be committed in their name [11,17].

The Cyber-attacks are reported by business ISP Beaming to have cost UK businesses as much as £30 billion in 2016. This claim was backed up by the Cyber Crime Assessment 2016 conducted by National Crime Agency (NCA) which estimates the cost of cyber-crime to the UK's economy in "billions of pounds per annum – and is growing [17].

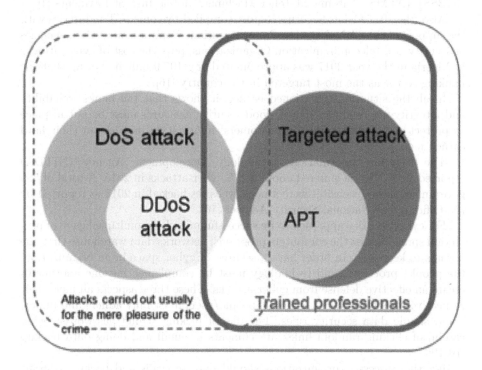

Fig. 1. Diagram of cyber attacks and theri relationship

Figure 1 depicts the categories of cyber-attacks, which include the targeted attacks geared at particular organizations, services, and individuals. The type of attack is usually carried out to obtain private, technical, institutional information or intellectual assets with vandalism intent or monetary gains. Targeted attacks include deploying a bonnet, spearfishing or subverting the supply chain others. The Advanced persistent threat (APTs) is a kind of targeted attack that continuously use variety of means in order to gain access through to their target. Then, there is the un-targeted attacks. In this the attackers target as many devices or users as they can, in search of different vulnerabilities. In doing so, exploring advantages brought about by the openness of the Internet. These advantages include Phishing, water holing, ransomeware, scanning etc. [11].

Financial loss through making false transaction is one of the major impacts cyber-attacks causes. The Cyber attackers can steal confidential information and sell it, or even use it for terrorism and spying. Attacker target customers through their organizations, which may result in customers' frustration or identity theft. Consequently, destructing organization's public image and labeling as insufficient in information security compliance [8].

Furthermore, cyber crime was rated by the Central Bank of Nigeria (CBN) as one of the biggest risk of the country's financial sector. The crime is threatening electronic payment solutions such as Nigeria Inter-bank Settlement System (NIBSS), (ATMS) Automated Teller Machines, Mobile Instant Payments [16].

Also, the 2017 Cyber Security Report compiled by some ICT industries with the support of the CBN, Nigerian Communications Commission (NCC), agencies of security and telecommunication Organizations, puts the cost of cyber-attacks in Nigeria in the year 2017 was approximated at N197.9 billion. Noting that the banking sector as the most targeted in the country [16].

In all the situations mentioned earlier, it shows that the banks' reliability and integrity are at stake. Hence, good security measures must be put in place to protect the confidentiality of customers' information and lost of their hard earned money [16].

The Nigerian Information Technology Development Agency (NITDA) reported that, Nigeria suffered about 2,175 cyber-attacks in 2015. A total of 585 government owned websites were among websites hacked in 2015 as reported by the Office of the National Security Adviser [16].

For cyber security approach to be successful must have multiple layers of protection spread across the computers programs, networks data warehouse that one intends to keep safe. In order have a secured of cyber space in an organization, the people, processes, and technology must be complementing one another to create an effective defense from cyber-attacks. These three aspects all have their respective roles to play. For example, people/users must fully adhere and understand simple data security rules. The like of picking strong passwords; being careful of clicking random links; attachments in email and doing data backup [10, 19].

For the processes, organizations should have firewalls and backup systems in place in event of possible failure. This minimizes the actual consequences of failure it occurred. The organizations must have a framework explaining how to identify attacks, protect systems, react to threats and recover from attacks. With the presence of system backup, mild breach would not prevent the business or organization from operating on the backup while the problem is addressed [6].

Then, when it comes to technology, the three main entities which must be protected are; endpoint devices (computers, Tablets, smart phoneand routers), networks and the cloud. The common technologies used to protect these entities are Domain Name Server filtering, malware protection, anti-virus software, next-generation firewalls, and email security solutions [10].

3 Methodology

3.1 Research Design

This study employs a cross sectional descriptive survey research method to collect data, modeled it, critically analyze the effects of cyber-attacks on electronic banking platforms in Nigeria.

As a survey research method, the target population provides responses to a series of statements in a questionnaire. The items for data collection was tied to the UTAUT model. The analysis was done using standardized statistical procedures of Cronbach's Alpha for reliability testing and Spearman's Rho correlation. Also, simple percentage was used for presenting the demographic analysis of the study.

3.2 Population of the Study

The population of the survey targeted users and stake holders of commercial bank offering e-banking. These number may not be easily arrived at. However, using the cochran formula Eq. 1 with population of 1000 and significant level of 5%, a total sample 286 respondents was arrive at. Twenty (20) persons from each commercial banks were randomly selected. The respondents consist of the both customers and employees of different the banks.

$$n = \frac{N}{1 + N(\delta)^2} \tag{1}$$

Where n is the size of sample, N is the total population and delta as the level of significance.

3.3 Data Collection

The instrument of data collection in this study was the questionnaire developed based on the study's three research questions. In essence, the questions asked are tailored to elicit the data using a 7 Likert scale rating. The questionnaires were administered both offline and online using Google forms. The respondents were presented with this link https://docs.google.com/forms to access the questionnaire.

3.4 Research Model

The research adopts the unified theory of acceptance and use of technology as the model of the study. From the past literatures based on this model, the following expectations was developed to investigate the influence of cyber-attacks on electronic banking platforms. The model will be used to evaluate if its acceptance and adoption is favorable or unfavorable to its users:

i. Performance Expectancy – The degree to which users believed using electronic banking help them gain job performance.

ii. Effort Expectancy – The degree of ease associated with use electronic banking

iii. Social Influence – The degree to which users perceive how important others believed they should use electronic banking.

iv. Facilitating Conditions - The degree to which users believe the an organizational and technical infrastructure exist supporting the use electronic banking

v. Attitude Factor – The degree to which users believed good and interesting is the idea of using electronic banking.

These factors are the ones that are relevant to the this study. They are contained in the generic UTAUT model depicted in Fig. 2.

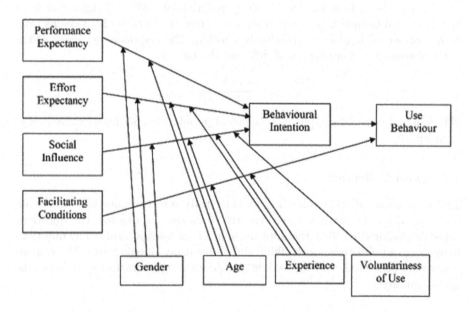

Fig. 2. Conceptual model of unified theory of acceptance and use of technology (UTAUT)

4   Result and Discussion

This section presents the results of the study, the research findings, implication and the analysis. This paper sought to presents the results as a test in achieving to the objectives of the study.

The first part of the result presentation gives the demographic distribution and analysis of the responders. This is done to highlight who participated in the study.

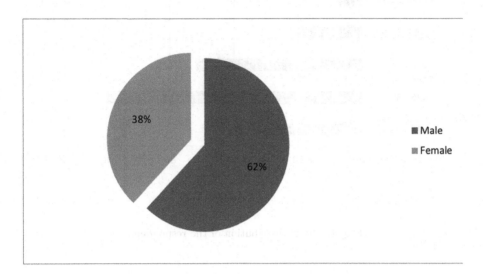

Fig. 3. Gender distribution of the respondents

Figure 3 shows the gender distribution of the responders. From the chart, it shows that there are 24% male respondents more than their female counterparts. This suggested that the male respondents are more conversant with electronic banking platforms compared to their female counterparts. This may also means that, the female users may be slow adopters of the technological advancement in the electronic means of banking and hence, so a huge number of them are not affected by cyber-attacks.

Also, Fig. 4 presents the age distribution of the respondents. The result shows that majority of the respondents belonged to the category of 26–35 years of age. Whereas the least among the respondents are those with 55 years of age and above with 4%. Majority of the response were gotten from the younger respondents. This implies that majority of the youth are conversant with emerging technologies and adapt easily to its usage.

From Fig. 5 which displays the qualifications of the respondents. The figure shows that the majority of the respondents representing 50% had Bachelor's Degree. While the minorities of the respondents were Ph.D. holders. This implies that, majority of the respondents were educated, technologically advanced, and hence, excellent adopters.

The second part of the result's presentation and analysis, was done using the UTAUT model. The presentation has two segments; the items reliability analysis and the correlation analysis. the reliability analysis was carried out using the Cronbach's Alpha reliability testing. While the correlation was tested using the

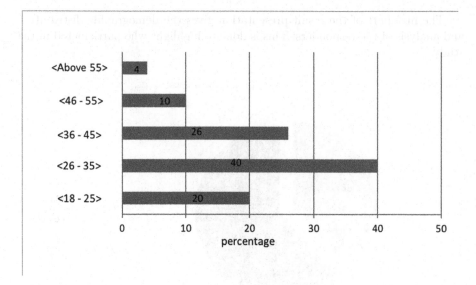

Fig. 4. Age of distribution of the respondents

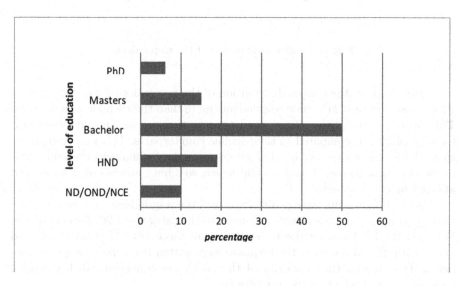

Fig. 5. Educational qualification of the respondents

Spearman's rho Correlation Analysis. Both tools were the recommended tools for use with the UTAUT.

Table 1 shows the result of the Cronbach's Alpha reliability test for the items of the questionnaire.

From Table 1 it can be seen that all UTAUT factors are having the Cronbach's Aplha value of 0.5 and above. This means that all the response given based on

Table 1. Reliability analysis of the utaut factors using cronbach's alpha

Item	Cronbach's alpha values	Number of varibles
Attitude	0.964	5
Effort expectancy	0.978	8
Social influence	0.948	6
Facility condition	0.544	5
Performance expectancy	0.760	6

Factor		Attitude	Effort Expectancy	Social Influence	Facility Condition	Performance Expectancy
Attitude	Correlation Coefficient		1.00	1.00	1.00	1.00
	Sig. (2-tailed)		0.0	0.0	0.0	0.0
Effort Expectancy	Correlation Coefficient	0.986**		1.00	1.00	1.00
	Sig. (2-tailed)	0		0.0	0.0	0.0
Social Influence	Correlation Coefficient	0.954**	0.958**		1.00	1.00
	Sig. (2-tailed)	0	0		0.0	0.0
Facility Condition	Correlation Coefficient	0.303**	0.291**	0.292**		1.00
	Sig. (2-tailed)	0.002	0.003	0.003		0.0
Performance Expectancy	Correlation Coefficient	0.701**	0.726**	0.764**	0.269**	
	Sig. (2-tailed)	0	0	0	0.007	

Fig. 6. Spearman's rho correlation analysis on the UTAUT factors

the items under each factor are reliable. The Effort Expectancy factor has the highest reliability and the Facility condition having the lowest. This was so, even though the factors' item variation are between 5 to 6. Thus, this shows that all the responses used are reliable.

Since, the responses to the UTAUT factors are found to be reliable, Then, the next thing is to test for correlation between each pair of the factors in order to see whether there is significant relation between them. Figure 6 presents the correlation analysis result in a matrix form. This is done for easy and better presentation instead of using individual table which was the norm.

Figure 6 displays the matrix for Spearman's rho Correlation Analysis for all the factors. The intersection of any pair of factors contain two values the correlation coefficient and Significant (2 tallied) values. The area shaded in green, are the intersection with correlation values that are more than the P value of 0.05. Hence, the correlation between the two intersecting factors is significant at the 0.01 level (2-tailed). This is the situation for all the pairs of the UTAUT factors tested. Moreover, this implied that all UTAUT factors used in the work have significant correlation and have together influence the way and manner in which cyber attack shaped the e-banking system in Nigeria.

Furthermore, the findings show that 87% of the respondents agreed that certain factors like knowledge gap, selfish business gain are among the factors contributing to the re-occurrence of cyber-attacks. Thus, there should be improvement in avoidance of security breaches and more efforts towards securing e-banking users personal details.

5   Conclusion

The study have find out that despite persistent cyber attack of different magnitudes and dimensions, e-banking system as emerging technology is gaining acceptance by users. The set objective of the study which were modeled with UTAUT show that there significant correlation amongst all the factor used. This in turn means, users behavior towards acceptance and use of the e-banking system is influenced by the individual and the group of the UTAUT's factors.

Also, the results of the study show that, cyber attacking is seen as a business opportunity to some people driven by selfish gain and profit. In addition, the absence of, or ineffective law enforcement efforts on computer related fraud encourages the violators to perpetuate cyber-attacks. Lastly, the low level of cyber literacy amongst e-banking users make them vulnerable to the cyber attacks.

Furthermore, the results suggested that for the extent of the effects of the cyber attacks, the respondents indicated reduced customer confidence in Online banking transactions. This affects the integrity and reputation of a bank; also, negatively impact the decisions of investors.

Notwithstanding, the respondents in general indicated acceptance and use of the e-banking system. Thus, the study observed and recommended the following: There should be a continuous increase of the security layers trough emerging security technologies such as firewalls, anti-virus software, intrusion detection systems (IDSs), data loss prevention (DLP), and effective cloud based backup and recovery systems. Also, the training and re-training of the ICT staff manning these improved technologies, should be frequent. In addition, a sustain advocacy, campaign and enlightenment for e-banking customers on how to avoid been vulnerable or compromising sensitive information should be keep constant.

References

1. Olumide, O.O., Victor, F.B.: E-crime in Nigeria: trends, tricks, and treatment. Pac. J. Sci. Technol. **11**(1), 343–355 (2010)
2. Olumoye, M.Y.: Cyber crime and technology misuse: overview, impacts and preventive measures. Euro. J. Comput. Sci. Inf. **1**(3), 10–20 (2013)
3. Maryanne, M.N.: Factors Contributing to Occurrence of Cybercrime on E-Banking in Commercial Banks in Kenya (2015)
4. Ali, L., Ali, F., Priyanka, S., Bindhya, T.: The effects of cyber threats on customer behaviour in e-banking services. Int. J. e-Education e-Business, e-Management e-Learning **7**(1), 70–78 (2016)
5. Liaqat, A.: Cybercrime a Constant Threat for the Business Sector and its Growth (2019)
6. Atmel, F.: Impact of Cyber-attacks on Financial Institutions. J. Internet Bank. Commer.(2018)
7. Ewepu, G.: Nigeria loses N127bn annually to cyber-crime - NSA (2016)
8. Mahmadi, F.N., Zaaba, Z.F., Osman, A.: Computer Security Issues in Online Banking (2016)
9. Jackson, J.T., Robert, W.E.: Cybercrime and the challenges of socio-economic development in Nigeria. JORIND **14**(2), 42–49 (2016)
10. Hassan, A.B., Lass, F.D., Makinde, J.: Cybercrime in Nigeria: causes, effects and the way out, arpn. J. Sci. Technol. **2**(7), 626–631 (2012)
11. Iroegbu, E.: Cyber-security: Nigeria loses over N127bn annually through Cyber-crime (2019). http://www.thisdaylive.com/index.php/2016/04/18/cyber-security-nigeria-loses-over-n127bn-annually-through-cybercrime/
12. Omotayo, F.O., Adebayo, A. K.: Factors influencing intention to adopt internet banking by postgraduate students of the University of Ibadan, Nigeria (2015)
13. Wada, F., Odulaja, G.O.: Electronic banking and cyber crime in Nigeria - a theoretical policy perspective on causation. Afr. J. Comp. ICT **5**(1), 69–82 (2014)
14. Prince, O., Juliet, U.: Nigeria: rising wave of e-frauds puts economy at risk. The Vanguard Newspaper Nigeria (2018)
15. Ojeka, S., Ben-Caleb, E., Ekpe, E.O.I.: Cyber security in the nigerian banking sector: an appraisal of audit committee effectiveness. Int. Rev. Manag. Market. **7**(2), 340–346 (2017)
16. Oteh, U.O., Iboka N.I., Nto C.P.O.: Adoption and Usage of E-Banking Channels in Nigeria: Implication for Deepening Financial Inclusion (2017)
17. Olasanmi, O.O.: Computer crimes and counter measures in the nigerian banking sector. J. Internet Bank. Commer. **15**(1), 1 (2010)
18. DeZabala, T., Baich, R.: Cybercrime: a clear and present danger. Combating the fastest growing security threat. pp. 4–6 (2010)
19. Nto, P.O.O., Nto, C.P.O., Mbanasor, J.A.: Socio-economic determinants of the adoption of electronic banking in Abia State. Nigeria. British J. Appl. Sci. Technol. **4**(7), 1089–1099 (2014)

Information Science and Technology

A Scoping Review of the Literature on the Current Mental Health Status of Developers

Ghaida Albakri[1] and Rahma Bouaziz[1,2(✉)]

[1] Computer Science Departement, Taibah University, Medina, Saudi Arabia
ghaydalbakri@gmail.com, rkammoun@taibahu.edu.sa
[2] ReDCAD, University of Sfax, Sfax, Tunisia

Abstract. Year after year the need for technical solutions increased, which made the role of software developers more important. However, researchers found that developers' productivity increased based on their happiness and unhappiness. In addition, focusing on the developer's happiness will provide more problem solvers with better abilities of analysis. To understand the happiness and unhappiness of software developers, we need to process in the behavioral software engineering (BSE) area. In this research, we gathered related problems and generate hypotheses that solve those problems. Besides, we specify a research plan for each hypothesis.

Keywords: Affect · Happiness · Software development life cycle · Qualitative research · Quantitative research · Open-ended questions · Closed-ended questions

1 Introduction

For years, researchers were seeking the link between software developer performance and happiness. The researchers declared that improving developer performance can be done by focusing on the following aspects: 1) the developers and their ability to exceed the process, 2) the fact that human factors dominate over the software development process 3) software development process is an intellectual complex process which can be achieved using the processing abilities, 4) the fact that software development process can't be engineered led to understanding the unpredictable development environment that affects the developers, 5) individuals emotions and moods (affects) influence process that made by sense, 6) in addition to, how the performance of problem-solving linked with other cognitive processes [1]. Finally, other factors i.e. job performance feedback and peer support [2]. The software development process is a sense-making process, which dominated by individuals' emotions and moods (affects) [1].

Many studies attempted to find the connection between affect and software developer performance. Therefore, there is a need for studying the developers experiencing either positive or negative feelings during the development process and its impact on performance and productivity during the software development process. The researchers categorize the happiness and unhappiness consequences mainly based on the mental

S. Misra and B. Muhammad-Bello (Eds.): ICTA 2020, CCIS 1350, pp. 485–496, 2021.
https://doi.org/10.1007/978-3-030-69143-1_37

well-being of the developer, the process of software development, and the artifacts that are produced [3].

In [3] researchers affirm that to increase productivity, we need to study the consequences of both happiness and unhappiness on the development process Productivity study is beneficial for companies to provide the right circumstances for the software developers. Also, to measure the productivity of each individual while understanding the cause behind it [4]. However, usually, quantitative, qualitative, or mixed-method research is used to study the case. Moreover, the research phases in order: forming questions, collecting the data, analyzing the data, interoperation, and validation [5]. In this research, we will investigate further the encountered consequences of happiness and unhappiness during the development process by software developers. Moreover, we gathered the problems related to this topic and suggest hypotheses that solve the problems. Besides, we provide a research plan relative to the gathered problems.

The rest of the article is organized as follows. Section 2 defines the preliminaries related to the topic. Section 3 discusses the selected topic and the motivation behind it. The gathered problems are represented in Part 4. Part 5 contains the hypnotists that solve the gathered problems. The research plan for each hypothesis in part 6. Part 7 concludes this report.

2 Preliminaries

2.1 Affect

Affect is defined globally as "a neurophysiological state that is consciously accessible as a simple, non-reflective feeling that is an integral blend of hedonic (pleasure – displeasure) and arousal (sleepy – activated) values" [6].

2.2 Happiness

Happiness is defined as experiential episodes sequences while being happy is related to experiencing the positive effect frequently. Moreover, [7] happiness denoted as subjective well-being, while denoted as psychological well-being [8]. However, an individual's happiness is associated with sensing of their effect [3] and can be accomplished by increasing pleasures and decreasing pain [9].

2.3 Software Development Life Cycle

The phases of constructing a software system. The phases include requirements gathering and planning, design, development, test, and deployment [10].

Figure 1 represents the 5 phases of the software life cycle in order.

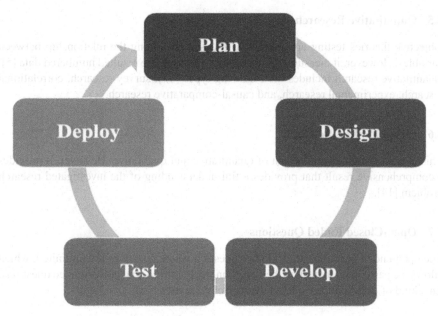

Fig. 1. Software development life cycle

2.4 Qualitative Research

The scientific inquiry aims to construct a full understanding of phenomena related to culture or society [7]. However, it can be done using one of the following types:

1. **Ethnography:** used for cultural understanding, observation & interviews used to collect the data. However, academic research and UX usually use it [11].
2. **Narrative:** used to grasp experience and sequence of individual, which can be applied to 1–5 participants. Moreover, typically data collected from individuals' stories and documents, while it is used to develop persona [11].
3. **Phenomenological:** used to gain people experience, while the number of participants from 5 to 25. However, the data collected through, it used to get the participation personal impact [11].
4. **Grounded Theory:** used to create a theory grounded in the data field, while the participant number is from 20–60. An interview is usually used to collect the data, then open and axial coding. Typically used for academic research [11]. However, this type usually relies on coding the data to be connected to generate theories out of it [12].
5. **Case Study:** used to elucidate an organization process, individual, or event, usually applied on one case or multiple. Moreover, data collected by interviews or reports, mainly used for education and research academics [11].

2.5 Quantitative Research

Objective theories testing approach, that focuses on finding the relationship between variables. However, it measures the variables to analyze the resulted numbered data [5]. Quantitative research includes the following types [13]: survey research, correlational research, experimental research, and causal-comparative research.

2.6 Mixed Method Research

This approach contains both data of quantitative and qualitative. However, it provides a comprehensive result that provides a full understanding of the investigated research problem [14].

2.7 Open-Closed Ended Questions

The open-ended questions are a kind of question where questions are unlimited, which allows the participant to declare their opinion freely [15]. About closed-ended questions, This kind of question have a fixed number of responses [15].

3 Related Works

Within the last decade, substantial research has been performed and published worldwide under the keywords "Developer mental health". The main focus is enhancing conditions of work and life quality, that can be achieved by the realization of a software developer's happiness and unhappiness. The study will be in the area of Behavioral Software Engineering (BSE), which is defined as "the study of cognitive, behavioral and social aspects of software engineering performed by individuals, groups or organizations" [16]. Many works are done on BSE as part of human factors in software engineering [17–19].

The latest researches in the field of behavioral software engineering focused on the link between the happiness of software developers and constructs that are related to work including productivity and performance, quality, developer's social interactions [3]. Many studies show that focusing on the developer's happiness will provide more problem solvers with better abilities of analysis. Therefore, the need to understand the happiness and unhappiness of developers increased [20].

We aim to investigate using the same area for many reasons including that a few researchers found that understand the developer's experienced consequence of happiness, which consider an important one. Also, an opportunity for increasing the developer's happiness to increase productivity, which can be done by happiness and unhappiness study. Moreover, researches in the area of developer happiness use a sample usually from all over the world, not taking into consideration that it might differ based on the region, gender, and experience. Also, helping the organizations to build the right environment that enriches the work conditions and life quality, which in turn increases the performance of the developers all over the world [20]. Finally, gaining a better understanding of the developer's happiness and unhappiness to help other researchers of worker happiness [3].

Based on the search we will classify the related problems according to the used approach, research sample, and test during one or more software development phases. Each of the items contains sub-items related to it, we will discuss sub-items regarding problems and why we consider it as problems.

The problems in Table 1 are considered promising since they contain important aspects of research approaches. Addressing these problems related to qualitative, quantitative, or mixed-method approach would produce more relevant and improved results.

Table 1. Problems of the used approach

Items	Sub-items	Results	References	Comment future scope
Approach	Qualitative approach	–	–	Good area to be study
	Quantitative approach	Programmer's ability to discover and correct errors increased depending on their level of being activated/deactivated	[21]	Questioner contains closed-ended questions
		Programming task productivity increased by the positive effects of developers	[22]	Using SAM questioners
	Mixed method approach	Categorize the happiness and unhappiness consequences mainly based on the mental well-being of the developer, the process of software development, and the artifacts that are produced	[3]	Questioner contains open-ended and close-ended questions, qualitative coding could be enhanced
		Positive effect on performance and happiness at work	[9]	Interview and questioners

The problems in Table 2 are considered promising since most of the papers facing a common problem. Addressing these problems related to the research sample size and data type would produce more relevant and improved results.

Table 2. Problems of the research sample

Items	Sub-items	Results	References	Comment future scope
Research sample	317 developers	42 unhappiness consequences, while 32 happiness consequences	[3]	Good sample size, gender-biased, need enhancement in a matter of developer work type also apply to a specific region
	12 Under graduation student	In 48 h, the software developer affects dramatically change	[23]	Could be enhanced, apply on developers Small sample size
	49 developers	Productivity enhanced by positive effects, while it decreased by negative affect	[24]	Small sample size, need enhancement in a matter of developer work type (employed or free-lancer)
	4 student and 4 developers	Self-assessed productivity of a programming task increased by positive effects of developers	[22]	Small sample size, gender-biased 7 out of 8 were men
	56 developers	The positive effect and productivity in design increased by using music	[25]	Developers from four different companies Gender biased

The problems in Table 3 considered promising since it contains important aspects related to software development stages. Addressing these problems related to the five stages would produce more relevant and improved results.

Table 3. Problems of software development. t phases.

Items	Sub-items	Results	References	Comment future scope
Software development phases	Requirements gathering phases	The final requirements raise a high effect of happiness in comparison to the non-final requirements	[26]	No need for enhancement
	Design phase	The positive effect and productivity in design increased by using the music	[25]	Could be enhanced by applying it to all phases
	Programming phase	Found the positive and negative emotions triggered while the software development process	[27]	Could be enhanced by applying it to all phases
	Debugging phase	When the positive affects increased it enhance the debugging performance	[28]	Could be enhanced by applying it to all phases
		Level of developer excitement affect error finding in the debugging phase	[21]	Debugging problems weren't from a real program could be enhanced
	All phases	At the beginning of the project, team emotions were positive which didn't affect the processes, while negative emotions dominate over the project life while affecting the processes	[29]	Good results no enhancement

4 Development of Hypotheses

This section offers our hypothesis for the related problem presented earlier in this paper. For each hypothesis, we explain the reason behind specifying it and the research plan.

Each research plan discusses the way to apply each hypothesis. All the research plans we offer can be achieved nowadays; so, they only need to be tested on real data.

To decrease the time of qualitative data coding and provide more accurate results, machine learning is used [30]. However, [30] declared that the researchers of this kind of approach usually lack the knowledge of machine learning basics; therefore, they need to be associated with machine learning researchers to apply the text analysis. Our hypothesis valuable since it enhances the result of the qualitative coding process, besides it will decrease the coding time. Apply ground theory qualitative approach, using open-ended questions. However, the coding of the collected data will be done by machine learning using the text analysis. The research should answer the following questions: Q1 what are the encountered consequences of happiness during the software development process that developers face? Q2 what are the encountered consequences of unhappiness during the software development process that developers face? As an alternative to applying the qualitative coding on the qualitative data, we analyze faster and more accurate using machine learning, to extract the encountered consequence of happiness and unhappiness of developers.

In [3, 24] the sample was from all over the world, which considered too general in a matter of applying the study. Since each region in the world has its condition and limitation, which could affect developer happiness and unhappiness. Thus, each region should be tested to extract the developer's related consequences of happiness and unhappiness. Our hypothesis aimed to study each region's consequences of happiness and unhappiness results by applying the study on developers, to provide more inclusive results of each region. Using a mixed-methods approach we divide the research into two studies, including a quantitative approach with closed-ended and the qualitative approach with open-ended questions survey. The research should answer the following questions: Q1 what are the encountered consequences of happiness during the software development process that developers face? Q2 what are the encountered consequences of unhappiness during the software development process that developers face? Q3 what are the encountered consequences of happiness related to religion that developers face during the software development process? Q4 what are the encountered consequences of unhappiness related to religion that developers face during the software development process? Then categorize the qualitative data to be analyzed by open and axial coding to extract the consequence of happiness and unhappiness of Saudi developers.

A limitation is specified in [3, 22, 25] that the sampling size is biased toward the male. Since both genders are occupying the developer job both should be integrated within the study equally. According to [31] gender differs in the level of happiness, where males with full-time jobs encounter positive feelings and females encounter negative feelings. However, based on the results in [31] we conclude that there is a difference between male and female happiness, which needs to be considered. Our hypothesis aimed to study each gender consequences of happiness and unhappiness results by applying the study on each gender separately or on both genders with equal numbers of participation, to provide more inclusive results of each gender. Apply the study on gender separately. Using a mixed-methods approach by dividing the research into two studies one for each gender, including a quantitative approach with a closed-ended question and a qualitative approach with open-ended questions survey. The research should answer the following questions: Q1 what are the encountered consequences of happiness during the software development process that male developers face? Q2 what are the encountered consequences of unhappiness during the software development process that male developers face? Q3 what are the encountered consequences of happiness during the software development process that female developers face? Q4 what are the encountered consequences of unhappiness during the software development process that female developers face? Then categorize the qualitative data to be analyzed by open and axial coding to extract the consequence of happiness and unhappiness of developers based on gender.

In [3, 24] the sample of developers included both employed and free-lancers. The researchers in [32] found that the work satisfaction of self-employed individuals is higher than the employed. Also, the results include the pay impact and working hours [32]. Therefore, in [33] the researchers clarify that the self-employed encounter positive effect in comparison with employed developers, which vary based on region. Our hypothesis considers it important to gain a comprehensive result of both employed and free-lancer developer's consequences of happiness and unhappiness. To test the real consequences of happiness and unhappiness, testing should be done in a real environment unlike, the way it was applied in [21]. The real environment means working on a real project to experience real consequences. Thus, a real use case of developers working dedicated to actual code should be used to trigger the actual consequences of happiness and unhappiness. Our hypothesis is valuable because it aims to trigger the real consequences that developers encounter using real debugging code, then compare it with the consequences in countered when using any other debugging code. Apply the study on employed and free-lancer developers separately. Using a mixed-methods approach by dividing the research into two studies one for employed and the other for free-lancer, including a quantitative approach with closed-ended questions and a qualitative approach with open-ended questions survey. The research should answer the following questions: Q1 what are the encountered consequences of happiness during the software development process that employed developers face? Q2 what are the encountered consequences of unhappiness during the software development process that employed developers face? Q3 what are the encountered consequences of happiness during the software development process that free-lancer developers face? Q4 what are the encountered consequences of unhappiness during the software development process that free-lancer developers face? Then analyze using open and axial coding to extract the consequence of happiness and unhappiness of free-lancer and employed developers.

The researchers in [29] provide a comprehensive result while applying the study over the full life cycle of software development, unlike applying it on one phase only as it is declared in [25, 27, 28]. However, at the beginning of the project team emotions were positive which didn't affect the processes, while negative emotions dominate over the project life while affecting the processes. Thus, we need to pay attention to the negative emotions that dominate all phases and study it further, which allows us to extract the consequences more deeply. Our hypothesis is valuable because it will enhance the result by applying the study to every phase. However, applying the study over the 5 phases (information gathering, analysis, design, implementation and, maintenance) separately, will provide a result of each phase combining all will provide a comprehensive result of the consequences. Using a quantitative approach with closed-ended questions. Moreover, the research will be divided into two parts, the first part will be applied to developers using any debugging code, while the second part will be applied during a real project debagging stage. In both parts, the following question will be asked: Q1 what are the encountered consequences of happiness during the fake debugging stage that employed developers face? Q2 what are the encountered consequences of unhappiness during the fake debugging stage that employed developers face? Q3 what are the encountered consequences of happiness during the real debugging stage that developers face? Q4 what are the encountered consequences of unhappiness during the real debugging stage that developers face? Then analyze the data to extract the consequence of happiness and unhappiness of developers in the real and the fake debugging stage. Using a qualitative approach including open-ended questions over each phase of the software development life cycle, to trigger the experienced consequences in each phase. Q1 what are the encountered consequences of happiness during the fake debugging stage that employed developers face? Q2 what are the encountered consequences of unhappiness during the fake debugging stage that employed developers face? Then analyze using open and axial coding to extract the consequence of happiness and unhappiness of developers encounter in each phase.

5 Conclusion

In this report, we discussed the importance of happiness and unhappiness of software developers. However, researchers have found that the productivity of developers has improved based on their happiness and unhappiness. In addition, focusing on the satisfaction of the creator would provide more problem solvers with improved analytical capabilities. We need to process behavioral software engineering (BSE) in order to recognize the happiness and unhappiness of software developers. Thus, we gathered the problem related to this topic to be solved by the proposed hypotheses. In this study, we have collected related problems and developed hypotheses that solve those problems. In addition, we define a research strategy for each hypothesis. Moreover, we offer a research plan for each discussed hypothesis. The future work will include applying the proposed research plans, test them, analyze and evaluate their results .

Acknowledgments. We would like to thank Dr. Masud Hasan for his valuable comments and helpful suggestion.

References

1. Graziotin, D., Wang, X., Abrahamsson, P.: Software developers, moods, emotions, and performance. arXiv preprint arXiv:1405.4422. 17 May 2014
2. Murphy-Hill, E.: What predicts software developers' productivity? IEEE Trans. Softw. Eng. (2019)
3. Graziotin, D., Fagerholm, F., Wang, X., Abrahamsson, P.: What happens when software developers are (un) happy. J. Syst. Softw. **140**, 32–37 (2018)
4. Sadowski, C., Zimmermann, T.: Rethinking Productivity in Software Engineering. Springer, Berlin (2019)

5. Creswell, J.W., Creswell, J.D.: Research Design: Qualitative, Quantitative, and Mixed Methods Approach. Sage publications, California (2017)
6. Russell, J.A.: Core affect and the psychological construction of emotion. Psychol. Rev. **110**(1), 145 (2003)
7. Zelenski, J.M., Murphy, S.A., Jenkins, D.A.: The happy productive worker thesis revisited. J. Happiness Stud. **9**(4), 521–537 (2008)
8. Wright, T.A., Cropanzano, R.: The happy/productive worker thesis revisited (2007)
9. Dorp, T.V.: Agile Teams: Experienced Work Characteristics and Their Effects on Employees' Perceived Job Performance and Happiness at Work (Master's thesis) (2019)
10. Leau, Y.B., Loo, W.K., Tham, W.Y., Tan, S.F.: Software development life cycle AGILE vs traditional approaches. In: International Conference on Information and Network Technology, vol. 37, no. 1, pp. 162–167 (2012)
11. Work, E.Y.: Qualitative research (2018)
12. Astelin, P.K.: Qualitative research designs: a conceptual framework. Int. J. Soc. Sci. Interdiscipl. Res. **2**(1), 118–124 (2013)
13. Sukamolson, S.: Fundamentals of quantitative research. Language Institute at Chulalongkorn University (2007)
14. Van Griensven, H., Moore, A.P., Hall, V.: Mixed methods research–The best of both worlds? Man. Ther. **19**(5), 367–371 (2014)
15. Reja, U., Manfreda, K.L., Hlebec, V., Vehovar, V.: Open-ended vs close-ended questions in web questionnaires. Develop. Appl. Stat. **19**(1), 159–177 (2003)
16. Lenberg, P., Feldt, R., Wallgren, L.G.: Behavioral software engineering: a definition and systematic literature review. J. Syst. Softw. **1**(107), 15–37 (2015)
17. Ibrahim, A., Misra, S., Cafer, F.: The role of leadership cognitive complexity in software development projects: an empirical assessment. Hum. Factors Ergon. Manuf. Serv. Ind. **21**(5), 443–525 (2011)
18. Fernández-Sanz, L., Misra, S.: Influence of human factors in software quality and productivity. In: Murgante, B., Gervasi, O., Iglesias, A., Taniar, D., Apduhan, B.O. (eds.) Computational Science and Its Applications, vol. 6786, pp. 257–269. Springer, Heidelberg (2011). https://doi.org/10.1007/978-3-642-21934-4_22
19. Misra, S., Akman, A.I.: Cognitive Model for Meetings in the process of Software developments. Hum. Factors Ergon. Manuf. Serv. Ind. **24**(1), 1–13 (2014)
20. Graziotin, D., Wang, X., Abrahamsson, P.: Happy software developers solve problems better: psychological measurements in empirical software engineering. Peer J. **2**, e289 (2014)
21. Khan, I.A., Hierons, R.M., Brinkman, W.P.: Moods and programmers' performance. In: PPIG, p. 2 (2007)
22. LNCS Homepage. https://www.springer.com/lncs. Accessed 21 Nov 2016
23. Khan, I.A., Hierons, R.M., Brinkman, W.P.: Moods and programmers' performance. In: PPIG, p. 2 (2007)
24. Graziotin, D., Wang, X., Abrahamsson, P.: Are happy developers more productive? In: Heidrich, J., Oivo, M., Jedlitschka, A., Baldassarre, M.T. (eds.) Product-Focused Software Process Improvement, vol. 7983, pp. 50–64. Springer, Heidelberg (2013). https://doi.org/10.1007/978-3-642-39259-7_7
25. Shaw, T.: The emotions of systems developers: an empirical study of affective events theory. In: Proceedings of the 2004 SIGMIS Conference on Computer Personnel Research: Careers, Culture, and Ethics in a Networked Environment, 22 April 2004, pp. 124–126 (2004)
26. Wrobel, M.R.: Emotions in the software development process. In: 2013 6th International Conference on Human System Interactions (HSI), 6 June 2013, pp. 518–523. IEEE (2013)
27. Lesiuk, T.: The effect of music listening on work performance. Psychol. Music. **33**(2), 173–191 (2005)

28. Colomo-Palacios, R., Hernández-López, A., García-Crespo, Á., Soto-Acosta, P.: A study of emotions in requirements engineering. In: Lytras, M.D., Ordonez de Pablos, P., Ziderman, A., Roulstone, A., Maurer, H., Imber, J.B. (eds.) WSKS 2010. CCIS, vol. 112, pp. 1–7. Springer, Heidelberg (2010). https://doi.org/10.1007/978-3-642-16324-1_1

29. Girardi, D., Novielli, N., Fucci, D., Lanubile, F.: Recognizing developers' emotions while programming. arXiv preprint arXiv:2001.09177 (2020)

30. Khan, I.A., Brinkman, W.P., Hierons, R.M.: Do moods affect programmers' debug performance? Cogn. Technol. Work 13(4), 245–258 (2011)

31. Peslak, A.R.: Emotions and team projects and processes. Team Perf. Manag. Int. J. 11(7), 251 (2005)

32. Chen, N.C., et al.: Challenges of applying machine learning to qualitative coding. In: ACM SIGCHI Workshop on Human-Centered Machine Learning (2016)

33. Hori, M., Kamo, Y.: Gender differences in happiness: the effects of marriage, social roles, and social support in East Asia. Appl. Res. Quality Life 13(4), 839–857 (2018)

Gamifying Users' Learning Experience of Scrum

Guillermo Rodriguez[1,3]($\boxtimes$), Alfredo Teyseyre[2,3], Pablo Gonzalez[1], and Sanjay Misra[4]

[1] UADE-INTEC Business School, Buenos Aires, Argentina
{guirodriguez,pablogonzalez}@uade.edu.ar
[2] Universidad Nacional del Centro de la Provincia de Buenos Aires, Tandil, Argentina
alfredo.teyseyre@isistan.unicen.edu.ar
[3] ISISTAN (UNICEN-CONICET) Research Institute, Tandil, Argentina
[4] Covenant University, Ota, Nigeria
ssopam@gmail.com

Abstract. Serious games have arisen to boost users' interaction and efficiency as they reach a particular objective, integrating with the game's mechanics, thus producing a very enticing mission. The use of serious games in Software Engineering to increase the participation of developers has been studied with great interest to train potential professionals to encounter situations they may face in the development of software. This paper introduces *ScrumGame*, a serious game to train both students in Software Engineering and software practitioners in Scrum. The game was tested with users who use Scrum in their everyday work using pre-test-post-test style. The SIMS and MSLQ tests were used for this, which were both performed by the users before and after the game was played. We aimed at assessing how game use affects learning strategies and motivation. Backed up with evidence for statistical significance, findings indicate that *ScrumGame* has had a positive effect on the students.

Keywords: Scrum · Serious game · Software engineering education · M-learning · SIMS · MSLQ

1 Introduction

In recent years, the use of agile methodologies such as Scrum has grown significantly. According to a 2019 survey conducted by Forbes Insights and Scrum Alliance [1], 81% of executives consider agility as the most important characteristic of a successful organization, due to its ability to respond to changing priorities and the visibility of your projects. Furthermore, 76% of surveyed companies use Scrum or hybrid approaches involving Scrum [2]. These results provide several insights about Agile are nowadays the de-facto methodologies in the software industry. This issue implies a clear need for workers prepared to adapt to this development methodology.

Along this line, universities and educational entities are including the teaching of agile methodology within their study plans [13], for which they employ different learning strategies. Thus, universities need to effectively provide students with the skills needed to succeed in current software organizations. In particular, experience-based learning

© Springer Nature Switzerland AG 2021
S. Misra and B. Muhammad-Bello (Eds.): ICTA 2020, CCIS 1350, pp. 497–509, 2021.
https://doi.org/10.1007/978-3-030-69143-1_38

techniques, such as games, have been widely used. Among these, the use of a LEGO-based simulation game to teaching Scrum [3]; Scrum-X, a spreadsheet-based simulation game for teaching Scrum [4]; Scrumi, an electronic board serious game for teaching concepts inherent to the SCRUM framework [5]; and a gamified system oriented to mobile platforms that allows applying the Scrum process from the Scrum Master's viewpoint [6], among others.

In this work, we have built *ScrumGame*, a serious game to train both software engineering students and software practitioners in Scrum by exploiting gamification design and ubiquity. To validate the game, user tests were carried out with 10 employees of a software development company focused on the development of mobile games that use Scrum in their daily work. We aimed to analyze psychological variables, such as motivation and learning-oriented strategies. For this analysis, two validated questionnaires were used: the SIMS (Situational Motivation Scale) [7] and the MSLQ (Motivated Strategies for Learning Questionnaire) [8], both carried out before and after using the application, with the intention of observing how the use of the game impacts on the variables under study. As main results, it was obtained that most of the variables under study in both tests showed positive changes. These insights showed that the use of our game generated a positive impact on the users, both in the learning strategies as motivation, which are crucial issues in the development of self-managed education.

The remainder of this paper is structured as follows. Section 2 describes the background. Section 3 reports the related work. Section 4 introduces our serious game approach. Section 5 reports the assessment of the approach. Section 6 presents the results obtained during the study. Finally, Sect. 7 concludes our work and identifies future line of research.

2   Background

Scrum is a framework by which people can tackle complex adaptive problems, where requirements are changing or poorly defined, while delivering incremental value products. According to the last annual survey carried out by the State of Agile in 2020 [2], Scrum is the most used agile methodology with 66%, which, considering also the hybrid combination Scrum and other frameworks, give a total 76%. This methodology consists of teams and their associated roles, events, artifacts, and rules. Each component within the framework serves a specific purpose and is essential to the success of a software application. Scrum ensures that knowledge comes from experience and from making decisions based on what is known. From there, its iterative and incremental approach optimizes predictability and risk control.

Gamification is a term that refers to the use of techniques, elements and dynamics typical of games in non-recreational systems in order to enhance motivation, to reinforce behavior to solve a problem, and to improve productivity [9]. Furthermore, gamification is used to improve user experience and the level of commitment and participation of users [10]. More specifically, according to [11] the importance of its application has several reasons, such as activation of the motivation for learning, constant feedback, facilitation of more meaningful learning, commitment to learning, more measurable results such as levels, points and medals, generation of adequate skills, digital alphabetization, generation of autonomous learners, and development of competitiveness as well as collaboration, among others.

Serious games were conceived within the variety of games for a primary purpose beyond mere fun [14]. They aim at a wide variety of audiences, from primary and secondary school students to professionals and consumers. Serious games can be of any genre, use any game technology and be developed for any platform. They are made to provide a context of entertainment and self-empowerment with which to motivate, educate and train users. These games seek to improve learning; they aim to strike a balance between studio content and the gameplay and ability of the player to retain and apply that content in the real world. They are also widely used in the business world to improve employee skills.

3 Related Work

The use of serious games in Software Engineering to increase the participation of developers has been widely studied with the aim of train potential professionals to encounter situations they may face in the development of software. In [15], the authors use games to accompany the teaching of Software Engineering concepts, especially in students of other Engineering careers with little or no knowledge of software. The authors have presented *CodeCombat* to teach concepts of the Object Oriented Paradigm.

Along this line, in [16] the authors introduced an approach to teaching Scrum concepts in practice, simulating Sprints, while incrementally planning and developing a *LEGO* brick product. The students showed commitment and enthusiasm when learning in a playful way in contrast to traditional teaching. It was observed that even the most experienced students reported having learned new concepts. Likewise, in [4] the authors have presented *Scrum-X* for teaching Scrum, with the objective of comparing education based on simulations and games against traditional education. *Scrum-X* is a game created in a spreadsheet, which simulates the application of Scrum. It was observed that this type of teaching might have a positive impact on the student's motivation to learn, while providing an engaging and enjoyable learning experience.

In [17], the authors have presented the development and validation of *SCRUMI*, with the aim of teaching concepts inherent to Scrum. The proposed game aims to help students understand content related to the Project Management discipline as well as the dissemination of the use of serious games with the intention of increasing their use in education. The authors concluded that the use of games and their mechanics could be more exploited in the teaching of Project Management and other disciplines, since they provide a different and enjoyable experience, compared to the contents seen in the traditional classroom.

In [18], the authors presented the teaching of Scrum in a practical way with gamification, using the *Minecraft* game. The authors worked in university classes with approximately 110 students in 2 different periods. Previously, the students received, as a theoretical framework, the following information: general introduction to Project Management and its organization, external presentations by three Project Managers, a study by the students themselves on obstacles encountered in real-life projects in companies, a presentation of a general approach to agile project management, a presentation of Scrum and a video of its application in companies.

In [19], the authors have proposed a game-based learning for Scrum, using Trello. Although it is not a Scrum tool, its characteristics allow it to be used for project development. The authors concluded that learning in a playful and interactive way turns out to be more successful in contrast to traditional education, considering Scrum learning as the main aspect and other soft skill such as presentation, communication and teamwork.

In [20], the authors have proposed a game called *Scrum Master*. The system was implemented using Unity and guides the user, explaining the basic concepts of Scrum, its roles, artifacts and events. To evaluate usability, a questionnaire was carried out on different aspects, seeking to obtain descriptive data from the system.

Most of the aforementioned games have exploited gamification tools to improve learning experience and students'perception of agile methologies. Nevertheless, none of the approaches have assessed the motivation and learning strategies by using the SIMS and MSQL tests to corroborate the positive impact of the game on the users.

4 ScrumGame

This section presents the approach used to develop the *ScrumGame* application. This game aims to support Scrum teaching and training both in academic fields and professional contexts. To deal with this issue, a mobile application was implemented, using gamification, serious games and game-based learning concepts. Figure 1 depicts a snapshot of *ScrumGame* in action. It is worth mentioning that the *ScrumGame* user interface is in Spanish.

Fig. 1. Snapshot of *Scrum Game* in action.

The structure of the game content will be presented as follows. *ScrumGame* has a series of levels, which will divide the information into the main topics. Each topic has a series of sub-levels, which divide the content of the level into sub-themes within the main theme. Each sub-level is divided, in turn, into two main parts. On the one hand, the theory shows the theoretical information of the topic within a sub-level. The theory is presented in pages. Each page, like a page of a book, shows the data that the user will need to face the game. On the other hand, a sub-level is divided into games, which are presented in different formats to enrich users' learning experience.

A level has certain information to provide the user with a context. The level highlights the title of the topic, the number of sub-levels necessary to complete to advance to the next one, and the percentage of completeness of the level. This value is obtained by analyzing the percentage of completeness of the contained sub-levels. In addition, the level contains a state, which shows its current situation, namely locked, started and finished.

Each sub-level also has a title, a status and a percentage of completion. Each sub-level is made up of theoretical information on the sub-topic discussed, which is presented to the user in the first instance. Furthermore, a sub-level also contains a series of games where the user can put into practice the concepts learned in the theoretical section, as well as give rise to possible more interpretative theoretical derivations. The completeness of the theoretical concepts and the number of successfully completed games of a sub-level will be used to compute the percentage of completeness that will be presented to the user.

The theory module has a control to advance or go back the pages of the game, showing different options depending on the page where the user is. This movement can also be achieved by performing a lateral slide, also known as swipe left/right. In addition, the concept of "Jump" is introduced, which allows users to go directly to the Games module, if they prefer. This definition stems from the need to avoid being pushed to revisit concepts by experienced users. The theoretical section will be considered complete if a user presses the play button or the skip button at the end of the section. The sub-level games section consists of a set of games prepared to give a user a way to validate the concepts learned in the theoretical section, presented in an attractive and motivating way.

Figure 2 illustrates two games developed in *ScrumGame*. Some games are based on multiple-choice (Fig. 2a) or drag-and-drop (Fig. 2b) strategies, among others. All the games aim to assess Scrum concepts according to the knowledge level gained by the user along the game. Particularly, games depicted in Fig. 2 propose to train users in the life-cycle of Scrum and the artifacts and events used along the methodology. The goal in the game (b) is to drag the components (Scrum artifacts or event) and drop them in the correct place of the Scrum framework.

Once the user submits a correct response, the game notifies the main controller so that it can stop the game timer. Meanwhile, it shows the user a message that the game was completed successfully and waits for their interaction. When the user agrees to continue, the main controller is notified to prepare for the next game, and also sends the "correct answer" and "total game time" events to the server. Finally, the main controller removes controller for the recently completed game, leaving room for the next game. It should also be noted that when completing each game within the sublevel, the main controller

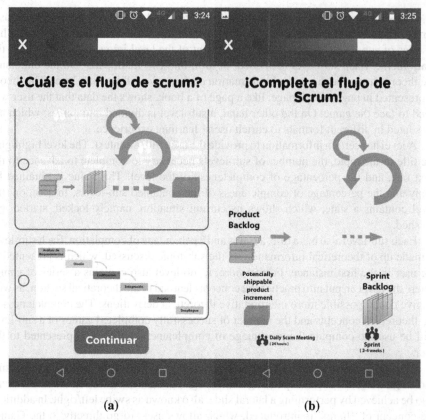

(a)   **(b)**

Fig. 2. Example game strategies developed in *ScrumGame*: (a) Multiple-choice (b) Drag-and-drop.

sends the progress data for storage. For its local save, *ScrumGame* uses Realm (https://realm.io/), while for its persistence in the cloud, the game uses Firebase (https://firebase.google.com/?hl=en).

5   Experimental Results

The goal of the evaluation is to measure the impact of *ScrumGame* on learning experience and motivation of users. To meet our objective, we used a pre-test-post-test design. To do this, two different tests were utilized: the SIMS [7] and the MSLQ [8]. Before playing, the users participating in the evaluation completed the tests and, after experiencing a given scenario with *ScrumGame*, the users completed the same tests again.

5.1   Setup

For the development of the experiment, 10 users took part in the experience, of whom 7 were men and 3 women. All participants are employees of a software development company focused on the development of mobile games. They are in the age range of 25–40 years old and the distribution of roles is described as follows: Project Manager (1), UX/UI Designers (2), Technical Leader (2), Developers (2), Product Owner (2), DevOps Leader (1). Particularly, in this company, knowledge of Scrum is not a mandatory requirement, since each team is organized with the methodology that best suits their projects and members. This allowed the participants to have different initial background of Scrum when conducting the experiment.

5.2 Pre-test and Post-test

Two of the important psychological variables to consider in self-managed education are motivation and the learning strategies. In this work, 2 instruments were used: the MSLQ and SIMS tests. The former is a self-report instrument that has been used in research to assess students' motivation and beliefs, among other aspects. This information is useful for evaluating strengths and difficulties of a student and, according to these, optimizing learning. The latter is a situational questionnaire, used to measure motivation. It seeks to judge the constructions of intrinsic motivation, identified regulation, external regulation and amotivation.

To answer the questionnaires, a Likert scale was used, which is the most widely used psychometric scale in research surveys, mainly in the social sciences. When answering a question from a questionnaire developed with the Likert scale, the level of agreement or disagreement with a statement is specified [12]. In our experiment, participants were asked to agree with a statement giving a value from 1 (does not correspond at all) up to 7 (totally corresponds) for SIMS.

In our case, the Motivation and Learning Strategies Questionnaire Short Form – CMEA FC [7] was used, which is the result of the translation and adaptation into Spanish of the MSLQ, in its reduced and validated version. The short form consists of 40 items with a Likert scale of 5 points, which goes from 1 (Never) up to 5 (Always). The short form is structured as follows with the corresponding dimensions (i.e. items): Motivation variable is determined by three items that evaluate the assessment of the task and four items that assess the anxiety under examination situations. Regarding the Learning Strategies variable, the cognitive and metacognitive strategies, resource management strategies and intrinsic orientation were organized in the following way: five items to evaluate the elaboration strategies, four items to consider organization strategies, three items to assess critical thinking, and seven items to take into account self-regulation to metacognition. The Resource Management Strategies are defined as follows: six items to evaluate study time and habits, six items to talk about self-regulation of effort. And finally two items evaluate the goals of intrinsic orientation.

The SIMS test seeks to judge the constructions of intrinsic motivation, identified regulation, external regulation and amotivation, in a short and versatile way, both in field and laboratory studies [8]. It corresponds to 16 statements that the user must assess, according to the Likert scale, as detailed in the following section. These 16 statements are structured as follows along with the corresponding dimensions: Intrinsic motivation (4 items), Identified regulation (4 items), External regulation (4 items) and Amotivation (4 items).

5.3 Psychological Variables Under Study

For our analysis, six psychological variables were taken into account during the experiment: two variables from MSLQ (Learning Strategies and Motivation) and four variables from SIMS (Intrinsic Motivation, External Regulation, Identified Regulation, and Amotivation).

- Learning Strategies: it talks about the imposition of own goals, distribution of time and effort, repetition, organization, critical thinking, and other cognitive processes that determine the acquisition of information, its processing and recovery. This variable is ranged from 33 to 165.
- Motivation: this variable consists of all the internal determinants that stimulate action. Motivation activates, directs and maintains a behavior. In this factor, micro variables such as the assessment of the task to be carried out and the management of anxiety are evaluated. This variable ranges from 7 to 35.
- Intrinsic Motivation: it is a motivation originated within the individual, and is directed by the needs of exploration, experimentation, curiosity and manipulation, which are considered motivating behaviors in themselves. That is, those behaviors that are carried out in the absence of any apparent external contingency are considered intrinsically motivated. The range of this variable is [4...28].
- External regulation: is a prototype of motivation not generated by one. Externally regulated behaviors are carried out to obtain a reward or satisfy external demand. The range of this variable is [4...28].
- Identified Regulation: represents an extrinsic motivation that is internalized and autonomous. They are behaviors regulated by personally important aspects. The range of this variable is [4...28].
- Amotivation: lack of motivation causes individuals to experience a lack of contingency between their behaviors and their results. Unmotivated behaviors are the least self-determined because there is no sense of purpose and there are no expectations of reward or possibility of changing the course of events. The range of this variable is [4...28].

5.4 Hypothesis Statement

For all variables under study, we defined null hypothesis and alternative hypothesis as follows. Null hypothesis (H_0) states that there is no significant difference between the pre-test and post-test values for the variable under study ($p\text{-}value \geq 0.05$). The alternative hypothesis (H_1) states that there is a significant difference between the pre-test and post-test values for the variable under study ($p\text{-}value < 0.05$). The hypotheses were corroborated by utilizing the two-tailed Student t-Test with SPSS tool.

6 Analysis of Results

This section reports the results obtained after conducting both tests and analyzing the means for each pair of psychology variables (before-after). All the null hypotheses were rejected and consequently the alternative hypotheses accepted ($p\text{-}value < 0.0001$).

Table 1 shows that External Regulation slightly decreased from 17.6 to 16.4. In other words, all those motivational behaviors driven by strictly external stimuli decreased in the post-test, after using *ScrumGame* (Table 2). Regarding the Amotivation, Table 3 shows decay after the post-test (from 12.4 to 7.5). Positively, the lack of motivation fell in the post-test. This variation could mean that the users found a sense of purpose within the game (Table 4). As can be seen in Table 5, Intrinsic Motivation has risen after using the game (from 20.1 to 23.8), and this impact is backed up statistically is illustrated in Table 6.

Table 1. Comparison of means of the variable External Regulation in pre-test and post-test.

	N	Mean	Std. deviation	Std. deviation mean
1 - TOTAL external regulation	10	17.6	3.65	1.15
2 - TOTAL external regulation	10	16.4	3.37	1.06

Table 2. Statistical Student t-test of External Regulation in pre- and post-test.

	Test value = 0					
	t	df	Sig. (2-tailed)	Mean difference	95% confidence interval of the difference	
					Lower	Upper
1 - TOTAL external regulation	15.21	9	.000	17.60	14.98	20.21
2 - TOTAL external regulation	15.37	9	.000	16.40	13.98	18.81

Table 3. Comparison of means of the variable Amotivation in pre-test and post-test.

	N	Mean	Std. deviation	Std. deviation mean
1 - TOTAL amotivation	10	12.40	6.73	2.13
2 - TOTAL amotivation	10	7.50	2.95	.93

Similarly, the Identified Regulation, understood as those external motivations that users understand and accept as their own, increased slightly in the post-test (from 23.8 to 22.8) as shown in Table 7 and Table 8. With regard to Motivation, Table 9 illustrates that the values slightly decreased after using *ScrumGame* (from 28.0 to 27.7). In this case, the variables related to the assessment of the task and anxiety management decreased in the post-test (Table 10). This unfavorable result could be attributed to the lack of

Table 4. Statistical Student t-test of Amotivation in pre- and post-test.

| | Test value = 0 | | | | | |
| | t | df | Sig. (2-tailed) | Mean difference | 95% confidence interval of the difference | |
					Lower	Upper
1 - TOTAL amotivation	5.82	9	.000	12.40	7.58	17.21
2 - TOTAL amotivation	8.03	9	.000	7.50	5.38	9.61

Table 5. Comparison of means of the variable Intrinsic Motivation in pre-test and post-test.

	N	Mean	Std. deviation	Std. deviation mean
1 - TOTAL intrinsic motivation	10	20.1	4.22	1.33
2 - TOTAL intrinsic motivation	10	23.8	2.78	0.87

Table 6. Statistical Student t-test of Intrinsic Motivation in pre- and post-test.

| | Test value = 0 | | | | | |
| | t | df | Sig. (2-tailed) | Mean difference | 95% confidence interval of the difference | |
					Lower	Upper
1 - TOTAL intrinsic motivation	15.03	9	.000	20.1	17.07	23.12
2 - TOTAL intrinsic motivation	27.06	9	.000	23.8	21.81	25.78

psychological preparation in games and in the application in general, to improve key concepts that affect this variable, such as competition and anxiety management.

Table 7. Comparison of means of the variable Identified Regulation in pre-test and post-test.

	N	Mean	Std. deviation	Std. deviation mean
1 - TOTAL identified regulation	10	22.8	2.09	0.66
2 - TOTAL identified regulation	10	23.8	1.75	0.55

As for Learning Strategies, Table 11 shows that this variable has increased in the post-test (from 163.4 to 169.2). The micro variables related to this aspect, such as the

Table 8. Statistical Student t-test of Identified Regulation in pre- and post-test.

	Test value = 0					
	t	df	Sig. (2-tailed)	Mean difference	95% confidence interval of the difference	
					Lower	Upper
1 - TOTAL identified regulation	34.37	9	.000	22.8	21.29	24.3
2 - TOTAL identified regulation	42.97	9	.000	23.8	22.54	25.05

Table 9. Comparison of means of the variable Motivation in pre-test and post-test.

	N	Mean	Std. deviation	Std. deviation mean
1 - TOTAL motivation	10	28	7.78	2.46
2 - TOTAL motivation	10	27.7	7.68	2.43

Table 10. Statistical Student t-test of Motivation in pre- and post-test.

	Test value = 0					
	t	df	Sig. (2-tailed)	Mean difference	95% confidence interval of the difference	
					Lower	Upper
1 - TOTAL motivation	11.36	9	.000	28	22.42	33.57
2 - TOTAL motivation	11.39	9	.000	27.7	22.19	33.2

imposition of own goals, distribution of time and effort, among others, improved after playing *ScrumGame* (Table 12).

Table 11. Comparison of means of Learning Strategies in pre- and post-test.

	N	Mean	Std. deviation	Std. deviation mean
1 - TOTAL learning strategies	10	163.4	16.08	5.08
2 - TOTAL learning strategies	10	169.2	15	4.74

Table 12. Statistical Student t-test of Learning Strategies in pre- and post-test.

	Test value = 0				95% confidence interval of the difference	
	t	df	Sig. (2-tailed)	Mean difference		
					Lower	Upper
1 - TOTAL learning strategies	32.15	9	.000	163.4	151.89	174.9
2 - TOTAL learning strategies	35.66	9	.000	169.2	158.46	179.93

7   Conclusions

In this work, we presented a serious game for optimizing users' learning experience of Scrum. After the evaluation carried out through a pre-test-post-test design experiment with 10 users, we concluded that most of the psychological variables under study showed positive changes after the post-test. We can affirm that the use of *ScrumGame* significantly showed a positive impact on users, both in learning-related strategies and motivation.

As future work, firstly, we propose to generate new games with a psycho-pedagogical perspective, in order to fulfill the Scrum learning with crucial concepts such as management of waste [21] and Scrum of Scrum [22]. Secondly, we plan to incorporate more games to simulate real complex situations, serving as practice for specific scenarios in professional contexts. Thirdly, by using the users' feedback, we will work on improving techniques and components related to gamification issues, in order to generate higher commitment, fun and motivation from users. Finally, we aim to apply analytics to the data generated along the game sessions to discover knowledge and assist users in their learning experience.

References

1. The Elusive Agile Enterprise. https://www.scrumalliance.org/forbes/the-report
2. 14th Annual State of Agile Survey, State of Agile. https://explore.digital.ai/state-of-agile/14th-annual-state-of-agile-report
3. Paasivaara, M., Heikkilä, V., Lassenius, C., Toivola, T.: Teaching students scrum using LEGO blocks. In Companion Proceedings of the 36th International Conference on Software Engineering, pp. 382–391 (2014)
4. Lee, W.L.: SCRUM-X: an interactive and experiential learning platform for teaching scrum (2016)
5. De Souza, A.D., Seabra, R.D., Ribeiro, J.M., Rodrigues, L.E.D.: SCRUMI: a board serious virtual game for teaching the SCRUM framework. In: International Conference on Software Engineering Companion (ICSE-C), pp. 319–321 (2017)
6. Angarita, L.B., Hernández, J.A.G.: Sistema gamificado para el aprendizaje del proceso de desarrollo Scrum. In: Iberian Conference on Information Systems and Technologies (CISTI), Coimbra, Portugal (2017)

7. Sabogal Tinoco, L.F., Barraza Heras, E., Hernandez Castellar, A., Zapata, L.: Validación del Cuestionario de Motivación y Estrategias de Aprendizaje Forma Corta-MSLQ SF, en estudiantes universitarios de una institución Pública-Santa Marta. Psicogente **14**(25), 36–50 (2011)
8. Martín-Albo, J., Núñez, J., Navarro, J.: Validation of the Spanish version of the situational motivation scale (EMSI) in the educational context. Spanish J. Psychol. **12**(2), 799–807 (2009)
9. Zichermann, G., Cunningham, C.: Gamification by Design: Implementing Game Mechanics in Web and Mobile Apps. O'Reilly Media, Sebastopol (2011)
10. Deterding, S., Sicart, M., Nacke, L., O'Hara, K., Dixon, D.: Gamification. Using game-design elements in non-gaming contexts. Extended Abstracts on Human Factors in Computing Systems (CHI EA 2011), pp. 2425–2428. ACM, New York (2011)
11. Borrás Gené, O.: Fundamentos de la gamificación. GATE-Universidad Politécnica de Madrid, Madrid (2015)
12. Burns, A., Burns, R.: Basic Marketing Research, 2nd edn., p. 245 Pearson Education, New Jersey (2008)
13. Rodríguez, G., Soria, Á., Campo, M.: Measuring the impact of agile coaching on students' performance. IEEE Trans. Educ. **59**(3), 202–209 (2016)
14. Alvarez, J., Djaouti, D.: An introduction to Serious game Definitions and concepts. Serious Games Simul. Risks Manage. **11**(1), 11–15 (2011)
15. Alatrista-Salas, H., Nunez-Del-Prado, M.: Teaching software engineering through computer games. In: 2018 IEEE World Engineering Education Conference (2018)
16. Paasivaara, M., Heikkilä, V., Lassenius, C., Toivola, T.: Teaching students scrum using LEGO blocks. In: Companion Proceedings of the 36th International Conference on Software Engineering, pp. 382–391 (2014)
17. De Souza, A.D., Seabra, R.D., Ribeiro, J.M., Rodrigues, L.E.D.S.L.: SCRUMI: a board serious virtual game for teaching the SCRUM framework. In: International Conference on Software Engineering Companion (ICSE-C), pp. 319–321. IEEE (2017)
18. Schäfer, U.: Training scrum with gamification: lessons learned after two teaching periods. In: Global Engineering Education Conference (EDUCON), pp. 754–761. IEEE (2017)
19. Naik, N., Jenkins, P.: Relax, It's a game: utilising gamification in learning agile scrum software development. In: IEEE Conference on Games (CoG), pp. 1–4 (2019)
20. Angarita, L.B., Hernández, J.A.G.: Sistema gamificado para el aprendizaje del proceso de desarrollo Scrum. In: Iberian Conference on Information Systems and Technologies (CISTI), Coimbra, Portugal (2019)
21. Correia, A., Gonçalves, A., Misra, S.: Integrating the scrum framework and lean six sigma. In: Misra, S., Gervasi, O., Murgante, B., Stankova, E., Korkhov, V., Torre, C., Rocha, Ana Maria A.C., Taniar, D., Apduhan, Bernady O., Tarantino, E. (eds.) ICCSA 2019. LNCS, vol. 11623, pp. 136–149. Springer, Cham (2019). https://doi.org/10.1007/978-3-030-24308-1_12
22. Mundra, A., Misra, S., Dhawale, C.A.: Practical scrum-scrum team: Way to produce successful and quality software. In: 13th International Conference on Computational Science and Its Applications, pp. 119–123. IEEE (2013)

Visualizing Multilevel Test-to-Code Relations

Nadera Aljawabrah[1]([⊠]), Abdallah Qusef[2], Tamás Gergely[1], and Adhyatmananda Pati[3]

[1] University of Szeged, Szeged, Hungary
{nadera,gertom}@inf.u-szeged.hu
[2] Princess Sumaya University for Technology, Amman, Jordan
a.qusef@psut.edu.jo
[3] Odisha, India

Abstract. The test-to-code traceability (TCT) links play an important role in the process of software maintenance and re-engineering. However, the main issue is how to visualize these links efficiently and effectively to support the comprehension and maintenance of these links. In this work, a visualization approach is presented that displays the TCT links in two levels, class-level, and method level. Visualization traceability links at a method-level provide detailed information of the traceability links that support the development of software in different tasks such as, software maintenance, refactoring, and change impact analysis. The visualization approach is implemented using our visualization tool namely TCTracVis. The presented tool is evaluated on a real simple project and the achieved results confirm that the proposed approach and tool are efficient to support several tasks in software development.

Keywords: Traceability links visualization · TCT links · Software comprehension · Class-level · Method-level

1 Introduction

Unit testing is a vital part of software development to ensure software quality [26], however, maintaining a precise representation of the relations between the tests and tested code is essential. Traceability links can provide an intuitive model to describe these relations. TCT links help to improve the process of software engineering in several ways: facilitating program comprehension, system changing safely, artifacts reusing easily [1]. For example, TCT links can be used to determine which tests should be checked after the code changes which helps in reducing regression tests generation [25]. Different techniques have been developed to recover high-quality test-to-code-traceability links [3, 16], however, the main issue is how to support the comprehension and maintenance of these links efficiently and effectively? Visualization of TCT links is an approach that effectively supports understanding test-to-code relations and helps various tasks in the software development life cycle (SDLC) [2]. It can provide a detailed description of how tests and tested code are connected. Moreover, visualization can improve the maintenance of TCT links by reducing the submitted effort in understanding software

© Springer Nature Switzerland AG 2021
S. Misra and B. Muhammad-Bello (Eds.): ICTA 2020, CCIS 1350, pp. 510–519, 2021.
https://doi.org/10.1007/978-3-030-69143-1_39

[10], however, all current test-to-code traceability links techniques and support tools have the disadvantage of visualization support [11].

Previous research of TCT link recovery has focused on the class level, where test classes are connected to their tested classes [4–6, 16]. Despite the fully realized benefits of appropriate information of traceability lie in the identification of method level, where unit tests are connected to their tested methods, only a small portion of work has been done on the method level [7–9]. Our particular interest in this work is to provide visualization support of traceability links between tests and tested code on the two levels.

In this work, we provide a multilevel visualization approach that presents a detailed overview of TCT links on the class level and method level simultaneously. The hierarchical tree visualization technique is applied to display the traceability links in a traced system. The approach is implemented using the TCTracVis visualization tool [17]. Our approach and its implementation aim to improve and ease the development process in several ways: helps comprehension, interact search, and impact analysis when something needs to be changed. The results of the evaluation confirm that the proposed approach is efficient to support several tasks in software development.

The remaining of this paper is organized as follows. In Sect. 2, we introduce our visualization approach. Section 3 describes the implementation of the approach with simple real examples and the possible uses in practice. Related work is presented in Sect. 4. Section 5 presents the evaluation of our visualization approach. Section 6 presents the conclusion and future work.

2   Visualization Approach

To provide an efficient visualization of traceability links, we have developed an approach supporting multi-level of traceability links representation that displays a thorough overview of each link. Our approach shows which artifacts are related, visualizing links between test artifacts and tested artifacts at different levels, class-level, and method-level. As we are establishing links on the class-level as well as on the method-level, we use the terms class-under-test (CUT) when referring to a tested class (TC), and the terms tested method or method-under-test (MUT) for the method-level. Furthermore, a tested class is tested by one or more test classes on the class level, on the method level, a tested-method is tested by one or more test methods (TM).

To create the TCT links, we applied two existing test-to-code recovery techniques, Naming convention [16], and the Last Call Before Assert [16], as they support our approach' goal and perform well in several situations [6, 16]. For example, NC supports the established links more in class-level, while LCBA performs better at method-level. We adopt the hierarchal tree visualization technique to display the detailed dependency artifacts in both views. We use left-to-right hierarchal tree visualization [22, 23] (see Fig. 1). Once the traceability links of a selected node are established and retrieved, a hierarchical tree graph is built to show links that are related to the selected node. When a specific node in the tree is selected, the tree is expanded to show all related nodes and links of a selected node.

Traceability links can be shown in two types of view, "class-level-view" which shows the traceability links for a specified tested class with all related test classes, and "method-level-view" which shows the traceability links for a specified test class with its related test methods, tested class and tested methods. More details about the views will be provided in the next section.

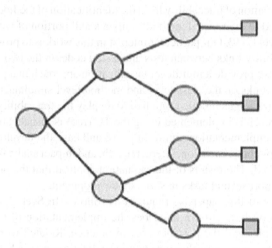

Fig. 1. Hierarchal tree visualization

3   Implementation and Possible Usage

The overview of our approach is presented in Fig. 2. In Fig. 2, it can be observed that the traceability data files with candidates' artifacts (test classes, CUT, test methods, MUT) and traceability links are the input for the approach. As mentioned above, the traceability links are retrieved using well-known recovery techniques, NC and LCBA as they have been described in several books and tutorials (e.g. [3, 16]) which is an indication of their widespread usage in different contexts. The input files are stored in a specific format defined using XML. Then the input files are loaded into visualization generators which support two types of views, class view, and method view.

Our approach is implemented using "TCTracVis" [17], a traceability visualization tool developed as a stand-alone desktop application that runs in MS Windows and supports the visualization of TCT links. The tool is evaluated using HR system, a human resources information system developed by ITG with enough unit tests for implementation and evaluation purposes.

1. Class-level-view.
    In this view, as the traceability links have the advantages of being bidirectional, links can be visualized in two directions:

    – **TC-to-CUT.** The test class is selected, then all related tested classes, which a selected test class was written to evaluate, are displayed. Figure 3 shows an

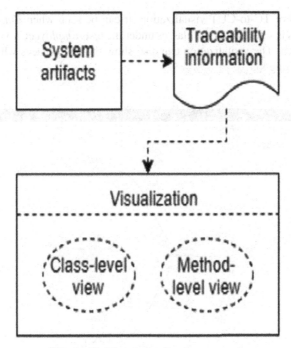

Fig. 2. Multilevel visualization approach

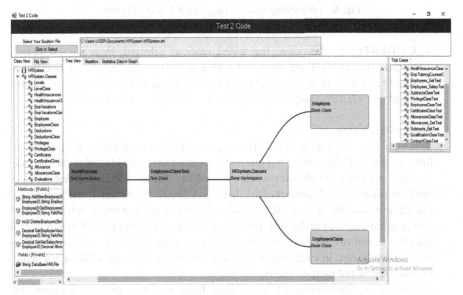

Fig. 3. Traceability links of EmployeeClassTest test class in TCTracVis

example of TC-to-CUT visualization. It can be seen when *EmployeeClassTest*
test class is selected, all the classes under the test; *EmployeeClass* and *Employee*,
are shown. The visualization can also show the namespaces where the TC and
CUT belong to.

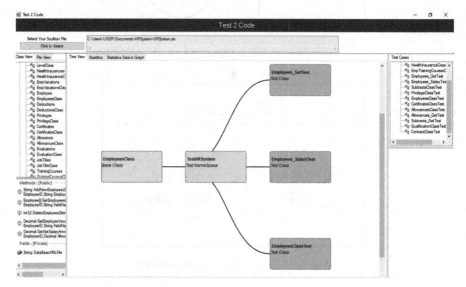

Fig. 4. Traceability links of EmployeeClass (CUT) class

– **CUT-to-TC.** In this view, the tested class is selected, then all test classes
which evaluate CUT are displayed with namespaces that belong to. See Fig. 4,
EmployeeClass is a tested class which is evaluated by three test classes,
Employee-GetTest, *Employee-SalaryTest*, and *EmployeeClassTest*.

2. Method-level-view
This view provides a more detailed overview of TCT links. It shows the traceability
links established between a class test and its related test methods and methods under
tests that the test methods were written to evaluate. Figure 5 shows all test methods
and their related tested methods of the *PrivilegeClassTest* class test. It can be observed
that the test class has several test methods where each method test is written to check
one or more methods under test. For example, the test method *AddNewPrivilege* is
intended to test two methods, the *privilege class* method, and the *addNewPrivilege*
method. Moreover, in each node of the tested method, the name of the CUT which
includes the tested method can be shown.
Multilevel representations of traceability links facilitate the development and
improve the evolution of software. It can empower consistency between continuous
code changes and tests. Our visualization approach supports these goals. It is mainly
intended to serve software development activities. It provides a better understanding
of different traceability link levels between tests and tested code. It contributes to

interactive search, more precise impact analysis, and a cost-effective maintenance process.

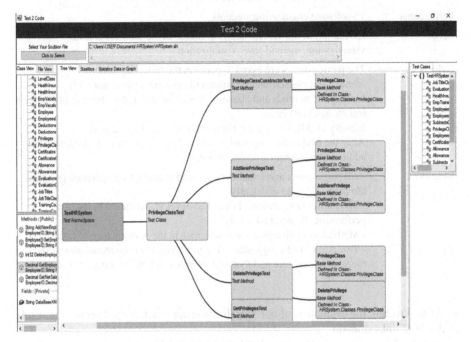

Fig. 5. Method level representation

4 Evaluation

The evaluation of our visualization approach was conducted through a HR system solution; a human resources information system developed by ITG[1] with enough unit tests for implementation and evaluation purposes. The system has 31 production classes, 180 base methods, 15 test classes, and 109 test methods. Table 1 summarizes the evaluation process of the traced system.

Based on evaluation results, we observed that participants can easily find a specific CUT in the hierarchal tree and it's all related tested classes. This kind of visualization can support developers in the analysis of impact change; if a class needs to be changed, all related classes which could be affected can be easily identified. Furthermore, method-level visualization made it simple for participants to understand the structure of the traced system and display the detailed information of links of a selected class; all related tested methods, as well as all methods under test that tested methods, was written to

---

[1] Integrated Technology Group (ITG) https://github.com/rayyad79/HRSystem.git.

Table 1. Evaluation strategy

Target	Analysis and validation of multilevel TCT links visualization approach
Solution	HR system; a human resources information system
Participants	15 software engineering students
Scope	Evaluation of the visualizations available in the tool: class-level visualization, method-level visualization
Evidence sources	The participants were asked to perform the following tasks: Identify test classes that are written to evaluate a particular CUT Identify all methods and classes that may be affected in the case of change a test method\ test class Identify all MUT that are related to a particular test method After the evaluation, the participants were asked to provide feedback and additional information on our approach
Results	- All participants agree that the proposed visualization approach performs the proposed tasks efficiently - The participants indicated that class-level visualization helps in performing the first task easily - Method-level visualization is adequate in the performance of tasks 2 and 3 - Two participants suggested using more visualization techniques to show the system structure and thorough analysis of links in a traced system

evaluate. Overall, the evaluation of our visualization approach gained promising results in the TCT links domain.

While many visualization approaches have been developed that support visualizing traceability links between artifacts of software [9, 14, 24], visualization support for TCT links is limited in the literature. Research on TCT links is mostly interested in the methods used to recover the links between code and tests artifacts [9]. While many of the approaches were proposed to establish TCT links [6, 9, 16, 20], none of these approaches support the visualization of these links [11]. Visualization can be an important part of traceability, as it provides enhanced process visibility and helps engineers, developers, and testers to verify the quality of TCT links [19, 21]. These issues motivated the authors of this paper to propose a novel visualization approach that enhances understanding and maintaining TCT links.

5   Related Work

Several visualization tools and methods are proposed depending on the intent of visualization and the form of traceability information to be visualized, for example, understand software artifacts relationships and dependencies, their interactions, and how they support document links among several types of artifacts in a software (e.g. tests. Requirements).

Four well-known visualization techniques [matrix, graphs, lists, and hyperlinks] were analyzed and compared in [18] to discover in which context these visualization methods can be properly used. ADAMS [12] is developed to support identifying traceability links between pairs of software artifacts. Traceability links are arranged in a graph where nodes are the artifacts and edges represent traceability links. In [27] Multi-Viso generates four visualization techniques: Sunburst, matrix, tree, and graph depending on the scope in which the traceability is being applied. The visualization displays a global structure of traceability and a detailed overview of each link.

A hierarchical graphical structure is presented by Cleland-Huang and Habrat [13] to visualize links between requirements information, where requirements are represented as leaf nodes while internal nodes represent titles and other hierarchical information. Merten et al. [15] present interactive Sunburst and Netmap representations as a way to visualize traceability links between the elements of requirements knowledge. Sunburst promotes the visualization of the structure of the project to be traced hierarchy. In [14], a hierarchical graphical tree is applied as a supplemental for tree-map visualization to provide more detailed information about each link between a class in source code and sections in documents.

There is not much interest in the literature being reviewed in visualizing TCT links. This infers that works on the visualization of testing are still practically restricted. Recently, in more important projects, developers can not miss testing. However, they omit traceability because, during the development process, they do not feel the need for it. Therefore, they do not spend effort on it.

6 Conclusion and Future Work

Many techniques have been developed to recover high-quality test-to-code-traceability links; however, it is a major challenge to support the comprehension and maintenance of these links efficiently and effectively. Visualization is intended to solve such a problem. In this paper, we present an efficient visualization approach that supports the comprehension of TCT links in two levels: class-level, which shows the links between the class under test and all related tested class and vice versa, and method-level, which provides detailed information about the test methods and all related methods under test.

The evaluation results show that TCTracVis can provide hierarchal tree visualization to display TCT links. Our Visualization approach is mainly intended to serve the software development activities. It provides a better understanding of different traceability link levels between tests and tested code. It contributes to an interactive search and more precise impact analysis. Moreover, the results confirm that our visualization approach can help to ease the development process and make maintenance and evolution more cost-effective processes. Our future work is to extend our visualization system to include one overall overview visualization of all traceability links for the whole project. Moreover, we are working on extending the tool to supports several TCT link recovery methods to automatically retrieved TCT links.

References

1. Winkler, S., von Pilgrim, J.: A survey of traceability in requirements engineering and model-driven development. Softw. Syst. Model. 9(4), 529–565 (2010)

518   N. Aljawabrah et al.

2. Roman, G.-C., Cox, K.C.: Program visualization: the art of mapping programs to pictures. In: Proceedings of the 14th International Conference on Software Engineering (1992)
3. Qusef, A., et al.: Scotch: slicing and coupling based test to code trace hunter. In: 2011 18th Working Conference on Reverse Engineering. IEEE (2011)
4. Csuvik, V., Kicsi, A., Vidács, L.: Evaluation of textual similarity techniques in code level traceability. In: Misra, S. (ed.) ICCSA 2019. LNCS, vol. 11622, pp. 529–543. Springer, Cham (2019). https://doi.org/10.1007/978-3-030-24305-0_40
5. Csuvik, V., Kicsi, A., Vidács, L.: Source code level word embeddings in aiding semantic test-to-code traceability. In: 2019 IEEE/ACM 10th International Symposium on Software and Systems Traceability (SST). IEEE (2019)
6. Qusef, A., et al.: Recovering test-to-code traceability using slicing and textual analysis. J. Syst. Softw. **88**, 147–168 (2014)
7. Ghafari, M., Ghezzi, C., Rubinov, K.: Automatically identifying focal methods under test in unit test cases. In: 2015 IEEE 15th International Working Conference on Source Code Analysis and Manipulation (SCAM). IEEE (2015)
8. Hurdugaci, V., Zaidman, A.: Aiding software developers to maintain developer tests. In: 2012 16th European Conference on Software Maintenance and Reengineering. IEEE (2012)
9. White, R., Krinke, J., Tan, R.: Establishing multilevel test-to-code traceability links. In: 42nd International Conference on Software Engineering (ICSE 2020). ACM (2020)
10. Koschke, R.: Software visualization in software maintenance, reverse engineering, and re-engineering: A research survey. J. Softw. Maintenance Evol. Res. Pract. **15**(2), 87–109 (2003)
11. Parizi, R.M., Lee, S.P., Dabbagh, M.: Achievements and challenges in state-of-the-art software traceability between test and code artifacts. IEEE Trans. Reliab. **63**(4), 913–926 (2014)
12. De Lucia, A., et al.: Adams re-trace: a traceability recovery tool. In: Ninth European Conference on Software Maintenance and Reengineering. IEEE (2005)
13. Cleland-Huang, J., et al.: Best practices for automated traceability. Computer **40**(6), 27–35 (2007)
14. Chen, X., Hosking, J., Grundy, J., Amor, R.: DCTracVis: a system retrieving and visualizing traceability links between source code and documentation. Autom. Softw. Eng. **25**(4), 703–741 (2018). https://doi.org/10.1007/s10515-018-0243-8
15. Merten, T., Jüppner, D., Delater, A.: Improved representation of traceability links in requirements engineering knowledge using Sunburst and Netmap visualizations. In: 2011 4th International Workshop on Managing Requirements Knowledge. IEEE (2011)
16. Van Rompaey, B., Demeyer, S.: Establishing traceability links between unit test cases and units under test. In: 2009 13th European Conference on Software Maintenance and Reengineering. IEEE (2009)
17. Aljawabrah, N., Qusef, A.: TCTracVis: test-to-code links visualization tool. In: Proceedings of the Second International Conference on Data Science, E-Learning and Information Systems, pp. 1–4 (2019)
18. Li, Y., Maalej, W.: Which traceability visualization is suitable in this context? A comparative study. In: Regnell, B., Damian, D. (eds.) REFSQ 2012. LNCS, vol. 7195, pp. 194–210. Springer, Heidelberg (2012). https://doi.org/10.1007/978-3-642-28714-5_17
19. Meedeniya, D.A., Rubasinghe, I.D., Perera, I.: Traceability establishment and visualization of software artefacts in DevOps practice: a survey. Int. J. Adv. Comput. Sci. Appl. (IJACSA) **10**(7), 66–76 (2019)
20. Gergely, T., Balogh, G., Horváth, F., Vancsics, B., Beszédes, Á., Gyimóthy, T.: Differences between a static and a dynamic test-to-code traceability recovery method. Software Qual. J. **27**(2), 797–822 (2018). https://doi.org/10.1007/s11219-018-9430-x
21. Aljawabrah, N., Gergely, T., Kharabsheh, M.: Understanding test-to-code traceability links: the need for a better visualizing model. In: Misra, S. (ed.) ICCSA 2019. LNCS, vol. 11622, pp. 428–441. Springer, Cham (2019). https://doi.org/10.1007/978-3-030-24305-0_32

22. Kamalabalan, K., et al.: Tool support for traceability of software artifacts. In: 2015 Moratuwa Engineering Research Conference (MERCon). IEEE (2015)
23. Klochkov, Y., et al.: Classifiers of nonconformities in norms and requirements. In: 2016 5th International Conference on Reliability, Infocom Technologies, and Optimization (Trends and Future Directions) (ICRITO). IEEE (2016)
24. Kugele, S., Antkowiak, D.: Visualization of trace links and change impact analysis. In: 2016 IEEE 24th International Requirements Engineering Conference Workshops (REW). IEEE (2016)
25. Singhal, S., Suri, B., Misra, S.: An empirical study of regression test suite reduction using MHBG_TCS tool. In: Proceedings of International Conference on Computing Networking and Informatics (ICCNI), pp. 1–5, October 2017
26. Misra, S., Adewumi, A., Maskeliūnas, R., Damaševičius, R., Cafer, F.: Unit testing in global software development environment. In: Panda, B., Sharma, S., Roy, N.R. (eds.) REDSET 2017. CCIS, vol. 799, pp. 309–317. Springer, Singapore (2018). https://doi.org/10.1007/978-981-10-8527-7_25
27. Rodrigues, A., Lencastre, M., Gilberto Filho, A.D.A.: Multi-VisioTrace: traceability visualization tool. In: 2016 10th International Conference on the Quality of Information and Communications Technology (QUATIC), pp. 61–66. IEEE (2016)

Privacy Preservation in Mobile-Based Learning Systems: Current Trends, Methodologies, Challenges, Opportunities and Future Direction

Muhammad Kudu Muhammad(✉), Ishaq Oyebisi Oyefolahan,
Olayemi Mikail Olaniyi, and Ojeniyi Joseph Adebayo

Federal University of Technology, Minna, Nigeria
{muhammad_kudu,o.ishaq,mikail.olaniyi,ojeniyia}@futminna.edu.ng

Abstract. The adoption of mobile technologies in education are evolving like in the business and health sectors. The design of user-centric platform to enable individuals participate in the activities of learning and teaching is currently area of research. The Learning Management Systems (LMS) area assists learners and academic activities but, it continues to fall short of desired impact due to huge demands of the application. More importantly, the mobile applications offer enormous convenience not without the possibility of eavesdropping and maliciously exploiting data about users. The original structure of mobile learning requires that data and processing heads have centralized entity, which is not possible in wireless application arrangements due to communication overhead of transmitting raw data to central learning processor. This led to the use of distributed mobile learning structure, which preserve privacy of learners. This study discusses the challenges, current trends, methodology, opportunities and future direction of privacy preservation in mobile-based learning systems. The study highlighted the use of learners' private data and behavioral activities by LMS especially in understanding the needs of learners as well as improvement of their experiences. But, it raises concerns about the risks of learners' privacy on LMS due the mining processes of learners, which were not considered in existing related studies in literature.

Keywords: Mobile learning · Mobile-based learning system · Privacy preservation · Learning management system developers

1 Introduction

The LMS have been adopted by higher level of education (such as universities) in order to improve the practice of educators and learners, and provides learning management functionalities for these institutions [1]. One concern features prominently, which is the protection of the privacy of users. The problem of privacy continues to attract the attention of users and developers. Third parties find easy to determine actions, transaction consummated, traffic data, and location information of users for potential security and privacy compromises [2].

© Springer Nature Switzerland AG 2021
S. Misra and B. Muhammad-Bello (Eds.): ICTA 2020, CCIS 1350, pp. 520–534, 2021.
https://doi.org/10.1007/978-3-030-69143-1_40

The progression in vast computing and communication effectiveness of the devices and systems; there is an unprecedented ease in storing, retrieving and processing of big volumes of information [3]. In LMS, there is argument that data mining can be carried in a secure way to support private information preservation for private learning activities. Learning systems make use of data mining approaches in order to detach strong data emanating from diverse sources though certain information considered grungy is expected to be removed to protect privacy and security of individual users including identifiers, names, conveys and location information [4].

There are immersed opportunities available to several fields such as education, for harvesting and gaining valuable insight into learners' private information, which puts enormous risks on them. The Chun attributes analysis performed by operators on public database infrastructure further makes learners' data vulnerable to unrestricted invasion of privacy. The solution is to scrutinize the attributes of users' in the dataset to determine excusive and private or sensitive data requiring preservations [5]. Studies in [6–9] have confirmed the use of learners' private data and behavioural activities in LMS for the purpose of understanding the needs of learners as well as enhance their experiences. The privacy and security lapses caused by these mining processes of learners were not considered.

Therefore, this study presents a review to examine the trends of the published articles as a synthesis onto privacy preservation in mobile-based learning systems under subsections such as current trends, methodology, challenges, opportunities and future direction. This article makes the following contributions:

1. Presents the current applications and trends of mobile-based learning systems in pedagogy achievements of learners;
2. Investigate the existing problems and challenges of mobile-based learning systems inhibiting successful widespread implementation;
3. Identify the methodologies and solutions to the problems and challenges of privacy preservation of mobile-based learning system;
4. Further examine the opportunities of mobile-based learning systems;
5. Recommend on future research directions on the privacy preservation in mobile-based learning systems.

The remaining parts of the review are arranged as follows: Sect. 2 explains the previous related studies and the differences of the new study and existing studies. Section 3 presents the review methodology for the articles selection and data collection processes. Section 4 is the results presentation of data collected. Section 5 is the concluding part of the review.

2   Literature Review

The differences and similarities between the present study and the review of selected studies or articles, which serve as the justifications of this study is presented in Table 1.

Table 1. The differences between the existing related studies selected and this study.

Author(s)	Domain of study	Type of article	Privacy and security considerations
[6]	Adaptive e-learning system	Systematic Literature Review	Only offers personalised and self-directed learning environment without considerations for privacy and security
[7]	Learning Management System	Review	Highlights use of LMS for teaching and learning in institutions. Provide less considerations for privacy
[13]	E-Learning Systems	Systematic Literature Review	Individual and social sustainability meta-requirements of e-learning systems
[11]	Learning Management System	Review	-Blurred data elements for privacy of learners was reported and behavioural patterns of learners are a key to LMS
[15]	Learning Management System	Review	Provides the information necessary to develop highly adaptive and person-centred LMS and uses unified theory of acceptance and use of technology (UTAUT) to mine learners' data, without considerations for privacy and security
[12]	Smart Big Data Analytics in Healthcare	Systematic Literature Review	The video-based continuous tracking of human activities through cameras deployed in rooms raises privacy issues
[14]	Learning Management System	Full-article	Only highlights behaviour of teachers to LMS in universities, trust and UTAUT 2 approaches were used to identify factors impacting acceptance without considerations for privacy and security
[8]	Learning Management System	Review	Explores learners' interactions and behaviours patterns with LMS and focuses on learning analytics and educational data mining as key part of LMS without considerations for privacy and security
[10]	Knowledge Sharing	Systematic Literature Review	Explain social media sites without considerations for privacy and security

From Table 1, there are opening for further investigations on ways of evolving novel learning analytics approaches grounded on secure learning process mining for better learning situations through the use of learners' data [8]. There is no definite consideration on the concerns posed by security and privacy issues about platforms, and tools applicable for knowledge sharing [10]. There are quite a number of confirmations on the use of learners' private data and behavioral activities by LMS especially in studying and understanding the needs of learners as well as improvement of their experiences. The data assists in situating technology for educational purposes; it increases in the risks of learners' information on LMS. Specifically, the privacy and security lapses caused by these mining processes of learners were not considered by [6–9]. There is general consensus on the fact that learners' behavioral patterns and personal data are often harvested by many LMS deployed for teaching and learning in educational setups. This learner information mining is a veritable process for the proper functioning of LMS. This study focuses on the issues arising from legitimate use of learners' data for providing better learning experiences using selected studies in the next section.

2.1 Related Studies

In recent time, many studies were conducted to review and survey the conventional learning management system (LMS) domain. Amongst earlier significant works of [9] who introduced a review on the mobile-based learning systems. The authors analyzed and explore learners' interactions and behaviors patterns with LMS advantages and limitations related to learning analytics and educational data mining as key part of LMS. However, the review do not consider the issues of privacy and security.

Many other SLR studies in privacy preservation in mobile-based learning systems were also presented. For instance, [10] in knowledge sharing domain conducted a SLR and ascertain there is lack of focus on the impact of security and privacy concerns about platforms, and tools applicable for knowledge sharing through social media sites. A related work in [11] reported on there are review that there is blurred data elements for privacy of learners and behavioral patterns of learners are a key to LMS. With remarkable SLR of [12] in Smart Big Data Analytics in Healthcare with video-based tool continuous tracking of human activities through cameras deployed in rooms detecting privacy issues.

However, [12] is on health application area which also be applied in educational area particularly in distance learning environment. Also, the SLR of [6, 13] both in e-learning domain described the personalized learning environment, self-directed, individual and social sustainability meta-requirements of e-learning systems as its related to privacy. Recently, [14] highlights behavior of teachers to LMS in universities. Trust and UTAUT 2 approaches were used to identify factors impacting acceptance (privacy preservation metrics). [7, 15] both reviewed they are articles in LMS domain with similarities in their strengths and weaknesses. According to the [7] the use of LMS for teaching and learning in institutions globally is the strength while missing of virtual laboratory from the review of the LMS is a limitation.

The later [15] provides the information necessary to develop highly adaptive and person-centered LMS and uses unified theory of acceptance and use of technology (UTAUT) to mine learners' data. Similarly, [9] SLR in Digital Technology based learning and education domain identifies ways of deepening technology in educational sector and improve students-teacher experiences. Hence, the review uses search strategy and selection criteria following the guidelines used by Preferred Reporting Items for Systematic Reviews and Meta-Analysis (PRISMA) technique. Next section explained the justification for this study.

2.2 Mapping of the Study

The mapping justifies the highest influence and association to the present study as realized from the connected papers' prior and derivative studies graph built illustrated in Fig. 1.

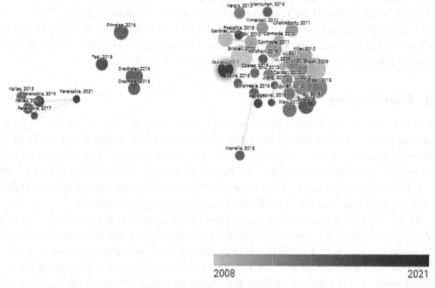

Fig. 1. Privacy-preserving learning analytics: challenges and techniques.

In Fig. 1, this study included studies outside of the scope of the mapping article especially including post-2020 era. This present review paper is a derivative work encompassing fresh subjects related to privacy of mobile learning systems and Big Data applications. It serves as the reason for embarking on this study in order to cover for the gaps in the existing studies.

3 Review Methodology

This study discusses the research questions and the methodology for conducting the Systematic Literature Review (SLR) using the Preferred Reporting Items for Systematic Reviews and Meta-Analysis (PRISMA) technique.

3.1 Research Questions

This survey makes use of the following research questions:

1. What are the current applications and trends of mobile-based learning systems in pedagogy achievements of learners?
2. Are there existing problems and challenges of mobile-based learning systems inhibiting successful widespread implementation?
3. What are the best methodologies and solutions to the problems and challenges of privacy preservation of mobile-based learning system?
4. Are there opportunities of mobile-based learning systems?
5. What are the future research directions on the privacy preservation in mobile-based learning systems?

The purpose of the review is to systematically develop the concise stages for the proposed research. This method of study involves Planning and specifying research questions, conducting the review (that is, an identification of search string and data sources, selecting studies, quality assessment, and data extraction and finally reporting the review [16]. In order to achieve this, the preferred reporting items as reported by [13, 16]. The inclusion and exclusion criteria include all published peer reviewed articles from five major criteria established for this study as shown in Fig. 2. The criteria for data extraction or inclusion in this study include:

1. Articles details the first author, country and type of paper.
2. Articles in the categories of technical reports, journals, conference proceedings and reviews/surveys.
3. Articles published with the timeline of January 2013 to January 2020.
4. Articles related to the keywords or concepts of this study such as Mobile Learning, Privacy and Security, Big Data Mining Procedure, and Data Management for Learners.
5. Articles written in the English Language.

The manual and autonomous search for this study involves a series of search strings across the titles, the abstract, and keywords fields of the articles in digital libraries as follows: (privacy and security in mobile learning systems) AND (data mining techniques in learning management systems) AND (challenges and issues of mobile learning management systems) AND (electronic or learning management systems) AND (privacy and security solutions to learners' data mining). The records sources for the study include: ResearchGate, Springer Link, ACM Digital Library, Scopus, Wiley, Thompson Reuters, IEEExplore Digital Library, Google Scholar, and Elsevier.

From Table 2, the research area enjoys biggest activities in the years covering 2018 and 2019 with 38.71% and 19.35% respectively. The trend revealed popularity of the technology in pedagogy in teaching and learning especially in the year 2018 but decreased considerable afterwards due to several challenges of security and privacy of learner's data mining for legitimate and unapproved usages in year 2019 according this new study.

The timeline for the study and quantity of records returned in terms of percentages matching the year are presented in Table 2.

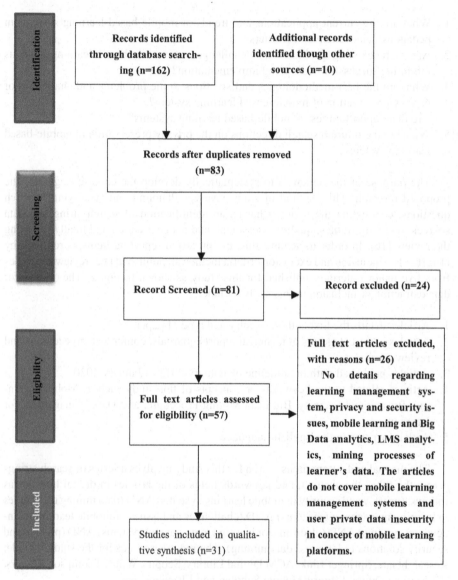

Fig. 2. The review workflow with PRISMA.

Table 2. Timeline of published articles.

Year of publication	Quantity returned	Percentage (%)
2020	1	3.23
2019	6	19.35
2018	12	38.71
2017	5	16.13
2016	5	16.13
2015	0	0.00
2014	1	3.23
2013	1	3.23
Total	31	100

4   Results and Discussion

The answers to the research questions (that is, research questions 1–5) are presented in the next subsections as follows:

4.1   Current Trends

The current trends of this study explain the period of research activities from year 2013 to 2020 as depicted in Fig. 3.

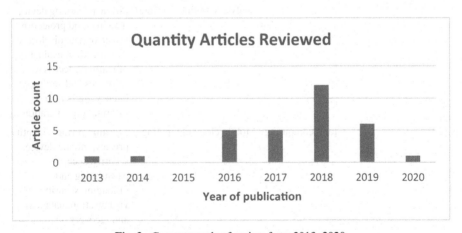

Fig. 3. Current trends of review from 2013–2020.

From Fig. 3, the research activities were most pronounced in the year 2018, but reduced significantly in the year 2019. These changes can be explained as general acceptance of technology for the business of teaching and learning in higher institutions but, the privacy and security issues of learner's data during analytics exposed more risks of learning management systems supported by mobile and handheld devices on the basis of this new study.

4.2 Challenges and Issues of Mobile-Based Learning System and Its Applications

This study identified issues related to mobile-based learning system and its applications domain as presented in Table 3.

Table 3. The challenges and issues of mobile-based learning system.

Author(s)	Domain	Application area	Issues identified
[1, 5, 17–21, 26–34]	Big Data	E-Security, E-Health, E-Leaning systems, data analytics, online merchandize, cyberspace, Human Computer Interaction	Privacy, security, large dataset, identity/attributes disclosure, storage, authentication, usability, unauthorized access, data sharing, technology integration, verification, data collection, poor framework, large communication overheads, and third-party services
[23–25]	Educational	Mobile learning, learning analytics, online learning	Privacy, threats to physical learning devices, data in cloud protection, sensitive data disclosure, data tracking, evaluation of learners, access to resources and services, latency, outliers and information generation
[22]	Cloud computing	Mobile cloud computing	Location privacy, identity privacy, mobile device security, security, partitioning and offloading security, visualisation, data loss and recovery

From Table 3, the general setups for m-learning needs safeguards mechanisms to preserve private and sensitive data concerning actors (or learners) [1, 23–25, 28, 31]. A number of these private sensitive data of learners have been identified including

[24]: name, gender, birth data, address, credit card details, biometric characteristics of actors, mobile phone number, email address, location data, IP address, IMEI, location data, service usage data, e-mail, call record and web-browsing log files and history, and security credentials. According to the study in [18], the birth of Big data has given rise to several issues of security and privacy due to the need to perform analytics and mining of private and sensitive data of users' datasets for diverse applications such as medicals, educational, etc. There are the general concerns about users losing their privacy rights regardless of the fact that the enormous datasets have potential benefits to the society and improving application effectiveness. In addition, several quantities of data concerning users are available on Big Data applications including: Internet activity, demographic information, content usages, private data, which are harvested and analyzed by several organizations for surveys. These activities are highly harmful to the users and data providers because sensitive data and identity of users can be divulged [17]. Individuals become sensitive to the need for privacy of their health information in cases of terminal and serious illness disclosure [29].

4.3 Existing Methodology and Solutions to Privacy and Security

There are several of methodologies and solutions to privacy and security of Big Data and its applications (that is, mobile-based LMS) in different domains along with weaknesses are presented in Table 4.

Table 4. The methodologies and solutions to privacy and security of Big Data.

Author(s)	Domain	Methodology/solution	Weakness
[1, 5, 17, 18, 26–34]	Big Data	- Encryption, cryptosystems and intrusion detection systems - Personalised services	- Re-identification - Private data access - Convergence
[23–25]	Educational	- Data mining, visual data analysis techniques	- Privacy, ethical and risks to learners' data
[21, 22]	Cyberspace	- Infrastructure security layers, cryptography, data provenance, secure and distributed computing, access controls	- Vulnerable to attacks during data usages
[22]	Cloud computing	- Data partitioning strategy (sensitive and non-sensitive), secure socket layer, encryption and cryptography, strong authentication and access control schemes	- Computational and performance degradation - Cloud and mobile device integration complexities

From Table 4, the privacy of data during storage, access and manipulations pose major challenges which is gaining interests. There are no privacy guarantees for private data elements in users' dataset during the process of content mining for diverse applications. A number of anonymization techniques make use of machine learning analysis to isolate and mask personal identifiers in datasets to enforce privacy of users. Cryptographic, encryption, data partitioning strategy, intrusion detection systems are often used to mitigate privacy and security issues in Big Data and its applications.

4.4 Opportunities and Future Directions

The popularity and dominance of Big Data, have opened the opportunities for improving teaching and learning activities, and the learning situations in LMS and mobile-based LMS as presented in Table 5.

Table 5. The opportunities of mobile-based LMS.

S/N	Author (s)	Opportunities for mobile-based LMS
1	[7, 8, 11, 14]	Data acquisition
2	[7, 8, 11]	Storage
3	[6–8, 11, 14, 35]	Data analysis
4	[6–8, 11, 35]	Data visualization
5	[6–9, 11, 14, 15, 35]	Learning process
6	[6–9, 14, 35]	Learning achievements

This study found from literatures that, many researchers and scholars have identified the needs to increase security requirements of Big Data and mobile-based LMS to support data analysis, transfer, acquisition and storage while overcoming data leakages [18, 28]. There are needs to ascertain the effectiveness of common privacy preservations schemes identified by this study for Big data and its applications (or micro-data) including cryptography, perturbation, anonymization, randomized response and condensation [5, 17, 29]. The future data privacy schemes must investigate inherent capabilities of machine learning algorithms in protecting mobile-based LMS private user data [18, 32]. More so, the masking techniques should not only add noise and decrease quality, but dimensionality decrement too to fit into prevailing bandwidth and storage requirements of mobile-based LMS [30, 33].

4.5 Future Directions

The concerning issues relating to LMS its applications, and suggestions for further probing are highlighted on the bases of selected studies and articles in Table 6.

From Table 6, researchers and scholars have identified the needs to focus attention on authentication and authorization schemes for Educational and its applications (such as

Table 6. The issues of Big Data and its applications for future directions.

S/N	Author	Domain	Solution proposed of future investigations
1	[1, 5, 17–21, 26–33]	Big Data	- Monitoring of network traffic to detect suspicious behaviours fast - Transferable data must be encrypted with proper standard in accordance: data type - Users and devices need to be granted access to be able to use resources - All communications should take place over secure channels - Personal data should be masked prior to the publish of the dataset
2	[23, 24, 25,]	Educational	- Data privacy is a problematic. Despite progress in s technical solutions, there are still complexities in defining privacy and inherent limitations of privacy-preserving mechanisms
3	[22]	Cloud Computing	- There is need to reduce overheads during communication and computation for improved mobile devices effectiveness

mobile-based LMS) because of their capabilities to protect privacy of application users and other private dataset through anonymizations and encryption methods. In fact, there is need to increase security requirements of Big Data and mobile-based LMS to support data analysis, transfer, acquisition and storage while overcoming data leakages [18].

The anonymization schemes have recognised as effective in providing k-anonymity and its operators in order to protect micro-data. The main idea is to make user private data elements or attributes indistinguishable, which can be applied in education and medicine [17]. There is need to investigate machine learning pre-processing approach such as dimensionality minimisation and sampling which can be integrated in to appropriate data masking techniques for preserving privacy. More so, the masking techniques should not only add noise and decrease quality, but dimensionality decrement too to fit into prevailing bandwidth and storage requirements of mobile-based LMS [30].

5 Conclusion

This study found that a number of terminologies have been given to the process of deploying technology to share knowledge including mobile learning, digital learning, and electronic learning. The learning management system make use of pedagogical infrastructures, human interaction, learning content and evaluation support to enhance teaching and learning events in higher institutions of learning.

There is quest at present to meet the needs of learners when it comes to the learning process and content distributions. The Learning Management System and its applications have become commonplace procedures for storing, analyzing, integrating and visualizing of large data of users in easier ways. One of the main applications of Big Data in education is the mobile-based LMS that support distrusted and learner-centered learning process.

There are efforts to protect learner's data from unauthorized and inordinate exposure of privacy which have raised security concerns about mobile based learning management systems [5]. The future works are to consider the best ways of performing mining operations on learner's data without fear of privacy compromises. Also, there is need to determine the private elements of learner's data using machine learning algorithms alongside appropriate privacy preservation approaches.

References

1. Singh, H., Miah, S.J.: Design of a mobile-based learning management system for incorporating employment demands: case context of an Australian University. Educ. Inf. Technol. **24**(2), 995–1014 (2018). https://doi.org/10.1007/s10639-018-9816-1
2. Wang, Y., Zheng, N., Xu, M., Qiao, T., Zhang, Q., Yan, F.: Hierarchical identifier: application to user privacy eavesdropping on mobile payment app. Sensors **19**(14), 1–9 (2019). https://doi.org/10.3390/s19143052
3. Ketthari, M.T., Rajendran, S.: Privacy preserving data mining using hiding maximum utility item first algorithm by means of grey wolf optimisation algorithm. Int. J. Bus. Intell. Data Min. **14**(3), 401–418 (2019)
4. Mohanrao, M., Karthik, S.: Privacy preserving for global data using ensemble approach. In: International Conference on Computer Vision and Machine Learning, vol. 1228, pp. 1–7 (2019). https://doi.org/10.1088/1742-6596/1228/1/012046
5. Nagaraj, K., Sharvani, G.S., Sridhar, A.: Encrypting and preserving sensitive attributes in customer churn data using novel dragonfly based pseudonymizer approach. Information **10**(9), 1–21 (2019)
6. Normadhi, N.B.A., Shuib, L., Nasir, H.N., Bimba, A., Idris, N., Balakrishnan, V.: Identification of personal traits in adaptive learning environment: systematic literature review. Comput. Educ. **130**, 168–190 (2019). https://doi.org/10.1016/j.compedu.2018.11.005
7. Aldiab, A., Chowdhury, H., Kootsookos, A., Alam, F., Allhibi, H.: Utilization of learning management systems (LMSs) in higher utilization of learning management systems in higher education system: a case review for Saudi Arabia. Energy Procedia **160**, 731–737 (2019). https://doi.org/10.1016/j.egypro.2019.02.186
8. Juhanak, L., Zounek, J., Rohlíkov, L.: Using process mining to analyze students' quiz-taking behavior patterns in a learning management system. Comput. Hum. Behav. J. **92**, 496–506 (2017). https://doi.org/10.1016/j.chb.2017.12.015
9. Sarker, N.I., Wu, M., Cao, Q., Alam, G.M.M., Li, D.: Leveraging digital technology for better learning and education: a systematic literature review. Int. J. Inf. Educ. Technol. **9**(7), 453–461 (2019). https://doi.org/10.18178/ijiet.2019.9.7.1246
10. Ahmed, Y.A., Ahmad, M.N., Ahmad, N., Zakaria, N.H.: Social media for knowledge-sharing: a systematic literature review. Telematics Inform. **37**, 72–112 (2018). https://doi.org/10.1016/j.tele.2018.01.015
11. Cantabella, M., et al.: Analysis of student behavior in learning management systems through a big data framework. Future Gener. Comput. Syst. **90**, 262–272 (2019). https://doi.org/10.1016/j.future.2018.08.003
12. Ismail, A., Shehab, A., El-Henawy, I.M.: Healthcare analysis in smart big data analytics: reviews, challenges and recommendations. In: Hassanien, A.E., Elhoseny, M., Ahmed, S.H., Singh, A.K. (eds.) Security in Smart Cities: Models, Applications, and Challenges. LNITI, pp. 27–45. Springer, Cham (2019). https://doi.org/10.1007/978-3-030-01560-2_2

13. Alharthi, A.D., Spichkova, M., Hamilton, M.: Sustainability requirements for eLearning systems: a systematic literature review and analysis. Requirements Eng. **24**(4), 523–543 (2018). https://doi.org/10.1007/s00766-018-0299-9

14. Antonius, H., Widjaja, E., Santoso, S.W., Petrus, S., Cahyadi, J.: The enhancement of learning management system in teaching learning process with the UTAUT2 and trust model. In: 2019 International Conference on Information Management and Technology, vol. 1, pp. 309–313. IEEE (2019)

15. Garone, A., et al.: Clustering university teaching staff through UTAUT: implications for the acceptance of a new learning management system. Br. J. Educ. Technol. **50**(5), 2466–2483 (2019). https://doi.org/10.1111/bjet.12867

16. Kaur, A., Kaur, K.: Systematic literature review of mobile application development and testing effort estimation. J. King Saud Univ.-Comput. Inf. Sci. (2018). https://doi.org/10.1016/j.jksuci.2018.11.002

17. Karle, T., Vora, D.: PRIVACY preservation in big data using anonymization techniques. In: 2017 International Conference on Data Management, Analytics and Innovation, pp. 340–343 (2017). https://doi.org/https://doi.org/10.1109/ICDMAI.2017.8073538

18. Bashari, B., Akbarzadeh, N., Ataei, P., Khakbiz, Y.: Security and privacy challenges in big data era. Int. J. Control Theory Appl. **9**(43), 437–448 (2016)

19. Fatt, Q.K., Ramadas, A.: The usefulness and challenges of big data in healthcare. J. Healthc. Commun. **3**(2), 1–4 (2018). https://doi.org/10.4172/2472-1654.100131

20. Simo, H.: Big data: opportunities and privacy challenges, pp. 1–21 (2018)

21. Kaushik, M., Jain, A.: Challenges to big data security and privacy. Int. J. Comput. Sci. Inf. Technol. **5**(3), 3042–3043 (2014)

22. Baqer, M., Azad, A.K., Vasilakos, A.: Security and privacy challenges in mobile cloud computing: survey and way ahead. J. Netw. Comput. Appl. **84**, 38–54 (2017). https://doi.org/10.1016/j.jnca.2017.02.001

23. Avella, J.T., Kebritchi, M., Nunn, S.G., Kanai, T.: Learning analytics methods, benefits, and challenges in higher education: a systematic literature review. Online Learn. **20**(2), 13–29 (2016)

24. Kambourakis, G.: Security and privacy in m-learning and beyond: challenges and state-of-the-art. Int. J. U- and E-Serv. Sci. Technol. **6**(3), 67–84 (2013)

25. Gursoy, M.E., Inan, A., Nergiz, M.E., Saygin, Y.: Privacy-preserving learning analytics: challenges and techniques. IEEE Trans. Learn. Technol. **114**, 1–4 (2018)

26. Manogaran, G., Thota, C., Lopez, D.: HCI Challenges and Privacy Preservation in Big Data Security. The Advances in Human and Social Aspects of Technology (AHSAT) Book Series, pp. 1–23 (2018). https://doi.org/https://doi.org/10.4018/978-1-5225-2863-0.ch001

27. Kabassi, K., Alepis, E.: Learning analytics in distance and mobile learning for designing personalised software. In: Virvou, M., Alepis, E., Tsihrintzis, G.A., Jain, L.C. (eds.) Machine Learning Paradigms. ISRL, vol. 158, pp. 185–203. Springer, Cham (2020). https://doi.org/10.1007/978-3-030-13743-4_10

28. Niknam, S., Dhillon, H.S., Reed, J.H.: Federated learning for wireless communications: motivation, opportunities and challenges, pp. 1–6 (2019). arXiv:1908.06847v3

29. Esmaeilzadeh, P.: The effects of public concern for information privacy on the adoption of health information exchanges (HIEs) by healthcare entities. Health Commun. **34**, 1202–1211 (2018). https://doi.org/10.1080/10410236.2018.1471336

30. Torra, V., Navarro-Arribas, G.: Big data privacy and anonymization. In: Lehmann, A., Whitehouse, D., Fischer-Hübner, S., Fritsch, L., Raab, C. (eds.) Privacy and Identity Management, vol. 498, pp. 15–26. Springer, Cham (2016). https://doi.org/10.1007/978-3-319-55783-0_2

31. Merceron, A.: Educational data mining/learning analytics: methods, tasks and current trends. In: 2015 Proceedings of DeLFI Workshops, pp. 101–109 (2015)

32. Wang, Y., Tian, Z., Zhang, H., Su, S., Shi, W.: A privacy preserving scheme for nearest neighbor query. Sensor **18**(8), 1–4 (2018). https://doi.org/10.3390/s18082440
33. Hadioui, A., Faddouli, N.E., Touimi, Y.B., Bennani, S.: Machine learning based on big data extraction of massive educational knowledge. IJET **12**(11), 151–167 (2017)
34. Plamondon, R., Pirlo, G., Anquetil, É., Rémi, C., Teulings, H.-L., Nakagawa, M.: Personal digital bodyguards for e-security, e-learning and e-health: a prospective survey. Pattern Recogn. **81**, 633–659 (2018). https://doi.org/10.1016/j.patcog.2018.04.012
35. Omolade, A.O.: Predictors of use of mobile applications by university students in Oyo State, Nigeria. J. Inf. Sci. Syst. Technol. **1**(1), 34–48 (2017)

Drug Verification System Using Quick Response Code

Roseline Oluwaseun Ogundokun[1]([✉]) [ID], Joseph Bamidele Awotunde[3] [ID],
Sanjay Misra[2], and Dennison Oluwatobi Umoru[1]

[1] Department of Computer Science, Landmark University, Omu Aran, Nigeria
Ogundokun.roseline@lmu.edu.ng
[2] Department of Electrical and Information Engineering, Covenant University, Ota, Nigeria
[3] Department of Computer Science, University of Ilorin, Ilorin, Nigeria

Abstract. Drug errors and abuses are the most frequently reported deficiencies in the healthcare sector worldwide. In the US alone over $3.5 billion has been expended on treatment related to drug errors that concern more than 1.5 million individuals. The drug is an important part of livelihood has faced the problem of authentication because medicines have to be tested to differentiate between the real and the fake. Drug code detection will reduce the risk of these mistakes by supplying the first responders with accurate information that can quickly decode this information using a code scanner on their smartphones and thus take the necessary steps against their use. The previous study implemented a desktop application system that checks for standardized drugs by scanning the Quick Response codes on the pack. Recently, lots of improvements have taken place in terms of smartphone development with various tools like cameras, which can be used to scan drug barcode. Therefore, the study developed a mobile application to scan the drugs' barcode and verify authenticity. The application designed using an integrated database for real-time drug authentications. The application was implemented using SQL running on a server and interacted with an Application Programming Interface (API) to serve as an intermediary between the application and the browser API built with an Object-relational mapping (ORM) called Sequelize. After code is scanned to gets its serial code, the API validates the serial code and releases a quick response code through a JavaScript Object Notation (JSON). The proposed system can be used by doctors, pharmacists and patients for the identification of fakes and harmful drugs, hence reduced the calculations of fakes or harmful drugs.

Keywords: Drugs · Quick response · Bar code · Healthcare · Consumption · Verification · Mobile · Android

1 Introduction

Substandard or illegal drugs pose a major danger to global public safety [1]. According to the Global Health Organisation (WHO), under-standard or falsified drugs force 10.5 per cent of low- and middle-income counterproductions, costing an additional US$ 30.5

© Springer Nature Switzerland AG 2021
S. Misra and B. Muhammad-Bello (Eds.): ICTA 2020, CCIS 1350, pp. 535–545, 2021.
https://doi.org/10.1007/978-3-030-69143-1_41

billion annually [2]. As a result of global policies such as the EU Falsified Medicines Directive and the US Pharmaceutical Supply Chain Protection Act [3], pharmaceutical producers and suppliers are working to follow a structured brand labeling scheme to help patient traceability and fight medication counterfeiting. Current authentication strategies use two main approaches: 1) tamper-evident or – resistant packaging; and 2) packaging serialization (i.e. two-dimensional (2D) barcode printing [4, 5]. However, such techniques will actually only be effective in the presence of standardized packaging for certain drugs which are processed en masse. Falsified antimalarials are estimated to contribute up to an additional 267,000 deaths annually in sub-Saharan Africa alone [6]. It is clear that successful counterfeit measures need to be built to ensure patient protection around the product supply chain [7, 8].

The main value of adoption of drug verification and identification reduces hospital injuries caused by prescription mistakes, known as preventable side effects, harmful and fake drugs. Barcodes are commonly used for marking items for identification [9–11]. For example, barcodes are used for marking a product or part to permit the identification of the product or part and retrieval of information about the product or part. For instance, barcodes can be used to mark packages to facilitate automated tracking and sorting of the packages during shipment. A barcode can identify a package, such as the shipping address, destination address among others, and use the information for routing the package. Also, allow for a tracking and sorting system to retrieve information about the package. There are several ways of using barcode standards. A barcode standard provides a mapping between barcodes conforming to the standard and the data encoded by the barcodes.

Quick Response codes, commonly abbreviated as QR codes, started as an alternative to the regular Universal Product Code (UPC) barcode widely used in retail and manufacturing [12–15]. Unlike a 1-D barcode, a QR code is a 2-D matrix code that transmits information in columns and rows by arranging its dark and light elements [16, 17]. You will access the data in a QR code by taking a picture of the QR code and using a QR code scanner to decode it [18, 19]. The QR code itself is simply an array of bits that a scanner must identify [13, 14, 20]. Bits are allocated for the scanner to define and orient the file, as well as for the details regarding version and size [21, 22].

Barcode, a printed arrangement of equal bars or lines of various widths utilized to input information into a PC framework [23–26]. The bars on a white foundation are generally dark, and their width and amount differ as indicated by use [25, 26]. The bars are utilized to speak to the double digits 0 and 1, groupings from which, in actuality, numbers from 0 to 9 can be deciphered and prepared by a computerized personal computer (PC) [27, 28]. The machine peruses the nearness or nonappearance of a bar of a specific width in a given situation in an arrangement as either a 0 or 1.

An optical (laser) scanner which is a piece of a PC framework peruses the standardized identification data [29]. A handheld scanner or standardized identification pen is pushed over the code, or a scanner incorporated with a checkout counter or other surface moves the code itself by hand. The central favorable position of the barcode is that at the moment the barcode is scanned, they permit clients to process data [30], as opposed to just store data for result handling.

The word QR code represents the Code of Rapid Response. QR codes are square scanner tags (two-dimensional standardized identifications) created and first utilized in Japan [31–33]. Similarly, as with some other standardized identification, a QR code is just an approach to store data in an optical mark decipherable by the machine [34, 35]. The information that a QR code contains can be anything from straightforward content to email addresses, telephone numbers among others [36]. QR codes store information, arranged in a square grid, uses black mark shapes and white space [19, 37]. This study, therefore, designed a QuickCheck smartphone application that combines Quick Response (QR) and Barcode readers to check whether a drug is fake or not. This application will tackle and assist in detecting counterfeit drugs, and check the expiration of drugs to avoid bad drugs.

2 Related Works

There are many researches works on the use of barcode in the areas of product recognitions, but little or no research has been the focus on drug verifications.

Han et al. [7], implemented the integration of microtaggant into drugs. Such microtaggants contain QR codes that provide the authentication of the drug when the drug is scanned with a mobile phone. The QR-coded microtaggant is lithographically processed in a microfluidic channel with one single exposure to patterned UV light. The advanced capable functions of high capacity and error correction not only allow the medication to be authenticated but also monitor the details such as supplier and expiry date, which is included in the individual unit-of-dose dosage type.

Imam, [38] implemented a personal health card that requires a barcode and QR code scanning to send details of patients through a secure means. Poor coordination of treatment may result in increased medical costs, adverse patient care outcomes, or risk of hospital readmissions. That architecture incorporates a personal health card to use the QR coding technology to access general medical details.

Al-Khalifa, [39] implemented a 2D barcode and QR code scanner for mobile phones to aid the visually impaired people in which texts are converted to codes and then transmitted through audio means to the person. The method is based on the idea of using QR codes (two-dimensional barcode) that are connected to an object and checked using a camera phone that is fitted with a QR scanner.

Purushothaman & Sujithra [40] built a system that could scan QR codes of drugs, check the expiry date, and then bills the customer based on the prescription of the doctor. The main motive is to make the procedure efficient. One of the major problems in the medical industry is that drugs are discontinued beyond their expiry date and as a consequence, there is a huge loss of human health and life.

Uzun & Bilgin, [41] evaluated and implemented a system that serves an identity tag to identify patients, their records, the drugs they currently on, and other functions. Its system provides critical identity warnings dependent on QR code, and an identification system for patients in hospitals. A special QR Code Tag is given to each medical system employee; the QR Code Identification Tag may be worn as a watch or necklace or used as an ID card to facilitate alerts regarding patient identification. Patients should always have QR code Identification bracelets in-hospital. Those QR code bracelets link to the

QR Code Identification page where you store accurate information; the code can be checked using a mobile or standalone QR code scanner.

Tseng & Wu [42], implemented an online drug management support system that utilizes QR code and elderly outpatient web services. This system was based on the prescription of drugs by doctors in QR codes and monitoring its delivery. The system proposed consists of architecture on three levels: front-end stage, desktop tier, and server tier. The smartphone group will house on mobile devices the customized drug safety service system which offers multiple primary functions including prescription alerts, pill-dispensing aid, dosage tracking, product placement, and older outpatient drug notes.

Barasa [43], implemented a mobile phone solution for systematically identifying and reporting non-standardized medicinal by the use of QR codes that are on the pack on the drugs. This situation provides unparalleled resources that researchers can use to improve the current manner in which counterfeit products are detected and published. This dissertation provides the human population in Kenya and globally an overview of the production and impact of illicit products with an emphasis on the emerging markets.

Dube, Ndlovu, Nyathi & Sibanda [44], implemented a medical health record transmission that was based in QR codes for security. This involves records of people admitted, discharged, and other detailed information. The logging of these patient health card information makes them vulnerable to tempering, losing, misinterpretation, and prone to confidentiality breaches.

Rahman, Rahman, Seyal & Timbang, [45] implemented a mobile application QR code for wellbeing verification to book appointments, get drug prescriptions, and get notifications on health issues by access to the hospital's database. The QR code created and that the need to retain all the information.

Leza, Emran & Ghani [46], developed a system for Improving the usability of data using the QR Code in healthcare. Here, patients scan a particular QR code specialized for them to gain access to their knowledge servers, which is also usually included in QR code to improve security. The model adopts QR code technologies to gain access to their knowledge database, which is typically also in QR code to improve security. The platform follows QR code technology as a tool that allows multi-platform access points to the data.

The work done by Barasa in 2016 served the nation of Kenya in terms of drug verification to reduce deaths per year. Barasa implemented a system that identifies non-standardized medicinal drugs by using QR codes. Therefore, this paper enhanced the work by implementing a mobile application that identifies harmful and fake drugs built on a better and newer platform and also includes the ability to scan on sight instead of taking the picture. The system is fast, secure, accurate, reliable, and informative. The proposed system will also report any identified harmful or fake drugs to pharmaceutical companies and allow users to give feedback.

3 Proposed Mobile Application Framework

QR code drugs verification mobile systems reduce harmful and fake drugs by electronically verifying the drugs. The design process of the QR code drugs verification is depicted in Fig. 1. The system comprises three major elements, the users, the data submission, and the drug verification. The workflow of this mobile application deduced that;

1. A customer uses his/her mobile phone's camera to scan QR barcodes and select the name of the company.
2. Data submitted would have access to the company's database and therefore data analysis and interpretation of results are made.
3. If the drug is original, it gets verified and the customer gets the results alongside the information of such drug but if fake, the customer gets notified about such drug not useful.

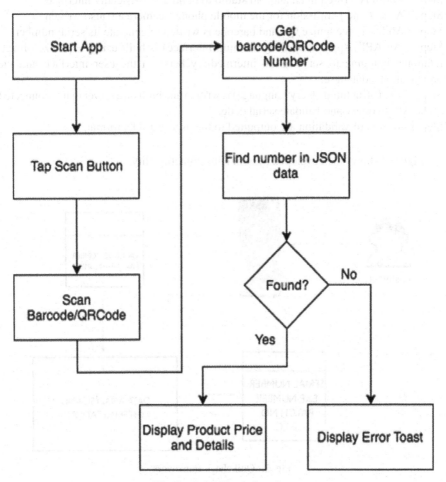

Fig. 1. QuickCheck flowchart

4 Proposed Mobile Application Requirements

The mobile application which is useful in drug verification can only be used when requirements to use the applications are met both physically and non-physically. Physical requirements are in terms of the type of mobile phone and its specifications which include most importantly he camera, a capable operating system, and others. The non-physical requirement part of it is phases and mediums it passes through to finally get to the final stage which in this case includes only the customer.

4.1 System Algorithm

Step 1: Kotlin is written in an android studio to build a user-friendly interface.
Step 2: Access and permission for the mobile phone's camera are also written.
Step 3: Ability to recognize QR and barcode is written to generate its serial number.
Step 4: An API (Application Programming Interface) is built using sequelize object-relational mapping to serve as an intermediary between the user interface and the organization's database.
Step 5: SQL (Structured Query Language) is written and built on a server that is connected to the API to query and validate serial code.
Step 6: Results of validation are outputted to the user in JSON format.

Figure 2 shows the developed system entire functionality.

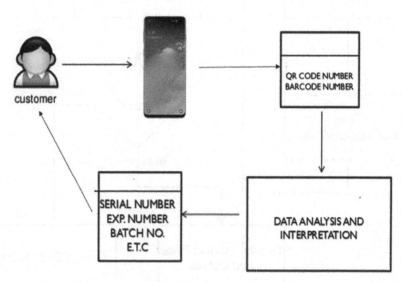

Fig. 2. Quikcheck framework

4.2 System Algorithm

The study used mobile development tools provided by android studio, although there are others mobile development tools [47–49] but android studio proved more useful than others one, and many of the available mobile operating system are running on android OS [50–52]. The mobile application system has an integrated database which has been implemented using SQL running on a server and it is interacted with an API to serve as an intermediary between the mobile application and the browser. The API is built with an ORM called Sequelize. After code is scanned to gets its serial code, the serial code with the aid of the API gets validated and releases a response through a JSON.

5 Implementation

The mobile application, after selecting both the name of the organization and scanned code, it matches them and looks them up in the database for analysis. Implementation involves an integration of an Application Programming Interface (API) to have access to an organization's database and also the integration of java code for the mobile to be able to scan codes.

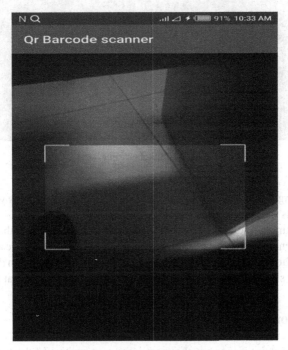

Fig. 3. Quikcheck interface

This mobile Application interface as shown in Fig. 3 above, after requesting permission to use the mobile phone's camera following the java code written, accesses the

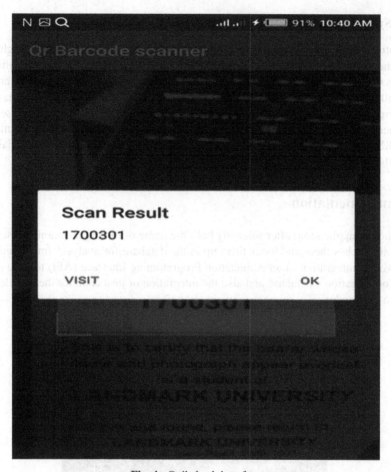

Fig. 4. Quikcheck interface

camera intending to find a QR or barcode to scan. The java program is written such that nothing interests the camera than either the QR code or the bar code.

After the camera finds the QR code or barcode to scan on sight, the corresponding java program generates the corresponding code that is behind such code and therefore by popping up as shown in Fig. 4 above, the visit button is clicked and then drug verification is done thereby showing you all necessary information concerning that particular drug.

6 Conclusion

Security and its maintenance are the most important entities in the technology world today. This code scanning systems have served as one of the most reliable forms of security for data and other measures amongst other security systems. This could be in the form of hardware or software depending on the number of resources at hand. The software mostly consists of the use of mobile phones and their camera system according to its program code. The system has proven to be of high-quality security in terms of its access to database and results encryption.

Throughout the research conducted, it was been discovered that several companies and NGO's are also planning to implement such software, but in specialized categories, this idea is one that can be appropriately termed as a "disruptive idea" as this would be the first of its kind to incorporate all aspects of the present technology under a single application.

7 Future Work

In the future, this work can be improved in the area of scan on sight. This area should be faster because some mobile phone cameras can't quickly scan on sight. After scanning, the results could be popped up immediately without any delay in accessing the database. Speed should be the main focus in all areas of the mobile application system.

References

1. Trenfield, S.J., et al.: Track-and-trace: novel anti-counterfeit measures for 3D printed personalized drug products using smart material inks. Int. J. Pharm. **567**, 118443 (2019)
2. Kelesidis, T., Falagas, M.E.: Substandard/counterfeit antimicrobial drugs. Clin. Microbiol. Rev. **28**(2), 443–464 (2015)
3. Berger, J.: European market assessment for the main organic export products from Armenia, Moldova, and Ukraine (2018)
4. Bansal, D., Malla, S., Gudala, K., Tiwari, P.: Anti-counterfeit technologies: a pharmaceutical industry perspective. Sci. Pharm. **81**(1), 1–14 (2013)
5. Lee, K.S., et al.: Combating sale of counterfeit and falsified medicines online: a losing battle. Front. Pharmacol. **8**, 268 (2017)
6. Naughton, B.: The Future of Falsified and Substandard Medicine Detection: Digital Methods to Track and Authenticate Pharmaceutical Products (2018)
7. Han, S., et al.: Lithographically encoded polymer microtaggant using high-capacity and error-correctable QR code for anti-counterfeiting of drugs. Adv. Mater. **24**(44), 5924–5929 (2012)
8. You, M., et al.: Three-dimensional quick response code based on inkjet printing of up conversion fluorescent nanoparticles for drug anti-counterfeiting. Nanoscale **8**(19), 10096–10104 (2016)
9. Liu, Y., Tao, X., Wang, Y.P.: U.S. Patent No. 9,111,159. U.S. Patent and Trademark Office, Washington, DC (2015)
10. Bell, T., Duncan, C., Rainer, A.: What is coding? In: Creating the Coding Generation in Primary Schools, pp. 3–21. Routledge (2017)
11. Perret, E., Vena, A., Tedjini, S., Boutant, Y., Halope, C.: U.S. Patent No. 9,697,446. U.S. Patent and Trademark Office, Washington, DC (2017)
12. Winter, M.: Scan me everybody's guide to the magical world of QR codes. West song Publishing (2011)
13. Tiryakioglu, B., Kayakutlu, G., Duzdar, I.: Medical device tracking via QR code and efficiency analysis. In 2016 Portland International Conference on Management of Engineering and Technology (PICMET), pp. 3115–3128. IEEE, September 2016
14. Naik, N., Kadam, N., Bhalekar, M.: A technique to hide encrypted data in QR codes using EK-EQR algorithm. Int. J. Comput. Appl. **161**(12), 25–28 (2017)

15. Adeniyi, A.E., Amusan, E.A., Olagunju, M., Ogundokun, R.O.: Application of smartphone QR code scanner as a means of authenticating student identity card. Int. J. Eng. Res. Technol. **13**(1), 48–43 (2020)
16. Picard, J., Landry, P.: U.S. Patent No. 9,594,993. U.S. Patent and Trademark Office, Washington, DC (2017)
17. Yan, B., Xiang, Y., Hua, G.: Improving Image Quality in Visual Cryptography. Springer, Singapore (2020). https://doi.org/10.1007/978-981-13-8289-5
18. Vazquez-Briseno, M., Hirata, F.I., Sanchez-Lopez, J., Jimenez-Garcia, E., Navarro-Cota, C., Nieto-Hipolito, J.: Using RFID/NFC and QR-code in mobile phones to link the physical and the digital world. Interactive Multimedia, pp. 219–242 (2012)
19. Brodie, K., Madden, L.L., Rosen, C.A.: Applications of quick response (QR) codes in medical education. J. Grad. Med. Edu. **12**(2), 138–140 (2020)
20. Kumar, A., Kumar Nigam, A.: A Comparative Analysis of uses of 1-D and 2-D Barcodes. Int. J. Adv. Res. Comput. Sci. **5**(6) (2014)
21. Li, C.M., Hu, P., Lau, W.C.: Authpaper: protecting paper-based documents and credentials using authenticated 2D barcodes. In: 2015 IEEE International Conference on Communications (ICC), pp. 7400–7406. IEEE, June 2014
22. Nazemzadeh, P., Fontanelli, D., Macii, D., Palopoli, L.: Indoor localization of mobile robots through QR code detection and dead reckoning data fusion. IEEE/ASME Trans. Mechatron. **22**(6), 2588–2599 (2017)
23. Burian, A., Kangas, J.A., Vehvilainen, M.: U.S. Patent No. 7,946,491. U.S. Patent and Trademark Office, Washington, DC (2011)
24. Zhao, Y., Chapman, E., Wang, S.G., Hoover, M.E., Eschbach, R.: U.S. Patent No. 8,261,988. U.S. Patent and Trademark Office, Washington, DC (2012)
25. Gallo, O., Manduchi, R.: U.S. Patent No. 9,098,764. U.S. Patent and Trademark Office, Washington, DC (2015)
26. Bachelder, I.A., Vaidyanathan, S.: U.S. Patent No. 9,361,499. U.S. Patent and Trademark Office, Washington, DC (2016)
27. Knudson, E.B., Rodriguez, T.F.: U.S. Patent No. 8,620,021. U.S. Patent and Trademark Office, Washington, DC (2013)
28. Hsu, J.Y.: Computer Architecture: Software Aspects, Coding, and Hardware. CRC Press, Boca Raton (2017)
29. Mullani, J.J., Sankar, M., Khade, P.S., Sonalkar, S.H., Patil, N.L.: OCR based speech synthesis system using labview: text to speech conversion system using OCR. In: 2018 Second International Conference on Computing Methodologies and Communication (ICCMC), pp. 7–14. IEEE, February 2018
30. Someswar, G.M., Reddy, M.M.: Design and development of a suitable identity management framework in heterogeneous internet of things. Compusoft **7**(3), 2716–2732 (2018)
31. Falas, T., Kashani, H.: Two-dimensional bar-code decoding with camera-equipped mobile phones. In: Fifth Annual IEEE International Conference on Pervasive Computing and Communications Workshops (PerComW 2007), pp. 597–600. IEEE, March 2007
32. Soon, T.J.: QR code. . Synth. J. **2008**, 59–78 (2008)
33. Xu, F.: QR Codes and library bibliographic records. Vine (2014)
34. Ecker, M., Pretsch, T.: The durability of switchable QR code carriers under hydrolytic and photolytic conditions. Smart Mater. Struct. **22**(9), 094005 (2013)
35. Guenter, E., Maresh, M.E., Mazzeo, T.S., Nolan, C., Vargas, J.F.: U.S. Patent No. 8,794,537. U.S. Patent and Trademark Office, Washington, DC (2014)
36. Weir, M.: QR Codes and Mobile Marketing for the Small Business Owner. Michael (2010)
37. Sahu, S.K., Gonnade, S.K.: Encryption in QR code using steganography. IJERA Int. J. Eng. Res. Appl. **3**(4) (2013)

38. Imam, K.: Personal Health Card: Use of QR Code to Access Medical Data (2018)
39. Al-Khalifa, H.S.: Utilizing QR code and mobile phones for blinds and visually impaired people. In: Miesenberger, K., Klaus, J., Zagler, W., Karshmer, A. (eds.) ICCHP 2008. LNCS, vol. 5105, pp. 1065–1069. Springer, Heidelberg (2008). https://doi.org/10.1007/978-3-540-70540-6_159
40. Purushothaman, M.V., Dhanalakshmi J., Sujithra, K.: QR code inbuild prescription modules for effective pharmacy billing application **119**(15), 45–58 (2018). https://www.acadpubl.eu/hub/
41. Uzun, V., Bilgin, S.: Evaluation and implementation of QR code identity tag system for healthcare in Turkey. SpringerPlus **5**(1), 1–24 (2016). https://doi.org/10.1186/s40064-016-3020-9
42. Tseng, M.H., Wu, H.C.: A cloud medication safety support system using QR code and Web services for elderly outpatients. Technol. Health Care **22**(1), 99–113 (2014). https://doi.org/10.3233/THC-140778
43. Barasa, M.M.: A Mobile phone solution for systematically identifying and reporting nonstandardised medicinal drugs in Nairobi, Kenya (Doctoral dissertation, Strathmore University) (2016)
44. Dube, S., Sihwa, S., Nyathi, T., Sibanda, K.: QR code based patient medical health records transmission: Zimbabwean case. In: Proceedings of the 2015 InSITE Conference, pp. 521–530 (2015). https://doi.org/10.28945/2233
45. Rahman, M.N.A., Rahman, A.A., Seyal, A.H., Timbang, I.: QR code for health notification mobile application (2015). https://doi.org/10.15242/iae.iae0215004
46. Leza, M., Emran, F.N., Ghani, N.A.: Improving Data Accessibility Using QR Code in Healthcare Domain. E-Proceeding of Software Engineering Postgraduates Workshop (SEPoW) Innovative Software Engineering for Creative and Co-Organizer, pp. 119–123 (2013)
47. Adeniyi, E.A., Awotunde, J.B., Ogundokun, R.O., Kolawole, P.O., Abiodun, M.K., Adeniyi, A.A.: Mobile health application and COVID-19: opportunities and challenges. J. Crit. Rev. **7**(15), 3481–3488 (2020)
48. Sadiku, P.O., Ogundokun, R.O., Habib, E.A.A., Akande, A.: Design and implementation of an android based tourist guide. Int. J. Modern Hosp. Tour. **1**(1), 1–33 (2019)
49. Kayode, A.A., Adeniyi, A.E., Ogundokun, R.O., Ochigbo, S.A.: An android based blood bank information retrieval system. J. Blood Med. **10**, 119 (2019)
50. Odusami, M., Abayomi-Alli, O., Misra, S., Shobayo, O., Damasevicius, R., Maskeliunas, R.: Android malware detection: a survey. In: Florez, H., Diaz, C., Chavarriaga, J. (eds.) ICAI 2018. CCIS, vol. 942, pp. 255–266. Springer, Cham (2018). https://doi.org/10.1007/978-3-030-01535-0_19
51. Osho, O., Mohammed, U.L., Nimzing, N.N., Uduimoh, A.A., Misra, S.: Forensic analysis of mobile banking apps. In: Misra, S., et al. (eds.) ICCSA 2019. LNCS, vol. 11623, pp. 613–626. Springer, Cham (2019). https://doi.org/10.1007/978-3-030-24308-1_49
52. Aungst, T.D., Clauson, K.A., Misra, S., Lewis, T.L., Husain, I.: How to identify, assess and utilise mobile medical applications in clinical practice. Int. J. Clin. Pract. **68**(2), 155–162 (2014)

A Novel Approach to News Archiving from Newswires

Bilkisu Larai Muhammad-Bello[1,2](✉) ⓘ, Mudi Lukman[2], and Mudi Salim[2]

[1] Computer Science and Electrical Engineering G.S.S.T,
Kumamoto University, Kumamoto, Japan
[2] Federal University of Technology Minna, Minna, Niger, Nigeria
bilkisu_bello@futminna.edu.ng, {lukman.mudi,
salim.mudi}@st.futminna.edu.ng

Abstract. A news archive is the core operational tool a media relations team depends on in order to effectively feed a data-hungry organization. An ingrained approach to news archiving in existence is the use of a relational database. As a consequence, integrating search engines that support full-text search is practically impossible due to the strict data schema that is defined in relational database systems. Therefore, there is a need for news archives that support full-text search with relevance ranking of news. In this paper, an approach that supports full-text search is proposed. The process is started by crawling newswire websites for news that are relevant with respect to some predefined keywords and extracting them. Then, they are stored in a data structure known as an inverted-index which supports full-text search, aggregation, and relevance ranking of search results. Search results are ranked and returned to a user in the order of decreasing relevance to the search term. We were able to provide a software solution written in java, the jsoup library for HTML parsing, and an elasticsearch implementation of a search engine. We tested our solution on nine newswires using ten keywords and were able to retrieve a total of 42 relevant news matching seven keywords. The approach proposed in this paper when compared to the manual approach performed better in terms of retrieval speed and accuracy. We conclude that three main components are important in a good digital archive: relevance, extraction, and search. This work is an integration of a good relevance marking technique, an extraction method, and a search engine.

Keywords: Web content extraction · Press review archiving · News extraction from newswires · Search engines as archives

1 Introduction

Newswires syndicate news regarding events, individuals, or organizations which are of interest to specific consumer profiles such as media relation teams, data analysts, scientific researchers, and journalists among others. The periodic avalanche of news generated by these newswires can be used in serving different information needs such as press reviews and news archives. On the one hand, generating a press review does

© Springer Nature Switzerland AG 2021
S. Misra and B. Muhammad-Bello (Eds.): ICTA 2020, CCIS 1350, pp. 546–559, 2021.
https://doi.org/10.1007/978-3-030-69143-1_42

not necessarily require a retrospective of news while on the other hand, news archives must store both past and present news in order to support various tasks such as insight generation through analytics and search engine integration.

Information technology has seen a huge adoption from the digital news industry over the years due to the rapid increase in the amount of information on the internet and how effective, efficient and budget-friendly it supports information delivery [1, 2]. Several web content extraction tools and approaches have been developed in order to successfully and effectively extract the relevant content from webpages. Content extraction from webpages is an intricate task due to the dynamic and ever-evolving nature of webpages and by extension, newswires. Programs known as wrappers specialized for the purpose of extracting relevant content from web sources and mapping them with structures or formats that define a similar or compatible relation are faced with the challenge of recognizing the relevant content from noisy ones [3]. Once extracted, this news can be adapted to support different tasks; news extraction can be applied to generate news highlight sentences that capture the main topic within a news article [4]. Also, the fast and effective extraction of content from webpages could be used to adapt webpages for small screen devices [5] and as proclaimed [6], if we can extract the relevant content of a webpage rapidly, many semantic applications such as search engines can be developed by leveraging this.

In this paper, we present a novel approach to archiving digital news extracted from newswires. Our approach introduces a news archive that extracts news from newswires via tag IDing using predefined keywords. The extracted news is formatted for appropriate storage and indexed in Elasticsearch.[1] We used the jsoup[2] Java[3] library to determine and extract the relevant content. A brief overview of the problem that motivated this work is presented in the next subsection. The novelty of combining a relevance marking approach, content extraction approach, and a search engine as an archive is the crux of this paper and shall be expounded in the following sections.

This paper comprises five main sections. The rest of this paper is organized as follows: a discussion of several existing works on content extraction are presented in Sect. 2; Sect. 3 is the materials and methods section. It presents a discussion of our relevance algorithm and news extraction approach along with details of the search engine. Section 4 presents the results and discussion with a detailed experiment and an evaluation of our approach in comparison with the manual-labor approach. Lastly, we conclude the paper in Sect. 5 with a summary of our work and a brief note on how our approach can be adapted for further work.

1.1 Problem Statement

Several organizations and institutions have specific departments i.e. media relations team whose sole responsibility is to provide members of staff with a summary of work-related news that is of interest to the organization at large (press reviews). This is often achieved through the use of specialized software packages for extracting, formatting,

---

[1] https://www.elastic.co/.

[2] https://jsoup.org/.

[3] https://www.java.com/en/.

disseminating, and archiving news periodically. This information grows and gradually forms a plethora of news that requires proper maintenance. An ingrained approach to building digital archives in existing works is the use of a relational database that defines a schema. In relational models of databases, all data is technically structured within named relations called tables. Each table is composed of named attributes known as columns. The set of all columns describing a record within a table sums up to what is known as a row. This model was first proposed in 1970 by E. F. Codd in his paper titled A relational model of data for large shared data banks. The concept of normalization was introduced in his paper which in simple terms involves creating relations that have no repeating groups [7].

A major problem surfaces when the need for archived news arises yet they cannot be retrieved even after spending an inordinate amount of time walking through an entire corpus of documents and even putting certain jobs at risk. This is due to the fact that when working with relational databases, search queries are always short in expressive power and features such as context suggestion cannot be leveraged effectively. Therefore, there is a need for a search engine as archive that provides search engine level features such as query autocomplete, context suggestion, analytics support, and provides search results ranked based on their relevance to the search term in real time. In general, features like query suggestion are useful for query term disambiguation and dealing with typographical errors among others [8]. This search engine as archive solution will improve an organizations' business process by saving a sizeable amount of time spent on information retrieval. It will also serve as a fault tolerant solution due to the distributed nature of the underlying search engine implementation presented herein as it allows for replication of multiple copies of data on different machines.

2 Related Work

The goal of content extraction is to produce structured data ready for post-processing, which is relevant in both Web data mining and information retrieval systems [9]. News webpages are made up of varying components such as navigation links, advertisements, social media pointers, and the relevant content of interest as shown in Fig. 1. The speed of information retrieval (IR) can greatly be enhanced through the use of a good document clustering approach. A Modsup-based term frequency and Rider Optimization-based Moth Search Algorithm (Rn-MSA) [10] is presented. It serves as a good document clustering approach that enhances the efficiency of corpus navigation. Content extraction is achieved using the term frequency-inverse document frequency algorithm (TF-IDF) and Wordnet features. Wordnet ontology is used to derive two relations between words: synonyms and hyponyms. Noisy and redundant terms are reduced by removing stop words and stemming inflected words to their root word. Document clustering is performed based on their similarity using the proposed Modsup and Rn-MSA.

An intelligent information system that extracts and archives generic topics from newswires on weekly basis that adapts the term frequency * proportional document frequency algorithm (TF*PDF) is presented in [11]. The TF*PDF of a term is the frequency of the term within a webpage and its frequency within different newswires concurrently.

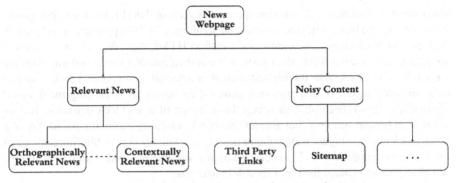

Fig. 1. Classification of contents of a news webpage

The topics containing those terms with high weights are labeled main topics. this approach is not designed to serve press reviews that take keywords into account as such, it is more suited for a popularity ranking use-case as opposed to a relevance ranking one.

Content extraction is being adapted for the extraction of news article narrative [12]. Natural language processing (NLP) methods were employed to enable the analysis and extraction of information from text. These methods were used in extracting individual accounts from news articles by dividing the problem into three steps, namely, named entity recognition, event extraction, and attribute extraction. Named entity extraction was achieved using trained machine learning-based models. A hybrid approach was developed and used to achieve event extraction. Lastly, a dependency parser and Levin's verb classes were used in achieving attribute extraction. CoreEx, a simple heuristic algorithm [5] that extracts the main content from webpages of newswires was developed with an approach that eschewed: the problems associated with structure-dependent approaches e.g. changes in page structure; problems associated with machine learning approaches e.g. re-training as dataset evolves; problems associated with natural language processing (NLP) approaches e.g. their computational expense for large datasets. However, it sometimes excludes the title of a news from the extracted content due to node distance.

A main content extraction algorithm based on node characteristics such as text density and hyperlink density along with neighbor node characteristics was introduced [6]. In abstraction, the algorithm involves six steps: document object model (DOM) generator which is responsible for generating an object model for a webpage, DOM processor does the "housekeeping" of the raw DOM such as extensible hypertext markup language (XHTML) formatting and removal of noisy tags, node fusion uses a similarity algorithm to merge similar nodes, node characteristics analyzer classifies all nodes according to the text density and hyperlink density, node filter filters the noisy nodes, and finally content generator returns the extracted content.

Based on the notion that newer webpages are eschewing the use of structural tags and are adopting an architecture that makes use of stylesheets for structural information, a content extraction technique which was called Content Extraction via Tag Ratios (CETR) [13] was developed in order to keep up content extractors with the aforementioned architectural change. Tag ratio is used to determine content tag by picking the tag with the highest tag ratio from an array of tags based on each tags' content-text value. A template-independent news extraction approach was created in [14] for news aggregators by exploiting the block-oriented structure of webpages. In this approach, a webpage is divided into blocks based on some criteria such as HTML tags. Weights are calculated for each block by considering their textual size and calculating their similarity with the page title. The block with the highest weight is selected as the news block. The use of a similarity model in this approach makes it an outlier from existing block-based approaches. This is because it increases the accuracy of news block detection. It does not rely on textual size only, but also on title-block similarity due to the possibility of a noisy block having a higher weight than a news block with fewer text. Multithreading and recursion were applied in [15] to design a highly scalable bytecode-based java archive search engine to manage the rapid growth in data size.

The application of text ranking cuts across different application areas, primarily used in IR; text ranking is being used also for NLP. In [16], an overview of a framework for text ranking using transformers is presented. Transformers are a kind of neural network architecture for text ranking. The exact type of transformer employed is a bidirectional encoder representation from transformers (BERT) by Google [17].

3 Materials and Methods

3.1 Relevance Marking

In our approach, a news can be either orthographically relevant, contextually relevant or both. If the set of tags that qualify the news as relevant contains only acronyms and abbreviations, then the news is simply classified as orthographically relevant e.g. "Sec." could mean "Securities and Exchange Commission" or just an abbreviation of "Secondary". Finally, if the set of tags that qualify the news as relevant contains at least one jargon, noun, or phrase, it is classified as both orthographically and contextually relevant as shown by the dashed arrow in Fig. 1. Relevant news articles can become less relevant as more documents are added to a search engine over time. This can be due to poor-quality content being added and the daily refresh interval of what users view as up-to-date [18]. The relevance scoring function for documents relevant to a query cannot always be ran for all documents in a large scale search engine due to the impact of the corpuses size on computational cost [19]. Both arguments have a huge impact on news relevance marking. A news webpage always contains both the relevant content i.e. title and body and the noisy content which includes elements such as external links, sitemaps, advertisements, comment blocks, etc. Advertisements can be removed from web pages during the parsing process using the common and efficient approach of analyzing HTML tag attributes. Our focus is on the relevant content so we restrict the discussion of noisy content to what has been mentioned earlier. Tags or keywords which represent topic of interest are used to determine whether a news is relevant or not. As described, there exists a dichotomy between semantic matching and relevance matching [20]. On the one hand, sematic matching involves identifying the language level meaning of text and the language level relationship existing between two homogenous texts. On the other hand, relevance matching involves determining whether a document is relevant to a given query term.

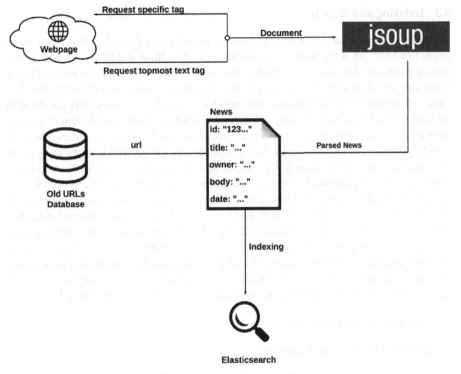

Fig. 2. Key stages in our news archive system

3.2 News Extraction

In order to accomplish an effective extraction of the relevant news, rather than reinventing the wheel, our approach employs the jsoup (version 1.12.1) extraction library. We used a selector-syntax to mark specific HTML tags of familiar newswire webpages i.e. < div.entry-content > tag was used as with the following: 'String body = newsContent.select("div.entry-content").first().text();' while for unfamiliar newswires, we simply select the topmost text tag from the DOM tree of its webpage. The extracted news is then associated with some attributes to reference it in memory i.e. a unique ID to uniquely identify each instance of a news, a title attribute that stores the news title, an owner attribute that stores the uniform resource locator (URL) of the newswire from which the news was extracted, a body attribute that stores the actual text of the extracted news, and a date attribute that stores a timestamp for the extracted news for future reference or to enable tasks like sorting of news in chronological order. The URL of the extracted news is added to a list of old URLs backed by a permanent storage location in order to avoid duplication of effort in subsequent extractions by skipping all URLs in the list of old URLs. The extraction process is completed by sending the extracted news to Elasticsearch for indexing as shown in Fig. 2.

3.3 Indexing and Search

Google ranks pages based on their popularity among other pages i.e. how many other pages link to it. As at the time of this writing, Google, Bing, Baidu, Naver, and Yahoo among others are the most used search systems across the globe [21]. An inverted index is the core of all modern-day search engines. An inverted index is a data structure that creates a mapping between unique tokenized terms and their associated information such as to which document do they belong and at what position in the document do they appear. This data structure is a popular choice with search engine designers due to its speedy provision of search results. Our approach uses Elasticsearch as the archive for all extracted news. Even though it is almost an indispensable choice of search engine implementation for our work, the key motivation to why we preferred and used it is its speed and distributed nature. These powerful characteristics it has can be leveraged in the future to scale a platform to very large number of server machines and data flow with minimal effect on performance [22, 23]. User expectation from search engines with regards to response time has greatly increased, owing to factors like increase in network speed and user shrewdness [24]. As the reader may have guessed, Elasticsearch also relies on the use of an inverted index as the data structure for storing input data. A sample text and its corresponding inverted index is presented below. (Table 1)

"Take care of five before five"

Assuming the document name is 1;

Table 1. The inverted index built for the sample text

Term	Document:Position
Take	1:1
care	1:2
of	1:3
five	1:4, 1:6
before	1:5

Before the indexed news can be searchable, a pseudo-schema (lazily enforced) has to be defined to map all the attributes of the news i.e. id, title, body, owner, and date to a specific data type. For this, we map the id, title, body, and owner attributes to a string data type and map the date attribute to a date data type. Our software implementation[4] communicated with Elasticsearch through Elasticsearch's Java high level REST client 6.3 library and data is being sent and received in JavaScript object notation (JSON) format.

---

[4] https://github.com/MudiLukman/news-archive.

4   Results and Discussion

4.1   Implementation

Our approach was implemented in Java using the IntelliJ[5] version 2017.2.2 integrated development environment (IDE) bundled with the Java Development Kit version 8 (JDK 8). The experiment was carried out on a computer with an Intel Pentium B960@2.20 GHz CPU with 5 GB of main memory on a 64-bit windows 7 ultimate environment. The primary reason Java was chosen as the language of choice is its portability. Java programs are portable in that, they allow programmers write and deploy the same codebase on different types of machine architecture in a technique that employs the use of a bridge language known as bytecode. These bytecode instructions can run on any machine that has the Java Virtual Machine (JVM) installed. Although, the notion of universal portability of Java is not entirely correct due to recent platform-dependent evolution of some APIs as is the case with some classes in the New I/O (NIO) API in recent versions of Java [25, 26]. Elasticsearch 6.3.0 configured to use the *multi match* full-text search query which allows us search multiple fields in a single pass, say *title* and *body* was used. The default analyzer i.e. standard analyzer was not altered in any form. We briefly describe the visual interface of our implementation below.

User Interface
The first point of interaction between the system and a user is the login page which leads to the window depicted in Fig. 3. This is the final stage in the initial installation process

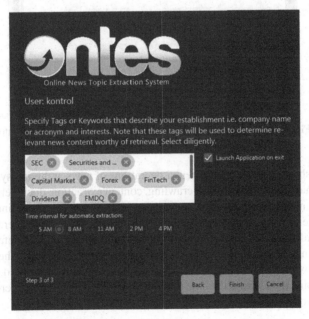

Fig. 3. Specifying keywords and tags at the installation stage

_____
[5] https://www.jetbrains.com/idea/.

where a user is prompted to sets the various tags (which includes topics, acronyms, words, initials and trending topics) or keywords that best represents the interests of the organization. The default time interval for automatic news content extraction is also set as depicted in Fig. 3.

Figure 4 depicts the window where information regarding data sources are collected. The system requires a default news aggregator source to fetch daily news content to be displayed. A minimum of one newswire source is required to create a pathway for data that is required to be fetched from the internet. The data is then parsed, and indexed in the search server.

Fig. 4. Collecting data sources and specifying a Default Aggregator

Figure 5 shows the core fundamental operations of news archiving system at work. The operational stages include: web crawling, content extraction, document parsing, and archiving in an inverted index. The content area depicted in Fig. 5 continues to display all news contents as they are being extracted from the web and considered relevant. A topic is considered relevant if it contains at least one of the tags or default keywords specified during the installation stage. Clicking on the Archive button at the bottom-right corner of the window saves all the extracted news contents in an inverted index while a click on the plus icon allows the user to input web links to news documents considered to be index-worthy.

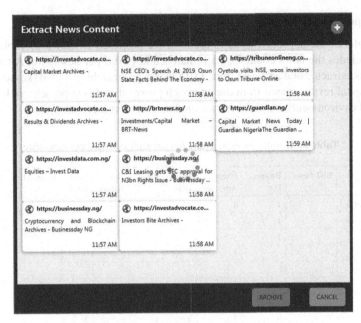

Fig. 5. Content area of the news archiving system

4.2 Experimental Data Source

We used 3,018 webpages from 9 newswires and 10 keywords to test the effectiveness of our approach. The basic information of the experimental newswires is shown in Table 2.

Table 2. A list of the experimental newswires used

Newswire	URL	Number of traversable links
BRT-News	http://brtnews.ng/	332
Invest Data	https://investdata.com.ng/	106
Invest Advocate	https://investadvocate.com.ng/	201
Business Day	https://businessday.ng/	473
Punch	https://punchng.com/	155
The Nation	https://thenationonlineng.net/	731
Daily Trust	https://www.dailytrust.com.ng/	218
Independent	https://www.independent.ng/	499
New Telegraph	https://www.newtelegraphng.com/	303
Total	9	**3,018**

4.3 Experimental Results

The results of the approach to news archives we proposed is shown in Table 3. This result includes the news count for each matched keyword per newswire. A total of 42 news was extracted and archived from 3,018 webpages matching 7 of 10 keywords. The experimental results drawn from our approach proves that this approach can be used in practical environments for news extraction due to its accuracy

Table 3. Results for news extracted for each keyword per newswire

Keywords	BRT-News	Business Day	Invest Advocate	Invest Data	Punch	The Nation	Daily Trust	Independent	New Telegraph
Capital Market		1	4	1		1			
Cryptocurrency		1							
Dividends		1	3						
Equities			1			2			
FinTech									
Forex									
Investors			2	1					
SEC	1	3	7	2	1	3	3		3
Securities and Exchange Commission								1	
Stock Market									
Total	1	6	17	4	1	6	3	1	3

An important, if not mandatory characteristic of an algorithm is that it is effective in solving the problem for which it was designed [27]. However, some newswires refused to accept incoming connections and a request-timeout error was returned. So, no news was extracted from these newswires.

As shown in Table 3, seven news webpages matching the keyword "**Capital Market**" were extracted from four different newswires; one each from *Bussinessday*, *InvestData*, and The Nation while four from *InvestAdvocate*. This includes news that contains the keyword within either its title, body, or both. one webpage matching the keyword "**cryptocurrency**" was marked as relevant and was extracted from *Businessday*. Four webpages from two newswires (one from *Businessday* and three from *InvestAdvocate*) matching the keyword "**Dividends**" were marked as relevant and were consequently extracted. Three webpages were found matching the keyword "**Equities**" from two sources; one from *InvestAdvocate* and two from The Nation. a total of three webpages matching the keyword "**Investors**" were extracted from two sources; two from *InvestAdvocate* and one from *InvestData*. A total of twenty-three news webpages matching the keyword "**SEC**" were found and extracted from eight sources; one each from BRT-News and Punch, three each from *Businessday*, The Nation, Daily Trust, and New Telegraph, two from *InvestData*, and seven from *InvestAdvocate*. finally, one news webpage matching the keyword "**Securities and Exchange Commission**" was found and extracted from independent.

4.4 Evaluation

To measure the performance of our approach in terms of its effectiveness, we used the following criterion to evaluate our experimental result. To accomplish this, we first carried out news extraction manually. Our approach is used afterwards. We assign a score of 1 for every correct extraction made on each side. In the end, the manual approach had a total of 34 points, while our approach had a total of 42 points.

To measure the efficiency of our approach, we also recorded the total execution time for news extraction using our approach in comparison with that of the manual approach. Our program had an execution time of 270 s while the manual process took 3,360 s to complete. The results obtained above shows that our approach outperforms the manual approach to news extraction.

5 Conclusion

News extraction and archiving is important in businesses and to organizations. We presented a novel approach that combines an extraction method for news webpages with a search engine as an archive to support information retrieval with a nice architecture, providing an analytics platform, eliminating the likelihood of errors resulting from human intervention in news extraction and archiving, a profound usage of multithreading and parallel computing techniques, avoiding duplication of effort by skipping archived news during extraction, and consequently affecting business processes positively. Multithreading and recursion were applied to design a highly scalable bytecode based java archive search engine to manage the rapid growth in data size. We therefore recommend that the approach to news archives presented herein be put into practical use by organizations and news aggregators that work with real time news wherever applicable.

In further works, our approach can be extended to support real time dispersal of extracted news to subscribed clients at periodic intervals.

References

1. García, R., Perdrix, F., Gil, R.M.: Ontological infrastructure for a semantic newspaper. In: Proceedings 15th World Wide Web Conference on Semantic Web Annotations for Multimedia (SWAMM), pp. 1–12 (2006)
2. Crescenzi, V., Mecca, G., Merialdo, P.: RoadRunner: towards automatic data extraction from large web sites. In: VLDB 2001 - Proceedings of 27th International Conference on Very Large Data Bases, pp. 109–118 (2001)
3. Laender, A.H.F. Ribeiro-Neto, B.A., da Silver, A.S., Teixerira, J.S.: A brief survey of web data extraction tools. ACM SIGMOD Rec. 31(2), p. 84 (2002). https://doi.org/10.1145/565 117.565137
4. Wong, K.-F. et al.: Utilizing microblogs for automatic news highlights extraction. In: Series on Language Processing, Pattern Recognition, and Intelligent Systems. Social Media Content Analysis, pp. 277–296 (2017). https://doi.org/10.1142/9789813223615_0019
5. Prasad, J., Paepcke, A.: {CoreEx}: content extraction from online news articles. In: CIKM 2008 Proceeding 17th ACM Conference on Information and Knowledge. Management. pp. 1391–1392 (2008). https://dl.acm.org/doi/10.1145/1458082.1458295

6. Liu, Q., Shao, M., Wu, L., Zhao, G.: Main content extraction from web pages based on node characteristics. J. Comput. Sci. Eng. **11**(2), 39–48 (2017). https://doi.org/10.5626/JCSE.2017. 11.2.39

7. Connolly, T., Begg, C.: Database Systems: A practical Approach to Design, Implementation and Management (Sixth Edition). Pearson, Boston (2014)

8. Dehghani, M., Rothe, S, Alfonseca, P., Fleury, P.: Learning to attend, copy, and generate for session-based query suggestion. In: Proceedings of the 2017 ACM International Conference on Information and Knowledge Management, pp. 1747–1756 (2017). https://doi.org/10.1145/ 3132847.3133010

9. Negm, N., ElKafrawy, P., Salem, A.B.: A survey of web information extraction tools. Int. J. Comput. Appl. **43**(7), 19–27 (2012). https://doi.org/10.5120/6115-8296

10. Yarlagadda, M., Gangadhara Rao, K., Srikrishna, A.: Frequent itemset-based feature selection and Rider Moth Search Algorithm for document clustering. J. King Saud Univ. Comput. Inf. Sci. (2019). https://doi.org/10.1016/j.jksuci.2019.09.002

11. Bun, K.K., Ishizuka, M.: Topic extraction from news archive using TF*PDF algorithm In: Proceedings of the Third International Conference on Web Information Systems Engineering WISE 2002, IEEE, pp. 73–82 (2002). https://doi.org/10.1109/wise.2002.1181645

12. Zhang, H., Boons, F., Batista-Navarro, R.: Whose story is it anyway? automatic extraction of accounts from news articles. Inf. Process. Manag. **56**, 1837–1848 (2019). https://doi.org/10. 1016/j.ipm.2019.02.012

13. Weninger, T., Hsu, W., Han, J.: CETR - content extraction via tag ratios. In: Proceedings of the 19th International Conference on the World Wide Web, WWW 2010. pp. 971–980 (2010). https://doi.org/10.1145/1772690.1772789

14. Yenicag, A., İnternet, H., İçin, S., İçerik, S-B., Yöntemi C.: A Template-Independent Content Extraction Approach for News (2012)

15. Karnalim, O.: Improving scalability of java archive search engine through recursion conversion and multithreading. CommIT (Commun. Inf. Technol.) J. **10**, 15–26 (2016). https://doi. org/10.21512/commit.v10i1.832

16. Lin, J., Nogueira, R., Yates, A.: Pretrained Transformers for Text Ranking: BERT and Beyond (2020)

17. Devlin, J., Chang, M.W., Lee, K., Toutanova, K.: BERT: pre-training of deep bidirectional transformers for language understanding. In: NAACL HLT 2019 – 2019 Conference North American Chapter of the Association for Computational Linguistics Human Language Technologies - Proceeings Conference volume 1, pp. 4171–4186 (2019)

18. Croft, W.B., Metzler, D., Strohman, T.: Search Engines Information Retrieval in Practice. Pearson, Prentice Hall (2015)

19. Nakamura, T.A., Calias, P.H., de Castro Reis, D., Lemos, A.P.: An anatomy for neural search engines. Inf. Process. Manag. **480**, 339–353 (2019). https://doi.org/10.1016/j.ins.2018.12.041

20. Guo, J., Fan, Y., Ai, Q., Croft, W.B.: A deep relevance matching model for Ad-hoc retrieval. In: Proceedings of the 25th ACM International Conference on Information and Knowledge Management, pp. 55–64 (2016). https://doi.org/10.1145/2983323.2983769

21. Liu, B.: Web data mining: exploring hyperlinks, contents, and usage data. In: Carey, M.J. and Ceri, S. Data Centric Systems and Applications. (Second Edition). Springer, Berlin (2015). https://doi.org/10.1007/978-3-642-19460-3

22. Dixit, B., Kuć, R., Rogoziński, M., Chhajed, S.: Elasticsearch A Complete Guide. Packt Publishing, Sebastopol (2017)

23. Gormley, C., Tong, Z.: Elasticsearch: The Definitive Guide: A Distributed Real-Time Search and Analytics Engine. O'Reilly Media, Sebastopol (2015)

24. Brutlag, J.D. Hutchinson, H., Stone, M.: User preference and search engine latency. In: JSM Proceedings, Quality and Productivity Research Conference, American Statistical Association, vol. 12, pp. 1–13 (2008)

25. Schildt, H.: Java The Complete Reference (Eleventh Edition). McGraw-Hill, New York (2018)
26. Liang, Y.D.: Introduction to Java Programming Comprehensive Version. Pearson, Prentice Hall (2016)
27. Cormen, T.H., Leiserson, C.E., Rivest, R.L., Stein C..: Introduction to Algorithms. MIT Press (3rd Edition), Cambridge (2009)

Mobile Application Software Usability Evaluation: Issues, Methods and Future Research Directions

Blessing Iganya Attah[(✉)], John Kolo Alhassan [iD], Ishaq Oyebisi Oyefolahan,
and Sulaimon Adebayo Bashir

Federal University of Technology, Minna, Nigeria
blessingiganya@gmail.com, {jkalhassan,o.ishaq,
bashirsulaimon}@futminna.edu.ng

Abstract. Recently, the growth and advancement in mobile technology (such as mobile devices, smartphones, mobile wireless networks) have cushioned everyday lives of peoples across the globe. Interestingly, this can be attributed to the greater ease of developing mobile applications for diverse usages such as healthcare, finance, and agriculture. Another reason for this is that, there is the quest to rollout mobile device tailored application software having lower budget, quicker time of delivery, and top-quality product from the developers and the end-user's perspectives. The challenges of appropriate designs frameworks; and the understanding of the needs of users (that is, the end users) have persisted long after their eventual rollouts. The concept of mobile app usability and accessibility evaluation were developed to enable developers to ascertain the level of usages and relevance of mobile applications in-use or prior release under diverse criteria such as maintainability, understandability, comprehensibility, as well as parameters specified by Usability Standards of ISO 9241-11 (that is, effectiveness, efficiency, and satisfaction). This study undertakes a systematic literature review (SLR) to discuss the subject of mobile application software usability under the specific scope of issues, methods and future research directions. To achieve these, a total of forty (40) peer-reviewed articles from diverse databases/sources of records were selected. The outcomes of this study revealed that, mobile applications usability evaluations and processes are domain-specific (or locality-dependent). Also, there are no generic approaches identified or developed for performing usability and accessibility of mobile applications due to the non-deterministic nature of the domain, and context-of-use.

Keywords: Usability · Mobile application · Mobile devices · Quality · Software product · Users · Developers

1 Introduction

Mobile application is type of software application built particularly for use on small and wireless computing devices such as tablets and smartphones [1]. According to estimates for 2020 by [2], mobile applications are projected to produce nearly $189 billion in

© Springer Nature Switzerland AG 2021
S. Misra and B. Muhammad-Bello (Eds.): ICTA 2020, CCIS 1350, pp. 560–573, 2021.
https://doi.org/10.1007/978-3-030-69143-1_43

proceeds from app stores and in-app commercials. The outburst of mobile apps spans a wide range of industries including media, retail, education, travel, finance, healthcare, and social [1, 3]. This is attributable to the use of mobile apps to deliver services with improved access, high quality, reduced cost, and increased safety. But, the attitudes of users and end-users towards these new technology needs to assessed urgently in order to redress it [3]. Software quality evaluation is an activity targeted at maintaining, managing and controlling a piece of software. The usability evaluation of software has been directly linked to the levels of software usability [4].

Besides, usability attributes are dissimilar, the mobile Apps lay more emphasis on the usage and accessibility when compared to conventional desktop applications. Again, the range of users as well as scope is larger in mobile apps than conventional application. The number of apps developers and builders are on the increase across the globe, but the prospective users continue to diminish over the years owing to several issues to include: proof of product claims unsupportive, behavioral changes, unsupportive of existing media, poor human touches and app features [5].

The International Standard Organization (ISO) established five core characteristics in which every mobile application is built upon including: reliability, usability, portability, maintainability, and accessibility. Ideally, usability relies on what the user wants to do and their goals in the context of the user's action [6]. Usability models for mobile applications are relatively unexplored and unproven, still evolving, isolated or disintegrated [7]. Mobile Apps have huge pervasiveness in e-commerce, financial solutions, and mobile shopping experiences, as well as diverse integration and support for several lifestyle applications such as health, banking, fashion, etc. [8, 9].

This paper investigates the following research questions including:

1. What is the present state of usability evaluation of mobile applications?
2. What usability and accessibility evaluations models or methods are identified in existing studies?
3. What are the problems with usability and accessibility evaluation of mobile applications?
4. What is the future focus of mobile application usability?

The remaining four sections include: literature review, research methodology, results of the study, and conclusion.

2   Literature Review

2.1   The Concept of Software Usability

The quest to create good quality software products is evolving over time in the field of software engineering. A number of factors have been specified in the efforts to ascertain the quality of software products by ISO including: reliability, usability, effectiveness, efficiency, etc. [10]. In general, software products are referred to as top quality after using factors such as functionality, reliability, efficiency, usability, portability, and maintainability. According to study in [4], usability is the most profound quality factors of software products, which are expected to be strictly observed during the developmental phase of software. Usability is coined from the concept of user-friendliness that is often used among software professionals to explain the ease of use, satisfaction, efficiency and effectiveness, learnability, and remembrance of man-made items such as website, software application, machine, tool, process, book, and any object with capability of interacting with humans. The tasks of conducting usability assessments on software products are performed by usability experts, writers, end-users, marketing personnel, technical writers, designers, etc.

Though, majority of usability models rely largely on the perspectives of end-users with regards to the functionalities and operations of certain parts of the application [8]. According to the study in [11], the context of use is essential for assessing usability of mobile apps, which involves efforts capable of affecting quality of interactions of end-users with the mobile apps [11]. Again, user interface is regarded as key metric of software system, which directly impacts on the subsequent effectiveness. The usability concept is often related to user-friendliness and ease of use of a software system. As a result, the efforts of usability evaluation are geared towards the design of intuitive user interfaces in order to make software system effective, satisfaction, and efficiency by relying on the user's perspective [12–14]. In fact, the human-computer interaction (HCI) community has evolved several usability concepts including: inspection methods, frameworks, and heuristics approaches for the purpose of improving the understanding, measure and assess usability that targets the eventual delivery high quality software products and software quality assurances [9, 15]. The benefits of usability evaluation include [8, 9, 11, 16, 17]:

1. To enable better human computer interaction in which end-users of a software product have ease communicating and utilizing the functions of software systems.
2. To promote loyalty and acceptance of customers and Apps respectively.
3. To evolve better versions of mobile Apps and experience of end-users.
4. To improve on the sales and usages of the mobile Apps.
5. To report bugs and areas of negative concerns.
6. To enable HCI practitioners to concentrate on the basic components of software, this can be problematic for end-users.
7. To enhance the software quality assurances for present and future projects.
8. To create online business opportunity for marketers and consumers.

The common usability standards consider software systems [1, 18]; software product [10, 18, 19]; and service and information systems [20, 21]. These standards provide guidelines for developing systems and application software for optimal user experience and continuous relevance of the software product for both desktop and mobile platforms. The process and practice of software usability evaluation models were derived from basic attributes defined by the ISO 1924-11 standards for conducting usability evaluations of mobile applications similar to desktop applications. The metrics focus on the users' experiences [4] the developers and external experts [11, 13] to measure the successes or failures during usage or prior releases. Msweli & Mawela in [16] identified usability enablers of financial mobile apps to include: Perceived value, perceived ease of use, convenience, and consumer attitudes. The barriers are trust, privacy, security, personalization, and technical knowledge of users.

2.2 Mapping Studies

The mobile applications usability testing and evaluation ensure the effectiveness on the users' perceptive with regards to satisfactions of the running application. it affords users the capability to identify and address issues during the course of the developmental processes [22]. The majority of the studies surveyed cover healthcare and related mobile apps [22–25]. While, few of the mapping articles discussed usability characteristics

Table 1. The differences between connected papers and studies to the new study.

S/No.	Author(s)	Title of the article	Type of article	Period of study	Category of study
1.	[1]	Usability of Mobile Applications: A Systematic Literature Study	SLR	1990–2018	Derivative work
2.	[16]	Enablers and Barriers for Mobile Commerce and Banking Services Among the Elderly in Developing Countries: A Systematic Review	SLR	2009–2019	Derivative work
3.	[9]	A mixed-methods measurement and evaluation methodology for mobile application usability studies	SLR	1992–2018	Derivative work
4.	[31]	Set of Usability Heuristics for Quality Assessment of Mobile Applications on Smartphones	SLR	1932–2018	Prior work
5.	[32]	A Systematic Literature Review: Opinion Mining Studies from Mobile App Store User Reviews	SLR	2000–2015	Prior work

under general scope including the mobile websites and apps, mobile computing [12], software development, and mobile software development [26–28].

Weichbroth [1] identified the most widespread usability attributes including: efficiency, satisfaction, effectiveness (adapted from usability definition of ISO 924-11); fewer occurring attributes were learnability, memorability, cognitive load, errors; and least occurring attributes are simplicity, and ease of use.

The concepts of eWOM and UX provide valuable information for the purpose of evaluating the usability of mobile apps using a number of criteria [29]. Mixed methods usability approaches were adopted to guarantee software quality assurances of the present and future projects in a more reliable and valuable manner [9]. Jha et al. in [30] identified software maintainability as a performance or usability attribute of software product, which can be adopted for mobile apps developments. Recently, the deep learning approaches have found to hold great potentials in accurately and autonomously predicting maintainability of software. A study in by Msweli and Mawela [16], key enablers for financial mobile apps usability were found to include: satisfaction, usefulness, attitude, accessible, suitable, understanding, familiarity, easy to use, prior experience and user-friendliness.

2.3 Justification for the New Study

The justification for the new study is generated from the connected papers prior and derivative works graph built indicating the influence and connection is shown in Fig. 1.

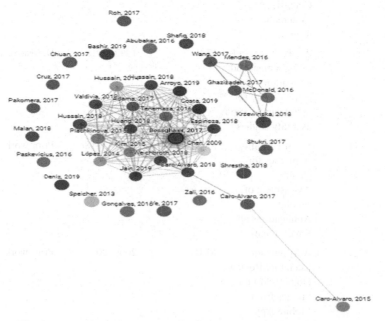

Fig. 1. Towards usability evaluation of hybrid mobile user interfaces [14].

The distinctions between connected papers or articles and the new study in terms of author(s), title of article, type of article, period of study, and category of work are presented in the Table 1.

In Table 1, the new study covers the period from between 2019–2020, which is not reviewed in the prior and derivative works obtainable. This provides the justification for a new study in the subject area uncovered by previous studies.

3 Research Methodology

This study presents a systematic literature review on peer reviewed and published journals using comprehensive searches of record sources/databases. A total of fifty-two (52) papers out of the initial search of 1550 were identified to have direct answers to the questions of usability and assessments of mobile applications usability and accessibility, models for conducting mobile application usability and accessibility, and research areas of mobile application in the future time. This study is to provide answers to the following research questions (RQ):

RQ1. What is the present state of usability evaluation of mobile applications?

RQ2. What usability and accessibility evaluations models or methods are identified in existing studies?

RQ3. What are the problems with usability and accessibility evaluation of mobile applications?

RQ4. What is the future focus of mobile applications usability?

The purpose of the Systematic Literature Review (SLR) is to orderly chart the concise phases of the proposed research. The method including Planning and specifying research questions, conducting the review (that is, an identification of search string and data sources, selecting studies, quality assessment, and data extraction and finally reporting the review [28]. In order to achieve this, the preferred reporting item as reported by [28] was adopted. The review procedure adopted the Preferred Reporting Items for SLRs and Meta-Analyses (PRISMA) statement [33] in conjunction with the standard guidelines for conducting computer science SLRs by [34] as illustrated in Fig. 2.

From Fig. 2, the item selection was divided into phases with associated criteria as shown in Table 2. The Identification phase collected 1550 peer-reviewed from different database listed in Table 4 and other sources. The screening phase used 420 articles for identifying and removing of duplicate from previous phase to arrive at 320 screened articles. Eligibility phase considered 131 eligible articles and excluded 79 due to no details regarding design, development of usability evaluation or usability issues of mobile apps. The articles do not cover mobile apps usability and assessment testing. The last phase is the Included phase that provided items or articles included in the qualitative synthesis of the new study.

The inclusion and exclusion criteria include all published peer reviewed articles from five major criteria established for this study as indicated in Table 2.

Data extraction is concerned with opinion mining for search strings for the distinct research questions RQ1, RQ2, RQ3, and RQ4. The information synthesis took account of the findings and methods, repetition, contradictions, and inconsistencies. The main criteria for data extraction process include:

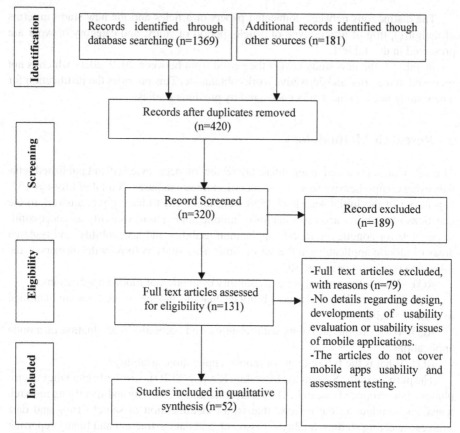

Fig. 2. The process of study using Preferred Reporting Items for Systematic Reviews and Meta-Analysis (PRISMA).

1. The studied details of the first author, country and type of article.
2. Description of the methods for mobile application usability and accessibility.
3. Application areas of mobile applications and prospects in real world.
4. The issues and gaps of usability and accessibility of mobile apps.

This study generated diverse data from various records sources including: Research-Gate, Clarivate WoS, SpringerLink, ACM Digital Library, AISeL, ScienceDirect, Google Scholar, Connected Papers, and Semantic Scholars. The different records included in this study are generated from distinct word/phrases or keyword search using the criteria of keyword, year, article title, abstract and subject area as presented in Table 3.

This study generated diverse data from various records and corresponding URL addresses are under-listed in Table 4.

Table 2. Criteria Inclusion and Selection and Matching Justification.

S./No	Criteria	Justification for Inclusion/Exclusion in the Study
1.	Titles of articles	To investigate and eliminate studies unrelated to the present area of research
2.	Abstract and keywords	To review abstract and keywords in studies from above step to ensure information provided is relevant to the study
3.	Clearly stated findings to the research questions set for the study	The primary studies offer analysis of mobile apps trends, methods, issues and future directions
4.	Reference list	To cross-check the reference list of the mapping studies to find supplementary studies relevant to the records searches
5.	Language of articles	To review articles written in English, that is, authors' language of communication for the study
6.	Peer-reviewed articles	To review articles such as presentations, blog posts, books, journals, conference papers

Table 3. Records word/phrases/keyword or search strings.

S./No	Subject area	Search string
1.	Mobile applications	((mobile apps) OR (mobile applications))
2.	Software development	((software application) OR (software lifecycle) OR (software development))
3.	Usability evaluation	((definition of usability) OR (standards for usability evaluation) OR (usability assessment techniques))
4.	Accessibility	((mobile accessibility techniques) OR (methods of mobile accessibility))
5.	Financial mobile apps	((what is financial mobile apps, what are problems of financial mobile apps?) OR (Issues of financial mobile apps usability) OR (issues of financial mobile apps accessibility))
6.	Usability Methods	((methodology of usability and accessibility evaluations) OR (trends in usability evaluations) OR (main usability evaluation methods))

Table 4. Record sources and databases

S/No.	Source/Database of Articles	URL address
1.	ResearchGate	https://www.researchgate.net/
2.	Clarivate WoS	http://wokinfo.com/
3.	SpringerLink	https://link.springer.com/
4.	ACM Digital Library	https://dl.acm.org/
5.	AISeL	https://aisel.aisnet.org/
6.	ScienceDirect	https://www.sciencedirect.com/
7.	Google Scholar	https://scholar.google.com/
8.	Connected papers	https://www.connectedpapers.com/
9.	Semantic scholars	https://www.semanticscholar.org/

4   Results of the Study

4.1   Present State of Mobile Application Usability Evaluation

This subsection answers the RQ1 which reveals the popularity of concept of usability evaluations researches over the period under review as shown in Fig. 3.

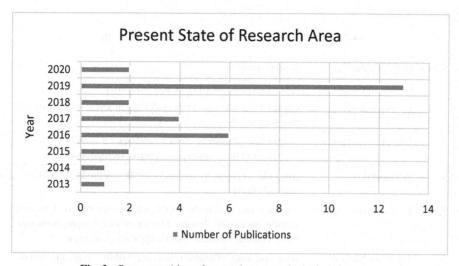

Fig. 3. Current position of research area on the included studies.

From Fig. 3, the popularity of the concept of usability evaluations of mobile apps is most in year 2019 due to the growth of mobile computing and technology. The studies are still evolving especially in the current of review or study in which more studies are expected by end of the year after ease of lockdowns.

4.2 Usability and Accessibility Evaluation Methods

This study found a list of the usability models measures for the categories of mobile apps as presented in Table 5.

Table 5. The usability and accessibility evaluation models.

S./No	Author(s)	Category	Methods
1.	[3, 9, 24, 27, 29, 35, 37, 42]	Product	ISO 9241-11 and SIO/IEC 25010 usability guidelines, Product usability guidelines, Use case point, Mobile Apps user development model, Mobile Apps Rating Scale (MARS), Accessibility evaluation and reporting using visualisation of bugs identified in the source code, Electronic word of mouth (eWoM), Mixed-methods methodology for mobile application usability measurement (3 M$MAUME)
2.	[23, 36]	Expert	5-Point Likert scale, Maintainability Index (MI) model, Expert evaluation of usability and accessibility
3.	[22, 25, 39]	User	Classical Test Theory (CTT), Agile model of user experience, Frame mode using questionnaire, Machine learning models for user behavioural traits of interactions, Mobile Apps user ratings with a 5-star scale, Automatic and manual/visual analytical tools for user experience of mobile app, Affect-Behaviour-Cognition (ABC) model, User dimension-based usability testing; SUS to assess the experience of user
4.	[26, 30, 32, 40, 41]	Heuristic	People at the Centre of Mobile Application Development (PACMAD), PACMAD UE framework, App store spam review detection, Hybrid of Experience Sampling Method and logging methods, Extending usability Heuristics for smartphone apps, Deep learning for software maintainability metric prediction, Cognitive walkthrough and Heuristic evaluation/expert reviews

From Table 5, the methods for evaluating usability and accessibility of mobile apps are broadly categorized into four with associated models/techniques/methods. These include: product, user, expert and Heuristic, which answers the RQ2.

4.3 Problems of Usability and Accessibility Evaluation of Mobile Applications

The main challenges facing usability evaluation processes for three categories of mobile apps (namely: native apps, web apps and hybrid apps) are presented in Table 6.

Table 6. The challenges identified with usability and accessibility of mobile applications.

S./No	Author(s)	Specific issues
1.	[3, 28, 35, 36]	No formal model or technique for usability testing. Subjective appraisal-based model
2.	[23, 26, 42]	Omission of usability on the part of the developers on the part of the benefactors
3.	[9, 14, 16]	Compatibility of mobile platforms and user interface designs arising from bugs, errors, designs and performance
4.	[1, 9, 24]	Majority of models targeted at user experience contexts such as product quality, user beliefs, preferences, and emotions. There is little on developers
5.	[22, 38–40]	Metrics/methods are incomprehensive and unreflective of user experience and behaviours towards Apps due to poor communication and large budgets incurred during tests
6.	[25, 30]	Non-compliance with standards such as WCAG 2.1 due to difficulty in choosing relevant metrics
7.	[16, 30]	Trust, security, digital literacy, access to electronic services, complicated menu, fears and privacy

From Table 6, the main issues militating against the practice of usability and accessibility evaluation of mobile apps include: perception of users, metrics/parameters inadequacies, over-reliance on user experience alone, omission of developers or benefactors in the process, product compatibility, lack of well-defined model or technique for conducting tests and the subjective appraisal approach deployed by many usability evaluations. These provided the answers to the RQ3.

4.4 Future Focus of Mobile Applications Usability Evaluations

This subsection explained the answer to the RQ4. Recently, models of usability assessments for mobiles apps favor the autonomous and self-regulated approaches rather than the traditional or manual approaches for effectiveness of process. Hence, new research works must consider new measuring attributes concerning users' interactive and behavioral characteristics (user logs and interactions with mobile apps).

Again, new studies should create new parameters and design usability evaluation model, which are dynamic, automated and comprehensive (machine learning supportive) for increased usability evaluation of mobile applications [42, 43].

Developing usable application software remains daunting challenges because of peculiarity of conditions of environment, networks, sizes and controls. Then, there is need to establish a common ground for the theory and practice of mobile applications usability assessments [1]. There is need to consider mixed methods of usability evaluation in order to enhance obtainable software quality assurance schemes [9].

There is need to perform usability evaluation on more mobile apps especially within their local contexts [43]. And, the usability heuristic should be developed for domain-specific situation in order to effectively detect issues in the user interfaces and functionality [36]. A study on financial mobile applications among adult population shows drastically poor usages and adoption. This is expected to be redressed to benefit maximally from the potentials of mobile applications [16].

5 Conclusion

This paper found that, the general usability of mobile applications depends on the continuous users' feedbacks, which are valuable for designers in adjusting the product for the purpose of accommodating user's behavioral issues. Shah et al. in [24] argued that usability evaluation or measures must take into account user behavior issues, motivation retention to unceasingly utilize mobile applications through the provision of the right and optimal services.

The usability and accessibility of mobile applications approaches cover diverse user experiences which are inconsistent with the present-day reality. Actors such as designers/developers and external usability experts are tremendously valuable, which has led to new kinds of approaches to enable appropriate estimation of usability before release of system or software products.

Usability evaluation of software product or system increases its quality assurances, and improved user experiences. However, there is no consensus on the generic usability measurement method for mobile apps. Therefore, a number of usability methods are developed from prior techniques or for domain-specific. The next generation of usability techniques must leverage on the user behaviors by adopting advanced machine learning or modeling models [30] for faster, accurate and appropriate outcomes.

References

1. Weichbroth, P.: Usability of mobile applications: a systematic literature study. IEEE Access 8, 55563–55577 (2020)
2. Swaid, S.I., Suid, T.Z.: Usability of mobile apps: an integrated approach usability heuristics for M-commerce apps. In: International Conference on Applied Human Factors and Ergonomics, pp. 79–88 (2018)
3. Sereda, M., Smith, S., Newton, K., Stockdale, D.: Mobile apps for management of tinnitus: users' survey, quality assessment, and content analysis. JMIR mHeakth uHealth 7(1), e10353 (2019)
4. Gupta, D., Ahlawat, A.K., Sagar, K.: Usability prediction & ranking of SDLC models using fuzzy hierarchical usability model. Open Eng. 7(1), 161–168 (2017)
5. Evans, S.H., Clarke, P., Glovinsky, J.: A consumer health app works well. but, diffusion is not so easy. J. Technol. Behav. Sci. 5(2), 164–170 (2019)
6. Dur, M.A.: Usability heuristics for mobile applications a systematic review. In: ICEIS, pp. 978–989 (2018)

7. Hoehle, H., Venkatesh, V.: Mobile application usability: conceptualization and instrument development. MIS Q. **39**(2), 435–472 (2015)
8. Hussain, A., Mkpojiogu, E.O.C., Jamaludin, N.H., Moh, S.T.L.: A usability evaluation of Lazada mobile application. In: AIP Conference Proceedings, vol. 1891, no. 1, pp. 020059 (2017)
9. Weichbroth, P.: A mixed-methods measurement and evaluation methodology for mobile application usability studies. Architecture **43**(44), 45 (2019)
10. ISO, W. 9241–11.: Ergonomic requirements for office work with visual display terminals (VDTs). The international organization for standardization, vol. 45 (1998)
11. Joyce, G., Lilley, M., Barker, T., Jefferies, A.: Mobile application usability heuristics: decoupling context-of-use. In: Marcus, A., Wang, W. (eds.) DUXU 2017. LNCS, vol. 10288, pp. 410–423. Springer, Cham (2017). https://doi.org/10.1007/978-3-319-58634-2_30
12. Islam, M.N., Bouwman, H., Islam, A.K.M.N.: Evaluating web and mobile user interfaces with semiotics: an empirical study. IEEE Access **8**, 84396–84414 (2020)
13. Sagar, K., Saha, A.: Qualitative usability feature selection with ranking: a novel approach for ranking the identified usability problematic attributes for academic websites using data-mining techniques. Hum. Centric Comput. Inf. Sci. **7**(1), 29 (2017)
14. Bessghaier, N., Soui, M.: Towards usability evaluation of hybrid mobile user interfaces. In: 2017 IEEE/ACS 14th International Conference on Computer Systems and Applications, pp. 895–900 (2017)
15. Weichbroth, P.: Delivering usability in IT products: empirical lessons from the field. Int. J. Softw. Eng. Knowl. Eng. **28**(07), 1027–1045 (2018)
16. Msweli, N.T., Mawela, T.: Enablers and barriers for mobile commerce and banking services among the elderly in developing countries: a systematic review. In: Conference on e-Business, e-Services and e-Society, pp. 319–330 (2020)
17. Tavakoli, M., Zhao, L., Heydari, A., Nenadi, G.: Extracting useful software development information from mobile application reviews: a survey of intelligent mining techniques and tools. Expert Syst. Appl. **113**, 186–199 (2018)
18. ISO.: ISO/IEC 9126-1:2001 Software engineering – Product quality- Part 1: Quality model. ISO/IEC JTC 1/ SC 7 Software and systems engineering, vol. 25 (2001)
19. ISO.: ISO/DIS 9241-171:2008 Ergonomics of Human-System Interaction – Part 171: Guidance on software Accessibility. Technical report, International Organization for Standardization (2008)
20. Radatz, J., Geraci, A., Katki, F.: IEEE standard glossary of software engineering terminology. IEEE Std. 610.12-1990. Computer Society of the IEEE (1990)
21. European Union.: Directive (EU) 2016/2102 of the European Parliament and of the Council of 26 October 2016 on the accessibility of the websites and mobile applications of public sector bodies (2016)
22. Nathan, S.S., Hussain, A., Hashim, N.L.: Usability evaluation of DEAF mobile application interface: a systematic review. J. Eng. Appl. Sci. **13**(2), 291–297 (2018)
23. Arnhold, M., Quade, M., Kirch, W., Arnhold, M.: Mobile applications for diabetics: a systematic review and expert-based usability evaluation considering the special requirements of diabetes patients age 50 years or older. J. Med. Internet Res. **16**(4), e104 (2014)
24. Shah, U.M., Chiew, T.K.: A systematic literature review of the design approach and usability evaluation of the pain management mobile applications. Symmetry **11**(3), 400 (2019)
25. Medina, J.L.P., Acosta-Vargas, P., Rybarczyk, Y.: A systematic literature review of usability and accessibility in tele-rehabilitation systems. In: Assistive and Rehabilitation Engineering. IntechOpen, pp. 1–20 (2019)
26. Harrison, R., Flood, D., Duce, D.: A systematic literature review of usability and accessibility in tele-rehabilitation systems. J. Interact. Sci. **1**, 1–16 (2013)

27. Shitkova, M., Holler, J., Heide, T., Clever, N., Becker, J.: Towards usability guidelines for mobile websites and applications. In: Proceedings of 2015 Wirtschaftsinformatik, vol. 107, pp. 1603–1617 (2015)
28. Kaur, A., Kaur, K.: Systematic literature review of mobile application development and testing effort estimation. J. King Saud Univ. Comput. Inf. Sci. (2018). https://doi.org/10.1016/j.jks uci.2018.11.002
29. Weichbroth, P., Baj-rogowska, A.: Do online reviews reveal mobile application usability and user experience? The case of WhatsApp. In: Proceedings of the Federated Conference on Computer Science and Information Systems, vol. 18, pp. 747–754 (2019)
30. Jha, S., et al.: Deep learning approach for software maintainability metrics prediction. IEEE Access 7, 61840–61855 (2019)
31. Da Costa, R.P., Canedo, E.D., De Sousa, R.T., Albuquerque, R.D.O., Villalba, L.J.G.: Set of usability heuristics for quality assessment of mobile applications on smartphones. IEEE Access 7, 116145–116161 (2019)
32. Genc-nayebi, N., Abran, A.: A systematic literature review: opinion mining studies from mobile app store user reviews. J. Syst. Softw. 125, 207–219 (2016)
33. Moher, D., Liberati, A., Tetzla, J., Altman, D.G.: Preferred reporting items for systematic reviews and meta-analyses. Ann. Intern. Med. 151(4), 264–269 (2009)
34. Kitchenham, B., Charters, S.: Guidelines for Performing Systematic Literature Reviews in Software Engineering. Software Engineering Group, Keele (2007)
35. Kaur, A., Kaur, K.: Suitability of existing software development life cycle (SDLC) in context of mobile application development life cycle (MADLC). Int. J. Comput. Appl. 116(19), 1–6 (2015)
36. Khowaja, K., Al-Thani, D., Aqle, A., Banire, B.: Accessibility or usability of the user interfaces for visually impaired users? A comparative study. In: Antona, M., Stephanidis, C. (eds.) HCII 2019. LNCS, vol. 11572, pp. 268–283. Springer, Cham (2019). https://doi.org/10.1007/978-3-030-23560-4_20
37. Behnamghader, P., Boehm, B.: Towards better understanding of software maintainability evolution. In: Adams, S., Beling, Peter A., Lambert, James H., Scherer, William T., Fleming, Cody H. (eds.) Systems Engineering in Context, pp. 593–603. Springer, Cham (2019). https://doi.org/10.1007/978-3-030-00114-8_47
38. Reddy, B.R., Ojha, A.: Performance of maintainability index prediction models: a feature selection based study. Evol. Syst. 10(2), 179–204 (2019). https://doi.org/10.1007/s12530-017-9201-0
39. Liu, X., Ai, W.E.I., Li, H., Tang, J., Huang, G., Feng, F., Mei, Q.: Deriving user preferences of mobile apps from their management activities. ACM Trans. Inf. Syst. 35(4), 1–32 (2017)
40. Saleh, A.M., Ismail, R.B.: Usability evaluation frameworks of mobile application: a mini-systematic literature review. In: Global Summit on Education, pp. 1–10 (2015)
41. Nur, M., Sulaiman, S., Aman, S.: Heuristic evaluation: comparing generic and specific usability heuristics for identification of usability problems in a living museum mobile guide app. In: Advances in Human-Computer Interaction (2018)
42. Feiner, J., et al.: A new approach to visualise accessibility problems of mobile apps in source code. In: Proceedings of the 20th International Conference on Enterprise Information System, vol. 2, pp. 519–526 (2018)
43. Adewumi, A.O., Omoregbe, N.A., Misra, S.: Usability evaluation of mobile access to institutional repository. Int. J. Pharm. Tech. 8(4), 22892–22905 (2016)

Perception of Social Media Privacy Among Computer Science Students

Adebayo Omotosho[1]([✉]) [iD], Peace Ayegba[2] [iD], and Justice Emuoyibofarhe[1] [iD]

[1] Mobile and E-Computing Research Group, Department of Computer Science and Engineering, Ladoke Akintola University, Ogbomosho, Nigeria
bayotosho@gmail.com
[2] Department of Computer Science, Landmark University, Kwara, Nigeria

Abstract. People meet at different places and for different reasons, and those with common interests usually interact and have something to share – this is the traditional model of social networking. Although social networking occurs in a virtual world, it has positively transformed communication in several aspects of our life like education, business, healthcare, government and so on. However, social networking has increased the exposure of private lives, the nuisance of unsolicited chat messages, and unhealthy cyber monitoring. This study aims to investigate the privacy concerns and awareness of social media privacy policies amongst computer science students by presenting a review of some of the privacy challenges with using social networking applications. We further carried out an online survey to collect data on their views by investigating their understanding and usage of privacy settings on their preferred platforms. Our participants were found to mostly use Facebook, WhatsApp, and Instagram, and results show that only 23.8% read the privacy agreement. About 30.1% and 13.3% accept friend requests from the friend of friends and strangers respectively. Also, 89.2% of users have their privacy features enabled and 82.9% indicates satisfaction with the current privacy settings available on their social media sites which may be the reason only 54.2% of users show a high level of concern about their privacy.

Keywords: Social media · Privacy settings · Social networking · Computer science students

1 Introduction

The popularity of Internet-enabled devices has contributed to the growth in the use of social media. Nowadays, youths spend more time on social networking sites and applications than real-life social interactions. One study on the impact of social networking sites on the social life of college students showed that there is a significant relationship between social network application usage and social relationship, and that gender has no influence on the use of social media [1]. Nevertheless, it is increasingly becoming difficult to draw clear lines of safety around social networks because it encompasses interactions between people who are assumed to be trusted associates. Whereas, this circle of trusted groups can transmit malicious content which may breach the user's device

© Springer Nature Switzerland AG 2021
S. Misra and B. Muhammad-Bello (Eds.): ICTA 2020, CCIS 1350, pp. 574–587, 2021.
https://doi.org/10.1007/978-3-030-69143-1_44

or steal their personal information. Some threats common to social network services include viruses, social engineering attacks, identity theft, third-party applications, and public comments [2]. Social media users continuously and, most times, voluntarily share an enormous volume of personal information with their social network, and it appears some of them are not aware of the consequences of private information sharing with mixed audiences in their friends' list. As of 2012, only about one-third of adult Internet users were not using social networking sites. According to [3], most of the remaining active two-third were reported to be using the privacy settings on their social network accounts to increase their accounts' confidentiality, more than in the past years. The use of privacy features is becoming a norm irrespective of age differences when using social networking sites. Features such as deleting people from friends' networks, deleting comments, deleting names from tagged images and making account private have been used more by younger users.

It is however bizarre, that many young college users find it challenging and have one or more complaints about using some of the privacy settings on their profiles. This may be due to unclear privacy policies, from a legal perspective as investigated by [4]. Facebook was used as their case study because it is one of the most popular social networking sites, and it is also known for constantly modifying its privacy settings. The authors criticized Facebook constantly changing privacy settings as it is responsible for the ambiguity users experienced when using their privacy tools. The author emphasizes the deployment of the Data Protection Directive fairness principle that does not put users under obligation to supply personal data and support transparent use of data. [5] reported that permission settings on Facebook are misleading and users are always underinformed about permission granted to apps accessing their personal data. 116 of the 120 participants in their study expressed some degree of concern for their Facebook privacy, and yet many of them are still guilty of oversharing their information online. Their findings showed that none of the 120 participants has a full understanding of how their personal information is shared with Facebook apps. Social network service providers are known to make money through the monetization of users' data via targeted advertising [6]. This option is usually embedded in the privacy policies – which describe how user data is handled and then presented to users to use their service. Some of these policies have been found to have some forms of intrusions on user's privacy. Therefore, users might get reluctant accepting policies that will make them disclose their personal information in the future, this, in turn, could reduce data monetization and revenue of the provider.

Several studies have focused on investigating the privacy perception on the use of social media amongst adults [7], and some others recommend the use of social media for enhancing academic development and collaborative learning in students [8, 9]. However, only a few studies have focused on the privacy perception of social media sites amongst students particularly students in Computer Science. In Landmark University, the department of computer science is one of the most populated department, with over 500 students across all levels. The students in this department are often taught with online tools and technologies and are often exposed to various social media platforms. As highlighted by [10], a students' major in the university and the classroom technology adopted, often predisposes these students to various social media platforms.

Mobile phones and other smart gadgets are now part of household devices, and this has increased the preference for mobile social networks. Smartphones, in particular, are equipped with several features such as a global position system, multiple sensors, and radios which have made them to easily enhance our conventional social networks [11]. Since mobile social networks also require an online presence, issues regarding the privacy of data used in online interaction is also a concern as malicious and untrusted culprits might abuse residual personal data for harm or personal gain. Also, the concept, meaning, and coverage of online privacy itself are contextual, therefore, understanding the circumstances surrounding the usage of the term is important. The different understanding of privacy by different online users that defines intrusive use was presented by [12]. The general deduction is that privacy concerns depend on how personal an application is, and that is why social media and debit card applications create more privacy anxiety than less personal applications like email and search engines. This paper presents an exploration of privacy awareness using social networking applications and websites. The first objective is to investigate the privacy concerns and perception of social media privacy policies and the second objective is to evaluate the level of satisfaction and usage of the privacy settings in the most used social media sites amongst computer science students.

The remaining part of this paper is divided into the following sections: related work, methodology, results and discussions, and conclusion.

2 Related Work

Adebo [13] underlined some of the positive effects of social media, in education it gives students the ability to interact for assignments and class activities, digital and productive citizenship, and easy feedback. Some of the negative effects were also mentioned and these include the exchange of false information, privacy issues, and time-wasting. Also, identity theft, phishing, and brute force attacks are among the top security issues while privacy includes cyberstalking, bullying, and profile cloning [14].

Social media privacy concerns cut across users of all demographics and it has a strong influence on user's attitudes and behaviours. Surveys and experimental research have been the most used and effective methods employed to approach this, though susceptible to the limitation of unreliable reports from the participants [15]. Nearly 65% of adults in the United States use social networking sites according to [16]. In their study, an analysis of social media usage based on 27 surveys and 47,000 interviews was carried out amongst adults between the years 2005 and 2015. In their findings, 2% of seniors used social media in 2005 and 35% used social media networks in 2015. In 2005, 12% of young adults between ages 18 to 29 used social media whereas, in 2015, 90% used social media. Also, 76% of social media tools have been adopted in colleges and high schools. [17] evaluated the use of social media by medical students and faculty at the Albert Einstein College of Medicine in New York. They made use of survey monkey in computing social media sites usage frequency, and 496 medical students and 614 faculty members responded to the survey. Reports indicated that 34.1% of students used social media 6 or more hours per week,15.9% used social media less than an hour per week or do not use it at all, and 95% of these students have their privacy settings turned on.

One can conclude from their study that the frequency of social media use is inversely proportional to age. [18] studied the privacy leakages from mobile social networks by comparing the results of users' shared location with the user's real location. A 3-week experiment on 30 participants was carried out using direct sharing, indirect sharing, and ground truth traces to infer the similarities. They found that direct and indirect location sharing revealed 16% and 33% of the users' real points of interests respectively. Results of a structured attack showed that the age, gender, occupation, living place, and education level can be inferred 69.2%, 73%, 53.8%, 54.5% and 76% of the time respectively.

[19] performed a survey on the various approaches in tackling privacy issues on social networks. The approaches were categorized into methods addressing user participation, security automation, and privacy preservation using a decentralized architecture. Under user participation, they recommended privacy policy collaboration and sharing to combat users' challenges in maintaining the policies. [20] worked on user's behaviour in online social networks and their study was categorized four aspects of a social graph - connectivity and interaction, traffic activities on online social networks, mobile social behaviour, and malicious behaviour. However, they also concluded that a decentralized online social network can protect sensitive information although difficulties will arise in convincing users to switch to a decentralized social network. [21] presented various technologies that are suitable for the privacy and security of information shared on social media networks. They also outlined classic and modern threats, with solutions to mitigate them. Classic threats include malware, phishing attacks, and internet fraud. Modern threats include fake profiles, clickjacking, in-formation and location leakages.

[22] proposed a system called the Face/Off app which makes use of facial recognition functionality in social networks as a control mechanism in accessing pictures of individuals shared online. The system can determine which faces in the pictures are restricted to other users and blur them. They introduced this technique to handle cases where interested parties have conflicting interests regarding photos shared, that is, the privacy setting of one user overrides the privacy settings of another. Because many relationship-based access control methods are limited to a single user's decision in granting access or sharing media on social media, [23] proposed a method that detects conflicts in these relationship-based policies and resolves the conflicts using a negotiation mechanism. However, the number of conflicts that needed to be resolved grows exponentially, and to deal with the complexity, they developed heuristics. Results showed that the negotiation mechanism is unreasonable without the use of heuristics, and the Greedy BnB heuristic offered results fast enough to be used in real-world infrastructures which would greatly enhance auto-mated privacy negotiations in social media shared items.

Other selected works on specific social media usage and their privacy risks are summarized in Table 1.

Table 1. Summary of related works.

Author	Social media	Methods and findings
[24]	Facebook	They performed qualitative research on the role of social media in teenage patients. An interview with 20 patients within age 12–18 was performed at the children's hospital in eastern Ontario, Canada. It was found that all 20 patients used Facebook and its privacy settings. Also, only a few patients disclose their personal health information with their friends on Facebook. This work showed the need for privacy awareness in using social media networks and guidelines on patient's communication on social media networks provided
[25]	Facebook, Twitter, and Google plus	The author reviewed the effects of social media on users' privacy, focusing on Facebook, Twitter and Google plus, and compare both negative and positive aspects of their privacy policies. All three social media networks have different policies though lengthy; they do not describe the policy in detail. Google plus explains the policies, but users must accept the privacy policies of both Gmail and YouTube first. They concluded that social media applications do not provide information on how information is retrieved or sent. Also, they urge users to be more aware of privacy issues

(continued)

Table 1. (*continued*)

Author	Social media	Methods and findings
[26]	Facebook and others	They investigated the level of user awareness in protecting private information on social networks. They analyzed the types of information that are most important to users in protecting their privacy, the difficulties they face in choosing privacy settings and suitable methods for privacy settings on mobile devices. A survey conducted amongst 18- and 45-years old participants at the University of New England and University of Dumman showed that 32% of respondents had Facebook accounts and 45% had more than one social network account. Also, 66% of respondents were concerned with the misuse of their personal information. Of 71% of respondents who receive invitations from unknown users, 68% reject them. They then proposed a predictable wizard system for privacy settings supported on all mobile devices
[27]	Facebook	They investigated the social factors, perceived costs, and benefits that affect self-disclosure in social networking sites. First, they reviewed the factors that affect face-to-face and online self-disclosure on the sites which revealed that perceived privacy cost and the benefit is a common factor for online self-disclosure. Then, they came up with a model that examined the roles of perceived cost-benefits and social influence on self-disclosure on Facebook. Some of the perceived benefits include maintaining existing relationships, enjoyment and building new relationships, with the perceived cost being privacy risks. Their model revealed a 49% variance in self-disclosure of Facebook whereas perceived cost and benefits do not have any impact

(*continued*)

Table 1. (*continued*)

Author	Social media	Methods and findings
[28]	Facebook, Foursquare Gowalla and Loopt	They provided an overview of the privacy issues associated with online social networks and their inherent limitations. Daily, about 100,000 tweets are sent on Twitter, 684,478 pieces of content are shared on Facebook and 3,600 photos are shared on Instagram. They classified social network sites into location-based networks, social media sharing sites and social media networking sites. Users of location-based social networks face situations where the information they publicize can be used to track their location. Examples of these sites are Foursquare, Gowalla and Loopt. This study also outlines steps like the use of login, HTTPS encryption, avoiding malicious links and third-party applications, in protecting users on these sites

3 Methodology

An online questionnaire designed with Google Forms was used to capture information about social media sites' privacy awareness among computer science students of Landmark University. Unlike in previous works, this survey is narrowed to computer scientists view and their satisfaction with social privacy settings, and if they would prefer an improved mechanism. Also, more than one social networking site or application used by these students were considered in this study. The social sites captured include, LinkedIn, Twitter, Google+, WhatsApp, Facebook, Snapchat, Instagram, Tumblr, and Pinterest. Brief consent information was presented to interested students and this has to be acknowledged for their opinions to be accepted. A total of 20 questions were answered which covered key characteristics of the respondent, interaction with social media applications and sites, and privacy issues. Most of the questions were multiple choices and 4-point Likert scale choices. A total of 84 computer science students from Landmark University completed the survey which took 30 days. SPSS Statistical tool was used for the analysis.

4   Questionnaire Analysis

4.1   Characteristics of Respondents

Of the 84 students that responded to the questionnaire, 78.6% were male students and 21.4% female students, within ages 15–25. 75% were within ages 15–20 and 25% within ages 20–25.

4.2   Type of Device Owned

41% of users have been registered on social media for more than 6 years, 27.7% for 2–4 years, 22.9% for 4–6 years while the rest have been on a social media site for 2 years or less. Students were asked to specify the devices majorly used for social media activities. Amongst the devices specified, laptops and phones were the most frequently used devices indicated.

4.3   Frequency of Use

Students were asked to identify the sites commonly visited from several specific social media sites. 78.6%, 94% and 91.7% of users generally use Facebook, WhatsApp, and Instagram respectively. 60.7% use Twitter, 25% use LinkedIn, 48.8% use Snapchat, 4.8% use Tumblr, 39.3% use Google+ and the least used sites, Pinterest and IMessage with 1.2% users both. Figure 1 presents the most used site of all the sites specified. Although the majority of students (89.3%) report 'Not addicted' to the use of social media sites, 53% report visiting a social media site every day, 39.8% visit at least once a week and 7.2% visit at least once a month. Figure 2 shows the number of hours a day spent by students on social media sites. Also, 88.1% of users never send broadcast messages, but the majority receive unwanted broadcast messages as shown in Fig. 3.

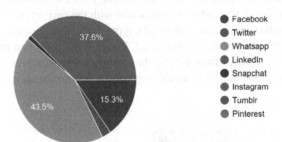

Fig. 1. Most used social media site.

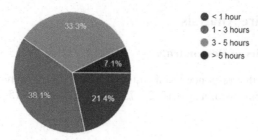

Fig. 2. Number of hours spent on social media daily

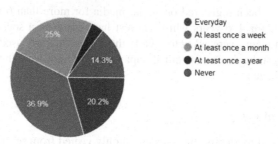

Fig. 3. The frequency at which broadcast messages are received.

4.4 Privacy Policies and Settings

Figure 4 shows the number of users who read and understand the privacy policies of applications before use. A vast majority of users rarely read or understand these policies, and this could be associated with long words or the use of too many technical words in stating the policies. With the use of a 5-point Likert scale where 1 = Not concerned all and 5 = Very concerned, students rated their level of concern on social media privacy, 54.2% users indicate a high level of concern although 89.2% of users have their privacy features enabled and 81.9% indicate satisfaction with the current privacy settings available on social media sites. Figure 5 shows the type of friend request accepted by students depending on familiarity with the individual. Figure 6 indicates that more users do not receive or accept messages from people they hardly know, however, we found that as many as 45.8% of users are often added to groups without their consent.

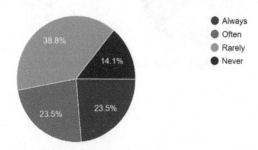

Fig. 4. Users who read and understand privacy policies

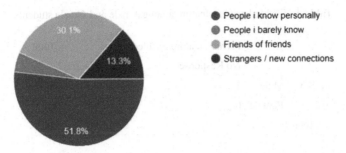

Fig. 5. Types of friend requests accepted by users

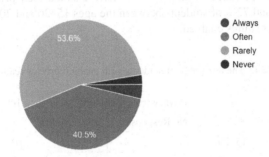

Fig. 6. Frequency of messages received from unknown individuals

4.5 Students' Gender and Social Media Privacy Features

A cross-tabulation in Table 2 showing the privacy concerns amongst the respondents indicates 61% of female students and 52% of male students had high concerns on the information privacy policies on social media sites. However, in Table 3, we see that 89.5% of male students have enabled privacy features on their devices while 77% of female students enabled theirs.

Table 2. Privacy concerns amongst students

		Rate of concern					Total
		Very low	Low	Neutral	High	Very high	
Sex	Male	1	0	16	15	35	67
	Female	0	2	2	3	11	18
Total		1	2	18	18	46	85

Table 3. Enabled privacy feature amongst male and female students

		Privacy feature enabled			Total
		No Response	Yes	Neutral	
Sex	Male	1	0	35	67
	Female	0	2	11	18
Total		1	2	46	85

4.6   Students' Age Range and Enabled Privacy Settings

Table 4 shows the age range of students who have enabled their privacy features on social sites. 92% and 72% of students between the ages 15–20 and 20–25 respectively have their privacy features enabled.

Table 4. The age range of students with enabled privacy features

		Privacy feature enabled			Total
		No Response	Yes	Neutral	
Age	15–20	1	58	4	63
	20–25	0	16	5	21
	Below 15	1	0	0	1
Total		2	9	74	85

4.7   Most Used Social Media Site and Privacy Settings

In relating the most popularly used social sites and the privacy features enabled in Table 5, we see that the highest number of students enabled privacy settings on WhatsApp followed by Instagram, Facebook and Twitter. This could, however, be subject to the fact that WhatsApp and Instagram are the most used social media sites amongst the respondents.

4.8   Discussion of Findings

From the results shown above, it can be seen that the privacy concerns amongst computer science students are relatively high, particularly in male students. Although a majority of the students are concerned about their privacy on social media, a large percentage of students fail to read privacy policies of the social sites before agreeing to the terms and conditions.

A study by [29] showed that ordinary users of these sites are not able to understand the data collection and legal privacy policies as these policies are very ambiguous and

Table 5. Social media sites and privacy feature settings.

		Privacy feature enabled			Total
		No Response	Yes	Neutral	
Most used social site	WhatsApp	0	2	35	37
	Instagram	1	4	27	32
	Facebook	1	1	11	13
	Twitter	0	1	1	2
	Snapchat	0	1	0	1
Total		2	9	74	85

not effectively communicated to users. In this study, only 51.8% of respondents accept friend requests from people they are familiar with, and 41.8% of students are often added to groups without their consent. Recent privacy restrictions on group requests have been implemented on social sites like WhatsApp and Instagram whereby users' have the option to accept or reject such requests. Privacy options like location sharing, photo tagging, audience and tagging, data sharing policies as well as discoverability settings have now been implemented on most social sites and there is a need for awareness. Users' of these sites need to be aware of such options and be acquainted with the types of personal private information they have willingly consented to sharing.

5 Conclusion

Social media has become a household name but despite its popularity, this mode of social interaction is not exempted from the privacy and security issues facing other internetwork applications like e-health, e-government, e-banking and so on [30]. This paper presents a study that shows that it would be an inaccurate assumption to think students studying computer science have an off the chart perception of online privacy. Only a meagre 23.8% reads and understands social media privacy agreement although most of the participants, about 89.2%, enabled their application-specific security settings. Recently, studies on various methods of analyzing large social networks have been introduced to be able to gain insights and patterns on users' online behaviours [31–33]. This study also confirms that there is a significant rise in the use of privacy features embedded in social networking sites and applications such as Facebook, Instagram, and WhatsApp, as it appears their security features have improved over time, going by the 81.9% level of satisfaction. However, there still exist privacy concerns on the data exchange and legal policies associated with these sites which should be carefully considered in future works.

References

1. Kumari, A., Verma, J.: Impact of social networking sites on social interaction-a study of college students. J. Hum. Soc. Sci. **4**(2), 55–62 (2015)

2. Salama, M., Panda, M., Elbarawy, Y., Hassanien, A., Abraham, A.: Computational social networks: security and privacy. In: Abraham, A. (ed.) Computational Social Networks, pp. 3–21. Springer, London (2012). https://doi.org/10.1007/978-1-4471-4051-1_1

3. Madden, M.: Privacy management on social media sites. Pew Internet Report, 1–20 (2012)

4. Kuczerawy, A., Fanny C.: Privacy settings in social networking sites: is it fair? In: Fischer-Hübner, S., Duquenoy, P., Hansen, M., Leenes, R., Zhang, G. (eds.) IFIP Prime Life International Summer School on Privacy and Identity Management for Life, pp. 231–243. Springer, Heidelberg (2010). https://doi.org/10.1007/978-3-642-20769-3_19

5. Golbeck, J., Matthew, M.: User perception of Facebook app data access: a comparison of methods and privacy concerns. Future Internet 8(2), 9–12 (2016)

6. Gerlach, J., Thomas, W., Peter, B.: Handle with care: How online social network providers' privacy policies impact users' information sharing behavior. J. Strateg. Inf. Syst. 24(1), 33–43 (2015)

7. Dumbrell, D., Steele, R.: Privacy perceptions of older adults when using social media technologies. In: Cyber Law, Privacy, and Security: Concepts, Methodologies, Tools, and Applications, pp. 1748–1764. IGI Global (2019)

8. Al-Rahmi, W., Othman, M., Yusuf, L.: The role of social media for collaborative learning to improve the academic performance of students and researchers in Malaysian higher education. Int. Rev. Res. Open and Distr. Learn. 16(4), 117–204 (2015)

9. Wandera, S., James-Waldon, N., Bromley, D., Henry, Z.: The influence of social media on collaborative learning in a cohort environment. Interdisciplinary J. e-Skills Life Long Learn. 12, 123–143 (2016)

10. Williams, D., Crittenden, V., Keo, T., McCarty, P.: The use of social media: an exploratory study of usage among digital natives. J. Public Affairs 12(2), 127–136 (2012)

11. Hu, X., Chu, T., Leung, V., Ngai, E., Kruchten, P., Chan, H.: A survey on mobile social networks: applications, platforms, system architectures, and future research directions. IEEE Commun. Surv. Tutor. 17(3), 1557–1581 (2014)

12. Bergström, A.: Online privacy concerns: a broad approach to understanding the concerns of different groups for different uses. Comput. Hum. Behav. 53, 419–426 (2015)

13. Shabnoor, S., Singh, T.: Social media its impact with positive and negative aspects. Int. J. Comput. Appl. Technol. Res. 5(2), 71–75 (2016)

14. Patel, R., Bhagat, R., Modi, P., Joshi, H.: Privacy and security issues in social online networks. In: National Conference on Latest Trends in Networking and Cyber Security (IJIRST), pp. 130–134 (2017)

15. Kokolakis, S.: Privacy attitudes and privacy behaviour: a review of current research on the privacy paradox phenomenon. Comput. Ssecur. 64, 122–134 (2017)

16. Perrin, A.: Social media usage. Pew research center, pp. 52–68 (2015)

17. Kitsis, E., Milan, F., Cohen, H., Myers, D., Herron, P., McEvoy, M., Grayson, S.: Who's misbehaving? Perceptions of unprofessional social media use by medical students and faculty. BMC Med. Educ. 16(1), 1–7 (2016)

18. Li, H., Zhu, H., Du, S., Liang, X., Shen, X.: Privacy leakage of location sharing in mobile social networks: attacks and defense. IEEE Trans. Dependable Secure Comput. 15(4), 646–660 (2016)

19. Li, D.: Privacy protection in social networking services. In: T-110.5290 Seminar on Network Security (2010)

20. Jin, L., Chen, Y., Wang, T., Hui, P., Vasilakos, A.: Understanding user behavior in online social networks: a survey. IEEE Commun. Mag. 51(9), 144–150 (2013)

21. Sangeeta, K. Singh, S.: A critical analysis of privacy and security on social media. In: 5th International Conference on Communication Systems and Network Technologies, IEEE, India, pp. 602–608 (2015)

22. Ilia, P., Polakis, I., Athanasopoulos, E., Maggi, F., Ioannidis, S.: Face/off: preventing privacy leakage from photos in social networks. In: Proceedings of the 22nd ACM SIGSAC Conference on Computer and Communications Security, ACM, USA, pp. 781–792 (2015)
23. Such, M., Rovatsos, M.: Privacy policy negotiation in social media. ACM Trans. Autonom. Adapt. Syst. (TAAS) 11(1), 1–29 (2016)
24. Beigi, G., Liu, H.: Privacy in social media: identification. Mitigation Appl. 9(4), 1–36 (2018)
25. Ralph, G., Acquisti, A.: Information revelation and privacy in online social networks. In: Proceedings of the 2005 ACM Workshop on Privacy in the Electronic Society, ACM, USA, pp. 71–80 (2005)
26. Nahier, A., Watson, C., Sajeev, A.: Personal information privacy settings of online social networks and their suitability for mobile internet devices. Privacy Int. J. Secur. Trust Manage. (IJSPTM) 2(2), 1–7 (2013)
27. Cheung, C., Lee, Z.W.: Self-disclosure in social networking sites: the role of perceived cost, perceived benefits and social influence. Internet Res. Electr. Networking Appl. Pol. 25(2), 7–12 (2015)
28. Neier, S., Zayer, L.: Students' perceptions and experiences of social media in higher education. J. Mark. Educ. 37(3), 133–143 (2015)
29. Bonneau, J., Preibusch, S.: The privacy jungle: on the market for data protection in social networks. In: Moore, T., Pym, D., Ioannidis, C. (eds.) Economics of Information Security and Privacy, pp. 121–167. Springer, Boston (2010). https://doi.org/10.1007/978-1-4419-696 7-5_8
30. Omotosho, A., Emuoyibofarhe, J., Meinel, C.: Ensuring patients' privacy in a cryptographic-based-electronic health records using bio-cryptography. Int. J. Electr. Healthcare 9(4), 227–254 (2017)
31. Kumari, A., Behera, R.K., Shukla, A.S., Sahoo, S.P., Misra, S., Rath, S.K.: Quantifying influential communities in granular social networks using fuzzy theory. In: Gervasi, O., et al. (eds.) ICCSA 2020. LNCS, vol. 12252, pp. 906–917. Springer, Cham (2020). https://doi.org/10.1007/978-3-030-58811-3_64
32. Kumar Behera, R., Kumar Rath, S., Misra, S., Damaševičius, R., Maskeliūnas, R.: Distributed centrality analysis of social network data using MapReduce. Algorithms 12(8), 161–172 (2019)
33. Rafique, N., Ishaq, A., Shoaib, M., Misra, S., Oluranti, J., Ahuja, R.: Uses and impact of social media on work performance of low literate people. In: Chillarige, R., Distefano, S., Rawat, S. (eds.) International Conference on Advances in Computational Intelligence and Informatics, pp. 381-387. Springer, Singapore (2019). https://doi.org/10.1007/978-981-15-3338-9_43

An Efficient Holistic Schema Matching Approach

Aola Yousfi[(✉)], Moulay Hafid El Yazidi, and Ahmed Zellou

Software Project Management Research Team, ENSIAS,
Mohammed V University in Rabat, Rabat, Morocco
aola.yousfi@gmail.com, {my-hafid.elyazidi,ahmed.zellou}@um5.ac.ma

Abstract. Schema matching allows a certain way of communication between heterogeneous, autonomous and distributed data sources. We choose the matching approach depending on the number of sources we wish to integrate: pairwise matching approaches for a small to a medium total number of data sources, and holistic matching approaches for a big to a huge number of data sources. Nevertheless, current matching approaches were proven to achieve a very moderate matching accuracy. Moreover, holistic matching approaches operate in a series of two-way matching steps. In this paper, we present hMatcher, an efficient holistic schema matching approach. To execute holistic schema matching, hMatcher captures frequent schema elements in the given domain prior to any matching operation. To achieve high matching accuracy, hMatcher uses a context-based semantic similarity measure. Experimental results on real-world domain show that hMatcher performs holistic schema matching properly, and outperforms current matching approaches in terms of matching accuracy.

Keywords: Holistic schema matching · Semantic similarity measure · Matching accuracy

1 Introduction

Schema matching has got a lot of attention from the research community over the past three decades (see [10,18] for surveys). It is very critical for applications that manipulate data across schemas of distinct data sources, examples of areas where this kind of applications are used include mainly data integration on the World Wide Web, data warehousing, e-commerce, scientific collaboration and bioinformatics. Another reason that makes schema matching very important is that it hides the semantic and syntactic heterogeneity between different schemas and makes the latter looks like one single integrated schema, which facilitates significantly access to data.

Schema matching and schema mapping are often used interchangeably, however they in fact refer to two different things. The former refers to the process of searching for semantically corresponding elements (also called matches or semantically similar elements [4,21,22]) in multiple, heterogeneous, autonomous and

S. Misra and B. Muhammad-Bello (Eds.): ICTA 2020, CCIS 1350, pp. 588–601, 2021.
https://doi.org/10.1007/978-3-030-69143-1_45

scattered schemas of data sources. Figure 1 illustrates an example of the schema matching problem: given two schemata S_1 and S_2 (for the sake of clarification, we depict them as trees) describing film information, we aim to determine the matches (indicated by dotted lines), which identify schema elements representing the same concepts in the two. The latter however refers to the process of defining the relationship between elements of different schemas. Also, schema matching takes place right before schema mapping, as the output of the former is used by the latter; also schema mapping cannot work without schema matching which again emphasizes the big importance and criticality of schema matching.

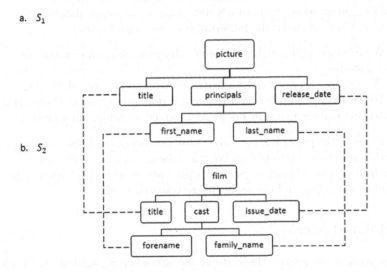

Fig. 1. Example of the schema matching problem

Researchers grouped schema matching approaches into two major categories: pairwise matching and holistic matching. The former aims at identifying the matches between two schemas at a time, which appears to be insufficient when it comes to matching a huge number of schemas. Thus, the latter came to place as it aims to match multiple schemas simultaneously, which intends to overcome the aforementioned limitations faced by pairwise schema matching approaches.

Current holistic schema matching approaches, also called collective schema matching approaches [15], (see Sect. 2) often proceed in a series of two-way matching steps which contradict with the initial goal of holistic schema matching as they do not necessarily match schemas simultaneously, but instead they match schemas incrementally: they first combine two schemas into one integrated schema using the matches between them, and then matches one schema at a time to the combined schema (e.g. PORSCHE).

Current matching approaches often reach moderate matching accuracy. This implies a continuous human assistance to correct the final results: remove false matches and add missed matches; which impacts the overall performance of the matching system in question.

The main concrete challenges, we addressed when working on this research project, are listed below:

a. Define an appropriate approach to capture frequent schema elements.
c. Define a method to reduce the total number of rare schema elements.
d. Come up with an efficient approach to holistic schema matching.

In this paper, we introduce hMatcher, an efficient holistic schema matching approach. The main idea of hMatcher is to (1) execute holistic schema matching; and (2) reach a high matching accuracy. To do so, hMatcher employs a semantic similarity measure, uses the transitivity principle, and exploits a hierarchical lexical dictionary along with an abbreviations & acronyms database.

In summary, we make the following concrete contributions:

a. We propose an algorithm to identify frequent schema elements in a particular domain.
b. We propose an approach to match multiple schemas holistically.
c. We evaluate hMatcher on a real-world domain and show that it is able to match multiple schemas at once and produce high matching accuracy.

The rest of the paper is structured as follows. Section 2 discusses related work. Section 3 defines the problem of holistic schema matching. Section 4 describes the architecture of hMatcher. Section 5 presents experimental results. Section 6 concludes this paper and discusses future research work.

2   Related Work

In this section, we review the state of the art schema matching methods that are most relevant to our work.

AgreementMakerLight (AML) [6] is an ontology matching approach. It derives from AgreementMaker [2]. AML consists of two key modules: the ontology loading module and the ontology matching module. The ontology loading module loads the ontologies and the external resources, and then generates the ontology objects. The ontology matching module main objective is to align the ontology objects generated by the previous module.

ALIN [17] is a human-interactive ontology matching approach. It takes as input two ontologies and outputs a set of alignments. It goes through two key steps. First, it defines the initial mappings. Second, it waits for human expert feedbacks and changes the mappings accordingly so as to improve the quality of the final results. The second step is repeated till experts run out of suggestions.

ALOD2Vec [14] uses the WebIsALOD database of hypernym relations extracted from the Web. It also employs both element-based information and label-based information. In order to determine the similarity score between nodes of the knowledge graph (WebIsALOD is viewed as a knowledge graph), ALOD2Vec applies RDF2Vec which transforms RDFs into vectors.

Deep Ontology MatchEr (DOME) [7] uses doc2vec and exploits large texts that describe the concepts of the ontologies. To deal with the main issue of matching similar large texts, DOME exploits topic modeling for instance Latent Semantic Analysis (LSA) and Latent Dirichlet Allocation (LDA).

FCAMapX [1] is an automated ontology alignment system. It is based on Formal Concept Analysis, which is a mathematical model for analyzing individuals and structuring concepts.

KEPLER [9] is an ontology matching system which takes advantage of the expressiveness of the Web Ontology Language (OWL) statements by means of six complementary steps: parsing, partitioning/translation, indexing, candidate mappings identification, filtering and recovery, and alignment generation.

Lily [19] is an ontology alignment approach. Its main advantage is that it is able to process normal ontologies, weak informative ontologies, ontology mapping debugging and ontology matching tuning [20].

LogMap [8] is a scalable and logic-based ontology matching approach. It uses lexical indexation, logic-based module extraction, propositional horn reasoning, axiom tracking, local repair and semantic indexation to match two given ontologies. LogMapLt is a lightweight variant of LogMap, which essentially applies string-based matching techniques.

Simulated ANnealing-based Ontology Matching (SANOM) [12] uses the notorious Simulated Annealing (SA) [13] to discover semantically similar elements between two input ontologies, which results on a potential intermediate alignment. The evolution of that alignment needs the use of both lexical similarity metrics and structural similarity metrics.

Holontology [16] is a holistic ontology matching approach based on the Linear Program for Holistic Ontology Matching (LPHOM) approach [11]. It exploits a combination of several similarity measures and dissimilarity distances: exact match, Levenstein, Jaccard and Lin to match two ontologies or multiple ontologies at once after it converts them into an internal predefined format. Then, Holontology converts the results into alignments exported by RDF.

Current holistic schema matching methods face several challenges. First, they are unable to perform collective schema matching properly: they match schemas incrementally in a series of two-way matching steps. Second, they reach a moderate matching accuracy (see Sect. 5 for more details). Finally, they are human-dependent.

In the next section, we will state the problem we are working on in this paper and present related definitions.

3   Problem Statement

In this section, we first provide definitions related to the problem we are working on in this paper; we then state the research question; and finally we display the notations used throughout this paper.

Definition 3.1. (Set of words). A set of words $\theta = \{w_1, w_2, \ldots, w_{|\theta|}\}$ includes words extracted from a schema element e. In Sect. 4, we will describe thoroughly the process of generating a set of words.

Remark. All the words' sets generated from a schema S are denoted by Θ.

Definition 3.2. (Semantically corresponding elements). Let S_1, S_2, S_3 be three given schemata. Semantically corresponding elements φ is a tuple (E_1, E_2, E_3), where E_1, E_2 and E_3 are three subsets of schema elements from S_1, S_2 and S_3 respectively.

Definition 3.3. (Learning schemas). The learning schemas are the schemas we use to identify the initial set of frequent schema elements in the given domain. We denote the set of learning schemas by $\mathbb{S}_{Learning}$.

Definition 3.4. (Testing schemas). The testing schemas are the schemas we want to match using the frequent schema elements. We denote the set of testing schemas by $\mathbb{S}_{Testing}$.

Definition 3.5. (Frequent schema element.) Given a schema S, let f be an element from S. f is a frequent schema element if and only if it has duplicates in a certain number of schemas describing the same domain. Note that the duplicates of f can either be f as well or semantic corresponding elements of f. We denote the set of frequent schema elements by $\mathbb{F}$.

Definition 3.6. (Rare schema element). Given n schemas $S_1, S_2, \ldots, S_n$ we wish to match. Let E be the set of elements contained in $S_1, S_2, \ldots,$ and S_n, and let $\mathbb{F}$ be the set of frequent schema elements. A rare schema element $r \in E$ is a schema element that does not belong to $\mathbb{F}$. We denote the set of rare schema elements by $\mathbb{R}$.

Definition 3.7. (Problem statement). Given n input schemas $S_1, S_2, \ldots, S_n$ we wish to match. Our goal in this paper is to identify the semantic correspondences $\Phi = \{\varphi_1, \varphi_2, \ldots, \varphi_{|\Phi|}\}$ between $S_1, S_2, \ldots, S_n$ as a result of matching $S_1, S_2, \ldots, S_n$ simultaneously (rather than two at a time). The matching approach also has to ensure superior matching accuracy.

The list of symbols used throughout this paper is given in Table 1.

Table 1. Symbols used throughout this paper

Symbol	Description
S, e	Schema, schema element
Θ, $|\Theta|$, θ, $|\theta|$	Sets of words, cardinality of Θ, a set of words in Θ, cardinality of θ
$\mathbb{S}_{Learning}$, $|\mathbb{S}_{Learning}|$	Learning schemas, cardinality of $\mathbb{S}_{Learning}$
$\mathbb{S}_{Testing}$, $|\mathbb{S}_{Testing}|$	Testing schemas, cardinality of $\mathbb{S}_{Testing}$
$\mathbb{S}$	$\mathbb{S} = \mathbb{S}_{Learning} \cup \mathbb{S}_{Testing}$
Φ, φ	Matches, a tuple of matches in Φ
$\mathbb{F}$, f, $|\mathbb{F}|$	Frequent elements list, a frequent schema element, cardinality of $\mathbb{F}$
$\mathbb{R}$, r, $|\mathbb{R}|$	Rare elements list, a rare schema element, cardinality of $\mathbb{R}$

In the next section, we will describe the hMatcher solution to the problem described in Definition 3.7.

4   The hMatcher Approach

The hMatcher architecture (see Fig. 2) is composed of three different components: the frequent elements generator, the schema matcher and the rare elements matcher. Let $\mathbb{S}_{Learning} \in \mathbb{S}$ be the learning schemas. First, the frequent elements generator takes as input $\mathbb{S}_{Learning}$, utilizes both a hierarchical lexical dictionary and an abbreviations & acronyms database, and provides as output the frequent schema elements $\mathbb{F}$. Let $\mathbb{S}_{Testing} \in \mathbb{S}$ be the testing schemas. The schema matcher then takes in $\mathbb{S}_{Testing}$, employs the frequent schema elements, and provides as output the matches Φ. Finally, the rare elements matcher reuses the results to find out new potential matches in the rare schema elements $\mathbb{R}$.

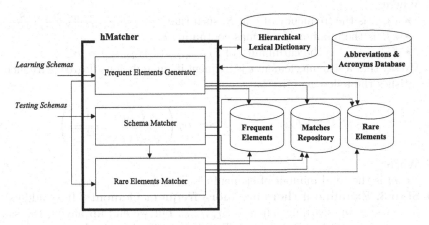

Fig. 2. The hMatcher Architecture

In the rest of this section, we first present the frequent elements generator (see Sect. 4.1), we then describe the schema matcher (see Sect. 4.2), and finally, we introduce the rare elements matcher (see Sect. 4.3).

4.1   The Frequent Elements Generator

Let $\mathbb{S}_{Learning} = \{S_1, S_2, \ldots, S_p\} \in \mathbb{S}$ be the learning schemas, the frequent elements generator employs the pre-processing method presented in [23–25] in order to extract from each schema element e a words set θ that represents its meaning. That pre-processing method proceeds as follows. It first extracts words from the schema elements using the lexical dictionary. It then substitutes abbreviations and acronyms with their corresponding full forms using the abbreviations & acronyms database. It next generates words sets. Finally, it identifies the meaning of words based on their context (a word often changes its meaning in different contexts). Note that the words sets generated from S_1 are denoted by Θ_1, the words sets generated from S_2 are denoted by Θ_2, etc. Later, the frequent elements generator operates in three different steps:

- **Step 1: Capture the matches.** Let $e_1 \in S_1$ and $e_2 \in S_2$ be two elements, and let $\theta_1 = \{w_{1,1}, w_{1,2}, \ldots, w_{1,|\theta_1|}\}$ and $\theta_2 = \{w_{2,1}, w_{2,2}, \ldots, w_{2,|\theta_2|}\}$ be their respective words sets. The frequent elements generator uses the measure (CSSM) in [24] to see whether θ_1 and θ_2 are semantically similar or not.
- **Step 2: Determine frequent schema elements.** Let $S \in \mathbb{S}_{Learning}$ be a schema and let e be an element from S. We use *EF–SF* (Element Frequency-Schema Frequency) (1) to find the degree of frequency of e.

$$EF - SF_{e \in S, \mathbb{S}_{Learning}} = EF_{e,S} \times SF_{e,\mathbb{S}_{Learning}} = e^{ef_{e,S}} \times e^{\left(\frac{sf_e}{|\mathbb{S}_{Learning}|}\right)} \quad (1)$$

Where:
- $ef_{e,S}$ is the frequency of e in S, such that $ef_{e,S} = \frac{count\ of\ e\ in\ S}{number\ of\ elements\ in\ S}$.
- sf_e is the number of schemas containing e.
- $|\mathbb{S}_{Learning}|$ is the cardinality of $\mathbb{S}_{Learning}$ ($|\mathbb{S}_{Learning}| = p$).

We say that a schema element e is frequent if and only if its degree of frequency satisfies the following criteria:

$$\lfloor EF - SF_{e \in S, \mathbb{S}_{Learning}} \rfloor >= log\left(\frac{\sqrt[2]{(m^4 + 1)}}{\sqrt[2]{|\mathbb{S}_{Learning}|^2 - 1}}\right) \quad (2)$$

Where:
- m is the total number of elements in $\mathbb{S}_{Learning}$.
- **Step 3: Examine if there are more frequent elements.** If we add extra schemas to the learning schemas $\mathbb{S}_{Learning}$ but we end up having the same exact frequent schema elements ($|\mathbb{F}| = constant$), then the frequent elements generator stops. Otherwise, it repeats both steps 1 and 2.

Algorithm 1 summarizes this.

4.2 The Schema Matcher

Let $\mathbb{S}_{Testing} = \{S_{p+1}, S_{p+2}, \ldots, S_n\}$ be the testing schemas, and let $\Theta_{p+1}, \Theta_{p+2}, \ldots, \Theta_n$ be the words sets generated from $S_{p+1}, S_{p+2}, \ldots, S_n$, respectively. The schema matcher proceeds as follows (summarized in Algorithm 2).

- **Step 1: Compute the semantic similarity.** It compares the words sets $\Theta_{p+1}, \Theta_{p+2}, \ldots, \Theta_n$ to the frequent schema elements $\mathbb{F}$ according to the semantic similarity measure in [24].
- **Step 2: Find out new matches.** Every set $\theta_i \in \{\Theta_{p+1}, \Theta_{p+2}, \ldots, \Theta_n\}$ that has a semantically corresponding element f_i in $\mathbb{F}$, its schema element e_i will be added to the matches list Φ such that $\varphi \leftarrow \varphi \cup e_i$, where $f_i \in \varphi$ and $\varphi \in \Phi$.

Algorithm 1. FrequentElementsGenerator($\Theta_1, \Theta_2, \ldots, \Theta_p$)

Input:
   $\Theta_1, \Theta_2, \ldots, \Theta_p$: *The sets of words generated from* $S_1, S_2, \ldots, S_p$
Output:
   $\mathbb{F}$: *The frequent schema elements*

   $\mathbb{F} \leftarrow \emptyset$
   Generate the matches Φ between $\Theta_1, \Theta_2, \ldots, \Theta_p$ according to the measure in [24]
   FOR each φ in Φ

   IF ($e \in \varphi$ AND $\lfloor EF - SF_{e \in S, \mathbb{S}_{Learning}} \rfloor >= log\left(\frac{\sqrt[2]{(m^4+1)}}{\sqrt[2]{|\mathbb{S}_{Learning}|^2 - 1}} \right)$) THEN

   $\mathbb{F} \leftarrow \mathbb{F} \cup e$ /* $\mathbb{F}$ *stores one single element e in* φ */
   END IF
   END FOR
return $\mathbb{F}$

Algorithm 2. SchemaMatcher($\Theta_{p+1}, \Theta_{p+2}, \ldots, \Theta_n$)

Input:
   $\Theta_{p+1}, \Theta_{p+2}, \ldots, \Theta_n$: *The words sets generated from* $S_{p+1}, S_{p+2}, \ldots, S_n$
Output:
   Φ : *The matches*

   FOR each Θ in $\{\Theta_{p+1}, \Theta_{p+2}, \ldots, \Theta_n\}$
   Generate the matches Φ between Θ and $\mathbb{F}$ according to the semantic similarity
measure in [24]
   END FOR
return Φ

4.3 The Rare Elements Matcher

Theorem 1. (Transitive relation). A binary relation $\Re$ is transitive over a set A if and only if it satisfies the following criteria:
   $\forall \, x, y, z \in A, (x\Re y \land y\Re z) \implies x\Re z$, i.e. for all elements x, y, z in A, whenever $\Re$ relates x to y and y to z, then $\Re$ also relates x to z.

Let S_1 and S_2 be two schemas, let $r_1 \in \mathbb{R}$ and $r_2 \in \mathbb{R}$ be two rare schema elements from S_1 and S_2, respectively; and let $\mathbb{F} = \{f_1, f_2, \ldots, f_q\}$ (where $q \in \mathbb{N}^*$) be the set of frequent schema elements. Using the transitive relation, we have the following:

$$\forall \, i \in \{1, 2, \ldots, q\}, CSSM(r_1, f_i) = CSSM(r_2, f_i) \pm 0.05 \implies r_1 \text{ and } r_2 \text{ are matched.}$$

If r_1 (or r_2) satisfies (2), then the frequent schema elements list is updated as follows:
$$\mathbb{F} \leftarrow \mathbb{F} \cup r_1 \text{ OR } \mathbb{F} \leftarrow \mathbb{F} \cup r_2 \text{ (not both).}$$

And the list of rare schema elements is updated as follows:
$$\mathbb{R} \leftarrow \mathbb{R} \setminus r_1 \text{ AND } \mathbb{R} \leftarrow \mathbb{R} \setminus r_2.$$

Algorithm 3 summarizes this.

Algorithm 3. RareElementsMatcher($\mathbb{R}$, $\mathbb{F}$)

Input:
   $\mathbb{R}$: *Rare schema elements*
   $\mathbb{F}$: *Frequent schema elements*
Output:
   Φ, $\mathbb{F}$, $\mathbb{R}$: *The matches; the frequent schema elements; the rare elements*

   FOR each r_1 and r_2 in $\mathbb{R}$
   IF $(CSSM(r_1, f) = CSSM(r_2, f) \pm 0.05, \forall f \in \mathbb{F})$ THEN
   $\varphi \leftarrow \varphi \cup r_1$ /* $\varphi \in \Phi$ *is the tuple that includes the matches of* r_1 */
   $\mathbb{F} \leftarrow \mathbb{F} \cup r_1;$ $\mathbb{R} \leftarrow \mathbb{R} \setminus r_1;$ $\mathbb{R} \leftarrow \mathbb{R} \setminus r_2$
   END IF
   END FOR
return $(\Phi, \mathbb{F}, \mathbb{R})$

---

5 Experiments and Evaluations

In this section, we evaluate hMatcher in terms of matching accuracy and compare the results to other matching approaches.

5.1 Datasets

We evaluated hMatcher on the *Conference* dataset which contains 16 ontologies describing the domain of organizing academic conferences. The ontologies were used in OAEI 2019 and are publicly available on the Web[1]. The *Conference* dataset has been used by the research community for over thirteen years. It has 21 reference alignments composed from 7 out of 16 real domain ontologies.

5.2 Measures

We first exploit *Precision* (3), *Recall* (4), *Overall* (5) and *F − Measure* (6) to evaluate the matches generated by hMatcher on the *Conference* dataset.

$$Precision = \frac{Correct\ Matches}{Correct\ Matches + Incorrect\ Matches} \tag{3}$$

(3) is the probability of correct matches among all matches returned by the matching system.

$$Recall = \frac{Correct\ Matches}{Missed\ Matches + Correct\ Matches} \tag{4}$$

(4) is the probability of correct matches returned by a matching system among the reference matches.

$$Overall = Recall \times (2 - \frac{1}{Precision}) \tag{5}$$

---

[1] http://oaei.ontologymatching.org/2019/.

(5) measures the amount of manual post-effort required to remove false matches and add missed matches. Unlike *Precision* and *Recall*, *Overall* can have negative values if *Precision* < 0.5. Note that if *Overall* < 0 then most matches must be produced manually, concluding that the matching system is not interesting.

$$F - Measure = \frac{2 \times Precision \times Recall}{Precision + Recall} \tag{6}$$

(6) is the harmonic mean of *Precision* and *Recall*.

We then compare the results obtained on the *Conference* dataset against previously published results of twelve well-known and high-accuracy ontology matching systems (SANOM [12], AML [5], LogMap [8], XMap [3], KEPLER [9], ALIN [17], DOME [7], Holontology [16], FCAMapX [1], LogMapLt [8], ALOD2Vec [14] and Lily [19]). The evaluations are based on nine combinations of variants with crisp reference alignments: *ra1-M1, ra1-M2, ra1-M3, ra2-M1, ra2-M2, ra2-M3, rar2-M1, rar2-M2* and *rar2-M3* (*ra1* is the original reference alignment; *ra2* is an extension of *ra1*; and *rar2* is an updated version of *ra2* that deals with the violations of conservativity). *ra1-M1, ra2-M1* and *rar2-M1* are used to evaluate alignments between classes; *ra1-M2, ra2-M2* and *rar2-M2* are used to evaluate alignments between properties; and *ra1-M3, ra2-M3* and *rar2-M3* are used to evaluate both alignments between classes and properties.

5.3   Results and Discussions

Figs. 3, 4, 5, 6, 7, 8, 9, 10 and 11 depict the new and previously published results on the *Conference* dataset.

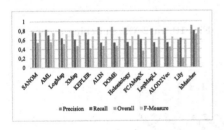
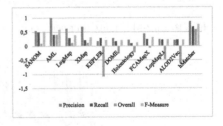

Fig. 3. ra1-M1: matching accuracy   **Fig. 4.** ra1-M2: matching accuracy

On the one hand, the previously published findings indicate visible changes for *Precision, Recall, Overall* and *F-Measure*. They achieved high matching accuracy when evaluated based on *ra1-M1, ra1-M3, ra2-M1, ra2-M3, rar2-M1* and *rar2-M3*; and low matching accuracy even null in some situations (e.g. Lily and ALIN) with *ra1-M2, ra2-M2* and *rar2-M2*. On the other hand, hMatcher reached superior matching accuracy, which implies that it surpassed current matching systems almost every time with the exception of *ra1-M2* and *ra2-M2* where AML surpassed it slightly (*Precision* = 1).

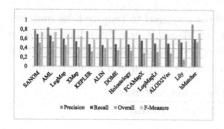

Fig. 5. ra1-M3: matching accuracy

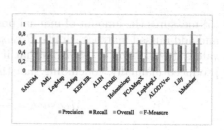

Fig. 6. ra1-M2: matching accuracy

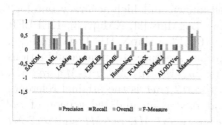

Fig. 7. ra2-M2: matching accuracy

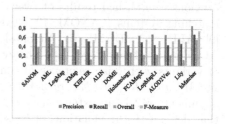

Fig. 8. ra1-M3: matching accuracy

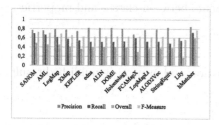

Fig. 9. rar2-M1: matching accuracy

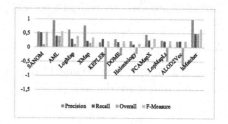

Fig. 10. rar2-M2: matching accuracy

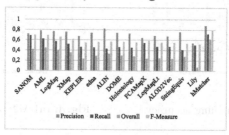

Fig. 11. rar2-M3: matching accuracy

Lily and ALIN match only classes, as a result, they failed to reach a high-matching accuracy with *ra1-M2*, *ra2-M2* and *rar2-M2*; SANOM, AML, LogMap and XMap match some but not all properties which explains their negative *Overall* with *ra1-M2*, *ra2-M2* and *rar2-M2*; KEPLER, DOME, Holontology,

FCAMapX, LogMapLt and ALOD2Vec match very few properties which justifies their negative *Overall* and inferior *Precision, Recall* and *F-Measure* with
ra1-M2, ra2-M2 and *rar2-M2*; and hMatcher matches both classes and properties which justifies its positive *Overall* and high *Precision, Recall* and *F-Measure*
with *ra1-M1, ra1-M2, ra1-M3, ra2-M1, ra2-M2, ra2-M3, rar2-M1, rar2-M2* and
rar2-M3. Thus, we sum up that: (1) SANOM, AML, LogMap, XMap, KEPLER,
ALIN, DOME, Holontology, FCAMapX, LogMapLt, ALOD2Vec and Lily work
well with the reference alignments that consider either classes or both classes
and properties. Nonetheless, they fail to match correctly with the reference
alignments that consider only properties; and (2) hMatcher accomplishes better
results as it achieves a superior matching accuracy regardless of the reference
alignments it is compared to.

6 Conclusion and Future Work

We showed that carefully defining a holistic schema matching approach is mandatory to deliver accurate results and match a huge number of schemas. Current
matching approaches often reach low matching accuracy and thus require human
assistance to correct the matches; moreover, existing matching approaches are
more likely to match two schemas at a time rather than many at once.

Let $\mathbb{S}_{Learning}$ be the learning schemas and $\mathbb{S}_{Testing}$ be the testing schemas,
hMatcher generates frequent schema elements $\mathbb{F}$ from $\mathbb{S}_{Learning}$. It then uses $\mathbb{F}$
to capture new matches Φ in $\mathbb{S}_{Testing}$. At the end, hMatcher reuses previous
results to identify new matches among the few rare schema elements we are left
with.

We evaluated hMatcher on the conference dataset, the results show a high
matching accuracy reached by hMatcher on the one hand; and on the other hand,
an inferior matching accuracy obtained by current matching approaches.

Future interesting research directions include mainly the following:

- **Consider situations where schemas are represented using different lexical languages.** In this dissertation, we focused mainly on schemas
  expressed in the same lexical language. An interesting future research direction would be to match schemas regardless of the lexical language they are
  expressed in. A way to do that would be to implement a translator.
- **How does hMatcher impact data source selection and ordering?**
  Prior to returning the answer to the user, the system selects a subset of data
  sources that are more likely to include the answer or a piece of the answer to
  the user query, this process is what we call source selection; then, the system
  orders data sources in a descending order of their coverage (source coverage
  is the amount of answers to a particular query contained in the data source),
  this process is called source ordering. So, a future research direction would
  be to study the relationship between hMatcher and data source selection and
  ordering.

References

1. Chen, G., Zhang, S.: Fcamapx results for OAEI 2018. In: Proceedings of the 13th International Workshop on Ontology Matching co-Located with the 17th International Semantic Web Conference, OM@ISWC 2018, Monterey, CA, USA, 8 October 2018, pp. 160–166 (2018) http://ceur-ws.org/Vol-2288/oaei18_paper7.pdf
2. Cruz, I.F., Antonelli, F.P., Stroe, C.: Agreementmaker: efficient matching for large real-world schemas and ontologies. PVLDB 2(2), 1586–1589 (2009). https://doi.org/10.14778/1687553.1687598, http://www.vldb.org/pvldb/vol2/vldb09-1003.pdf
3. Djeddi, W.E., Yahia, S.B., Khadir, M.T.: Xmap: results for OAEI 2018. In: Proceedings of the 13th International Workshop on Ontology Matching co-located with the 17th International Semantic Web Conference, OM@ISWC 2018, Monterey, 8 October 2018, pp. 210–215 (2018). http://ceur-ws.org/Vol-2288/oaei18_paper15.pdf
4. El Yazidi, M.H., Zellou, A., Idri, A.: Towards a fuzzy mapping for mediation systems. In: 2012 IEEE International Conference on Complex Systems (ICCS), pp. 1–4 (2012)
5. Faria, D., et al.: Results of AML participation in OAEI 2018. In: Proceedings of the 13th International Workshop on Ontology Matching co-located with the 17th International Semantic Web Conference, OM@ISWC 2018, Monterey, CA, USA, 8 October 2018, pp. 125–131 (2018). http://ceur-ws.org/Vol-2288/oaei18_paper2.pdf
6. Faria, D., Pesquita, C., Santos, E., Palmonari, M., Cruz, I.F., Couto, F.M.: The AgreementMakerLight ontology matching system. In: Meersman, R. (ed.) OTM 2013. LNCS, vol. 8185, pp. 527–541. Springer, Heidelberg (2013). https://doi.org/10.1007/978-3-642-41030-7_38
7. Hertling, S., Paulheim, H.: DOME results for OAEI 2018. In: Proceedings of the 13th International Workshop on Ontology Matching co-located with the 17th International Semantic Web Conference, OM@ISWC 2018, Monterey, CA, USA, 8 October 2018, pp. 144–151 (2018). http://ceur-ws.org/Vol-2288/oaei18_paper5.pdf
8. Jiménez-Ruiz, E., Grau, B.C., Cross, V.: Logmap family participation in the OAEI 2018. In: Proceedings of the 13th International Workshop on Ontology Matching co-located with the 17th International Semantic Web Conference, OM@ISWC 2018, Monterey, CA, USA, 8 October 2018, pp. 187–191 (2018). http://ceur-ws.org/Vol-2288/oaei18_paper11.pdf
9. Kachroudi, M., Diallo, G., Yahia, S.B.: KEPLER at OAEI 2018. In: Proceedings of the 13th International Workshop on Ontology Matching co-located with the 17th International Semantic Web Conference, OM@ISWC 2018, Monterey, CA, USA, 8 October 2018, pp. 173–178 (2018). http://ceur-ws.org/Vol-2288/oaei18_paper9.pdf
10. Köpke, J.: Annotation paths for matching xml-schemas. Data Knowl. Eng. 122, 25–54 (2019). https://doi.org/10.1016/j.datak.2017.12.002
11. Megdiche, I., Teste, O., Trojahn, C.: An extensible linear approach for holistic ontology matching. In: Groth, P. (ed.) ISWC 2016. LNCS, vol. 9981, pp. 393–410. Springer, Cham (2016). https://doi.org/10.1007/978-3-319-46523-4_24
12. Mohammadi, M., Hofman, W., Tan, Y.: SANOM results for OAEI 2018. In: Proceedings of the 13th International Workshop on Ontology Matching co-located with the 17th International Semantic Web Conference, OM@ISWC 2018, Monterey, CA, USA, 8 October 2018, pp. 205–209 (2018). http://ceur-ws.org/Vol-2288/oaei18_paper14.pdf

13. Mohammadi, M., Hofman, W., Tan, Y.: Simulated annealing-based ontology matching. ACM Trans. Manage. Inf. Syst. **10**(1), 3:1–3:24 (2019). https://doi.org/10.1145/3314948
14. Portisch, J., Paulheim, H.: Alod2vec matcher. In: Proceedings of the 13th International Workshop on Ontology Matching co-located with the 17th International Semantic Web Conference, OM@ISWC 2018, Monterey, CA, USA, 8 October 2018, pp. 132–137 (2018). http://ceur-ws.org/Vol-2288/oaei18_paper3.pdf
15. Rahm, E., Peukert, E.: Large-scale schema matching. Encyclopedia of Big Data Technologies (2019). https://doi.org/10.1007/978-3-319-63962-8_330-1
16. Roussille, P., Megdiche, I., Teste, O., Trojahn, C.: Holontology: results of the 2018 OAEI evaluation campaign. In: Proceedings of the 13th International Workshop on Ontology Matching co-located with the 17th International Semantic Web Conference, OM@ISWC 2018, Monterey, CA, USA, 8 October 2018, pp. 167–172 (2018). http://ceur-ws.org/Vol-2288/oaei18_paper8.pdf
17. da Silva, J., Revoredo, K., Baião, F.A.: ALIN results for OAEI 2018. In: Proceedings of the 13th International Workshop on Ontology Matching co-located with the 17th International Semantic Web Conference, OM@ISWC 2018, Monterey, CA, USA, 8 October 2018, pp. 117–124 (2018). http://ceur-ws.org/Vol-2288/oaei18_paper1.pdf
18. Sutanta, E., Wardoyo, R., Mustofa, K., Winarko, E.: Survey: models and prototypes of schema matching. Int. J. Electr. Comput. Eng. (2088–8708) **6**(3), 1011–1022 (2016)
19. Tang, Y., Wang, P., Pan, Z., Liu, H.: Lily results for OAEI 2018. In: Proceedings of the 13th International Workshop on Ontology Matching co-located with the 17th International Semantic Web Conference, OM@ISWC 2018, Monterey, CA, USA, 8 October 2018, pp. 179–186 (2018). http://ceur-ws.org/Vol-2288/oaei18_paper10.pdf
20. Yang, P., Wang, P., Ji, L., Chen, X., Huang, K., Yu, B.: Ontology matching tuning based on particle swarm optimization: preliminary results. In: Zhao, D., Du, J., Wang, H., Wang, P., Ji, D., Pan, J.Z. (eds.) CSWS 2014. CCIS, vol. 480, pp. 146–155. Springer, Heidelberg (2014). https://doi.org/10.1007/978-3-662-45495-4_13
21. Yazidi, M.H.E., Zellou, A., Idri, A.: FMAMS: fuzzy mapping approach for mediation systems. IJAEC **4**(3), 34–46 (2013). https://doi.org/10.4018/jaec.2013070104
22. Yazidi, M.H.E., Zellou, A., Idri, A.: Fgav (fuzzy global as views). AIP Conf. Proc. **1644**(1), 236–243 (2015)
23. Yousfi, A., El Yazidi, M.H., Zellou, A.: hmatcher: Matching schemas holistically. Int. J. Intell. Eng. Syst. **13**(5), 490–501 (2020)
24. Yousfi, A., Elyazidi, M.H., Zellou, A.: Assessing the performance of a new semantic similarity measure designed for schema matching for mediation systems. In: Nguyen, N.T., Pimenidis, E., Khan, Z., Trawiński, B. (eds.) ICCCI 2018. LNCS (LNAI), vol. 11055, pp. 64–74. Springer, Cham (2018). https://doi.org/10.1007/978-3-319-98443-8_7
25. Yousfi, A., Yazidi, M.H.E., Zellou, A.: xmatcher: Matching extensible markup language schemas using semantic-based techniques. Int. J. Adv. Comput. Sci. Appl. **11**(8), 655–665 (2020). https://doi.org/10.14569/IJACSA.2020.0110880

AnnoGram4MD: A Language for Annotating Grammars for High Quality Metamodel Derivation

Hamzat Olanrewaju Aliyu[1]([⊠]) and Oumar Maïga[2]

[1] School of Info. & Comm. Tech., Federal University of Technology, Minna, Nigeria
hamzat.aliyu@futminna.edu.ng
[2] Université des Sciences, Techniques et Technologies, Bamako, Mali
maigababa78@yahoo.fr

Abstract. The quests for transfers of software artifacts between the model ware and grammar ware technical spaces have increased in recent decades. Particularly, the need to port grammar-based concepts into the model ware space has birthed efforts to synthesise Ecore-based metamodels from Extended Backus Naur Form (EBNF)-based grammars. However, automatic derivation of high-quality metamodels from grammars is still a challenge as existing solutions produce metamodels containing either superfluous classes or anonymous classifiers or both, making the results less useful. AnnoGram4MD addresses these issues by adding special annotations to the grammar as complementary information to guide the derivation algorithm towards producing high-quality metamodels. A comparison of AnnoGram4MD with existing solutions when applied to a sample grammar reduced the number of EClassifiers by 52% and without anonymous EClassifiers in the generated metamodel.

Keywords: Grammar to metamodel · EBNF to MOF · Reverse engineering

1 Introduction

Metamodels and grammars define software languages in the modelware and grammarware technical spaces (TSs) respectively [1, 2]. Thus, "metamodel" and "grammar" occupy equivalent meta positions in the two orthogonal TSs. Researches in Model-Driven Engineering (MDE) [3, 4] have prompted the need to establish equivalences between the two TSs to facilitate the exchange of specified domain concepts between them. In fact, bridging the two TSs is considered a prerequisite to several MDE activities [5] especially in reverse engineering and/or model-driven software evolution [6] where codes are transformed to high-level models for use in the modelware TS. For example, a "semantic-preserving" grammar-metamodel translation is needed to reuse Z language-based specifications [7, 8] in the modelware TS. The three most significant deficiencies of the metamodels obtained using the existing grammar-metamodel translation techniques are:

© Springer Nature Switzerland AG 2021
S. Misra and B. Muhammad-Bello (Eds.): ICTA 2020, CCIS 1350, pp. 602–617, 2021.
https://doi.org/10.1007/978-3-030-69143-1_46

- Superfluous Eclassifiers (Classes and Enums) and EReferences.
- Presence of poorly named or anonymous Eclassifiers and EReferences.
- Missing elements due to incomplete extraction of concepts from grammars.

To address these issues, we view the challenges from two perspectives:

Difference in the Goals of Grammars and Metamodels: An EBNF grammar [9] specifies both the abstract and concrete syntaxes of a language while a metamodel defines only the former. Thus, the mechanism for deriving metamodels from grammars must be able to filter out those concrete syntax elements that will add noise to the output.

Difference in the Details Required to Specify Languages in the Two TSs: Grammars use fewer details than metamodels to define clear language elements. e.g., "Exp := Exp1 + Exp1;" is understood once the token Exp1 is defined in the grammar. However, a metmodel must define the roles of each operand wrt the operator "+". Thus, a mechanism to infer a metamodel from the grammar must have a deterministic way to augment the limited information in the grammar to derive a complete metamodel.

This paper presents the Annotated Grammar for Meta-model Derivation (Anno-Gram4MD), a language for annotating grammar specifications as directives for auto-mated derivation of "high-quality" metamodels. AnnoGram4MD defines special anno-tations which guide the metamodel derivation algorithm to filter out "noisy" concrete syntax elements and add extra information where necessary.

Section 2 lays the foundation for subsequent sections and presents a running exam-ple to illustrate the approach. AnnoGram4MD's syntax and semantics are presented in Sects. 3 and 4 respectively with applications to the running example at different stages. Section 4 discusses the related works before the conclusion in Sect. 5.

2 Background

2.1 Elements of a Software Language

We assume the reader has a basic knowledge of the elements of a software language specification; hence they are not discussed here due to space constraints. If necessary, interested readers may consults [10–12] for detailed descriptions of the elements.

2.2 Grammars

A (context-free) grammar specifies a language by defining all the keywords and con-crete symbols to render its sentences in specified patterns [12]. They are used to define programming languages, and to formalise other string-processing applications. Mathematically, a grammar, G, can be defined as in Eq. (1) [13]:

$$G = \langle V, T, P, S \rangle; V \cap T = \emptyset. \tag{1}$$

V, T and P are finite sets of variables, terminals and production rules respectively. While $t \in T$ is an irreducible element of the language, $v \in V$ describes an independent entity in the language vocabulary, which is defined recursively in terms of other variables and/or terminals by production rules. $S \in V$ is the root variable called the starting symbol; every other element (variable or terminal) must be reachable from S.

EBNF [9] uses the model in Eq. (1) to formally specify grammars. An EBNF description is an unordered list of EBNF (production) rules, each having three parts: a left-hand side (LHS), a right-hand side (RHS), and the special character ":=" (read as "is defined as") separating the two sides. The LHS, a variable $v \in V$, is defined by the RHS which contains elements of $(V \setminus \{S\}) \cup T$ in four major configurations [9]:

- *Sequence.* An ordered list of zero or more variables and/or terminals from left-to-right. For example, the RHS of the rule $v := v_1 t_1 v_2$ is a sequence.
- *Selection.* Two or more independent definitions (choices) separated by the "stroke" character (|) from which exactly one is chosen. e.g., $v := v_1 | t_1 | v_2$.
- *Option.* An element appearing zero or one time at its specified location
- *Repetition.* One or more successive appearances of an element in a rule. *Optional repetition* implies zero or more successive appearances of an element in a rule.

Listing 1 is an excerpt from syntax of the Z specification language [14], which serves as a running example in this paper. The starting variable of the excerpt is *Predicate*.

Listing 1. A sample grammar

```
Predicate:= ∀ SchemaText • Predicate |∃ SchemaText • Predicate
|∃₁ SchemaText • Predicate |Predicate1;
Predicate1:= Expression Rel Expression |SchemaRef |Predicate1 ∧ Predicate1
|Predicate1 ∨ Predicate1 |Predicate1 ⟹ Predicate1
|Predicate1 ⟺ Predicate1;
Expression:= Expression InFun Expression |Expression2;
Expression2 := SetExp |⟨Expression,..., Expression⟩ |⟦ Expression,..., Ex-
pression ⟧ |(Expression, ..., Expression);
SetExp:={Expression,..., Expression /} |{SchemaText/ • Expression/};
Rel:=equal_to|not_equal|greater_than|less_than|greater_or_equal; | less_or_equal
| member_of | contains;
InFun:=plus|minus|mult|div|mod|union|intersection|difference;
```

2.3 Metamodels

"A metamodel is a model of a modelling language" [1]. It defines the abstract syntax (set of domain concepts and their legal relationships) of a modelling language. A metamodel may be described using a subset of the Unified Modeling Language (UML)'s class diagram [15].

2.4 Annotations

Annotations are special metadata that provide additional information about program/model elements during processing without altering their semantics [16]. They are used in programming languages like Java for documentations and to associate specific properties with program artefacts. In the modelware, annotations are used in UML to aid code syntheses. They are also used sparingly in grammarware to filter undesired grammar elements or add role information to grammar elements [17]. In AnnoGram4MD, we adopt the Java convention [16] to annotate EBNF grammar rules. This convention can be described in general using EBNF as:

```
Annotation:= @annotationType[(param₁ = 'value₁',..., paramₙ = 'valueₙ')]
```

3   AnnoGram4MD

This section presents the key elements of AnnoGram4MD language specification; i.e., the syntaxes, syntax mapping, semantics domain and semantics mapping.

3.1   Abstract and Concrete Syntaxes

The metamodel in Fig. 1 shows the abstract syntax of AnnoGram4MD. The language combines major grammar concepts with annotations embedded in production rules. Therefore, the abstract syntax has two parts with one describing grammar elements as summarized in Sect. 2.2 and the other describing the proposed abstract annotations.

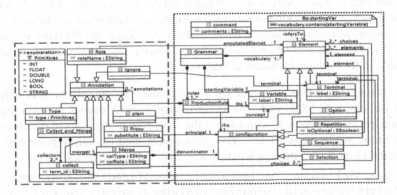

Fig. 1. Abstract syntax of AnnoGram4MD

Grammar Concepts in AnnoGram4MD. This part is contained within the dotted box on the right side of Fig. 1. A grammar (Class Grammar) has a vocabulary which is a set of named Elements. An element may be a Variable, Terminal or any of the different configurations described previously in Sect. 2.2.

AnnoGram4MD Annotations. They are specified in the dashed box on the left side of Fig. 1. A productionRule (i.e., in the grammar concepts) may contain some annotations attached to it. The various kinds of annotation in AnnoGram4MD are:

Ignore Annotation. It is used to filter tokens that serve only as concrete syntax elements in the grammar and, as such, are to be excluded from the generated metamodel. Given that a rule defines a set as "$S := \{a, b\};$", metamodelling simply sees S as comprising a and b while all other symbols on the RHS are concrete syntax elements. We represent the annotation as "@ign" preceding a token. In the rule "SetExp" in Listing 1, the curly brackets "{" and "}" in the two choices and the bullet symbol "●" are not needed in the metamodel. These can be removed by annotating the rule as follows:

```
SetExp:=@ign{[Expression,...,Expression]@ign}
|@ign{SchemaText[@ign●Expression]@ign};
```

Role Annotation. It is used to precise the role of an element in a sequence configuration. The grammar only indicates the presence of each element at certain locations in a sequence without any clue its role. This becomes more important when a particular element appears at different positions in the sequence. While the role is intuitive in the grammar, it will be difficult to differentiate them when translated to a metamodel. Therefore, this annotation adds unique role names to variables and terminals where necessary. It is denoted by @role('roleName'). We illustrate its application on one of the choices in the selection that produces the variable Expression in Listing 1:

```
Expression:=@role('lhs')Expression1 @role('op')InFun @role('rhs')Expression1;
```

In this example, the production rule describes an infix operator "InFun" with two operands each of type "Expression1". When translated into a metamodel, each element in this sequence will be a kind of structural features (e.g., attribute or reference) of class "Expression" which should have a "name" and a "type". Since only the types are explicit in the grammar, this annotation provides the "roleName" to complement the available information for a complete metamodel derivation.

Plain Annotation. It indicates variables whose productions are selections of only terminal choices; e.g., "Rel" and "InFun" in Listing 1. Such entities are expressed in metamodels as enumerations with each of the choices as a literal; more details of this will be provided in the semantics. The annotation is used by simply placing @plain before the variable. By applying it to the "Rel" and "InFun" variables, we have:

```
@plainRel:=equal|neq|greater|memberOf|geq|leq|contains;
@plainInFun:=plus|minus|mult|div|mod|union|intersection;
```

Proxy Annotation. We can see from Fig. 1 that the outer-most configuration presented by the RHS of a productionRule may embed some other configurations. e.g., embedding sequences within selections. While this enhances the compactness of the grammar, it also leads to shortage of information when translating the grammar to metamodel, thereby leading to the creation of anonymous Eclassifiers in the metamodel. To address this problem, we define a variable, "substitute", through a proxy annotation to replace the embedded configuration while itself (substitute) is defined by the "principal" configuration being replaced. It is applied by preceding a configuration to be replaced with @prox('substitute'). We apply it to the rule SetExp in Listing 1, thus:

```
SetExp:= @prox('EnumeratedSet'){[Expression,...,Expression]}
        |@prox('SetBuilder'){SchemaText[●Expression]};
```

After processing the annotations, the rule will be broken into simpler rules as follows:

```
SetExp := EnumeratedSet|SetBuilder;
EnumeratedSet := {[Expression,...,Expression]};
SetBuilder := {SchemaText[●Expression]};
```

Type Annotation. Recall from Sect. 2.2 that terminals are indivisible elements in a grammar which are usually expressed in metamodels as attributes of primitive types like integer, boolean etc. Given a grammar describing a domain, a domain expert may intuitively decipher the group to which a terminal belongs but this must be explicitly defined in a metamodel. We use the type annotations to add type information to terminals where necessary. It is denoted by @type('type') preceding a terminal. Given an hypothetical production rule, `Article := name value;` describing an article in a store where terminals "name" and "value" refer to the article's name and price respectively. While a reader can intuitively respectively assign types string and double to the terminals, a transformation algorithm must be told. We apply the annotation as:

```
Article := @type('string')name @type('double')value;
```

Collect-and-Merge Annotation. This is a combo annotation that provides directives for refactoring a particular pattern of definition by providing a simple general equivalent definition for a group of choices in a selection. It is used to tell the parser that a group of two or more choices in a selection configuration can actually be collected and merged into one choice as a common denominator in a metamodel. There are two requirements to be met by all choices in the group to merit being merged:

i. All choices in the group are described by a sequence of same elements in the same order; the only difference being the terminals at one particular position in each sequence
ii. The distinguishing terminals at the specific position must be semantically suitable to be grouped into one category in the domain being described.

For instance, given a production rule describing the mathematical expression as `Exp:=Exp1 + term|Exp1 - term|Exp1 * term|Exp1 div term;`, all the four choices in the selection are expressed as sequences of same elements in same order with the only difference being the middle terminals (+, -, * and div). Interestingly, these terminals can be semantically grouped into a category 'ArithOps', i.e., Arithmetic operators. If we generate a metamodel from this rule as is, it will give four superfluous sub-classes of Exp, each denoting the different operations. However, it is sufficient to merge the four choices into one by replacing the middle terminals with a variable 'ArithOps'. In that way, the rule can be replaced by the following two rules:

```
Exp := Exp1 ArithOps term;
ArithOps := +|-|*|div;
```

Similarly, the first three choices in the production of variable Predicate in Listing 1 typifies this situation; the differences between the three choices are the terminals ∀, ∃ and $\exists_1$ in the first position of each sequence. Semantically, the three terminals belong to the group of "Quantifier" and so can be collected and merged in a variable. Collect-and-Merge combines two annotations, @merge and @col, which are defined as:

@merge(colRole='role',colType='varName',denomintor='replacement')(choice$_1$|...|choice$_n$)

choice$_1$|...|choice$_n$ are the choices to be merged. The collect parts of the annotation, denoted by @col('term$_i$'), identify the unique terminals in their respective choices. The parameter "colType" of @merge specifies the name of the general variable to replace the unique terminals while "colRole" specifies its role name in the refactored grammar and "denominator" defines a general replacement for the merged of choices.

After processing the directives given by this group of annotations, (choice$_1$|...|choice$_n$) will be replaced by @role('role') varName replacement; in the original rule and a new rule varName:= term$_1$|...|term$_n$; is created. We illustrate this combo-annotation by applying it to the production rule of Predicate in Listing 1.

```
Predicate:= @merge(colRole='quantifier',colType ='Quantifier',
denominator='Quantifier SchemaText● Predicate')(@col('forAll')
∀SchemaText ● Predicate|@col('exists') ∃SchemaText ● Predi-
cate |@col('unique') ∃₁SchemaText ● Predicate) | Predicate1;
```

The @merge part of the annotation covers the first three choices of the selection configuration while the @col parts provide the identities to distinguish the terminals. Therefore, after processing these directives, the rule will be refactored as follows:

```
Predicate := @role('quantifier') Quantifier SchemaText● Predicate
|Predicate1;    Quantifier := forAll | exists | unique;
```

Consequently, instead of having three superfluous classes - each describing one of the merged choices - in the resulting metamodel, we will have one class with an attribute, quantifier, of type Quantifier while Quantifier itself will generate an enumeration with literals "forAll", "exists" and "unique".

3.2 Case Study

Listing 2 presents the application of appropriate annotations to the entire grammar in Listing 1. Note the applications of multiple annotations on the same elements. The semantics will be provided in the next section.

Listing 2. AnnoGram4MD Annotated Grammar

Predicate:= @*prox*('*QuantifiedPred*')@*merge*(*colRole* = '*quantifier*', *colType* = '*Quantifier*', *denominator*='*Quantifier SchemaText @ign • Predicate*')(@*col*('*forAll*')∀ SchemaText • Predicate | @*col*('*exists*') ∃ SchemaText • Predicate | @*col*('*unique*') ∃₁ SchemaText • Predicate) |Predicate1;

Predicate1:= @*prox*('*SimplePred*') @*role*('*lhs*')Expression @*role*('*op*') Rel @*role*('*rhs*')Expression |SchemaRef

| @*prox*('*ComplexPred*')@*merge*(*colRole*='*connective*', *colType* = '*LogicalConnective*', *denominator*=' @*role*('*lhs*')Predicate1 LogicalConnective @*role*('*rhs*') Predicate1)(Predicate1 @*col*('*and*') ∧ Predicate1

|@*col*('*or*') ∨ Predicate1 |Predicate1 @*col*('*implies*') ⟹ Predicate1 |Predicate1 @*col*('*equiv*') ⟺ Predicate1);

Expression:= @*prox*('*ArithExp*') @*role*('*lhs*') Expression @*role*('*op*') InFun @*role*('*rhs*')Expression |Expression2;

Expression2 := SetExp | @*prox*('*Sequence*') @*ign*⟨*/*Expression*,...,* Expression*/* @*ign*⟩ | @*prox*('*Bag*') @*ign*⟦*/* Expression*,...,* Expression *]*@*ign*⟧ | @*prox*('*Tuple*') @*ign*(Expression, ..., Expression @*ign*);

SetExp:= @*prox*('*EnumeratedSet*') @*ign*{ */*Expression*,...,* Expression *]*@*ign*} | @*prox*('*SetBuilder*') @*ign*{SchemaText*/* @*ign*• Expression*/* @*ign*};

@*plain*Rel:=equal|neq|greater|memberOf|geq|leq|contains;

@*plain*InFun:=plus|minus|mult|div|mod|union|intersection;

3.3 Semantics Domain

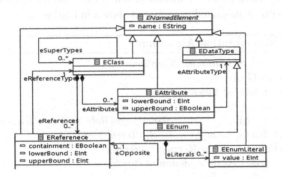

Fig. 2. Abridged Ecore Kernel

The semantics of AnnoGram4MD is based on the Ecore, an implementation of the Object Management Group (OMG)'s Essential Meta-Object Facility (EMOF) [18] for the Eclipse Modeling Framework (EMF) [19]. Ecore contains a part of the UML class that is sufficient to create abstractions of classes and class structures.

Figure 2 is an abridged Ecore kernel that defines the semantics of AnnoGram4MD. ENamedElement is the base class of all uniquely named elements in a metamodel. EClass describes an independent entity which may have some attributes (eAttributes) and/or references (eReferences) as structural features and may inherit from other Eclasses by referencing them as its superTypes. Every attribute has a type that is defined by a data type or an Enumeration. The allowable limits of occurrence of an attribute or reference in a class are defined by lowerBound and upperBound.

3.4 Semantics Mapping

The semantics mapping occurs in two phases: normalization and derivation. The derivation phase generates metamodel from the normalized annotated grammar by mapping its elements to the corresponding elements of the Ecore.

Normalization. In AnnoGram4MD, a normalized grammar is one in which:

i.   There are no concrete syntax-specific symbols except those for recognising configurations and the separators ';' that mark the ends of production rules.
ii. No selection has any other configuration embedded in any of its choices
iii. No sequence has a selection embedded within it
iv. No option or repetition has any other kind of configuration embedded in it
v.   No selection contains choices that may be merged into a compact choice

Condition (i) can be satisfied by processing all @ign annotations in the grammar, conditions (ii)–(iv) by processing all @prox annotations while condition (v) is satisfied by processing the @merge-and-@col annotations. Algorithm 1 presents the normalization algorithm to process all occurrences of the aforementioned annotations in the grammar in the normalization phase. A normalization of the annotated grammar in Listing 2 produces a normalized annotated grammar as shown in Listing 3.

Algorithm 1 Normalization Algorithm

1: *function normalize (AnnotatedGrammar G)*
2: **for all** @*ign in G* **do**
3:     delete the annotated token
4: **end for**
5: **for**   all   @*merge(colRole, colType, denominator)(choice_1 | ... |choice_n); @col_1('term'_1), ..., @col_n('term'_n) in G* **do**
6:     create *colType := term_1|term_2| ... |term_n*
7:     substitute @*role('colRole')denominator* for
        (*choice_1| ... |choice_n*) *in G*
8: **end for**
9: **for all** @*prox('substitute') element in G* **do**
10:    create *substitute := element*
11:    replace '*element*' with '*substitute*' in *G*
12: **end for**
13: **return** *normalized G*
14: *end function*

Listing 3. Normalized Annotated Grammar

```
Predicate := QuantifiedPred | Predicate1;
QuantifiedPred:= @role('quantifier') Quantifier SchemaText Predicate;
Quantifier:= forAll | exists |unique;
Predicate1 := SimplePred | SchemaRef | ComplexPred;
SimplePred := @role('lhs')Expression @role('op') Rel @role('rhs')Expression;
ComplexPred:= @role('lhs') Predicate1 @role('connective') LogicalConnec-
tive @role('rhs') Predicate1;
LogicalConnective := and | or | implies | equiv;
Expression := ArithExp | Number| Expression2;
ArithExp := @role('lhs')Expression @role('op')InFun @role('rhs')Expression;
Expression2 := SetExp| Sequence | Bag | Tuple;
Sequence:= [Expression,..., Expression];
Bag:= [Expression,..., Expression];
Tuple := [Expression,..., Expression];
SetExp := EnumeratedSet | SetBuilder;
EnumeratedSet:= [Expression,..., Expression];
SetBuilder := SchemaText [Expression];
@plainRel:=equal|neq|greater|memberOf|geq|leq|contains;
@plainInFun:=plus|minus|mult|div|mod|union|intersection;
```

Derivation. The derivation phase maps the elements of the normalized annotated grammar obtained in the previous phase to Ecore elements to generate metmodels. The derivation process follows two general rules:

i. Every lhs variable with @plain annotation translates into an EEnum such that the choices at the rhs of the production become the eLiterals of the EEnum.

ii. Every lhs variable without a @plain annotation translates into an EClass.

Table 1 provides a summary of how the rhs elements are translated to build the EClass obtained from the lhs following from these rules, henceforth; we refer to variables with and without the @plain annotation as enum variables and class variables respectively. In Table 1, 'L' represents the EClass generated from the class variable on the lhs of the production rule.

Algorithm 2 gives the details about the implementation of the rules in the table. Function *derive(Variable V, AnnotatedGrammar G)* takes two parameters; V and G (where V is a variable in G) and returns a metamodel EClass or EEnum derived from the description of V in G. In the process of building the metamodel representation of a variable, the function recursively builds the corresponding metamodel elements of all variables and terminals that define its production rule. The result obtained by processing the normalized grammar in Listing 1.3 with the derivation algorithm is shown in Fig. 3(a). The R@role and R@type clauses in the derive function refer to the information attached to R by the @role and @type annotations respectively.

Table 1. Mapping table for productions of class variables *Assume L to be the EClass generated for variables

Configuration	Element	Annotation	Ecore Element
Sequence	class variable C	@role("rolename")	A reference of L with name "rolename", cardinality '1..1' and type C. If no @role annotation, reference name same as C in lowercase
	enum variable E	@role("rolename")	An attribute of L with name "rolename", cardinality '1..1' and type E. If no @role annotation, reference name as L in lowercase
	terminal T	@role("rolename") @type("typename")	An attribute of L with name "rolename", cardinality '1..1' and type @type("typename"). If no @role annotation, reference name as T in lowercase
Selection	$C_1|C_2|...|C_n$	N/A	EClasses $C_1, C_2,..., C_n$ are subclasses of L
Option	Same as in Sequence but with cardinality '0..1'		
Repetition	Same as in Sequence but with cardinality '1..*'		
Optional repetition	Same as in Sequence but with cardinality '0..*'		

There are other smaller functions called within the function derive() which we cannot provide their detailed definitions due to space constraint. We will however provide brief descriptions. newClass(V) returns an EClass named 'V' if already created, it creates and returns a new class named 'V' if otherwise. newEnum(V) is similar to newClass(V) except that it returns an EEnum instead. addAttribute(C, word, T, mult) adds an attribute 'word' of type 'T' with cardinality 'mult' to EClass 'C'. addLiteral (E, word) adds an eLiteral named 'word' to an EEnum 'E'. connectSubClass(C1, C2) creates an inheritance relationship between classes C1 and C2 with the former as the superType of the later. Finally, compose(C1, C2, role, mult) creates a composition association named 'role' with cardinality 'mult' between classes 'C1' and 'C2' with the former as the container. Algorithm 3 describes the main transformation function that cascades the normalization and derivation processes. It takes a raw annotated grammar and its starting variable as input to generate an equivalent metamodel.

Algorithm 2 Derivation Algorithm

```
 1: function derive (Var V, AnnotatedGrammar G)
 2: V := R ← getRule(V, G) {get the definition of V in G}
 3: if R is a selection (R = R₁|R₂|...|Rₙ) then
 4:    if V has @plain annotation then
 5:       M ← newEnum(V) {create empty enum V}
 6:       for all Rᵢ ∈ R₁, R₂, ..., Rₙ do
 7:          addLiteral(M, Rᵢ)
 8:       end for
 9:    else {i.e., R₁, ..., Rₙ are all variables}
10:       M ← newClass(V) {create empty class V.}
11:       for all Rᵢ ∈ R₁, R₂,..., Rₙ do
12:          connectSubClass(M, derive(Rᵢ))
13:       end for
14:    end if
15:    return M
16: else
17:    M ← newClass(V) {create empty class named V}
18:    if R is a sequence (R = R₁, R₂,..., Rₙ) then
19:       for all Rᵢ ∈ R₁, R₂,..., Rₙ do
20:          if Rᵢ is a repetition (Rᵢ = (R')+) then
21:             if R' is a terminal then
22:                addAttribute(M, R', R'@type,' mult')
23:             else if R' is an enum variable then
24:                addAttribute(M, Rᵢ@role, R'.' mult')
25:             else { i.e., R' is a class variable}
26:                compose(M, derive(R', G), Rᵢ@role,' mult')
27:             end if
28:          else if Rᵢ is an optional repetition (Rᵢ = (R')*) then
29:             if R' is a terminal then
30:                addAttribute(M, R', R'@type,' optMult')
31:             else if R' is an enum variable then
32:                addAttribute(M, Rᵢ@role, R',' optMult')
33:             else { i.e., R' is a class variable}
34:                compose(M, derive(R', G), Rᵢ@role, 'optMult')
35:             end if
36:          else if Rᵢ is an option (Rᵢ = (R')?) then
37:             if R' is a terminal then
38:                addAttribute(M, R', R'@type,' opt')
39:             else if R' is an enum variable then
40:                addAttribute(M, Rᵢ@role, R',' opt')
41:             else { i.e., R' is a class variable}
42:                compose(M, derive(R', G), Rᵢ@role,' opt')
43:             end if
44:             else
45:                if R' is a terminal then
46:                   addAttribute(M, R', R'@type,' single')
47:                else if R' is an enum variable then
48:                   addAttribute(M, Rᵢ@role, R'.' single')
49:                else {i.e., R' is a class variable}
50:                   compose(M, derive(R', G), Rᵢ@role,' single')
51:                end if
52:          end if
53:       end for
54:    else if R is a repetition (R = (R')+) then
55:       if R' is a terminal then
56:          addAttribute(M, R', R'@type,' mult')
57:       else if R' is an enum variable then
58:          addAttribute(M, R'@role, R',' mult')
59:       else {i.e., R' is a class variable}
60:          compose(M, derive(R', G), R'@role,' mult')
61:       end if
62:    else if R is an optional repetition (R = (R')*) then
63:       if R' is a terminal then
64:          addAttribute(M, R', R'@type,' optMult')
65:       else if R' is an enum variable then
66:          addAttribute(M, R'@role, R',' optMult')
67:       else { i.e., R' is a class variable}
68:          compose(M, derive(R', G), R'@role,' optMult')
69:       end if
70:    else if R is an option (R = (R')?) then
71:       if R' is a terminal then
72:          addAttribute(M, R', R'@type,' opt')
73:       else if R' is an enum variable then
74:          addAttribute(M, R'@role, R',' opt')
75:       else {i.e., R' is a class variable}
76:          compose(M, derive(R', G), R'@role,' opt')
77:       end if
78:    else if R is a terminal then
79:       addAttribute(M, R, R@type,' single')
80:    else
81:       Invalid grammar
82:    end if
83:    return M
84: end if
85: endfunction
```

Algorithm 3 Main Transformation Algorithm

```
1: function transform (Var S AnnotatedGrammar G) {S is the starting variale of G}
2: Gₙ ← normalize(G)
3: Metamodel_G ← derive(S, Gₙ)
4: return Metamodel_G
5: endfunction
```

4   Related Works

Alanen and Porres [20] made one of the earliest proposals that gave impetus to further studies of this subject. The idea is to map each token in a sequence configuration to ordered unidirectional composite properties (references and attributes). Properties generated for successive tokens in a sequence are numbered in increasing alphabetical orders to document their order of occurrences in the source grammar. The rules for generating the cardinalities of such properties are similar to that used in our approach. For every terminal symbol (including the concrete syntax-specific elements), an enumeration is created having the string value of the terminal as its only literal, then an attribute is added to the class with this enumeration as its type. When a selection configuration is encountered, a class is generated with an automatically generated nomenclature and it is sub classed by the classes generated for all choices in the selection. Similar automatically-named classes are generated for repetitions and options which are then connected to the corresponding classes under them according to the rule for sequence configuration. An attempt to use this approach has shown that it will produce a metamodel that is very difficult to (re)use. There are issues such superfluous classes, properties and enumeration. Another aspect that needs improvement in this approach is the area of nomenclature of metamodel elements which is also acknowledged by the authors; the use of alphabets in ascending order as names of metamodel elements will not help the user to understand the domain being modeled. Using this approach, the metamodel derived from the grammar in Listing 1. is shown in Fig. 3(b). When compared with the metamodel generated by AnnoGram4MD in Fig. 3(a), we observe that the latter generated a total of 20 classes and enums compared to 42 in the latter; that is about 52.4% reduction in the size of the output. Moreover, out of the 42 classifiers in Fig. 3(b), only 9 have comprehensible names while others bear some anonymously generated identities. This is also compounded by the generated references, which all have anonymous identities.

AnnoGramm4MD proffers solutions to these drawbacks as shown in the Fig. 3(a) with the metamodel elements bearing names extracted from the source grammar and the embedded annotations. Due to space constraint, we cannot do side-by-side comparisons of the metamodel generated by AnnoGramm4MD and every other work in the literature; nevertheless, we present as much of such comparisons as possible in the rest of this section.

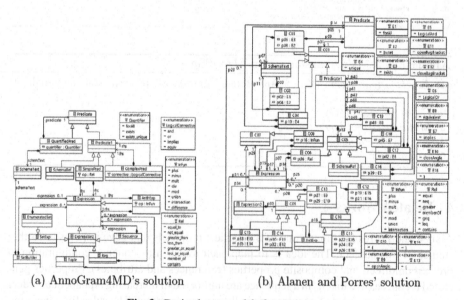

(a) AnnoGram4MD's solution   (b) Alanen and Porres' solution

Fig. 3. Derived metamodels from grammars

Wimmer and Kramler [21] have also proposed solutions to some of the drawbacks of [20]. They proposed a three-stage process to generate high-quality MOF-based meta-models from EBNF grammars. The first stage, parsing stage, generates what is referred to as a raw metamodel from a given EBNF grammar. It generates a stereotyped class for every kind of configuration encountered (e.g., sequence, repetition) that has the appropriate references to the metamodel elements generated from the grammar tokens they encapsulate.

Having recognized the possibility of the raw metamodel having exaggerated number of classes, the second - optimization- stage removes undesired elements while documenting the changes made in a "change model". The result obtained from the second stage is called the "condensed metamodel".

The third - customization - stage adds annotations to the condensed metamodel to provide additional semantics that are not expressed in the original EBNF grammar. From the annotated condensed metamodel, a "customized" metamodel is automatically generated which is considered to be of high quality.

While this is an interesting approach especially considering the fact that it uses the native annotation techniques in the target MOF, we are of the opinion that unless a strict measure is taken, the user may have to redo the annotation in the event that the grammar (source) changes and existing annotations are overwritten during regeneration. Moreover, the user will most likely have to redo the optimization and customization processes as many times as changes are made in the grammar. AnnoGram4MD add annotations to the grammar itself and automates all other processes to avoid the possible situations of repeated work at the different stages when some changes are made in the grammar since they will all be automated. Another advantage of doing the annotation at the source is that it allows for building the metamodel directly from the knowledge of grammar; even someone with only the knowledge of grammars can play with the annotations and obtain a usable metamodel of the domain.

A more recent approach by Kunert [17] proposed another interesting multistage solution. The author is also of the opinion that it will be more convenient to add abstract concepts directly to the grammar as the user will have only one source file to contend with; an opinion that arguably gives more credence to the approach proposed in the current paper. Kunert [17] however did not propose a complete solution to this hypothetical problem. Though the paper also uses annotations in the grammar, its use is limited to identifying grammar specific concrete syntax elements that are not required in a metmodel; it used a special character '!' to annotate concrete syntax elements such as delimiters and identifiers in the grammar to prevent them from being transferred to the generated metamodel. The annotated grammar is then fed into a parent compiler that produces what is called the "simple metamodel" which is considered to be of low quality. The simple metamodel is processed further in a second stage by removing unwanted classes and providing additional annotations to provide information such as alternative class names to produce a "good metamodel". The paper identifies the need for annotating only grammars and automating all other processes, though it did not provide a complete solution to the problem. It, however, provides the motivation for further contributions such as AnnoGram4MD.

5   Conclusions

We have presented the AnnoGram4MD, a language that formally blends java-like annotations with grammar concepts to facilitate the addition of complementary information to EBNF-based grammars for automated synthesis of equivalent domain metamodel of high quality. This has become necessary particularly to facilitate the reuse of grammar-based formal specification languages in the MDE environments. This paper documents the syntax and semantics of the language as well as a case study to illustrate its usability in a step-by-step application of the different techniques. AnnoGram4MD offers the means to underscore grammar elements that are not desired in metamodels as well as add domain-specific information not captured in the grammar concepts but required to build useful metamodels while the metamodel derivation process can be completely automated.

It is however important to state here that our current solution does not directly provide support for adding information that could be used to derive constraints for static semantics as is sometimes required to complement a metamodel. But it supports the derivation of usable Ecore-based metamodels. Moreover, unlike most of the existing solutions, there is currently no support for bidirectional transformation between grammars and metamodel though our grammar to metamodel track claims some important advantages compared to many other proposals. We believe the documentation provided in this paper can serve as guide towards the implementation of supporting tools for the language.

References

1. Favre, J.-M.: Foundations of meta-pyramids: Languages vs. metamodels–episode ii: Story of thotus the baboon1. In: Dagstuhl Seminar Proceedings. Schloss Dagstuhl-Leibniz-Zentrum für Informatik (2005)
2. Favre, J.-M.: Towards a basic theory to model model driven engineering. In: 3rd Workshop in Software Model Engineering (2004)
3. Schmidt, D.C.: Model-driven engineering. Comput. IEEE Comput. Soc. **39**(2), 25 (2006)
4. Brambilla, M., Cabot, J., Wimmer, M.: Model-driven software engineering in practice. Synth. Lect. Softw. Eng. **3**(1), 1–207 (2017)
5. Bergmayr, A., Wimmer, M.: Generating metamodels from grammars by chaining translational and by-example techniques. In: 1st International Workshop on Model-driven Engineering By Example (2013)
6. Cánovas Izquierdo, J.L., García Molina, J.: Extracting models from source code in software modernization. Softw. Syst. Model. **13**(2), 713–734 (2012). https://doi.org/10.1007/s10270-012-0270-z
7. Smith, G., The Object-Z Specification Language, vol. 1. Springer, Berlin (2012)
8. Spivey, J.M., Abrial, J.: The Z notation. Prentice Hall, Hemel Hempstead (1992)
9. Feynman, R.: EBNF: a notation to describe syntax. Режим доступа, 1–19 (2016). http://www.ics.uci.edu/pattis/misc/ebnf2.pdf
10. Kolovos, D.S., et al.: Bridging the epsilon wizard language and the eclipse graphical modeling framework. In: Modeling Symposium, Eclipse Summit Europe, Ludwigsburg, Germany (2007)
11. Kleppe, A.: A language description is more than a metamodel. In: 4th International Workshop on Software Language Engineering (2007). http://www.megaplanet.org

12. Kleppe, A.: Software Language Engineering: creating Domain-specific Languages using Metamodels. Pearson Education, Prentice Hall (2008)
13. Hopcroft, J.E., Motwani, R., Ullman, J.D.: Introduction to automata theory, languages, and computation. ACM Sigact News **32**(1), 60–65 (2001)
14. Spivey, J.M.: Understanding Z: A Specification Language and its Formal Semantics, vol. 3. Cambridge University Press, Cambridge (1988)
15. Booch, G.: The Unified Modeling Language User Guide. Pearson Education, Prentice Hall (2005)
16. Cazzola, W., Vacchi, E.: @ Java: Bringing a richer annotation model to Java. Comput. Lang. Syst. Structures **40**(1), 2–18 (2014)
17. Kunert, A.: Semi-automatic generation of metamodels and models from grammars and programs. Electron. Notes Theor. Comput. Sci. **211**, 111–119 (2008)
18. OMG: OMG Meta Object Facility (MOF) Core Specification. Object Management Group (2019)
19. Steinberg, D., et al.: EMF: Eclipse Modeling Framework. Pearson Education, Prentice Hall (2008)
20. Alanen, M., Porres, I.: A Relation Between Context-Free Grammars and Meta Object Facility Metamodels (2003)
21. Wimmer, M., Kramler, G.: Bridging grammarware and modelware. In: International Conference on Model Driven Engineering Languages and Systems. Springer (2005)

Design and Implementation of an IoT Based Baggage Tracking System

Olamilekan Shobayo, Ayobami Olajube$^{(\boxtimes)}$, Obina Okoyeigbo, and Jesse Ogbonna

Covenant University, KM 10, Idiroko Road, Ota, Ogun State, Nigeria
ayobami.olajube@covenantuniversity.edu.ng

Abstract. Missing pieces of baggage, loss of luggage, and damage to customers' belongings are the common flaws faced in the aviation industry around the world. Passengers in other transportation sectors are also at risk of luggage theft as they transit from location to another. Therefore, a system needs to be designed and developed to combat these problems. The system has a GSM/GPS module that is integrated into the tracking system to keep it actively connected at all times. Also, an Arduino microcontroller is added to the system for information processing. The system provides the location of luggage on a map for real-time tracking and, that can be achieved when the GPS module retrieves the location coordinates of the bag and sends it to the microcontroller for processing. Afterward, the processed information is sent as an SMS through the GSM module, which provides a connection between the bag and the passenger using the GSM communication system. This IoT based device gives passengers the advantage of seeing the current location of their baggage from anywhere in the world. And, if implemented, this system will reduce the stress experienced by both passengers and the aviation industry in locating missing, misled, or stolen suitcases.

Keywords: Baggage tracking · IoT · Arduino · Map · GPS module

1 Introduction

Internet of Things (IoT) is the networking of physical objects that integrate electronics embedded in their structure to communicate and detect interactions between themselves or concerning the external environment. It is a network of objects such as structures, cars, etc. equipped with sensors, electronics, and other things related to the system that help these objects gather and exchange information. IoT allows objects to be sensed and managed from a remote access point, maximizing financial benefit, precision, and performance. This involves devices like smart homes, car tracking, health management [1], monitoring and regulating home appliances, and, eventually, smart cities as IoT is paired with sensors. Everything is distinctive and recognizable, and easily accessible when extended by the internet and computer infrastructure [2]. IoT-based technology will provide robust service quality in the future, practically changing our daily lives and adding to them. In this project work, a device that is smart and connected using IoT based technology is developed for tracking missing bags. This will help resolve the issue of cases involving luggage and assets mishandling, theft, or loss in the travel sector.

© Springer Nature Switzerland AG 2021
S. Misra and B. Muhammad-Bello (Eds.): ICTA 2020, CCIS 1350, pp. 618–631, 2021.
https://doi.org/10.1007/978-3-030-69143-1_47

Luggage loss can occur with anyone irrespective of circumstances and conditions. Baggage misplaced, mislaid baggage, and damage to a customer's belongings are the most common shortcomings encountered in the aviation industry. With more than 2 billion passengers registered annually, the airline industry is the most effective means of international transport and inter-state transport in most countries around the world. More than 31 million passengers and 34 million bags are impacted each year by baggage mishandling, which has resulted in a loss of up to $3.3 billion in the airline industry. A passenger is also losing about 1.7 days of his holiday or business trip waiting for the mishandled bag [3]. Some of the lost luggage is identified after several hours of monitoring and tracking, while other items are confirmed to be permanently lost. Huge resources are drawn upon in airports and airlines to trace and return the lost luggage to passengers at a high price [4]. This is a constant source of stress for passengers, as well as waiting for the baggage claims to wonder if their bag in the aircraft might be very frustrating [5]. Passenger satisfaction is the most crucial factor for any airport in its facilities. As stated by the airport authorities, the time is taken to gain access to their baggage is typically not a satisfactory factor for passengers [6]. This delay could emanate from a number of reasons such as lack of facilities and equipment, insufficient personnel, sluggish operations and procedures, and information flow delay [7]. This also affects the passengers waiting for the conveyor system to pick their luggage. Although individuals and some organizations have taken many approaches to provide luggage monitoring, a completely homogeneous tracking system is far from being implemented.

Luggage and bags with relevant documents or valuable objects such as keys, money, credit cards, probably medication, cell phones, etc. can be misplaced or stolen, such that people can lose these essential things. In general, people are frequently robbed in public areas, such as train stations, bus stands, and other public and private areas. People often seem to forget their bags and luggage, which may have essential and vital items inside. Therefore, in case of loss and robbery, it is very important to track the bags down [8].

To confront this issue, a tracking device that is based on IoT is developed in this project, which can be embedded in travel bags in order to aid passengers using the travel sector or victims of luggage theft or loss to locate their luggage with the possibility of real-time monitoring on a map. This article is divides into sections starting with the introduction. Section 2 gives the brief background of the baggage tracking technologies; Sect. 3 gives a critical literature review of the IoT based baggage tracking systems with the comprising technologies such as the RFID, IoT, the related works, and the problem we want to solve, Sect. 4 provides the system description, the components and how the device works, Sect. 5 describes the materials and the methodology, Sect. 6 shows the testing of the device and the results obtained while the last part gives the conclusion, acknowledgment, and the references.

2 Background

Even though there has been a reduced rate of luggage mishandling reported in Airports over the years, millions of passengers are still affected. It is vital for people to know the location of their luggage at all times so that when cases of mishandling, theft, or loss occur, passengers can have some control over the situation. Anyone can be a victim. Intelligent baggage or smart bag systems have been implemented using the capacity of the raspberry pi processor to retrieve data from tracked objects as implemented in [9] for plate number identification, to build smart luggage carrying robot according to [10]. The authors in [11] developed an intelligent school bag that utilizes the RFID, Raspberry Pi, and the GPS to maintain and modify the lists of books according to the daily school activities.

Other authors in [12] also presented a graphical user interface (GUI) model to control different smart devices automated by Bluetooth in conjunction with the IoT. IoT has the capacity to connect vast devices all over the world to a central database using sensors. Data are collated from these databases to achieve a special objective or make a vital decision in various forms of intelligent systems.

3 Literature Review

Present technological advancements like the Internet of Things (IoT) have paved the way for fully functioning smart cities worldwide. However, this will require the simultaneous enhancement of infrastructure and facilities in many sectors, such as industries, education, and governments. Communication between the real world and the virtual world is an essential part of the so-called Internet of Things (IoT) smart systems. The sample data collected is transformed into insightful data to be used for real data. This increases the exchangeable data usage between different sectors [13, 14]. There are, however, a few categories that lack the use of IoT. One such area is the aviation industry.

Airport baggage management is a crucial part of the aviation industry. However, many bags are mishandled every year for many reasons, which costs the aviation industry a lot of money and causes annoyance and dissatisfaction for the passenger. Common baggage malfunctions are: left behind at the airport of origin, missed connecting flight, loss of luggage, a wrong destination for the package, etc. A bag must go through several measures when moving to the final destination from the airport of origin. These measures include check-in, inspection, sorting, paying, airport transit switch, arrival, etc. Mismanagement at either of these stages may be the explanation for the mishandling of the container. Diverse innovations such as IoT have been introduced to reduce baggage mismanagement in the aviation sector, and it is predicted to reduce by 10% when fully implemented in the industry [15].

3.1 Internet of Things (IoT)

The Internet of Things (IoT) is known to offer connectivity to everything at any time and in any location. We are moving into a world with the advent of technology, where all and everyone will be connected [16]. The IoT is known to be a potential Internet evaluation, which carries out machine-to-machine (M2M) learning [17]. The fundamental concept of IoT is to enable safe and free communication between devices and applications [18] and to share data among real-world devices. It can be viewed as a global network that allows for connectivity and interaction between human-to-human, human-to-things, and things-to-things. This is done by providing a unique identifier for each object [19]. Like any other system, the Internet of Things needs a few required components to allow communication between devices and objects. It includes gadgets, sensor devices, communication networks, computer units, and processing units that can be set up on the cloud. Decision-making and action invoking systems are also required [20]. IoT has found application in all facets of human existence enabling communication between humans and smart devices. Some of these applications are in the health sector [1], the agricultural sector for the smart irrigation systems [21], object tracking systems [22], road navigation systems [23], and the vehicle tracking and identification systems [9, 24].

3.2 Radio-Frequency Identification (RFID)

RFID is listed among the most successful fields for research in recent years and has been increasingly attracted attention. The three primary components of an RFID device include a Transponder/Tag, Editor, and Backend Function. The tag is made up of an antenna, and a data storage microchip where details such as price, period, date, manufacture, and composition of the product can also be stored. For identifying the object, a unique serial number is allocated. The most significant purpose of RFID technology is for all physical objects to join the virtual environment formed by an RFID networked system. The RFID tags can also be identified as a unique unit in the Internet of Things infrastructure [25]. A great number of researchers implemented the RFID technology in their methodologies in an attempt to resolve the issue of baggage mishandling, loss, or theft. In [26], the authors proposed a system that involves an interactive digital bracelet that is worn around the passenger's arm to support the RFID in a baggage-tracking device. In this method, the RFID signal is processed, and text messages are sent to the passenger bracelet when the baggage moves from station to station. A button is installed in the bracelet from which the passenger may use to send an emergency message. The authors in [27] proposed a smart bag designed to deliver information on the bag location in real-time. The proposed system will consist of a RASPBERRY PI, which collects the location information through different modules and forwards the information to the surveillance station, where it stores the data in the database and displays the information in a user-friendly graphical user interface (GUI).

3.3 Related Studies on IoT Based Baggage Tracking System

Sarkar et al. (2017) designed a radio-frequency identification (RFID) based smart bag tracking system using microcontrollers. This device automates the process of luggage tracking by attaching the RFID tag containing the owners' information to the luggage with an appropriate feedback mechanism to ascertain if the parcel has reached its destination or not. However, the system saves time and cost, but the lack of IoT in the setup that allows for device-to-device communication signifies the need for improvement [28]. Singh (2016) used RFID tags containing the owners' details to identify and track luggage to prevent loss or theft. The product improved security and efficiency over the contemporary barcode-based enabled over the UHF range. The weakness of this product was its inability to support mobile devices due to the lack of IoT in the setup [4]. Other RFID-based tracking systems have been identified in [29–32]. In the aforementioned tracking systems, there were security concerns that could be figured out from the tags, and there was also an issue of tracking during transit due to a limited range.

The limitations of the above RFID based tracking systems have been addressed over the years by the combination of the RFID technology with IoT, according to [33, 34]. The IoT based tracking technologies saved cost, improved efficiency, enables flexibility, support mobile device to device communications, and human-to-device communication.

3.4 The Problem

The problem developed with the loss or mishandling of luggage at any customer baggage-oriented place is a huge matter of consent. Every year, 1% of the luggage is lost in Airline travel itself, which is a huge stat in the aviation industry. Passengers wondering whether their bags got in the right place at the right time after releasing their luggage for processing and loading at any customer baggage-oriented site can be very frustrating. Many bags are mishandled every year for many reasons, which costs the aviation industry a lot of money and causes annoyance and dissatisfaction for the passenger. Common baggage malfunctions are: left behind at the airport of origin, missed connecting flight, loss of luggage, a wrong destination for the package, etc. This project intends to help passengers monitor their luggage at all times to prevent such from happening and reduce further baggage mishandling or loss faced by the travel sector in the coming years. This project also addresses baggage theft and loss, which occur in other travel sectors.

4 System Description

The system is built using GSM/GPS module, which activates after the system finishes initializing; the GSM module sends a message to the end-user requesting whether to retrieve the luggage location. The GPS module retrieves the luggage location when the end-user sends the right command, which will be discussed later on. It then sends the information, which is the luggage location, to the Arduino Nano microcontroller for processing. After processing the information, the microcontroller sends the information to the GSM module, which receives it and sends it to the end-user via SMS (Short Message Service). The end-user can use the information displayed on the device, preferably a mobile phone, to find the location of the luggage on Google Maps or other mapping APIs preferred by the end-user. This process is shown in Fig. 1 below;

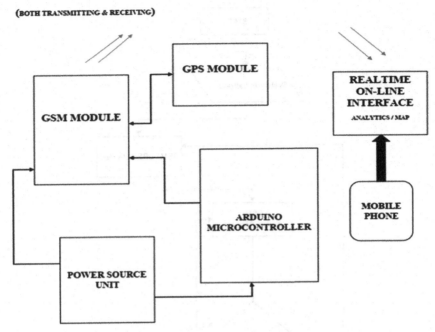

Fig. 1. Proposed system block diagram.

5 Materials and Methods

The system consists of four major components working together to achieve the intended function. The major components include an Arduino Nano Microcontroller, A GSM SIM900 Module, A DC Power Supply Unit, and a GPS Module. Figure 2 below shows the block diagram of the methodological flow diagram of the system.

5.1 Circuit Design and Simulation

Luggage refers to bags that hold personal belongings of passengers while in transit. This signifies the portability and the ease of conveyance of these pieces of luggage. Incorporating an AC power supply into the bag will cause a lot of inconveniences for the passenger. For example, the system will not function unless it is plugged into an AC supply outlet. Also, it will be substantial, thereby causing additional weights that the passenger may not welcome. Hence, during circuitry designing of the system, which was carried out using proteus software, a 36 V lithium-ion battery, which acts as a DC supply unit, was used to power the system. However, an Arduino Nano Microcontroller only needs as little as 5 V to perform its intended function. Therefore, to regulate the

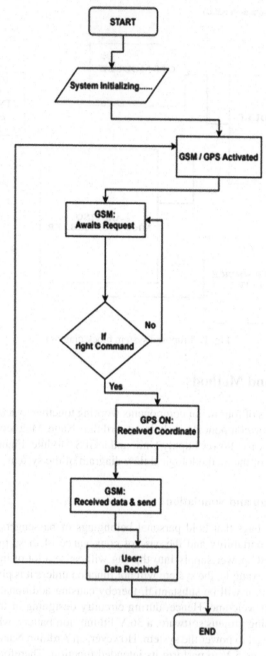

Fig. 2. Methodological flow chart.

voltage generated from the battery to 5 V, a 7805 5 V voltage regulator was added to the circuit. To power, the Arduino Nano microcontroller, the input pin of the microcontroller is connected to the voltage output of the regulator, where an input voltage of 5 V is supplied to the system. The GSM module requires a SIM card that must be inserted to establish an active connection between the GSM communication system. The TXD pin of the SIM900D GSM module, which is used for transmitting, is connected to the Digital Pin 2 of the microcontroller. The pin for receiving RXD is connected to digital pin 3 of the microcontroller. The GPS module TX pin is connected to pin 4 of the microcontroller as shown above to complete the circuit. The schematics diagram for the system is shown below (Fig. 3):

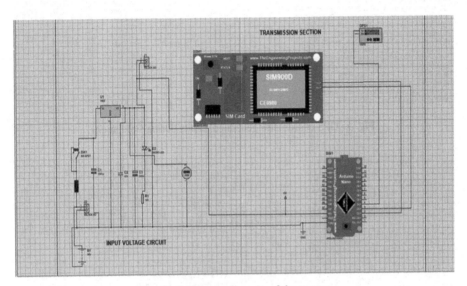

Fig. 3. Schematic diagram of the system

After completing the circuit design using Proteus 8 software, simulations were carried out to ensure proper circuit connection and functionality of the system. During the simulation, the voltmeter in the circuit showed a reading of 5 V, which verifies the voltage regulation from 36 V to 5 V. The GPS module activates, showing the location coordinates on the simulation logs, as shown below. Furthermore, A virtual map that uses Google API displays the location of the luggage on a map as the project simulation continues, as shown in Fig. 4 below (Fig. 5).

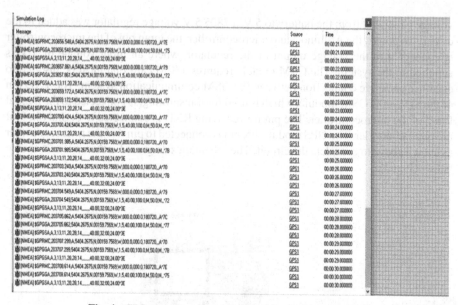

Fig. 4. GPS coordinates generated results during simulations

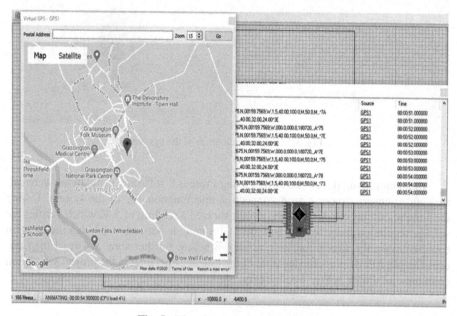

Fig. 5. Virtual map during simulations

6 Testing and Results

The system testing was carried out after construction to ensure its functionality and accuracy. The GSM/GPS module in the system was initialized by the Arduino microcontroller when the system was switched on (Fig. 6).

Fig. 6. Welcome screen before initialization during system testing

This was done to ensure the components were functioning as intended before proceeding to the next step. After initialization, the system remained on standby for the next instruction, which involved sending an SMS to the phone number registered to the GSM module in the device (Fig. 7).

Fig. 7. GSM module during testing stage

When the Arduino receives the SMS from GSM module, it prompts the GPS module to retrieve the luggage coordinates as instructed. These coordinates were sent back to the Arduino, which processes the information and proceeds to generate an SMS containing a google map link of bag's location. Through the GSM module, the SMS was sent back to the device, as shown in the diagram below. Furthermore, the google map application is opened when the link was clicked. It showed the current location of the bag as the blue dot indicates the current location of the bag owner while the red pin indicates the current location of the bag (Fig. 8 and Fig. 9).

Fig. 8. SMS showing a link that directs the user to google map application software to view the location on a map.

Fig. 9. User's location and bag's location shown on google map application software

7 Conclusion

There has been an alarming rate of luggage location confusion, misplacement, misman-agement, delay, and theft at the airports of most developing economies like Nigeria before planes are boarded by passengers or on arrival. This often leads to customer dis-satisfaction and frustration. Hence, the IoT based luggage tracking device will help to completely eradicate these hitches and provide a first view of the luggage coordinate and identification. It will effectively combat luggage mishandling, misplacement, and theft, thereby conserving time and forestalling stress experienced by travelers. The sys-tem utilizes the GSM communication system using the GSM module, which keeps the luggage's location on the map at all times. It can be accessed using a smartphone from anywhere in the world. The device has been appropriately tested and can be installed at strategic points of the airport close to scanning machines and load conveyors to ensure efficient luggage tracking on arrival or departure.

Acknowledgment. The authors gratefully adore covenant university for sponsoring this research article.

References

1. Hassanalieragh, M., et al.: Health monitoring and management using internet of things (IoT) sensing with cloud-based processing: opportunities and challenges. In: IEEE International Conference on Services Computing (2015)
2. Shreya, R., Kilari, K., Saran, A., Kiranmayee, T.S., Nadu, T.: IoT based airport baggage tracing system. J. Netw. Commun. Emerg. Technol. **8**(4), 382–385 (2018)
3. Wong, E.Y.C., Wong, W.H.: The development of reusable luggage tag with internet of things for mobile tracking and environmental. MDPI Sustain. **9**(58), 1–12 (2017)
4. Singh, A., Meshram, S., Gujar, T., Wankhede, P.R.: Baggage tracing and handling system using RFID and IoT for airports. In: International Conference on Computational Analysis and Security Trends (CAST), pp. 466–470 (2017)
5. Aarthi, S., Jaiswal, A., Singh, H.V., Velumani, N.: Architectural optimization of luggage tracking system. Int. Res. J. Eng. Technol. (IRJET) (2018)
6. Ghazal, M., Ali, S., Haneefa, F., Sweleh, A.: Towards smart wearable real-time airport lug-gage tracking. In: IEEE International Conference Industrial Informatics and Computational Science, (CIICS) (2016)
7. Senthilkumar, S., Jain, M.: Luggage tracking system using IoT. Int. J. Pure Appl. Math. **117**(17), 49–55 (2017)
8. Ye-Won, L., Yong-Lak, C.: Proposal for air- baggage tracking system based on IoT. In: Proceedings of 9th International Conference on Future Generation Communication and Networking, FGCN 2015, 2020, pp. 25–28 (2016)
9. Shobayo, O., Olajube, A., Ohere, N., Odusami, M., Okoyeigbo, O.: Development of smart plate number recognition system for fast cars with web application. Hindawi J. Appl. Comput. Intell. Soft Comput. (2020)
10. Dipali, K., Pallavi, K., Tabbasum, M., Hameed, P.: Smart luggage carrying robot using raspberry Pi. Int. Res. J. Eng. Technol. (IRJET) 4(4), 2019
11. Anand, A.P., et al.: Smart school bag. Int. J. Eng. Sci. Comput. (IJESC), **6**(5) (2016)

12. Hernandez, J., Daza, K., Florez, H., Misra, S.: Dynamic interface and access model by dead token for IoT systems. In: Florez, H., Leon, M., Diaz-Nafria, J.M., Belli, S. (eds.) ICAI 2019. CCIS, vol. 1051, pp. 485–498. Springer, Cham (2019). https://doi.org/10.1007/978-3-030-32475-9_35

13. Jimenez, C.E., Solanas, A., Falcone, F.: E-government interoperability: linking open and smart government. Computer **47**(10), 22–24 (2014)

14. Scholl, H., AlAwadhi, S.: Pooling and leveraging scarce resources: the smart city government alliance. In: Proceedings of 48th Hawaii International Conference of Systems Science, (HICSS) 2015, pp. 2355–2365 (2015)

15. Shuaibu, S.S., Salleh, M.A., Shehu, A.Y.: The impact of the Boko Haram insurgency on Nigerian national security. Int. J. Acad. Res. Bus. Soc. Sci. **5**(6), 254–266 (2015)

16. Zheng, J., Simplot-Ryl, D., Bisdikian, C., Mouftah, H.: The Internet of Things. IEEE Commun. Mag. **49**(11), 30–31 (2011)

17. Huang, Y., Li, G.: Descriptive model for Internet of Things. In: IEEE International Conference Intelligent Control Information Proceedings (ICICIP) 2010 (2010)

18. Fan, T., Chen, Y.: A scheme of data management in the Internet of Things. In: 2010 2nd IEEE International Conference on Network Infrastructure and Digital Content (2010)

19. Aggarwal, R., Lal Das, M.: RFID security in the context of Internet of Things. In: Proceedings of Ist International Conference on Security of Internet of Things, Kerala, pp. 51–56 (2012)

20. Yu, Y., Wang, J., Zhou, G.: The exploration in the education of professionals in applied internet of things Engineering. In: 4th International Conference on Distance Learning and Education, (ICDLE) (2010)

21. Adenugba, F., Misra, S., Maskeliūnas, R., Damaševičius, R., Kazanavičius, E.: Smart irrigation system for environmental sustainability in Africa: an Internet of Everything (IoE) approach. Math. Biosci. Eng. **16**(5), 5490–5503 (2019)

22. Zhang, H., Zhang, K., Zhang, L., Yang, Y., Kang, Q., Sun, D.: Object tracking for a smart city using IoT and edge computing. MDPI Sensors **19**(1987), 1–23 (2019)

23. Samuel, V., Misra, S., Nicholas, O.: Internet of Things (IoTs) and its application to road navigation and usage problem. In: Asia-Pacific World Congress on Computer Science and Engineering APWC CSE 2014 (2014)

24. Alrifale, M.F., Harum, N., Othman, M.F.I., Roslan, I., Shyaa, M.A.: Vehicle detection and tracking system IoT based: a review. Int. Res. J. Eng. Technol. (IRJET) **5**(8), 1237–1241 (2018)

25. Ozelkan, E.C., Sireli, Y., Munoz, M.P., Mahadevan, S.: A decision model to analyse costs and benefits of RFID for superior supply chain performance. In: Technology Management for Global Future, (PICMET), Istanbul, Turkey, pp. 610–617 (2006)

26. Sennou, A.S., Berrada, A., Salih-Ali, Y., Assem, N.: An Interractive RFID-based bracelet for airport luggage tracking system. In: 4th International Conference on Intelligent Systems, Modelling and Simulation (2013)

27. Abhang, A.L., Mahale, C.L., Desai, V.R., Biswas, P.: Smart bag. Int. J. Sci. Res. Sci. Technol. (IJSRST) **4**(7), 227–231 (2018)

28. Sarkar, S., Manna, S., Datta, S.: Smart bag tracking and alert system using RFID. In: 2017 International Conference on Electrical, Electronics, Communication, Computer, and Optimization Techniques (ICEECCOT) 2017, 2018, pp. 613–616 (2018)

29. Bi, H.H., Lin, D.K.J.: RFID-enabled discovery of supply neworks. IEEE Trans. Eng. Manage. **56**(1), 129–141 (2009)

30. Blass, E.O., Elkhiyaoui, K., Molva, R.: Tracker: security and privacy for RFID-based supply chains. In: Proceedings of the 18th Annual Network and Distributed System Security Symposium, pp. 29–36 (2011)

31. Elkhiyaoui, K., Blass, E.O., Molva, R.: CHECKER: on-site checking in RFID-based supply chains. In: Proceedings of the 5th ACM Conference on Security and Privacy in Wireless and Mobile Networks, pp. 173–184 (2012)
32. Ouaf, K., Vaudenay, S.: Pathchecker: an RFID application for tracing products in supply-chains. In: Proceedings of the 5th Workshop on RFID Security, pp. 1–14 (2009)
33. Kumar, T.P., Sri, Y.S., Pravallika, D., Harshavardhan, A.: Iot for baggage tracking in smart cities. Int. J. Eng. Adv. Technol. **8**(4), 887–890 (2019)
34. Poonkodi, M.: IoT Based smart object tracking system. Int. Res. J. Eng. Technol. 929 (2008)
35. Zhang, H., Zhang, Z., Zhang, L., Yang, Y., Kang, Q., Sun, D.: Object tracking for a smart city using IoT and edge computing. Sensors (Basel) **19**(9), 1–23 (2019)

Validation of Computational-Rabi's Driver Training Model for Prime Decision-Making

Rabi Mustapha[1]($\boxtimes$), Muhammed Auwal Ahmed[2], and Muhammad Aminu Ahmad[1]

[1] Department of Computer Science, Kaduna State University, Kaduna, Nigeria
rabichubu@gmail.com, muhdaminu@kasu.edu.ng
[2] Department of Computer Science, Kaduna Polytechnic, Kaduna, Nigeria
horare10@gmail.com

Abstract. This paper explains the validation of Computational-Rabi's Driver Training (C-RDT) model for Primed Decision-making. To prove the workability of this model, evaluation using validation is indispensable. Hence, validation is a method used to ensure the logical correctness of the model. Therefore, evaluating the model by validation method is yet to be achieved in literature. Hence, this study bridged this gap by providing it, and it serves as the novelty of this study. To validate the C-RDT model, experimental method was adopted whereby an experiment was conducted using human. An adapted game driving simulator features were mapped with the external factors of the awareness component of the model, and the instrument used for the validation was also designed based on the external and temporal factors of the training component of the model. Only a post-test experiment involved to examine the effectiveness of the model factors. The experiment determines the effect of the training with the game simulator on the automaticity of the driver to make effective prime decision. For the experiment, participants were divided into control and experimental groups. The experimental group were trained while the control group were not trained. Two hypotheses were set based on the outcomes of training: H0 and H1. The results obtained has shown that the experimental group participants have better decision-making skill as compared to control group. This supports the alternative hypothesis (H1), which implies that training factors in the model improved the driver's prime decision-making during emergency and this proved the validity of the model.

Keywords: Computational-rabi's driver training model · Prime decision-making · Game simulator · Instrument

1 Introduction

Prime as the name implies means "rapid or fast" and decision-making is the internal processes by which the driver selects a course of action or inaction from a set of alternatives [1]. Therefore, prime decision-making is a concept introduced by Gary Klein [2, 3] in naturalistic decision model named Recognition Primed Decision (RPD). As an illustration of rapid decision-making a driver may observe information and quickly make intuitive and unconscious decisions when something is suddenly about to happen while

© Springer Nature Switzerland AG 2021
S. Misra and B. Muhammad-Bello (Eds.): ICTA 2020, CCIS 1350, pp. 632–644, 2021.
https://doi.org/10.1007/978-3-030-69143-1_48

driving. This is by taking-decisive actions, such as swerving to a safer part of the road, or sudden braking action in a congested traffic or stopping rapidly to avoid any hazard from happening, as such, a prime decision or decision-making has been made. From these examples, it can be concluded that prime decision-making is the reaction of the driver at that particular time to avoid unwanted consequences/experiences. According to [4], sudden swerve to another direction and panic stops are the two critical decisions.

The C-RDT model [5] is an enhancement of the integrated decision model (IDM) proposed in [6], that is used for prime decision -making in the driving domain. To prove the workability of this model, validation is crucial; because the result of validated model proved that the inclusion of training factors in the model improved driver's prime decision making during the experiment [5, 7].

Section 2 presents the methodology of the study under which other sections such as Sects. 2.1, 2.2, 2.3, 2.4 and 2.5 are to be discussed Sect. 3 present results and the discussions. Simulator analysis is to be presented in Subsect. 3.1, while Subsect. 3.2 discusses questionnaire analysis. Then, Sect. 4 the conclusion.

2 Method

2.1 Computational-Rabi's Driver Training (C-RDT) Model

The C-RDT model has thirty-one (31) driver's training factors as against twelve (12) factors for the IDM. The 31 training factors identified were categorized into three viz.

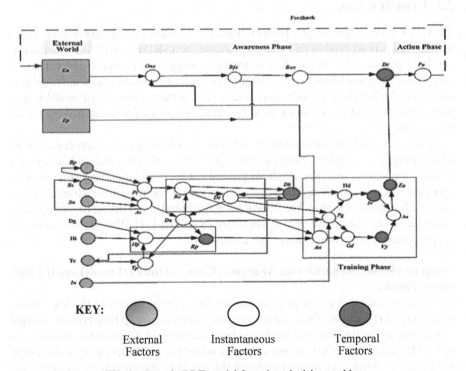

Fig. 1. Generic RDT model for prime decision-making

external, instantaneous and temporal factors as shown in Fig. 1. however, the detailed explanation of this model factors, their relationship, formalization and simulation are found in this study [5]. The causal relationships of the training factors produced the conceptual Rabi's driver training (RDT) model. The generic conceptual model is shown also in Fig. 1.

Figure 1 shows the generic model, where the training factors as constructs are not well expanded.

2.2 Validation of C-RDT Model

To validate the Computational-RDT model, an experimental design was conducted based on this study [8]. The experimental design in this study involves only a post-test experiment. The purpose of the post-test is to examine the effectiveness of model factors in order to see if the simulation scenarios based on the model factors matches the behavior of the driver in real life domain. The experiment determines how these factors affect drivers' prime decision-making during emergencies. That is, it determines the influence of the training with the game simulator on the automaticity of the driver to make effective prime decision particularly during emergencies, which eventually enhances the drivers' performance of action. For the validation process, the game simulator and the instrument are used, the procedures, and the data analysis for the experiment are also presented.

2.3 Game Simulator

The City Car Driving Simulator Home Edition [9], which is a car simulator game called 3D instructor, is adapted in this study to validate the C-RDT model. The simulator is designed to assist users to feel the car driving in a big city or country under different conditions. The game simulator is a commercial application incorporated in the desktop computers for the participants to play to ascertain if the computational model is proportional to the real behaviour of the driver in terms of rapid decision-making during emergencies.

The game simulator uses advanced car physics to achieve a realistic car feeling and a high-quality render engine for graphical realism. Pedestrians, cars, and roads are created to make the players feel they are driving a real car in a real city. The justification for choosing the City Car Driving Simulator is that it has several strengths or advantages over other shelf simulators such as The Open Racing Car Simulator TORCS [10] and Systems Technology Inc. Interactive driving simulator (STISIM) [11]. The adapted simulator supports many real driving features and conditions.

Mapping Driving Scenarios with Awareness factors of the RDT model and the Simulator Features

The game simulator features were mapped to the external factors of the SA components of the RDT model. There are three driving scenarios set up based on the external factors that are in line with the three simulated scenarios in a simulation environment using MATLAB. The three driving scenarios set up are good driving conditions (low risk), average driving conditions (moderate risk) and bad driving conditions (high risk)

[12, 13]. The three different driving scenarios consist of different conditions in driving environment that includes road, traffic, obstacles, car condition and visibility.

Scenarios for the Awareness Component
In simulating the awareness component of the RDT model, simulations conditions were used based on the five inputs factors (*road, traffic, obstacles, car condition, and visibility*) of the awareness component of the RDT model.

The scenario conditions were presented in the form of 0's and 1's values. One (1) means good and (0) means bad/poor for all the factors except obstacle in which the reverse is the case. This means that in case of obstacle, 1 means there is obstacle and 0 means no obstacle.

Simulator Stages
The City Car Driving Simulator Home Edition has two main stages: The free driving stage (where drivers drive under various conditions without training) and the career driving stage (where drivers are trained).

The Free Driving Stage
In the free driving stage, the driver drives in a virtual city based on the scenario set up to achieve the study objective. The driving scenarios are set up based on the model external factors particularly the awareness model external factors. The free driving is used for both experimental and control groups in this study.

The Career Driving Stage
In the career driving stage, the drivers are assumed to be receiving training lessons in a virtual driving school. In the simulator, there are tasks to be achieved, such as car starting and shifting of gear (training), slalom (zigzag), U-turn, garage, turns, hills, track test and city driving test. However, for this study, city driving test is chosen to train the experimental group participants. It is one of the training tasks used in city car driving simulator. A driver is trained in the virtual city. The virtual instructor gives the trainee the driving directions to follow; when the trainee completes the task and parks the car at the finished point without violating the driving rules and regulations and without exceeding the permissible violation score, then, the driver is said to be successful. This gives the trainee (driver) the achievement "city driving test". Then, the three driving scenarios was mapped with the game driving simulator.

2.4 Instrument

In order to validate the Computational-RDT model, for effective prime decision-making during emergencies, a questionnaire was designed as the instrument. The instrument was adapted from the validated items derived from previous studies. The instrument consisted of eleven (11) factors having sixty-six (67) items and it is divided into two different sections. Details about the instrument is found in this study [7].

2.5 Experimental Procedures

The validation procedures were conducted using validation protocols based on User-Centred Design (UCD) approach. The UCD approach is a process in which the needs, wants, and limitations of the end user of a product are given large attention at each stage of the design process. The protocol follows the approach stated in Fig. 2 to carry out the human experiment.

Participants

In experimental research, the focus is the representativeness of participants ahead of other randomization technique [14], Babbie added that in experimental research design, representativeness of participants is more crucial than the sample size. Therefore, to ensure representativeness of participants in this study, 20 participants (18 males, and 2 females) were selected [8, 15, 16] using criteria, namely valid driving licence, driving experience of more than 5 years for experienced drivers, and less than 1 year for inexperienced drivers, and minimum driving covering 5,000 km mileage per year. In addition, the participants were middle-age drivers (23 to 53 years old), having knowledge of computer, video gaming, driving game simulator, and having willingness to play the game simulator. These criteria were in line with prior studies [15, 17]. For this purpose, fifty (50) questionnaires were distributed at the College of Arts and Sciences (CAS), Universiti Utara Malaysia to select participants who fulfilled the aforementioned criteria. Hence, the sample of the questionnaire for selecting participants is written in English and Bahasa Malay. They were all brought to Human-Centered Computing Research Lab (HCCRL) Universiti Utara Malaysia for the experiment.

The experiment room was very quiet, conducive and convenient for the participants for the smooth interaction with the game application. The participants were grouped into two thus; experimental and control groups using simple randomization technique. The experimental group participants were trained using city-driving test during the experiment while the control group were not trained; they played the free driving test in the game simulator.

Participants Interaction with Game Simulator

At this point, the participants (drivers) interacted with the game simulator. The game simulator has two main stages, career driving and free driving. The game simulator simulates series of fictitious driving, experiences and scenarios (good, average and bad driving conditions). These driving conditions (scenarios) are based on the simulation scenarios used in MATLAB. Each of these scenarios was labelled A, B, and C and configured into six different PCs that the participants used, with each PC having a scenario configured based on the model external factors mapped inside the game simulator.

The experimental group played both the career and free driving stages, while the control group played only the free driving stage. The career driving test is main for training the participants, while the free driving is for normal driving routine. After the two groups of participants had interacted and played the different scenarios configured in the game simulator, instrument based on the external and temporal factors of the RDT model were administered to the participants. Given that the experimental group

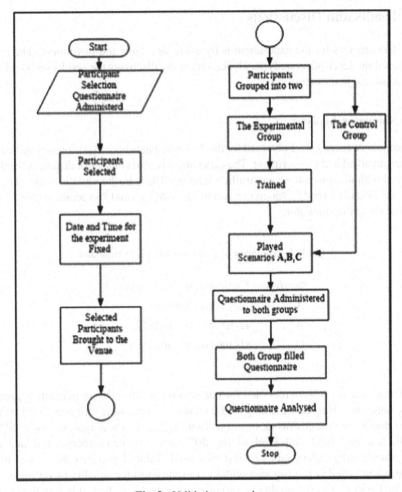

Fig. 2. Validation procedures

participants were trained, it is likely that they were to perform better than the control group participants. Thus, this study states two hypotheses with respect to the outcomes of training:

H0: Training does not improve driver's prime decision making.
H1: Training improves driver's prime decision making.

The participants then filled in the instrument based on their experiences and interactions with the game simulator. See this study (7) for the sample of the post-test instrument. The instrument was analyzed using SPSS.

3 Results and Discussions

The data analysis for the experiment is by using simulator and instrument. The results are based on descriptive analysis. Hence, the study discusses the results obtained from simulator and instrument.

3.1 Simulator Analysis

The simulator results were obtained for the 20 participants both experimental and control groups involved in the experiment. The experiment record consists of distances the driver covered without committing any traffic violation. These traffic violations are classified into "no violations (NV)", "no major violations (NMV)", and "no accident (NA)" while driving the game simulator.

Table 1. Summary of scenarios settings in simulator

Scenarios	Traffic density measurement (%)
A	0–20 (Low Traffic)
B	41–60 (Average Traffic)
C	81–100 (High Traffic)

These violations were recorded for one session because the participants played the game only once. Hence, the setting of the scenarios in the simulator was based on their traffic density measurements as shown in Table 1. The data was analysed using SPSS.

To test the significant level of the difference between experimental and control groups, independent-sample t-test was used. Table 2 presents the results of the independent sample t-test together with the Levene's test for equality of variance.

The Levene's test of equality of variance suggests that if the test is significant at the 5% level, it means that the assumption of equal variance is violated and the "equal variance not assumed" is used. Equally, if the significant value of Levene's Test for Equality of Variances is not significant at the 5% level, one can conclude that the assumption of equal variances is not violated and for this reason, "equal variances assumed" are used (18–20). The test is used to determine the significant difference between the experimental and control groups in relation to 'No Violation', 'No Major Violation' and 'No Accident' for scenarios A, B and C.

The results in Table 2 for scenario **C** suggested that the significant value of Levene's Test for Equality of Variances indicated the P- value 0.009 for 'NV'. Since this value is <5% it can be concluded that the assumption of equal variances is violated and for this reason, equal variances not assumed are used. The corresponding result of t-test = 7.479 with the significant value = 0.000. The significant value is also <5%, it was concluded that there was significant difference in 'NV' between the experimental and control groups. Also, for same scenario, Levene's Test for Equality of Variances is significant at 5% level (p-value 0.031) for 'NMV' suggests that the assumption of equal

Table 2. Participants' simulator results for test of mean difference

Violations	Groups	Participants	Mean	Levene's test for equality of variances		t-stat	p-value
				F	Sig.		
NV (A)	Experimental	10	0.457	2.793	0.112	1.849	0.081
	Control	10	0.347				
NMV(A)	Experimental	10	0.672	0.653	0.430	0.134	0.895
	Control	10	0.638				
NA (A)	Experimental	10	1.476	4.220	0.055	0.871	0.395
	Control	10	0.818				
NV (B)	Experimental	10	0.342	0.517	0.481	1.014	0.324
	Control	10	0.275				
NMV(B)	Experimental	10	0.628	4.352	0.051	−0.396	0.697
	Control	10	0.700				
NA(B)	Experimental	10	0.930	0.182	0.675	0.178	0.861
	Control	10	0.876				
NV(C)	Experimental	10	0.613	8.571	0.009	7.479	0.000
	Control	10	0.258				
NMV(C)	Experimental	10	0.593	5.484	0.031	2.629	0.017
	Control	10	0.384				
NA(C)	Experimental	10	1.050	1.843	0.191	2.247	0.037
	Control	10	0.486				

Note: The tests are performed for Scenarios, A, B and C

variances is violated and therefore, equal variances not assumed are used. Based on the t-test and significant values, the significant value, <5%, suggests that there is significant difference in 'NMV' between the 2 groups.

For same scenario **C**, Levene's Test for Equality of Variances is insignificant at 5% with p- value equals to 0.191 for 'NA'. This means that there is no violation of the assumption of equal variances and hence equal variances assumed are used. The t-test value and p-value indicated in Table 2 shows that there was a significant (at the 5% level) difference in 'NA' between the 2 groups.

However, the values on mean scores showed in Table 2 between the 2 groups for scenarios A, B and C respectively, it can be concluded that the experimental groups performed better than the control group participants in terms of longer distance covered without violation of traffic.

With respect to the measurement of "NMV" in traffic for the 3 scenarios as shown in Table 2. Based on the distance mean scores for the two groups, the experimental group participants covered longer distance with "NMV" committed compared to the control group participants under scenarios **A** and **C**. However, the distance means scores covered with "NMV" for control group participants under scenario **B** is longer than that of the experimental group participant. This result is not surprising because scenario **B** is operated under normal conditions. Therefore, any of the participants from the 2 groups has the tendency to perform better under this scenario.

As regards to the measurement of "NA" in traffic for the 3 scenarios. Based on the mean scores shown in same Table 2, it can be concluded that experimental group covered longer distance with "NA" committed under scenarios A, B and C. Generally, it can be concluded that the experimental group participants performed better than the control group participants in terms of longer distances covered without committing MV in traffic.

3.2 The Questionnaire Analysis.

The analysis of participants' responses obtained through questionnaire designed based on the external and temporal factors of the training part of the model for the two groups are analysed using SPSS as well, and the results of the independent sample t-test for the comparison between the two groups in relation to the following factors: Basic Skills (Bs), Basic Practice(Bp), Sensory Ability (Sa), Driving Goals (Dg), Driving Intention (In), Potential Hazardous Information (Hi), Exposure for Task Complexity (Tc), Risk Perception (Rp), Driving Knowledge (Dk), Involuntary Automaticity (Iv), and Voluntary automaticity (Vy) are presented in Table 3.

The results in Table 3 indicates that the values of Levene's Test for Equality of Variances are not significant at 5% for all the factors, suggesting that there is no violation of assumption of equal variances. Hence, equal variances assumed are employed. The corresponding values of t-test for almost all the factors are >5.0, indicating that they are significant at 1% level. This suggests that there is significant difference in each of the factors between the experimental and the control groups.

Same Table also show the mean scores of the participants in experimental group and the control group, respectively for each of the 11 factors based on the items used to measure them. According to the results presented in the table, there were clear indications that the mean scores values for all the factors for the experimental group are higher than that of the control group participants. This suggested that training given to the experimental group participants reflected in their responses to the questionnaire. For instance, in the case of driving knowledge, the mean score (9.15) of the experimental group participants is higher (6.58) than that of the control group. In addition, the driving knowledge as a factor had the highest mean score among all the factors in the experimental group. The higher mean value obtained from the driving knowledge indicated that the experimental group participants had a clear understanding of traffic rules, traffic signs and signals, that minimized the risk of accident. This evidence was consistent with the argument of [21] that abiding by traffic rules could lead to less or no accident. Therefore, training of drivers is important for prime decision making, in particular during emergency.

Similarly, the risk perception mean score of the experimental group participants is higher than that of the control group participants. This indicates that the experimental group participants have a higher tendency to avoid, recognize, and handle risk [22].

Table 3. Results of independent sample test

Factors	Group	Participants	Mean	Levene's test for equality of variances		t-test for equality of means	
				F	Sig.	t-stat	p-value
Bs	Experimental	10	7.29	0.001	0.982	4.50	0.000
	Control	10	5.89				
Bp	Experimental	10	6.57	1.546	0.23	6.81	0.000
	Control	10	5.18				
Sa	Experimental	10	5.08	0.626	0.439	5.29	0.000
	Control	10	3.64				
Dg	Experimental	10	8.60	0.58	0.456	7.84	0.000
	Control	10	6.47				
In	Experimental	10	8.50	1.618	0.22	7.42	0.000
	Control	10	6.47				
Hi	Experimental	10	8.08	0.773	0.391	5.10	0.000
	Control	10	6.53				
Tc	Experimental	10	8.10	0.463	0.505	7.43	0.000
	Control	10	6.15				
Rp	Experimental	10	7.72	0.69	0.417	7.77	0.000
	Control	10	6.11				
Dk	Experimental	10	9.15	0.771	0.391	20.6	0.000
	Control	10	6.58				
Iv	Experimental	10	7.55	0.000	1.000	5.37	0.000
	Control	10	6.40				
Vy	Experimental	10	2.45	0.000	1.000	−5.37	0.000
	Control	10	3.60				

Note: Independent Sample Test comparing experimental and control group participants

However, the results for the voluntary automaticity factor, that captured the conscious automaticity of the participants, revealed that the experimental group had lower mean score compared to the control group participants because for any prime decision making, the participant needed to operate independent of conscious control. Hence, training enhances the automatic actions of the participants (e.g., matching of clutch and changing of gear) during driving. Furthermore, the mean score for the driving goal of the experimental group participants is higher than that of the control group participants. This is because the experimental participants can manage multiple goals (e.g., safety and time saving) while driving. This is in line with this study [23] that made the assertion that drivers' behaviours are regulated with their goals of which safety has the highest priority.

Same participants' exposure to task complexity for the experimental group participants has higher mean score than the control group. This revealed that the participant in the experimental group could handle complex tasks [24]. In fact, the ability of the experimental group to handle task complexity enables drivers to attain multiple goals.

Furthermore, for all the factor shown in Table 3, the mean scores for the experimental group were higher than those for the control group. This shows that participants' responses based on questionnaire indicated the influence of training on the experimental group participants made them have better decision-making skill as compared to control group participants.

4   Conclusion

This paper presented a validation of C-RDT model for Primed Decision-making by proving the applicability of the model in real life domain using human experiment. This was accomplished by using an adapted application (game driving simulator). The game driving simulator features were mapped with the external factors of the awareness component of the model. In addition, a questionnaire was designed based on the external and temporal factors of the training component of the model to validate the model.

The simulator results suggested that scenario C being the high-risk scenario requires the expertise of the participants. Whereby the influence of training is important because of the complexity of the scenario. The results indicated that in scenario C, the mean scores for 'NV, 'NMV and 'NA' were greater for experimental group than for the control group participants. This shows that training plays an important role in making better decision by drivers in experimental group. Similarly, the results from the analysis of participants' responses based on instrument indicated the influence of training on the experimental group participants made them have better decision-making skill compared to the control group participants. The result supported the alternative hypothesis (H1). Therefore, this shows that training is a determinant for an effective prime decision-making of a driver particularly during emergency. It implies that including of training factors in the C-RDT model improved driver's prime decision-making during emergency and this proved the validity of the model.

One the limitations of this study that, the game driving simulator (City Car Driving) is an off -the -shelf. Hence, the configuration of the model features in the simulator is constrained only to the available features to validate the model. However, an appropriate software (driving simulator) should be developed rather than off-the-shelf software that restricts the personalized mapping of all the factors. This allows seamless factors integration and adaptation to future enhancement of the model.

The future work of this study is the evaluation of the C-RDT model using both the verification and validation methods.

References

1. Smith, J.: Decision-making in midwifery: a tripartite clinical decision. Br. J. Midwifery [Internet]. **24**(8), 574–580 (2016)
2. Klein, G.: Naturalistic decision making. Hum. Factors Ergon. Soc. **50**(3), 456–460 (2008)
3. Klein, G.: A naturalistic decision making perspective on studying intuitive decision making. J. Appl. Res. Mem. Cogn. [Internet]. **4**(3), 164–168 (2015)
4. Leland, F.: Critical decision making under pressure. Homel. Secur. Rev. [Internet]. **3**(1), 43–74 (2009)
5. Mustapha, R., Yusof, Y., Aziz, A.A.: Computational-Rabi's driver training model for prime decision-making in driving. J. Theor. Appl. Inf. Technol. **97**(13), 3540–3563 (2019)
6. Noyes, J.: Automation and decision making. In: Noyes, J., Cook, M., Masakowski, Y. (eds.) Decision Making in Complex Environments. Ashgate Publishing, Ltd., UK, pp. 113–122 (2012)
7. Mustapha, R., Ahmad, M.A., Daniel, A., Ahmed, M.A., Hussaini, M.: Validating measures of driver behavior's training factors for prime decision-making. Sci. World J. **15**(1), 102–112 (2020)
8. Liu, Y.F., Wang, Y.M., Li, W.S., Xu, W.Q., Gui, J.S.: Improve driver performance by experience of driver cognitive behavior model's practice. In: IEEE Intelligent Vehicles Symposium, Proceedings, pp. 475–80. IEEE (2009)
9. City Car Driving S. City Car Driving [Internet]. 2017.
10. Wymann, B., Dimitrakakis, C., Sumner, A., Espié, E.: TORCS: The Open Racing Car Simulator (2015)
11. Allen, R., Stein, A., Aponso, B., Rosenthal, T.: Low-Cost Part Task Driving Simulator using microcomputer technology [Internet] (1990)
12. Mustapha, R., Yusof, Y., Aziz, A.A.: A Computational Agent Model of Automaticity for Driver's Training. In: International Research and Innovation Summit (IRIS2017) [Internet]. IOP Publishing (2017)
13. Mustapha, R., Yusof, Y., Aziz, A.A.: Computational model of situation awareness for decision making in driving. Adv. Sci. Lett. [Internet]. **24**(2), 1244–1248 (2018)
14. Babbie, E.: The Practice of Social Research, 12th edn. Thomson Wadsworth, Belmont (2010)
15. Bellet, T., Mayenobe, P., Bornard, J., Paris, J.: Human driver modelling and simulation into a virtual road environment [Internet]. In: Pietro, C.C., Magnus, H., Andreas, L., Costanza, R. (eds.) Human Modelling in Assisted Transportation, pp. 251–262. Springer (2011). https://doi.org/10.1007/978-88-470-1821-1_27
16. Kaber, D., Zhang, Y., Jin, S., Mosaly, P., Garner, M.: Effects of hazard exposure and roadway complexity on young and older driver situation awareness and performance. Transp. Res. Part F Traffic Psychol. Behav. [Internet]. **15**(5), 600–611 (2012)
17. Hjälmdahl, M., Shinar, D., Carsten, O., Peters, B.: The ITERATE Project—Overview, theoretical framework and validation [Internet]. In: Pietro, C.C., Magnus, H., Andreas, L., Costanza, R. (eds.) Human Modelling in Assisted Transportation, pp. 97–106. Springer (2011). https://doi.org/10.1007/978-88-470-1821-1_10
18. Coakes SJ. SPSS : analysis without anguish : version 20 for Windows. John Wiley and Sons, Australia (2013)
19. Field, A.: Discovering Statistics Using SPSS, 3rd edn. Sage Publications, London (2009)
20. Pallant, J.: SPSS Survival Manual: A Step by Step Guide to Data Analysis Using SPSS, 4th edn. Open University Press/McGraw-Hill, New York (2013)
21. Zaidi, S., Paul, P., Mishra, P., Srivastav, A.: Risk perception and practice towards road traffic safety among medical students. Int. J. Community Med. Public Heal [Internet]. **4**(1), 9–14 (2017)

22. Rosenbloom, T., Shahar, A., Elharar, A., Danino, O.: Risk perception of driving as a function of advanced training aimed at recognizing and handling risks in demanding driving situations. Accid. Anal. Prev. **40**(2), 697–703 (2008)

23. Dogan, E., Steg, L., Delhomme, P.: The influence of multiple goals on driving behavior: the case of safety, time saving, and fuel saving. Accid. Anal. Prev. [Internet]. **43**(5), 1635–1643 (2011)

24. Grill, T., Osswald, S., Tscheligi, M.: Task complexity and user model attributes. Comput. Help People with Spec Needs [Internet] **642–9** (2012)

Efficient Approaches to Agile Cost Estimation in Software Industries: A Project-Based Case Study

Shariq Aziz Butt[1]([✉]), Sanjay Misra[2], Diaz-Martinez Jorge Luis[3], and De la Hoz-Franco Emiro[3]

[1] University of Lahore, Lahore, Pakistan
Shariq2315@gmail.com
[2] Covenant University, Ota, Nigeria
sanjay.misra@covenantuniversity.edu.ng
[3] Department of Computer Science and Electronics, Universidad de La Costa,
Barranquilla, Colombia
{jdiaz5,edelahoz}@cuc.edu.co

Abstract. Agile was invented to improve and overcome the traditional deficiencies of software development. At present, the agile model is used in software development very vastly due to its support to developers and clients. Agile methodology increases the interaction between the developer-client, and it makes software product defects free. The agile model is fast and becoming more popular because of its features and flexibility. The study shows that the agile software development model is an efficient and effective software development strategy that easily accommodates user changes, but it is not free from errors or shortcomings. The study shows that COCOMO and Planning Poker are famous cost estimation procedures, but are not ingenious for agile development. We conduct a study on real-time projects from multinational software industries using different estimation approaches to estimate the project's cost and time. We thoroughly explain these projects with the limitations of the techniques. The study has proven that the traditional and modern estimation approaches still have limitations to accurate estimation of projects.

Keywords: Agile · Agile project cost and time estimation · Estimation technique · Software

1 Introduction

Researchers are going on for improving software development methodologies, and in results, various development techniques and methods are available in the literature. Various comparison amongst different development methodologies are available in multiple pieces of research [1, 2]. Agile software development (ASD) is the preference of numerous companies and gained more attention, even facing difficulty during COVID-19 [3]. It is because Agile software development is treated as the development of knowledge management and creativity [4]. Further, ASD offers various methods, and amongst them,

© Springer Nature Switzerland AG 2021
S. Misra and B. Muhammad-Bello (Eds.): ICTA 2020, CCIS 1350, pp. 645–659, 2021.
https://doi.org/10.1007/978-3-030-69143-1_49

the popular ones are Scrum [5] and extreme programming [6]. Further researches are coming up by combining multiple agile methods [7] to improve the development process. Due to popularity and its practical advantages, agile methods are being applied in various places for obtaining efficiency in organizations [6–10].

The agile model is a comparatively new and essential model for efficient development in software development [2]. The agile model encourages the customer to give change demand at any phase of the project. Rather than such a large number of highlights and prevalence, the agile model additionally has few disadvantages. The change request from client is the most complicated component that over changes demands from the customer, that cause of time and cost increment. The cost and time can cause project disappointment. The cost and time increase impacts negatively on the reputation of a developer or vendor. In this study, we visited some software industries to examine the cost estimation techniques still in use in their projects. From this line of research, we find 2 cost estimation techniques that are vastly in use for estimation in the scrum projects, and to also interact with different development teams. The cost and time estimation techniques such as COCOMO and Planning Poker, but these techniques do not aid the understanding of issues for agile programming improvement. Our targeted industries that are using the agile model for software development and the traditional or modern cost estimation technique for projects. We also presented the reasons why these estimation techniques are adopted by industries and ways to enhance improvement and efficiency.

The paper is organized as follows. The second section provides the literature review. Methodology and experimentations are given in the Sect. 2. The discussion and analysis is given in Sect. 4, and the conclusion drawn is summarized in the last Sect. 5.

2   Related Work

Agile methodologies are becoming the preferable model for software development due to its robustness and scalability. However, it can be limited by the size of the project and the number of programmers involved. The agile model is very attractive for the development of applications for software companies and the development of software by modules, obviously without neglecting the quality and guaranteeing the updating of the documentation. In 2001, 17 people representing alternative forms of software development decided to unite their methodologies under an umbrella called Agile Software Development as a way to reach most software developers. In addition to the common name that serves as a brand, they published a Manifesto consisting of 4 values and 12 principles, which allow limiting who can use the brand [11–13]. These 17 innovators were: Kent Beck, Mike Beedle, Arie van Bennekum, Alistair Cockburn, Ward Cunningham Martin Fowler, James Grenning, Jim Highsmith, Andrew Hunt, Ron Jeffries, Jon Kern, Brian Marick, Robert C. Martin, Steve Mellor, Ken Schwaber, Jeff Sutherland, and Dave Thomas. Currently, there are several proposals on the market on how to implement the values and principles mentioned above, to which the different authors add their personal touch depending on their experience or need. Among the most recognized agile methodologies are SCRUM, Crystal Methodologies, Dynamic Systems Development Method (DSDM), Adaptive Software Development (ASD), Feature-Driven Development (FDD), Lean Development (LD), XP, and Kanban [14–16]. Different Agile methodologies are now available because of several fairly traditional models in which the client was not involved in the process, and their actions were minimal, which caused many delays in developing the software. The client must work together with the development team, which will help to build software according to what the client wants, this is one of the challenges that arise in various companies at the time to implement the agile scrum manifesto [17–19]. as shown in Fig. 1. However, the client's requirements are changing, and therefore, the building of software must align with the changing environment and market dynamics. Today's software is now made to pass the test, which has been previously established concerning the client's requirement to meet the requirements of the user. Considering the above, it is important to mention that in the mid-1990s, most of the software processes developed were being criticized as slow bureaucratic and few easy to adapt to change. So a reaction was generated to these heavyweight software methods, in which the market was changing and needed to demand faster results which allowed organizations to develop rapidly [20–22].

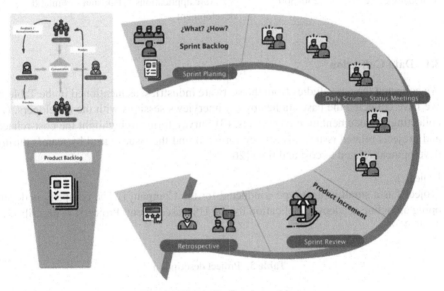

Fig. 1. The Agile Scrum working.

3   Methodology

Data collected through primary and secondary sources. Primary data were generated through Expert Opinion, Scrum Methodology, Planning Poker, COCOMO as shown in Table 1, and onsite visitation/survey of industries as seen in Table 2. These techniques have limitations to measure the accurate cost and time for agile software development with a change request from the client [23–25]. While secondary data were generated from journals and other publications for review of literature.

Table 1. Motivational technique

Techniques	Motivational work
Expert opinion	Expert judgment about project
Scrum methodology	Daily meeting session
Planning poker	Expert opinion
COCOMO	SLOC based estimation

Table 2. The Industries information on collected projects.

Companies	Projects	No. employees	Type of services	Location	Sub-locations
Company 1	1	300–400	IT Business Solutions	Pakistan	Dubai
Company 2	2	250–300	Software applications development	Pakistan	Finland

3.1 Data Collection

We collected the case studies from the software industries, as mentioned in the Table 2. We have collected the case studies by (1) interviews sessions with the developers, (2) collecting of documentation of projects, (3) Survey forms to highlight the cost-related and projects related issues, (4) Survey forms to find the issues faced by team/s during development related to cost and time [26–28].

Project 1
Project 1 is a small project type conducted for the Company1. The company is developing an online academic application for the US-based client. Project 1 is described in Table 3:

Table 3. Project description

Project description	Company 1
Project size	Small
Project nature	Online academic system
Team size	4
KLOC	25
No. modules	6
Completion time	18 months
Already developed modules	0
Project cost	35000 $

Project 2

Project 2 is a small project type conducted for Company 2. The company is developing a Property Estate Business application for the UK based client. Project 2 is described in Table 4:

Table 4. The Project 2 description.

Project description	Company 2
Project size	Small
Project nature	Property estate system
Team size	3
KLOC	20
No. modules	3
Completion time	16 months
Already developed modules	0
Project cost	27500 $

Project 1 Modules: The project Modules are explained in Fig. 2.

Project 1: The project's 1six modules are mentioned below. Project 1 is an online academic application system.

1. Student Login: In this module, the student can Log in and check his account, can view its all-academic activities.
2. Examinations: This module deal with the examination department. The exams schedule, updating, etc.
3. Administration: With the use of modules, the Admin department can manage the student's account, fee, results, academic activates, etc.
4. STD Lectures: Students can view and see their subject lectures on this phase of the application.
5. Course Selection: Students select courses which he wants to read in his/her current semester through this module access.
6. Assignments: The students can view their assignments through this module. They can submit their assignment, can checkmarks of assignments.

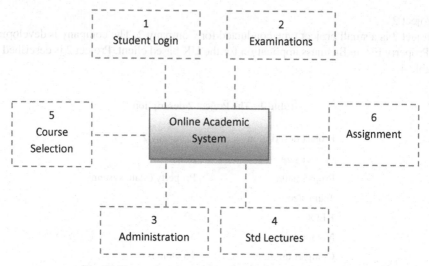

Fig. 2. The project 1 complete description with modules.

Project 2: The project's 2 four modules are mentioned in Fig. 3:

1. User Login: Users can log in and view the updated properties on rent, sale, etc.
2. Booking: Through this module, the client can book any property on sale and rent.
3. Administration: The owner of the app can update the properties on the Web and manage the client and block the accounts.
4. Payment: the client can pay through it.

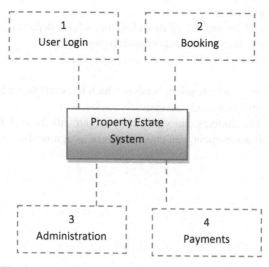

Fig. 3. Project 2 completes the description with modules.

Most Change Request on Project's Modules:

In **project 1** the change request comes from the client on modules are:

1. **Course Selection:** In this module, the, again and again, change request comes from the client because the courses to prescribed and related program students are showing correctly. Non-related program course show in the student portal. There is also course selection and saved issues the client is facing.
2. **Administration:** Admin Department facing the issue of the student no updated data and shuffling of student's data. The admin facing that when delete or update any student data then the data delete some more entities in data.
3. **Assignments:** In this module, students need to submit their assignments, but when they try to upload then the system creates an error.

   In **project 2** the change request comes from the client on modules are:

1. **User Login:** In this module when the user login and want to see its updated data mean in the form of payments, booking, etc. then some data become miss.
2. **Administration:** The administration is facing the issue that the updated data is not showing as of when customer book or pay against any property then the data or transactions is not showing to the admin of some clients.

   Project 1.

   The results obtained with the application of the COCOMO model on project 1. The project description and detail explained above in section Implementation. The team Size is 4 as the agile works with the small team. Due to project 1's 25 KLOC the project fall within the Organic Mode, therefore, the Co-efficient values used here are $a = 2.4$ & $b = 1.05$ & $c = 0.38$.

   By using the COCOMO formula:

Effort $= MM = a(KDSL/KLOC)b$
Effort $= MM = 2.4 \times (25)^{1.05} = 70.4$ **Person $-$ Months**
Person Per months $= 70.4 \div 18$ *Months* $= 3.8$ (Approx 4) Persons Per Months
Time $= TDEV = 2.5 \times MM^c$
By putting the values of project 1 data.
Time $= TDEV = 2.5 \times 70.4^{0.38} = 12$ **Months**
Cost $= 4$ Persons Per Months $\times$ Salary $= 1800\$$.
Total Cost of the Project $= 1800 \$ \times 12 = 21600\$$.

The Table 6 is explaining the difference between the project's description data and COCOMO implementation results. In the results, there is a distinction between the times and cost values mentioned in the project data and COCOMO results. The distinction between the values is without the consideration of change request comes from the client. Due to, again and again, change request comes from the client on modules course selection, administration, and assignment. The SLOC code of the whole project become increases due it the cost of the projected increase. The new Data of the complete project 1 is showing Table 5:

Effort $= MM = a(KDSL/KLOC)b$
Effort $= MM = 2.4 \times (17)^{1.05} = 47$ **Person $-$ Months**

Table 5. The new added no of modules in Project.1.

No of modules	3
Average SLOC	17000

As the equation of person per month is showing that 4 persons per month needed for project completion hence by putting values:

Time $= 47 \div 4 = 11.75$ (Approx 12 Moths)
Cost $= 180,000 \times 12$ Months $= 21600\$\ldots\ldots2$

Therefore the new cost and time of project 1 from Eq. 1 and 2 become:

Cost $= 21600\$ + 21600 \$ = 43200\$$
Time $= 12$ Moths $+ 12$ Months $= 24$ Months
Sloc $= 25$ kloc $+ 17$kloc $= 42$ Sloc

Hence exceed in time, SLOC and Costs of project 1 are shown in Table 6. The increment in the cost and time is because of again and again change request comes from the client. The change in the values of time, SLOC, and the cost is an assurance that the COCOMO model is not ingenious when the client gives change request in Agile Software Development.

Table 6. Results Project 1 Data Comparison with the COCOMO without the change request from client

	Project 1 Data	COCOMO	Distinction Rate
Team Size	4	4	0
KLOC	25	25	0
Time	18 months	12 months	6 months
Cost	35000$	21600$	13400$

In Table 7, the Actual values are showing the data described in the above Table 5. The final values are the values that the project manager gets after the completion of project 1. The incremented data is explaining the values which exceed after again and again change request from the client.

Table 7. Project 1 Cost, Time and SLOC Increment

	Actual	Final	Incremental
KLOC	25	25	0
Time	18 months	12 months	6 months
Cost	35000$	21600$	13400$

Project 2

Project 2 was implemented by using the most useful technique Planning Poker in the agile scrum cost estimation. As indicated by this procedure, colleagues examine expense and exertion estimation. Every part has various necessities concerning estimation; all colleagues take part in the conversation and trade their prerequisites in regards to the estimation process. After a concise conversation meeting, colleagues finished the estimation procedure and necessities by contrasting and every part prerequisites. This strategy is valuable to guarantee colleague communication [22, 31, 33]. This method has less experimental proof concerning exactness and less material in the programming industry. This procedure isn't a prescient base. Presently we depict the highlights and issues of existing estimation techniques. This depiction helps get summed up and fitting data about existing estimation methods initially. Figure 4 shows the story cards utilized for the estimation in the Planning Poker estimation method [34, 35, 37]. Figures 5 and 6 depict the working of project sprints in the industry for the estimation of time and cost regarding the Project 2.

Fig. 4. The cards used for estimation in Planning Poker.

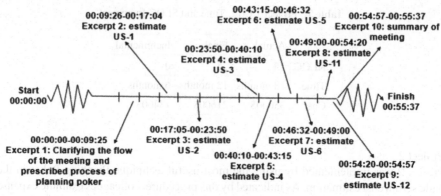

Fig. 5. Timeline Meeting 1.

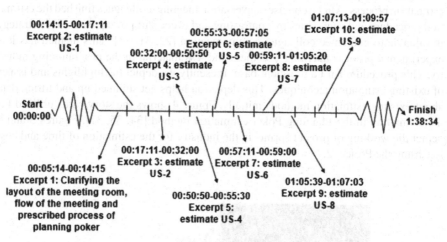

Fig. 6. Timeline Meeting 2.

As seen in Table 8, the **Actual values** are showing the data described. The **final values** are the values that the project manager gets after the completion of the project. The **incremented data** is explaining the values which exceed after again and again change request from the client.

Table 8. Project 2 Cost, Time, and SLOC Increment.

	Actual	Final	Incremental
KLOC	20	30	10
Time	16 months	20.5 months	4.5 months
Cost	27500$	31775$	4275$

Figure 7 is presenting the complete comparative analysis of project 1 and project 2.

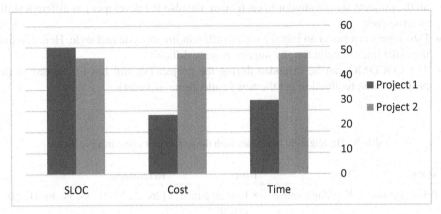

Fig. 7. The Accumulative results of Project.1 and Project 2.

4 Discussion and Analysis

There are 2 estimation techniques that are now in use in the software industries. Both techniques adopted due to the traditional way of estimation and the modern way of estimation of the project in terms of cost and time were mentioned in Table 9. However, the identified issues with the estimation techniques while being used for agile project development are as follows [38, 39, 48]:

- Planning poker is less precise when there is an absence of experience for comparable current ventures.
- Anchoring (for example oblige the senior/manager for anything) impact is another issue of arranging poker which means construct own supposition by utilizing beginning snippet of data and aptitudes as a base. It resembles a thought that surfaces from the introductory conversation and have a profound effect and impact on the rest of the piece of conversation.
- Domination is additionally another issue of arranging poker. In the meeting, when a most experienced part selects a card with an irregular number of client stories, test objects, determinations, prerequisites, experiments or bugs, and so on then the staying all individuals with less experience follow the same example of picking the card. This impacts the outcomes.
- Like master estimation arranging poker additionally required contribution of exceptionally broad versus gifted and experienced people who speaks to an assortment of perspectives.
- In arranging poker like master judgment, the judgment might be one-sided by unimportant and deceiving data, and arranging poker don't give as such strategy or methodology that can be reused.

- COCOMO is still in use method in the software industries due to its support on estimation based on previous project data. It is the main drawback of the technique as all the projects are not similar to each other and also the developer has different skills to write code.
- Developers can finish an inquiry with a different line of code and style. Hence to find the exact lines of code for any inquiry is quite difficult.
- The COCOMO can be extended during the project but still has limitations as the project's code required to get the new results (time and cost).

Table 9. Highlighting the issues with the techniques using in agile scrum

Method	Type	Issues	References
Poker planning	Non-Algorithmic	• Less empirical evidence regarding the accuracy • Less applicable • No reusability • Biased by providing misleading data	[26, 27, 29–31, 33, 34, 36, 41, 42]
COCOMO	Algorithmic	• Empirical evidence (Project SLOC) • Wrong Accuracy • Less applicable • Extensive skills required • Biased by providing misleading data	[23, 37, 40–47]

5   Conclusion

Agile was invented to improve and overcome the traditional deficiencies of software development and is getting popularity due to its unique features that include the client and developer interaction and connection. The agile model allows the client to give a change request at the stage of the project. Still, the software industries are using the COCOMO and Planning Poker cost estimation techniques. We selected some software industries that are suing the agile model and one of these estimation techniques for the project's estimation. We collected the project's data with the interview session with the team leaders, developers and project managers. In our results, we found that both techniques are not ingenious for the agile development since the changes solicitation comes then the estimations gone wrong and expanded from calculated values. Therefore in the agile development, there is still need a more appropriate estimation method to deal with the change request.

References

1. Misra, S., Omorodion, M., Fernández-Sanz, L., Pages, C.: A brief overview of software process models: benefits, limitations, and application in practice. In: Agile Estimation Techniques and Innovative Approaches to Software Process Improvement, pp. 258–271. IGI Global. https://doi.org/10.4018/978-1-4666-5182-1.ch015
2. Patel, A., et al.: A comparative study of agile, component-based, aspect-oriented and mashup software development methods. Tehnicki Vjesnik **19**(1), 175–189 (2012)
3. Butt, S.A., Misra, S., Anjum, M.W., Hassan, S.A.: Agile project development issues during COVID-19. In: Przybyłek, A., Miler, J., Poth, A., Riel, A. (eds.) Lean and Agile Software Development. LASD 2021. Lecture Notes in Business Information Processing, vol. 408. Springer, Cham (2021). https://doi.org/10.1007/978-3-030-67084-9_4
4. de la Barra, C.L., Crawford, B., Soto, R., Misra, S., Monfroy, E.: Agile software development: It is about knowledge management and creativity. In: Murgante, B., et al. (eds.) ICCSA 2013. LNCS, vol. 7973, pp. 98–113. Springer, Heidelberg (2013). https://doi.org/10.1007/978-3-642-39646-5_8
5. Mundra, A., Misra, S., Dhawale, C.A.: Practical scrum-scrum team: way to produce successful and quality software. In: 2013 13th International Conference on Computational Science and Its Applications, pp. 119–123. IEEE, June 2013
6. Misra, S.: Pair programming: an empirical investigation in an agile software development environment. In: Przybyłek, A., Miler, J., Poth, A., Riel, A. (eds.) Lean and Agile Software Development. LASD 2021. Lecture Notes in Business Information Processing, vol. 408. Springer, Cham (2021). https://doi.org/10.1007/978-3-030-67084-9_13
7. Correia, A., Gonçalves, A., Misra, S.: Integrating the scrum framework and lean six sigma. In: Misra, S., et al. (eds.) ICCSA 2019. LNCS, vol. 11623, pp. 136–149. Springer, Cham (2019). https://doi.org/10.1007/978-3-030-24308-1_12
8. Pham, Q.T., Nguyen, A.V., Misra, S.: Apply agile method for improving the efficiency of software development project at vng company. In: Murgante, B., et al. (eds.) ICCSA 2013. LNCS, vol. 7972, pp. 427–442. Springer, Heidelberg (2013). https://doi.org/10.1007/978-3-642-39643-4_31
9. Zamudio, L., Aguilar, J.A., Tripp, C., Misra, S.: A requirements engineering techniques review in agile software development methods. In: Gervasi, O., et al. (eds.) ICCSA 2017. LNCS, vol. 10408, pp. 683–698. Springer, Cham (2017). https://doi.org/10.1007/978-3-319-62404-4_50
10. Rodriguez, G., Glessi, M., Teyseyre, A., Gonzalez, P., Misra, S.: Gamifying users' learning experience of Scrum. In Proceedings of ICTA 2020, CCIS, Springer, Heidelberg (2020)
11. Lindsjørn, Y., Sjøberg, D.I., Dingsøyr, T., Bergersen, G.R., Dybå, T.: Teamwork quality and project success in software development: a survey of agile development teams. J. Syst. Softw. **122**, 274–286 (2016)
12. Dingsøyr, T., Lassenius, C.: Emerging themes in agile software development: introduction to the special section on continuous value delivery. Inf. Softw. Technol. **77**, 56–60 (2016)
13. Hofmann, C., Lauber, S., Haefner, B., Lanza, G.: Development of an agile development method based on Kanban for distributed part-time teams and an introduction framework. Proc. Manufact. **23**, 45–50 (2018)

14. Vinodh, S., Devadasan, S.R., Vimal, K.E.K., Kumar, D.: Design of agile supply chain assessment model and its case study in an Indian automotive components manufacturing organization. J. Manufact. Syst. **32**(4), 620–631 (2013)

15. Miranda, F.A., Subramanyam, G., Van Keuls, F.W., Romanofsky, R.R., Warner, J.D., Mueller, C.H.: Design and development of ferroelectric tunable microwave components for Kuand K-band satellite communication systems. IEEE Trans. Microw. Theory Tech. **48**(7), 1181–1189 (2000)

16. Glaiel, F.: Agile Project Dynamics A Strategic Project Management Approach to the study of Large-Scale Software Development Using System Dynamics. Composite Information Systems Laboratory (CISL), June 2012

17. Dingsøyr, T., Nerur, S., Balijepally, V.G., Moe, N.B.: A decade of agile methodologies: Towards explaining agile software development. 1213–1221. ELSEVIER (2012)

18. Amir, M.K., Khalid, K..A., Khan, M.N.A.: An appraisal of agile software development process. Int. J. Adv. Sci. Technol. **58**(56), 75-86 (2013)

19. Schett, N.M.: COCOMO (Constructive Cost Model). Seminar on Software Cost Estimation University of Zurich, Switzerland (2003)

20. Sommerville.: Software Engineering Edition 8th (2007)

21. Butt, S.A., Jamal, T.: Frequent change request from user to handle cost on project in agile model. Asia Pacific J. Multidiscipl. Res. **5**(2), 26-42 (2017)

22. Moe, N.B.: A teamwork model for understanding an agile team: a case study of a scrum project. Inf. Softw. Technol. **52**(5), 480-491 (2009)

23. Kaur, I., Narula, G.S., Wason, R., Jain, V., Baliyan, A.: Neuro fuzzy—COCOMO II model for software cost estimation. Int. J. Inf. Technol. **10**(2), 181–187 (2018). https://doi.org/10.1007/s41870-018-0083-6

24. Kushwahal, N., Suryakane.: Sofware cost estimation using the improved fuzzy logic framework. In: Conference on IT in Business Industry and Government (CSIBIG), India (2014)

25. Choudhari, J., Suman, U.: Story Points based effort estimation model for software maintenance. Proc. Technol. **4**, 761–765 (2011)

26. Rosa, W., Madachy, R., Clark, B., Boehm, B.: Early phase cost models for agile software processes in US DoD. In: ACM/IEEE International Symposium on Empirical Software Engineering and Measurement (ESEM) (2017)

27. Ahmed, A.R., et al.: Impact of story point estimation on the product using metrics in scrum development process. (IJACSA) Int. J. Adv. Comput. Sci. Appl. (2017)

28. Coelho, E., Basu, A.: Effort estimation in agile software development using story points. Int. J. Appl. Inf. Syst. **3** (IJAIS) (2012)

29. Williams, L., Nagappan, N.: Scrum + engineering practices: experience of three microsoft teams. Softw. Eng. IEEE (2011)

30. Caballero, E., Calvo-Manzano, J.A., San Feliu, T.: Introducing Scrum in a very small enterprise: a productivity and quality analysis. In: O'Connor, R.V., Pries-Heje, J., Messnarz, R. (eds.) EuroSPI 2011. CCIS, vol. 172, pp. 215–224. Springer, Heidelberg (2011). https://doi.org/10.1007/978-3-642-22206-1_19

31. Trendowicz, A., Jeffery, R.: Software Project effort estimation. Springer, Cham. (2014). https://doi.org/10.1007/978-3-319-03629-8

32. Zhang, Z.: The benefits and challenges of planning poker in software development: Comparison between theory and practice. Auckland University of Technology (2017). https://hdl.handle.net/10292/10557

33. Lavazza, L., Morasca, S., Taibi, D., Tosi, D.: Applying SCRUM in an OSS development process. Springer, International Conference on Agile (2010) https://doi.org/10.1007/978-3-642-13054-0_11.

34. Desharnais, J.M., Buglione, L., Kocaturk, B.: Using the COSMIC method to estimate agile user. In: Proceedings of the 12th International Conference on Product Focused Software Development and Process Improvement, pp. 68–73 (2011)
35. Hayata, T., Han, J.: A hybrid model for IT project with scrum. In: Proceedings of IEEE International Conference on Service Operations, Logistics and Informatics (2011)
36. Popli, R., Chauhan, N.: Cost and effort estimation in agile software development. In: International Conference on Reliability Optimization and Information Technology (ICROIT). IEEE (2014)
37. Raslan, A.T., Darwish, N.R., Hefny, H.A.: Towards a fuzzy based framework for effort estimation in agile software development. Int. J. Comput. Sci. Inf. Secur. (IJCSIS), 13(1), 37 (2015)
38. Torrecilla-Salinas, C.J., Sedeno, J., Escalona, M.J., Mejias, M.: Estimating, planning and managing agile web development projects under a value-based perspective. J. Syst. Softw. 61, 124-144 (2015)
39. Moharreri, K., Sapre, A.V., Ramanathan, J., Ramnath, R.: Cost-effective supervised Learning models for software effort estimation in agile environment. In: 40th Annual Computer Software and Applications Conference (COMPSAC). IEEE (2016)
40. Prakash, B., Viswanathan, V.: A Survey on software estimation techniques in traditional and agile development models. Indonesian J. Electr. Eng. Comput. Sci. (2017)
41. Litoriya, R., Sharma, N., Kothari, A.: Incorporating cost driver substitution to improve the effort using agile COCOMO II. In: 2012 CSI Sixth International Conference on Software Engineering (CONSEG), pp. 1–7. IEEE (2012)
42. Raslan, A.T., Darwish, N.R.: An enhanced framework for effort estimation of agile projects. Int. J. Intell. Eng. Syst. 11(3), 205–214 (2018)
43. Butt, S.A.: Analysis of unfair means cases in computer-based examination systems. Pac. Sci. Rev. B: Hum. Soc. Sci. 2(2), 75–79 (2016)
44. Khalid, A., Butt, S.A., Jamal, T., Gochhait, S.: Agile scrum issues at large-scale distributed projects: scrum project development at large. Int. J. Softw. Innov. (IJSI) 8(2), 85–94 (2020)
45. Butt, S.A.: Study of agile methodology with the cloud. Pac. Sci. Rev. B: Hum. Soc. Sci. 2(1), 22–28 (2016)
46. Boehm, B.W.: Software cost estimation meets software diversity. In: IEEE/ACM 39th International Conference on Software Engineering Companion (ICSE-C), pp. 495–496. IEEE (2017)
47. Nguyen, V., Boehm, B., Huang, L.: Determining relevant training data for effort estimation using window-based COCOMO calibration. J. Syst. Softw. 147, 124–146 (2019)
48. Butt, S.A., Abbas, S.A., Ahsan, M.: Software development life cycle & software quality measuring types. Asia. J. Math. Comput. Res. 11(2), 112–122 (2016)

Efficient Traffic Control System Using Fuzzy Logic with Priority

Ayuba Peter[1]([✉]) [iD], Babangida Zachariah[2] [iD], Luhutyit Peter Damuut[3] [iD], and Sa'adatu Abdulkadir[2] [iD]

[1] Department of Mathematical Sciences, Kaduna State University, Kaduna, Nigeria
ayubng@kasu.edu.ng
[2] Department of Computer Science, Kaduna State University, Kaduna, Nigeria
{babangida.zachariah,saa.abdul}@kasu.edu.ng
[3] Department of Computer Science, Plateau State University, Plateau, Nigeria
talk2pdamuut@gmail.com

Abstract. The increase in the number of vehicles on the road is evident by the rate of traffic congestions on daily basis. Problems of traffic congestions are difficult to be measured. Emission of dangerous substances are some of the worrisome effects on weather, theft and delays to motorist are other effects. More and better road network connections have been found to be effective. However, road networks often have intersection(s) which introduces conflicts to right-of-way. These are solved using road traffic light control systems. In this work, an attempt to improve upon an existing programmed stationary road traffic light control system of the Kaduna Refinery Junction (KRJ) is considered. The KRJ is the major road connection to Kaduna main town from the southern part of the state. During working days, motorist from other parts of the country, public and private servants, students, business men, etc. traveling to other parts of the country through the southern part of the state, meet at the KRJ. Trucks conveying petroleum products from the Kaduna Refinery, and vehicles transporting workers, and business men affect the flow of traffic at the junction. An efficient model of fuzzy logic (FL) technique is developed for the optimal scheduling of traffic light control system using TraCI4MATLAB and Simulation of Urban Mobility (SUMO). An average improvement of 2.74% over an earlier result was obtained. Considering priority for emergency vehicles, an improvement of 66.79% over the static phase scheduling was recorded. This shows that FL can be effective on traffic control system.

Keywords: Fuzzy logic · Traffic light control system · Dynamic phase traffic light system · Membership functions · Fuzzy sets

1 Introduction

Currently, traffic congestion and efficient traffic control system has become a generic problem for most urban cities. This is due to the high demand for the

S. Misra and B. Muhammad-Bello (Eds.): ICTA 2020, CCIS 1350, pp. 660–674, 2021.
https://doi.org/10.1007/978-3-030-69143-1_50

transportation of people, goods, and services within the shortest time possible [1]. The high demand in road transportation has led to the increase in the number of motorist. Though, several efforts have been put in place to mitigate the rise in demand by motorist in urban areas, there is no corresponding increase in the number and capacities of the road networks.

Road networks introduces intersections and roundabouts where different vehicular flows have conflicting right of way. In certain instances, this may result in deadlocks that could cause the possibility of crashes, emission of carbon monoxide and other harmful substances from the vehicles to the environment, and unnecessary high waiting times for commuters. There is need to optimally control traffic signals at such an intersection for efficient utilization of the intersection and minimize the environmental effects [2]. In an economy like Nigeria, many urban towns face such problems. Kaduna Refinery Junction (KRJ) which leads to the Refinery Petrochemical Company (RPC) is seriously affected by traffic congestions especially on working days. The KRJ is the major road connection to Kaduna main town from the southern part of the state. During working days, motorist from other parts of the country, public and private servants, students, business men, etc. traveling to other parts of the country through the southern part of the state, meet at the KRJ. Trucks conveying petroleum products from the Kaduna Refinery, and vehicles transporting workers, and business men affect the flow of traffic at the junction.

There are several works in the area of traffic responsive control strategies of traffic congestion problem. These researches employ different techniques such as Mathematical programming [3], dynamic programming (DP) [4], physics methods [5] and agent-based methods [6], fuzzy logic control approaches [7,8], expert systems [9–11], etc. to model and control traffic congestion problem. Each of these techniques has shown improvement over the classical approaches (manual or fixed-time approaches) of traffic management.

Traffic control problems are usually saddled with a lot of uncertainties, such as, the high dynamics of vehicles arrival, travel time, topology of road networks, interactions of other entities with the traffic flow, ambiguous and subjective perception of the road networks, departure time, distance travel, driving speed, weather conditions, personal preferences, roadwork information, etc. These uncertainties require an efficient tool that can deal with the dynamics of the traffic flows appropriately. Fuzzy logic is one of the best mathematical tools that can be very useful in modelling systems with uncertainties [12,13]. Fuzzy logic models a problem into sets whose membership is to a degree, using rules such as, IF queue Length is Long AND waiting Time is Large THEN Phase Duration is Long. The aggregation of such rules are evaluated for an action every time fuzzy inference system is executed.

The problem of emergency was addressed in [14] by designing and implementing smart traffic flow system for a smart city. The system equally addressed issues such as traffic flow adaptation, support of sound driving and message broadcasting. This system cannot be effective at the KRJ because it is solely developed for smart cities. An optimal allocation algorithm using fuzzy logic (FL) was proposed in [15] and reported an average performance of 65.35% improvement. The work in [16] improved upon the work in [15] and reported an average performance of 72.07%. However, the need for improvement on the results, especially in terms of minimal waiting time, queue length, emission of poisonous gases and emergency situations are yet to be fully accomplished.

In this paper, an efficient model is proposed that improves upon the average performance reported in [16] and considered emergency situation using fuzzy logic. The membership functions (MFs) and FL rule base (FLRB) are tuned in modeling a dynamic traffic light control system for the KRJ. The remaining paper is organized as follows: review of literatures and contributions to optimization of traffic control systems with emphasis on FL approaches are presented in Sect. 2. In Sect. 3, materials and methods are presented. Simulation and discussion of results are presented in Sect. 4, and the paper is concluded in Sect. 5 with future research direction.

2 Literature Review and Contributions

Samuel et al. in [17] reported that a major challenge of Africas urban areas, especially those in Nigeria is that of unpredicted traffic flows and the state of the roads. They proposed the application of the technology of internet of things (IoTs) for the enhancement of navigation on roads. However, they do acknowledge the following problems: there are routes without alternative way, poor internet accessibility, epileptic electricity supply, poor internet infrastructures and frequent failure of networks in Nigerian urban towns, to mention but a few that could make the implementation not realize its objectives. The need to implement traffic control systems that use instant data of the queue length and waiting time at an intersection in other to schedule the appropriate phase duration to vehicles is expedient. Dynamic approaches that use Computational Intelligence (CI) approaches are reported to be cost effective and efficient at handling uncertainties experienced at intersections during traffic congestions. In agreement to the need for effective and efficient traffic control management in urban areas; Jin et al. in [18] used SUMO to develop a computational frame work that optimizes traffic flow at two intersections. SUMO was also used by Lee et al. in [19] to model a road intersection by employing the idea of directed graph to create a function between the road network and the traffic flow network. The work reported an improvement on the number of vehicles that passes the intersection per unit time. Yin & Menendez in [20] used SUMO to model vehicles and pedestrians movements in a traffic flow by using DP technique. The results showed that the approach has the capability to control traffic flow. Yu et al. in [21] used Integer Linear Programming (ILP) approach to simulate a road network intersection in an automated vehicle technical environment traffic signal control. The simulation considered left and right turns as well as straight movement of vehicles. The approach attempts to optimize phase allocation, cycle length of the traffic light, vehicles changing lane behavior and the influx of vehicles to reduce the waiting period. The results showed that the Newells technique can track vehicles better than an earlier classical approach in connection to delays, discharge of harmful substances and the junction magnitude. However, the current work utilizes four-way intersection with three lanes each and FL approach in optimizing traffic light control system as compared to the two and one intersections, respectively, DP approach, and ILP which may not be able to adequately represent the complexity in a traffic flow system as they are not known to handle problems associated with uncertainties in complex situations.

In other to reduce traffic congestion at an intersection, Torabi et al. in [22] developed a system using Reinforcement Learning (RL) that was validated and simulated using a road network of 128 intersections. They claimed the system is better than the classical system. Zhang et al. in [23] reported a work using RL in managing traffic control signal wisely. They claimed the model can lower the average waiting period of vehicles at any junction. RL is known to take very long before it rewards or penalized an action as reported by Konar in [24]. Wang et al. in [25] proposed a model of signal assemblage optimization. The developed model consists of a chance component for determining the probability of conflict and a sign for safety innovation consisting of time with mobile energy for calculating the extent of conflict. The simulated results obtained proved that the model can be made operational. Probability approaches are not very good in dealing with uncertainties in complex environments. Emergency situations are considered in modeling traffic light control systems using fuzzy logic in the works reported by Salehi et al. in [26] and Mohit & Shailja in [7] with improvements recorded as compared to fixed traffic control system. However, in this work, four-way intersection with three lanes each is simulated and the inputs to the FL controller (FLC) is modeled using Gaussian membership functions as well as in the output.

Palandiz et al. in [27] applied FL technique to simulate the optimization of a five leg intersection of an automated setting. The results showed that 15.9% fuel usage can be reduced when compared to the traditional approaches. Webster, Elimination pairing and Transyt 14 were compared by Eriskin et al. in [28] for the optimization of a congested traffic flow condition of an intersection. They reported that Transyt 14 and Elimination Pairing generated a superior results and suggested the use of Elimination Pairing approach in a congested traffic situation. A work done by Jia et al. in [29] reported the use of Particle Swarm Optimization (PSO) approach for optimizing traffic light control signal of road intersections in urban areas. Parameters such as emission of poisonous substances, cost incurred for waiting on queues, and the capacity of the intersection are considered as the objectives of the research. The traffic flow considered was a normal traffic flow and not mixed flow. Yao et al. in [30] utilized a simulated automated situation in comparing a well ordered optimization algorithm for phases and a developed two-level progressive model of optimization on a real time adaptive signal timing mechanism of an uncertain traffic flow situation. The work aimed at minimizing the hindrance length of the higher layer and the average waiting time of motorist at the junction. They claimed to achieved 17.95% significant reduction of the average waiting time of motorist. A minimization concept of mathematics which uses

Quadratic Programming (QP) was developed by Raviraj & Daundasekera in [31] using MATLAB tool box for optimization to model an intersection of four lanes. Their objective is to reduce traffic congestion at the intersection. They claimed to have reduced the overall time spent at the intersection during traffic jams when compared to the existing approaches. Techniques such as PSO, Genetic Algorithm (GA), IRACE, and Differential Evolution were implemented by Ferrer et al. in [32] for traffic flow congestions at an intersection. They suggested that a combined approach is better, however, IRACE outperformed the other approaches. Gao et al. in [33] proposed an optimization technique using cells for resolving bad attitudes commonly displayed by motorist in a deregulated economy. The behavior of traffic rule violations when the green wave is assigned to the lane with the right of way. Left or right turns at a junction without being allowed by the traffic light is commonly behavior practiced by motorist. The designed technique had suitable plans in controlling the timing that takes care of conflicting conditions. Wide experimental coverage was done as well as validation in actual life situations. The obtained results when compared to TRANSYT-7F, proved a promising prospect for the model. Zhang in [34] proposed ways in which travelers will enjoy undisrupted and peaceful journeys by using optimization of aggregated road intersections. Travelers were advised to travel in buses and their transportation fairs be reduced and other incentives be provided. Cyclist are encouraged to use their bicycles in other to improve upon their health status. In a nutshell, government can equally participate by ensuring that traffic rules and regulations are adhered to strictly. Li et al. in [35] proposed a model of linked traveling time distribution technique that uses the summation of vehicle movement period as an objective. The time of traffic light signal were simultaneously optimized together with green time slice by the model. These simulations mimicked different scenarios from the current work.

The British Transport and Road Research Laboratory technique and the Australian Road Research Board method were compared with the distribution model and the outcome showed that the linked traveling distribution approach gave a lower number of stoppage by 15%, the total travel period by 0.5%, and reduced the system disruption frequency. Neural Network (NN) and Evolutionary Algorithm (EA) were model by Bernas et al. in [36] to optimize the decentralization policy of traffic light control with two modules. In the first module, sensor information from different road junction were gathered. In the second module, evaluation of priority scheme for deciding on which of the intersection should be given the green wave signal light is performed. GA was developed by Wang et al. in [37] for the optimization of urban road intersection using many parameters. The results show a lowering in the following indicators: 34.03% decrease in the traffic flow, 28.79% decrease in stopping time, 48.73% decrease in vehicle disruption, and 28.04% decrease in the discharge of vehicles at most. The road capacity increase proportionately by 15.67% and the road usage capacity by 7.74% at most. All of these approaches are simulated on different traffic light control systems whose intersections are quite different from the one considered in the current work.

The Fixed Time Traffic Light System (FTTLS) cannot manage different traffic flow with different capacities. In the design of FTTLS safety issues are not put into account. Sometimes, safety issues come as a result of conflict between vehicles taking right or left turn while cyclist are going straight and the failure of clearance that occur as a result of phase change. In an effort to address these problems, Xu et al. in [38] solve the problems of vehicle speed way and traffic signal period simultaneously by developing a combined model approach. The model optimizes traffic signal period and an inherent speed switch for balancing the power of the engine and brake force. This reduces the fuel intake of vehicles.

3   Materials and Method

The materials used for the simulation are the Traffic Light System (TLS) designed in SUMO, the Fuzzy Logic Controller (FLC) designed on MATLAB, and the instant traffic data from SUMO. The TLS manages the intersection by making decisions as to which lane(s) is/are to be allocated right of way be assigning the green wave signal. The TLS is modeled on SUMO displaying the intersection and vehicles as they approach the junction. The TraCI4MATLAB which is a flexible Application Programming Interface quite suitable for use with MATLAB creates an interface between the FLC and the instant traffic data from SUMO.

In this work, a four-way intersection having three lanes each (see Fig. 1 for the different possible traffic turnings at the KRJ) is simulated using simulation of urban mobility (SUMO) interfaced by TraCI4MATLAB on MATLAB R2018a running on Windows7 Ultimate 64-bit Operating system with a RAM size of 8.00 GB and Intel Core(TM) i7, 2620M CPU @2.70 GHz processor. The FL system is modeled using queue length and waiting time as inputs of five fuzzy sets (very low, low, medium, high and very high traffic flows (see Fig. 2)) of Gaussian MFs each and phase duration as output with same MFs. Twenty-five fuzzy rules are formed using the model

$$I^M \tag{1}$$

where, I is the number of fuzzy sets and M is the number of inputs. The surface plot of the design is Fig. 3.

Once a vehicle enters the service facility by passing the first buried loop which is 100 m from the TLS it is assigned an arrival time and a counter keeps track of the number of vehicles in the queue. If the number of vehicles in the service facility wait beyond 10 s, the information is used in the FLC to determine the waiting time of each vehicle and queue length of the vehicles. The FLC receives instant traffic data (waiting time and queue length) via TraCI4MATLAB, evaluates for the maximum waiting time and queue length and decides the optimal schedule for the phase duration (green wave). This is so because the queue discipline is on the basis of first come first serve except for priority case. When a lane has been awarded the green wave signal the data used are discarded after passing the second loop and at the end of the phase duration. These process continues as long as the system detects that the service facility is keeping vehicles waiting beyond 10 s without been assigned the right of way.

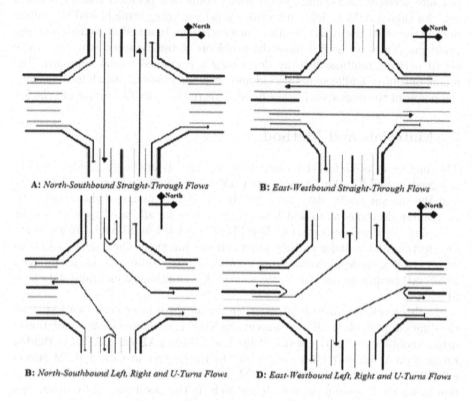

A: *North-Southbound Straight-Through Flows*   B: *East-Westbound Straight-Through Flows*

B: *North-Southbound Left, Right and U-Turns Flows*   D: *East-Westbound Left, Right and U-Turns Flows*

Fig. 1. Isolated intersection traffic flows

4   Simulations, Results and Discussions

The simulation was done for four-way high density, two-way high density, and one-way high density traffic flows and the average waiting time at the intersection was determine for each setup as shown in Table 1 for no priority. The vehicle with the maximum waiting time on each flow was obtained and the flow with the maximum waiting time is assigned the green wave. The maximum waiting time and the queue length is supplied to the FIS and the optimal phase duration is computed and used to set the traffic light for the current phase of the controller. Detectors (inductive loops) are used for obtaining real-time data of queue length and waiting time at the intersection.

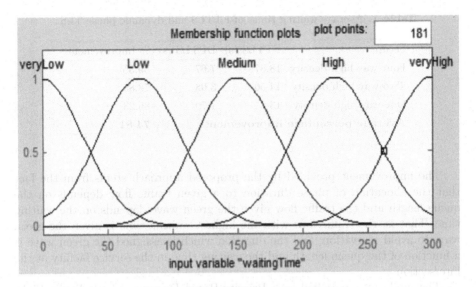

Fig. 2. Fuzzy logic membership functions

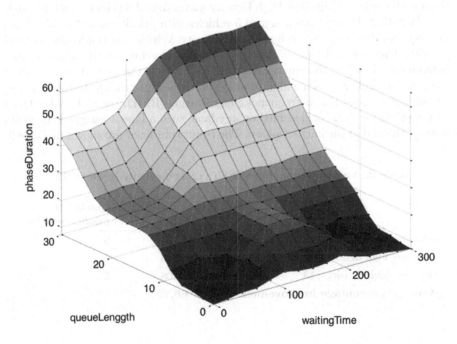

Fig. 3. Fuzzy logic control surface

Table 1. Average waiting times of FTTLS and dynamic phase TLS.

Setup	FTTLS (s)	DPTLS (s)	% Improvement
Four-way high density	18.87	7.67	59.35
Two-way high density	14.56	3.08	78.85
One-way high density	13	1.79	86.23
Average percentage improvement			**74.81**

The improvement provided by the proposed approach stems from the fact that the allocation of phase duration to a given traffic flow depends on the queue length and the traffic flow given the green wave depends on the waiting time. That is, the traffic flow with the highest waiting time is given the green wave to avoid starvation; and the duration which is assigned the green wave is a function of the queue length and the waiting time in the service facility at the intersection.

The model was modified to a Priority-Based Dynamic Phase Traffic Light System (PBDPTLS) to consider vehicles that are on emergency and assigned them with priority. Four-Way High Density was assigned 6 vehicles with priority, Two-Way High Density was assigned 5 vehicles with priority and One-Way High Density was also assigned 5 vehicles with priority. Vehicles are randomly assigned priority. The lane and time of arrival of a vehicle having priority is not known beforehand. However, the number of priority vehicles in the simulation were fixed as shown in Table 2. When a high priority vehicle is approaching the intersection, it is identified using Radio Frequency Identification (RFID) tag and reader. Once a high priority vehicle is identified on any lane, such a lane is assigned the green wave at the end of the current phase. The results obtained are shown in Table 2.

Table 2. Average waiting times of FTTLS and priority-based DPTLS.

Setup	SPSTLS (s)	PBDPSTLS (s)	% Improvement	Number of priority vehicles
Four-way high density	18.87	10.54	44.14	6
Two-way high density	14.56	4.49	69.16	5
One-way high density	13	1.68	87.08	5
Average percentage improvement		**66.79**		

4.1 Simulation Graphs

One-Way Scheduling Graphs

(a) Vehicle accumulation on Refinery Road

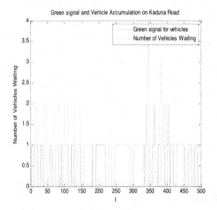

(b) Vehicle accumulation on Kaduna Road

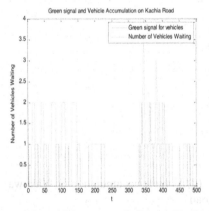

(c) Vehicle accumulation on Kachia Road.

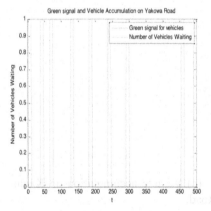

(d) Vehicle accumulation on Yakowa Road

Fig. 4. Vehicle accumulation on four different roads using one-way scheduling graphs.

Figure 4a and Fig. 4d, have no waiting vehicles. The traffic flows in those routes are usually mild. Figure 4b and Fig. 4c shows that about two vehicles are waiting at early hours of the day and about three to four vehicles wait at the evening hours of the day in Kaduna and Kachia roads. This is due to high traffic flow in this route, though one-way scheduling.

Two-Way Scheduling Graphs

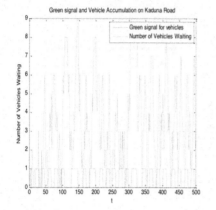

(a) Vehicle accumulation on Kaduna Road

(b) Vehicle accumulation on Refinery Road

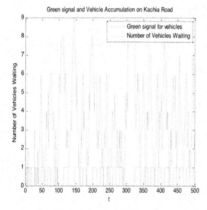

(c) Vehicle accumulation on Kachia Road.

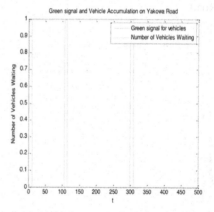

(d) Vehicle accumulation on Yakowa Road

Fig. 5. Vehicle accumulation on four different roads using two-way scheduling graphs.

In Fig. 5a and Fig. 5c, representing accumulations of vehicles at Kaduna and Kachia routes respectively, shows that there are about two to nine vehicles waiting. This is due to the high traffic flows at such routes. Figure 5b and Figure 5d shows no waiting vehicles through the period, this is due to low traffic flow in this routes.

In Fig. 6a and Fig. 6d below, representing accumulations of vehicles at Refinery and Yakowa roads have the maximum of ten vehicles waiting in their respective routes. This is a better representation of the situation at the intersection due to the high traffic flows at such routes. Figure 6b and Fig. 6c below, represents Kachia and Kaduna roads with the usual traffic flows at all period. However, the number of vehicles waiting for a four-way scheduling are still higher as compared to the two-way scheduling. This also reflects the condition obtainable at the intersection.

Four-Way Scheduling Graphs

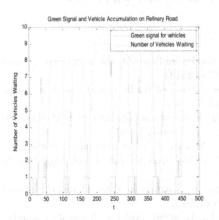

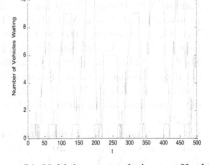

(a) Vehicle accumulation on Refinery Road

(b) Vehicle accumulation on Kachia Road

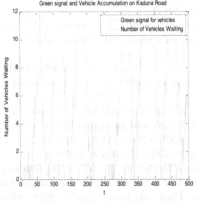

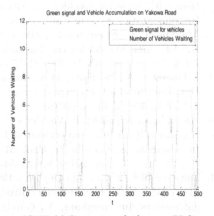

(c) Vehicle accumulation on Kaduna Road.

(d) Vehicle accumulation on Yakowa Road.

Fig. 6. Vehicle accumulation on four different roads using four-way scheduling graphs.

5   Conclusions and Future Research Direction

In this work, an improved dynamic phase scheduling of traffic light control system (DPSTLCS) using fuzzy logic as a modeling tool was done. The results obtained showed an average percentage improvement of 2.74%. When priority was considered a drop in the improvement was recorded. Future research direction, is to consider a combination of Gaussian membership function with a different membership function for both the cases of priority and non-priority.

References

1. Kumar, A.B., Baruah, N.: Minimum cut maximum flow of traffic in a traffic control problem. Int. J. Math. Arch. 4(1), 171–175 (2013)
2. Yan, G.: A two-stage fuzzy logic control method of traffic signal based on traffic urgency degree. Model. Simul. Eng. (2014)
3. Sheffi, Y.: Urban transportation networks: Equilibrium Analysis with Mathematical Programming Methods. Prentice-Hall, New Jersey (1985)
4. Asthana, R., Ahuja, N.J., Darbaari, M., Shukla, P.K.: A critical review on the development of urban traffic models and control systems. Int. J. Sci. Eng. Res. **3**, 16 (2012)
5. Liao, G., Shang, P.J.: Scaling and complexity-entropy analysis in discriminating traffic dynamics. Fractals **20**(03), 233–243 (2012)
6. Jiang, B., Yan, C., Yamada, T., Terano, T.: An agent model with adaptive weight-based multi-objective algorithm for road-network congestion management. Int. J. Comput. Inf. Technol. **03**(06), 1188–1198 (2014)
7. Mohit, J., Shailja, S.: Design of fuzzy logic traffic controller for isolated intersections with emergency vehicle priority system using MATLAB simulation. Control Instrumentation System Conference. ariXiv (2014)
8. Thompson, T., Sowunmi, O., Misra, S., Fernandez-Sanz, L., Crawford, B., Soto, R.: An expert system for the diagnosis of sexually transmitted diseasesESSTD. J. Intell. Fuzzy Syst. **33**(4), 2007–2017 (2017)
9. Falamarzia, A., Borhana, M.N., Rahmata, R.A., Cheraghib, S., Javadic, H.H.S.: Development of a fuzzy expert system to prioritize traffic calming projects. Jurnal Teknologi **78**(2), 43–53 (2016)
10. Azeez, N.A., Towolawi, T., Van der Vyver, C., Misra, S., Adewumi, A., Damaševičius, R., Ahuja, R.: A fuzzy expert system for diagnosing and analyzing human diseases. In: Abraham, A., Gandhi, N., Pant, M. (eds.) IBICA 2018. AISC, vol. 939, pp. 474–484. Springer, Cham (2019). https://doi.org/10.1007/978-3-030-16681-6_47
11. Lawanya Shri, M., Ganga Devi, E., Balusamy, B., Kadry, S., Misra, S., Odusami, M.: A fuzzy based hybrid firefly optimization technique for load balancing in cloud datacenters. In: Abraham, A., Gandhi, N., Pant, M. (eds.) IBICA 2018. AISC, vol. 939, pp. 463–473. Springer, Cham (2019). https://doi.org/10.1007/978-3-030-16681-6_46
12. Peter, A., Tella, Y.: Fuzzy logic system for indoor real-time symbolic location tracking using Wi-fi access point received signal strength indication values. Int. J. Artif. Intell. Mechatron. **3**(5), 254–262 (2015)
13. Kumari, A., Behera, R.K., Shukla, A.S., Sahoo, S.P., Misra, S., Rath, S.K.: Quantifying influential communities in granular social networks using fuzzy theory. In: Gervasi, O. (ed.) ICCSA 2020. LNCS, vol. 12252, pp. 906–917. Springer, Cham (2020). https://doi.org/10.1007/978-3-030-58811-3_64

14. Lee, W., Chiu, C.: Design and implementation of a smart traffic signal control system for smart city applications. Sensors **20**(508), 1–8 (2020)
15. Babangida, Z., Peter, A., Luhutyit, P.D.: Optimization of Traffic light control system of an intersection using fuzzy inference system. Sci. World J. **4**(4), 27–33 (2017)
16. Peter, A., Babangida, Z., Luhutyit, P.D.: Modification of fuzzy logic rule base in the optimization of traffic light control system. Sci. World J. **13**(2), 6–11 (2018)
17. Samuel, V., Misra, S., Nicholas, O.: Internet of things (IoTs) and its application to road navigation and usage problem. In: Asia Pacific World Congress on Computer Science and Engineering, pp. 1–5. IEEE (2014)
18. Jin, J., Ma, X., Kosonen, I.: A stochastic optimization framework for road traffic controls based on evolutionary algorithms and traffic simulation. Adv. Eng. Softw. **000**, 1–13 (2017)
19. Lee, S., Younis, M., Murali, A., Lee, M.: Dynamic local vehicular flow optimization using real-time traffic conditions. IEEE Access Multi. Rapid Rev. Open Access J. **7**, 28137–28157 (2019)
20. Yin, B., Menendez, M.: A reinforcement learning method for signal control at an isolated intersection with pedestrian flows. Retrieved from ASCE Library.org by University of Western Ontario on 8th, April 2019, CICTP, pp. 3123–3135 (2019)
21. Yu, C., Feng, Y., Liu, H.X., Ma, W., Yang, X.: Integrated optimization of traffic signals and vehicle trajectories at isolated urban intersections. Transp. Res. Part B **112**, 89–112 (2018)
22. Torabi, B., Wenkstern, R.Z., Saylor, R.: A collaborative agent-based traffic signal system for highly dynamic traffic conditions. Auton. Agents Multi-Agent Syst. **34**(1), 1–24 (2020). https://doi.org/10.1007/s10458-019-09434-w
23. Zhang, R., Ishikawa, A., Wang, W., Striner, B., Tonguz, O.: Intelligent traffic signal control: Using Reinforcement Learning with Partial Detection. arXiv: 1807.01628v2 [cs.AI], pp. 1–12 (2019)
24. Konar, A.: Computational Intelligence: Principles. Techniques and Applications. Springer, Berlin (2005) https://doi.org/10.1007/3-540-27335-2_1
25. Wang, F., Tang, K., Li, K., Liu, Z., Zhu, L.: A group-based signal timing optimization model considering safety for signalized intersections with mixed traffic flows. J. Adv. Transp. **1–14**, (2019)
26. Salehi, M., Iman, S., Yarahmadi, M.: TLCSBFL: a traffic lights control system based on fuzzy logic. Int. J. of U E-Serv. Sci. Technol. **7**(3), 27–34 (2014)
27. Palandiz, T., Senol, R., Bayrakci, H.C.: Optimization of traffic signalization for complex roundabout by fuzzy logic according to various parameters. Int. J. Comput. Exp. Sci. Eng. (IJCESEN) **5**(1), 27–30 (2019)
28. Eriskin, E., Karahancer, S., Terzi, S., Saltan, M.: Optimization of traffic signal timing at oversaturated intersections using elimination pairing system. In: 10th International Scientific Conference Transbaltica: Transport Science and Technology, Elsevier, ScienceDirect, Procedia Engineering, vol. 187, pp. 295–300 (2017)
29. Jia, H., Lin, Y., Luo, Q., Li, Y., Miao, H.: Multi-objective optimization of urban road intersection signal timing based on particle swarm optimization algorithm. Adv. Mech. Eng. **11**(4), 1–9 (2019)
30. Yao, Z., Wang, Y., Xiao, W., Zhao, B., Peng, B.: A two-level rolling optimization model for real-time adaptive signal control. MDPI, Algorithms **12**(38), 1–10 (2019)
31. Raviraj, Y., Daundasekera, W.: Real time traffic control to optimize waiting time of vehicles at a road intersection. Int. J. Res. Eng. Sci. (IJRES) **6**(4), 25–33 (2018)

32. Ferrer, J., Lo?ez-Ibaez, M., Alba, E.: Reliable simulation-optimization of traffic lights in a real world city. Appl. Soft. Comput. (2019). https://doi.org/10.1016/j.asoc.2019.03.016

33. Gao, Y., Liu, Y., Hu, H., Ge, Y.E.: Signal optimization for an intersection with illegal permissive left-turning movement. Transportmetrica B Transp. Dyn. (2018). https://doi.org/10.1080/21680566.2018.1518734

34. Zhang, H.S.: Traffic organization optimization of urban road combined Intersection. J. Transp. Technol. **9**, 325–330 (2019)

35. Li, M., Xue, H., Shi, F.: Optimization of traffic signal parameters based on distribution of link travel time. J. Cent. S. Univ. **24**(2), 432–441 (2017). https://doi.org/10.1007/s11771-017-3445-5

36. Bernas, M., Placzek, B., Smyla, J.: A neuroevolutionary approach to controlling traffic signals based on data from sensor network. Sensor **19**, 1–24 (2019)

37. Wang, Q., Wang, K., Zhou, S., Shi, Q., Zhang, Q., Sun, H.: Signal timing optimization model of urban road intersection based on multi-factor. MATEC Web Conf. **259**(02004), 1–7 (2019)

38. Xu, B., et al.: Cooperative method of traffic signal optimization and speed control of connected vehicles at isolated intersections. IEEE Trans. Intell. Transp. Syst. **1–14**, (2018). https://doi.org/10.1109/tits.2018.2849029

An Enhanced WordNet Query Expansion Approach for Ontology Based Information Retrieval System

Enesi Femi Aminu[1]([⊠]), Ishaq Oyebisi Oyefolahan[2], Muhammad Bashir Abdullahi[1], and Muhammadu Tajudeen Salaudeen[3]

[1] Department of Computer Science, Federal University of Technology Minna, Minna, Nigeria
{enesifa,el.bashir02}@futminna.edu.ng
[2] Department of Information and Media Technology, Federal University of Technology Minna, Minna, Nigeria
o.ishaq@futminna.edu.ng
[3] Department of Crop Production, Federal University of Technology Minna, Minna, Nigeria
mtsalaudeen@futminna.edu.ng

Abstract. Ontology-based information retrieval is described as a cutting-edge approach capable to enhance the returns of semantic results from documents. This approach works better when similar and relevant terms are added to user's initial query terms using data sources such as wordnet; such technique is known as query expansion. However, the precision of the added term(s) tends to be inaccurate because of the existing WordNet's deficit to handle inflected forms of words. In lieu of this development, this research aims to design Rule based Web Ontology Language (OWL) Information Retrieval System with an enhanced wordnet for query expansion but only limited to the noun subnet database. A combined ontology development methodology was implored; and OWL-2 to develop the ontology for a novel domain of maize crop considering primarily soil, fertilizer and irrigation knowledge. Its rule-based ontology because Competency Questions were modeled using First-Order-Logic (FOL) and encoded with Semantic Web Rule Language (SWRL). Similarly, the wordnet was enhanced on python environment considering the lemmatization's lookup table and the third party modules of Natural Language Tool Kits (NLTK), pattern.en and enchant. Therefore, in this research, the improved wordnet can handle inflected word without stemming it to the root word. It also correctly suggested related words in the case of user's wrong spelt word thereby; reduces minimally time wastage and fatigue. This development invariably aids ontology validation along with the other forms of validations carried out. The research ultimately offers an effective ontology-based information retrieval system based on the proposed algorithmic framework.

Keywords: Inflected words · Maize ontology · Query expansion · Soils fertilizer and irrigations knowledge · WordNet

© Springer Nature Switzerland AG 2021
S. Misra and B. Muhammad-Bello (Eds.): ICTA 2020, CCIS 1350, pp. 675–688, 2021.
https://doi.org/10.1007/978-3-030-69143-1_51

1 Introduction

In this present age, while the exponential growth of data across different repositories is described as heartwarming development; but on the other hand, it also present a challenge for efficient retrieval of relevant information [1]. No doubt that the evolution of semantic based Information Retrieval (IR) is gradually negating the syntactic forms of IR. This development is attributed to the word-based depiction of initial query and corpus documents in repositories of syntactic techniques, which is seen as its pitfall [2]. Based on literature, the challenges of retrieving relevant results as to user's intent is most often characterized by unstructured formats of data that is, data are not machine represented. Thereby, making it difficult for machine to understand and gives due meaning to user's query. To this end, literature have identified a cutting-edge technology known as semantic approach as a proven and possible solution [3]. Semantic search is a type of IR system that operate based on linguistic and knowledge models to proffer solutions to the limitations of keyword based search; that is, syntactic approach [4]. Semantic approach, on one hand entails ontology; and information retrieval technique on the other hand [5]. As a matter of emphasis, ontologies largely utilize semantic web's technologies for modeling [6]. While ontologies provide the platform of representing knowledge in a structure format, information retrieval on the other hand focuses on providing (additional) meaning of data about data in order to achieve relevant hit of information.

Ontology has many definitions but one of the most acceptable definitions according to literature is Gruber [7], which states that ontology is a formal and explicit specification of a shared conceptualization. Similar to standard software development, ontology development equally follows some laid down procedures otherwise known as ontology development methodologies. Examples are Fox and Gruninger, Methontology, Uschold and Kings and Food and Agriculture Organization of United Nations (FAO) Based methodologies. However, the scenario ontology developed in this research work to incorporate the proposed enhanced information retrieval technique is developed based on adoption of combined methodologies as proposed in the review literature of [8]. The adopted methodology consists of six activities or processes, which are collection of domain knowledge; specification of ontology's terminologies; definition of competency questions for ontology's purpose and scope; ontology formalization; ontology evaluation and ontology evolution. Thus, task-based or rule ontology has been developed for this proposed system. It is beyond domain ontology because Semantic Web Rule Language was implemented and the domain under consideration is primarily soil, fertilizer and irrigation knowledge for maize crop as an OWL rule-based ontology. And based on literature covered, the domain is considered novel to be ontologically design.

Information Retrieval is described as science of retrieving data or information relevant to user's need. Therefore, the challenge is no longer availability of information, but retrieving the relevant information according to user's intent [9]. This research issue is commonly attributed to the natural language ambiguities or word mismatch issue, for instance; synonyms and polysemy [10]. Naturally, words are synonymous that is; different words with a common meaning such as maize, corn or *zea may*. Similarly, most natural words are equally polysemous that is; a word that gives more than one descriptions. For example; ear which means the sense organ for hearing or fruiting spike of a cereal plant (maize). Obviously, these words ambiguities make it difficult for existing methods to retrieve accurate and balanced information without much compromise on recall and precision of results. Therefore, to proffer solutions to this issue, the technique of extending initial query constructs otherwise known as query expansion considering the query input's similarity or relatedness has been reliably considered in the literature of information retrieval.

Technically, literature [11] and [12] defined Query Expansion as process of adding useful terms to initial query terms manually, interactively or automatically. Essentially, the addition of meaningful terms is carried out and derived from data sources or knowledge collections such as wordnet, domain ontologies and the likes [13, 14]. In this research work, an enhancement of wordnet for query expansion is considered for the proposed framework of the ontology-based information retrieval system. The motivation of this improvement is as a result of the notable issue of the existing wordnet which lacks capacity to precisely output the correct results of word inflected forms [15]. Word inflected forms are parts of speech (for instance, noun) that can stem out existence in various forms such as addition of s, es, to form the plural forms of regular noun and different plural forms entirely for irregular noun from the root word. The existing wordnet works by only assume the root singular word. This issue clearly affects the precision and recall of additional terms from the wordnet to perform query expansion.

Therefore, this research work aims to design an OWL rule ontology-based information retrieval framework of an enhanced WordNet for query expansion approach. The remaining sections of this paper is organized as follows: Sect. 2 dealt with related studies of the subject matter and Sect. 3 presented the framework of the proposed system. The improvement of wordnet for query expansion was accounted for in Sect. 4. While Sect. 5 discusses the results, conclusion and suggested future work was presented in Sect. 6.

2   Related Works

Ontology-based information retrieval is described as a reliable approach that is capable of improving returns from sematic documents [16]. Besides the relevant methodology to develop ontology for information retrieval system, knowledge representation languages such as RDF/S, OWL [17]; and Protégé, TopBraidComposer [18, 19] as editors are equally required to formalize ontology. Despite the emergence of other document collections such as Wikipedia for query expansion, the relevance of wordnet in IR remains steady however, not without notable gap such as its capability to handle inflected forms of words. WordNet, a lexical resource is considered to be one of the global largest word collection corpus that offer a hierarchical structure of Synset (set of one or more synonyms) and semantic properties of every words [20, 21]. Wordnet has three databases. These are noun, verb, adjective and adverb but this research is limited to noun database.

In the research work of [22], a framework was proposed to enhanced query expansion for efficient information retrieval on ontology-based system. The aspect of enhancement was particularly on wordnet's issue of effectively handling inflected forms of word. However, it was not implemented and the algorithm for the system does not take into account ontology evolution. In the quest of noticeable gaps to expand query semantically, [23] carried out a survey research on query augmentation with the aid of sematic data sources. Incidentally, issue of increase in the number of expansion terms was identified for mixed mode technique despite being described to optimally perform. Therefore, the proposed research has duly considered it. The work of [2] observed that some concepts such as proper nouns, new words and other technical terms are not contained in wordnet and domain ontologies. The research therefore, proposed a new approach of obtaining a more accurate semantic search by considering Wikipedia along with wordnet and domain ontology. However, the issue of synsets, inflected terms and technical terms of both proper and improper nouns of wordnet remain unsolved. Similarly, reference [10] implored Wordnet and Wikipedia as a more effective data sources and novel technique for query reformulation in order to gain more results that are relevant. However, the issue of synsets to be selected for query expansion when search term reflects in several synsets remain unresolved. A technique of candidate concepts expansion not only from the set of synonyms of the user query, but also considered the synsets of the synsets was proposed. However, not all concepts form set of synonyms in wordnet.

Furthermore, [1] carried out a recent and well extensive survey work on the application of query expansion approach for retrieval of relevant information spanning from the year 1960 to 2017. The techniques reviewed covered both the old approaches such as relevance feedback and the recent and trending approaches (wordnet and Wikipedia). Specifically, data sources, semantic similarity functions and user participation and application were the factors considered to drawn their position for their comparisons and variances. In the end, the survey opened up several field of studies where query expansion could be applied. For example, in the area of Information retrieval systems since there is always a desire to personalize query results owing to user's query and intended results. Consequently, there is also need for IR systems to be manipulated by personalize query argumentation techniques. Hence, the researchers submitted that in the nearest future personalization of web search hits would offer a significant role in the research of Query Expansion (QE) technique. In addition, the importance of QE is also crucial in ontology mapping when used for information retrieval. For example, the precision of relevant results in the robust research works of [24, 25] could also be enhanced when the technique is implored. Finally, the accuracy and efficiency of this technique can be judged by considering precision and recall metrics of IR [26].

3 Framework of Ontology Based Information Retrieval (IR) System

In this research work, the proposed ontology based retrieval system is on maize crop domain but primarily limited to its soils, fertilizers and irrigation knowledge as shown by Fig. 2 following the adopted ontology development methodology. Figure 1 presented schematic representation of the proposed system in a conceptual framework. The ontology is designed to be rule based as clearly shown by Table 1. More importantly, the component shown in blue colour by Fig. 1 signifies the improved corpus collection (wordnet) in the aspect of handling word inflected forms for expansion of initial user's query. It would mitigate the issue of recall and precision metrics of information retrieval when fully implemented with the entire system. At this point, it is good to mention that the work is in progress and nearly at the point of evaluation.

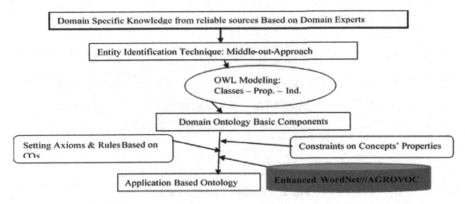

Fig. 1. Conceptual framework of ontology based IR system. (Color figure online)

From Fig. 1, data were collected from reliable research articles and books, published authoritative online data sources, trusted institutes such as CMMYT, IITA, The Institute for Agricultural Research (IAR), Zaria. Subsequently, the collections were validated by domain experts. Middle-out-approach is implored as concept identifying technique; because it first identify the most important concepts; then generalized, and specialized into other concepts. The next step formalized the concepts using OWL, the most highly expressive language that comprises of three major components as Classes, Properties and Individuals but denoted in the figure as *classes, prop and ind* respectively. These processes lead to domain ontology. However, the ontology based information retrieval in this research work goes beyond the development of domain ontology or light weight ontology. It is extended by making it tasking and more intelligent by enforcing high-level constraints on concepts' properties (object and data properties of classes) and considered rules and axioms. First-Order-Logic is used to model the competency questions based on contextual information provided by the group of domain experts for axioms and rules; implemented in protégé editor of 5.5.0 via SWRL. Table 1 presents some CQs that were encoded in SWRL and as well query with SQWRL. More importantly, in order to ensure credible information retrieval, an enhanced wordNet that is adequately capable to handle inflected forms of user's query was developed. This is to ensure balanced query augmentation for the proposed system.

The core concepts of the ontology designed includes but not limited to *Maize-Crop/MaizeSeeds* with super class *Crop, Soils, SoilClassificationMethods Fertilizers, FertilizerApplication_Methods, Irrigation, Irrigation_Methods,* as evidently shown in Fig. 3 by OntoGraf of protégé. All the core concepts are subclasses to the main super class *owl:Thing*.

The core concepts of the ontology is well represented by Fig. 2 such as *Soils, Fertilizers, Irrigations* and their related concepts. Currently, the ontology has a total of 4999 OWL axioms, 309 OWL Classes, 423 OWL Object properties, 174 Data properties, 386 Individuals and over 60 SWRL rules based on CQs.

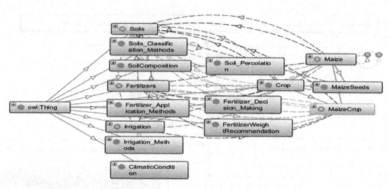

Fig. 2. Ontology's core concepts

The Table presented some samples of the CQs encoded with SWRL and expectedly query with SQWRL. Each of the rule is executed successfully with Drool engine and transferred back the inferred axioms to OWL model that evidently depict the rule richness of the ontology.

Table 1. Querying of rule based ontology

Input Query (Informal CQs)	Semantic Web Rule Language (SWRL)	Semantic Query-Enhanced Web Rule Language (SQWRL)
What is the best soil PH (range) for maize cropping?	Soils(?s)^SoilPHvalues(?p)^ MaizeCrop(?c)^MaizeSeeds(?e)^ Maize_Varieties(?v) ^ SoilFertility(?f) -> canGrowWellOn-TheRangeOf(?c,5-7_PHvalues)^ underWhichMaizeCanGrowdependsOn(?p, ?e) ^ underWhichMaizeCanGrowdependsOn(?p, ?v) ^ underWhichMaizeCanGrowdependsOn(?p, ?s) ^ underWhichMaizeCanGrowdependsOn(?p, ?f) ^ mayBeUsedToCorrect(?p, Liming)	SoilPHvalues(?p). sqwrl:makeSet(?s1, ?p). sqwrl:size(?d,?s1)^SoilFertility(?f)^Maize-Seeds(?e) . sqwrl:makeSet(?s2, ?e). sqwrl:size(?z, ?s2) ^ areInVariousRangesSuitableToGrow(?p, ?e)-> suitable-OrBestAreVariesToGrow(?p, ?e) ^ sqwrl:select(?p)
Which type of fertilizer is suitable for maize cultivation/ what is the best fertilizer type for maize?	Fertilizers(?f)^OrganicFertilizers(?o) InorganicFertilizers(?i)^MaizeCrop(?m)^Urea(?u)^NPK_Fertilizer(?n)^ isAheavyFeederOf(?m,Nitrogen)^strictlyContains(?u,Nitrogen)^containsGoodProportionOf(?n, Nitrogen)^ isAveryRich-FormsOf(PoultryDropping, ?o)^containsAlotOf(PoultryDropping, Nitrogen) ->isTheMostSuitable(PoultryDropping, ?o) ^ isTheMostSuitableForCultivating(?n, ?m) ^ isTheMostSuitableForCultivating (?u, ?m)	Fertilizers(?f).sqwrl:makeSet(?s1, ?f) ^ MaizeCrop(?m) ^ sqwrl:makeSet(?s2, ?m) ^ Urea(?u) ^ NPK_Fertilizer(?n) ^ isAheavyFeederOf(?m, Nitrogen) ^ containsMainlyNitrogen(?u, Nitrogen) ^ containsGoodProportionOf(?n, Nitrogen) ^ containsAlotOfNitrogen(?a, Nitrogen) ^ AnimalManures(?a)^containsAlotOfNitrogen(PoultryDropping,Nitrogen)-> isA_SuitableFertilizerToGrow(?a, ?m) ^ isA_SuitableFertilizerToGrow(?n, ?m) ^ isA_SuitableFertilizerToGrow(?u, ?m) ^ sqwrl:select(?n) ^ sqwrl:select(?u) ^ sqwrl:select(?a)
How many times can irrigation be carried out in maize crop?	Soils(?s)^Irrigation(?i)^Soil_Percolation(?p)^Water(?w)^MaizeCrop(?m)^ SoilNutrient(?n)^ClimaticCondition(?c)^ Season(?e)^ dependsOnAvaliabilityOf(?i, ?w)->mayDetermineTheNumbersOf(?p, ?i)^ mayDetermineTheNumbersOf(?c, ?i)^ mayDetermineTheNumbersOf(?e, ?i)	Soils(?s)^Irrigation_Numbers(?i)^ makeSet(?s1, ?i) ^Soil_Percolation(?p)^MaizeCrop(?m)^ClimaticCondition(?c)^ Season(?e) -> mayDetermineTheNumbersOf(?p, ?i)^ mayDetermineTheNumbersOf(?c, ?i)^ mayDetermineTheNumbersOf(?e, ?i) sqwrl:select(?i)

Furthermore, Algorithm1 duly represents the framework and effectiveness of information retrieval from the ontology. An aspect of uniqueness in this proposed algorithm has to do with the combination of the enhanced Wordnet (as shown by Algorithm2) and the proposed popular Agriculture Vocabulary (AGROVOC) database to serve as data sources to perform query expansion. Besides, the algorithm has the capacity to autonomously perform what we called ontology evolution. Valid concepts that form part of user's query but not in the ontology would be automatically added to it. The rationale behind the combination of the two data sources for query expansion is borne out of the fact that AGROVOC would be able to cover up for the Wordnet. That is, some query's concepts that are not single word cannot be handled by wordnet. And more interestingly, considering the local characteristics or peculiarities of the ontology's domain (agriculture), wordnet is deficit to handle such domain solely.

Algorithm1: A Proposed Ontology Based Information Retrieval Algorithm
Input: User's Query
Output: Semantic Results
Parameters: Query-Q (Competency Question); Enhanced WordNet; AGROVOC; DomainOntology; SeedVariables: Maize-M, Soils-S, Fertilizers-F and Irrigations-I; CandidateTerms-C = y, y is data structure that stores the candidate terms
Procedure:
Step1: *For Each* Input Q
Step2: *Tokenize* Q string
Step3: *While* (i = ! n) { //i and n represent counter and numbers of tokens in a given string respectively
    Preprocessed n *further* to extract C // y is created to count and store C
      /* During preprocessing, unwanted terms and punctuations are
      Eliminated. Candidate Terms-C are extracted based on matching the
      Derived terms (Initial Token minus unwanted terms) to the Domain On
      tology.... */
    ForEach x executes using enhanced WordNet and AGROVOC /* x stands
      for each candidate terms which is expanded using the data sources*/
    Store x on y //y is a candidate terms data structure
    Repeat Execution Until i = = y;
    }
    End Loop
    End For
Step4: Query Expansion (QE) formed = {a, b} or {i_1, i_2, i_3 ...i_n, a_1, a_2, a_3 ...a_e} /* a and b represents the candidate terms and new terms added for expansion. Then TF-IDF applies... */
Step5: *Execute* the QE and If successful, Goto 13.
Step6: *If* QE ≠ {a, b}
Step7: *Then* C do not contain >= two (2) seedVariables of owl:Thing
Step8: *ElseIf* C contain one (1) seedVariable of owl:Thing
Step9: *Then* system suggest one or more seedVariable of owl:Thing to form relation. Goto step5
Step10: *ElseIf* C contain >= two (2) seedVariable of owl:Thing and step4 still not formed.
Step11: *Then* activate ontology evolution and Goto step5.
Step12: *Else* input string is out of subject granularity
Step13: *Output* Semantic Result obtained.
EndFor.

In order to have an efficient ontology-based information retrieval, Algorithm1 proposes the framework. From step1 to 5, user input query gets tokenize. For example, a query as *what is the best soil to grow maize?* Breaks down into tokens as what, is, the, best, soil, to, grow, maize,?, so as to pave way for preprocessing where irrelevant concepts or terms and symbols such as *what, is, the, to,?*, in the first instance are discarded. This is as a result of matching the input tokens against the ontology. More so, in order to mitigate the effects of word mismatch (synonyms), the candidate terms are expanded using the two data sources: enhanced Wordnet and AGROVOC. Thus, the expanded relevant terms known as candidate terms are formed and stored in the data structure. At this point, TF-IDF algorithm is implored to assigns weight and ranked the new terms added (as denoted as b in step 4) to finally store out the best ranked. And thereby, execution of {a, b} follows and output the results accordingly.

Step 6 to 12 suggest that if query expansion do not form, the algorithm assumes that the candidate terms considering core knowledge of the ontology which is coded as seedVariable of owl: Thing are not equal to or greater than two so as to form relation. In that case, it is either the candidate terms contain only one term which cannot form relation (step 8) or the relation is formed (step 10) but terms not in the ontology. In the case of step 8, step 9 suggest that the system would add term(s) to form relation and execute. While for step 10 the system would automatically add the terms for the ontology to evolves. Finally, in a situation where the query terms are confirmed to be totally out of ontology purpose and scope, the algorithm would output message that suggest it.

4 Enhanced Wordnet Query Expansion

The use of WordNet, one of the largest corpus collections as data source for query expansion in IR remains highly significant despite its limitations. It has a long-standing history in the area of text processing or natural language processing. However, aside from its limitation to process compound words like Wikipedia, it is also defected in recognizing word in its inflected forms. It only assumes every word based on their root or stem form which inadvertently affects the expected precision of additional terms in query expansion. Therefore, the identified gap motivated the drive to enhance the wordnet considering its enormous advantages in the area of information retrieval.

In this research, Query Expansion (QE) is mathematically defined as follows:

$$QE = \{i_1, i_2, i_3 \ldots i_n, a_1, a_2, a_3 \ldots a_e\} \tag{1}$$

This equation one is derived from the second equation below.

$$QE = \{((i_1, i_2, i_3 \ldots i_n \cup u_1 \ldots u_m) - (u_1 \ldots u_m)) + (a_1, a_2, a_3 \ldots a_e)\} \tag{2}$$

Where set $\{i_1, i_2, i_3 \ldots i_n \cup u_1 \ldots u_m\}$ represents the initial user's query; set $\{u_1, u_2, u_3 \ldots u_m\}$ represents unwanted terms m which is/are contain(s) in n. However, the scenarios of m in n may occur as follows: m may be equal, greater or less than n (that is, $m > n$, $m > n$, $m > n$). The implication of these scenarios tells the computational overhead (cost) associated with query expansion approach. And lastly, set $\{a_1, a_2, a_3 \ldots a_e\}$ represent the augmented terms. That is, the required relevant and similar terms from the data sources.

In the first instance, the set difference (denoted as -) of the set of initial query terms and the unwanted terms is processed to find the required terms in accordance to the ontology. The unwanted terms consist of stop words, punctuations and the likes. Naturally, initial query terms others known as competency question is a composition or union of relevant and irrelevant query terms. As soon as this first step is achieved, the result (that is, relevant terms otherwise known as candidate term) of the set difference operation is autonomously tagged with similar words from the enhanced wordnet and AGROVOC for query expansion.

Lemmatization technique is implored in improving the inflected forms of word or term taken advantage of its generic lexical lookup table for word's singular and plural. Python environment is used for its implementation considering the NLTK, pattern.en and enchant modules. They make natural language processing easier to modify and improve upon. Figure 3 gives a conceptual representation of how the enhanced wordnet for query expansion is developed.

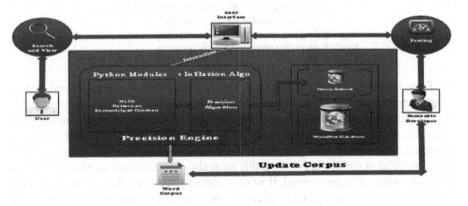

Fig. 3. The enhanced wordnet architecture

The developer accessed the existing wordnet (word corpus) in the python environment via the pattern.en module and NLTK. More so, enchant module was also considered to aid user for cross check spelling in the enhanced version. To deal with the main issue of inflected words, an algorithm named precision was designed as shown by Algorithm2 to finally developed the wordnet. As earlier stated in the previous section, it is only noun subnet or database that is being considered in this research. In addition, an interface was designed to enable end user input search word.

Algorithm2: Word Inflected Forms of (Noun Subnet) Wordnet Algorithm
Procedure:

    Step 1: import list of English words
    Step 2: initialize list of all English words
    Step 3: initialize singular and plural list [data structure]
    Step 4: input word and pass through Step1-3
    Step 5: if word is not == _exit
    Step 6: check singular list
        If Found in singular list
    Step 7: print -> word is singular
    Step 8:   if word is spelt correctly
    Step 9: return true and print dictionary data
        Else
    Step 10: get possible suggestion and print suggested words
    Step 11: identify Inflection
        If Found in plural list
    Step 12: repeat step 8 – 11
        If Not Found in both singular and plural list
        If user input not spelt correctly
    Step 13: initialize possible suggestion word
    Step 14: print suggested words and execute
    Step 15: stop

From step 1–4, through the modules of python programming language and lemmatization technique implored, the algorithm ab initio works by importing and initialize all list of English words in data structure. Then at step 4 user inputs word and the algorithm automatically repeat the previous steps against the inputted word. Step 5–14 checks the existence of the noun word in the lookup table of lemmatization approach and verify if it is in singular or plural words list. At this point also, correctness of word is verified a to ascertain inflected forms of word. If word is correctly spelt out, the system would print out the dictionary meaning and if otherwise, the system suggested possible words. The same processes would be undergone by any forms of inflected word.

5   Results and Discussion

In this research, the OWL rule ontology aspect of the proposed information retrieval system has been duly developed based on the domain. As stated earlier over 60 CQs have been formalized using FOL and as well encoded as rules with the aid of SWRL of protégé 5.5.0 version. All the rules were successfully executed with Drool engine and queried using SQWRL. For example, Fig. 4 depicted the result of querying rule2 of Table 1.

The queried rule in Fig. 4 refers to the second sample rule of Table 1 of the best fertilizer for maize. The question did not specified which of the fertilizer classes (organic or inorganic) consequently, the rule encoded in the ontology thus returns the best fertilizer for inorganic (that is, *NitrogenPhosphorusPotassium_Fertilizer* and *Urea_Fertilizer*) and organic (that is, *PoultryDropping*) from the ontology files as shown in the figure. Letters *n*, *u* and *a* at the output (that is, at the bottom of Fig. 4) are the variables used in the rule.

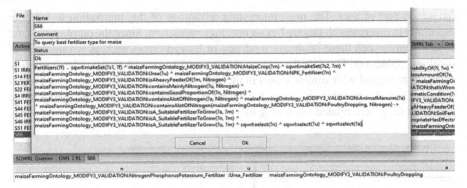

Fig. 4. The SWRL rule output

Furthermore, the proposed algorithm1 serves as a framework in which the ontology-based information retrieval system would be developed. As earlier stated, the development is already in good measures of progress before evaluation.

The results of Algorithm2's implementation in comparison with the existing wordnet are shown by Fig. 4 and Fig. 5.

Figure 4 shows the outputs of the existing and enhanced wordnets by left hand and right-hand sides respectively. The intent of the user's query is crops in inflected (plural) forms. However, while the existing wordnet returns results by working with the root word; the enhanced system works with the original inflected word and also returns appropriate results. Therefore, stemming input string to its root word as does by the existing wordnet can inadvertently affects its capability to provide a precise means of query expansion. Besides, as stated earlier; the enhanced wordnet has the strength to aid user with respect to wrong spelling of input word as shown by Fig. 5.

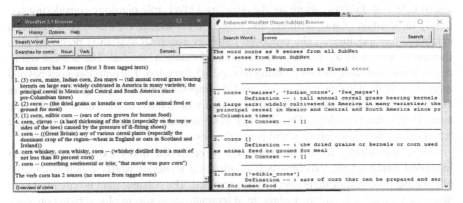

Fig. 5. Wordnets' output

Figure 5 shows a wrong spelling of fertilizer as *fertelizer*. The existing wordnet at left hand side shows no response. But the enhanced wordnet at the right-hand side suggested some correctly spelt related words to assist user. This constantly saves time wastage and fatigue on part of user. The most interesting advantage of this innovation to wordnet especially in this research largely lies on ontology validation. Since the ontology is hand coded from scratch there is always tendency of human errors such as wrong spell of ontology's concepts. Thus, on the course of query expansion, where candidate terms are expected to tagged with similar words in the data source and variance occur as a result of wrong coded concept in ontology; the enhanced wordnet would be able to trap it and generates suggested related terms.(Fig 6)

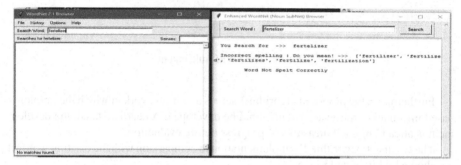

Fig. 6. Wordnets' input string spelling capability

6 Conclusion and Future Work

Query Expansion technique of Ontology-Based Information Retrieval may be designed in three forms. These are query expansion technique using independent knowledge model (WordNet); query expansion technique using domain-specific ontologies and combination of techniques. In this research, the combination of domain ontology and WordNet which is lexical database. More so, the developed OWL rule ontology considering primarily the domain of soil, fertilizer and irrigation knowledge for maize crop implored combined methodologies. The proposed ontology based IR system is premised on a framework shown by algorithm1 for effective information retrieval. The domain ontology is developed based on OWL2 using protégé 5.5.0 version. The ontology goes beyond mere classification in that, some set of verified competency questions (CQs) from domain experts were modeled using FOL, and encoded with SWRL of the editor. Hence, the named OWL Rule ontology. The ontology was validated by experts and also evaluated based on ontology's vocabulary and competencies.

More importantly in this research, the wordnet for query expansion has been improved based on the existing issue of inflected forms of words which is capable of affecting precision of input query to be expanded. The enhancement is only limited to noun subnet database, and the technique of lemmatization was implored based on algorithm2. It was implemented using python programming language taken the advantages of the third party modules of pattern.en, enchant and NLTK. Therefore, the enhanced wordnet has the capability to aid user in suggesting correctly related terms when wrong spelt word occurs. Thereby, reduces minimally user's time wastage and fatigue. This development equally aids in ontology validation. However, the AGROVOC proposed in the framework is yet to be implemented. More so, interested researchers may work on the other databases of WordNet. Besides, a technique can be devised to reduce the issue of computational costs associated with query expansion approach as rightly indicated in Sect. 4 of this research. It is also important to mention that the implementation of the framework (algorithm1) for the ontology-based information retrieval system is in good progress. Therefore, complete evaluation of the system will be carried out upon completion in due course.

References

1. Azad, H.K., Deepak, A.: Query expansion techniques for information retrieval: a survey. Inf. Process. Manage. **56**, 1698–1735 (2019)
2. Jiang, Y.: Semantically-enhanced information retrieval using multiple knowledge sources Cluster Comput. **23**, 1–20 (2020)
3. Sánchez, D., Batet, M., Isern, D., Valls, A.: Ontology-based semantic similarity: a new feature-based approach. Expert Syst. Appl. **39**, 7718–7728 (2012)
4. Thangaraj, M., Sujatha, G.: An architectural design for effective information retrieval in semantic web. Expert Syst. Appl. **41**(18), 8225–8233 (2014)
5. Sánchez, D., Isern, D., Millan, M.: Content annotation for the semantic web: an automatic web-based approach. Knowl. Inf. Syst. **27**, 393–418 (2011)
6. Shadbolt, N., Berners-Lee, T., Hall, W.: The semantic web revisited. IEEE Intell. Syst. **21**(3), 96–101 (2006)
7. Gruber, T.R.: A Translation Approach to Portable Ontology Specifications. Knowl. Acquisition **5**(2), 199–220 (1993)
8. Aminu, E. F., Oyefolahan, I. O., Abdullahi, M. B., Salaudeen, M. T.: A review on ontology development methodologies for developing ontological knowledge representation for various domains. Int. J. Inf. Eng. Electron. Bus. **2**, 28–39 (2020)
9. Yi, M.: Information organization and retrieval using a topic maps-based ontology: result of a task-based evaluation. J. Am. Soc. Inf. Sci. Technol. **15**(12), 1898 – 1911 (2008)
10. Azad, H.K., Deepak, A.: A new approach for query expansion using Wikipedia and WordNet. Inf. Sci. **492**, 147–163 (2019)
11. Bhogal, J., Macfarlane, A., Smith, P.: A review of ontology based query expansion. Inf. Process. Manage. **43**, 866–886 (2007)
12. Francesco, C., Massimo D. S., Luca, G., Paolo, N.: Weighted word pairs for query expansion. Inf. Process. Manage. **51**, 179–193 (2014)
13. Rayner, A., et al.: Ontology based query expansion for supporting information retrieval in agriculture. In: The 8th International Conference on Knowledge Management in organizations, Springer proceedings in Complexity (2014)
14. de Boer, M., Schutte, K., Kraaij, W.: Knowledge based query expansion in complex multimedia event detection. Multimedia Tools Appl. **75**(15), 9025–9043 (2015). https://doi.org/10.1007/s11042-015-2757-4
15. Fawei, B., Pan, J.Z., Kollingbaum, M., Wyner, A.Z.: A semi-automated ontology construction for legal question answering. New Gener. Comput. **37**(4), 453–478 (2019)
16. Baziz, M., Boughanem, M., Aussenac-Gilles, N.: Conceptual indexing based on document content representation. In: International conference on conceptions of library and information sciences, pp. 171–186. Springer (2005)
17. Allemang, D., Hendler, J.: Semantic Web for the Working Ontologist: Effective Modeling in RDFS and OWL. Elsevier, Waltham (2011)

18. Chujai, P., Kerdprasop, N., Kerdprasop, K.: On transforming the ER model to ontology using protégé OWL tool. Int. J. Comput. Theor. Eng. **6**(6), 484 (2014)
19. Alatrish, E.S.: Comparison some of ontology. J. Manage. Inf. Syst. **8**(2), 018–024 (2013)
20. Raja, B., John, P., Chakravarthi, B.R., Arcan, M., Mccrae, J.P.: Improving wordnets for under-resourced languages using machine translation (2018)
21. Uthayan, K.R., Mala, G.S.A.: Hybrid ontology for semantic information retrieval model using keyword matching indexing system. Sci. World J. **2015** (2015)
22. Aminu, E. F., Oyefolahan, I. O., Abdullahi, M. B., Salaudeen, M. T.: Enhanced query expansion algorithm: framework for effective ontology based information retrieval system. I-Manager's J. Comput. Sci.,**6**(4), 1–11 (2019)
23. Raza M,A, Mokhtar, R, Ahmad N, Pasha M, Pasha, U.: Taxonomy and survey of semantic approaches for query expansion. IEEE Access **7**, 17823–17833 (2019)
24. Arogundade, O.T., Abayomi-Alli, A., Misra, S.: An ontology-based security risk management model for information systems. Arab. J. Sci. Eng. **45**(8), 6183–6198 (2020). https://doi.org/10.1007/s13369-020-04524-4
25. Sowunmi, O.Y., Misra, S., Omoregbe, N., Damasevicius, R., Maskeliūnas, R.: A semantic web-based framework for information retrieval in E-learning systems. In: International Conference on Recent Developments in Science, Engineering and Technology, pp. 96–106 (2017)
26. Abioye, T. E., Arogundade, O.T., Misra, S., Akinwale, A. T., Adeniran, O. J.: Toward ontology-based risk management framework for software projects: an empirical study. J. Softw. Evol. Process, **32**(12), p. e2269. (2020)

Design of a Robotic Wearable Shoes
for Locomotion Assistance System

Bala Alhaji Salihu, Lukman Adewale Ajao[✉] [iD], Sanusi Adeiza Audu,
and Blessing Olatunde Abisoye [iD]

Federal University of Technology, Minna 92011, Nigeria
ajao.wale@futminna.edu.ng

Abstract. The inability of a patient to move freely or one part of the body paralysis is an indication of stroke disease or symptoms. This challenge resulted in locomotion of body impairment. In this research, a robotic wearable locomotion assistance system in a pair of shoes is developed using closed-control of mechatronic and embedded system approach. This is to render assistance for the patient impairment locomotion, to improve the passive control and design of orthoses for the structural support of the people with moderate lower-limb weaknesses. The adaptation of this system is varied in position during motion instantaneously and to manage the stiffness of the joint. This wearable robotic shoe helps the paralytic leg (prosthesis) to track the position of the non-paralytic leg using awareness of the sensor and transceivers to establish the communication between the foot posture and support. It also helps the stroke patient with orthoses or prostheses of (foot and leg) to walk linearly in an upright position (maintaining alignment of foot and leg), improving balance, and support the arch and heel of the patient. This system prototype was implemented and tested, and the results show high accuracy in linear tracking and alignment.

Keywords: Assistance system · Embedded system · Paralytic leg · Robotics · Wearable device

1 Introduction

The recent advancement in the robotic system and embedded wearable devices using wireless sensor networks (WSN) has been widely developed for the rehabilitation, human disability assistance, and monitoring health status in biomedical professionals [1, 2]. These systems are sophisticated mechatronic technology equipped with sensors and powerful processing units to exploit real-time information that facilitates independent training during the exercise or enable patient-tailored assistance for locomotion [3, 4]. A wearable robotic system is an innovative rehabilitation insight for individuals (patients) with disabilities [5]. This includes muscle weakness, neurological or muscular disorders [6, 7], stroke, and spinal cord injury which ends-up with loco-motion difficulty (walking or arm movements). Stroke is one of the major and com-mon disability diseases among people of this age that required serious attention to rehabilitation. This disease is seriously

© Springer Nature Switzerland AG 2021
S. Misra and B. Muhammad-Bello (Eds.): ICTA 2020, CCIS 1350, pp. 689–702, 2021.
https://doi.org/10.1007/978-3-030-69143-1_52

affecting humans as a result of poor flowrate in the blood to the brain. The stroke challenges can be Ischemic (inadequate or poor flow rate of the blood to the brain ensued from thrombosis and embolism). The second is hemorrhagic (bleeding) caused by intracerebral or subarachnoid hemorrhage. It is affirmed that stroke affects about 795,000 individuals every year in the USA and recorded as the third disease that leading to emergency death [8, 9].

The stroke disease consequences include body locomotion inability, part of the body paralyzes, speaking difficulty, dizziness, and loss of vision [10]. The National Health Interview Survey (NHIS) data reveal that people with ischemic stroke challenge increases among adolescents and young adults between 5–44 years [11]. It is discovered that about 10% of people between 18–50 years of age were affected with stroke, while the percentage of the people above 50 years are very high and rampant. This symptom can either be temporary or permanent in human if urgent medical attention is not taken. It can result in poor locomotion in humans, stammering, and many others [12]. Therefore, this condition can be improved or supported by taking advantage of the existence of the neuro-rehabilitation robotic system.

A mechatronics system is a typical robotic or an embedded system-on-chip (ESoC) that preferences change in signals from the environment using sensors, process it for the output response using controllers [13, 14], and transform such signal to the motion or actions (actuator). This digitally controlled system usually comprises mechanical systems, sensors, actuators, and microcontroller chips [15].

The design of a mechatronics system (robotics) for neuro-rehabilitation therapy de-pends on the embedded microchip technology [16]. It plays a fundamental role in neuroscience and promotes the recovery of the brain that is utilized for body control. This human mechanism assisting and guiding in the disability of humans to perform some tasks during sensory and coordination in the body system. The motivation of robotic-aided neuro-rehabilitation system design in this research was due to recent scientific evidence in neuroscience that described a physical exercise in the movement action [17]. It promotes a significant effect on the process of neurogenesis by speeding up basic mechanisms that are involved in neural plasticity [18, 19]. The rehabilitation robotic-aided design (RRAD) needs to meet users' requirements, adapt to human performance and guarantee safety, robustness, reliability, comfort, and freedom of movement while pursuing the effectiveness of the treatment. Numerous research efforts have been made towards neurorehabilitation assistance for stroke patients, tremor disorders in huntingtin disease and locomotion impairments development [20].

2   Related Work

A single-joint wearable robotic knee orthosis (RKO) for adult stroke survivals is developed for stroke patients' locomotion. A preliminary report on the efficacy of a hybrid assistive limb in post-stroke hemiplegic patients is proposed for post-stroke assistance [21]. This hybrid assistive limb and a knee-ankle foot orthosis system were tested with 16 stroke patients, which prove efficient during training and the result shows that it improves walking ability and speed.

A locomotive control of a wearable lower exoskeleton for walking enhancement was presented in [22]. This system used an inner and outer exoskeleton to stabilize human walking ability while carrying a payload. The system muscular function improved on the power compensation but cannot automatically move the non-active leg. Hassan et al. proposed the feasibility of synergy-based exoskeleton robot control on inter-limb locomotion [23, 24]. This system generates a motion pattern from a non-paretic leg to aid assistance. The system was tested on patients and results showed an improved spatial symmetry ratio and more consistent step length.

An emerging area of neurorehabilitation is the use of robotic devices to enhance the efficiency and effectiveness of lower extremity physical therapy post-stroke [25]. The mobility training of post-stroke chronic patients using a bionic knee orthosis shows an improved gait speed of (10-m walk), stride length, and walking endurance (6-min walk). But the system cannot automatically move a paralytic leg. Since the mobile robot architecture must include sensing, planning, and locomotion which are tied together by a model.

In this research, a robotic wearable shoe that provides autonomous assistance to stroke patient with walking shoe impairment is develop and implemented for this common human disability using the approach of mechatronics and embedded system designed. This proposed robotic shoe system will align with the affected patient's legs locomotion automatically when the healthy foreleg of a human change in position. However, the application of wearable robotic shoe design includes support for the independent mobility of the elderly with muscle weakness, stroke patients, and people with impaired motor function as well as support for nursing care that involves heavy laborious work [26]. The remaining parts of the paper are arranged as Sect. 3 discussed materials and methods, Sect. 3.1 discussed modeling the architecture of hu-man-robotic joint alignments using linear control loop technique for the controller designed. Section 4 explained the hardware system design and implementation, Sect. 5 is results and discussion and Sect. 6 concludes the research with future re-search expectation.

3 Materials and Methods

The design of neuro-rehabilitation robotics wearable shoes for stroke patient locomotion assistance is proposed using the synergistic approach of combining closed-loop control of mechatronics with embedded system technology. The system model consists of software coding using C-language in the Arduino IDE and hardware system integrations. The hardware architecture for an intelligent robotic shoe impairment of human locomotion assistance includes sensing, planning, and locomotion which all are embedded in a single-on-chip controller system. The neuro-rehabilitation wearable robotic shoe prototype is designed and implemented to assist human disability locomotion as found in stroke patients. The workability principle and flowchart of the system (see Fig. 1).

3.1 A Modeling Architecture of Human-Robotic Joint Alignments

The human sensory part of the brain plays a significant role in motion that controls the arbitrary way of muscle movement Xd and serves as a feedback control-loop in the body system [27]. The motor control of the output signal is generated and sent to the muscle for joint torque F (see Fig. 2). The wearable robotic system can be achieved by

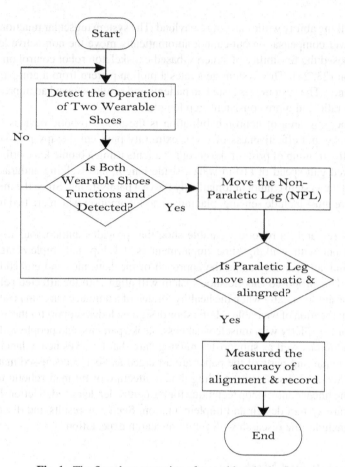

Fig. 1. The flowchart operation of wearable robotic shoes.

sending the received input signal from human motion (human-robot interface) through a muscular tissue (force sensors) and relay information to the embedded controller for the control (actuator). This signal will be processed to generate an assistance motion (torque Fa) to the muscle-skeletal body system accordingly [28, 29]. The closed-loop control system of the human wearable robotic locomotive system (see Fig. 3).

The impedance of the system can be expressed in the Laplace domain as the second-order transfer function $Z(s)$ relating the net force $F(s)$ to the position $X(s)$ as given in Eq. (1). The parameters of M, B, and K denote the mass (Kg), damping coefficient, and stiffness of the system respectively.

$$Z(s) = \frac{F(s)}{X(s)} = Ms^2 + Bs + K \tag{1}$$

In the control of the robot and actuator force $Fa(s)$, the actual dynamic behavior of the system can be modified and replaced by a set of virtual (or desired) parameters as Md, Bd, and Kd. This parameter form of control is referred to as the impedance or called admittance control. The acting force $F(s)$ of the system is subject to the actuator effort $Fa(s)$ generated by the motor. The admittance control can be used to adjust the actuator's force $Fa(s)$ with different impedance as defined in Eq. (2). The parameters of $Md, Bd,$ and Kd are the desired mass, damping coefficient, and stiffness.

$$Z_d(s) = M_d s^2 + B_d s + K_d \tag{2}$$

The measured position of $X(s)$ is used as an input to an impedance control that contains the impedance parameters chosen in the form $Zd(s)$. This system control (impedance) produces the desired force $Fd(s)$ as expressed in formula (3). The actuator force $Fd(s)$ selected and the actual kinematic trajectory $X(s)$ are purposely designed for robot control through the control inner force loop.

$$F_d(s) = \left(M_d s^2 + B_d s + K_d\right)[X_d(s) - X(s)] \tag{3}$$

Therefore, the design of a neurological impaired wearable robotic shoe system required an understanding of human motor control mechanisms [30] and related effects (injury). This is due to its principle of operation that is based on motion in the sagittal plane (front-to-back or back-to-front) through the center of the body [31]. An impedance control with adjustable parameters has been implemented for this assistive control system using derived formula in (4) and (5).

$$\tau = B(q)y + F_v q + F_s sign(q) \tag{4}$$

$$y = M_d^{-1}(M_d q_d + K_p q + K_d q) \tag{5}$$

where τ is the torque command, B is the inertia matrix, $F_v q$ and $F_s sign(q)$ is the dynamic and static friction torques respectively.

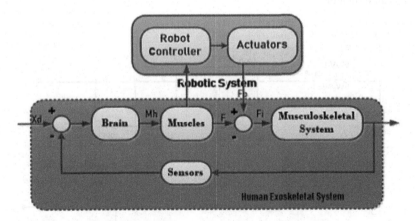

Fig. 2. The human-robot interaction control system.

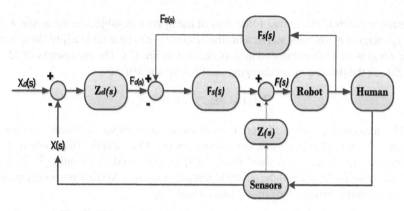

Fig. 3. The closed control loop impedance controller system.

3.2 Hardware System Design and Implementation of Human-Robotic Shoes

The robotic shoe system is a pair of footwear consisting of ultrasonic sensors (distance sensors), electric motors, tires, roller, microcontrollers, transceiver, power supply circuit, and some other electronic components. The (ATmega 328) is utilized as a microcontroller to process the input signal data sent to control the paralytic robotic shoe. The walking process depends on the paretic leg (robotic) to keep tracking and aligning with the non-paretic leg during human movement.

Power Supply Unit. The voltage supply of 5 V output is generated from the regulation of the 9 V battery (see Fig. 4). The positive terminal of the 9 V battery is connected to a switch in series while the negative terminal of the battery is grounded. The other terminal of the switch is connected to the input voltage (Vin) of the IC regulator (LM7805) and the output voltage (Vout) is then connected in parallel to a smoothening capacitor and LED as an indicator.

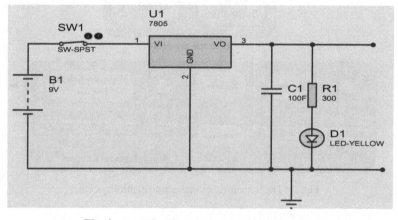

Fig. 4. A regulated power supply circuit diagram.

Position Awareness and Detection Unit. The ultrasonic distance sensor is implemented for non-contact distance measurement. It consists of a transmitter and receiver (Trigg and Echo) that are used to transmit and receive signals. The focus is to measure the time of flight of ultrasonic sound wave from the sensor to detect an object. Therefore, the distance between the transmitter and the object is calculated using simple computation by considering the time taken by the ultrasonic sensor wave to travel from the transmitter to the received end. The measurement range of the sensor is up to 20 m [32, 33] which continuously produces a sound wave that can reflect any surface material. The time it takes the wave to travels back from a reflector is related by the expression in (6) and (7).

$$T_{f(ref)} = D/k.V_s \tag{6}$$

if, $T_f \neq T_{f(ref)}$ then,

$$d = \begin{cases} V_m \times \tau \pm \varphi, T_f \neq T_{f(ref)} \\ 0, T_f = T_{f(ref)} \end{cases} \tag{7}$$

where, $T_{f(ref)}$ is reference time of an ultrasonic pulse to cover distance D in (m), V_s is the velocity of sound in air (m/s), K is constant close to 0.5 which depends on the sensor geometry, D is twice the distance between the legs, d is the distance to be covered by the motor for alignment in (m), T_f is the time of flight when the legs are not aligned, V_m is the velocity of a motor in (m/s), ϕ is the adjustment constant.

Therefore, the navigation is introduced to maintain the distance between the legs and position, thus D is kept constant within range as in formula (8).

$$V_N = D/T_f \tag{8}$$

Since the ultrasonic sensor has four pins which are trigger (Trig), echo, power (Vcc), and ground (GND) port. The Vcc is connected to the 5 V supply, Trig, and echo ports are connected to the microcontroller pins, and the ground is connected to the 0 V. Thus, the distance between the legs can be estimated and the absence of one leg can be detected.

Communication Module. The radio frequency (RF) transceiver is operating at 433 MHz with a data speed of 10 Kbps and is used to establish communication between the pair of robotic shoes. The ultrasonic sensor and the transceiver input signal are processed by a microcontroller to send a command to the dc electric motors. This transmitter utilizes the radio wave link to transmit signals in the form of radiofrequency. The communication distance range depends on the voltage input of (3.5–5 V) of the transmitter. The higher the power input the higher the range but the shorter the life span of the battery. Therefore, the supply voltage of the 0.7 V signal diode is connected in series with the 5V to limit the input power of the transmitter to 4.3 V.

Locomotive System Unit. The two pairs of mini-tires are connected to a pair of 5 V DC-motors with a no-load speed of 200 revolutions/minutes, load-speed of 152 revolutions/min, and torque of 1.0 Kg.cm output which in turn connected to ULN2830. The ULN2830 is connected to four pins of the Microcontroller to transmit and receive commands and is powered by a 5 V power supply. The locomotive circuit design of the wearable robotic system (see Fig. 5 and 6).

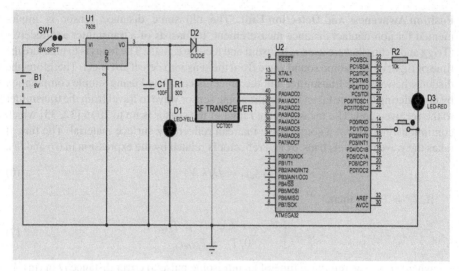

Fig. 5. A circuit design for non-paralytic robotic shoe.

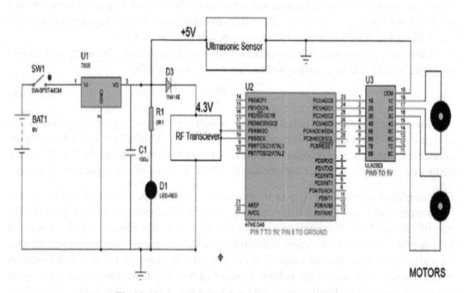

Fig. 6. A circuit design for paralytic robotic shoe.

4   Results and Discussion

The neuro-rehabilitation wearable robotic shoe prototype is designed and implement-ed to assist human disability locomotion as found in stroke patients. This system is tested by observed the position of the non-paretic leg (NPL). Whenever this NPL is lifted or move from point A, then the paretic leg (PL) at position B will automatically sense the change in position A and move to align with it. This process continues the same way to assist the stroke patients in moving the paretic leg automatically (see Fig. 7). The alignment accuracy of the system was tested and recorded during movement at a distance of (10, 20, 30, 40, and 50) meters apart. The result is presented in Table 1, and Table II contains error occurrence at different distances of locomotion.

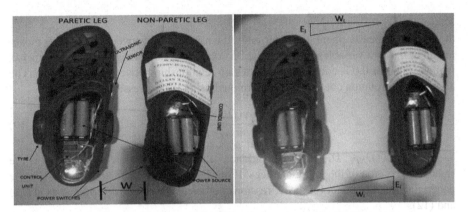

Fig. 7. A design prototype for the robotic wearable shoe.

The horizontal distance between the two legs is W, the forward distance move by the non-paretic leg and the paretic leg are DNPL and DPL respectively. During the movement, we observed differences at 15 cm distance apart between the legs W, while the non-paretic leg has moved a distance of 10 cm, the paretic leg tracked and aligned with a difference of 0.05 cm. Also, at the same distance apart, while the non-paretic leg has moved a distance of 20 cm, the paretic leg aligned with 0.06 cm error as contained in Table 1.

Table 1. Alignment accuracy of a wearable robotic shoes testing.

W = 15 cm		W = 20 cm	W = 25 cm
D_{NPL}(cm)	D_{PL} (cm)	D_{PL} (cm)	D_{PL} (cm)
10	9.95	9.95	9.94
20	19.94	19.94	19.94
30	29.92	29.91	29.90
40	39.92	30.90	39.85
50	49.90	49.90	49.85

4.1 System Performance Evaluation

The performance of this system is evaluated based on the alignment metric using the correlation coefficient between two wearable robotic shoes. The correlation coefficient is

Table 2. Error differences in the locomotive alignment testing.

Distance D_{NPL} (cm)	10	20	30	40	50
Error (e)		0.05	0.06	0.08	0.08	0.10

the statistical measurement that determines the relationship between the relative movements of the two variables. The correlation coefficient value ranges from -1.0 to 1.0, while a value of 0.0 is coefficients denotes no relationship between two variables. The alignment correlation coefficient is determined using the expression in (9).

$$p = \frac{Cov(D_{NPL}, D_{PL})}{\sigma_{NPL}\sigma_{PL}} \tag{9}$$

where $Cov(D_{NPL}, D_{PL})$ is the covariance of the two legs while $\sigma_{NPL} and \sigma_{PL}$ is the standard deviation of the individual legs. If our linear model characteristics is (10), the uncertainty measurement for the regression coefficient (μ) can be determined as in (11) and (12).

$$\gamma = \alpha_0 + \alpha_1 . \beta \tag{10}$$

$$\mu^2(\alpha_1) = \frac{n}{n \sum_{i=1}^{n} \beta_i^2 - (\sum_{i=1}^{n} \beta_i^2)^2} . \sigma^2 \tag{11}$$

$$\mu^2(\alpha_0) = \frac{\sum_{i=1}^{n} \beta_i^2}{n \sum_{i=1}^{n} \beta_i^2 - (\sum_{i=1}^{n} \beta_i^2)^2} . \sigma^2 \tag{12}$$

The covariance $cov(\alpha_0, \alpha_1)$ between the regression coefficients estimation is (13), and the standard deviation σ of distance (γ_i) can be estimated with residual variance is (14).

$$\mu(\alpha_0, \alpha_1) = cov(\alpha_0, \alpha_1) \frac{-\sum_{i=1}^{n} \beta_i}{n \sum_{i=1}^{n} \beta_i^2 - (\sum_{i=1}^{n} \beta_i^2)^2} . \sigma^2 \tag{13}$$

$$\sigma^2 MSE = \frac{1}{n - 2 \sum_{i=1}^{n} [w_i - (\alpha_1 . \beta + \alpha_0)]} \tag{14}$$

The alignment accuracy was conducted and the results are presented (see Fig. 10, 11 and 12). The error difference in alignment testing results in a positive correlation between the two legs (see Fig. 13).

4.2 Evaluation Analysis

The testing of the experimental robotic wearable pair of shoes for the human/patient locomotive disability assistance system was measured and the performances are evaluated using the correlation coefficient to determine the error occurrence during ambulation. At a distance of 10, 20, 30, 40, and 50 m covered during ambulation testing, the error

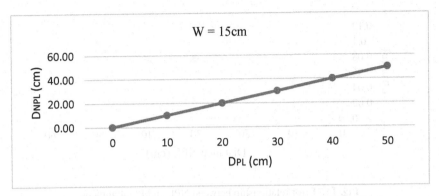

Fig. 8. A relationship between NPL and PL Alignment at W = 15 cm.

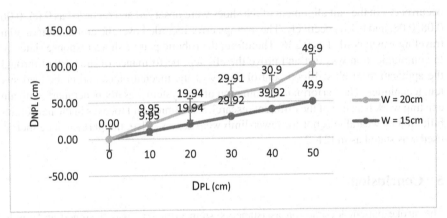

Fig. 9. A relationship between NPL and PL Alignment at W = 15 and 20 cm.

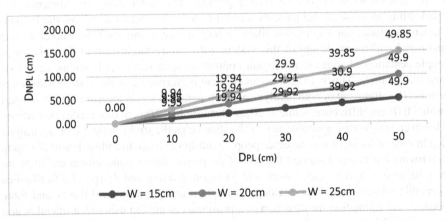

Fig. 10. A relationship between NPL and PL Alignment at W = 15, 20 and 25 cm.

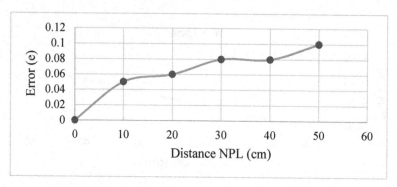

Fig. 11. Error relationship between NPL and PL alignment.

occurrences in the gait alignment of the shoes were observed and recorded as 0.05, 0.06, 0.08, 0.08, and 0.1 respectively. The average error recorded over the ambulation of 50 m traveling was recorded as 0.236. Therefore, the robotic pair of shoes response (latency) to communication was fast and prove the efficient performance of the system through the application of closed-loop control theory of the mechatronics and embedded system techniques. The performance evaluation of the system was not benchmark with any existing work because of the different researcher's opinion and focuses in the neurorehabilitation of wearable robot for lower-limb weaknesses. Also, the performance metrics used was stated as in [21–24].

5   Conclusion

The stroke patient locomotion assistance system prototype was designed and implemented. This system was tested and observing that it is working effectively with mi-nor correlation errors in the pair of shoe alignment. The result shows its efficiency and workability to assist stroke patients' disability to walk linearly and limit the humanitarian assistance for locomotion likewise help in exercising the legs. Therefore, the industrial realization design of this system will require the hi-tech and sophisticated implementation of sensors, intelligent controllers with fuzzy applications, actuators, and many others. This is to achieve an efficient performance of the system with fewer errors. The alignment of both paralytic and non-paralytic legs is measured at 10 cm apart with a 0.05 cm difference, while at 20 cm distance has 0.06 cm differences in position. However, this robotic wearable pair of the shoe helps the stroke patient with a paralytic leg in ease of locomotion and other people with lower limb disability. It will also help improving balance and support the heel of the patient for easy movement and to maintain balance. Future research work will focus on molding and design of a full-bodied wearable robotic pair of shoes using the Laplace domain of control theory and force localization estimation for detection of a prosthesis in motion using an artificial neural network (ANN).

References

1. Jarrassé, N., Proietti, T., Crocher, V., Robertson, J., Sahbani, A., Morel, G.: Robotic exoskeletons: a perspective for the rehabilitation of arm coordination in stroke patients. Front Hum. Neurosci. **8**(2014), 947 (2014)

2. Aliyu, A., Ajao, L.A., Agajo, J., Olaniyi, M.O., Umar, B.U.: Human vital physiological parameters monitoring: a wireless body area technology-based Internet of Things. Jurnal Teknologi dan Sistem Komputer (JTSiskom) **6**(3), 115–121 (2018)

3. Herr, H.: Exoskeletons and orthoses: classification, design challenges and future directions. J. Neuro Eng. Rehabil. **18**(6), 21–25 (2009)

4. Matsuki, H., Nagano, K., Fujimoto, Y.: Bilateral drive gear-a highly back drivable reduction gearbox for robotic actuators. IEEE/ASME Trans. Mechatron. **24**(6), 2661–2673 (2019)

5. Abisoye, B.O., Kolo, J.G., Ajao, L.A., Jimoh, N.O., Abisoye, O.A.: Development of an SMS-based wearable fall detection system. In: IEEE 1st International Conference on Mechatronics, Automation and Cyber-Physical Computer System, pp. 339–345. IEEE, Nigeria (2019)

6. Patel, S., Park, H., Bonato, P., Chan, L., Rodgers, M.: A review of wearable sensors and systems with application in rehabilitation. J. Neuroeng Rehabil. **9**(1), 21–23 (2012)

7. Wong, C.K., Bishop, L., Stein, J.: A wearable robotic knee orthosis for gait training: a case-series of hemiparetic stroke survivors. Prosthet. Orthot. Int. **36**(1), 113–120 (2012)

8. Runchey, S., McGee, S.: Does this patient have a hemorrhagic stroke: clinical findings distinguishing hemorrhagic stroke from ischemic stroke. JAMA **303**(22), 2280–2286 (2010)

9. Jibril, I.Z., Agajo, J., Ajao, L.A., Kolo, J.G., Inalegwu, O.C.: Development of a medical expert system for hypertensive patient's diagnosis: a knowledge-based rules. Adv. Electr. Telecommun. Eng. J. **1**, 23–29 (2018)

10. Stroke, https://en.m.wikipedia.org/wiki/stroke#cite_note-HLB2014W-5. Accessed 10 Jun 2019

11. Mozaffarian, D., et al.: Heart disease and stroke statistics-2016 update a report from the American heart association. Circulation **133**(4), 38–48 (2016)

12. Kriegman, D., Triend, E., Binford, T.: A mobile robot: sensing, planning and locomotion. In: IEEE International Conference on Robotics and Automation **4**(1), 402–408 (1987)

13. Ajao, L.A., Abisoye, B.O., Agajo, J., Ajao, A.O., Mua'zu, M.B., Salami, A.F.: Automated multiple water tanks control systems using ATMEGA and FPGA technology. In: 2019 IEEE 1st International Conference on Mechatronics, Automation and Cyber-Physical Computer System, 346–353, IEEE, Nigeria (2019)

14. Agajo, J., Ajao, L.A., Okahifoh, J., Alao, E.O., Bolaji, A.: Development of a mobile robot for remote monitoring for multimedia and data acquisition. Black Sea J. Eng. Sci. **3**(3), 1–9 (2020)

15. Mustafa, E.: Embedded controller design for mechatronics system. IntechOpen **1**(1), 1–7 (2017)

16. Ajao, L.A., Agajo, J., Kolo, J.G., Adegboye, M.A., Yusuf, Y.: Learning of embedded system design, simulation and implementation: a technical approach. Am. J. Embed. Syst. Appl. **3**(3), 35–42 (2016)

17. Nudo, R.J.: Recovery after brain injury: mechanisms and principles. Front Hum. Neu-rosci. **7**(2013), 887 (2013)

18. Simonetti, D., Tagliamonte, N.L., Zollo, L., Accoto, D., Guglielmelli, E.: Bio-mechatronic design criteria of systems for robot-mediated rehabilitation therapy. Bio-medico (Elsevier), chapter 3, 29–46 (2018)

19. Villa-Parra, A.C., Lima, J., Delisle-Rodriguez, D., Frizera-Neto, A., Bastos, T.: Stance control with the active knee orthosis all or for post-stroke patients during walking. Springer Nature. **22**, 196–200 (2019). https://doi.org/10.1007/978-3-030-01887-0_38

20. Maskeliunas, R., Lauraitis, A., Damasevicius, R., Misra, S.: Multi-class model MOV-OVR for automatic evaluation of tremor disorders in huntington's disease, pp. 1–12. Springer

21. Low, K.H., Liu, X., Goh, C.H.: Locomotive control of a wearable lower exoskeleton for walking enhancement. J. Vib. Control 12(12), 1311–1336 (2006)

22. Hassan, M., Kadone, H., Ueno, T., Hada, Y., Sankai, Y., Suzuki, K.: Feasibility of synergy-based exoskeleton robot control in hemiplegia. IEEE Trans. Neural Syst. Rehabil. Eng. 26(6), 1233–1242 (2018)

23. Young, A.J., Arbor, A., Ferris, D.P.: State of the art and future directions for lower limb robotic exoskeletons. IEEE Trans. Neural Syst. Rehabil. Eng. 25(2), 171–182 (2017)

24. Byl, N.N.: Mobility training using a bionic knee orthosis in patients in a post-stroke chronic state: a case series. J. Med. Case Rep. 6(1), 216 (2012)

25. Maeshima, S., et al.: Efficacy of a hybrid assistive limb in post-stroke hemiplegic patients: a preliminary report. BMC Neurol. 11(1), 116 (2011)

26. Kong, K., Tomizuka, M.: Control of exoskeletons inspired by the fictitious gain in human model. IEEE/ASME Trans. Mech. 14(6), 689–698 (2009)

27. Chen, W.-H., Yang, J., Guo, L., Li, S.: Disturbance-observer-based control and related methods: an overview. IEEE Trans. Ind. Electr. 63(2), 1083–1095 (2016)

28. Masia, L., Xiloyannis, M., Khanh, D.B., Wilson, A.C., Contu, S., Yongtae, K.G.: Actuation for robot-aided rehabilitation: design and control strategies. Nanyang Technological University, Singapore (Elsevier), chapter 4, 47–61 (2018).

29. Perry, J.C., Rosen, J., Burns, S.: Upper-limb powered exoskeleton design. IEEE/ASME Trans. Mechatron. 12(4), 408–417 (2007)

30. Song, S., Geyer, H.: Evaluation of a neuro-mechanical walking control model using disturbance experiments. Front. Comput. Neurosc. 11(15) 2017

31. Kelemen, M., et al.: Distance measurement via using of ultrasonic sensor. J. Autom. Control 3(3), 71–74 (2015)

32. Emmanuel, O.A., Abdusalam, M.O., Ajao, L.A.: Embedded system-based radio detection and ranging (RADAR) system using arduino and ultra-sonic sensor. Am. J. Embed. Syst. Appl. 5(1), 7–12 (2017)

33. Aliyu, S., Yusuf, A., Umar, A., Hafiz, M., Ajao, L.A.: Design and development of a low-cost gsm-bluetooth home automation system. Int. J. Artif. Intell. Appl. 9(8), 41–50 (2017)

Design of Cash Advance Payment System in a Developing Country: A Case Study of First Bank of Nigeria Mortgages Limited

Saka John[1], Jacob O. Mebawondu[2]([✉]) [iD], Ajayi O. Olajide[3], and Mebawondu O. Josephine[2]

[1] Department of Computer Science, Nasarawa State University, Keffi, Nigeria
johnsaka78@yahoo.com
[2] Department of Computer Science, Federal Polytechnic, Nasarawa, Nasarawa, Nigeria
mebawondu1010@gmail.com, jpmebawondu@gmail.com
[3] Department of Computer Science, Adekunle Ajasin University, Akungba, Ondo State, Nigeria
olushola.ajayi@aaaua.ng

Abstract. As Nigeria's economy continues to improve, an automated cash advance payment system can be achieved by adopting the automated Cash Advance Payment System (CAPS). The aim is to promote -good Corporate Governance, thereby increasing stakeholders' confidence in the day-to-day activities of the Bank. CAPS is a system designed to assist organizations in managing and administering cash advances to her employers and other related parties. The motivation for this work are challenges faced by the method of processing cash advance manually, which are prone to error or fraud, undue long hours in the computation of cash advance, and poor tracking of employee records. Insider abuse of cash advance and expense mismanagement has been the major contributor to this menace. This paper presents the design of a cash advance payment system that curbs non-repayment and prevents fraud. For this study, the languages of choice for implementation are PHP and MySQL. While PHP takes care of the client frontend, MySQL serves as the backend. Use case diagram was employed. The developed system stores information with ease, allows easy retrieval of cash advance details, eliminates cash advance fraud and generates reports, which can be printed from any date and year as hard copy for management review and audit purpose. The paper recommends that an automated cash advanced system can be deployed to overcome the observed and highlighted problems inherent in manual cash advanced systems.

Keywords: Mortgage · Credit loan · Financial institutions · Standard Operating Procedure · Cash advance · Payment system

1 Introduction

The banking sector has experienced automation in almost all its operations. Both internal and inter banking operations are now automated. So, automated receipts and payments at

© Springer Nature Switzerland AG 2021
S. Misra and B. Muhammad-Bello (Eds.): ICTA 2020, CCIS 1350, pp. 703–714, 2021.
https://doi.org/10.1007/978-3-030-69143-1_53

international levels; foreign exchange transactions are commendable. The exciting aspect of today banking is mobile banking that enables customers to enjoy banking services at home or any place without visiting the banking hall. However, most of the cash advance to staff for personal and official operations is not automated. Therefore, the existing manual operations lead to fraud, low debt recovery rate, more time used to manage the cash advancement, diversion of funds, and other sharp practices. Besides, the lack of effective control, poor cash advance management, and cash retirement challenges justify the CAPS system's needs. Corruption through fraud is economic cancer that destroys most nations' political, social, and economic sectors. Regrettably, financial frauds are committed through cash and banking transactions. The paper proffers solution by developing a framework for digital identity [1].

A cash advance is an advance payment to an employee that covers legitimate business and traveling expenses. It is a service provided by many organizations, companies, and credit card issuers that allow ATM cardholders to withdraw an amount of money directly from a bank or other financial agency. Cash advance disbursed to an employee of an organization for legitimate business expenses is typically interest-free, but the amount disbursed is to be retired after the assignment has been carried out. Other types of cash advances such as salary cash advance and credit card cash advance attract higher interest rates. Also, the interest begins to accrue immediately the cash is effected. On the other hand, cash advances are quick and easy to obtain without undue stress [2]. A common medium of cash withdrawal is ATM. In an attempt to minimize security in the banking payment system through the usage of ATM, using simulation approach, the work proposed enhanced ATM using a modified biometric security system [3]. The work also evaluated the proposed system; this work carried out CAPS evaluation. The challenge is that there are no fully developed systems to manage cash advancement. Some Cash advance incur fee, although this fee is sometimes waived if the account is in a credit or the applicant is a staff of the organization. Cash advances are short-term loans that one can take against a credit card, up to a certain amount as stipulated by the organization's cash advance policy. The client can collect cash by going to an ATM or a bank to get the cash [2, 3].

Automation of core banking services to customers are reported [3, 4]. Nevertheless, cash advance to staff for either personal or official purposes are not automated, hence, the challenge of high debt recovery rate of cash advance recorded in the financial institutions. Besides, some of the staff divert the cash / loan granted to purposes different from the approved purpose. The other challenges are management need regular update information of cash advanced like the other loans granted for its managerial functions. Automated Cash Advance Payment System (CAPS) will make financial transaction to be transparent, in the public sector; cash advance management system could help save millions, billions and trillions naira being fraudulently loss at local, state and federal levels respectively. The same is applicable to the private sector. An automated system will minimize the corruption experience in the current practice especially when the developed system is evaluated on metric such as precision, accuracy, true and false positive rates. That is global practice.

So, the review literatures highlights that there is need for purpose driven system, avoidance of diversion of cash advance granted to other purpose and the need for management to get up-to-date regular information that will enable management achieve its corporate goals. In addition, good system will reduce corruption and improve debt recovery rate hence increase dividend to stakeholders because financial loss will be minimized. The mentioned challenges justify the need for cash advance payment system in the financial institutions as well as other sector of the nation economy. An automated Cash Advance Payment System (CAPS) is a system designed to organization in the management and administration of cash advances to her employers and other related parties. The research work has five sections. Literature review, materials and method, system implementation, conclusion and recommendation are in Sects. 2, 3, 4, and 5, respectively.

2 Literature Review

According to FBN Mortgages (2006) Standard Operating Procedure (SOP), there are five essential means by which cash advance payment can be executed, namely regular cash advance, particular cash advance, credit card cash advance, merchant cash advance and overdraft cash advance. FBN Mortgages (2006) opined Standard Operating Procedure (SOP) for effective monitoring and policing policy [2, 4, 5].

The key benefit of a digital system is the way it allows organizations to manage expenses policy. Rather than policy being a static document, it can become an active part of the work routine. As more staff of financial institutions start to adopt the new approach, it creates an environment in which cash advance or expenses management is healthy and minimized fraud [6].

There are three primary reasons to request a cash advance, the first and second reasons are advanced monies needed for project and an extended stay in a remote location. The last reason is salary cash advance for customer or staff of the same organization. However, granting and utilization of cash advances need general guidelines for the granting and utilization of cash advance; for instance, no Cash advance shall be given unless for a legally specific purpose specified by the organization policy [4, 7], so a system that will keep tract of cash advance given is important to avoid diversion of fund for other purposes.

There is necessary procedure for obtaining cash advance using CAPS. Obtaining Cash Advances (Travel Advances, Remote Stay Funds, Expense, or Salary Advance), cash advances are requested and reconciled through the system. To receive a cash advance, the staff must first set up as eligible for CAPS. To request a specific cash advance, the staff must log in to the system and request the advance amount needed. The cash advance payment system is part of the expense management system [2, 7]. The Nigerian business environment offers many challenges and opportunities. Various programs and policies have been put in place by both the private and corporate organizations to enhance transparency and buy the confidence of the stakeholders amongst these are Cash Advance Policies [7]. In order to minimize security in banking payment system through the usage of ATM, the work proposed enhanced ATM using modified biometric security system [2]. The work also carried out evaluation of the proposed system, this work carried out CAPS evaluation.

The Design of CAPS ensure that there is transparency in the affairs and running of an organization that disburses cash advances to either their staff or customer. Cash is a scarce commodity. For transparency's sake, the disbursement of cash advance to staff and customers, an automated cash advance system is inevitable to provide a reliable means of carrying out the transaction. CAPS entails how money is being issued to staff and customers of an organization to meet specific needs or requests for funds. It is a general belief that the money is meant to be retired at a specified date, as stated in the organization policy statement for cash advance payment [8].

Regarding the framework for digital identity work, the researcher [1] used unified modeling language diagram (UMLD) technique to model identify features for the system, and the program developed is web-based. Like in the banking sector, where demand for money is more than an available fund, the education sector also faced serious challenges; there are limited lecture halls and laboratories to meet the need of an ever-growing student in high institutions. The researchers made attempt to resolve the challenge by proposing a timetabling that optimizes and laboratories' resources for stakeholders [9]. The developed system is effective and efficient in timetabling and has provision to remind the student of lecture time and place. Software engineering principles applied for system development [10].

According to the Standard Operation Procedure First Bank of Nigeria Mortgages 2016 [4, 11], cash advance settlement should be within 48 h of cash receipt from Finance Department except for traveling purposes where it will be settled 48 h after returning from the trip. Failure to retire due outstanding cash advance shall attract appropriate sanctions and recovery from the next salary and allowances of the affected staff. In the case of mortgage loan, recovery is about ten years [12]. To avoid intruders or unauthorized person to gain access to system, the paper reported security measures to be taken using neural network technique [13]. Currently, First Bank of Nigeria Mortgages Limited operates a manual system for her cash advance payment. The current problems being faced by manually processing cash advance are enormous, which are: late retirement, prone to error or fraud, undue long hours in the computation of cash advance, poor tracking of employee's record. The other factors are: inconsistencies in cash advance payment process, unfavorable and unfortunate policy implementation, and time-consumption.

The alarming increase in examination malpractices and fraud justify the need for online examination and exam marking, especially essay questions. A research paper [14] proposed a system that can mark both objectives and theory questions. The system could mark an exam in record time and is transparent to all candidates. The researchers used query features in the SQL tool for keywords march, which is used for marking essay questions. This research used SQL query features in CAPS to query or get information and report the client's cash advance transactions.

The motivation for carrying out this research was primarily an interest in undertaking the challenges in the cash advance payment system and the opportunity to be derived in the new system. Cash and expense fraud are acknowledged as one of the principal threats to the development of many organizations, and the banking sector in Nigeria is not an exception. Insider abuse of cash advance and expense mismanagement has been the major contributor to this menace. This work is to eliminate or reduce these challenges by implementing an automated cash advance payment system in order to reduce processing costs seen in the manual system. It will also improve compliance to corporate governance and reduce the reimbursement cycle time from weeks to days. It will again eliminate manual tasks, paperwork, time delay, and help reduce the risk of fraud.

This study attempted to design a cash advance payment system that curbs non-repayment and prevents fraud. Specifically, this study is to develop an automated cash advance payment system that will; eliminates manual processes and time delays in cash advance processing, improves compliance to corporate cash advance and expense policies, and reduces the entire reimbursement cycle time. The study concentrates on First Bank of Nigeria Mortgages Limited, a subsidiary of First Bank as part of the financial institutions whose cash advance payment system is the same as that of its parent Bank. The Bank and its subsidiary are guided and audited by the same internal and external policy, and they operate a consolidated same balance sheet. The choice of First Bank of Nigeria was made from available Banks in Nigeria since it is a general belief that the Bank has the highest staff strength and branch network in Nigeria.

Therefore, the review literature highlights the need for purpose-driven systems, avoidance of diversion of cash advance granted to other purposes, and the need for management to get up-to-date, regular information that will enable management to achieve its corporate goals. Besides, a sound system will reduce corruption and improve the debt recovery rate, increasing the dividend to stakeholders because the financial loss is minimized. The mentioned challenges justified the need for a cash advance payment system in financial institutions. The next section discusses how to achieve the set goals.

3 Materials and Method

System Design. This study adopted the structured analysis and design method. In this, stakeholders of the system and the system under investigation, Financial Control Department (FINCON) of FBN Mortgages Ltd, were adequately carried along and needed interviews were conducted to fetch data/information [13]. Samples of existing documents of the current manual cash advanced system were requested for study. To understand the information and data gathering process, upon receipt, sufficient time was taken to evaluate the system. To further ensure adequate evaluation of the system procedure, observations were made to see the running of the existing system further.

Conceptual Model of the New System. A conceptual model is how the user view interface. The model helps the users predict what will happen next and make appropriate decisions about what to do next, and they need a mental model of how the software works. A conceptual model of the interface conveys to users a working model that they can use to form their mental model as illustrated in Fig. 1 [15, 16].

The Fig. 1 depicts a data flow diagram of the Mortgage Cash Advance System. Fig. 2 illustrates the interrelationship between each unit in the systems.

Figure 2 illustrates the Data Flow Diagram of the New System, the password security check is in place to authenticate the user, and all unauthorized access are denied. This data flow is a process by which the CAPS is used to depict the flow of data through the system and the work/processing of all the operations. There are four groups of symbols; the first is predefined process symbol, which represents work to be done. The second

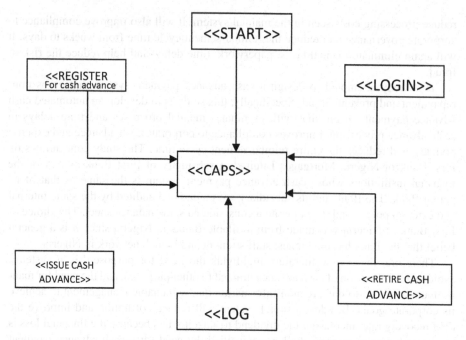

Fig. 1. Data flow diagram of the new system

is the internal storage/data and file storage symbol, which stands for data stores or databases that can be accessed by internal and external agents (e.g. financial control, bursary unit, audit unit etc.). The third is display and terminating symbols, which stands for outputting info and quitting system operations respectively; lastly, the arrows stand for data/operational flow.

Use Case Model. The use case model explains the proposed functionality of the new system, and it is also used to represent a discrete unit of interaction between human beings and the system. The use case also describes the system in terms of actors, but looking at the proposed system, we have three actors involved: the administrator, the user, and the database.

The administrator function is to issue a user name and a password or login details for each user of the system, for easy access into the portal. The administrator will be the only one to create this login detail for other branches. The admin will have access to upload new branches or newly created ones to the database, which is their location and other essential information people will have to know about the branch. The administrator manages database for proper management and maintenance of all reports or information that must have been stored from various branches and departments using the system.

Figure 3 shows the use case system for applicant and applicant's supervisor: A use case uses a system by all categories of users (applicants, supervisors or administrators) to carry out a process on the CAPS. Figure 3 describes the sequence of events of the users called actors of CAPS. Each of the Use Case captures the entire pieces of functional

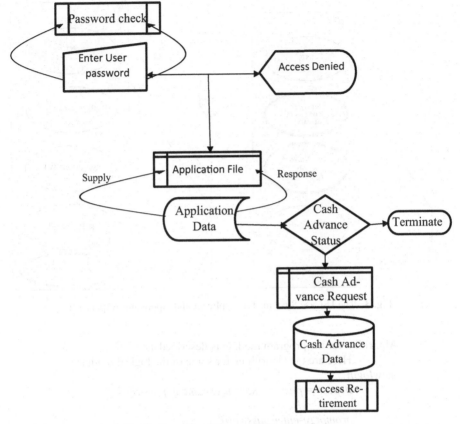

Fig. 2. Data Flow Diagram of the New System

requirements for the users. The entire U-Case altogether describe the overall functional requirements of the CAPs.

Users are the people operating the system from various branches; they will have a unique login detail provided by the administrator from the head office. The login detail used to access the web portal; if successful, the user will be permitted to sign in to the system, create a new record, print report, and view other transactions. The user could also view whether his supervisor and other approval bodies have approved his/her cash advance. After each transaction has been completed, there will be a logout button or exit button so that no other person can quickly access the portal after use. Figure 3 present the U-Case model for this study, showing the various actors.

Automate cash advance and expense management processes, generations of an automated report and are the strengths of the automated cash advance payment system. Other reasons for the systems are management of expense in real-time; cash flow planning assists management in audit processes and prevents the organization from the compliance risk and regulatory sanctions.

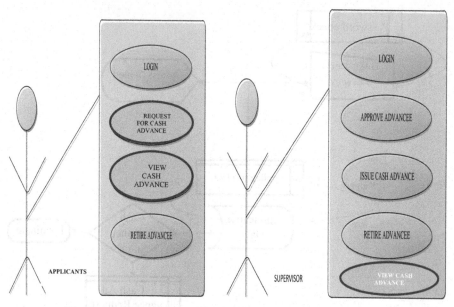

Fig. 3. The U-Case Systems for Applicant and Applicants Supervisor

Algorithm for the program module is described as:

Here are the algorithms for some of the logical modules.

-newlogin

> *Ifcpass = pass => save username & password*
> *else*
> *prompt re-enter password*

Programming Language. For this study, the languages of choice for implementation are PHP and MySQL. While PHP takes care of the client frontend, MySQL serves as the backend. The motivation for PHP and MySQL choice boils down to the fact that; both applications are open source and PHP combined with MySQL are cross-platform (which can be developed in Windows and serve on a Unix platform). Also, PHP is an efficient server scripting language and a powerful tool for making dynamic and inter-active Web pages.

4 System Implementation and Evaluation

Having done the review of the existing cash advance payment systems and the new system's modeling and design, the next thing is to implement the system using the requirements. The new system is fulfilling standard requirements, at the same time, being friendly to the end-users, and presenting precise and complete specifications to the computer programmers and technicians.

4.1 The New System Analysis

The Cash Advance Payment System is divided into modules where each module is described below.

Input / Output Specifications. This section demonstrates the various input and output designs of the proposed system.

Input Specification. Below Are the Various Backend and Frontend Input Forms.

   User's Login Design: the User's Login interface for the Cash Advance Payment Systeis based on the login level, the user is provided with various facilities and functionalities according to job function or assigned duties and responsibilities within the organization.

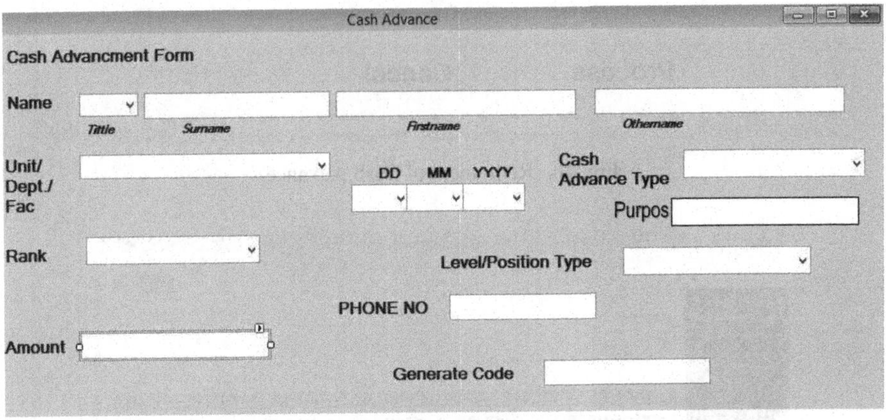

Fig. 4a. Application form for Cash Advance.

Application Form for Cash Advance Module. In Fig. 4a, the module the user an application form to fill all the vita details and information about the user and purpose of the transaction.

   Retirement of Cash Advance Module. In Fig. 4b, the opportunity to retire his/her cash advances by keying the necessary information provided by the system.

Interface Specification

The Retirement Status Interface: This is where all the cash advances listed for administrative review and management shown in Fig. 4c. Also, there is an u*ser' s/add user interface.*

CAPS Performance Evaluation

The work was subject to an integrity test [17]; that is, the program tested in 16 financial institutions in the country. The results of the testing are in Table 1. Users' grading system are excellent, good and fair. Thirteen and three were correctly and wrongly classified, respectively. Performance evaluation of the CAPS was carried out with the aid of the confusion matric tool.

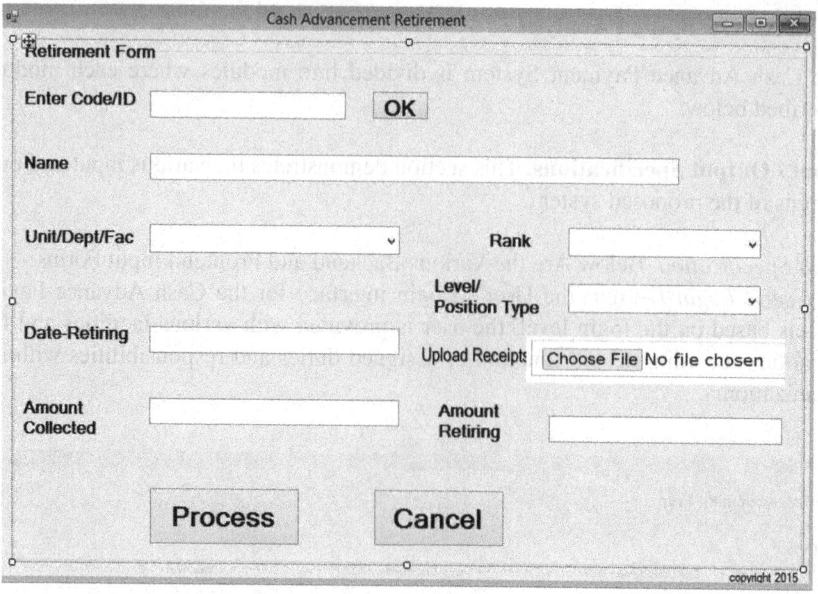

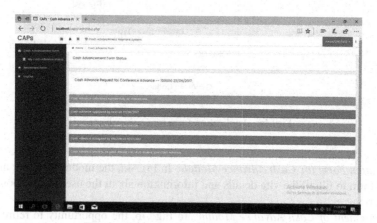

Fig. 4b. Retirement of Cash Advance.

Fig. 4c. Retirement Status Interface Design.

Table 1. Confusion Matrix

Excellent	Good	Fair	
9	1	1	**Excellent**
1	3	0	**Good**
0	0	1	**Fair**

Table 2 depicts the summary of CAPS evaluation. The FP and TP rates are 14.6% and 85.61%, respectively. That means the system is efficient for financial institutions. Similarly, precision and accuracy are 83.33% and 81.25%, respectively, which is another basis to confirm the CAPS system's reliability and efficiency.

Table 2. CAPS Performance evaluation results

Datasets	Correct Classifications	FP rate	TP rate	Precision	Accuracy
CAPS	13	14.6%	85.61%	83.33%	81.25%

5   Conclusion and Recommendation

Conclusion. There is indeed no doubt that the majority of financial institutions have taken advantage of IT for efficient service delivery. Indigenous banks have been rapidly transformed from being just a bank to a one-stop-shop financial solutions provider. As the economy of Nigeria continues to improve, the need for an automated cash advance payment system can be achieved by adopting the automated Cash Advance Payment System (CAPS) to promote good Corporate Governance, thereby increasing stake-holder's confidence in the day-to-day activities of the Bank. The system stores infor-mation with ease, allows easy retrieval of cash advance details, eliminates cash advance fraud, and generates a report which can be printed from any date and year as hard copy for management review and audit purpose.

Recommendation. The system is recommended for implementation in every organi-zation where cash advance payment is being used as part of their daily operational ac-tivities. The system testing and performance evaluation results show excellent improve-ment in the existing cash advance system. Therefore, cash advanced payment automation and implementation of this system is recommended to overcome the ob-served and highlighted problems inherent in manual cash advanced system. It is rec-ommended that anybody wishing to modify this work should dwell more on incorpo-rating an alert component that will instantaneously alert the advance for retirement cases. The need to integrate the CAPS system to banking software is recommended.

References

1. Adewumi, A., Igbinedion, D., Misra, S.: Design and development of a digital identity frame-work for Nigeria. Int. J. Control Theor. Appl. **9**(23), 355–362 (2016) Accessed 25 Oct 2020
2. Lauren, M.: The Evolution of Expense. https://www.tripit.com/blog/2014/05/the-history-of-expense-reports-a-look-at-how-expenses-have-evolved-throughouttime.html. Accessed 23 Feb 2020

3. Adewale, O.S., Mebawondu, J.O., Suleiman, M.N., Mebawondu, O.J.: A Simulation Model for Cardless Automated Teller Machine Transaction, i-manager's Journal on digital signal processing, vol. 6 Issue. 2, pp. 1–8 (2018). https://doi.org/https://doi.org/10.26634/jdp.6.2. 15588. Accessed 20 Jul 2020

4. First Bank of Nigeria Mortgages- Standard Operating Procedure. Accessed 2 May 2020

5. Acharya, V., Berger, N., Roman, A.: Lending implications of US bank stress tests: costs or benefits. J. Fin. Intermediation **34**, 58–90 (2018)

6. Raymond, B.: Expense Management for Ascend CFO. Publisher: CFO Research Services. https://www.ascendcfo.com/pdfFiles/Expense Management Article.pdf (2009). Accessed 17 Mar 2020

7. Duruechi, H., Ojiegbe, N., Chigbu, S.: An impact assessment of regulatory policies on bank lending in Nigeria. International Journal of Education, Science and Public Policy in Africa (IJESPPA) (2014)

8. Ojiegbe, J.: Credit Analysis, Lending and Administration, Owerri. Ben-Son Publishes. Accessed 2 Jul 2020

9. Adewumi, A., Obinnaya, L., Misra, S.: Design and implementation of a mobile based timetable filtering system. Int. J. Control Theor. Appl. **9**(23), 371–375 (2016). Accessed 25 Oct 2020

10. Mebawondu, J., Dahunsi, F., Adewale, O.: Hybrid intelligent model for real time assessment of voice quality of service, Scientific African journal homepage: www.elsevier.com. Accessed 7 Feb 2020

11. Kadge, S., Khan, U., Thange, A.: Sales and invoice management system with analysis of customer behaviour. Int. J. Comput. Appl. Willey & Sons, Inc. **136**(10), 1–7 (2016)

12. Duruechi, H., Ojiegbe, N. Chigbu, S.: An impact assessment of regulatory policies on bank lending in Nigeria. International Journal of Education, Science and Public Policy in Africa (IJESPPA) (2014)

13. Mayer, C.: Developing the Rules for Corporate Governance. Business Day. Accessed 23 Jun 2020

14. Adewumi, A., Adia, F., Misra, S.: Design and implementation of an online examination system for grading objective and essay-type questions. Int. J. Control Theor. Appl. **9**(23), pp. 363–370 (2016). Accessed 25 Oct 2020

15. Chen, C., Geng, L., Zhou, S.: Design and implementation of bank CRM system based on decision tree algorithm. Neural Comput. Appl. (2020). https://doi.org/https://doi.org/10.1007/s00521-020-04959-8

16. Dasaradh, K.: Gate and Pgecet for computer science and information technology Pgs. 9.3, Publisher, PHI Learning Private Limited, Delhi, 110092 (2014)

17. Dahunsi, F.M., Mebawondu, J.O., Adewale, O.S.: Performance evaluation and modeling of internet traffic of an academic institution in Nigeria: a case study of FUTA. Published in FUT Minna Journal 2015 Publication (2014)

Users' Perception of the Telecommunication Technologies Used for Improving Service Delivery at Federal University Libraries in Anambra and Enugu State

Rebecca Chidimma Ojobor[✉]

University of Nigeria, Nsukka, Nigeria
rebecca.ojobor@unn.edu.ng

Abstract. The study examines users' perception of the telecommunication technologies used for improving service delivery at federal university libraries in Anambra and Enugu States of Nigeria. Its specific objectives are to determine users' awareness and satisfaction on the use of telecommunication technologies in service delivery and also to highlight the roles and challenges associated with the use of the facilities in service delivery in the libraries under study. The paper adopts a descriptive survey design. Its target population was 11609 registered library users. A proportionate random sampling technique was used to select 5% (580 respondents) of the population as sample for the study. A self-developed questionnaire was used for data collection. The data collected were analyzed using mean and standard deviation. The result of the study reveals that users were aware of the use of some telecommunication technologies, but were not satisfied with the functional state of most of the technologies used for service delivery. However, the study identifies various challenging factors that undermined effective use of telecommunication technologies to improve service delivery in the study area. Among the identified challenges were poor funding, lack of competent personnel, irregular power supply and lack of internet connectivity. Suggestions are made to improve the functional state of the facilities to ensure prompt and efficient service delivery.

Keywords: Users' perception · Telecommunication technologies · Service delivery

1 Introduction

A library is a central unit of educational institutions especially in institutions of higher learning. It promotes the advancement of knowledge to enhance teaching, learning and research process through the provision of information resources and services to achieve its set objectives. The objectives of establishing libraries are centered on satisfying users' information needs; and were achieved in the pre-computer age using conventional media. Currently, it is difficult if not impossible to achieve the set goals of the library using the

© Springer Nature Switzerland AG 2021
S. Misra and B. Muhammad-Bello (Eds.): ICTA 2020, CCIS 1350, pp. 715–726, 2021.
https://doi.org/10.1007/978-3-030-69143-1_54

same media because of the varied forms and fast rate in which modern information appears. For the library to achieve its objectives of satisfying the informational, recreational and reference needs of patrons, there is need to incorporate computer and other information facilities and resources as their invention will bring several products and services to the scene more than what has been accessible in the pre-computer age [1]. This coincides with [2] that conventional media technologies can no longer meet the information needs of the users; hence, they should be replaced with the emerging technologies in the globe.

The 21st century is characterized with large volume of information resources in multiple formats; varied nature of information seeking-behaviour; and advent of new technologies for acquiring, processing, storing, accessing and disseminating the information to the end-users. Due to the global revolution resulting from the advent of Information and Communication Technology (ICT), the library assumes new dimension in philosophy, model and information service delivery, which result in reoccurring changes in library functions. The emergence of Information and Communication Technologies (ICTs) and the increase in the quest for their use in educational institutions does not only affect the structure of university education or the way teaching and learning is done in the institutions but has also affected the mode of rendering services in their attached libraries [3]. The wide-reaching trend necessitated the changing mode of information provision and service delivery in library from the traditional models to electronic and web-based formats [4].

The new trends in library services are not exempted in Festus Aghagbo Nwako Library, Nnamdi Azikiwe University (NAU) and Nnamdi Azikiwe library, University of Nigeria, Nsukka (UNN) which signify the Federal University Libraries in Anambra and Enugu State respectively. As the collections of these libraries increase exponentially in both forms and formats; processing, organizing and providing access to information resources especially the e-resources constitute serious challenges to service providers (librarians). Again, the rapidly changing preference and emergence of multiple users with diverse information needs suppress the ability of librarians in meeting the ever-increasing demand of information seekers due to the inefficiency of the conventional media used in service delivery. Although, the conventional media as observed by [5] contributed a lot in the past when ICTs had not taken over virtually every aspect of human endeavour, yet the media could neither expose library resources adequately nor assist users satisfactorily in accessing and retrieving information in modern libraries due to the massive volumes and forms of information sources in this era. To this effect, adopting innovative technologies particularly telecommunication technologies for library services becomes a fundamental approach through which the libraries could overcome the excessive burnout on service delivery and correct the adverse effect of users' perception in using the libraries and their resources. Users' perception in this study refers to their feelings and attitudes towards the utilization of telecommunication technologies in service delivery in the concerned libraries.

Telecommunication is an aspect of Information and Communication Technology (ICT) which includes telephone, radio, and television [6]. It is a worldwide transmission of information from one person to another within or outside a geographical area through electronic devices like the phones, radio, television, computers, and internet. The emergence of telecommunication technology has influenced the system of education and improve the mode of communication and service oriented. Information technology precisely the mobile phone as perceived by [7] is popularly use in primary and university education [8]. The positive influence of the technology also extends to libraries. It has improved the mode of information packaging; the dissemination of information resources is faster and more efficient. Currently, the world of information and communication is rapidly changing and today their convergence can be seen more than ever as information is transferred quickly and made available to users all over the world [9].

It is one thing to adopt the innovative technologies and quite another to ensure their effective utilization. A library may be of a good structure, well equipped with information resources, have related technologies and librarians, but when proper utilization of these facilities is not upheld, service delivery may be dreary or ineffectual. Therefore, to ensure appropriate standards on information provision and service delivery in libraries, evaluations to assess the strength and weakness of service delivery are necessary; as this is one of the ways in which libraries can remain relevant to the communities they serve. It is based on this that this paper seeks to examine users' perception of the use of telecommunication technologies for service delivery at federal university libraries in Anambra and Enugu State with specific reference to:

- Determine the level of users' awareness of the telecommunication technologies used for services delivery in federal university libraries of Anambra and Enugu State.
- Assess the level of users' satisfaction with the functionality state of the telecommunication technologies used for services delivery in the federal university libraries under study.
- Identifying users perceived challenges associated with the use of telecommunication for service delivery in federal university libraries of Anambra and Enugu State.

Significantly, the findings of the study are expected to be of immense important to the library, librarians, parent institutions, library users and researchers. Through the findings of the study, libraries will realize the need for proper functioning of telecommunication technologies to improve service delivery, satisfy users' information needs and remain relevance in the community. The findings of the study will also expose the potentials of telecommunication technologies to the librarians, encourage its usage to enable them render prompt and efficient service delivery and be relief from numerous stress of using conventional media. The parent institution will also be encouraged by the findings of this study; to provide adequate fund for maintenance and provision of more telecommunication technologies to enhance library services which geared towards achieving the institutional objectives. Since the study centered on enhancing service delivery, its findings will be beneficial to users as they will no longer waste much time or stress so much to satisfy their information needs. Finally, the findings of the study will serve as a reference material to researchers who may wish to embark on a similar study.

For the fact that no previous study was found to have examined users' perception of the telecommunication technologies used for improving service delivery at federal university libraries in Anambra and Enugu States of Nigeria, hence, the need for the study. The paper has four sections. In the next Sect. 2, the review of related literature is provided. Section 3 presents the research methodology while the fourth section presents and analysis the data. The fourth section has three subsections; the first subsection discusses the major findings; the second subsection highlights the implications of the study while the last subsection concludes the paper.

2   Review of Related Literature

A university library is an intellectual resource centre of the university established to play a supportive role of enhancing knowledge frontier of students, teaching and non-teaching staff of the university [10]. The library is projected as an indispensable organ of the university as it is generally considered as the foundation, epicenter, and hub of information sources of its parent institution, which provide assorted forms of information resources to meet the information needs of its community of users. University libraries support and underpin the delivery of a wide range of information resources making a huge contribution, through the universal offers, to education and lifelong learning among its community of users [11].

This vivacious organ of the university has a dynamic nature and possibly adjust to changes relative to human ideology. It is on the basis of this that Ranganathan in his fifth law described it as a growing organism; and assumes that as human/organizational ideology and knowledge change, the library collections and services also need to be changed to meet with the pace of change in the era. With the prevailing changes in information format, retrieval system and mode of information dissemination resulting from the advent of ICTs, modern libraries especially university libraries need great change in their mode of operations and service delivery to meet with the changing needs of their end users.

Library users are the most important persons in the library setting because all activities of the library are geared towards satisfying their information needs. They are the character for whom the library exists, collects, organizes, packages and disseminates materials and information [12]. Satisfying their information needs is essential to the management of libraries as it is the only way to ensure library's continuity. For this reason, library mission statement always reflects the determination of the other components of the library to render excellent services to the library users [13].

Despite this preference set aside for library users, most libraries are presently losing much of their users to cybercafé and other information centers due to poor quality of service delivery. In respect to this, [14] suggest that adequate plans should be made by libraries to improve their service delivery. This, according to him, could be achieved by first ensuring strong and lasting relationship with their customers, which comprise researchers, faculty members and students. The essence of such relationship is to collaborate and partner with the users in order to design attractive services that will meet their specific information needs, and also be preferable to the services offered in other information centers [15]. For a library to ascertain whether a strong and lasting relationship has been created with its users, there is need to determine users' perception of the nature of service delivery in the library.

Service delivery in a library setting is the manner in which a library packages its services and resources to the users. It is concerned with what, when, and how a library delivers its services to the user and the manner in which the users perceive the services whether it is fair or unfair to them. When a library's service delivery is unfair in nature, it creates negative thinking, scares users and discourages them from patronizing the library and its resources. The reverse is the case when the service delivery is fair or satisfactorily to them. Effectiveness in service delivery entails doing the right things which measure indicators like user satisfaction, via speed, service quality, timing, and human interaction [16]. Libraries of this age can survive and retain their reputation only if they could redesign their services to attract users.

Service delivery concept enormously defines "what is being delivered", how is it packaged before delivery" and "when is it delivered"; and these mediate between the users' information needs and the library's strategic intent to achieve its mission [17]. Therefore, it is crucial for library's openness to new ideas and propensity to adapt to change through adopting new technologies, resources, skills and administrative experience as these will serve as a gateway to an improved service delivery. International Federation of Library Associations and Institutions (IFLA) encourages libraries to adopt high standards on provision and services delivery to ensure innovation in the system [18].

Innovation in service delivery is inevitable for library's success. Globalization and increasing market competitiveness have driven firms towards innovativeness in their operations to gain sustainable competitive advantage [19]. Like other firms, libraries repackage and design new service offerings from either the user's viewpoint or the management's viewpoint to increase the number of their potential users and remain relevant to their user community. According to [20] innovation could either be reactive or proactive in nature. In its reactive nature, it aims at addressing perceived abnormalities, inadequacies and inefficiencies as identified by internal or external users of the library. Such kind of innovation is problem oriented and would adopt a problem-solving approach. Reactive service delivery innovation is triggered by problems perceived by users and administrators, who will highlight problematic practices and routines that they are responsible to oversee [21]. The disparity between the library's strategic intent (what the library intends to provide) and the users information need is one of the problems that leads to reactive service delivery innovation. Perceived service delivery problem is inevitable in any organization that involves a high degree of personal interaction between staff and customer because they cannot avoid errors, mistakes, failures, and complaints in the process [22]. This implies that reactive service delivery innovation is fundamental in addressing existing problems in the library as identified by internal and external patrons.

Proactive service delivery innovation on the other hand is indispensable as it aims at enhancing the library's practices, procedures and process before problems occur. Authors in [20] reveal that the initiatives for proactive service delivery innovation focus on continuous performance and improvement in the organisation. Basically, the creative use of delivery modes is increasingly becoming a new source of differentiation and innovation for organisations today [23]. Therefore, to ensure that the service package and service encounter fit the needs of the users and the library's objectives, library should adhere to proactive measures to design and deliver their services.

The library has undergone various stages of evolution in response to different stages of human development in rendering services that match the trend in the community of users it serves. In all the stages, its mission to provide prompt and efficient information service to users remain unchanged. However, the device used for executing the services changes with time. In centuries ago, the library acquires, catalogues and circulates information resources manually through paper, pens, cards, books, newspapers, newspaper clippings, posters, pictures, films, slides, and microfilms/fiches [24]. These devices served for several centuries until the invention of ICTs, which generates various kinds of scientific knowledge in the society. Meeting the demands of information seekers on such new knowledge create problems for the librarians as the conventional device cannot be used to render effective services. The librarians' inability to render prompt and efficient services, together with other irregularities in the library negatively influence the users' perception of using the library and its resources.

However, with the growing demand and utilization of innovative technologies in education, libraries particularly university libraries need to be restructured to meet the present needs of its parent institution. In this regard, [25] inspires academic libraries in Nigeria to move with the current trend in the globe to maintain its status by adapting innovative strategies to introduce new ideas, methods and processes of doing new things in the library so as to measure up with their contemporaries in the developed countries; meet the information needs of patrons and above all remain relevant to their user environment. Efficiency in adopting information and communication technologies can take different forms; which ranges from limiting errors, enhancing consistency via automating standard tasks to reducing costs by restructuring service delivery via e-applications [26].

Although the development of ICTs in the library improves the existing practices and transformed the library's mode of service delivery to a more prompt and efficient manner yet the innovation creates several challenges to the library and its patrons. It is a well-known fact that most library activities in this era are information technology (IT) dependent. This is a great challenge to both the library and its patrons because IT requires fund and basic skills (which every library staff is compelled to acquire) for its usage. Besides, the unprecedented increase in the volume of digital information available in e-books, e-journals, databases, archives and other digital information sources require some basic skills for easy retrieval and dissemination of such information to the end-users. Due to low level of ICT skill, poor funding and epileptic power supply effective use of telecommunication facilities in Nigerian university libraries is hindered [27]. Furthermore, technostress resulting from the misuse of ICTs is another hinderance to effective use the technologies to improve service delivery [28]. Other impediments to effective application of information technologies to enhance service delivery in libraries include insufficient IT facilities [29]; lack of training, poor infrastructure and high cost of usage [30].

Research Methodology
The study adopts a descriptive survey research design, with a target population of eleven thousand six hundred and nine (11,609) registered library users of the two federal university libraries under study. A sampling fraction of 5% was used to select a sample size of 580 respondents using the proportionate random sampling technique. Out of five hundred and eighty (580) copies of the questionnaire administered to the respondents, five hundred and sixty-seven (567) copies fully filled were retrieved and used for the

study. The data were analyzed using mean and standard deviation. Items with mean scores between 2.50 and above were accepted while items with mean scores below 2.50 were rejected.

3   Presentation and Analysis of Data

Table 1. Descriptive statistics on the level of users' awareness of the telecommunication technologies used for services delivery in federal university libraries in Anambra and Enugu State

No	Item statement	Highly aware	Aware	Less aware	Not aware	Mean	Standard deviation	Decision
1	Computer	382	176	9	0	3.65	0.51	HA
2	Internet	298	267	2	0	3.52	0.51	HA
3	Telephone	211	226	93	37	3.07	0.89	A
4	E- mail	236	148	108	75	2.96	1.07	A
5	Satellite dish	165	184	141	77	2.77	1.02	A
6	Radio	21	43	402	101	1.97	0.63	LA
7	Television	24	43	190	310	1.61	0.8	NA
8	Teleconferencing facilities	12	8	289	258	1.60	0.63	NA
9	Fax machine	0	6	260	301	1.48	0.52	NA
10	Telex	6	15	204	342	1.44	0.6	NA

Table 1 discloses the mean and standard deviation on the level of users' awareness of the telecommunication technologies used for service delivery in federal university library in Anambra and Enugu State. The respondents reveal that they are highly aware of the use of computer (3.65) and Internet (3.52); aware of telephone, e-mail and satellite dish with means scores of 3.07, 2.96 and 2.77 respectively for service delivery in the libraries under study. The table also shows that the respondents are less aware of the use of radio and were not aware of the use of items nos 7–10 for service delivery. This is because the mean scores of the items fall below the criterion mean of 2.50.

Table 2 above reveals the mean responses and standard deviation of users on their level of satisfaction with the functionality state of the telecommunication technologies used for service delivery in the libraries under study. The data displayed on the table show that the respondents were highly satisfied with the functionality of computer (3.63); they were equally satisfied with the functionality state of telephone and e-mail with a mean score of 3.37 and 3.30 respectively. The table also reveals that the respondents were not satisfied with the functionality state of items nos 4–10 as the mean scores of these items fall below the criterion mean of 2.50.

Table 2. Descriptive statistics on the level of users' satisfaction with the functionality state of the telecommunication technologies used for services delivery in federal universities libraries in Anambra and Enugu State.

No	Item statement	Highly satisfy	Satisfy	Less satisfy	Not satisfy	Mean	Standard deviation	Decision
1	Computer	388	157	15	7	3.63	0.60	HS
2	e-mail	340	127	70	30	3.37	0.89	S
3	Telephone	197	346	22	2	3.30	0.56	S
4	Satellite dish	96	143	202	126	2.37	1.01	LS
5	Internet	38	261	82	186	2.27	0.99	LS
6	Radio	88	110	206	163	2.22	1.03	LS
7	Television	70	43	144	310	1.78	1.03	NS
8	Teleconferencing facilities	31	43	235	258	1.73	0.82	NS
9	Telex	35	42	173	317	1.64	0.87	NS
10	Fax machine	22	6	238	301	1.56	0.71	NS

Table 3. Descriptive statistics on users perceived challenges associated with the use of telecommunication technologies for service delivery

No	Item statement	Strongly agree	Agree	Disagree	Strongly disagree	Mean	Standard deviation	Deci-sion
1	Irregular power supply	420	108	32	7	3.66	0.64	SA
2	Lack of competent personnel	324	209	30	4	3.50	0.63	SA
3	Inadequate technological facilities	354	155	38	20	3.49	0.77	SA
4	Poor functionality state of the facilities	273	212	70	12	3.32	0.77	A
5	Frequent change in technology	194	277	96	0	3. 17	0.69	A
6	Poor quality of the facilities	196	231	87	53	3.01	0.94	A
7	Poor network/internet connectivity	133	279	97	58	2.86	0.89	A
8	Poor funding	173	216	95	83	2.84	1.02	A
9	Lack of maintenance	156	236	75	100	2.79	1.03	A
10	Insecurity in the library	67	85	229	186	2.06	0.97	DA

Table 3 shows the challenges associated with the use of telecommunication technologies in service delivery as perceived by users of federal university library in Anambra and Enugu State. The users' responses did not discriminate widely across the numerous challenges encountered in using telecommunication technologies for service delivery. In spite of this, irregular power supply (mean = 3.66), lack of competent personnel (mean = 3.50) and inadequate technological facilities (mean = 3.49) were the greatest challenges encountered. The respondents also identify poor functional state of the facilities, frequent change in technology, poor quality of the facilities, poor network/internet connectivity, poor funding and lack of maintenance with the mean scores range from (3.32–2.79) as other limiting factors while insecurity in the library with (mean = 2.06) is a minor constraint to the use of telecommunication technologies in service delivery in the study area.

4   Discussion of Major Findings

From the data collected and analyzed in Table 1, it was discovered that the respondents were aware of the use of most of the telecommunication technologies like computer, Internet, telephone, e-mail and satellite dish for service delivery in the libraries under study. However, they were not aware of the use of television, fax machine and telex for service delivery in the libraries. These findings could be because most libraries commonly use computers, internet, telephone, e-mail and satellite dish in their public service unit, where the users are allowed to make use of the technologies. Whilst radio, television, fax machine and telex are usually kept and used in the administrative offices were users are not exposed to their usage. This finding agrees with [31] who observe that some available ICT facilities in most libraries are not readily accessible by library patrons as the facilities are kept in the administrative offices. The finding is also in consonance with [32] that the users were neither aware of, nor exposed to many multi-media resources boasted of by most libraries.

Another finding was that the respondents were satisfied with the functional state of computers (3.63), telephone (3.37) and e-mail (3.30). The finding disagrees with [33] who in their study realized that the users were only satisfied with the library space, fans, air conditions, lightings and ventilations and express greater dissatisfaction towards the photocopier facility and computers. However, the finding agrees with [13] who in their study discover that e-mail services, and online reference services satisfied users at a high extent.

The study also found out that the users were not satisfied with the functional state of facilities like internet, radio, telex and fax machine etc. This finding is in line with [13] that facilities such as the fax machine, computer web cameras, projectors and bulletin boards show no satisfaction to users. However, the researchers admit that the facilities were not available in the library at the time of the study.

Finally, the study identified several factors impeding adequate use of telecommunication technologies for service delivery in the study area. The identified factors amongst others are irregular power supply, lack of competent personnel, inadequate technological facilities, poor functionality state of the facilities, poor network/internet connectivity and poor funding. The finding relates with the findings of [27] that inadequate funds, inadequate power supply, lack of government sponsorship, time constraint, irregular organization of IT programmes, inadequate Internet cafes, among others are the challenges facing the effective use of computer systems and technologies in libraries. The finding also agrees with [29] that, the major inhibition to the use of Information technologies is insufficient facilities as well as electricity failure. Furthermore, [34] identified inadequate or slow bandwidth, inadequate computers, network problems, lack of ICT skills, and lack of formal training in internet use, server slowness and frequent breakdown as factors hindering the use of ICT in libraries. Besides, a study conducted by

[30] identified lack of training, poor infrastructure and high cost of usage as obstacles to proper and full application of ICT in libraries.

Implications of the Study

The findings of the study show that although the users of federal university libraries in Anambra and Enugu State were aware of most of the telecommunication technologies used for service delivery, they were not adequately satisfied with the functional state of majority of the facilities as it leads to excessive burnout on service delivery. This implies that users may develop negative attitude towards the use of the library which may consequently leads to neglect and underutilization of the library and its resources.

5 Conclusion

Based on the research findings, the paper concludes that the functional state of most telecommunication technologies in the libraries under study are not encouraging. However, various challenges factors depressing effective functioning of the technologies were identified. Among the challenges are poor funding, lack of competent personnel, irregular power supply and lack of internet connectivity.

Necessary actions should be taken to improve the functional state of telecommunication technologies in these libraries, for prompt and efficient service delivery to the users.

Acknowledgement. It is a pleasure to acknowledge the support provided by Nnamdi Azikiwe Library, University of Nigeria Nsukka through its digital section popularly known and (MTN Library). My thanks also go the numerous authors whose works contributed immensely to the writing of this article.

References

1. Onuoha, J., Chukwueke, C.: Emergent trends in library services delivery: the application of information and communication technologies in academic libraries. Libr. Philos. Pract. (e-journal), 2602 (2019). https://digitalcommons.unl.edu/libphilprac/2602
2. Oshinaike, A.B., Adekunmisi, S.R.: Use of multimedia for teaching in Nigerian university system: a case study of university of Ibadan. Libr. Philos. Pract. **682** (2012). https://unllib.unl.edu/lpp/
3. Utulu, S.C., Alonge, A.: Use of mobile phones for project-based learning by undergraduate students of Nigerian private universities. Int. J. Educ. Dev. Inf. Commun. Technol. (IJEDICT) **8**, 4–15 (2012)
4. Eje, O.C., Dushu, T.Y.: Transforming library and information services delivery using innovation technologies. Libr. Philos. Pract. (e-journal) 2036 (2018). https://digitalcommons.unl.edu/libphilprac/2036
5. Anyim, W.O.: Multimedia instructional resources for effective library user education programme in universities in North- Central, Nigeria. Libr. Philos. Pract. (e-journal) 1821 (2018). https://digitalcommons.unl.edu/libphilprac/1821

6. Egoeze, F., Misra, S., Maskeliunas, R., Damasevicius, R.: Impact of ICT on universities administrative services and management of students' records: ICT in university administration. Int. J. Hum. Capital Inf. Technol. Professionals (JHCITP) **9**(2) (2018)

7. Zaranis, N.: The use of ICT in kindergarten for teaching addition base on realistic mathematics education. Educ. Inf. Technol. **21**(3), 589–606 (2016)

8. Ojino, R., Mich, L.: Mobile applications in university education: the case of Kenya. J. E-learning Knowl. Soc. **14**(1), 111–125 (2018)

9. Sakineh, S.: The impact of information and communication technology (ICT) on the firms export behaviour in manufacturing firms of Iran using Tobit and Heckman method. Int. Bus. Manage. **10**(6), 908–916 (2016)

10. Anyim, W.O.: Improving reference services in federal university libraries in southeast Nigeria using interpersonal communication mechanism. Rev. Inf. Sci. Technol. J. **2**(1), 27–38 (2017)

11. Manoj, K.V.: Changing role of library professional in digital environment. Int. J. Libr. Sci. **13**(2), 97–104 (2015)

12. Nwokocha, U.: Assessment of library user education programmes in Abia State university and federal university of technology, Owerri. Unpublished Ph.D thesis in the department of library and information science; faculty of education university of Nigeria, Nsukka (2012)

13. Ekere, J.N., Omekwu, C.O., Nwoha, C.M.: Users' perception of the facilities, resources and services of the MTN digital library at the university of Nigeria, Nsukka. Libr. Philos. Pract. (e-journal) 1390 (2016). https://digitalcommons.unl.edu/libphilprac/1390

14. Perera, P.A.S.H.: A study on the pattern of usage of library facilities at the medical library, university of Peradeniya. J. Univ. Libr. Assoc. Sri Lanka **9**, 41–61 (2005)

15. Folorunso, O., Njoku, E.: Influence of library environment and user education on undergraduates' use of library at the university of Ibadan Nigeria. Eur. Sci. J. **12**, 288–304 (2016)

16. Ewuim, N.C., Igbokwe-Ibeto, C.J., Nkomah, B.B.: Information and communication technology and public service delivery in Amuwo-Odofin local government council of Lagos State-Nigeria. Singaporean J. Bus. Econ. Manage. Stud. **5**(1), 13–25 (2016)

17. Goldstein, S.M., Johnston, R., Duffy, J., Rao, J.: The service concept: the missing link in service design research? J. Oper. Manage. **20**, 121–134 (2002)

18. IFLA World summit on the information society "Information for all: The role of libraries in the information society" Geneva, Switzerland (2003). https://unige.ch/bibio/ses/IFLA/rol/lib/030526.pdf

19. Verma, R., Jayasimba, K.R.: Service delivery innovation architecture:an empirical study of antecedents and outcomes. IIMB Manage. Rev. **26**(2), 105–121 (2014)

20. Ledimo, O., Martins, N.: The perceptions and nature of service delivery innovation among government employees: an exploratory study. J. Gov. Regul. **4**(4), 575–581 (2015)

21. Sijbom, R.B.L., Janssen, O., Van Yperen, N.W.: Leaders receptivity to subordinates' creative input: The role of achievement goal and composition of creative input. Eur. J. Work Organisational Psychol. **24**(3), 462–478 (2015)

22. Otham, Z., Zahari, M.S.M., Radzi, S.M., Ismail, T.A.T., Majid, H.N.A.: The effect of service delivery failure on service recovery: a causal study. Int. J. Acad. Res. Bus. Soc. Sci. **8**(15), 33–48 (2018)

23. Chen, J.S., Tsou, T.H., Huang, A.Y.: Service delivery innovation: Antecedents and impact on firm performance. J. Serv. Res. **12**(1), 36–55 (2009)

24. Iwhiwhu, B.E., Ruteyan, J.O., Eghwubare, A.: Mobile phones for library services: Prospect for delta state university library Abraka. Libr. Philos. Pract. (e-journal) 346 (2010). https://digitalcommons.unl.edu.libphilprac/346

25. Basahuwa, C.B.: Innovation in academic libraries in the 21st century: a Nigerian perspective. Int. J. Appl. Technol. Libr. Inf. Manage. **3**(1), 18–30 (2017)

26. Ainabor, A.E.: Effective service delivery and the imperatives of information and communication technology in Nigerian local government service. Niger. Public Adm. Rev. 3(3), 225–233 (2011)

27. Nwachukwu, N.V., Asom, F.: Utilization of computer technology for academic work by lecturers of university of Jos-Nigeria. Int. J. Libr. Inf. Sci. Stud. 1(2), 14–22 (2015)

28. Gaudioso, F., Turel, O., Galimberti, C.: The mediating roles of strain facets and coping strategies in translating techno stressors into adverse job outcomes. Comput. Hum. Behav. J. 69, 189–196 (2017)

29. Oyadonghon, J.C., Eke, F.M.: Factors affecting students use of information technology: a comparative study of federal university technology Owerri and Niger Delta university Amazoma. Library of philosophy and practice (2011). https://unlib.uni.edu/oyadonghan-eke.htm-39k

30. Akporhornor, B.A., Akpojotor, L.O.: Challenges confronting postgraduate library and information science student in the use of electronic resources in southern Nigeria. Libr. Philos. Pract. (e-journal) 1319 (2016). https://digitalcommons.unl.edu/libphilprac/1319

31. Bhukuvhani, C., Zezekwa, N., Sunzuma, G.: Students' preparedness to integrate information and communication technology tools and resources for the learning of organic chemistry. Int. J. Educ. Dev. Inf. Commun. Technol. (IJEDICT). 7(2), 27–37 (2013)

32. Ukonu, M., Wogu, J., Obayi, P.: Problems and challenges facing the university of Nigeria, undergraduate students in the use the UNN digital library. J. Humanities Soc. Sci. (JHSS) 3(2), 04–12 (2012)

33. Iwhiwhu, B.E., Okorodudu, P.O.: Public library information resources, facilities, and services: user satisfaction with the Edo state central library, Benin-city Nigeria. Libr. Philos. Pract. 5, 1–7 (2012)

34. Nwabueze, A.U., Urhiewhu, O.L.: Availability and use of digital information resources by undergraduates of universities in Delta and Edo States, Nigeria. Int. J. Digit. Libr. Serv. 5(2) (2015)

A Step by Step Guide for Choosing Project Topics and Writing Research Papers in ICT Related Disciplines

Sanjay Misra[1,2(✉)]

[1] Covenant University, Ota, Nigeria
Sanjay.misra@covenantuniversity.edu.ng
[2] Atilim University, Ankara, Turkey

Abstract. ICT is fast-growing and changing field. A lot of researches are being done in various area of ICT, and results are presented in various platforms like conferences, journal and books. This is common observations in the publications from developing countries (especially in sub – Saharan africa) are not being published in reputed and established publishers even their technical/experiments are good. This is due to lack of several factors including professional presentation, the novelty of the topic, quality of literature review etc. This work guides final year bachelor's students, PG students (masters and PhD) and young researchers, especially working in computing-related disciplines, on how to convert their project works into quality publications. The authors provide details on how these researchers can select suitable project topics, do a proper review, write up the key components of a paper and present their results in an appropriate form (that is, writing style starting from abstract to conclusion). This paper also presents and guides on how to write various types of review papers.

Keywords: ICT · Project topic selection · Paper writing · Structure of research paper · Review paper

1 Introduction

Most of the students in their final year of study at bachelor, master and PhD level need to submit project work. For completing these projects, students work hard and put in effort to ensure their project is both innovative and novel to an extent. Based on the requirements of their various disciplines, the form of projects may differ. For instance, engineering and computer science students are required to produce hardware/software products along with the thesis. After the completion and presentation of the project, most of the students leave the institution, and these project reports are often kept in the archives of the department and / or the university library. In most cases, nobody reads and adequately handles those projects for further processing.

One of the issues in bachelors and master's projects is that after submission and final defence (final examination), neither student nor supervisor care to transform the work into articles that can be published in appropriate outlets. As a result, every year, millions

© Springer Nature Switzerland AG 2021
S. Misra and B. Muhammad-Bello (Eds.): ICTA 2020, CCIS 1350, pp. 727–744, 2021.
https://doi.org/10.1007/978-3-030-69143-1_55

of bachelors and master's project reports are being wasted without any outcome in terms of publications. However, suppose proper attention is given to the publication of the outcomes of each of these projects, it will not only boost and encourage the students but also help the supervisors and affiliated institutions in increasing their research profile.

The second issue is the quality of publication from masters and PhD theses. One can easily observe especially in developing countries that quality of publications from Master and Ph.D thesis are in low profile outlets. By considering these pitfalls, this work presents how to motivate and guide the students starting from the beginning of the project to work systematically so that it will be easy for them to extract the work for quality publication from their project. This proposed work provides the guidelines for the students for ICT and computing-related disciples. Researchers from other disciplines can also follow these guidelines, but writing and presentation style differs from discipline to discipline.

The paper is structured in five sections. The next section describes how to choose research/project topics. Section 3 prescribes ways to start working on collecting useful literature for review. In Sect. 4, the various components of the paper are described in detail. Section 5 discusses the types of review papers, and Sect. 6 summarize how to search quality journals and conferences, and finally, Sect. 7 concludes the paper.

2   Selection of Topic/Area of Research

It is a general observation that students often struggle with the selection of topics. At this point, it is essential that while selecting the topics, students are careful to follow the points highlighted in this section when deciding on a topic. It should be noted that these points are applicable to all levels of students doing projects. However, depending on the degree to be obtained (bachelors, masters or PhD), the rigour of work required may vary.

2.1   Area of Interest – Should be of Your Interest

The student should identify his/her areas of interest in the emerging regions of their field. Projects at both bachelors and master's level will give students a chance to gain in-depth knowledge of the problem in a particular area. It is up to the students to explore by themselves the areas of their field where they can better perform and are interested in.

2.2   Problem depending on Duration of Project

Some of the projects take a long time to complete. So, it would help if students chose at a bachelors' level, a work they can complete in 3–4 months. At master's level, they should be able to complete it in 6–12 months, and for PhD, they should be able to complete in 4 years. Besides that,

- At bachelor level, the concentration may be more on product development and development of some framework and models.

- At Masters Level- the topic should be more specific. At this stage, the student is going to take a specialization in a particular domain. It is for this reason that students' proposal/work should be based on strong theoretical background and product development.
- Selection of topic at the PhD level is similar to the previous one (masters) except the depth of work done at PhD level will be much higher than master level. It is advisable that before selecting any topic at this level, students should ensure that they have a solid foundation of background knowledge or are willing to put in the effort to learn the same.

2.3 Hot Topics on Current Issues

It is crucial that students should choose problems in a current emerging area. It is highly advisable not to take a topic on which a lot of work has been done unless the student is certain they can make distinct contributions. In other words the student is fully certain what new outcomes will be produced that would make significant contribution to the existing body of knowledge.

2.4 Related to the Job Market

It is highly advisable to try to choose a project topic that is not only of interest but also an emerging area (hot topic). Students can also choose based on the job market especially where they target to apply their expertise. For example – some countries have more jobs in IT (Germany/USA) and computing than management (Canada). Most of the African countries require more attention to IT, health, security and education, good governance etc.

2.5 Long Term Vision for Your Carrier

This is a crucial point of consideration while choosing a topic at a master or PhD level. Several students prefer to select a topic in the research area of their supervisors. In such cases certainly, the supervisor would be more helpful in the whole duration of the work. However, it may not be beneficial to the student's future career, especially if the topic is not of little interest to the student. For example, while selecting a topic at master's level in computing-related disciplines, if a student plans to work in the industry then s/he may choose a topic related to a specific industry (IT, management, human resources even in the financial sector) instead of selecting a topic only to complete the project. In the future, a student can plan for an MBA or PhD in IT management. Similarly, for students in management information systems, social science, engineering at bachelor or master levels, they can choose Informatics for PhD.

2.6 Selection of Topic and Supervisor

Finally, and most important of all is for the student to find a suitable guide. The student must be careful, especially in a masters or PhD program. If you don't have proper synchronization with your guide – you may lose your motivation and focus on your work. You should not only check the area of research work of your supervisor but also need to know how much he is available and helpful for students during project work. Students must bear in mind that in all academic institutions, they may find three types of professors/academicians. The first type is those who are excellent teachers in terms of teaching and problem-solving skills but they may not be good researchers (in terms of product development and research publication). The second type of academicians may be expert in innovation and product development and may not be expert in converting their innovative ideas into publications. The third type may be good researchers- they know how to transform creative ideas in publications form. Apart from the above three categories, students may also find some exceptional academicians who are great at teaching, product development or research administrators. A student needs a supervisor who will not only train the students but also motivate and boost them to perform their best and achieve their goals. These young students are full of energy, and they are ready to do ground-breaking research, but they need proper guidance and mentorship. To get such supervisors, students should devote time to explore their perspective supervisors on various social media, e.g. Google Scholar, ResearchGate, LinkedIn, Scopus etc. One more very effective way is to talk with multiple people (predecessors, teachers, other members of the department) before taking the final decision on your topic and supervisor. Students should not rely on one feedback but instead should base their choice on various multiple feedback.

3   Review of Literature

In the previous stage, the student got to select the topic and area of research. Now they have to perform an exhaustive literature review. This stage is an important stage of the whole project. After a careful literature review, a student may decide to change the proposed title of his/her project – or even change the area of research altogether. This is because at this stage the student will be able to know the recent developments and the most important is to find out gaps in existing works which will become the base of the student's proposed project. If the literature survey is not done thoughtfully, it is highly possible that a similar work has already been done and that the student is not aware of. By considering the importance of the literature review, it is highly recommended to explore various databases systematically.

3.1   Prepare Search String – This Can Be Done in the Following Way

The search for relevant papers can be done based in the following way:

1. Obtain significant keywords from the research questions (Which you have prepared before starting review);
2. Recognize different spellings and synonyms for the keywords;
3. Identify keywords in relevant papers
4. Use Boolean "OR" or "AND" to relate significant terms.

3.2   Search Selection Procedure

The search should be done on major databases. We can divide the search engine (databases) into 3 categories:

1. General databases
2. Specific publishers' databases
3. Databases need subscription

General Search Engine/Databases

Google is the most popular search engine. However, it is highly advised not to use the search results on google but instead **Google scholar**. This is because Google scholar provides results only from scholarly literature available on the internet. On the other hand, Google provides everything (academic/nonacademic). In this way quality of results that would be obtained from Google scholar is much higher than results from google. The following are the recommended sites for searching for scholarly work.

1. Google scholar - https://scholar.google.com
2. DBLP (for computer science) - https://dblp.org
3. PubMed (for health and medical sciences) - https://pubmed.ncbi.nlm.nih.gov/adv anced/
4. PMC (is the free full text/open access branch of PubMed) - https://www.ncbi.nlm. nih.gov/pmc/advanced

There are several other search engines like Microsoft academic research, Academic info, etc. (https://www.lowcountrygradcenter.org/the-6-best-search-engines-for-academic-research/), which you can choose based on your requirements and need. Here, we are only providing some of the popular and useful ones. Authors can also find more in their specific areas.

Specific Publisher Databases

It is always good to perform your search on specific publishers' website, which is most appropriate for you. For example, computer science and engineering disciplines, IEEE Xplore, ACM, Science direct will be a right choice for search. Some of the most renowned publishers and their website are given below.

5. Science Direct/ Elsevier, https://www.sciencedirect.com
6. IEEE Xplore- https://ieeexplore.ieee.org/Xplore/home.jsp
7. ACM- https://dl.acm.org/search/advanced
8. Springer digital libraries- https://link.springer.com/advanced-search
9. Wiley- https://onlinelibrary.wiley.com/search/advanced
10. Taylor & Francis- https://www.tandfonline.com/search/advanced
11. Sage Journal- http://methods.sagepub.com/Search

You can find more databases for health/medical science search databases such as - (https://paperpile.com/g/research-databases-healthcare/).

Databases Need Subscription

There are some databases which are more for indexing (Like Scopus and Clarivate Analytics (Web of Science)) but can also be used for searching. The search outcome from these databases is guaranteed to return quality materials because each work in these databases is already indexed and already passed from some quality checks. Both SCOPUS and Web of Science includes scholarly works (research papers, books, conference papers) from all disciplines. One of the options to access (free) Scopus is to review a paper of any Elsevier journal, and you will get SCOPUS to access for one month. Or contact one of your lecturers who are active in academics- s/he should have access.

Below are the websites of Web of Science(Clarivate Analysi) and Scopus

12. Scopus www.scopus.com
13. Web of Science- http://login.webofknowledge.com

Apart from the above official websites, you can also search relevant papers on social sites like

14. ResearchGate (www.researchgate.net),
15. Academia (https://www.academia.edu)

You can get a lot of research papers on ResearchGate which you cannot download from the publishers' website due to subscription issue. Several publishers allow authors to upload the last version of the accepted article (not published one) to upload on their own webpage for academic purpose and researchers available on ResearchGate and academia upload their papers.

Some useful tips during the search

Select the Most Appropriate 5–7 Databases

We have suggested 15 search databases for search. It is worth mentioning that it is not required to search in all of them. Instead, select 5–7 databases, which are most appropriate for your area of research. For example, we suggest for ScienceDirect, Google scholar and Springer for everybody and after then select 2–5 other databases. For engineering disciplines and computer science- IEEE Xplore and ACM and for medical and health, PubMed are appropriate databases. Based on the type of study, authors can increase or decrease the number of search databases.

Carefully Select Keyword

This is crucial for consideration while searching on these databases. Select the most appropriate keywords for your searching, as also suggested in Sect. 3.1. You can see some of the studies of how the keywords are selected in Alli et al. (2019) [3] and Odusami et al. (2020) [13], Adewumi et al. (2016) [4].

Use the Advanced Search Option

It is recommended to use the search string for advanced search. See examples of advanced search option in IEEE Xplore, Taylor and Francis and Wiley in Figs. 1, 2 and 3. The same search should be done in other databases. Most of the renowned publishers have both options- search and advanced search. Without searching on advances search, you may not get the most relevant papers.

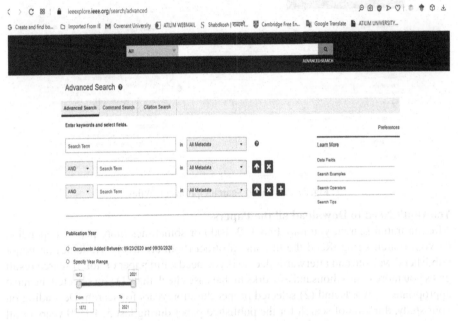

Fig. 1. Advanced search option on IEEE Xplore

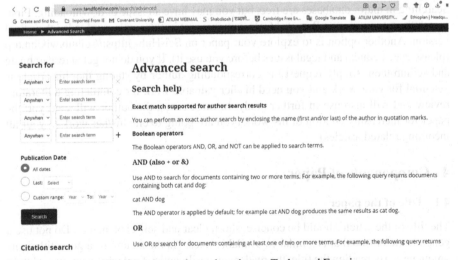

Fig. 2. Advanced search option on Taylor and Francis

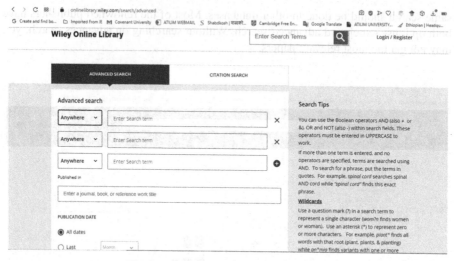

Fig. 3. Advanced Search Options on Wiley

You Don't Need to Download all the Papers

After an initial search, you may find 100–1000 or sometimes more papers depending on your search string. Read the title and abstract (both are freely available) on major publishers' website and afterwards decide if you need a full paper or not. If search result gives you more than a thousand of works in that case check that (1) you selected the most appropriate keywords and (2) selected proper duration/years for search. Depending on your study, duration of search for the published paper during last 5, 10, 20 years or all years.

Don't Worry if You Don't Have a Subscription

Searching in major databases are free, but you may have an issue of downloading. First, search the same paper on ResearchGate, you may get it if the author uploaded their final version. Another option is to explore your paper on Sci-Hub- https://scihub.wikicn.top (please check ethical and legal issues before you use it). If you do not get at researchgate and scihub then, simply request the corresponding author by stating that his article is essential for your work and you need his/her valuable work for completing a literature review and will also use in further study. In most cases, the author will send you the paper for increasing citation of his work (you are going to cite his/her work in your all incoming related articles).

4 Components of Paper

4.1 Title of the paper

The title of the article should be concise, short, clear and self-explanatory. Do not use a general title or one that is similar to available ones. As the beauty of a good title is its uniqueness. By reading the title, the reader can easily understand what a unique solution is provided in work. Avoid question mark and lengthy titles. In general, the title should be 4–12 words (not very strict) and also contain some keywords of the work.

4.2 Abstract

Usually, an abstract should not be too short or too long and should contain all the essential information. The typical size of an abstract should be of 200–300 words. However, it can vary from journal to journal and field of study. The following components should be contained in an abstract

Background- Provide 1–3 lines of the background and main reasons why you are doing that work (which existing problem you want to solve?).

Aim/Objective of paper- Clearly mention in 1–3 lines, the main aim/objectives of the paper.

Methodology- What methods are you applying to achieve your aim and objectives. The methodology may contain 1–4/5 lines depending upon the various methods/techniques used on the work.

Results- Provide quantitative results (if possible) which you got in your experimentation/study. This section should also be 1–3 lines.

Conclusion- What is the impact of your research.

Typically abstract should be written in one paragraph (200–300 Words) containing all the above components. The name of components may be changed in various disciplines, and types of papers (including review papers). It is a common observation that authors write 80% of the abstract as background, and in the last one-two lines, they write the aim of the paper, which is a bad practice. In all types of research papers abstract should contain purpose, and research problem, methods used to solve the problem, results and significant findings (similar to the provided headings). In summary, the abstract should show evidence to clarify the scientific contribution of the paper. Authors should include qualitative results that are investigated and conclusion based on it (results) so that the reader ends the abstract with the knowledge of what is the significant scientific contribution and the "concrete" conclusions.

Never do in the abstract:

- Citation of any reference
- Citation of any Table of Figures
- Avoid formula and abbreviation(s)

4.3 Introduction

The introduction is what and why the work is done. In general, the introduction should have 3–6 paragraphs depending on the type and length of the paper.

- In the first paragraph, you can introduce the topic by providing the background and write why this topic is important?
- In the second paragraph, you should provide a brief review of previous researches (relevant literature). You should always paraphrase relevant facts from the scientific literature, citing the sources to support each statement. You should also provide the gaps in the existing works.

- In the next paragraphs (3–5)- you should provide the different techniques and works and identify why are they used and what are the gaps in existing works. **Based on the gaps, you should give solid reasons(motivations) why you took/worked this project. It is always recommended to summarize your aim and objectives and provide research questions to be addressed in the work/project** (depending on the type of work) in the introduction section.
- In the last paragraph, always summarize the structure of the whole work. For example, in the present work, Sect. 2 summaries how to select the topics. Section 3 provides a systematic way of searching in various databases. Section 4 provides the various components of a normal paper.

4.4   Literature Review/State of the art

A literature review follows by a brief description of collections of articles with their pros and cons and finally the conclusion which also reflects gaps in the field (in general)- which becomes your motivation – reason of the proposed work. However, if the literature itself is the main topic of the project/work, you should require a different approach for presenting the complete literature review. Additionally, various types of review papers exist in the literature, which is summarized in the next Sect. 5. In this section- we present the writing style of literature review which are part of standard research articles.

In the introduction section, you have summarized the brief review on most important literature on the topic and gaps in the field in general. In this section (literature review), the student should provide all the available related works bearing in mind that s/he has to present the pros and cons of each work in the student's own words with proper citation.

It is always better to summarize the findings of the literature review in table form. The table should provide a quick and fast view of the student's review work. All the relevant and significant points of each considered article should be the content of the table.

At the end of the literature review section, the student should conclude the significant outcomes of the literature review. Here, the student can also mention the gaps in the field of research and based on that, his/her major reason for the proposed work.

Note- this section can also be sifted after methodology/ experimentation section where you will provide related work and then compare with your findings with others.

4.5   Materials and Methods/ Research Methodology/Proposed Work/Solution (Design/Framework/Model)

After the literature review section, this section will present the student's significant contributions. This section is the heart of any paper and demonstrates how the student has solved the problem.

The proposal and implementation/experimentation of a student's work depends upon the type and field of work. Also based on the type of paper, this section can be structured differently. For example, in theory, papers, the student would have to present a formal/mathematical proof. However, in empirical papers, the student provides quantitative and qualitative analysis and, in some product development papers show algorithms, prototype implementation. Please search and follow some article in your area on ScienceDirect(https://www.sciencedirect.com)

Simple tips/suggested steps-

Demonstrate the research methodology- A design of the flow of whole activities of your work.

Demonstrate your proposed method- Framework, algorithms, design of your proposed method

Demonstrate the experimentation and implementations – provide all experiments and implementations

4.6 Evaluation and Validation

After presenting your proposed model and implementation, you have to evaluate and validate your work. The way of evaluation and validation again depends on the area of research and type of article. For example, for software engineering experimental works- a student would have to prove theoretically (based on some established criteria) and empirically (mostly from practitioners). In computing related research, usability evaluation is one of the criteria for assessment and validation.

4.6.1 Comparison and Related Work

The worth of any work cannot be proved if it is not compared with other similar works. In this section first, you have to summarize the existing works which are very close to your work, and then you will compare your proposed work with similar studies and show how your work is better than the existing works. Demonstrate clearly what is similar and what are differences. Also never try to criticize negatively other's work to prove your work as best- this is a bad practice- your comparison should be made objectively and in natural ways.

Note-It is possible that you can provide related works here instead of giving the same after the Introduction section.

Simple Tips/Steps-

- Provide a table which will evaluate all similar works with your proposal.
- Provide a comparison of experimental results by tables and graphs.
- Explain the comparative results shown in tables and figures.

4.6.2 Result and Discussion and Limitation of work

In this section, you need to discuss the experimental results, comparison and prove that your proposal (solution) solved not only the problem but also contributed in the field.

Limitation of your study and work should be outlined in this section.

Note- You may find specific guidelines for presenting experimental works and evaluation and validation. For example, to present the case studies – Runeson and Host 2009) [15] presented specific guidelines which are applied in several papers (Misra et al. 2014 [9]).

4.7 Conclusion and Future work

This section concludes your whole work. Be specific and point out your key findings. Bear in mind that the conclusion should be based on quantitative findings (not only theoretical findings).

Usually a conclusion should have 2–3 paragraphs. First and second paragraphs contains significant findings and achievements of your work, and in the last paragraph, you have to give ideas about future work. Future work can include your incomplete work, an extension of your work or some major task in another similar area of research. The future work always gives a chance to other researchers to glean ideas from what you have done and possibly extend your work.

4.8 References

This section typically (mostly) comes without numbering (of this section) so do not give any number to this section. You have to cite all references in order based on a specific style, e.g., MLA, APA, IEEE and several other styles based on journal and publishers where you plan to submit.

Simple Tips-

- Always use some referencing software. There are several available free and by subscription (https://elearningindustry.com/12-best-free-online-bibliography-and-cit ation-tools).
- If you cannot find any referencing software on internet, please use inbuilt MS-OFFICE Reference.
- Don't use Wikipedia as referencing.
- Avoid using references of local newspapers, local websites and contents from blogs unless they belong to reputed organizations- like IBM, Microsoft.
- Always mention last accessed whenever you give reference to a website.

4.9 Appendix

This is an optional section and can usually be used if there are some extra materials which are required for the paper but could not be accommodated in the main text. The contents in the Appendix may be supporting documents or some Figures and Tables containing useful information which could not be included in the main text can also be part of this section.

5 Types of Review Papers

While you start working on a project, your first job is to do an exhaustive review to know the real gaps in the field of your proposed topic. Based on experience, there is a huge possibility that if you are seriously reviewing the literature, you may publish several papers as review articles. Based on this, we are giving some examples of various types of review papers, e.g. comment paper (Misra and Kilic 2006) [10], review paper (Misra,

2010 [12]. Misra and Adewumi 2014) [11], meta-analysis (Odusami 2020) [13], survey (Oliveira et al. (2019) [14], systematic literature review (Adewumi et al. (2016) [4]. There are specific guidelines for review papers in each discipline (Tawfik et al. (2019) [16], Denyer and Tranfield, (2009) [7], Kitchenham, 2007, Biolchini et al.(2005) [6]). For the ease of students -a framework of the systematic way for the selection of articles is given in Appendix Fig. 4.

Example/Case Study - We are taking an example of an author (Dr. Adewole Adewumi) how he was able to publish various review papers during his PhD work.

5.1 Comment Paper

On the serious evaluation of literature, you may find some serious gaps in the field, and if you are smart enough, you can publish a paper on these gaps. See the following example of a comment paper. In this paper the author's main focus was to develop a complete framework for the evaluation and validation of software measures. In initial studies (reviews) they observed that measurement theory which is based on fundamental principles of mathematics and physics could not be applied in software engineering and authors publish a comments paper on the same.

Misra, S., and Kilic, H. (2006). Measurement theory and validation criteria for software complexity measures. ACM SIGSOFT Software Engineering Notes, 31(6), 1–3. https://www.researchgate.net/publication/220630991_Measurement_theory_and_validation_criteria_for_software_complexity_measures.

Note- if you are not confident and do not have strong evidence for criticizing already exiting theory, do not try to do it.

5.2 Review/Analysis Paper Paper

Usually, a researcher can start writing the review paper. As soon as the researcher goes into the depth of the subject, s/he will gain more and more knowledge and expertise in the field. At this stage, s/he starts evaluating papers and can present his observations in terms of a research paper – called a review paper. However, the review paper does not mean that you can accumulate 20–30 articles and summarize their significant work and present. **Still, you have to evaluate the articles critically and present your novel outcomes which are not provided in previous reviews.**

Some useful tips-

- Always use several Tables for summarizing your findings and comparison of articles.
- Create some criteria for evaluation on which you will evaluate each paper. These criteria may be your major contribution to the review paper.
- Include 30–50 references for normal review papers (Total no of words 5000–7000).

As we mentioned earlier that we take a case study/example of an author for his journey to complete his PhD thesis. In his initial reviews, he presented a comparative study of 4 open-source software quality models and published in Elsevier conference.

*"Adewole Adewumi, Sanjay Misra, Nicholas Omoregbe & Luis Fernandez-Sanz' A Review of Models for Evaluating Quality in Open Source Software', Proceedings of 2013 International Conference on Electronic Engineering and Computer Science, IERI Procedia Vol 4 (2013) 88–92 (**Elesvier**).* http://www.sciencedirect.com/sci ence/article/pii/S2212667813000178 ".

In the second review paper, he evaluated the existing open-source quality models against ISO 25010.

"Adewole Adewumi, Sanjay Misra, and Nicholas Omoregbe, Evaluating Open Source Software Quality Models Against ISO 25010. Proc 15ᵗʰ IEEE International Conference on Computation and Information Technology, pp.872– 877, 2015. https://www.researchgate.net/publication/308848262_Evaluating_O pen_Source_Software_Quality_Models_Against_ISO_25010 ".

In his third review paper, he added more models and based on the evaluation of models; he proposed a new framework/criterion for selecting the best quality model.

"A. Adewumi, S. Misra, and N. Ikhu-Omoregbe, 'Quantitative Quality Model for Evaluating Open Source Web Applications: Case Study of Repository Software', 2013 IEEE 16th International Conference on Computational Science and Engineering (Sydney Australia), pp.1207–1213."

https://www.researchgate.net/publication/261661037_Quantitative_Quality_M odel_for_Evaluating_Open_Source_Web_Applications_Case_Study_of_Repository_ Software.

5.3   Meta-Analysis and Survey

Meta-analysis is generally applied for medical, health and in bioinformatics research. This is also a type of systematic review and extracts quantitative results from the reviews. In these days, computer scientists also use meta-analysis for their reviews (Modupe et al. 2020). Haidich(2010) defined meta-analysis as "**Meta-analysis** is a quantitative, formal, epidemiological study design used to systematically assess the results of previous research to derive conclusions about that body of research. Typically, but not necessarily, the study is based on randomized, controlled clinical trials."

In meta-analysis review papers, the depth of analysis is much higher than the review/analysis paper. Quantitative interpretation or review results are presented by several tables and graphs.

Survey papers in computing disciplines are almost similar to meta-analysis. In both survey papers and meta-analysis, number of references are around a hundred, and results are presented by several Tables (10–20) and Figures (10–20).

Examples of meta-analysis and survey paper in both medical and computing are given below [1, 2, 13].

"Adeloye, D., Sowunmi, O. Y., Jacobs, W., David, R. A., Adeosun, A. A., Amuta, A. O., Misra S,.... and Chan, K. Y. (2018). Estimating the incidence of breast cancer in Africa: a systematic review and meta-analysis. Journal of global health, 8(1). https://www.ncbi.nlm.nih.gov/pmc/articles/PMC5903682/".

"Odusami M, Misra S, Abayomi-Alli O, Abayomi-Alli A, Fernandez-Sanz L. A survey and meta-analysis of application-layer distributed denial-of-service attack. Int J Commun Syst. 2020;e4603. https://doi.org/10.1002/dac.4603 ".

5.4 Systematic Literature Review

A systematic literature review (SLR) is the final version of any review process. It requires an exhaustive literature review in a systematic way. Anders Kofod-Petersen (2015) [5] defines systematic literature review as 'A systematic literature review is a formal way of synthesizing the information available from available primary studies relevant to a set of research questions.' It is also similar to the meta-analysis type of review, which requires a quantitative presentation of review results in various presentation formats (Tables, Figures, Graphs, etc.). It is prevalent to use statistical analysis of review results in SLR written in computer science and software engineering fields. Although necessary steps like the selection of articles, research questions, quantitative analysis are common steps in writing SLR in all discipline; however, different approaches are developed for other domains.

You can find the criteria for writing SLR in different disciplines on the following sites. These are only a few examples. Writing SLR in all fields (even domain and sub-domains) are fast-growing. It is highly advisable for students to find the most recent articles and new criteria while writing SLRs.

1. Medicine- gent.uab.cat › sites › gent.uab.cat.diego_prior › files

   https://tropmedhealth.biomedcentral.com/articles/10.1186/s41182-019-0165-6

2. Engineering- https://www.researchgate.net/profile/Pablo_Torres-Carrion/public ation/323277902_Methodology_for_Systematic_Literature_Review_applied_to_E ngineering_and_Education/links/5b6f04f245851546c9fb6004/Methodology-for-Systematic-Literature-Review-applied-to-Engineering-and-Education.pdf
3. Software engineering- https://www.cin.ufpe.br/~in1037/leitura/systematicRevie wSE-COPPE.pdf
4. Business an dmanagement- https://link.springer.com/article/10.1007/s11301-018-0142-x
5. Education and social sciences- https://libraryguides.griffith.edu.au/c.php?g=451 351&p=3333115.

An example of systematic literature Review in computing/software engineering is given below [4]. Bear in mind that nowadays, analytics has become more advanced and most of SLRs in computing are using statistical and other modern techniques which are not used in this example.

"Adewumi, A., Misra, S., Omoregbe, N., Crawford, B., & Soto, R. (2016). A systematic literature review of open source software quality assessment models. SpringerPlus, 5(1), 1936."

6   After Completing Work-Searching of Conferences and Journal

Once you have completed paper, students are suggested to supplement their works with raw data, as well as uploading code to GitHub and following open research principle. There are several platforms provided by a renowned publisher like IEEE (https://www.ieee.org/about/ieee-dataport.html) and Elsevier who offer to upload your data.

Another significant issue is to where to publish your work. If you are only interested in publishing your work in quality outlets, then always search in the following databases:

- For Journals- search on the Web of Science- https://mjl.clarivate.com/search-results
- For Conferences and Journals- http://portal.core.edu.au/conf-ranks/

You can also search journals on SCOPUS, DBLP and other databases. Most of the renowned publishers also provide a Journal finder option where you can search an appropriate journal associated with a particular publisher. Some of links given below:

https://journalsuggester.springer.com
https://journalfinder.elsevier.com
https://authorservices.taylorandfrancis.com/publishing-your-research/choosing-a-journal/journal-suggester/
https://journalfinder.wiley.com/search?type=match
https://publication-recommender.ieee.org/home
https://www.pmid2cite.com/pubmed-journal-suggester

7   Conclusion

We have presented a simple systematic way of writing research paper extracted from MS and PhD thesis. These guidelines are only suggestions, and you have to apply them based on your type and size of paper and also area of research. Several section/subsections can be combined, for example, the literature review and introduction section, if you are writing a short paper. Similarly, proposed framework, experimentation/implementation, validation and comparative study can also be part of only one section if you are writing conference paper of 8–10 pages. You can also remove the literature survey and provide after your experimentation while making a comparison. You can also find several tips for writing papers on several websites.

Acknowledgement. The author appreciate the sponsorship from Covenant University through its Centre for Research, Innovation and Discovery, Covenant University, Ota Nigeria.

Disclaimer. Links and papers provided in the work is only given as examples. To leave any citation or link is not intentional.

Appendix

Systematic Way of Selection of Article for Review
The systematic review process and selection of the relevant articles at different stages is

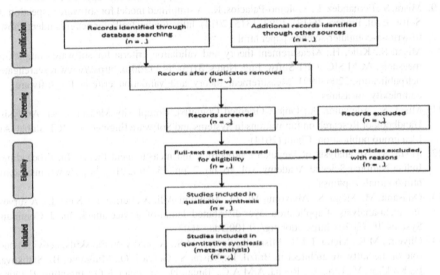

Fig. 4. PRISMA flow chart of the systematic review process and selection of the articles at different stages

illustrated in the PRISMA flow chart as shown in Fig. 4.

References

1. Adeloye, D., Sowunmi, O.Y., Jacobs, W., David, R.A., Adeosun, A.A., Amuta, A.O., Misra, S., Chan, K.Y.: Estimating the incidence of breast cancer in Africa: a systematic review and meta-analysis. J. Global Health, **8**(1) (2018). https://www.ncbi.nlm.nih.gov/pmc/articles/PMC5903682/
2. Adeloye, D., Adigun, T., Misra, S., Omoregbe, N.: Assessing the coverage of e-health services in sub-saharan africa. Methods Inf. Med. **56**(03), 189–199 (2017)
3. Abayomi-Alli, O., Misra, S., Abayomi-Alli, A., Odusami, M.: A review of soft techniques for SMS spam classification: methods, approaches and applications. Eng. Appl. Artif. Intell. **86**, 197–212 (2019). https://coek.info/pdf-a-review-of-soft-techniques-for-sms-spam-classification-methods-approaches-and-a.html

4. Adewumi, A., Misra, S., Omoregbe, N., Crawford, B., Soto, R.: A systematic literature review of open source software quality assessment models. SpringerPlus **5**(1), 1–13 (2016). https://doi.org/10.1186/s40064-016-3612-4
5. Anders, K.-P.: How to do a Structured Literature Review in computer science. https://www.researchgate.net/publication/265158913_How_to_do_a_Structured_Literature_Review_in_computer_science. Accessed 11 Oct 2020
6. Biolchini, J., Mian, P.G., Natali, A.C.C., Travassos, G.H.: Systematic review in software engineering. System Engineering and Computer Science Department COPPE/UFRJ, Technical Report ES, **679**(05), 45 (2005). https://www.cin.ufpe.br/~in1037/leitura/systematicRevie wSE-COPPE.pdf
7. Denyer, D., Tranfield, D.: Producing a systematic review. https://gent.uab.cat/diego_prior/sites/gent.uab.cat.diego_prior/files/. Accessed 11 Oct 2020
8. Haidich, A.-B.: Meta-analysis in medical research. Hippokratia **14**(Suppl 1), 29 (2010)
9. Misra, S., Fernández, L., Colomo-Palacios, R.: A simplified model for software inspection. J. Softw. Evol. Process **26**(12), 1297–1315 (2014). https://www.froihofer.net/en/students/how-to-write-a-computer-science-paper.html
10. Misra, S., Kilic, H.: Measurement theory and validation criteria for software complexity measures. ACM SIGSOFT Softw. Eng. Notes. **31**(6), 1–3 (2006). https://www.researchgate.net/publication/220630991_Measurement_theory_and_validation_criteria_for_software_complexity_measures
11. Misra, S., Adewumi, A.: Object-Oriented Cognitive Complexity Measures: An Analysis, Handbook of Research on Innovations in Systems and Software Engineering. IGI Global, An Idea group publication, Cham (2014)
12. Misra, S.: An analysis of Weyuker's properties and measurement theory. In: Proceedings Indian National Science Academy, vol. 76, no. 2, pp. 55–66 (2010). http://www.insa.ac.in/html/journals.asp#insa
13. Odusami, M., Misra, S., Abayomi-Alli, O., Abayomi-Alli, A., Fernandez-Sanz, L.: A survey and meta-analysis of application-layer distributed denial-of-service attack. Int. J. Commun. Syst. e4603 (2020). https://doi.org/10.1002/dac.4603
14. Oliveira, M.R., Vieira, F.J.R., Misra, S., Soares, M.S.: A survey on the skills, activities and role of the software architect in Brazil. In: Misra, S., Gervasi, O., Murgante, B., Stankova, E., Korkhov, V., Torre, C., Rocha, A.M.A.C., Taniar, D., Apduhan, B.O., Tarantino, E. (eds.) ICCSA 2019. LNCS, vol. 11623, pp. 43–58. Springer, Cham (2019). https://doi.org/10.1007/978-3-030-24308-1_4
15. Runeson, P., Host, M.: Guidelines for conducting and reporting case study research in software engineering. Empirical Softw. Eng. **14**(2), 131–164 (2009)
16. Tawfik, G.M., Dila, K.A.S., Mohamed, M.Y.F., Tam, D.N.H., Kien, N.D., Ahmed, A.M., Huy, N.T.: A step by step guide for conducting a systematic review and meta-analysis with simulation data. Tropical Med. Health **47**(1), 46 (2019)
17. Kitchenham, B., Stuart, C.: Guidelines for performing systematic literature reviews in software engineering. (2007). http://citeseerx.ist.psu.edu/viewdoc/download;jsessionid=C6B EB78617FB06E26F622C8A9890080C?doi=10.1.1.117.471&rep=rep1&type=pdf

Author Index